Dieterich Buxtehude

Eastman Studies in Music

Ralph P. Locke, Senior Editor
Eastman School of Music

Additional Titles on Music before 1800

*Aspects of Unity in J. S. Bach's
Partitas and Suites: An Analytical Study*
David W. Beach

*Bach and the Pedal Clavichord:
An Organist's Guide*
Joel Speerstra

*Bach's Changing World:
Voices in the Community*
Edited by Carol K. Baron

*The Chansons of Orlando di Lasso and
Their Protestant Listeners: Music, Piety,
and Print in Sixteenth-Century France*
Richard Freedman

*Explaining Tonality: Schenkerian
Theory and Beyond*
Matthew Brown

*French Organ Music from the
Revolution to Franck and Widor*
Edited by Lawrence Archbold
and William J. Peterson

*The Gardano Music Printing Firms,
1569–1611*
Richard J. Agee

*Historical Musicology: Sources,
Methods, Interpretations*
Edited by Stephen A. Crist and
Roberta Montemorra Marvin

*Substance of Things Heard: Writings
about Music*
Paul Griffiths

*Theories of Fugue from the Age of Josquin
to the Age of Bach*
Paul Mark Walker

A complete list of titles in the Eastman Studies in Music Series,
in order of publication, may be found at the end of this book.

Johannes Voorhout, "Musical Party," Hamburg, 1674 (Hamburg, Museum für Hamburgische Geschichte). Johann Adam Reincken sits at the harpsichord; the man playing the viola da gamba is probably Buxtehude.

Dieterich Buxtehude

Organist in Lübeck

KERALA J. SNYDER

 UNIVERSITY OF ROCHESTER PRESS

First published 1987 Schirmer Books, New York; Collier Macmillan, London.
Revised edition published 2007 by the University of Rochester Press.

University of Rochester Press
668 Mt. Hope Avenue, Rochester, NY 14620, USA
www.urpress.com
and Boydell & Brewer Limited
PO Box 9, Woodbridge, Suffolk IP12 3DF, UK
www.boydellandbrewer.com

ISBN-13: 978–1–58046–253–2
ISBN-10: 1–58046–253–7

ISSN: 1071–9989

Library of Congress Cataloging-in-Publication Data

Snyder, Kerala J.
    Dieterich Buxtehude : organist in Lübeck / Kerala J. Snyder. — Rev. ed.
        p. cm. — (Eastman studies in music, ISSN 1071-9989 ; v. 44)
    Includes bibliographical references (p.) and index.
    ISBN-13: 978-1-58046-253-2 (hardcover : alk. paper)
    ISBN-10: 1-58046-253-7
    1. Buxtehude, Dietrich, 1637–1707—Criticism and interpretation.   2. Music—
17th century—History and criticism.   I. Title.
    ML410.B99S6 2007
    780.92—dc22
    [B]

                                                                        2007003730

A catalogue record for this title is available from the British Library.

This publication is printed on acid-free paper.
Printed in the United States of America.

To Richard

Contents

Illustrations

Figures

Contents of the Accompanying Compact Disc

Tracks 1–2, 4, 9–16 courtesy of Dacapo Records, www.dacapo-records.dk

Track 3 courtesy of Intim Musik, www.intim-musik.se

Tracks 5–8 recorded on the North German organ in Örgryte Nya Kirka, Göteborg; courtesy of Loft Recordings, available at www.gothic-catalog.com

Preface to the Second Edition

The first edition of this book appeared in 1987 during the celebrations of the 350th anniversary of Buxtehude's birth. Since then, the Berlin wall has come down, new sources of Buxtehude's music have come to light, and a new generation of scholars has made substantial contributions to the literature. I, too, have done further work on the history of music in Lübeck, and the commemoration of the 300th anniversary of Buxtehude's death is at hand. Clearly it is time for a second edition.

Readers of the first edition will find much that is familiar: eleven chapters and six appendixes, all with the same titles; this is not a brand new book. But they will also find significant new material within these sections. Most important, many archival materials have returned to Lübeck from the former German Democratic Republic and Soviet Union. Following the bombing of 1942, seventy-five cases of rare books and manuscripts from the Lübeck library and the most important holdings of the Lübeck archives—including the account books of St. Mary's Church that Buxtehude kept as Werkmeister of the church—were stored for safekeeping in a salt mine in Bernburg, near Köthen. Following the war they were dispersed to various places, including Russia, Georgia, and Armenia. For the first edition I was able to consult Buxtehude's accounts through 1685, which were then in the German Democratic Republic; the rest were presumed lost. The account books and many other records from St. Mary's have returned to the Lübeck archives, but sadly numerous items from the library are still missing, including its unique copies of Buxtehude's printed occasional music. Excerpts from the St. Mary's accounts for the years 1686 to 1707 have now been added to appendix 4 (Section D7), and they contribute important new information on the organs of the church, with implications for their tuning, which is discussed in chapters 3 and 7.

The most exciting new source is surely J. S. Bach's copy of Buxtehude's *Nun freut euch lieben Christen gmein* (BuxWV 210), which he made as a young teenager even before he departed for school in Lüneburg in 1700; this is discussed in chapter 9. Other notable additions to the second edition include a reevaluation of the identification of Buxtehude in the famous painting *Musical Party* (frontispiece) in chapter 4, new information on the organ that Buxtehude played in Helsingør (chapter 1), more detailed discussions of the origins of the Lübeck Abendmusiken (chapter 2) and the musical repertoire and hymnody of St. Mary's in Lübeck (chapter 3), and a revised chronology (chapter 10). Finally, this second edition contains a compact disk with performances of works discussed in chapters 5, 7, 8, and 11.

During the twenty years between these two editions I have been closely associated with two institutions that have contributed greatly to my growth as a scholar: the Eastman School of Music and the Göteborg Organ Art Center (GOArt), and I am deeply indebted to my colleagues and students at both places. I would particularly like to thank Hans Davidsson, the founder of GOArt and now Professor of Organ at Eastman, who has facilitated the production of the CD for this book and has newly recorded four works on the North German mean-tone organ at Örgryte Nya Kirka in Gothenburg, Sweden, for it. I would also like to thank recording engineer Erik Sikkema; Roger Sherman, of Loft Recordings; Henrik Rørdam, of Dacapo Records; and Jan Johansson, of Intim Musik, for their contributions to the CD. A generous and much appreciated subsidy from the Eastman School of Music, Jamal J. Rossi, Interim Dean, has made its publication possible.

Following the first edition of this book, I received the Buxtehude Prize from the City of Lübeck, for which I am deeply grateful. Lübeck has continued to inspire my research and welcome me on my many visits, particularly at the Bibliothek der Hansestadt Lübeck, where Arndt Schnoor now serves as music librarian, and the Archiv der Hansestadt Lübeck, where Antjekathrin Graßmann still answers all my questions, although she has recently retired as director. To these worthy institutions I can now add a third locus for my research: the Archiv der Gesellschaft der Musikfreunde in Vienna, directed by Dr. Otto Biba, where the music from the old choir library of St. Mary's, Lübeck, is located. I have continued my work with the sources of Buxtehude's music at the University Library in Uppsala, Sweden, which has resulted in the recent publication of the *Düben Collection Database Catalogue*, in collaboration with Erik Kjellberg. And back at home, the fine staff of the Yale University Music Library, now led by Kenneth Crilly, continues to support my work from day to day. Since my retirement I have not had so many opportunities to work in the Sibley Music Library, headed by Daniel Zager, but it, too, has provided essential resources for my research.

This second edition has benefited greatly from my collaboration with Hans-Joachim Schulze, whose beautiful German translation of it appears under the title *Dieterich Buxtehude: Leben—Werk—Aufführungspraxis*, published by Bärenreiter Verlag, Kassel. I would also like to thank Ibo Ortgies for his help with my most recent research in the Lübeck archives and for making his collection of digital images available to me. Many other colleagues have assisted me by supplying materials, responding to my queries, or stimulating my thinking through discussions both in person and by e-mail. Among them are Ellen Beebe, Michael Belotti, Lars Berglund, David Boe, Ronald Broude, James David Christie, Pieter Dirksen, Mary Frandsen, Fred Gable, Ulf Grapenthin, Friedemann Hellwig, Joseph Herl, Gisela Jaacks, Ada Kadelbach, Sverker Jullander, Mads Kjersgaard, Eva Linfield, Henrik Fibiger Nørfelt, Christa

Rakich, Siegbert Rampe, Dorothea Schröder, David Schulenberg, Heinrich Schwab, Joel Speerstra, Harald Vogel, Paul Walker, Roland Wilson, Christoph Wolff, and Peter Wollny. To all of these colleagues, and to others I may have inadvertently omitted from this list, my most sincere thanks.

My special thanks go to the staff of the University of Rochester Press, led by Suzanne Guiod, who have worked so hard to bring this book out in time to commemorate the 300th anniversary of Buxtehude's death, and to Ralph Locke, who has done such a superb job of guiding the *Eastman Studies in Music* since its inception.

Finally, I wish to express my deep appreciation to my husband, Richard Snyder, for his constant support as I was trying to meet simultaneous deadlines from both sides of the Atlantic Ocean. I lovingly dedicate this book to him.

KJS
New Haven, Connecticut
February 2007

Preface to the First Edition

Dieterich Buxtehude (ca. 1637–1707) ranks as the leading composer in Germany between Heinrich Schütz and Johann Sebastian Bach. Buxtehude's organ praeludia, *avant-garde* compositions in their own day, were highly regarded by organists of succeeding generations and form part of the common repertory of organists today. His vocal compositions and sonatas, although less celebrated than his organ works, also represent outstanding contributions to their respective genres.

The time has certainly arrived for a new and comprehensive study of the life and works of Buxtehude. The first period of Buxtehude scholarship was a time of discovery, beginning with Philipp Spitta's lengthy discussion of Buxtehude in the first volume of his Bach biography, which appeared in 1873. André Pirro published the first book devoted exclusively to Buxtehude's life and music in 1913, and the wide acceptance that *Dietrich Buxtehude* enjoyed as the standard work on the composer led to its reprinting in 1976. The main emphasis of this first period was on the publication of Buxtehude's music, as new sources continued to come to light. A second phase, devoted to specialized studies, began in 1951 with Joseph Hedar's dissertation on Buxtehude's organ music. It included dissertations on Buxtehude's vocal music by Dietrich Kilian (1956), Søren Sørensen (1958), and Martin Geck (1965) and source studies encompassing Buxtehude sources by Friedrich Wilhelm Riedel (1960), Friedhelm Krummacher (1965), Bruno Grusnick (1964–66), and Jan Olof Rudén (1968). Georg Karstädt's publication in 1974 of a thematic catalogue of Buxtehude's works—the *Buxtehude-Werke-Verzeichnis*—ushered in a period of consolidation, to which my book belongs. Interest in specialized studies continues, however; four dissertations—by Lawrence Archbold, Sara Ruhle, Eva Linfield, and Christine Defant—were completed in the early 1980s.

This book is intended for all admirers of Buxtehude's music—listeners, performers, and scholars. Its first four chapters, which place Buxtehude's life and music in their historical, geographical, and social context, presuppose no technical knowledge of music on the part of the reader. Parts II and III—devoted to Buxtehude's works and their sources, chronology, and performance—are directed primarily toward performers and scholars, and I earnestly hope that the final chapter will engage members of both groups in discussions on the performance of Buxtehude's music.

Dieterich Buxtehude: Organist in Lübeck owes its title to a designation found in several manuscripts of Buxtehude's organ music (one can be seen in Figure 7-3) and its special character to the time that I spent in Lübeck during the early stage of the research upon which it is based. I went to Lübeck seeking a better understanding of the culture from which Buxtehude's music had sprung. I intended to write a book about Buxtehude's music, not his biography, believing at the time that I could not write much more about his life than I had already outlined in my article in *The New Grove Dictionary of Music and Musicians*. Once in Lübeck, however, I discovered that while I might not uncover any startling new facts concerning Buxtehude's life, a great deal remained to be written about the context in which that life was lived. The book underwent such a metamorphosis that the work I present here might be considered an introductory volume to the more analytical study that I originally intended to write. Much work remains to be done in the study of Buxtehude's music, and I hope that this book will inspire others to carry it forward.

The reader has no doubt noticed that I appear to have changed the spelling of Buxtehude's first name. But it is rather we who have written about him, edited his music, and placed it on musical programs, who have changed the spelling of his name, a practice that began in the eighteenth century. As my acquaintance with Dieterich Buxtehude grew closer, particularly through the study of his letters and the few remaining autograph manuscripts, I became convinced that his name ought to be spelled as he himself most often spelled it. Thus, I retained the various spellings of his name in all quotations and transcriptions from sources and documents, but I normalized it to "Dieterich" elsewhere. I trust this decision will not cause undue bibliographical confusion.

Because I hope to reach a broad audience with this book, I reduced the documentation within its main body to an absolute minimum. To my scholarly colleagues I offer as compensation six appendixes containing much information drawn from the primary sources on which my work is based. At the beginning of the notes to each chapter I list the most important literature on which I drew for that chapter. References to cited documents or literature usually appear within the text itself, and whenever the location is easily found—as, for example, in Walther's *Musicalisches Lexicon* or *Mattheson's Grundlage einer Ehrenpforte*—I include no extra note. The archival documents transcribed in Appendix 4 are entered in chronological sequence within each category.

The archival documents from Lübeck are introduced in two main categories, those that have remained in Lübeck and those in the custody of the German Democratic Republic. For reasons unknown to me, connected perhaps with my United States citizenship, I was permitted to study documents in the latter category that had previously been unavailable to scholars since their removal from Lübeck following the bombing of 1942. While this book was in press, an agreement for an exchange of archival documents was reached between the Federal Republic of Germany and the German Democratic Republic under which these

xvi ᴣᴀ PREFACE TO THE FIRST EDITION

documents will be returned to Lübeck. It may be some time before they are reintegrated into the Lübeck archives, however, and thus I allowed all references to these documents to stand, reflecting their location at the time of my research. The agreement does not extend to library materials, so the Lübeck tablature A 373 remains at the Deutsche Staatsbibliothek in Berlin for the forseeable future.

The research for this book took me on journeys that I recall with great pleasure, along with the names of many colleagues who helped me along the way. The book grew out of my article on Buxtehude for *The New Grove*, and I thank its editor, Stanley Sadie, for his encouragement at the earliest stage of my research. Georg Karstädt, music librarian emeritus at the Bibliothek der Hansestadt Lübeck, provided a constant flow of information and lively discussions throughout the evolution of this book, and he more than any other persuaded me to tackle Buxtehude's biography. His *Buxtehude-Werke-Verzeichnis* was my constant companion, along with *The New Grove*. My bibliography would be twice as long if I had listed all the separate articles in *The New Grove* that I consulted as I wrote.

My study of Buxtehude gave me an entrée to Scandinavia that afforded much of scholarly value and pleasure. Søren Sørensen, professor at Aarhus University, provided me with much of the Danish literature on Buxtehude and assisted my efforts to learn about the early part of Buxtehude's life in numerous ways. Inga Johannson, assistant librarian in the manuscript division of the Uppsala University Library, greatly facilitated my work with the Buxtehude manuscripts there and has always responded cheerfully to my requests for further information. Bo Lundgren, librarian emeritus of the Academic Music Library in Stockholm, Erik Kjellberg, professor at Uppsala University, and Per Rudén, cathedral organist at Lund, made numerous Swedish materials available to me; and Ole Kongsted, of the Music Historical Museum in Copenhagen, introduced me to the Danish archives there. The efforts and courtesy of these Scandinavian colleagues made it possible for me to give the Danish portion of Buxtehude's life the emphasis that I believe it deserves.

My work in Uppsala and my first stay in Lübeck were made possible by a Senior Faculty Research Fellowship from Yale University. My second stay in Lübeck came as part of the city's celebration of 800 years of music in Lübeck. Over six months, the city staged a series of lecture-concerts that brought to life its musical heritage from its beginnings to the present day. Thanks to a research grant from the city, I was able to participate in this festival, learn more about the broad musical heritage of which Buxtehude's music forms a part, and carry on further research for the book. So many people supported my work in Lübeck that I cannot possibly mention them all, but I must especially thank Bruno Grusnick, retired cantor of St. Jacobi Church; Armin Schoof, organist of St. Jacobi; Renate Schleth, music librarian of the Bibliothek der Hansestadt Lübeck; Antjekathrin Graßmann, director of the Archiv der Hansestadt Lübeck; Hans-Bernd Spies, also of the Lübeck Archives; Horst Weimann, director of the

Lübeck Church Archives; and Martin Botsch, professor of architecture at the Hochschule.

Lübeck provided not only the ideal location in which to learn about Hanseatic culture, but also a convenient point of departure for travel to other sources of information in Copenhagen, Berlin, and Bad Oldesloe. Dr. von Busch, organist of the Church of Sts. Peter and Paul in Bad Oldesloe, eased my way with the archives there, and Eveline Bartlitz, of the music division at the Deutsche Staatsbibliothek in Berlin, always enhances the pleasure of working at that library. Members of the musicological faculty at the University of Kiel, particularly Professors Friedhelm Krummacher, Arnfried Edler, and Heinrich Schwab, stimulated my thinking enormously, as did Professor Harald Vogel of the North German Organ Academy.

In addition to the benefits of working with primary sources and meeting with colleagues there, my European travels produced shelves of books, drawers of file folders, and seeming miles of microfilm. The remaining hard work of integrating their contents and writing this book was done at home. Here, too, I benefited from the stimulation, encouragement, and assistance of many colleagues. Professor Christoph Wolff, of Harvard University, supplied me with materials and gave me much-needed encouragement at an early stage in my work. Professor Harold Samuel, librarian of the Music Library at Yale University, together with his entire staff, provided the kind of support that every scholar desires. A number of colleagues read the book or portions of it and helped me with their critical comments—Professors Friedhelm Krummacher, of Kiel University; Fenner Douglas, of Duke University; Søren Sørensen, of Aarhus University; Reinhard Strohm, Claude Palisca, Charles Krigbaum, Eva Linfield, and Stephen Hefling, all of Yale University; Harald Vogel, of the North German Organ Academy; and Imanuel Willheim, of the Hartt School of Music, University of Hartford. Charles Krigbaum also helped me to obtain important materials. Two conferences on Buxtehude's music sponsored by the Westfield Center for Early Keyboard Studies provided opportunities for performers, scholars, and instrument builders to meet and learn from one another. My friends Fred Powledge and Roland Hoover shared with me their special expertise on the making of books, and my students over the years will recognize a number of projects on which they worked. Their questions stimulated me more than they could possibly know.

The actual writing of this book was supported by a fellowship from the National Endowment for the Humanities, and a grant from the Vincent Coffin Fund at the University of Hartford enabled me to set up a database for the information that I had gathered about Buxtehude's works and their sources. I was helped by an extremely talented crew of research assistants: Christopher Tietze, Catherine Liddell, Sara Snyder, and Gregory Hayes. Elsa Johnson and Leo McManus provided secretarial assistance, and without the help of XyWrite and Knowledgeman this book would not yet be finished. Maribeth Payne, senior editor of Schirmer Books, skillfully and cheerfully guided its publication, and I am grateful to all those at Schirmer Books who worked hard to make it possible for this book to appear in 1987 to celebrate the 350th anniversary of Buxtehude's birth.

The people I have named here, and many more whom I have not mentioned, helped me immeasurably with the research and writing of this book. But as I think about its genesis, I realize that it goes back to a time many years before I actually began to work on it, to the teachers who inspired me to become a scholar and guided my development as a musician: to Hubert Lamb, who infected me with his love of seventeenth-century music; to Magdalene Schindelin and Alexander Kessler, who introduced me to the wonders of German literature; to Claude Palisca, who taught me the musicologist's craft; and to Melville Smith and William Herrmann, who guided my first performances of Buxtehude's music in the chapel of Wellesley College. In that space—the same room that now houses the Fisk meantone organ—this book was conceived.

The writing of this book was inspired and sustained by the academic community, but I could never have completed it without the love and support of my family. Above all, I am deeply grateful to my husband, Richard Snyder, for welcoming Dieterich Buxtehude into our home and our lives.

KJS
New Haven, Connecticut
June 1987

Abbreviations

Pitch Identification

C · B   c · b   c' · b'   c" · g"

A	Alto
B	Basso
Bc	Basso continuo
Bom	Bombarde
BuxWV	Buxtehude Werke Verzeichnis
BWV	Bach Werke Verzeichnis
Cemb	Cembalo
Cn	Cornetto
com	complemento
Con	continuo part labeled as such
cto	concertato
Cym	Cymbalo
C1	soprano clef
C2	mezzo-soprano clef
C3	alto clef
C4	tenor clef
DKL	*Das deutsche Kirchenlied* [RISM]
Fg	Fagotto (dulcian)
fig	figured
Fl	Flute (recorder)
F2	bass clef
G2	treble clef
inc	incomplete
KB	Kritischer Bericht
Kbd	Keyboard
man	*manualiter*
m.p.	manu propria
NBA	*Neue Bach Ausgabe*
nf	nonfigured continuo part

Ob	Hautbois
Org	Organ
ped	*pedaliter*
O	Organo or Oberwerck
rip	ripieno
R	Rückpositiv
RISM	Répertoire international des sources musicales
S	Soprano
Sor	Sordino (mute)
Sp	Spinett
T	Tenore
tab	tablature
Th	Theorbo
Tm	Timpani
Tn	Trombone
Tr	Trombetta
V	Violin
Va	Viola
Vb	Viola da braccia
Vg	Viola da gamba
Vn	Violone
Vt	Violetta
[ ]	part is there but not named
/	choice of instruments indicated in source
&	both instruments contained consecutively in part
+	(between insts): both instruments play simultaneously
	(after period): following insts double essential parts to left of period
( )	added information RE: clefs, inst doubled, figuration, incomplete part, etc.
	NB: For sources in staff notation, Viola 1 parts are in alto clef and Viola 2 parts in tenor clef unless otherwise noted.

Library Sigla from the Répertoire Internationale des Sources Musicales

B	Berlin (West), Staatsbibliothek Preußischer Kulturbesitz
Bc	Brussels, Bibliothèque du Conservatoire Royal de Musique
DHgm	The Hague, Gemeentemuseum
Gs	Göttingen, Niedersächsische Staats- und Universitätsbibliothek
Hs	Hamburg, Staats- und Universitätsbibliothek
KAu	Kaliningrad (Königsberg), Universitetskaya Biblioteka
KA	Karlsruhe, Badische Landesbibliothek

Kj	Kraków, Biblioteka Jagiellonska
Kk	Copenhagen, Det Kongelige Bibliotek
L	Lund, Universitetsbibliotek
LEm	Leipzig, Städtische Bibliotheken – Musikbibliothek
Lr	Lüneburg, Ratsbibliothek
LÜh	Lübeck, Bibliothek der Hansestadt
N	Norrköping (Sweden), Stadsbiblioteket
NH	New Haven, Yale University Music Library
Ob	Oxford, Bodleian Library
Pn	Paris, Bibliothèque nationale
Uu	Uppsala, Universitetsbibliotek
Wgm	Vienna, Gesellschaft der Musikfreunde

Editions of Buxtehude's Music

BA	Bärenreiter Ausgabe, single works edited mainly by Bruno Grusnick
Ban	D. Buxtehude, *Klavervaerker*, edited by Emilius Bangert (Copenhagen, 1942); reprinted by Kalmus
BSS	B. Schott's Söhne, Mainz
CW	D. Buxtehude, *Collected Works*, edited by Kerala J. Snyder et al. (New York, 1987)
Dan	Samfundet til udgivelse af dansk musik, single works edited by Søren Sørensen
DdT	Denkmäler deutscher Tonkunst; vol. XIV edited by Max Seiffert (1903)
EB	Edition Breitkopf, keyboard works edited by Klaus Beckmann
EM	Edition Merseburger, single works edited by Dietrich Kilian
H	*Dietrich Buxtehudes Orgelwerke*, edited by Joseph Hedar (Stockholm, 1952)
HE	Hänssler-Edition, Stuttgart, single works, various editors
K	D. Buxtehude, *Orgelwerke*, introduction by Walter Kraft (Wiesbaden, 1952); reprinted by Kalmus
Lun	D. Buxtehude, *Vier Suiten*, edited by Bo Lundgren (Copenhagen, 1954)
Nor	Nordisk Musikförlaget, Stockholm, single works edited by Joseph Hedar
S	*Dietrich Buxtehudes Werke für Orgel*, edited by Philipp Spitta, rev. Max Seiffert (Leipzig, 1903–4)
S Erg.	*Dietrich Werke für Orgel*, edited by Max Seiffert, Ergänzungsband (Leipzig, 1939)
W	*Dietrich Buxtehudes Werke*, edited by Wilibald Gurlitt et al. (8 vols; Klecken and Hamburg, 1925–58; reprint New York, 1977)
WH	Wilhelm Hansen, Copenhagen, single works edited by Søren Sørensen

Events in the Life of
Dieterich Buxtehude

1680   Dedication of BuxWV 75 to Gustav Düben
        BuxWV 119 for marriage of King Charles XI of Sweden and Princess
        Ulrika Eleonore of Denmark
1681   BuxWV 122 for wedding of Joachim von Dalen and Catharine von
        Hachenburg
        Nicolaus Bruhns studies with D. B. in Lübeck
1683   25 March: baptism of daughter Dorothea Catrin
1684   Announcement of future publication of *Sonaten à 2 & 3 Violini & Viola da
        gamba, Himmlische Seelenlust auf Erden,* and *Das allerschröcklichste und
        allererfreulichste*
        Georg Dietrich Leiding studies with D. B. in Lübeck
1685   Music for wedding of Johann Adam Reincken and Anna Wagner (BuxWV 19?)
1686   7 April: baptism of daughter Maria Engel
1687   6 April: burial of daughter Maria Engel
        7 May: D. B. travels to Hamburg to test Schnitger's organ at St. Nicholas's
1688   Abendmusik based on parable of the prodigal son
ca. 1689 Friedrich Gottlieb Klingenberg studies with D. B. in Lübeck
1692   16 November: burial of daughter Helena Elisabeth; one Abendmusik
        performance cancelled
1694   Probable publication date for Sonatas, opus 1 (BuxWV 252–58), dedicated
        to Lübeck burgomasters and members of city council
1695   BuxWV 117 for wedding of Joachim Carstens and Anna Catharina Leopold
1696   Publication of Sonatas, opus 2 (BuxWV 259–65), dedicated to Johann Ritter
1698   BuxWV 121 for wedding of Benedict Winkler and Margaretha von Höveln
1699   Pachelbel dedicates *Hexachordum Apollinis* to D. B.
1700   1 January: music for *Hundertjähriges Gedicht für die Wolfahrt der
        Kayserlichen Freyen Reichs Stadt Lübeck*
        Abendmusiken: five mixed concerts
1703   17 August: Handel and Mattheson visit D. B. in Lübeck
1705   BuxWV 120 for wedding of Anton Winckler and Elisabeth Niemann
        Visit of Johann Sebastian Bach
        2 and 3 December: "extraordinary" Abendmusiken, *Castrum doloris* and
        Templum honoris
1707   19 March: last entry by D. B. in account book
        9 May: death of D. B.
        16 May: burial in St. Mary's, Lübeck

Part I

Buxtehude's World

Chapter One

Denmark

On the ninth day of May *Didericus Buxtehude* met with his last day. [He], if anyone, [was] a most skillful master of the art of music, and among us he [was] for thirty-eight years Director of the organ in the Church of Mary. Besides this, his name is known among connoisseurs of such things; a record is kept here and there in our *News*. He recognized Denmark as his country, from whence he was brought to our shores; he lived for about seventy years.

This obituary appeared in the July 1707 issue of *Nova literaria Maris Balthici et septentrionis*, a monthly literary journal for the Baltic Sea area published in Lübeck. The notice of Dieterich Buxtehude's death supplies the sole source for the approximate year of his birth—1637—and thus the story of his life begins there. The place of his birth is even less certain. Three cities come into question: Helsingør, Denmark, his home before his arrival in Lübeck and the place where his father, Johannes, served as organist for thirty-two years; Helsingborg, across the Øre Sound in what is now Sweden, the location of his father's previous employment; and Oldesloe, between Lübeck and Hamburg, the city from which his father had emigrated to Denmark. In none of these three cities do baptismal records extend as far back as 1637, but Helsingborg now appears to be the most likely choice for his birthplace.

Buxtehude's Birthplace and Ancestry

In the absence of documentary evidence, the search for Dieterich Buxtehude's birthplace can only focus upon the whereabouts of Johannes Buxtehude around 1637. Dieterich himself supplied valuable biographical information about his father on the title page of his funeral music, *Fried- und Freudenreiche Hinfahrt* (BuxWV 76), published in 1674:

> Peaceful and Joyful Departure of the old, faithful Simeon, on the occasion of the blessed death of the late, most honorable, greatly respected and artistic gentleman Johannes Buxtehude, organist for 32 years at the St. Olai Church in the royal city of Helsingör, who departed with peace and joy from this anxious and unpeaceful world in

the 72nd year of his life, on the 22nd of January of the year 1674, here in Lübeck, and was taken home by his Redeemer (for whom he had long waited with yearning), and then was buried in a Christian manner on the 29th of the same in the principal church of St. Mary. Performed out of dutiful honor and Christian praise for the blessed departed, his heartily beloved father, in two counterpoints by Dieterico Buxtehude, Organist of the principal church of St. Mary in Lübeck.

The first biographical sketch of Dieterich Buxtehude appeared in Johann Moller's *Cimbria literata* in 1744. Moller drew upon the information from Dieterich's obituary and Johannes's funeral music to conclude that Dieterich had been born in Helsingør:

Dietericus Buxtehude. Born in Helsingør in Zealand, Denmark, in the year 1637. [His] father [was] Johannes, organist of the church in that city. [D. Buxtehude] served in that same office at the church of Mary in Lübeck from the year 1669. [He] departed from the living at the age of 70 on May 9, 1707.

Two other documents, however, both unknown to Moller, place Johannes Buxtehude in Helsingborg in the year 1641. The organ in St. Mary's, Helsingborg, was renovated that year, and a commemorative plaque was attached to the organ. It read:

In the year of Christ 1641, when the councillor of the realm Christopher Ulfeldt, Lord of Rabelöf and Knight of the Order of Elephants, was royal governor, when Master Andreas Gemzö was pastor and dean, and when Kaspar Petersen W. and Jan Christian[sen] were burgomasters and Jacob Werber, Andreas Haggäsen, Matthew Matiesen and Thomas Jacobsen Gleg were city councillors, Christopher Fredriksen and Niels Larssen were teachers and Johan Buxtehude was organist, this organ was repaired and embellished, to the glory of Jehovah and the honor of the church.[1]

The Helsingborg organ was moved in 1849 to the parish church of Torrlösa, a village located between Helsingborg and Lund, where it still stands. The commemorative plaque is gone, but the organ still bears an inscription carved into a panel of the case by Johannes Buxtehude himself:

Johannes Buxtehude
Oldesloe: Holsat*us*
Organist: Helsinb:
1641[2]

From these documents it can be deduced that Johannes Buxtehude came from Oldesloe in the duchy of Holstein, that he was probably born in 1601, that in 1641 he was organist at St. Mary's in Helsingborg—at that time still part of the Kingdom of Denmark—and that he must have begun his employment in Helsingør after that date.

The archival records from Helsingør do not establish the date of Johannes Buxtehude's appointment as organist at St. Olai Church. His predecessor, Claus Feitter, was paid as organist for the year 1641–42. Feitter was still alive and bearing the title *Orgemester* in 1644, but he was dead in 1645. Johannes Buxtehude's presence in Helsingør is first documented with the baptism of his son Peter (Peiter) on 17 January 1645, but he could have been there earlier, for the city accounts from which his salary was paid are missing for the years 1642–45. Johannes Buxtehude appears to have retired from active service when his successor, Esaias Hasse, was appointed organist on 17 January 1671. The financial arrangement between them—whereby Johannes Buxtehude continued to receive the bulk of the organist's annual salary of 125 dollars—was recorded on 25 May 1671. They shared the salary for the years 1671 and 1672, but in 1673 Hasse received all of it. If Dieterich Buxtehude's statement that his father was organist in Helsingør for thirty-two years is to be taken literally, then both Claus Feitter and Johannes Buxtehude must have continued to enjoy the title of organist after their respective retirements, and Johannes Buxtehude must have first assumed his duties in Helsingør early in 1642. In any event, Helsingør appears to be excluded as Dieterich Buxtehude's birthplace.

The date of Johannes Buxtehude's arrival in Helsingborg is even less certain, since the account books begin with the year 1657 and the church record books not until 1680. His presence there is documented only for the year 1641, the year of the renovation of the organ. St. Mary's was the only church in the city at that time, and there may have been a change of organists there in 1633, since the new organist appointed that year at Our Lady's Church in Copenhagen had come from Helsingborg.

Johannes Buxtehude's presence in Oldesloe is not documented at all. Account books from the church there do exist for this period, but unfortunately many of the recipients of the payments recorded in it are named either incompletely or not at all. A new organ was built in 1624, and after that an unnamed organist is occasionally mentioned, but he did not receive a regular salary from the church, as did the schoolmaster and the calcant, or organblower. Only once, in 1631, did the organist receive a payment that may have been related to his duties, and this is the last mention of him for this period. The following year an *Orgelistken* (feminine) received 3 marks to help her take her things away. Perhaps she was the wife of an organist who had died or moved away. The vicissitudes of the Thirty Years War are reflected in these accounts by numerous small payments to pastors and others who were refugees.

During the years in which there was no regular organist in Oldesloe, the schoolmaster played the organ for the church, according to the Oldesloe historian Friedrich Bangert. Only the first name of the schoolmaster appears in the church accounts; Bangert listed one named Johannes for the years 1629–38 and again for 1640–42, and one named Friedrich for the year 1639. Shortly after Torsten Mårtensson's discovery of the "Johannes Buxtehude Oldesloe . . ."

inscription in 1928, Laurits Pedersen, a local historian in Helsingør, drew on Bangert's information to suggest in 1933 that Johannes Buxtehude and the schoolmaster Johannes in Oldesloe might be the same man. Any doubts that they might *not* be the same man had vanished by 1937, when Pedersen proposed the theory that since the schoolmaster Johannes had been in Oldesloe through 1638, Dieterich Buxtehude must have been born in Oldesloe. The Lübeck organist and writer Wilhelm Stahl rejected this theory at first but later embraced it,[3] and it appears in most later writings on Buxtehude, including Friedrich Blume's article in the first edition of *Die Musik in Geschichte und Gegenwart* and the original version of my article in *The New Grove Dictionary of Music and Musicians*. Niels Friis, however, raised the possibility that Johannes Buxtehude could have settled in Helsingborg as early as 1633, the year in which the unnamed Helsingborg organist—possibly Christoffer Schuler—moved to Copenhagen.

It might be thought that the phrase "patriam agnoscit Daniam" in Dieterich Buxtehude's obituary would shed some light on the question of his birthplace; unfortunately, it does not. The word *patria* can mean "native land," but it does not necessarily; it is derived from *pater*, father, and no matter where he was actually born, Dieterich Buxtehude would have considered Denmark—the place where his father was employed and where he grew up—as his homeland. Furthermore, the meaning of the word *Dania* could also be understood to include Oldesloe, for the king of Denmark was at that time also the duke of Holstein. Although the duchy of Holstein lay within the boundaries of the Holy Roman empire and was thus not actually part of *Dania*, some contemporary maps do show it that way. Johannes Buxtehude, however, wrote that he had come from *Holsatia*.

Although the place of Dieterich Buxtehude's birth cannot be finally settled, a review of the archival materials in Oldesloe and a consideration of Johannes Buxtehude's life in Denmark cast serious doubt on the theory that he had once been the schoolmaster in Oldesloe. The schoolmaster received 6 marks semiannually from the church from at least 1603 through the period in question, and a number of the entries indicate that he was being compensated for his services in regulating and oiling the church clock (*Seiger* in Low German). There is no mention in these accounts of any activity as an organist. Furthermore, it seems unlikely that a German schoolteacher who adjusted clocks on the side—and perhaps played the organ as well—would emigrate to Denmark and then become a respected organist there. And there can be no doubt that Johannes Buxtehude was well respected as an organist in Denmark. The commemorative plaque on the Helsingborg organ attested to that already in 1641, and records in Helsingør refer to him as a master of the organ. The congregations he served in Helsingborg and Helsingør were cosmopolitan, and their church buildings large and richly appointed, including good organs—among the better instruments in Denmark at the time. Finally, the poem that Dieterich Buxtehude wrote upon the death of his father, "Muß der Tod denn auch entbinden" (in BuxWV 76-2) clearly indicates that the son, an acknowledged master performer in 1674, respected his father's keyboard playing.

If Johannes Buxtehude was not the schoolmaster of Oldesloe, then there is no way to establish a date for his departure from that city. Possibly he was the Oldesloe organist last mentioned in 1631 or 1632, who could then have emigrated to Denmark and taken the position in Helsingborg when it became vacant in 1633. The fact that his name was inscribed on the plaque in 1641 suggests that he had been there a while, had perhaps even instigated the major renovation of that organ, as he would later do in Helsingør. He might have left Oldesloe much earlier, however, since it is doubtful that he could have received his training as an organist there. Oldesloe was an important transfer point in the trade between Hamburg and Lübeck, and both of those cities boasted superb organists with whom he might have studied, among them the Sweelinck students Jacob and Johann Praetorius in Hamburg and Peter Hasse in Lübeck. In either place he could have learned of the good opportunities for aspiring German organists in Scandinavia at that time. Whenever it was that he left Oldesloe, it seems unlikely that he was still living there after 1632 and quite probable that he was established in Helsingborg well before 1641. Helsingborg thus remains the most likely choice for Dieterich Buxtehude's birthplace.

The Buxtehude family, like many others who had settled in Scandinavia, was clearly of German origin. The family name comes from the city of Buxtehude, now part of the greater Hamburg orbit, but in the fourteenth century a small Hanseatic city in its own right. The Hansa was an association of German cities which dominated northern European trade during the late Middle Ages. Their shipping routes stretched through the Baltic and North seas from Russia and Scandinavia to Flanders and London and even into the Atlantic Ocean and the Mediterranean Sea. The contacts opened up by this trade resulted in the exchange of people and ideas as well as raw materials from the east and salt and manufactured goods from the west. The shores of the Baltic Sea (fig. 1-1)—the original home of the Hansa—played host to numerous German-speaking communities. Among the many Germans living in Helsingør in the early seventeenth century was one Franz Buxtehude, who was summoned before the authorities in 1619 for the unlawful serving of liquor in his house. There is no evidence to suggest that he was a member of the composer's family; he more likely belonged to another family that had once come from the city of Buxtehude. The same can be said for the families bearing that name who were established in Hamburg and Lübeck—the capital city of the Hansa—during the thirteenth and fourteenth centuries.

Since Johannes Buxtehude came from Oldesloe, we have little reason to doubt that he belonged to the Buxtehude family that had been living there since at least the early sixteenth century. A Dirick van Buxtehude is listed as a city councilman in the year 1517.[4] The names Frederick Buchstehude, Valentin Buxtehude, Bartold Buxtehude, Mychell Buxtehude, Hans Bucstehude, and

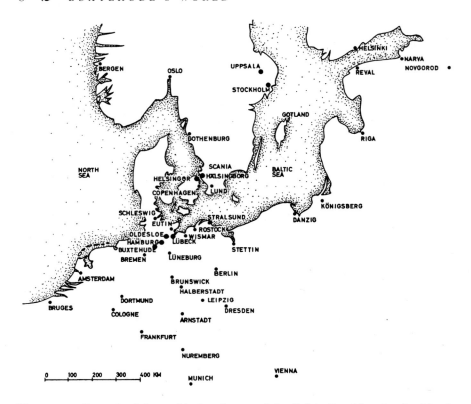

Figure 1-1. Buxtehude's world: the shores of the Baltic Sea (drawing by Martin Botsch).

Mouritz Bucstehude appear in various Oldesloe records during the sixteenth century, and the names Dirich Buxtehude, Gretye Buchstehude, Cathrina Buchstehude, and Diderich Buchstehude in the early seventeenth century.[5] When one considers that our Johannes Buxtehude, known as Hans, named two of his children Dieterich and Cathrina, the recurrence of the names Dieterich, Hans, and Catrin among the Oldesloe Buxtehudes is quite striking. Diderich Buchstehude died in 1624 and was buried with seven tolls of the church bell. Catrin Buxtehuden is listed as the owner of a house in 1626 and was still alive as a widow in 1636. Diderich and Catrin Buxtehude of Oldesloe were in all likelihood Dieterich Buxtehude's paternal grandparents.

In the Danish literature, Johannes Buxtehude is often named Hans Jensen Buxtehude. This name derives from the fact that the recipient of the organist's pay for the years 1650–51, 1651–52, and 1652–53 is listed variously as "Hanns Jensen," "Hens Jensen," and "Hanns Jennssen." By contrast, the organist goes unnamed in 1645–46 and is listed as "Hanss Buxtehude" in 1648–49 and "Hanß Orgemester" in 1649–50. In the other years prior to 1673 for which the accounts exist, the name Hans Buxtehude appears, with a variety of spellings for the last name. Of his three extant letters, two are signed "H. Buxtehude" and the third "Hans Buxtehude." The full name Hans Jensen Buxtehude appears nowhere in the seventeenth-century sources. If this was his full name, it would imply that his father's name had been Jens, not Diderich, which would conflict with what is known about the Buxtehude family in Oldesloe.

Several resolutions for this dilemma may be offered, none of which is particularly satisfactory. One possibility is that the organist Hans Jensen was actually someone else, but this explanation conflicts with Dieterich Buxtehude's statement that his father had been organist at St. Olai for thirty-two years. Another possibility is that Hans was the son of one Jens Buxtehude of Oldesloe, although no such person is known. A third possible explanation is that Hans had a double name that had nothing to do with the name of his father. The organ builder Hans Christoph Fritzsche, the son of Gottfried Fritzsche, is listed in the St. Mary's accounts of 1662 as Hanß Christofferßen. Like Gottfried Fritzsche, Hans Buxtehude's father was not personally known to the citizens of Helsingør. Finally, it should be mentioned that the city treasurer who paid the organist and kept the accounts was not a regular civil servant; the job was rotated yearly among ordinary citizens, usually two each year. Two men named Hans Jensen (or Jensøn) served as city treasurer during this period: one in 1645–46 and 1648–49, listed as a *Krydenerer*, and the other in 1665, a haulage contractor by trade (Hans Jensen is a common Danish name). Of Hans Buxtehude's German ancestry, however, there can be no doubt; he wrote fluent German, as attested by his his letter of 1648 (appendix 4, B8) to the patrons of "our Danish church."

Child in Helsingør

Helsingør was a prosperous city in the early seventeenth century, the second-largest city in Denmark. Its most famous landmark is the Kronborg—Hamlet's castle—which the kings of Denmark used to enforce their toll on shipping. The Øre Sound offered the most easily navigable connection from the Baltic to the North Sea, and it reaches its narrowest point between Helsingør and Helsingborg (fig. 1-2). The toll provided an important source of income for the royal treasury, and its collection formed the basis of Helsingør's economy. The city teemed with civil servants, soldiers, foreigners, and merchants who provided goods to the passing ships.

As a child growing up in Helsingør, Dieterich Buxtehude must have been aware of both his German heritage and his Danish surroundings. Indeed, his mother may have been Danish. We meet Hans Buxtehude's wife Helle, Jespers Daater (Jesper's daughter), for the first time at the baptism of their son Peter in

Figure 1-2. The Øre Sound in 1630, showing Helsingør with the Kronborg and Helsingborg (Helsingør Kommunes Museer).

Helsingør on 17 January 1645. Her Danish-sounding name provided a stumbling block for Stahl. In order to maintain that Dieterich Buxtehude was born in Oldesloe, he hypothesized that Dieterich's German mother had died on the trip to Denmark and that Helle was Hans Buxtehude's second wife. Both Helle and Jesper (spelled Jasper) are perfectly respectable German names, however, and at least two men named Jasper lived in Oldesloe during the seventeenth century. On the other hand, it is quite possible that Hans Buxtehude did not marry until he had secured his position in Helsingborg, in which case Dieterich's mother might well have been Danish. The family also included at least two daughters, Cathrina and Anna. Since they both appear as godparents in 1651, they were probably older than Dieterich. Cathrina may have been known later under the Danish equivalent Karren, who appears as a godparent in 1670. Dieterich himself changed the spelling of his name; he normally used the form "Diderich"—the Oldesloe spelling—in Helsingør and also in his early years in Lübeck, but later he regularly signed his name "Dieterich" in German or "Dietericus" in Latin.

Whether or not Buxtehude's mother was Danish, he undoubtedly grew up bilingual. The familial language appears to have been Danish; an invitation written in Danish by Hans Buxtehude to "Dear son Diderich" was recently found in a rat's nest during the restoration of St. Olai Church, and Dieterich wrote fluent Danish, as attested by three letters preserved from his Helsingør years. The fluency of his German, however, precludes his having learned it as an adult. His Danish seems to have faded once he moved to Lübeck; a letter of 1 September 1671 to the Helsingør burgomaster is written in German.

Among Dieterich Buxtehude's most vivid childhood memories must have been that of St. Olai, the church where his father was organist. St. Olai, named after the Norwegian saint Olaf, was the parish church of Helsingør, and it had been greatly enlarged during the fifteenth and sixteenth centuries to accommodate Helsingør's growth in population following the imposition of the Øre Sound toll in 1426. This elegant brick basilica, with its sturdy tower and tall steeple, is still one of the largest churches in Denmark. It was undoubtedly in this spacious and richly decorated church that Dieterich Buxtehude first heard the sounds of the organ and later began to play it under the tutelage of his father.

The St. Olai organ had been built, or perhaps rebuilt, in 1575 by Hans Brebos, the youngest member of the famous Flemish organ-building family. Fifty years later it had been rebuilt and enlarged by Johann Lorentz, organ builder to King Christian IV. Lorentz, like Hans Buxtehude, was a German immigrant, a native of Grimma, in Saxony. Before the 1625 renovation the St. Olai organ had seventeen stops; Lorentz added at least two stops, perhaps more. Its exact specifications are unknown; the only recorded details concern its decoration with paintings of the seven liberal arts and the nine muses. It was located high on the north wall of the nave, above the pulpit.

A major repair of the St. Olai organ in 1649–50 gave the young Dieterich Buxtehude an important opportunity to gain first-hand knowledge of the art of organ building. Hans Buxtehude had outlined its deficiencies in a letter of 27 January 1648 to the St. Olai Church Council. He wrote that the organ had been incomplete even before he had assumed his position.

> Although outwardly it has a cheerful and good appearance, first the Rückpositiv is completely mute; second, the Oberwerck is inwardly rather an inferior thing and, (God knows) needing a good renovation—in fact, it longs and sighs for it as the hart longs for flowing streams. Third, it is necessary to put some lead on the roof of the bellows room, so that the bellows can better be protected from rain and snow.

In vivid, indeed passionate German he pointed out that this was the principal church of the city, that many traveling foreigners visited it, and begged his patrons to "have mercy on this inwardly weak, very sick, indeed weeping organ and help to get it back on its feet." He invited them to come to the organ loft so they could see for themselves what the problems were.

The city fathers acceded to Hans Buxtehude's request, and Johann Lorentz was called to make the repairs in 1649. Dieterich Buxtehude was about twelve years old at that time, and one can easily imagine the interest with which he watched the master organ builder at work. Lorentz was by then about seventy years old, and he died in Helsingør during this renovation. He was buried in St. Olai on 18 June 1650, and his chief journeyman, Gregor Mulisch, completed the work. A close friendship must have existed between Lorentz and the elder Buxtehude; Hans Buxtehude participated in the settling of the estate, along with Lorentz's son, also named Johann, who had by then already achieved fame as the organist at St. Nicholas's Church in Copenhagen.

St. Olai Church owned a house for its organist, located adjacent to the churchyard on St. Anna Gade. This house, in which Dieterich Buxtehude grew up, is still standing (fig. 1-3). In its present remodeling, it is divided into two apartments; if Hans Buxtehude and his family occupied the entire house, their accomodations were spacious indeed.

The knowledge of Latin that Dieterich Buxtehude displayed in later life indicates that he must have attended a Latin school as a boy. The establishment of Latin schools for the teaching of the liberal arts and the Christian religion had

Figure 1-3. Buxtehude's house in Helsingør (Helsingør Kommunes Museer).

formed an important part of the Lutheran Reformation in Scandinavia as well as in Germany. The study of music found its place in the curriculum as part of the quadrivium, along with arithmetic, geometry, and astronomy. The instruction in music was both theoretical and practical; every pupil learned to sing. School and church were closely interrelated; the music that the pupils learned in school served both to educate them in music and Latin and to embellish the worship services in the local parish churches.

Helsingør had a good Latin school, according to Jens Lauritsøn Wolf's Danish almanac of 1654. With five classes, it was one of the larger Latin schools in Denmark; most had only two classes. Pupils began at about the age of six and progressed from one class to the next, not yearly but as they were ready to advance to the next stage of the curriculum. Pupils also remained in school for varying amounts of time; it was not uncommon for a young man of twenty still to be a pupil at a Latin school, particularly if he had a good voice or demonstrated the potential to become a teacher himself. Helsingør's Latin school employed a rector, a conrector, four teachers, and a cantor. From 1637 until 1654 the cantor at Helsingør was Johann Friccius, a German from Vollpurst, near Brunswick. Few Danish Latin schools had a cantor at that time; all the instructors were normally expected to teach music. In a school with five classes, the study of music normally began in the second class.

The Helsingør Latin school met in the former monastery of St. Mary, which had been built by the Carmelite order in the fifteenth century. This elegant complex of buildings still exists, offering the best-preserved example of monastic architecture in Denmark. Following the dissolution of the monastery at the time of the Reformation, its west wing (fig. 1-4) housed the classrooms of the Latin school, apartments for its teachers, and sleeping space for about thirty pupils who received free room and board. Boarding students came from as far away as Norway, Bornholm, and the Faroe Islands. The school was well endowed by gifts in the sixteenth century both from the king and from a wealthy citizen, Herlof Trolle. Trolle's endowment in 1577 had stipulated that the rector was responsible for leading the singing of the pupils at church, presumably monophonic music at the parish church, St. Olai. St. Mary's monastery church, forming the south wing of the complex, functioned as the church for the German-speaking community and was served by the cantor of the school. The church owned an excellent library of polyphonic music, which the pupils must have learned in school and performed in the church. Buxtehude would return to this church in 1660 to become its organist. The former monastery buildings also contained a home for aged and infirm men, providing a continuation of the social-service function that the monks had once performed.

A Danish treatise on music theory, *Heptachordum Danicum*, published in 1646, gives extraordinary insight into what Buxtehude's music education must have been like. Its author, Hans Mikkelsen Ravn, also known as Corvinus, was the rector of the Latin school in Slagelse, a city west of Copenhagen. He intended his

Figure 1-4. St. Mary's, Helsingør, west gable of the church and west wing of the Carmelite cloister, where the Latin school was located (Helsingør Kommunes Museer).

treatise to be used as a text book in Latin schools, and it probably represents the curriculum that he taught in Slagelse. Bengt Johnsson's commentary on this work has demonstrated that the *Heptachordum Danicum*, like most other compendia of its day, was almost entirely derived from other treatises, notably those of Seth Calvisius, Johannes Lippius, and Johann Crüger. These treatises are representative of the instruction in music at the Latin schools in Germany at the time, and if they were in use in Slagelse we can be quite sure that Friccius, who had presumably received his own education in Germany, used them in Helsingør as well. It is even possible that Buxtehude studied directly from the *Heptachordum Danicum*.

Ravn wrote the *Heptachordum Danicum* almost entirely in Latin, with occasional comments in Danish, particularly in chapters XX and XXI, which discuss musical terminology. He structured it as a textbook, beginning with the rudiments of notation, progressing through intervals, scales, melodies, and counterpoint, and ending with fifteen canons. The canons served as examples both for instruction in the theory and composition of music and for practice in singing. Both the title of the book and its subtitle, *Nova Solsisatio*, announced Ravn's emphasis on a modern solmisation system, which added a seventh degree to the old Guidonian hexachords, using the syllable *si* for a whole tone above the sixth degree and *sa* for a semitone. Ravn's discussion of the triad in chapter XII, based on Johannes Lippius's *Synopsis musicae* (1612), was also modern in outlook. The engraved title page of the book (fig. 1-5), however, illustrates the degree to which music was still perceived as a branch of mathematics. The *Logistica harmonica*, which Ravn appended to the *Heptachordum Danicum*—and which is not reproduced in the facsimile edition—is devoted entirely to a mathematical discussion of intervals and scales.

The approach to music articulated on the title page of *Heptachordum Danicum*—to teach the singing as well as the composition of both monophonic and contrapuntal music—reflected that of all Lutheran Latin schools. Its final chapter provides information on the cultivation of singing in the Danish Latin schools in the form of the rules for the practice of music in churches and schools written in 1573 by the rector of Our Lady's school in Copenhagen. Among them was the singing of both unison and figural music in the schools from twelve to one each day and the singing from door to door on the eves of certain feasts for the purpose of begging money. The singing from door to door included polyphonic music sung from notation, not from memory. Among the rules for deportment during this activity was the prohibition of snowball fights (*certamina cum niveis globiis*). The school choir, or half of it, could be hired to perform at weddings and funerals.

It is possible to reconstruct both the monophonic and the polyphonic repertoires from which Dieterich Buxtehude sang as a boy. Two publications from the sixteenth century—both available in modern facsimile reprintings—still defined the monophonic repertoire of the Danish church. Congregational singing in the vernacular was as important in Lutheran Denmark as it was in Germany, and the first great collection of Danish hymnody was Hans Thomissøn's *Den danske Psalmebog* of 1569. Of its 371 hymns, many are Danish translations of German hymns, but some are pre-Reformation Danish hymns and a few remain in Latin. As in Germany, some parts of the Latin liturgy were retained in Danish cities and Latin schools, and the Danish Protestant version of this Latin liturgical music is found in Niels Jespersøn's *Gradual* of 1573. It contains Latin introits, Alleluias, sequences, and responsories, and the "Te Deum" as well as a selection of Danish hymns. Ravn drew on both sources for musical examples in *Heptachordum Danicum*.

The polyphonic repertory of Buxtehude's youth can be found in an inventory of the music library of St. Mary's Church in Helsingør from the year 1659; it appears in its entirety in appendix 5A. The presence of one secular publication

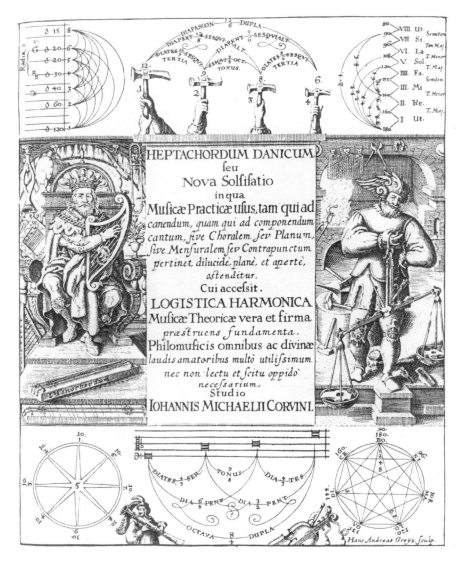

Figure 1-5. Hans Mikkelsen Ravn, *Heptachordum Danicum* (Copenhagen, 1646), Frontispiece (Copenhagen, Det kongelige Bibliotek).

on the list—Caspar Kittel's *Arien und Cantaten* (1638)—suggests that this collection of music was assembled for use in both the school and the church. Kittel, an instructor of the choirboys at the electoral court in Dresden, wrote in the foreword to *Arien und Cantaten* that choirboys could learn to sing powerfully and swiftly from the solos and duets in it. Since the cantor of St. Mary's served both the church and the Latin school, it would have been he who purchased and looked after the music for both institutions. A much shorter inventory of music belonging to the school itself in the year 1696 also exists and is given in appendix 5B. Although the works contained in it were probably purchased after Buxtehude's time as a pupil in the Latin school, some of them may have come into the collection during the years 1660–68, when he was organist at the church.

The music collection of St. Mary's, Helsingør, presented an extremely well-balanced repertoire to a schoolboy of the early 1650s. One is struck by the presence of both old and new music, Catholic and Protestant, Italian and German, many-voiced motets and few-voiced concertos. The old is represented by two venerable anthologies assembled by Caspar Hassler—the brother of Hans Leo Hassler—and Erhard Bodenschatz. Hassler's collections of sacred symphonies for from four to sixteen voices concentrated mainly on Italian composers of the late sixteenth century. Bodenschatz's famous *Florilegium Portense* collections represent the repertory used at the electoral school in Pforta, near Naumburg, during the early seventeenth century. His first volume, originally published in 1603, revised and enlarged in 1618, concentrates on motets of Jacob Handl (also known as Gallus), Orlando di Lasso, and Hieronymus Praetorius. The second *Florilegium* volume (1621) contains fifteen motets by Martin Roth, a cantor at Schulpforta who wrote in the style of Jacob Handl, but otherwise it is more Italianate in its selections than the first volume. It is not known which collection St. Mary's, Helsingør, owned, since both were published in nine partbooks, the only specification given in the inventory. Both volumes of the *Florilegium* circulated widely and continued to be reprinted until the middle of the eighteenth century; J. S. Bach twice ordered replacement copies for the St. Thomas School.

The vast majority of the motets of the *Florilegium Portense* are set to Latin texts and are scored for eight voices. Polychoral textures predominate, and it could have been through this collection that Buxtehude first became acquainted with the polychoral style, which he would later use so effectively in his Abendmusiken, performed from the six balconies of St. Mary's in Lübeck. Bodenschatz added a basso continuo to all the motets, most of which had originally been composed without one. Example 1-1 gives the *Florilegium* version of the beginning of Jacob Handl's "Hierusalem gaude," originally published in Handl's *Opus musicum* I (1586).[6]

A striking feature of the 1659 inventory of St. Mary's, Helsingør, is the fact that nearly two thirds of the publications listed in it appeared between 1640 and 1646. Much new music must have been purchased during the late 1640s and early 1650s, just the time when Buxtehude would have been a pupil at the Latin school there. Composers from North German coastal cities are prominently represented in these prints: Thomas Selle and Johann Schop from Hamburg, Caspar Movius and Johann Vierdanck from Stralsund, Paul Siefert from Danzig, and Johann Weichmann from Königsberg. The most popular composer of new

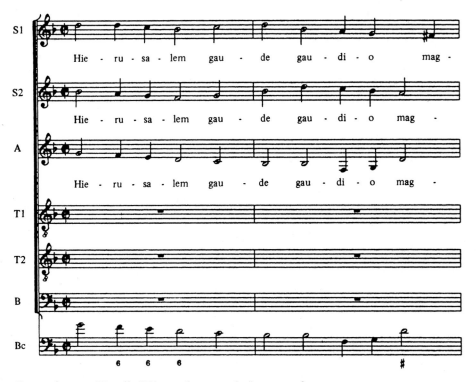

Example 1-1. Handl, "Hierusalem gaude," mm. 1–8.

music, however, was Andreas Hammerschmidt. St. Mary's owned four of his collections: parts II, III, and IV of the *Musicalische Andachten* (1641, 1642, 1646)
and the second part of the *Geistliche Dialoge* (1645). Hammerschmidt's popularity was not limited to Helsingør; he was the overwhelming favorite in all the
Danish Latin schools for which information exists. In Lübeck, too, his music
formed a basic component of the Latin-school vocal repertoire. In 1671, the
Lübeck partbooks of the *Musicalische Andachten*, part IV, needed rebinding
because they were "so torn from daily use." By contrast, the works of Heinrich
Schütz are conspicuously absent from the Danish school inventories, despite his
presence in Denmark as court Kapellmeister from 1633 to 1635 and again from
1642 to 1644.

The three volumes of Hammerschmidt's *Musicalische Andachten* found at
Helsingør contain a wide variety of motets, sacred concertos large and small,
and sacred madrigals, scored for one to twelve voices, with and without instruments, mostly set to biblical texts. Hammerschmidt's sacred dialogues are more
intimate in nature, and those of the second part contain settings of Martin

Example 1-1 (*continued*).

Opitz's poetic paraphrase of the Song of Solomon. These are not dramatic dialogues; they contain no recitative, but are rather arias for one and two voices. Where there are two voices, they alternate strophes or sing in duet style. Buxtehude's introduction to aria style, which would figure so prominently in his vocal works, could have come from a work such as example 1-2, the first section of number XI, based on Song of Solomon 7:1.

Johann Friccius was the first cantor to enjoy a long tenure at the Helsingør Latin school, and to judge from the library that he assembled, he must have given dynamic leadership to the school's music program during the years when Buxtehude was a pupil there. Accounts for the school exist only from the year 1674, a time when the city was not so prosperous as it had been, and two cantors had died in the preceding four years. Nevertheless, the outlays for music for the years 1674 and 1675 are impressive. The cantor received a small amount

Example 1-1 (*continued*).

each month, probably to pay singers and/or instrumentalists. Teachers were paid for singing in the choir. Hammerschmidt's *Kirchen und Tafelmusik* (1662) was purchased and bound into nine volumes in 1674. Purchases for the following year included some music in manuscript, paper bound into nine books for the purpose of copying music, and a new cornetto.

The Unknown Years of Apprenticeship

There can be little doubt that Buxtehude began his organ studies with his father and his academic studies at the Latin school in Helsingør, but how long he remained a pupil in Helsingør is completely unknown. No document records

Example 1-2. Hammerschmidt, "Wie schöne Fuß," mm. 1–22.

his presence anywhere until he is found in Helsingborg at the age of about twenty-one. André Pirro suggested that he might have gone to Copenhagen to study with the organist Johann Lorentz, Jr., soon after 1650, when the death of the organ builder Johann Lorentz, Sr., in Helsingør brought his son into contact with the Buxtehude family. Pirro also proposed a later apprenticeship for Buxtehude in Hamburg. Study in Lübeck with Franz Tunder would have been another possibility, and it is not out of the question that he could have completed his education in Helsingør.

Copenhagen lies only 46 kilometers south of Helsingør, and it had been an important center for the cultivation of music since the reign of Christian IV (1588–1648). This great patron of the arts had employed John Dowland as court lutenist from 1598 to 1606, had sent Mogens Pedersøn and other young Danes to study with Giovanni Gabrieli in Venice, and had twice called Heinrich Schütz to lead the music at his court. The king had recommended the appointment of Johann Lorentz, Jr., as organist of Our Lady's Church in 1629, when Lorentz was nineteen, and two years later had given him a scholarship for study in Italy and elsewhere. Lorentz returned to Copenhagen in 1634 and assumed the post of organist at St. Nicholas's Church, which he retained until his death in 1689. His study abroad must have included a stay in Hamburg, because in 1635 he married Gesa Praetorius, daughter of Jacob Praetorius, the esteemed organist of St. Peter's Church there. Lorentz was later offered that post following the death of Jacob Praetorius in 1651, but he chose to remain in Copenhagen. There he was considered the finest organist in the city; indeed, in 1670 Holger Jacobaeus wrote that as an organist he was second to none in Europe.[7] At St. Nicholas's he played an organ of about forty stops on three manuals that had been built by his father in the early 1630s. Its exact specifications are unknown, but in 1655 it was used as the model in drawing the plans for a new organ of forty stops to be built by Hans Christoph Fritzsche at Trinity Church.

The source of Johann Lorentz's fame lay in the concerts that he gave three times weekly at St. Nicholas's, which Wolf described in 1654:

> Mondays, Wednesdays and Fridays, from Easter until St. Michael's from four to five o'clock, and from St. Michael's to Easter from three to four o'clock on the same days, many beautiful pieces and hymns [are played], at which times, winter and summer, many distinguished people go to listen with pleasure.[8]

Already in 1634 the French embassy secretary Charles Ogier had praised these concerts, in which the organist "filled not only our ears, but the soul itself with the most beautiful sounds."[9] The practice of giving organ recitals apart from the liturgy was well established in the Netherlands, where Calvinist doctrine forbade the use of the organ during worship services. Jan Pieterszoon Sweelinck's students undoubtedly listened to him play many such concerts at the Oude Kerk in Amsterdam, and Lorentz would have learned of them from his father-in-law, who had studied with Sweelinck. No similar concerts are documented for Hamburg, but private arrangements may have existed between the organists and the leading businessmen, many of whom often traveled to Amsterdam. Such was the case in Lübeck, where Tunder gave concerts at St. Mary's for the business community on Thursdays before the opening of the stock exchange. Johann Lorentz's son Jacob, who had studied in Hamburg with Heinrich Scheidemann, also gave concerts three times weekly at the cathedral in Ribe, where he served as organist until 1659.

Since one would need a vast repertoire to fill three hours of concerts every week throughout the year, it is likely that Johann Lorentz's performances in Copenhagen included a great deal of improvisation. The compositions by Lorentz that survive are on a very modest scale, consisting largely of simple dance movements. They are preserved mainly in student copy books—one of which, *Uu* Ihre 285, also transmits four suites by Buxtehude—and the presence of numerous fingerings indicates that they were intended for teaching purposes, not concert performance. Only one praeludium reaches fifty measures, and it consists almost entirely of motivic interplay; there is no fugal writing. The remaining praeludia are much shorter; example 1-3, a praeludium given here in its entirety, demonstrates the paired fingering that Buxtehude would have learned as a youth, whether or not he actually studied with Lorentz. A piece such as this could have found no place on a concert program, and we must assume either that Lorentz's larger works are lost or that he never wrote them down as

Example 1-3. Lorentz, *Praeludium ex clave D* (*Uu* Ihre 284, pp. 46–47).

compositions. It is likely that his improvisations were modeled on the great wealth of organ music that was being composed in Hamburg, to which his family connections would have given him ample access.

That organ music from Germany—and that of Sweelinck's students in particular—was known in Copenhagen in the 1630s is documented by the fragments of works by Melchior Schildt, Jacob Praetorius, Heinrich Scheidemann, and others discovered in 1964 in the bellows of the organ at Clausholm castle. These music manuscripts, probably from Our Lady's Church, were used as scrap paper when the brothers Johan and Peter Petersen Botzen restored the organ in Copenhagen about 1700 before it was moved to Clausholm. This repertoire has been reconstructed and edited by Henrik Glahn and Søren Sørensen. Melchior Schildt had worked in Copenhagen as court organist from 1626 to 1629 and may have returned briefly in 1634 from his post in Hannover for the festivities surrounding the wedding of the Danish Prince Christian and Magdalena Sibylla of Saxony. The fact that Jacob Praetorius is the composer most strongly represented may indicate that Lorentz was instrumental in bringing these works to Copenhagen, but they then appear to have passed into general circulation.

As a composer, Buxtehude appears to have learned more from the works of the direct Sweelinck students, particularly Scheidemann, than from Lorentz, to judge from their surviving works. But it would most likely have been through Lorentz, acting either as mentor or as teacher, that Buxtehude first gained access to the organ works of the North German composers. And in the art of performing, he may have learned a great deal from Lorentz, either by studying with him directly or by attending his concerts. Buxtehude would himself later achieve fame as a presenter of concerts—the Lübeck Abendmusiken.

Buxtehude's presence in Copenhagen is documented for only one later occasion, in 1666, when he entered the city through its eastern gate, coming from Helsingør. The fact that the guards' journal contains no report of his having left the city at this time indicates that its records of those passing through the gates are incomplete; thus the lack of any earlier mention of Buxtehude in this journal cannot be understood to mean that he had not visited Copenhagen on previous occasions.

Whether in Helsingør or in Copenhagen, Buxtehude must have been aware of the musical trends at the Danish royal court even if he did not personally witness any court events. The time of his youth and young adulthood corresponds almost exactly to the reign of Frederick III (1648–1670). As a young prince, Frederick had spent some time in Paris, where he acquired a taste for French opera, ballet, and orchestral music. His queen, Sophie Amalia from Brunswick, was even more strongly inclined toward the French style, and their reign was characterized by lavish performances of operas and ballets, despite the fact that wars with Sweden were straining the royal budget. French singers, dancers, and string players found employment at their court. The Kapellmeister to the king during most of this time—from 1652 to 1655 and again from 1661 to 1667—was, however, a German who had been trained in Italy, Kaspar Förster, Jr. The larger works that he composed for the court are all lost, but some of his sacred concertos, oratorios, and sonatas for strings survive, and there can be no doubt that Buxtehude knew his music.

The possibility that Buxtehude may have studied in Hamburg, first suggested by Pirro, appears even more likely in the light of new information that was unknown to him: that Johannes Buxtehude was born in Oldesloe and that Dieterich Buxtehude later enjoyed a close friendship with the Hamburg composer Johann Adam Reincken. Johannes Buxtehude's birth in Oldesloe, together with the good possibility that he studied in one of the neighboring cities of Hamburg or Lübeck, increases the likelihood that he would have sent his son back to the place where he himself had received his training. This pattern can be seen in the families of other organists of German descent who were working in Scandinavia. Andreas Düben, Kapellmeister to the king of Sweden, sent his son Gustav at the age of about sixteen back to the Continent for study. Gustav Düben's sons in turn—Gustav, Junior, before the age of twenty-four and Anders at seventeen—also studied abroad. Johann Lorentz, Jr., born in Flensburg of a Dutch mother and a German father, studied in Hamburg himself at about the age of twenty-one and later sent his son Jacob there to study with Scheidemann.

From 1631 to 1651, the organists at all four of Hamburg's principal churches had been students of Sweelinck: Jacob Praetorius at St. Peter's, his brother Johann at St. Nicholas's, Scheidemann at St. Catherine's, and Ulrich Cernitz at St. Jacobi. Jacob Praetorius died in 1651, and when Johann Lorentz did not accept the position at St. Peter's, Johann Olfen was chosen. Matthias Weckmann, a student of Jacob Praetorius, succeeded Cernitz at St. Jacobi in 1655; Scheidemann remained at St. Catherine's until his death in 1663, when he was succeeded by his student Johann Adam Reincken. The most likely time for Buxtehude to have studied in Hamburg would have been from around 1654 until 1657. One can find the influence of both Scheidemann and Weckmann in Buxtehude's compositions, but Scheidemann is the more likely choice. The fact that Johann Lorentz sent his own son to study with Scheidemann suggests that he might have recommended the same course to Buxtehude; also, if Buxtehude arrived in 1654, Weckmann would still have been in Dresden. The year 1654 would have been a good time to leave Denmark, since a severe epidemic of plague occurred there that year.

Buxtehude's close friendship with Reincken, discussed in detail in chapter 4, is documented by a recently discovered painting by Johannes Voorhout (frontispiece) from the year 1674. Reincken probably studied with Scheidemann from 1654 to 1657, the most likely years for Buxtehude to have been in Hamburg. Buxtehude later demonstrated his familiarity with the treatise that circulated in Hamburg as the theoretical teaching of Sweelinck, one copy of which was written out by Reincken. The friendship between Reincken and Buxtehude and their common interest in learned counterpoint, symbolized by the canon in the Voorhout painting, could have been founded on a mutual experience as students of Scheidemann.

Lübeck would probably have appeared considerably less exciting than Hamburg to the young Buxtehude as a place to complete his musical education, but it must be considered as a possibility. The close business connections between Lübeck and Oldesloe can be seen in the fact that several Lübeck citizens contributed to the building of the new Oldesloe organ in 1624. If Johannes Buxtehude had studied with Peter Hasse in Lübeck, he might have encouraged his son to study with Hasse's successor, Franz Tunder. Tunder's compositions can be seen to have influenced Buxtehude's style, although as Tunder's successor Buxtehude would surely have become acquainted with them in any event.

In view of Buxtehude's later success, a first-class education such as Pirro proposed—beginning at the Latin school in Helsingør, progressing to study with Johann Lorentz in Copenhagen, and ending with further study with one of the great North German organists in Hamburg or Lübeck—remains a most attractive hypothesis. Johannes Buxtehude did not command a large salary, however, and the king does not appear to have been awarding stipends for foreign study at this time; the financial means may not have been available for Dieterich Buxtehude to travel to Hamburg or Lübeck to complete his education. It is thus important to recognize that the resources did exist for him to become a fully formed artist without ever leaving Denmark. Besides his father, there was another organist in Helsingør, Claus Dengel, probably only a few years older than Dieterich Buxtehude, who might have taught him. Dengel must have been a good musician; he served as organist at St. Mary's from 1650 to 1660, after which he returned to his native city of Schleswig to become organist at the cathedral there. In 1689 he succeeded Johann Lorentz at St. Nicholas's in Copenhagen, where he died in 1708.[10] Johann Lorentz was present in Copenhagen during Buxtehude's entire youth and would have been available as a teacher, mentor, or provider of music. And the compositions of Sweelinck's students, on which Buxtehude would base his own work, were available in Denmark for him to study.

Organist in Helsingborg

By late 1657 or early 1658, Buxtehude had completed his formal education, and he moved across the Øre Sound to Helsingborg to assume the same position as organist of St. Mary's Church that his father had occupied before coming to Helsingør. As its name implies, Helsingborg was the site of a medieval fortress— much older than the Kronborg in Helsingør—whose central tower still dominates the city. In the middle of the seventeenth century Helsingborg was a smaller city than Helsingør, but it too had enjoyed prosperity and growth during the first half of the century. Its population, like Helsingør's, was cosmopolitan. Just as the water route between the Baltic and North seas passed between these two ports, so the land route from the Scandinavian peninsula to the European continent led directly through them.

The two or three years during which Dieterich Buxtehude lived in Helsingborg marked one of the most difficult times in the history of the city. Denmark and Sweden had been locked in a contest for control of the Baltic Sea throughout the preceding century, and Sweden was definitely in the ascendancy. The Swedes had occupied Helsingborg from 1644 until 1645, following which the Danes had heavily fortified both the castle and the city. Denmark declared war in the summer of 1657, but its hopes for victory were dashed when the Swedish king Charles X Gustavus took advantage of an exceedingly cold winter and marched his army across the ice from Jutland to Zealand in February 1658. In the Peace of Roskilde, which was concluded shortly thereafter, Denmark ceded the province of Scania, which included Helsingborg, to Sweden. The Swedish king arrived in Helsingborg in March, and Buxtehude probably participated in the music for the welcoming ceremonies. The peace was not to last, however; hostilities broke out again in August, and the Swedes captured and occupied the Kronborg and besieged Copenhagen. The sound between Helsingør and Helsingborg was the scene of a fierce naval battle that October between the Swedes and the Dutch, who had sent a fleet to aid the Danes. The war continued until May of 1660, and at its conclusion Scania remained Swedish.

Helsingborg did not experience any actual fighting during this war, but its citizens had to quarter large numbers of soldiers—first Danish, then Swedish. Its economy suffered badly from the expense of the fortifications, the quartering of the soldiers, and the disruption of trade that resulted from the change to Swedish rule. Buxtehude does not appear to have harbored any ill feelings toward the Swedes as a result of this experience, however. A few years later he dedicated a composition (BuxWV 7) to the Swedish commissioner in Helsingør, and in 1680 he composed an aria (BuxWV 119) in honor of the marriage of King Charles XI, the son of the Swedish king who had taken possession of Helsingborg in 1658, to Princess Ulrika Eleonore of Denmark. Its text, probably written by Buxtehude himself, celebrates peace between the two countries with its refrain "the nordic lions are friends once again." In the last two strophes he expresses both his love for Denmark and his prayer for continued peace between the two countries:

4. *Freue dich, Schweden; dein Himmel geht offen.*	*Rejoice, Sweden, the sky opens up.*
Dennemarck jauchze; die güldene Zeit	*Denmark, exult, the golden time*
kömmet dir wieder vom Himmel getroffen.	*comes to you again by a stroke of heaven.*
Welchen nur lallen kann, freudig ausschreit:	*Whoever can speak, cry out joyfully:*
Die nordischen Leuen sind Freunde von neuen!	*The nordic lions are friends once again!*
Gnug ist mit Kugeln und Schwertern gekriegt;	*There has been enough fighting with cannon balls and swords;*

nun wird mit Grüssen und Küssen gesiegt.	*now victory will be achieved with greetings and kisses.*
Wo man mit sölchem Gewehre nur ficht,	*If one fights with only such weapons,*
Segen und Leben ganz reichlich aufbricht.	*Blessing and life burst out abundantly.*
5. Höchster, erhöre mein brünstiges Flehen,	*Almighty, hear my fervent prayer,*
welches aus Liebe zum Vaterland geht.	*which comes from love for my country.*
Himmelan lass diese Könige sehen,	*Up to the heavens let these kings see*
wie ihre Herrschaft in voller Blüt steht!	*how their government flourishes.*
Die nordischen Leuen müssen sich freuen!	*The nordic lions must rejoice!*
Segene dieses grossmächtigste Paar,	*Bless this most powerful couple,*
baue und mehre es Jahre für Jahr,	*build and strengthen it year after year,*
dass in der Bitte dir neulich vertraut,	*that, through recent prayer,*
Himmel und Königreich werden gebaut!	*Heaven and the kingdom may be built!*

Ironically, it was to be in Sweden that Buxtehude's music was most treasured and best preserved.

The exact date of Buxtehude's appointment in Helsingborg is not known. The oldest church accounts begin on 1 April 1657, and the organist who was paid a salary of 75 dollars (*Sletdaler*) for the year beginning on that date is not named. During the following year, according to S. A. E. Hagen,[11] "Dierich Organist" paid a rent of 12 shillings—apparently for the previous year—on a property owned by the church. As organist he was entitled to a free house, to be shared with the bellringer, but it needed repairs, perhaps because of vandalism by soldiers who had been quartered there. The accounts show that the church did make the repairs, but in 1659 someone else was living in the organist's house. Meanwhile, Buxtehude continued to pay 12 shillings in rent—a very small amount—for the other property. During this time he incurred a considerable debt of over 40 dollars to David Gjedde, a wealthy city councillor who loaned money to other musicians as well.

At 75 dollars per year, Dieterich Buxtehude earned considerably less than the 125 dollars that his father received in Helsingør. Three types of dollars were in use in Denmark at this time: ordinary dollars (*Sletdaler, Daler Möndt,* or simply *Daler*), worth 4 Danish marks or 64 shillings; *Courandtdaler,* worth 5 Danish marks or 80 shillings; and rixdollars (*Rigsdaler, Reichsthaler,* or *Speciedaler*) worth 6 Danish marks or 96 shillings. The relationship between Sletdaler and Courandtdaler is made explicit in the records of Johannes Buxtehude's pay for 1648: "Hanss Buxtehude is given each year before New Years Day in four payments, each payment 25 *Courandtdaler,* that is 125 *Dlr.*" In other words, 100 Courandtdaler and 125 Sletdaler were both equal to 500 Danish marks. The relationship between the rixdollar and the ordinary dollar is likewise shown in the payment to two organists for inspecting the completed renovation of the St. Mary's organ in 1663: together they were given 10 RDlr, making 15 Dlr, the equivalent of 60 Danish marks. The more valuable rixdollars in circulation were chiefly German Reichsthaler that had been collected in the Øre Sound tolls.

St. Mary's Church (fig. 1-6) stands in the center of the oldest part of Helsingborg, overlooking the harbor. This was the first of three churches named St. Mary's that Dieterich Buxtehude would serve during his lifetime; all three are situated near harbors and share the brick Gothic architectural style, which had spread from Lübeck throughout the Baltic area. St. Mary's, Helsingborg, had been built in the mid-fifteenth century in the form of a half basilica, with a nave and two aisles but without clerestory windows. Its richly decorated pulpit had been donated by King Christian IV of Denmark in 1615. Its altar still holds a double-winged triptych that was carved and painted in Stralsund at the time the church was built. We cannot be certain, however, that it was on display during the war years when Buxtehude served as organist.

The organ of St. Mary's that Buxtehude played was located in a gallery between two pillars of the north aisle, east of the pulpit. Abraham Hülphers listed its specifications in 1773:

Figure 1-6. St. Mary's Church, Helsingborg (Helsingborgs Museum).

Öfwerwerket	Positiw	Pedalen
Gedagt 8'	Gedagt 8'	Gedagt 16'
Principal 4' (facade)	Principal 4'	Principal 8'
Gedagt 4'	Gedagt 4'	Gedagt 8'
Nasat 3'	Qwinta 3'	Principal 4' (facade)
Octawa 2'	Super Octawa 2'	Qwinta 1½'
Wall Fleut 2'	Scharf III	Trompet 8'
Mixtur III	Dulcian 8'	Cornettin 2'
Scharf II		
Sexquialtera II		
Trompet 8'		

The organ had been renovated a number of times between 1660 and 1773, however, so Hülphers' specifications are probably not identical to those of the organ that both Johannes and Dieterich Buxtehude played. It does appear that the Rückpositiv had been added in the rebuilding of 1641, however, because changes were made to the gallery at that time.[12] Johann Lorentz was quite likely the builder responsible for that renovation. He had received an exclusive privilege in 1639 from King Christian IV to build and renovate organs in all of Denmark, and the organ case bears a striking resemblance to those of the Lorentz organs in Helsingør and Kristianstad.

Dieterich Buxtehude played this organ for only a short time before returning to Helsingør in 1660. His interest in the Helsingborg organ continued after that, however. In 1662, a major repair was completed, and Buxtehude was invited—and paid 18 dollars—to inspect it. Already, at the age of about twenty-five, he was recognized as an organ expert. The organ builder Hans Christoph Fritzsche received a large sum—681 dollars—for this work, so it may have included additions as well as repairs. This is an astounding figure, in view of the economic hardship that Helsingborg had so recently suffered. It is quite possible that Buxtehude had drawn up the plans for this renovation, but that it had been delayed because of the war. If this was the case, then some of the stops in Hülphers' list may have been installed at Buxtehude's suggestion. Fritzsche was the son of the famous Hamburg organ builder Gottfried Fritzsche; he had come to Copenhagen in 1655 to build a new, forty-stop organ for Trinity Church. He appears for a while to have filled the gap in Danish organ building left by Lorentz's death in 1650.

The old Helsingborg organ survives in part in the village church of Torrlösa, but it has suffered many indignities since Buxtehude's time, beginning with the theft of a large number of its lead pipes by the organist of the Helsingborg church in 1693. When it was installed in Torrlösa in 1850, it was rebuilt without its Rückpositiv. A restoration by the Frobenius firm in 1961–62 provided a new Rückpositiv in modernistic style (fig. 1-7) and replicated very closely the specifications given by Hülphers while extending the range to modern standards. The

Figure 1-7. Organ from St. Mary's, Helsingborg, now in Torrlösa (Th. Frobenius & Sønner).

old pipes in the organ suggest that its original manual compass contained forty-one notes, C–a″ with a short octave in the bass and lacking g♯‴, that its pedal comprised only eighteen notes, C–a with a short octave, and that it was originally pitched in Chorton. In its tonal characteristics it now resembles the aesthetic of the twentieth-century Organ Reform Movement more closely than that of Johann Lorentz or Hans Christoph Fritzsche. Meanwhile, in 2000 Robert Gustavsson and Mads Kjersgaard built a new choir organ for St. Mary's in Helsingborg that is based on a much better preserved organ, now in the Malmö Museum, that had been rebuilt by Hans Christoph Fritzsche in 1660, and that better matches the tonal qualities of the Helsingborg organ that Buxtehude played.

Organist in Helsingør

The position of organist at St. Mary's, Helsingør, became vacant in 1660, when Claus Dengel returned to his native city of Schleswig to become organist at the cathedral there. Buxtehude auditioned for the position in October of that year, along with one other applicant, a man from Landskrona, and each of them received an honorarium of 15 dollars. Dieterich Buxtehude was chosen. The Helsingør post carried a salary of 200 dollars per year, nearly three times what he had received in Helsingborg and considerably more than his father's salary of 125 dollars at St. Olai. That the organist's salary should be higher at the less important of the two churches in Helsingør seems surprising, but it is probably attributable to the fact that St. Mary's was financed in part directly by the king. Since Dieterich Buxtehude was still unmarried, the normal housing allowance of 40 dollars was cut in half, and he moved back into the St. Olai organist's house with his family. He appears to have taken over some of the responsibility for the maintenance of the house; his three preserved letters written in Danish, dated 1666 and 1667, concern repairs to this house.

When Buxtehude returned to the city of his youth in October 1660, the Swedes had only recently withdrawn from their occupation following the capture of the Kronborg in 1658. Helsingør had suffered even more than Helsingborg during this war. In addition to the heavy expenses incurred in the quartering of Swedish officers and troops, city buildings and the harbor had suffered damage during the battle for the Kronborg, and much property had been destroyed or stolen during the occupation. Furthermore, Helsingør's population had already declined during the epidemic of plague in 1654; the city did not soon return to the level of prosperity that it had enjoyed in the first half of the century.

St. Mary's Church, also known as the German church, served the foreign population of Helsingør, which included the garrison at the Kronborg, many of whom were mercenaries. The pastor of St. Mary's, traditionally a German, served also as chaplain to the Kronborg; German was the military language of the day. The pastor during Buxtehude's tenure was Just Valentin Steeman, from Hamburg. He had fled Helsingør during the Swedish occupation and had taken that opportunity to gain his licentiate degree from the university at Rostock, with a thesis entitled "Ecclesia Romana monstrum Triceps" (The Roman Church a Three-Headed Monster). A man of a definite intellectual bent, he later received doctor's degrees from both Rostock and Copenhagen.

St. Mary's, Helsingør, is the only one of the three churches Buxtehude served whose organ case can still be seen in its original place, on the west wall (fig. 1-8). Johann Lorentz, Sr., had built it as a new organ, with ManualWerk, UnterPositiv, and Pedal, around 1641. Buxtehude was apparently not satisfied with the instrument, however, for in 1662–63 Hans Christoph Fritzsche was paid 393 dollars "to make (*forfærdige*) the organ," soon after he had completed the repairs on Buxtehude's old organ in Helsingborg. Although he was paid less for the work in Helsingør, it included changing the Unterpositiv to a separate Rückpositiv and moving the console to the front of the organ, with a false Brustwerk containing two fields of wooden pipes. The organ that Buxtehude played after Fritzsche's renovation consisted of twenty-four stops, with a manual compass of CDEFGA–c‴ and a pedal compass of CDE–c′. Its specification has been reconstructed as follows:

Manualwerk	Rückwerk	Pedalwerk
Principal 8'	Gedact 8'	UnterSatz 16'
Gedact 8'	Principal 4' (facade)	Principal 8'
Octava 4'	Flöit 4'	Gedact 8'
Rohr Flöit 4'	Quint 3'	Octava 4'
Quint 3'	Octava 2'	RauschPfeiffe II
Octava 2'	Scharf III	Posaun 16'
Zifflöit 1 ½'	KrumbHorn 8'	Trompet 8'
MiksTur III–IV		Trompet 4'
Trompet 8'		
Manual coupler, Zimbelstern		

The pipework of this organ was removed in 1854 to make way for a new Marcussen organ; only the twenty-seven Principal 4' pipes in the facade of the Rückpositiv, no longer sounding, remained in place. In 1960 Frobenius built a neobaroque organ behind the old facade, including a Rückpositiv that allowed the old facade pipes to sound again. Finally, following extensive research, Marcussen & Søn reconstructed the Lorentz-Fritzsche organ in 1997, adding to the original specification a Sesquialtera in the Rückpositiv and a sounding Brustwerk with Gedact 8', Flöit 4', Gemshorn 2', Sedecima 1', and Regal 8'; the compass of the Rückpositiv and Pedal have been slightly expanded as well. The scaling, narrow and elegant, as well as the pitch—a' = 435 Hz—were derived from the original facade pipes. St. Mary's in Helsingør is now the only one of the three churches in which Buxtehude served as organist where we can gain both a tonal and a visual impression of the organ that he played.

As organist of St. Mary's, Buxtehude was expected to play at the beginning of the service while the pastor was robing himself; he and the cantor were to provide instrumental and vocal music for the church on feast days and at other times at the pastor's request. The cantor during Buxtehude's tenure was David Böeckel (1620–70), who had come from Wismar. The two men must have been on friendly terms, because Böeckel invited Buxtehude to be godfather to his son Fridericus, baptized on 1 November 1664. At the baptism of Peter Böeckel the previous year, one of the godparents had been Martin Böeckel (1610–88), a lawyer and *Ratssyndicus* from Lübeck and perhaps a cousin of the cantor, since his grandfather also had come from Wismar. Martin Böeckel had previously travelled to Copenhagen in 1648 as one of Lübeck's three delegates for the coronation of King Frederick III.[13] He was no longer in Lübeck when Buxtehude arrived in 1668, however; he had given up his position in 1666 and moved to Hamburg.[14] Nevertheless, it could have been through him that Buxtehude learned of Franz Tunder's death and the subsequent vacancy at St. Mary's, Lübeck.

Figure 1-8. Organ of St. Mary's, Helsingør (Photo [1998] by Marcussen & Søn).

Buxtehude appears to have taken his place as a good citizen in the Helsingør community. He stood several times as godfather in both St. Mary's and St. Olai Church, often with rather prominent members of Helsingør's bourgeois society. These included Henrik Henriksen, pastor of St. Olai; Gallas Glausen and David

Melvin, members of the city council; Major General Ejler Holck, commander of the Kronborg; and Sophia Schneider, the wife of the Swedish commissary Christoffer Schneider.

Buxtehude dedicated his sacred concerto *Aperite mihi portas justitiae* (BuxWV 7) to Christoffer Schneider. On its title page he describes Schneider as "his patron, a friend among few to the art of music." Buxtehude betrays himself in this ostentatious dedication as one proud of his position and of his mastery of Latin; he even slips in a Greek word as well.[15] Schneider was the Swedish postmaster in Helsingør until 1662, so Buxtehude must have composed this piece between 1662 and 1668, after which "Dietericus Buxtehude" was no longer "Ecclesiae, quae Helsingorae est Germanicae, Organista." This is Buxtehude's only extant composition that we can ascribe with certainty to the time when he was organist of the German church in Helsingør.

One of the leading musical intellectuals of Europe, Marcus Meibom, was a member of St. Mary's Church while Buxtehude was organist there. From 1664 to 1668 he held a high administrative post in Helsingør as director of customs. Prior to that he had briefly served Queen Christina of Sweden as assistant royal librarian and had also advised King Frederick III on the purchase of books for the Danish royal library. His personal library was extensive and comprehensive; an auction catalogue of part of it that he prepared in 1705 included books on theology, law, medicine, botany, philosophy, mathematics, history, geography, literature, and dictionaries of foreign languages. Books on music are listed in the mathematics division and include works by Glareanus, Zarlino, Zacconi, Artusi, Doni, Picerli, and Lippius.[16] His own major contribution to musical scholarship is his *Antiquae musicae auctores septem* (1652), which presents editions of Greek music theory translated into Latin. One can imagine that Buxtehude cultivated Meibom's acquaintance and learned from him.

When the opportunity arose for Buxtehude to go to Lübeck to fill one of the most prestigious organist's posts in Germany, he was ready. During his years in Denmark—possibly with an interlude in Hamburg or Lübeck—he had achieved a solid grounding in performance, organ construnction, and composition. As a youth in Helsingør, he had watched Johann Lorentz rebuild his father's organ; as a young organist, he had inspected one organ restored by Hans Christoph Fritzsche and had worked with him personally on the renovation of another. He had acquired experience playing church services for cosmopolitan congregations in Helsingborg and Helsingør. And he had learned the theory behind his art, first at the Helsingør Latin school and later perhaps from Meibom. On 16 March, 1668, his successor, Johan Radeck, was appointed at St. Mary's, Helsingør, "in the place of the previous organist, who has now been called to Lübeck."

Chapter Two

Lübeck: The City

Dieterich Buxtehude made Lübeck his home for nearly forty years, and it was there that he achieved his fame as a composer and performing musician; the designation "Organist in Lübeck" is found after his name in widely scattered manuscripts. The position of organist and Werkmeister at St. Mary's had become vacant upon the death of Franz Tunder on 5 November 1667. This was a much more prestigious and better-paying position than the one Buxtehude had held in Helsingør. The combined annual salary of organist and Werkmeister at St. Mary's, Lübeck, including a clothing and meat allowance, amounted to 923 Lübeck marks, or more than 307 rixdollars, the currency common to Lübeck and Denmark. This represented more than twice his Helsingør salary of 200 dollars, which was equivalent to just over 133 rixdollars.

Two other organists had auditioned before Buxtehude was chosen, Johann Schade from Hamburg in December and Johannes Stanislaus Boronski from Schönenberg in Poland early in February. Buxtehude's formal selection did not occur until 11 April 1668,[1] but he must have been assured of the post prior to that, since his successor in Helsingør had already been appointed on 16 March. Buxtehude was present in Lübeck no later than 19 March, when he acted as god-father for a child of the bell ringer Hanß Beede. Within a few months he took the two remaining steps that would establish him as a full member of this community: he became a citizen of Lübeck and a married man. In this chapter we will be concerned with the secular aspects of Buxtehude's life in Lübeck: his family, the larger environment in which he lived and worked, and his direction of those concerts so special to Lübeck, the Abendmusiken, an activity that lay outside his official duties as organist of St. Mary's. His work at St. Mary's will be the subject of chapter 3.

Citizen of Lübeck

Buxtehude swore the oath of citizenship on 23 July 1668, paying a fee of 7 rixdollars and displaying his armor for the defense of the city. His witnesses were Amelinck Hansen and Sebastian Spangenberg, both businessmen. Men were required to become citizens before they could marry, set themselves up in business, or become masters in a trade. As citizens, they were obliged to do watch duty, but in practice they often paid others to do it for them.

In 1668, Lübeck was already a city of great historical importance. From the time of its final founding in 1159 by Henry the Lion, duke of Saxony, it had been a center of trade, and the history of the German Hansa is sometimes considered to begin with the founding of Lübeck. The city's location at the most southwesterly point on the Baltic Sea suited it well for its role as the center of northern European trade in the late Middle Ages. No sooner had its Westphalian settlers completed the building of their houses than they built ships and sailed to the island of Gotland, where they made arrangements with the Gotlanders to participate in the trade with Russia. By the fourteenth century, the Hansa of German towns—among them Cologne, Dortmund, Bremen, Hamburg, Braunschweig, Rostock, Stralsund, and Danzig—had replaced the earlier association of individual merchants. Under the leadership of Lübeck, the Hansa had established *Kontore* in Novgorod, Bergen, Bruges, and London, where its merchants enjoyed significant trade privileges. It reached the height of its power in 1370 with the Peace of Stralsund, the conclusion of a war with Denmark that left the Hansa in control of the Øre Sound and the castles that defended it, including the one at Helsingborg.

Lübeck's prosperity had grown with that of the Hansa. In 1226 it had become an imperial free city, owing its allegiance directly to the Holy Roman emperor and not to any intervening lord. By the mid-thirteenth century its walls were in place, and its city hall and five large churches had risen in their earliest forms. Following devastating fires in 1251 and 1276, brick was the only building material permitted, and Lübeck's characteristic brick-Gothic cityscape began to emerge. Its wealthy businessmen built large, gabled houses that functioned not only as residences but also as offices and storerooms for their far-flung enterprises. The character of Lübeck's leadership changed during the fifteenth century, however, from one of bold initiative to a more conservative stance. Later, during the sixteenth century, changing trade patterns—particularly the ascendancy of the Dutch and English merchant marine—shattered the primacy of the Hansa in northern European trade.

When Buxtehude arrived in Lübeck in 1668, he found both the city and the Hansa in the midst of crisis. Lübeck had been spared any actual fighting during the Thirty Years War, but its economy had suffered and it had gone heavily into debt as a result of rebuilding its fortifications and maintaining its neutrality by making financial contributions to the opposing powers. The city council, then made up exclusively of patricians and the upper strata of businessmen, had imposed new taxes in 1661, and the rest of the population was in a state of rebellion against them. The matter was resolved in 1669 with a new constitution that gave the smaller businessmen, tradesmen, and handworkers some voice in the government. 1669 also marked the last meeting of a Hanseatic diet in Lübeck. As an association of cities subject to various political rulers, the Hansa had found itself unable to compete with the strong national powers that were emerging. Increasingly, its members were unable even to agree among themselves on economic policy. Of seventy large towns and over one hundred smaller ones that had formed the Hansa during the fifteenth century, only nine sent representatives to Lübeck in 1669, and their discussions proved inconclusive. A year after Buxtehude's arrival in Lübeck, the Hansa was dead; all that remained was a loose alliance among Lübeck, Hamburg, and Bremen, all three of which still proudly call themselves Hanseatic cities.

The strong contrast between the past glory and the present reality of Lübeck may have struck Buxtehude as it did William Carr, the English consul in Amsterdam, who left an account of his visit to Lübeck, which probably took place in the mid-1670s:

From Hambourg I went to Lubeck, which is also a Commonwealth and Imperiall town. It is a large well built city containing ten parish Churches; the Cathedrall dedicated to St. Peter being in length 500 foot, with two high spires all covered with brass, as the rest of the churches of that city are. In former times this city was the place, where the deputies of all the Hansiatick towns assembled, and was once so powerfull as to make war against Denmark and Sweden, and to conquer severall places and Islands belonging to those two Crowns, nay and to lend Ships to England and other Potentates, without any prejudice to their own trade, wherein they vied in all parts with their neighbours; but it is now exceedingly run into decay not onely in territories, but in wealth and trade also. And the reason of that was chiefely the inconsiderate zeal of their Lutheran Ministers, who perswaded the Magistrates to banish all Roman Catholicks, Calvinists, Jews, and all that dissented from them in matter of Religion, even the English Company too, who all went and setled in Hambourg, to the great advantage of that city and almost ruine of Lubeck, which hath not now above 200 Ships belonging to it, nor more territories to the State; than the city it self and a small part called Termond [Travemünde], about eight miles distant from it. The rest of there territories are now in the possession of the Danes and Swedes, by whom the burghers are so continually allarmed, that they are quite tired out with keeping guard and paying of Taxes. The city is indeed well fortified; but the government not being able to maintain above 1500 Soldiers in pay, 400 Burghers in two Companies are obliged to watch every day. They have a large well built Stathouse, and an Exchange covered, on the top whereof the globes of the world are painted. This Exchange is about fifty yards in length, and but fifteen in breadth; over it there is a Roome where the skins of five Lions which the burghers killed at the city gates in the year 1252, are kept stuft. The great market-place is very large, where a monumentall stone is to be seen, on which one of their Burgemasters was beheaded for running away whithout fighting in a sea engagement. The people here spend much time in their Churches at devotion, which consists chiefely in singing. The women are beautifull, but disfigured with a kind of Antick dress; they wearing cloaks like men. It is cheap living in this town; for one may hire a palace for a matter of 20 L. a year, and have provisions at very reasonable rates: besides the air and water is very good, the city being supplied with fountains of Excellent fresh water, which Hambourg wants; and good ground for cellarage, there being cellars here fourty or fifty foot deep.[2]

The "large well-built city" described by Carr can be seen in an etching from the workshop of Matthias Merian (fig. 2-1), published in 1641. Lübeck lies on a

Figure 2-1. Lübeck, view of the city from the west. Engraving by Matthäus Merian, 1641 (Museen für Kunst und Kulturgeschichte der Hansestadt Lübeck).

peninsula formed by a sharp turn southward by the river Wackenitz before it flows into the Trave. Merian's view is from the west, and the heavy fortifications on this side protected not only the city but also its harbor on the river Trave. The Trave flows into the Baltic at Travemünde, about twelve miles to the northeast; the two ships to the right in the picture are sailing upstream toward Oldesloe. Of the ten churches, only the five large ones had functioned as parish churches since the Reformation. The cathedral—dedicated to John the Baptist, not Saint Peter—is the twin-spired church farthest to the right; to its left are the single towers of St. Aegidien and St. Peter's. St. Mary's, the official church of the city council, stands with its two towers at the central and highest point in the city, rather like a sentry guarding the harbor. To its left is the monastery church of St. Catherine's, with a roof spire but no tower; since the Reformation this monastery building had housed Lübeck's Latin school, whose choir sang in St. Mary's. The remaining tower is that of St. Jacobi, the parish church of the seafarers and fishermen. These seven towers still define the skyline of Lübeck; the two churches to the north of St. Jacobi were torn down early in the nineteenth century.

Lübeck's harbor, the heart of its economy, is depicted in an ink drawing by C. H. Hustede from the mid-nineteenth century (fig. 2-2). On the quay in the foreground, lying between the harbor and the fortifications, we see the city lumberyard. Ingots of iron from Sweden are leaning against the city wall, which remained in place until 1853. Through it a small gate opens to Alfstraße, which leads up the hill to St. Mary's. Many similar gates cut through the wall, but there were only four main gates to the city through the outer fortifications. The Mühlentor to the south and the Hüxtertor to the east were removed during the nineteenth century, but the sturdy twin-towered Holstentor to the west and the graceful Burgtor to the north still command the entrances to the inner city from Hamburg and Travemünde.

The churches of Lübeck were both the principal attractions and the repositories for the antiquities and works of art that Conrad von Höveln described in a guidebook published in 1666 for the benefit of both inhabitants and visitors. A revised edition of the guidebook appeared in 1697 under the title *Die Beglückte und Geschmückte Stadt Lübeck*.[3] Besides the churches, the city hall (*Rathaus*), with its wine cellar, is the only building described in any detail. The city also boasted an armory containing rare weapons and beautifully polished armor, a shipbuilding yard, a variety of inns and pubs, a water system, a foundry, and a fireworks factory.

Carr ascribed Lübeck's state of decline to religious intolerance, which did in fact exist. Calvinists and Roman Catholics received the rights of citizenship only in 1811, and Jews not until 1848. Hamburg's reception of Calvinist religious refugees was a factor in its greater economic vitality at this time, but hardly the only one. Hamburg's greater proximity to the Atlantic was a distinct advantage as the modern age dawned, just as Lübeck's location on the Baltic had been

Figure 2-2. Lübeck, harbor at the lower Trave by Alfstraße. Drawing by C. H. Hustede, before 1848 (Museen für Kunst und Kulturgeschichte der Hansestadt Lübeck).

during the Middle Ages. Lübeck's economic stagnation could also be attributed to its general inability to adjust to new trade patterns, in particular its continued adherence to the old Hanseatic "guest law," which limited the rights of foreigners to trade within the city and forbade its citizens to enter into partnerships with foreigners. Although Lübeck had been second in population only to Cologne among medieval German cities, it was now only half the size of Hamburg; Carr lists the number of its houses at 6,500, compared with 12,500 for Hamburg.

Despite the undeniable decline from its peak of greatness during the thirteenth, fourteenth, and fifteenth centuries, Lübeck remained a city of considerable wealth and an important center for shipbuilding, shipping, and wholesale trade. Its population stood at about 27,000.[4] And among its businessmen were some who were innovative and forward-looking, such as Thomas Fredenhagen, who began to engage in extensive Atlantic trade in the late 1660s and thereby rose from fairly modest beginnings to become one of the city's wealthiest businessmen.[5] In 1697 he donated an elaborate marble high altar to St. Mary's Church, carved by the Antwerp artist Thomas Quellinus at a cost of 2,659 Lübeck marks, the largest gift to the church since the Reformation. Wholesale trade would continue to dominate Lübeck's economic, political, and social life into the nineteenth century, and nowhere is the social milieu of bourgeois Lübeck better depicted than in Thomas Mann's novel *Buddenbrooks*. The character Edmund Pfühl is said to be modeled closely on Hermann Jimmerthal, organist at St. Mary's from 1845 to 1886. In the novel, Gerda Buddenbrook engaged Pfühl to come to her house every Wednesday afternoon to accompany her violin playing on the piano. Pfühl also gave piano lessons to the young Hanno and invited him to the organ loft of St. Mary's to draw stops for him. Pfühl's relationship with the Buddenbrook family can be considered analogous to that of Buxtehude with his patrons in the Lübeck business community.

The florescence of music in seventeenth-century Lübeck must be considered remarkable in view of the fact that in every other area of intellectual and artistic endeavor, the city had lost the role of leadership it had formerly enjoyed. Lübeck's decline in intellectual leadership coincided with the fall of the Low German language from the lingua franca of the entire Baltic region to a dialect spoken mainly by the lower classes. Lübeck's Reformation had been carried out in Low German, but its literary monuments—Johann Bugenhagen's *Kirchenordnung* (1531) and translation of the Luther Bible (1534) and the hymnal of Hermann Bonnus (1545)—became the last great expressions of this language there. From about 1600, the Lübeck church used only High German. In Oldesloe, the church accounts of the 1630s were still being written in Low German, but Hans Buxtehude wrote High German, as did his son.

The conservatism that generally characterized Lübeck's economic affairs during the seventeenth century was even more pronounced in the realm of religion; Lübeck stood as a bastion of Lutheran orthodoxy until well into the eighteenth century. The chief religious leader of the city was the superintendent, defined by Bugenhagen as "a scholarly man, learned in the holy scriptures, to whom the entire city could turn in questions of conscience, if the other pastors and preachers are not able to instruct their parish members sufficiently."[6] The four superintendents who held office during Buxtehude's tenure were all learned men and staunch upholders of Lutheran orthodoxy. The first of them, Meno Hanneken, had studied theology at Wittenberg and had been a professor of theology at Marburg for twenty years before coming to Lübeck as superintendent in 1646. He concerned himself particularly with preserving the confessional unity of the city against dissidents of any kind. When he died in 1671, Buxtehude honored him with funeral music in strict contrapuntal style, a setting of the chorale "Mit Fried und Freud ich fahr dahin" in invertible counterpoint (BuxWV 76-1). For Hanneken's son, a theology student also named Meno, Buxtehude had already composed a contrapuntal work of a lighter nature, a canon with the text—in French—"let us divert ourselves today, let us drink to the health of my friend" (BuxWV 124). Buxtehude left no clues concerning his relationships with the later superintendents.

Below the level of the strict orthodoxy of its ministers, the first manifestations of the movement that would later be known as Pietism had appeared in Lübeck with the organization of conventicles in 1665 and again in 1666. In both cases these meetings had been outlawed by the city council, but a group of people—mainly women—who wished to enrich their spiritual lives by meeting together apart from the official church had identified itself. From 1675 to 1676 the theologian Johann Wilhelm Petersen (1649–1727), a native Lübecker, resided in the city, hoping to obtain a preaching position. He had close ties with Philipp Jakob Spener—author of the *Pia desideria* (1675), which later gave the Pietist movement its name—and Petersen transmitted Spener's ideas to the Lübeck spiritualists. Although he was soon forced to leave Lübeck, Petersen maintained his contacts there from his later positions in Eutin and Lüneburg. The famous Pietist leader August Hermann Francke (1663–1727) was also born in Lübeck; he returned briefly in 1690, hoping to be hired as a preacher, but was instead denounced as a heretic. He was nevertheless allowed to preach twice there, once at St. Mary's. Two years later Adelheid Sibylle Schwartz, a leader of the Lübeck Pietist group, was banished from the city as a result of her prophecies against the superintendent August Pfeiffer, an energetic opponent of Pietism.

Buxtehude was undoubtedly aware of the Pietist sentiments abroad in Lübeck, but it is unlikely that he ever became an active participant in the conventicles. Pietism remained an underground movement in seventeenth-century Lübeck, and Buxtehude's professional life required a good relationship with the religious establishment, which in Lübeck—unlike Hamburg and Lüneburg—included no pastors of Pietist persuasion. Nevertheless, a number of the texts that he set, including one by Petersen in BuxWV 90, reflect the intense spirituality cultivated by the Pietists. These texts are discussed in chapter 5, where the broader implications of the Pietist movement and Buxtehude's relationship to it are explored further.

Buxtehude's Marriage

Once he had become a citizen of Lübeck, Buxtehude was free to marry and set up his household. On the ninth Sunday after Trinity, 19 July 1668, the banns were read in St. Mary's for his marriage to Anna Margaretha Tunder. The wedding was celebrated on Monday, 3 August, at the home of Johann von Essen, a silk retailer who owned the house at 1 Mengstraße, across the street from St. Mary's. Daniel Baerholtz, a member of the Elbe-Swan Order literary society, composed a poem—lost since 1942—in honor of the occasion. There were seventy guests, twice the permissible number.

Wedding celebrations were carefully regulated by Lübeck's sumptuary laws, under which the number of guests at Buxtehude's wedding was limited to thirty-five and cake could be served but not wine. Lübeck's society was divided into six classes, of which Buxtehude belonged to the fourth, together with lesser wholesalers, retailers, and brewers. In the first class were the burgomasters, syndics, council members, and patrician families, the members of the Circle Society. Below them stood the company of leading businessmen, and in the third class the wholesalers organized into companies—such as *Schonenfahrer, Novgorodfahrer, Rigafahrer, Stockholmfahrer*—and also the cloth cutters. Ship captains and members of the four greater guilds—smiths, tailors, bakers, and shoemakers—belonged to the fifth class; the members of the lesser guilds, hucksters, and seamen belonged to the sixth. In addition to the number of guests and refreshments, the value of gifts between the bride and groom, the contents of the bride's trousseau and hope chest, and the number of musicians who could play at the wedding were regulated according to class.[7] Trumpeters and timpanists were permitted to play only for members of the first class. The *Spielgreve*, appointed by the city council, attended all weddings and enforced the law. Buxtehude would normally have been permitted no more than three musicians plus a player of the positive organ, but in view of his position as the leading musician in Lübeck, it would not be surprising if all seven municipal musicians were present.

Buxtehude's bride, Anna Margaretha Tunder, had been baptized in Lübeck on 11 August 1646 as the second daughter of Franz Tunder, Buxtehude's predecessor. It is possible that Buxtehude's willingness to enter into this marriage had been a factor in the decision by the church council to hire him, but it is unlikely that Tunder himself had laid down the condition, as Buxtehude would later do for his own successor. Had there been a prior agreement between him and Buxtehude, it is unlikely that the church would have auditioned other candidates.

It was by no means uncommon in that time and place for a man to marry the daughter or widow of his predecessor in his occupation. The great violinist Nathaniel Schnittelbach had married the widow of his predecessor, Paul Bruhns, when he became a municipal musician in Lübeck in 1655. An agreement appears to have existed between Johann Lorentz and Jacob Praetorius whereby Lorentz would receive his father-in-law's position at St. Jacobi, Hamburg, on the latter's death, although Lorentz later declined it. William Carr mentioned this practice in his account of his visit to Hamburg:

> I shall onely take notice of some peculiar customs they have, wherein they differ from Holland. When a Barber, shoe maker, or any other Artizan dies, leaving a widow and Children, another of the same trade is not admitted to set up for himself as a master; unless he compound with the widow for a piece of money, or else marry her, or a daughter of hers with her consent.[8]

Whether a formal requirement or not, the expectation that a young man would accept the responsibility for those left behind by his predecessor provided a form of social security at that time. Franz Tunder had left a widow and two unmarried daughters; his oldest daughter was already married to Samuel Franck, cantor of St. Mary's.

St. Mary's had a further policy for the care of the widows of its employees, much of it at the successor's expense. During the customary "year of grace" the widow received her late husband's entire salary. After that, as a stipulation of his contract of employment, the church required Buxtehude to pay Elisabeth Tunder 100 rixdollars yearly, which represented nearly one-third of his cash salary. Buxtehude repeatedly asked to be relieved of this heavy burden and finally reached a private agreement with his mother-in-law in 1678.

Dieterich and Anna Margaretha Buxtehude made their home in the Werkmeister's apartment in St. Mary's *Werkhaus*, a building on the south side of the church yard. Its location was the same as that of the present *Werkhaus*, which replaced the old one in 1903. A staircase led directly from the church yard to their apartment on the second floor. During the summer of 1675 the church built an addition to the *Werkhaus* in order to provide a study for Buxtehude. Their home was most conveniently located, adjacent to Weiter Krambuden, a small street leading directly to the central marketplace. A woodcut of the marketplace from about 1580 (fig. 2-3) depicts the bustling commercial activity at the center of the city. The imposing city hall, built in three distinct sections from the thirteenth through the fifteenth centuries, forms its northeast corner. Beneath its arcades twenty-six goldsmiths had their shops, an indication of the wealth remaining in Lübeck even in a time of decline.

Family and Social Life

Seven daughters were born into the Buxtehude family and baptized at St. Mary's. The first daughter, Helena, died in infancy, and the church records concerning her baptism and burial stand in conflict. The baptismal records of St. Mary's do not list the names of the children baptized before September

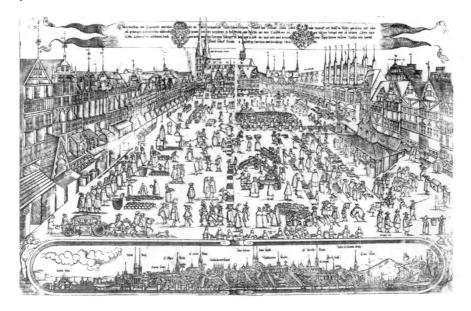

Figure 2-3. Lübeck, marketplace about 1580 (Museen für Kunst und Kulturgeschichte der Hansestadt Lübeck).

1669, but Diederich Buxtehude appears as the father of a daughter baptized on 24 July 1669. Baptisms of other children on 14, 17, and 22 July precede hers on the page. The church did not keep a register of deaths at this time, but all burials of parish members appear in the church accounts, since fees for burial provided a principal source of income for the church. For the week beginning Sunday, 11 July 1669, we read:

> Monday [12 July], with the approval of my lords the directors, I buried my little daughter Helena Buxtehude in the grave in the wall before the door, with the ringing of bells for a child.

Buxtehude himself kept the accounts as part of his duties as Werkmeister, and it is unlikely that he would have made an error concerning an event of this magnitude. Since she could not have been baptized nearly two weeks after she had been buried, the error must lie in the baptismal records, in which other irregularities occur at about this time. No baptisms are recorded between 27 August and 27 September 1669, and a note explains that this entire month had been left out through carelessness and lack of diligence, as had also been the case from 1668 to 1669. It seems quite possible that these baptismal records were entered after the fact, copied perhaps from separate sheets of paper, and that Helena was actually baptized in June rather than July. A second Buxtehude daughter was baptized the following year, and here too an irregularity occurs in the record. The name of the child baptized on 15 July 1670 was originally entered as Helena Elisabeth, but Helena is crossed out and replaced by Margreta, which in turn is crossed out and replaced by Magdalena. This daughter died in early adulthood and was buried as Helena Elisabeth on 16 November 1692.

Five other daughters were born to Dieterich and Anna Margaretha Buxtehude, of whom two died in early childhood: Anna Sophia, baptized on 8 April 1672, buried on 9 April 1675, and Maria Engel, baptized on 7 April 1686, buried on 6 April 1687. Three daughters lived in the Buxtehude household from their birth until after the death of their father: Anna Margreta, baptized on 10 June 1675, a second Anna Sophia, baptized on 30 August 1678, and Dorothea Catrin, baptized on 25 March 1683.

Buxtehude's family was enlarged by the arrival of his father, Hans Buxtehude, from Helsingør, probably in 1673. He had retired as organist of St. Olai in 1671, but he continued to receive part of his salary during 1672. His wife, Helle, died and was buried in Helsingør on 27 December 1671. He himself died in Lübeck on 22 January 1674 and was buried in St. Mary's a week later. His son Dieterich demonstrated the love and respect that he felt for his father by composing the words and music of an elegy (*Klag-Lied*) of seven strophes, "Muß der Tod denn auch entbinden," and publishing it together with the contrapuntal setting of the chorale "Mit Fried und Freud"—composed three years earlier for the funeral of Meno Hanneken—as his father's funeral music, both parts under the title *Fried- und Freudenreiche Hinfahrt* (BuxWV 76).

Dieterich Buxtehude's brother Peter, a barber by trade, moved to Lübeck from Helsingør in 1677. In November of that year he borrowed 300 Lübeck marks from St. Mary's Church at 5 percent interest in order to take over the barbershop of the late Berent Buck. He became a Lübeck citizen on 14 February 1678, with his brother standing witness for him, and a few days later he married Elisabeth Buck, widow of the barber whose business he had bought.

Buxtehude's extended family included his Tunder in-laws, with whom he had close working relations. His sister-in-law Sophia Augusta born in 1644, was married to the cantor Samuel Franck, Buxtehude's partner in music-making at St. Mary's. His brother-in-law Johann Christoph Tunder, born in 1648, had kept the accounts at St. Mary's following Franz Tunder's death and continued to do so during all of 1668, even after Buxtehude was appointed Werkmeister. Johann Christoph later studied law and worked as a notary; he also owned a brewery. Buxtehude's sister-in-law Dorothea Tunder, born in 1652, never married; she lived with her mother in the widow's apartment at the St. Mary's *Werkhaus* and continued to live there following Elisabeth Tunder's death in 1680. Perhaps she helped her sister Anna Margaretha in caring for the Buxtehude children.

We can gain a slight glimpse into the familial and social relationships of Dieterich and Anna Margaretha Buxtehude from the baptismal records of their daughters. Three persons regularly stood as godparents to every child, two women and a man for female children. Sophia Augusta and Samuel Franck, Dorothea and Johann Christoph Tunder, and Peter Buxtehude each acted once as godparent; only Elisabeth Buxtehude is unrepresented among the siblings and in-laws. The remaining godparents to Buxtehude's children were nearly all prominent members of the Lübeck business community, or more often their wives, since female godparents were in considerable demand for the Buxtehude family. St. Mary's was the parish church for the section of Lübeck in which the foremost families lived, and the four church directors always came from these families, often acting simultaneously as city councilmen or burgomasters, of which there were four. It is not surprising, then, to find these people acting as godparents to the children of the organist and Werkmeister of the church.

To meet some of the godparents of Buxtehude's children is to be introduced to the upper level of Lübeck society, to attend a wedding where wine and pastries were served and the musicians could include trumpet players. Matthäeus Rodde (1599–1677), a leading member of the business aristocracy, was a burgomaster and director of St. Mary's; his wife Catharina was godmother to Helena Buxtehude in 1669. His daughter Margreta Catrina and his son Matthäeus junior (1626–74), a director of St. Mary's, served as godparents to Anna Sophia in 1672. Another son, Adolf Matthäeus Rodde, was a lawyer and later a burgomaster; his wife, Engel, stood godparent to Maria Engel in 1686. Engel Rodde was the daughter of the burgomaster Johann Ritter, also a director of St. Mary's, whose wife was godmother to the second Anna Sophia in 1678. The syndic David Gloxin (1597–1671), burgomaster and director of St. Mary's, had masterminded the new constitution of 1669; his wife, Anna, was godmother to Helena Elisabeth in 1670. We have already met Thomas Fredenhagen; he served as a director of St. Mary's from 1681 to 1709, and his wife, Maria, was godmother to Maria Engel in 1686. Other members of prominent Lübeck families who served as godparents to the Buxtehude children included Margaretha Balemann, wife of the pastor of St. Mary's; their nephew Heinrich Balemann; Thomas and Margreta Plönnius; and Caspar von Deginck's wife, Margaretha.

We must not forget that Buxtehude belonged to the fourth class of Lübeck society. The fact that the godparents to his children were drawn from the leading families does not mean that he socialized with them as an equal. They did not invite him or his wife to be a godparent for their children. In performing this service for his family they were according him a measure of respect, but they probably never lost sight of the difference in their ranks. For his part, in inviting them to serve as godparents—and in some cases naming his children after them—Buxtehude was also cultivating their patronage for his musical enterprises. We can still see a small part of this patronage through the few surviving compositions that they commissioned from him, works such as *Auf, Saiten, auf!* (BuxWV 115) for the wedding of Caspar von Degingk's daughter Dorothea, or *Gestreuet mit Blumen* (BuxWV 118) for the wedding of Johann Ritter's daughter

Anna Margaretha. Ritter must have been an especially generous patron, for Buxtehude dedicated his second volume of published sonatas to him. The extent to which Buxtehude gave musical instruction to the children of the leading families and performed chamber music in their homes is unknown.

A letter that Buxtehude wrote to the burgomaster of Helsingør in 1671 reveals that he was a generous man who took his social responsibilities seriously. Margreta Fechter, the daughter of Claus Fechter (or Feitter), his father's predecessor at St. Olai, was living in Lübeck and had suffered serious illness and financial misfortune.

> So she had nothing with which to conserve her life and sought help from me, which out of Christian love I provided her time after time with money in cash, so that it has become fifty rixdollars as of 28 December 1670.

This was an enormous sum for a young father who was supporting his mother-in-law as well, and he enclosed her promissory note in hopes of restitution from her conservators in Helsingør.

Of the three children who survived him, Anna Margreta was the famous daughter for whom Buxtehude laid down the condition that his successor must marry her. She reached the age of thirty-two before her marriage to Johann Christian Schieferdecker, announced on the ninth Sunday after Trinity (21 August) and celebrated 5 September 1707. Anna Margreta gave birth to a daughter, Johanna Sophia, in 1708 but then died on 18 December 1709. Dorothea Catrin, the youngest Buxtehude daughter, married—without benefit of the marriage condition—an organist from Braunschweig, Johann Caspar Winkler, on 12 September 1707. The middle daughter, Anna Sophia, married a spice dealer, Johann Nicolaus Herman, in 1713 but was divorced from him three years later.

Buxtehude's descendents through his granddaughter Johanna Sophia Schieferdecker included several Lübeck musicians. Johanna married Jürgen Sandberg, organist of St. Aegidien Church and also a municipal musician, in 1734. Her son Gerhard Friedrich, born in 1743, became organist at St. Peter's. Her daughter Catharina Magdalena, born in 1736, married Johann Gottfried Kuntzen, son of the St. Mary's organist Johann Paul Kuntzen and successor to his father-in-law as organist at St. Aegidien. Among their children was Johann Carl Kuntzen, a great-great grandson of Dieterich Buxtehude, who worked as a private music teacher (*Informator in der Musik*) in Lübeck.

Musical Life in Lübeck

As organist of St. Mary's, Buxtehude commanded the most prestigious, best-paid musical post in Lübeck. As a skilled musician, however, he was not without peers;

Lübeck boasted an excellent band of municipal musicians who greatly enhanced the musical environment of the city. Without their participation in his musical enterprises, he could not have achieved the degree of fame that he enjoyed.

The seven municipal musicians, or *Ratsmusikanten*, together with two *Feldtrompeter*, one *Ratspfeiffer*, and a *Ratstrommelschläger*, formed the elite corps among Lübeck's instrumentalists, those who were directly employed by the city council. Although the salary from the city was not great—600 Lübeck marks per year to be divided among the seven municipal musicians—the positions were eagerly sought after because they carried with them the assurance of employment at numerous private affairs, particularly weddings. In addition, the municipal musicians received a separate salary from St. Mary's Church for their services there to the cantor and organist. Other instrumentalists also resided in Lübeck and were enrolled in the musicians' guild. They earned their living playing in the churches and at weddings, and for this reason they were known as the *Chor- und Köstenbrüder*.

Lübeck had been known as an important center of string playing since the appointment of Nikolaus Bleyer (1591–1658) as a municipal musician in 1621. Bleyer, himself a pupil of the English violinist and viol player William Brade, established himself as a renowned teacher during his long tenure in Lübeck until his death in 1658. His pupils included Paul Bruhns, who became a municipal musician in 1639, Johann Gabriel Schütze, who distinguished himself as a municipal musician in Nürnberg, and Nathaniel Schnittelbach, the greatest of the Lübeck violinists. Schnittelbach, born in Danzig in 1633, came to Lübeck in 1655 from the Swedish royal court to fill the position of municipal musician left vacant by the death of Paul Bruhns. Schnittelbach studied with Bleyer until the latter's death and achieved fame himself both as a virtuoso performer and as a teacher. The most important of his pupils were Thomas Baltzer, who studied only briefly with him before departing for England, and Nicolaus Adam Strungk, whose violin playing later impressed both Emperor Leopold I in Vienna and Corelli in Rome. With Schnittelbach's sudden death in 1667 at the age of thirty-four, the most notable phase of the Lübeck violin school had passed.

Although he did not arrive in Lübeck until after Schnittelbach's death, Buxtehude was nevertheless able to experience the legacy of the Lübeck violin school through Peter Bruhns, the one pupil of Schnittelbach who remained in Lübeck and became a municipal musician. Peter Bruhns, born in 1641, was the youngest son of Paul Bruhns and the grandson of Nikolaus Bleyer. He was at the same time the stepson of Schnittelbach, who had married Anna Bleyer Bruhns, the widow of his predecessor. Peter Bruhns served as a municipal musician from 1669 until his death in 1698. His playing must have pleased Buxtehude, for according to Mattheson "he achieved such skill on the viola da gamba, and especially on the violin, that he was very highly esteemed by all musicians who were alive at that time and knew him."[9] Peter Bruhns was in turn the uncle of Nicolaus Bruhns, who came to Lübeck in about 1682 at the age of sixteen to study violin with his uncle and organ and composition with Buxtehude. Although he is remembered chiefly as an organist, Nicolaus Bruhns was also a worthy member of the Lübeck violin school. Mattheson continues:

> Because he was very strong on the violin and knew how to play it with double stops, [making it sound] as if there were three or four of them, he had the custom now and then of making a variation at the organ, playing the violin simultaneously with an appropriate pedal part, all by himself, in a most pleasing manner.

The cultivation of extreme versatility is probably the attribute that most distinguishes the professional musicians of Buxtehude's day from those of our own. Perhaps the most versatile of all the musicians who worked with Buxtehude was Hans Iwe, one of the two municipal musicians whose special job it was to assist Buxtehude at the large organ in St. Mary's. In his initial application for a position as municipal musician in 1672, Iwe wrote that

> in the beginning I learned to play music on all kinds of instruments from Hinrich Höpfener, a municipal musician here, and afterwards I sang with the late Schnittelbach at weddings and other events, and I often substituted for the late Cronenberg on the bass violin. Otherwise, through the grace of God, I practiced my art so diligently, that I do not hesitate to play violin, viola da gamba, violone, all manner of woodwinds, cornetto, dulcian, trombone, bass trombone and flutes in a suitable manner; also if necessary I can serve with keyboard and vocal music.

He was not appointed immediately, but received an expectancy for the next position. The following year the position of municipal drummer was open, and Iwe wrote that "I also have a pair of kettledrums of my own, and I have practiced diligently to play them from written music, and without bragging I can say that I play them well." That position was given instead to Daniel Grecke, whose principal instrument was the violin. Iwe began to work with Buxtehude at St. Mary's in 1674 and was appointed a municipal musician in 1675, serving until his death in 1692.

The other musician who assisted Buxtehude regularly at the large organ was Johann Philip Roth. In applying in 1668 for the position vacated by the death of the lutenist Joachim Baltzer (brother of Thomas), Roth wrote that "I have served his late serene highness, Duke Augustus of Braunschweig-Lüneburg, for twenty-three years as lutenist and musician on the French and German lute, the viola da gamba, violin and pandora, together with several other instruments that I play." Roth served from 1669 until his death in 1712.

From 1678 until 1692—precisely those years from which the most of Buxtehude's music for voices and instruments survives—the membership of the corps of municipal musicians remained constant. In addition to the three already introduced—Bruhns, Iwe, and Roth—they included Hinrich Höppner, Jacob Hampe, Peter Zachow, and Christoffer Panning. Hinrich Höppner wrote in 1652 that he had studied with the Lübeck cornettist Hans Frese before leaving the city to work in other places, principally Stralsund. In a renewed application the following year he added trombone and violin to his list. He was probably appointed in 1655 and served until his death in 1702. Jacob Hampe was born in Lübeck in 1636, studied with the violone player Zacharias Cronenberg until the age of eighteen, and then "brought his art to perfection for eighteen years in Denmark, Norway, Holland, England and many other places in the [Holy] Roman empire." On Cronenberg's death in 1672 Hampe was working in Stralsund, and his brother Adam, a civil servant in Lübeck, applied for the position on his behalf. He was appointed in 1675 and served until his death in 1702. In his application of 1669 Peter Zachow wrote that "through the grace of God I have learned my art on all instruments, but principally on the cornettino, cornetto and trombone." No letter of application survives from Christoffer Panning, so his instruments are unknown. He served from 1672 until 1698.

At least two of these musicians, Hans Iwe and Peter Zachow, were active as composers. Between them they composed the melodies for the devotional songs in a collection of poems and songs written by Christian von Stökken and published in 1678 under the title *Klahre Andeutung Und wahre Anleitung. . . .* The complete title of this work may be translated:

> *Clear Indication and True Instruction to the Imitation of Christ, by Rejection of Worldly Vanity and Overcoming of Adverse Events by Considering the Divine Sweetnesses; Taken from Three Books of Thomas à Kempis in Such a Manner, also Decorated with Thirty-eight Devotional Songs, and Almost as Many New Melodies, That Henceforth All Can Be Read without Error, Understood without Hindrance and Profitably Used for the Practice of Devotion by True Protestant Christians.* By Christian von Stökken, Interim Court Preacher and Superintendent to His Serene Highness, the Bishop of Lübeck.

The court of the bishop of Lübeck was in Eutin, and the book was published in Plön. The devotional songs are reminiscent of earlier songs written by Johann Rist and set to music by Johann Schop, the leading municipal violinist in Hamburg from 1621 until his death in 1667.

Songs such as those of Rist-Schop and Stökken-Iwe-Zachow were associated chiefly with music making within the home. Although in many homes the music-making probably consisted only of devotional singing, that was certainly not the case in the homes of professional musicians. Mattheson tells in the *Ehrenpforte* of a visit by Rist—who lived in Wedel, east of Hamburg—to the home of Christoph Bernhard, in order to hear some professional house music:

> In the year 1666 the world famous Johann Rist came to Hamburg, really for the purpose of experiencing the delight of the renowned music there. An excellent concert was given for him in Bernhard's house, in which, among other things, a beautiful sonata by [Kaspar] Förster Jr. with two violins and one viola da gamba was played, in

which each had eight measures to play his free improvisations, according to the *Stylo phantastico.*

Samuel Peter von Sidon also played a solo on the violin, and Rist said that he surpassed Johann Schop by far. The degree to which this diversion pleased him can be read in his last Monthly Conversation, which appeared before his death, and also in the second part of the Rejection of Vanity and Pleasure of the World. The following year Rist died. . . .

In the same year 1667 the Kapellmeister Förster came to Hamburg and visited our Bernhard. They performed a Latin work of Förster's composition, A.T.B. He had brought the alto, a castrato, with him from Copenhagen. Bernhard sang the tenor; Förster [sang] the bass and played continuo at the same time.

The vocal work by Förster would have been a sacred concerto, not a devotional song. Similar performances of both vocal and instrumental music must have taken place in the homes of the professional musicians of Lübeck.

In addition to whatever private chamber music Buxtehude played with the Lübeck municipal musicians, he worked professionally with them in a number of ways: in the Abendmusiken, in performances during the services at St. Mary's, at weddings, and probably playing dinner music in the homes of the business aristocracy. One work in particular exploits the prized versatility of the municipal musicians: *Mein Gemüt erfreuet sich* (BuxWV 72). Its instrumental scoring calls for a seemingly large orchestra of four violins, four cornetti, two recorders, three dulcians, two trumpets, and three trombones; these instruments appear in succession, however, and the work could be played by five versatile instrumentalists. In like manner, when Buxtehude called for twenty-five violins to play in unison, as in the lost *Templum honoris,* he seems to have been counting on the fact that whatever their specialty, most professional musicians could also play the violin.

Buxtehude's working relationship with the municipal musicians appears to have been good; in any event, there is no record of complaints against him such as the municipal musicians brought against the St. Mary's organist Johann Paul Kunzen in 1736. They accused Kunzen of claiming a privilege in the composition of wedding serenades, of charging too high a price for them—a minimum of 100 Lübeck marks—and of assuming the character of a *Director musices* over the musicians. Both the musicians and Kunzen invoked Buxtehude's memory in their defense. The musicians wrote that Kunzen's excellent predecessors had charged only 30 to 36 Lübeck marks for a wedding serenade; Kunzen replied that Buxtehude had always called himself *Director* on the texts for his Abendmusiken.[10] This is not the case for the three printed texts that survive, however, in which Buxtehude designates himself simply as organist. On the title page of the sonatas, opus 2, and of the lost wedding serenade *Opachi boschetti* (BuxWV 121) he calls himself *Direttore dell' organo,* and the Latin equivalent of this expression appears in his obituary in the *Nova literaria Maris Balthici.*

Kunzen, on the other hand, called himself "*Direttore della Musica*" on the title page of his 1739 Abendmusik, *Belsazar*.[11]

That Buxtehude considered himself a partner in music making with the municipal musicians can be seen in the text that he composed for the wedding of Anton Winckler, the senior burgomaster, in 1705. The final lines of *O fröhliche Stunden, o herrlicher Tag* (BuxWV 120) read:

O möcht es gefallen nur was wir hie bringen	*O may what we bring here be pleasing;*
Die Gönner zu Ehre, wir treten hervor	*We step forward to honor the patrons,*
Ich Diener der Orgel, und mit mir das Chor.	*I servant of the organ, and with me the choir.*

The work consists of a strophic aria for soprano and continuo, followed by a ritornello for two oboes and continuo and preceded by a "Sonatina forte con molti Violini all unisono."[12] The word *Chor* clearly indicates a band of instrumentalists, including many players of the violin and perhaps the soprano soloist as well. In this context Buxtehude designates himself most modestly as the "servant of the organ."

The Abendmusiken

With respect to the presentation of the annual concert series in Lübeck known as the Abendmusiken, Buxtehude was definitely the director of all the music, even if he chose not to state that fact in the printed librettos that have survived. He organized the entire production, composed the music, raised the necessary funds, chose the singers and instrumentalists, and conducted the performances. In this aspect of his professional life he functioned as a musical entrepreneur, and his experience as Werkmeister of St. Mary's must have qualified him well to manage the business of producing the Abendmusiken. The people of Lübeck recognized him as the director of the Abendmusiken and took pride in the renown that he thereby brought to their city. In its tour of St. Mary's Church, the 1697 edition of the Lübeck guidebook makes this statement when it reaches the west wall:

> On the west side, between the two pillars under the towers, one can see the large and magnificent organ, which, like the small organ, is now presided over by the world-famous organist and composer Dietrich Buxtehude. Of particular note is the great Abend-Music, consisting of pleasant vocal and instrumental music, presented yearly on five Sundays between St. Martin's and Christmas, following the Sunday vesper sermon, from 4 to 5 o'clock, by the aforementioned organist as director, in an artistic and praiseworthy manner. This happens nowhere else.[13]

At this point in the original 1666 edition of the guidebook, von Höveln describes Franz Tunder as a "talented and widely praised master of the organ" but mentions nothing about the Abendmusiken. Tunder had in fact initiated the practice of presenting concerts in St. Mary's at least as early as 1646, but the format described in 1697—which was maintained in Lübeck until 1810—was the creation of Buxtehude.

The earliest account of the Lübeck Abendmusiken comes from Caspar Ruetz, cantor at St. Mary's from 1737 to 1755, in his engaging book *Refutation of Prejudices Concerning the Nature of Contemporary Church Music and the Life Style of Some Musicians*, published in 1752. As the only near-contemporary source, Ruetz is worth quoting at length; if he appears less than enthusiastic about his subject, it is because as cantor he had nothing to do with the Abendmusiken other than to allow the organist to use his choir from St. Catherine's school.

Since we have been considering theatrical music, it will not be out of place, nor disagreeable to the reader if I give here a short report about the so-called Lübeck Abendmusiken. These Abendmusiken, which are given every year in St. Mary's Church from the large organ, are not just theatrical, but a complete *Drama per Musica*, as the Italians say, and the singers would only need to act for it to be a sacred opera. The poet uses a biblical story as the basis and constructs it according to the rules of theatrical poetics, dividing it into five parts, which are performed on as many Sundays, namely on the last two Sundays of Trinity and on the second, third and fourth Sundays of Advent. In our times they have begun to observe the rules of theatrical poetics closely. Great poets have occupied themselves with the preparation of the Abendmusiken, among whom our famous Conrector Mr. Lange is now the usual Abendmusik poet. The composer has never failed also to give an artistic and beautiful setting. However, it cannot be denied that there is something unnatural about a performance in which a story that takes place within a day or even part of a day is brought to completion only after several weeks. But the conditions of the time will not allow otherwise, and neither the poet nor the composer is to blame. It is also a great inconvenience that the Abendmusiken are held at such an unfriendly and bleak time of year, namely in the middle of the winter, so that after one has already spent three hours in the cold one must freeze for a fourth hour as well. The atrocious noise of the mischievous young people and the unruly running and romping about behind the choir take away all the enjoyment that the music might have given, to say nothing of the sins and wickedness that takes place under cover of darkness and poor light.

One can learn nothing definite about the origins of the Lübeck Abendmusiken. I have tried for a long time in vain. Even in the most complete and extensive reports about Lübeck, such as our great historian Jacob von Melle has written, there is nothing about the origins of the Abendmusiken. I suspect, however, that they did not result from an explicit order of the authorities, nor do they appear to have any public function of the usual sort, because no one can show any particular reason or occasion as to why they should be held, especially at this time. There is no holiday that the church celebrates, no thanksgiving for particular divine favors, no birthday or anniversary of an emperor that would require such festivity. Nor can the Abendmusiken be considered part of public worship, because the worship service ends with the hymn "Nun Got Lob! es ist vollbracht" and with the Benedicamus Domino. . . .

I have spoken with a 90-year-old man who can remember that in his youth these concerts were held during the week, on a Thursday. According to this man, the noise and uproar during the music were even worse then than now. That was the reason why these concerts, doubtless with the permission of the authorities, were changed to the above-mentioned Sundays. This situation, namely, that these concerts were held during the week, on Thursday, gives some credibility to the tradition regarding the origins of the Abendmusiken. To wit: in former times the citizenry, before going to the stock market, had the praiseworthy custom of assembling in St. Mary's Church, and the organist [that would have been Tunder] sometimes played something on the organ for their pleasure, to pass the time and to make himself popular with the citizenry. This was well received, and several rich people, who were also lovers of music, gave him gifts. The organist was thus encouraged, first to add a few violins and then singers as well, until finally it had become a large performance, which was moved to the aforementioned Sundays of Trinity and Advent. The famous organist Diederich Buxtehude decorated the Abendmusiken magnificently already in his day. The oldest Abendmusik of his that I have seen is from 1681. His successor, Mr. Schiefferdecker, did not fail to maintain the reputation of these concerts and even augment it. But our admirable Mr. Kuntze has brought them to the highest level. He has gotten the most famous singers [both male and female] from the Hamburg opera; he has even employed Italian women. So if one is to believe this oral tradition, the Abendmusiken have grown to such greatness from humble beginnings. But whether their foundation lies in the Glory of God or in self interest; likewise, whether it might not be more pleasing to God if the resources that are used for the Abendmusiken were used for proper church music, so that it might be better and more important—these are questions that I would rather leave for someone else to answer.[14]

Although Ruetz's account of the origins of the Abendmusiken was admittedly based on shaky evidence, its main points can be substantiated by other information. The Lübeck stock exchange did in fact meet out of doors in the market from its founding in 1605 until 1673. The archives of the Schonenfahrer record the decision taken on June 13, 1672, that

a Börse be built out of the clothiers' guild hall, which is now empty, because that place will be very suitable for the purpose, so that the merchants may have a more comfortable place to hold the regular stock-exchange meeting, especially with the burning heat at midday in the summer, and the unpleasant snow, hail, rain and storms during fall and winter.[15]

With its location adjacent to the market, St. Mary's Church, the parish church for the leading businessmen in the community, would have been the logical place for them to assemble before the stock-exchange meetings before 1673. And one of the "rich people who were also lovers of music" who encouraged Franz Tunder to add instruments and voices to his concert offerings can in all likelihood be identified: Matthäus Rodde, a director of St. Mary's Church and godfather to Tunder's son Johann Christoph in 1648.

Rodde was one of the more progressive of Lübeck's businessmen, engaging early in the Atlantic trade, both in wine with Portugal and in whaling around Greenland. In late 1663 he formed part of a three-man Lübeck trade delegation to Stockholm, and in 1664 the earliest copies of Tunder's vocal music now in the

Figure 2-4. Lübeck, St. Mary's Church before 1942, showing northwest balcony built in 1669 (Kirchenkreis Lübeck der Nordelbischen Evangelisch-Lutherischen Kirche, Kirchenbauamt).

Düben Collection in Uppsala were made in Stockholm. It appears that Rodde brought the exemplars for these copies with him on that trip, thus beginning a commerce in music manuscripts between Lübeck and Stockholm that would later rise to mammoth proportions with the copying of the majority of Buxtehude's extant vocal works in Stockholm.

When Buxtehude assumed his position at St. Mary's, he not only inherited a tradition of church concerts in Lübeck established by Tunder, he also brought with him a familiarity with Johann Lorentz's concerts at St. Nicholas's Church in Copenhagen. Buxtehude must have had ambitious plans for concert-giving at St. Mary's from the very beginning of his tenure there. Within a year of his arrival he had had two new balconies installed near the large organ at the west end of the church, each paid for by a single donor. The north balcony, shown in figure 2-4, was donated by Jeronymus Moller, the south balcony by Peter Haecks. Neither man belonged to the church council. These new balconies, together with the four that were already there, could accommodate about forty singers and instrumentalists.

The balconies by the organ lay in the domain of the organist; they were used for the Abendmusiken and for the music that he directed during church services, principally during the distribution of communion. The normal liturgical music of the church services, however, was directed by the cantor and performed from the principal choir loft of the church, located above the rood screen at the east end. Four years after the completion of the new balconies, Buxtehude noted in the account book the purchase in November 1673, with the authorization of Matthäus Rodde Jr., of "two trumpets for the embellishment of the Abendmusik, made in a special way, the likes of which have not been heard in the orchestra of any prince, where otherwise everything in noble music is advanced." Since this was the same year that the stock exchange got its indoor quarters, this purchase may mark the shift of the Abendmusiken to Sundays in the Advent season. No later than 1675 a schedule of five Abendmusiken concerts must have been in place; a request was made to the church directors the following January that any new members appointed to the municipal musicians be required to play all five Abendmusiken from the large organ, at the organist's expense. Some of the dramatic Abendmusiken in the following years did not fill five evenings, so the remaining concerts may have consisted of performances of instrumental or mixed instrumental and vocal music, in the manner of the earlier stock-exchange concerts. In 1692 Buxtehude noted that only four performances had taken place; the first was canceled due to the death of his daughter Helena Elisabeth, who was buried on 16 November that year.

The first evidence for Buxtehude's presentation of a dramatic work in the Abendmusiken dates from the year 1678: the libretto for a two-part oratorio, *Die Hochzeit des Lamms*. Its complete title page (fig. 2-5) may be translated as follows:

The Wedding of the Lamb and the Joyful Reception of the Bride to It in the Five Wise [Virgins] and the Exclusion of the Ungodly from It in the Five Foolish Virgins, as It is Told by the Bridegroom

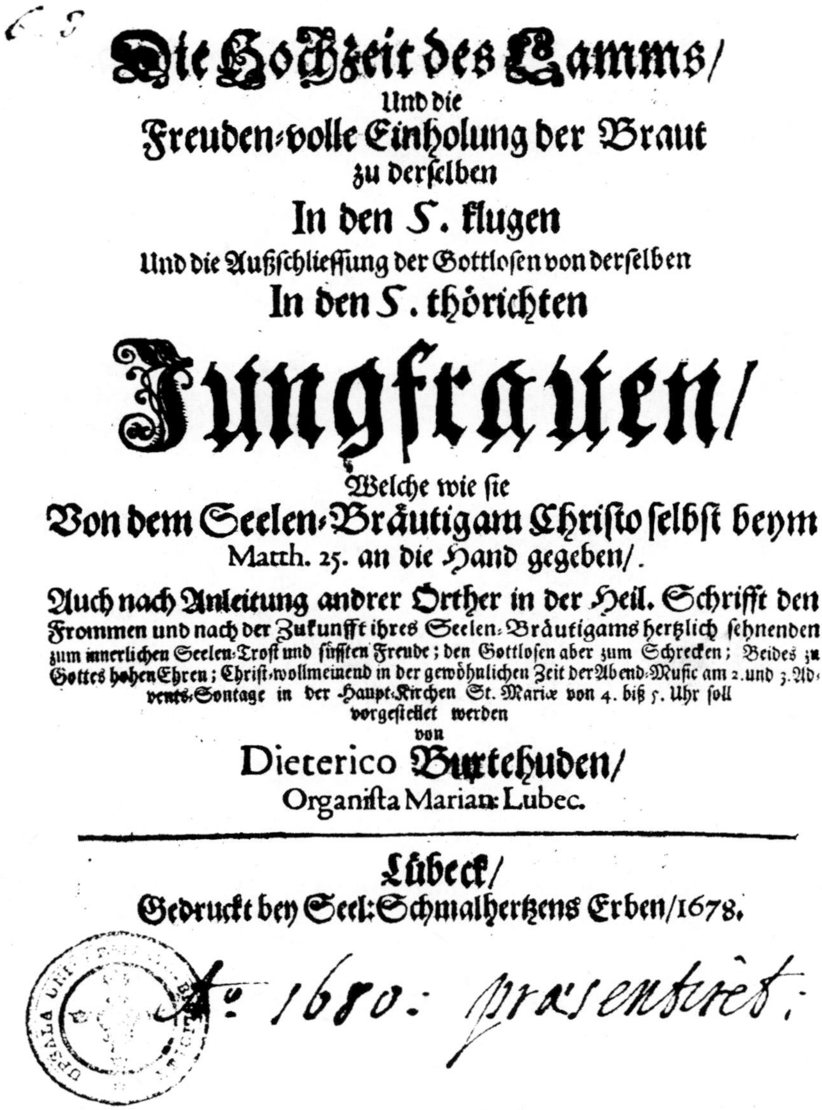

Die Hochzeit des Lamms/
Und die
Freuden-volle Einholung der Braut
zu derselben
In den 5. klugen
Und die Außschliessung der Gottlosen von derselben
In den 5. thörichten
Jungfrauen/
Welche wie sie
Von dem Seelen-Bräutigam Christo selbst beym
Matth. 25. an die Hand gegeben/.
Auch nach Anleitung andrer Orther in der Heil. Schrifft den Frommen und nach der Zukunfft ihres Seelen-Bräutigams hertzlich sehnenden zum innerlichen Seelen-Trost und süssten Freude; den Gottlosen aber zum Schrecken; Beides zu Gottes hohen Ehren; Christ-wollmeinend in der gewöhnlichen Zeit der Abend-Music am 2. und 3. Advents-Sontage in der Haupt-Kirchen St. Mariæ von 4. biß 5. Uhr soll vorgestellet werden
von
Dieterico Buxtehuden/
Organista Marian: Lubec.

Lübeck/
Gedruckt bey Seel: Schmalhertzens Erben/1678.

Ao 1680: praesentiret:

Figure 2-5. Buxtehude, *Die Hochzeit des Lamms,* 1678. Libretto (Uppsala Universitetsbibliotek).

of the Soul, Christ Himself, in Matthew 25, and in Other Passages of Scripture, [to provide] Inner Consolation of the Soul and Sweetest Joy to the Pious and Those who Heartily Long for the Future of their Bridegroom of the Soul, but Fright to the Ungodly; Both to the High Honor of God [and] in Christian Sincerity to be Presented by Dieterico Buxtehude, Organist of [St.] Mary in Lübeck, in the Customary Time of the Abend-Music on the second and third Sundays of Advent in the Main Church of St. Mary from four until five o'clock. Lübeck, Printed by the Late Schmalhertzen's Heirs, 1678.

The words "presented in the year 1680," handwritten by Buxtehude on the title page of the Uppsala copy of the libretto, suggest that this work was performed again in the Abendmusiken of 1680. Johann Moller cites a print of this work—presumably also a libretto—dated 1681. His source was a catalogue, however, and the date may be a misprint; it seems unlikely that Buxtehude would present the same work three times in four seasons. Furthermore, Moller also names a collection of librettos, *Abend-Musick in IX. Theilen. Lub. 1678–1687.* It apparently contained nine works from ten seasons, allowing for only one repeat performance.

The text of *Die Hochzeit des Lamms*[16] gives an embroidered version of the parable of the wise and foolish virgins, using a mixture of biblical passages, familiar hymn texts, and newly composed poetry. The characters are both biblical—Jesus, the wise virgins, the foolish virgins, the angels—and allegorical—the church. Some portions of the text are reflective and not assigned to any particular character, but only to a vocal part. The chorale texts are drawn from "Wie schön leuchtet der Morgenstern," "Jesu meine Freude," and "Wachet auf, ruft uns die Stimme." The new poetry includes a love duet for Christ and the Church, who is the bride:

Ich bin dein und du bist mein.	*I am thine and thou art mine.*
Du bist mein und ich bin dein,	*Thou art mine and I am thine,*
Ewig sol die Liebe seyn.	*Our love shall be eternal.*

Jürgen Heidrich has argued convincingly that Johann Wilhelm Petersen could have been the author of this libretto. While still a student at St. Catherine's school he had apparently composed a poem for Buxtehude's wedding,[17] He passed through Lübeck in the summer of 1678 on his move from Hannover to Eutin, and he later published a devotional treatise with nearly the same title, also based on the parable of the wise and foolish virgins.

The scoring calls for six solo voices, a heavenly choir, eleven violins, three violas, three viole da gamba, two trumpets, and trombones. A bass consistently sings the role of Jesus, two sopranos the wise virgins, and two altos the foolish virgins. The role of the church, however, is sung first by the entire chorus, then by an alto, and finally by a soprano. The angels vary from two sopranos to three voices. Among the instruments, the eleven violins playing at one time probably represent the total number of instrumentalists, given the versatility of the municipal musicians. The heavenly choir could have consisted of either all the vocal soloists or the cantor's choir from St. Catherine's school, making the total number of performers—apart from the continuo players—as few as seventeen or, with the *Cantorei*, considerably more. Among the continuo instruments was probably the 16′ regal that the church had purchased the previous January for Buxtehude's use in his music for feast days and his Abendmusiken.

The scope of the Abendmusiken expanded in 1679 both in length and number of performers. Buxtehude was unable to cover his costs with the donations from the business community, and St. Mary's Church contributed 100 Lübeck marks the following February to help him. He gratefully noted in the account book the receipt of the money

> for the recently held Abendmusik, in consideration of the extensive work and the great exertion, both in composing and in writing, which used up 400 bifolios; also the large number of assisting instrumentalists and singers, almost forty people, and other similar costs, which were poorly recompensed by the citizenry.

The instruments used in this work included three shawms and two recorders, which had been purchased from Hamburg in September for this purpose.

For the Abendmusiken of 1682, Buxtehude presented a work of more limited scope than he had originally intended. The first of ten preserved letters from Buxtehude to the administrators of the businessmen's collective treasury—the Lübeck Chamber of Commerce, as it were—dates from February, 1683:

> [Outer address:] To the most honorable, greatly respected and noble assembled Gentlemen, Seniors and Directors of the Spanish Collections, also Directors of the honorable businessmen's *Dröge* here. My most highly honored gentlemen and esteemed patrons:

> Most honorable, greatly respected and noble, especially honored gentlemen and esteemed patrons.

> To the same I say once again most dutiful thanks for the considerable assistance extended to me last year in compensation for the costs related to the Abendmusik at that time. Although in the most recent time [I] have not been able to present as complete a work as [I] wished and intended, on account of impediments which have occurred, nevertheless [I] have the most respectful confidence in my highly and widely honored gentlemen, that they will have kindly accepted the little that has been presented and will further manifest their good will toward me—already so laudably shown—for more encouragement of a fuller and larger work in the future, to demonstrate that such [good will] will stimulate me not only for the work desired of my office, but also for particular service to my most highly honored gentlemen, both collectively and individually. Committing myself to the protection of divine grace, [I] am and remain

> the most obliging servant of my highly honored gentlemen,

> Dieterich Buxtehude
> signed by his own hand

> Lübeck,
> 7 February 1683

This short letter (fig. 2-6), deemed too insignificant for publication by the first editor of Buxtehude's letters, contains a number of important facts: that Buxtehude considered the work performed in 1682 to have been smaller— probably both in length and in scoring—than he had wished; that the presentation of the Abendmusiken lay entirely or for the most part outside his official duties as organist of the church, being rather a "particular service" to his patrons in the business community; and that this patronage consisted of both a donation from the collective treasury and support by individuals.

The church accounts contain further information concerning the Abendmusiken of 1682:

> Inasmuch as . . . a bass by the name of Jean Carl Quelmaltz had to be brought from Hamburg for the recently presented Abendmusik, since the singers in the choir (*Cantorey*) of this school at the present time have been poor, and I could not use them, so I have paid 23 rixdollars in charges spent for the bill at the inn and also to content the aforementioned bass with a gratuity. But because this has caused great damage to my resources, in view of the present bad times and very small reimbursement by the citizenry, my highly honored directors have been so good as to come to my assistance with 10 rixdollars from the church, which is hereby accepted with grateful thanks and entered into the account.

The church's subsidy of 30 Lübeck marks for the 1682 Abendmusiken amounted to considerably less than the 100 Lübeck marks it had given for the extensive work of 1679.

Buxtehude's wish to produce a fuller and more complete work in the future may have been fulfilled in the Abendmusiken of 1683, which appear to have extended to five concerts. The lack of suitable singers in the school again made it necessary to import singers, this time a tenor and a bass from Kiel. One received free room and board in the home of Hanß Braschen; the other stayed in an inn, and in January 1684 the church reimbursed Buxtehude the 12 rixdollars that he had paid for seven weeks' lodging at the inn. Just over five weeks elapsed between the first concert on the penultimate Sunday in Trinity and the last on the fourth Sunday in Advent, the customary times for the Abendmusiken according to the later information from Ruetz. If this was the schedule followed in 1683, as seems likely, it would have left the singers an ample two weeks' rehearsal time before the first concert.

Corroborating evidence for a five-concert schedule in 1683 comes from the fact that in 1684 the spring catalogues of the book fairs in Frankfurt and Leipzig announced the forthcoming publication of two dramatic works in five parts by Buxtehude, *Himmlische Seelenlust auf Erden* and *Das allerschröcklichste und allererfreulichste*. The catalogue listings included some information concerning the style and scoring of these works:

> *Heavenly Joy of the Spirit on Earth over the Incarnation and Birth of Our Dearest Savior Jesus Christ*, in five separate acts, in opera style, with many arias and ritornelli, brought

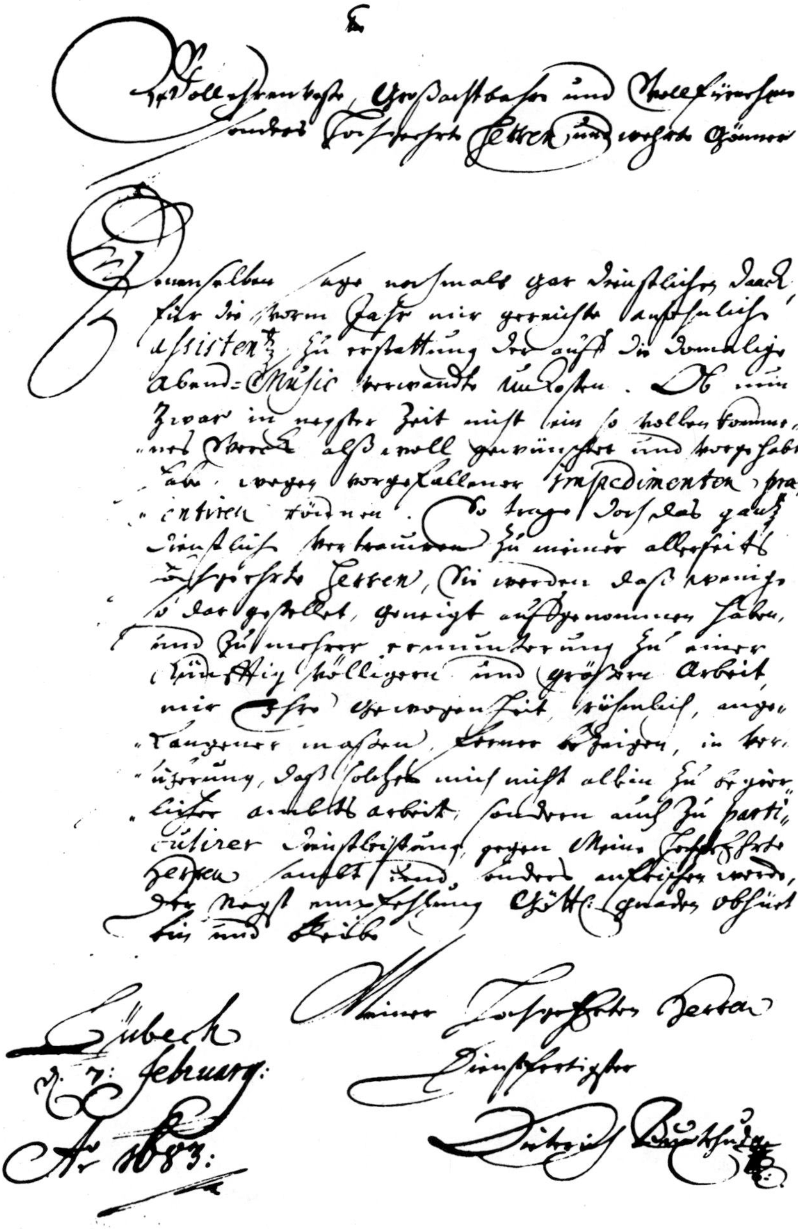
Lübeck d. 7. February Ao 1683.

Dietrich Buxtehude

Figure 2-6. Letter from Buxtehude to the directors of the Spanish Collections and businessmen's *Dröge,* 1683 (Archiv der Hansestadt Lübeck).

into a musical harmony for six concerted voices, various instruments and capella voices.

The Most Frightful and Most Joyful; Namely, the End of Time and Beginning of Eternity, in dialogue style, also shown in five scenes, for five concerted voices, instruments, etc.[18]

Neither libretto nor music for either work has come to light, and it may be that they never actually appeared in print. Nevertheless, assuming that both works had already been composed and performed by the spring of 1684, the most likely years for their performances would have been 1681 and 1683. The earliest Abendmusik by Buxtehude known to Ruetz dated from 1681; had this work departed from the five-part form that was normal in the eighteenth century, he probably would have noted the fact. In 1682, on the other hand, it appears from Buxtehude's letter that a shorter work may have been presented.

The employment of the police for watch duty during the Abendmusiken began in 1682 and is documented for later years. On these occasions they were paid for their attendance at the Christmas services as well, so the need for them was not limited to the Abendmusiken alone. It was probably related to the darkness at Lübeck's northern latitude during this time of year and to the large crowds that both the Abendmusiken and the Christmas services attracted. "The atrocious noise of the mischievous young people and the unruly running and romping about behind the choir" that Ruetz noted may have formed part of the problem.

Buxtehude's letters to his official patrons provide the chief source of information concerning his Abendmusiken for the remainder of the seventeenth century. Most of the letters follow the formula already seen in 1683 of beginning with thanks for the contribution of the previous year, followed by a solicitation for a renewed donation, with reference to the presentation just completed. He attached a brief financial statement to the letter of 1699:

As an official account I report that my musical
collections for this time have been: 182 Lübeck marks,
but the expenses required of them: 206 Lübeck marks
so at least this much more has been paid: 24 Lübeck marks

The "musical collections," called "reimbursement from the citizenry" elsewhere, were the donations that he received from individuals, usually around the New Year. From the letter of 1701 we learn that the customary contribution from the businessmen's collective treasury was 20 rixdollars, or 60 Lübeck marks. In 1699 he apparently received only half this sum, however, and in 1700, nothing at all. This led to a bitter complaint in 1701 that the love of noble music in Lübeck was diminishing and growing cold, enough to make many a man of his age die a miserable death. In the letters of 1687 and 1699 he emphasized the fact that it was the commercial guilds, businessmen, and citizens who had wished to have the Abendmusiken in the first place.

Buxtehude also included in these letters numerous expressions of pride in his accomplishments, and in in 1688 the subject of the work recently performed: the story of the prodigal son. The presentation of the Abendmusiken was "a praiseworthy work, and customary nowhere else" (1687), a "musical ornament" (1689), and "an incomparable ornament" (1698). Buxtehude used the word *Abendmusik* in both singular and plural, in a variety of spellings, usually to mean the concerts, but on occasion referring to the work itself. At times he was disappointed with the quality of the performance, as in 1684, when the singers did not meet his expectations, but at other times he was certain that his patrons had been well pleased. The claim by both Buxtehude and the 1697 Lübeck guidebook that the Abendmusiken were unique to Lübeck might be dismissed as an expression of parochial pride, but in truth no similar occurrence in North Germany during the seventeenth century has yet come to light.

Buxtehude's performances of theatrical music in the church—outside the liturgy, to be sure—never invoked criticism from the Lübeck ministry. Hinrich Elmenhorst, a preacher at St. Catherine's Church in Hamburg and a librettist for the Hamburg opera, commented on this fact in 1688 in his book *Dramatologia Antiquo-Hodierna*:

> Musicians understand the word *operas* to mean the compositions of poets and composers performed not only in theaters, but also in churches. . . . In this connection I must mention how the world-famous Lübeck musician Diedericus Buxtehude has performed more than one such opera in public churches there in the Abendmusik customary at a certain time of year, whose poetry has been published. Neither the highly praised magistrate of that place, nor the late Superintendent, nor the honorable ministry has disapproved, rejected or hindered this in any way.[19]

Elmenhorst wrote his *Dramatologia* in defense of the Hamburg opera, which was under attack at the time by the Pietist ministers Anton Reiser of St. Jacobi Church and Johann Winckler of St. Michael's. Hamburg's own tradition of oratorio performances, so strong in the eighteenth century, had not yet been firmly established.

The Abendmusiken of 1700 departed from the pattern of dramatic works that Buxtehude had instituted and consisted instead of mixed programs of vocal music. Buxtehude's failure to compose a new dramatic work could have been related to the fact that he had received no contribution from the businessmen's fund that year. The libretto from 1700—lost since 1942—showed that the first four concerts each included three vocal works: various settings of chorales, psalms and new poetic texts.[20] The last concert gave a repeat performance—at the request of Buxtehude's patrons—of a work that had been performed on the first of January of that year, "Hundred-year Poem for the Welfare of the Imperial Free City of Lübeck." This lost work must have been similar in nature to an earlier, shorter work by Buxtehude, *Schwinget euch himmelan* (BuxWV 96), the last four strophes of whose text follow:

5. *Bleibe, o Vater, ach bleibe genädig,*
Lübeck laß bleiben dein Liebesgerüst,
mache von sündlichem Wesen uns ledig,
werde mit heiligen Lippen geküßt.
Betet und ächzet, ächzet und lechzet:
Vater, ach Vater, dein heiliges Wort
lasse uns seliglich leuchten hinfort.

5. *Remain gracious, o father;*
let Lübeck continue to enjoy your love;
make us free from sinful ways;
be kissed with holy lips.
Pray and moan, moan and languish,
Father, oh Father, let your holy word
shine forth blessedly for all.

6. *Lasse die Obrigkeit glücklich regieren!*
Schlage die Laster durch diese ins Grab;
wollest das Rathaus mit Weisheit bezieren,
schütte viel Gnade auf dieses herab!
Betet und ächzet, ächzet und lechzet:
Herrscher, die Herrscher mit Segen beschütt,
alle vor Schaden und Feinden behüt.

6. *Let the authorities govern beneficially;*
through them throw wickedness into the grave.
Let the Rathaus be decorated with wisdom;
pour down your grace on it.
Pray and moan, moan and languish,
Ruler, cover rulers with blessing,
protect all from injury and enemies.

7. *Häufe das Käufen mit reichlichem Segen,*
Handel und Wandel uns wachse herzu,
lasse die Schiffe zum Segen bewegen,
stärke die Werker mit Leben und Ruh!
Betet und ächzet, ächzet und lechzet:
Vater, dein segenerfülleter Schoß
mache dein Lübeck erfreuet und groß.

7. *Pile rich blessing on business;*
let commerce and trade increase;
let the ships move profitably,
strengthen the workers with life and peace.
Pray and moan, moan and languish;
Father, from your blessing-filled bosom
make Lübeck happy and great.

8. *Treibe ganz ferne des Krieges Getümmel!*
Hunger und Seuchen von hinnen verfliehn.
Halte die Alten aus offenem Himmel,
lasse die Jungen zur Tugend erziehn!
Betet und ächzet, ächzet und lechzet:
Vater, vertreibe die schädliche Wut,
kröne mit Segen die Leiber, den Mut.
Amen.

8. *Drive far away the tumult of war;*
let hunger and plague disappear from here;
protect the aged from an open heaven,
let the young people be educated toward virtue.
Pray and moan, moan and languish;
Father, drive away harmful madness;
crown with blessing our bodies and spirits.
Amen.

Schwinget euch himmelan is scored for the same musical forces that Buxtehude had specified for the second of the Abendmusiken to be published in 1684: five concerted voices, instruments, and probably capella (the group of singers who reinforced the soloists in tutti passages). Its musical style is simple and direct, almost folklike (see exx. 5-15 and 5-16). The mixture of the sacred and secular embodied in the text of this work, especially its blessing of business, would have appealed to the businessmen who financed the Abendmusiken, and the music must have sounded quite at home in the old St. Mary's Church, whose walls were covered with the epitaphs of successful businessmen.

In the year 1705, on the second and third of December, Buxtehude presented two Abendmusik concerts that he termed "extraordinary," perhaps in part because they were given on Wednesday and Thursday instead of the usual Sunday. The first of them, *Castrum doloris*, or "Castle of Sorrow," commemorated the death of the Holy Roman emperor Leopold I; the second, *Templum honoris*, or "Temple of Honor," celebrated the accession of his successor, Joseph I. In honoring its emperors, Lübeck was also celebrating its own status as an imperial free city. The librettos for these two works survive,[21] and their descriptions of the decorations in the church for these performances are also extraordinary. *Castrum doloris* was given, as usual, from the large organ.

> In an illumination on the recently repaired and completely gilded large organ, now covered, and decorated with many lamps and lights, is presented the body of his highness the Kaiser in a coffin on the catafalque; at his head the imperial coat of arms, on both sides the royal Hungarian, Bohemian, and other royal coats of arms; above this, a beautifully decorated sky rests on four palm trees, hung with the imperial, royal and provincial coats of arms; many angels with lights keep watch around it. The two musical choruses by the organ are dressed in black; the trombones and trumpets are muted, and all the other instruments are also muted.

The other instruments are not further specified. The display for the following evening's performance of *Templum honoris* was at the opposite end of the church; there

> the temple of honor is beautifully decorated and illuminated, surrounded by a strong guard of brave heroes. The path to the temple is bordered with the virtues and the sciences. The folding doors stand open, and inside one can see on the altar the bust of His Holy Roman Imperial Majesty, before which are presented Joy and Gladness with their children, who carry all kinds of trophies, wreaths and flowers with palm and laurel branches.

The libretto specifies two choruses of trumpets and timpani—the church purchased two new kettledrums for the occasion—two choruses of concertizing horns and oboes, and twenty-five unison violins.

The vocal forces employed in these two works appear to have been extensive, but they are not specified in detail. *Castrum doloris* has a chorus of mourning women as well as other single choruses; *Templum honoris* employs a double chorus at the end, combined into a single chorus for refrains earlier. All of the characters in both works are allegorical, and the solo voices assigned to these roles are not named. There is no dramatic action in either work.

A brief report on the presentation of *Castrum doloris* and *Templum honoris* appeared in the April 1706 issue of *Nova literaria Maris Balthici*. Unfortunately, it does not provide a review of the performances or a description of the music, beyond the fact that the works were respectively mournful and joyful. The only information contained in it that is not supplied by the librettos themselves is the actual dates of the performances.

Three librettos, the titles of two dramatic works announced in 1684 and of thirteen shorter works performed in 1700, and the subject of one dramatic work from 1688: these are the only sure remains of Buxtehude's famed Abendmusiken. Of more than one hundred preserved vocal works by Buxtehude, not one matches these texts, titles, or theme, although among them several suggest themselves as good candidates for performance in an Abendmusik of the type presented in 1700. And among all the vocal works with sacred texts in German preserved from the latter part of the seventeenth century, only one work is of sufficient length to raise the possibility that it might be a dramatic Abendmusik by Buxtehude: an anonymous oratorio in three acts, untitled, with the opening text "Wacht! Euch zum Streit gefasset macht."

Wacht! Euch zum Streit is transmitted in a set of parts copied in the mid-1680s at the Swedish royal court in Stockholm, standing in close proximity to numerous vocal works by Buxtehude that were copied at the same time and place and preserved in the Düben collection at Uppsala.[22] Willy Maxton identified it with *Das allerschröcklichste und allererfreulichste*, rearranged its three acts into five parts while cutting out numerous arias, and published it as a work of Buxtehude under a new title, *Das jüngste Gericht*, in 1939. Claims for its authenticity as a composition of Buxtehude aroused considerable controversy. In the catalogue of Buxtehude's works, it stands among the doubtful works (BuxWV Anhang 3). The objections to its authenticity are discussed in chapter 5; in recent years, however, *Wacht! Euch zum Streit* has increasingly come to be accepted as an Abendmusik of Buxtehude, although not *Das allerschröcklichste und allererfreulichste*.

Wacht! Euch zum Streit consists of a short prologue followed by two longer acts of quasi-dramatic action and reflection. Its text is made up of biblical quotations, chorale verses, and new poetry, with the main emphasis on the new strophic poetry. It is scored for five or six vocal soloists, two violins, two violas, and continuo, with a brief and optional appearance for trombones. Its characters are all allegorical, to the extent that they are named at all. In the prologue, Avarice, Wantonness, and Pride (three sopranos) argue among themselves as to which is the most powerful, and the Divine Voice (bass) denounces them all with biblical words. No characters are named in acts II and III. The bass part continues to function as the Divine Voice, but Avarice, Wantonness, and Pride have disappeared as characters, although they are clearly the operative sins in the drama. Two new and strongly contrasting characters have appeared in the first and second soprano parts, which could be named the Pious Soul and the Ungodly Soul. A small tenor part can be identified as Jesus. A five-voice ensemble (SSATB) sings all the chorales and the reflective arias which frame each of the three acts.

The libretto of *Wacht! Euch zum Streit*[23] appears to have been compiled by a North German literary amateur and is admirably well qualified for a Lübeck Abendmusik. It shares with the *Hochzeit des Lamms* the same three textual components of biblical quotations, chorale verses and new poetry, the strong thematic contrast between the pious and the ungodly, the condemnation of the ungodly to the flames of hell, and the use of the chorale "Wie schön leuchtet der Morgenstern" to depict the joyful love between Jesus and the pious. With its division into three acts, it would have been well suited to performances on the second, third, and fourth Sundays of Advent. It departs from the *Hochzeit des Lamms* in its greater length, much greater number of arias set to new strophic poetry, and the worldliness of those arias that depict the depravity of the ungodly second soprano. These are all stylistic traits of opera, and the booksellers' announcement of 1684 indicates that Buxtehude was experimenting with the incorporation of operatic elements into his Abendmusiken at approximately the same time as the copying of the manuscript of *Wacht! Euch zum Streit*. Since it lacks the rich scoring and five-part structure associated with the works announced for publication in 1684, *Wacht! Euch zum Streit* could have been the work that Buxtehude presented in 1682, the one not so complete as he had wished and intended. Perhaps Jean Carl Quelmaltz was called from Hamburg to sing the role of the Divine Voice.

The historical importance of Buxtehude's leadership of the Lübeck Abendmusiken lies not only in his creation of a new musical genre but also in his mobilization of the business community to contribute funds for the presentation of concerts that were open to the general public free of charge. Buxtehude's five-part oratorio form, each part to be performed in a separate concert, was followed by his successors at St. Mary's until the abolition of the Abendmusiken in 1810 during the French occupation. It does not appear to have been imitated outside of Lübeck, however, unless J. S. Bach's division of his *Christmas Oratorio* into six separate performances can be said to reflect his visit to Buxtehude thirty years earlier. In cultivating the patronage of the business community to make music available to a wider public, however, Buxtehude's early fundraising efforts assume an importance that extends far beyond the walls of Lübeck and into our present musical life. When a corporation underwrites the broadcasting of opera on radio and television, it unwittingly participates in the tradition of the Lübeck Abendmusiken.

Then as now, astute fund raisers such as Buxtehude and his successors found ways to encourage patronage by reserving certain privileges for the donors. Buxtehude sent librettos to his patrons before the start of the series each year,[24] expecting a donation the following New Year. The choir loft above the rood screen at the east end of St. Mary's offered the best seats from which to see and hear the Abendmusiken, and these seats were reserved for the members of the council and other prominent citizens. In 1752, Johann Paul Kunzen began to allow his patrons to attend the dress rehearsals, held at first in the *Werkhaus* and later in the stock exchange. In time, the dress rehearsals became more fashionable than the public performances.

One of the most ardent supporters of Buxtehude's Abendmusiken was Peter Hinrich Tesdorpf (1648–1723), an importer of wines from the Rhine, France,

Spain, Portugal, and the Canary Islands. He belonged to two commercial guilds, the Schonenfahrer and the Stockholmfahrer, and used these offices to speak in behalf of the "Advent music in St. Mary's." He considered himself am admirer and true friend of Buxtehude and particularly enjoyed his organ playing. Tesdorpf's grandson recalled his saying that "in the ardor of his compositions, Buxtehude understood well how to give a foretaste of heavenly bliss."[25]

Beyond the walls of Lübeck—with the possible exception of Hamburg—Buxtehude's reputation lay chiefly in his skill as an organist and composer for the organ. Within the city, however, and particularly outside St. Mary's parish, he appears to have been even more greatly admired as the director of the Abendmusiken. An elegy for his funeral by Johann Caspar Ulich bears the title "The Undesired Silent Abend-Musique . . . presented for the last time the 16th of May, 1707."[26]

Chapter Three

Lübeck: St. Mary's Church

St. Mary's Church formed the locus for Buxtehude's professional activity in Lübeck, whether as director of the Abendmusiken or performer on the organ during church services or administrator of the church. His position as organist and Werkmeister of this venerable church conferred upon him the status that enabled him to raise money and present the Abendmusiken, and the church provided a magnificent space in which his performances could take place. Most important, St. Mary's church placed at his disposal one of the largest and most colorful organs in Germany, the instrument on which the most characteristic expression of his art manifested itself.

The Church Building

St. Mary's Church stands almost exactly in the center of Lübeck, at the point of its highest elevation, and its twin towers form the focal point of every depiction of this many-spired city. The central market place was part of the original plan for the city, and a modest wooden market church was built soon after the final foundation of Lübeck under Henry the Lion in 1159. The present structure, like most medieval churches, has a long and complicated architectural history. It began as a Romanesque basilica (ca. 1200), was rebuilt into an early Gothic hall church (ca. 1250), and achieved its final form, as a High Gothic basilica, during the years 1290–1350 (fig. 3-1). Its nave and choir rise high above the side aisles and ambulatory: the vaulting of the nave, supported by flying buttresses, is 38.5 meters high, "as high as the lighthouse in Travemünde," according to von Höveln's guidebook. This style had been developed in France, using stone; in Lübeck the normal building material was brick, and St. Mary's was one of the first brick churches built in the High Gothic style. It exerted a powerful influence in the spread of the "brick Gothic" style throughout the Baltic region.

The years of the building of St. Mary's correspond exactly to the time of greatest growth for both Lübeck and the Hansa. The large dimensions of the church—104 meters in length, 58 meters in width—and its up-to-date style represented the growing power, wealth, and self-confidence of its constituency, the merchant classes and city council, as opposed to the ecclesiastical power of the

Figure 3-1. Lübeck, St. Mary's Church before 1872, viewed from the market-place (Museen für Kunst und Kulturgeschichte der Hansestadt Lübeck).

bishop, whose seat was in the cathedral (Dom), the other double-towered church to the south. Although all parish churches were subject to the bishop and the cathedral chapter, in 1286 the city council gained the right to choose the head pastor of St. Mary's, which functioned as *its* church, the *Ratskirche*. The church bell called the council into session, and its members assembled in the church before proceeding as a group across the churchyard to the city hall. Much city business was carried on within the walls of the church: the burgomasters held audience there with the citizens, contracts were executed there in the presence of a council member, at their installation, new council members were seated in a large pew especially for the purpose, and all the treasures and important documents of both the city and the Hansa were kept in the treasury above the burgomasters' chapel. Public scribes were available in the chapel of indulgences for the recording of documents.

With the Reformation, which Lübeck officially adopted in 1530, the council gained even more power, since under the Lutheran system of church government it was now the head of all the churches in Lübeck. The city council appointed a theologian as superintendent to administer this responsibility; he also preached regularly at St. Mary's. The financial affairs of the church were managed by four directors, analogous to the four burgomasters who governed the city. Like the burgomasters and council members, the church directors were elected for life. Each year they audited and signed the account books that Buxtehude kept in his capacity as Werkmeister, and their coats of arms were displayed prominently near the organs that he played.

After more than seven hundred years of proud history, St. Mary's church was virtually destroyed by flames following the bombing of Lübeck on the night of 28–29 March 1942. Only its walls remained standing; its steeples, its roof, and nearly everything inside the church fell victim to the fire, including one of the organs that Buxtehude had played. The old church bells remain to this day embedded in the floor beneath the tower from which they fell.

St. Mary's has been rebuilt, and once again its twin steeples dominate the center of Lübeck. Its interior looked very different in Buxtehude's day, however; it was as profusely decorated then as it is plain now. The aesthetic goals of its rebuilding were partly to restore it to its medieval state and partly to make it appropriate for present-day worship; very little of the baroque remains. Formerly there were large and elaborately carved pews for the burgomasters, council members, and members of the various wholesalers' companies. Battle flags hung from the walls. Large, ornate memorials covered every available spot of the walls and pillars, lovingly described, one by one, in the 1697 guidebook. Many of these had been erected during Buxtehude's time, and some memorialized his known patrons, such as Senator Heinrich Balemann, godfather to Buxtehude's daughter Dorothea Catrin, and the burgomaster Heinrich von Kirchring, for whose wedding he had composed *Auf! stimmet die Saiten* (BuxWV 116). The ornately carved marble pulpit and the

Figure 3-2. Lübeck, St. Mary's Church, east end before 1942, showing the choir loft over the rood screen (Museen für Kunst und Kulturgeschichte der Hansestadt Lübeck).

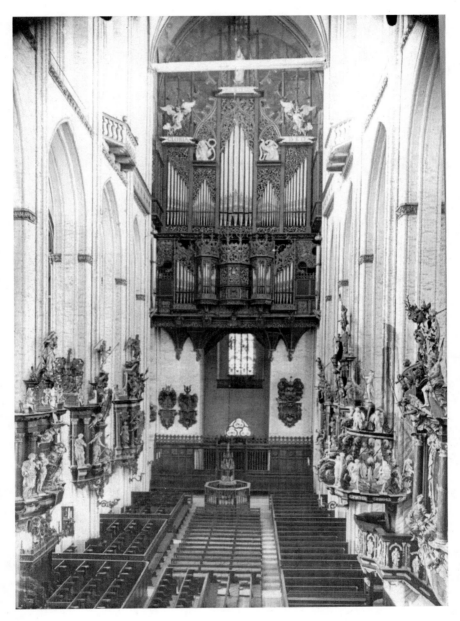

Figure 3-3. Lübeck, St. Mary's Church, west end before 1942, showing the large organ (Museen für Kunst und Kulturgeschichte der Hansestadt Lübeck).

Figure 3-4. Lübeck, St. Mary's Church, small organ in the Totentanz chapel before 1942 (Museen für Kunst und Kulturgeschichte der Hansestadt Lübeck).

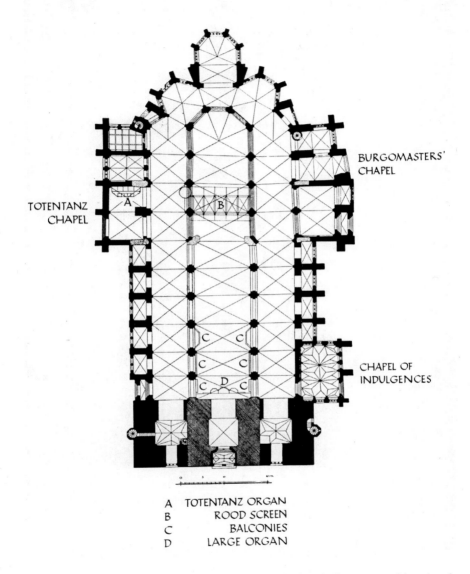

TOTENTANZ
CHAPEL

BURGOMASTERS'
CHAPEL

CHAPEL OF
INDULGENCES

A   TOTENTANZ ORGAN
B   ROOD SCREEN
C   BALCONIES
D   LARGE ORGAN

Figure 3-5. Lübeck, St. Mary's Church, ground plan before 1942 (drawing by Martin Botsch).

Figure 3-6. Lübeck, St. Mary's Church, large organ before 1850. From an anonymous oil painting (Museen für Kunst und Kulturgeschichte der Hansestadt Lübeck).

Fredenhagen altar also made their appearance during this time. The rood screen which divided the choir from the nave was a raised choir loft supported by five vaults (fig. 3-2). All of these furnishings and decorations provided an unintended benefit: They helped to damp the acoustics, now much too live, of this very large space.

In the ambulatory behind the high altar stood one of the marvels of the church—its astronomical clock—built in 1407. At its center was a planetarium in which the sun pointed to the correct time, the moon showed its phase, and the movements of the five known planets—Mercury, Venus, Mars, Jupiter, and Saturn—were displayed. This clock must have been of more than passing interest to Buxtehude, who composed a series of seven keyboard suites (BuxWV 251, now lost) that depicted the nature or quality of the planets. Below the planetarium was a calendar clock with the date and the signs of the zodiac, and above it a mechanical puppet show with a bell that struck the hours; at the hour of twelve a procession of electors emerged and bowed before the figure of Christ.

Organs

It was common for the Lübeck churches to have two organs, a large one for full services and a smaller one for devotional services and funerals. When Buxtehude arrived at St. Mary's in 1668, the church boasted two three-manual organs, a large instrument of fifty-two stops that hung on the west wall of the nave (fig. 3-3), and a smaller one of about forty stops (fig. 3-4) located on the east wall of the Totentanz chapel. Figure 3-5 shows the location of these instruments.

Buxtehude's large organ had been built as a two-manual instrument in 1516–18, with a magnificent two-story facade (fig. 3-6), which survived all subsequent alterations to the organ until the destruction of the church in 1942. Its upper level, divided into five fields, housed the Hauptwerk in its second and fourth fields and part of the pedal in the outer and middle fields, with its 32′ Principal in the facade. The remainder of the pedal was in the outer fields of the lower level, to either side of the two projecting towers that housed the large Positiv "im Stoell," or chair organ. A Brustwerk with a third manual, placed between those of the Hauptwerk above and the Positiv below, was added by the Hamburg organ builder Jacob Scherer in 1560–61. The organ was enlarged by Gottschalk Borchert and Jacob Rabe in 1596–98, rebuilt by Friedrich Stellwagen in 1637–41, and enlarged by two stops in 1704, yielding the specifications that Johann Mattheson listed in 1721[1]:

Werck	Rück-Positiv [Unterwerk]
1. Principal 16' [facade]	1. Principal 8' [facade]
2. Quintadena 16'	2. Bordun 16'
3. Octava 8'	3. Blockflöte 8'
4. Spitz-Flöte 8'	4. Sesquialtera II
5. Octava 4'	5. Hohl-Flöte 8'
6. Hohlflöte 4'	6. Quintadena 8'
7. Nasat 3'	7. Octava 4'
8. Rauschpfeiffe IV	8. Spiel-Flöte 2'
9. Scharff IV	9. Mixtura V
10. Mixtura XV	10. Dulcian 16'
11. Trommete 16'	11. Baarpfeiffe 8'
12. Trommete 8'	12. Trichter-Regal 8'
13. Zincke 8'	13. Vox humana 8'
	14. Scharff IV–V

Brust	Pedal
1. Principal 16' [sic; should be 8']	1. Principal 32' [facade]
2. Gedact 8'	2. Sub-Bass 16'
3. Octava 4' [facade]	3. Octava 8'
4. Hohlflöte 4'	4. Bauerflöte 2'
5. Sesquialtera II	5. Mixtura VI
6. Feld-Pfeiffe 2'	6. Groß-Posaun 24'
7. Gemshorn 2'	7. Posaune 16'
8. Sifflet 1½'	8. Trommete 8'
9. Mixtura VIII	9. Principal 16' [facade]
10. Cimbel III	10. Gedact 8'
11. Krumhorn 8'	11. Octava 4'
12. Regal 8'	12. Nachthorn 2'
	13. Dulcian 16'
	14. Krumhorn 8'
	15. Cornet 2'

Cimbel Stern
2 Trummeln
2 Tremulanten
16 Bellows

The console of the large organ shown in figure 3-6 is not the one from which Buxtehude played; it was added in a renovation of 1733–35, at which time the organ received new manuals and a new pedal board to accommodate an expanded compass. Prior to that time, it apparently lacked couplers, and all three manuals and pedals were equipped with only the short octave, according to Hermann Jimmerthal's manuscript chronicle of St. Mary's Church:

2. The three keyboards and pedal[board] were newly built, and the keyboard for the Hauptwerk, which formerly lay uppermost and far from the hand, was brought to the

middle; and couplers provided for the three manuals, which until then were lacking; also the stop knobs better arranged.

3. For all manuals and the pedal, where everywhere in the bass the pitches C♯, D♯, F♯, and G♯ were lacking, the three last pitches were added in all stops, besides the five pitches C, g♯″, b″ [b♭″], h″ [b♮″] and c‴ which were hitherto lacking in the Brustwerk.[2]

The entire works of the large organ were removed in 1851 when Johann Friedrich Schulze installed a new organ behind the existing facade, with its pipes extending into the two balconies closest to the organ (fig. 3-3).[3] At that time, Scherer's Brustwerk facade was removed and used to build a new positive organ for the choir loft on the rood screen, visible in figure 3-2, and the new ivory keyboards that had been made for the large organ in 1834 were installed on the small organ in 1853.[4] Following the destruction of 1942 and the subsequent rebuilding of the church, Kemper and Son of Lübeck installed a new large organ on the west wall in 1968; it is placed considerably higher than the old organ was and contains 101 stops on five manuals and pedal.

The small organ stood in the Totentanz chapel, which is somewhat analogous to the north transept of a cathedral, but with the height of the side aisle. Around its walls was a famous painting, *The Dance of Death* ("Totentanz"), executed in 1463 by Lübeck's most famous artist, Bernt Notke, following a serious epidemic of the plague. It depicted a skeleton dancing alternately with a member of every class of society, from the pope and the emperor down to a baby, with the city of Lübeck in the background. A poem underneath narrated the conversation between death and each of these persons. Above this painting the organ builder Johannes Stephani built a small organ, with one manual and pedal, in 1475–77.

The history of the small organ is poorly documented; the earliest known stop list, written by the Lübeck organ builder Theodor Vogt, dates from about 1845. The Rückpositiv appears to have been added in 1557–58 by Jacob Scherer, and Henning Kröger built the Brustwerk in 1621–22. Friedrich Stellwagen renovated the instrument in 1653–55; after that no further extensive changes were made until 1760–61. Vogt's stop list numbers thirty-nine stops, which he reduced to thirty-four in a renovation carried out in 1845–46. This organ naturally attracted attention during the organ revival of the 1920s and 1930s, and in 1937 the Lübeck organ builder Karl Kemper restored it, presumably to the state in which Buxtehude had played it. After this restoration, the organ expert Gustav Fock inspected it and wrote down the following stop list, together with his opinion concerning the builder of each of the stops:

Hauptwerk	Rückpositiv
Quintade 16′ (Stellwagen)	Principal 8′ (facade; partly Kemper)
Principal 8′ (facade)	Rohrflöte 8′ (Kröger)
Spitzflöte 8′ (Kröger)	Quintatön 8′ (Kröger)
Oktave 4′ (Kröger)	Oktave 4′ (probably Stellwagen)
Nasat 2 2/3′ (Kröger; partly Kemper)	Rohrflöte 4′ (Kröger)

Hauptwerk	Rückpositiv
Mixtur VI–X (Kröger; partly Kemper)	Sifflöte 1 1/3' (Stellwagen)
Rauschpfeife II (Kemper)	Scharf VI–VIII (Stellwagen; partly Kemper)
Trompete 8' (perhaps Stellwagen)	Sesquialter II (Stellwagen)
	Dulcian 16' (Stellwagen)
	Trichterregal 8' (Stellwagen)

Brustwerk	Pedal
Gedact 8' (Kröger)	Principal 16' (facade)
Quintade 4' (Kemper)	Subbaß 16' (Kröger, G-d')
Hohlflöte 2' (Kröger)	Oktave 8' (Stellwagen)
Quintflöte 1 1/2' (Kemper)	Gedackt 8' (Kröger)
Zimbel IV (Kemper)	Oktave 4' (Kröger)
Krummhorn 8' (Kröger; upper half new	Quintade 4' (Kemper)
resonators by Kemper)	Oktave 2' (Kröger)
Schalmei 4' (blocks, tongues, shallots old;	Nachthorn 1' (Kemper)
new resonators by Kemper)	Mixtur IV (Kröger)
	Zimbel II (Kemper)
	Posaune 16'
	Dulcian 16' (Kemper)
	Trompete 8' (Kröger)
	Schalmei 4' (Kröger; on new chest)
	Kornett 2' (Kemper; on new chest)[5]

Visitors to the Totentanz chapel in the postwar church will find the Dance of Death depicted by stained-glass windows instead of a mural and a new astronomical clock where the old organ used to be. A new "Totentanz" organ, built by Alfred Führer of Wilhelmshaven in 1985, presently hangs on the north wall of the ambulatory. Only one of Lübeck's baroque organs survived later replacement or destruction by the war: the small organ in St. Jacobi. Stellwagen had enlarged it in 1637 to specifications similar to those of the small organ in St. Mary's, but with a much smaller pedal division. This instrument was restored in 1977–78 by the Hillebrand firm of Hannover and offers a distinct echo of Buxtehude's tonal world.

Concerning the temperament of the St. Mary's organs, we know from documented evidence only that the large organ was tuned to equal temperament in 1782 and the small organ not until 1805. During the seventeenth century, the tuning system commonly in use throughout North Germany was quarter-comma mean tone, as described extensively by Michael Praetorius in his *Organographia* of 1618. In this system, all major thirds are pure and all fifths are tuned one quarter syntonic comma flat. Because eleven flattened fifths far exceed the number needed to close the circle of fifths, the final interval, likened to a howling wolf, is about one and two thirds commas sharper than a fifth, and enharmonic equivalence is impossible; only the twelve pitch classes ascending by fifth from E♭ to G♯ fall within the system (see table 3-1). Fewer than half of Buxtehude's

Table 3-1. Some tuning systems compared

PURE INTERVALS, RECKONED FROM C

proportions: tone,9:8 (D) · m3,6:5 (E♭) · M3,5:4 (E) · P4,4:3 (F) · P5,3:2 (G) · M6,5:3 (A)

proportions	C	D	E♭	E	F	G	A	C
cents	0	204	316	386	498	702	884	1200

1/4-COMMA MEAN-TONE   (Göteborg, North German organ; Stockholm, German Church Düben organ)

11 fifths 1/4 syntonic comma, or 5 cents, flat; 1 unusable ("wolf," = 36 cents sharp), normally G♯–E♭ on organs.
8 major thirds pure; 4 unusable (41 cents sharp), normally C♯–E♯, F♯–A♯, G♯–B♯ and B–D♯ on organs.

	C	C♯	[D♭]	D	[D♯]	E♭	E	F	F♯	[G♭]	G	G♯	[A♭]	A	[A♯]	B♭	B	C
cents	0	76	117	193	269	310	386	503	579	620	697	773	814	890	965	1007	1083	1200

A MODIFIED MEAN-TONE   (Harald Vogel 1975: Langwarden, St. Laurentius-Kirche)

8 fifths 1/4 syntonic comma, or 5 cents, flat; 3 fifths (C♯–G♯, E♭–B♭, B♭–F) pure; "wolf" fifth (G♯–E♭) 19.5 cents sharp.
5 major thirds pure; 3 good (6–11 cents sharp); 4 very sharp (B–D♯, 31 cents; F♯–A♯, 36 cents; A♭–C, 36 cents; C♯–E♯ 41 cents)

	C	C♯	D	D♯/E♭	E	F	F♯	G	G♯/A♭	A	B♭	B	C
cents	0	76	193	300	386	503	579	697	778	890	1001	1083	1200

WERCKMEISTER III, 1681   (Lübeck, St. Jacobi, Stellwagen organ, 1978)

4 fifths (C–G, G–D, D–A, B–F♯) 1/4 Pythagorean comma, or nearly 6 cents, flat; other fifths pure.
Major thirds vary from 1/4 to 1 comma sharp (F♯–A♯, D–F, A♭–C); all usable.

	C	C♯/D♭	D	D♯/E♭	E	F	F♯/G♭	G	G♯/A♭	A	A♯/B♭	B	C
cents	0	90	192	294	390	498	588	696	792	888	996	1092	1200

EQUAL TEMPERAMENT   (most organs)

All fifths 1/12 Pythagorean comma, or 2 cents, flat; all major thirds 14 cents, sharp.

	C	C♯/D♭	D	D♯/E♭	E	F	F♯/G♭	G	G♯/A♭	A	A♯/B♭	B	C
cents	0	100	200	300	400	500	600	700	800	900	1000	1100	1200

Syntonic comma (21.5 cents): the amount by which 4 pure fifths less 2 octaves exceed a pure major third.
Pythagorean comma (23.46 cents): the amount by which 12 pure fifths exceed 7 octaves.
Schisma (2 cents): the difference between Pythagorean and syntonic comma.
To evaluate any interval, subtract the smaller cents value from the larger and compare the difference with the cents value of the pure interval.

organ works stay strictly within these limits, and a number of his most ambitious compositions, such as the praeludia in E minor (BuxWV 142), D major (BuxWV 139), and—most impossible of all—F♯ minor (BuxWV 146), make prominent use of pitch classes outside the system: D♯, A♯, A♭, and E♯.

Andreas Werckmeister had published the first discourse on circulating, well-tempered tuning in 1681 in the first edition of his *Orgel-Probe*, with its subtitle announcing instruction in tempering and tuning a keyboard instrument "so that according to the contemporary manner one can hear all the transposed modes in a bearable and pleasant harmony." In it Werckmeister gives two unequal temperaments that close the circle of fifths, the first to be used for keys with many sharps and flats, the second favoring the regular modes. These are the first and second correct temperaments that Werckmeister discussed at length five or ten years later in *Musicalische Temperatur* and listed as numbers III and IV in its chart, where number I is the pure scale and number II the "incorrect temperament," quarter-comma mean-tone. Werckmeister's first correct temperament (no. III)—in which the fifths C–G, G–D, D–A, and B–F♯ are tuned one-quarter comma flat with the remaining fifths pure—provides a good solution to the problem posed by works such as BuxWV 139, 142, and 146. Indeed, Werckmeister could have written his 1698 defense of his new temperament with Buxtehude's music in mind:

> Since through the grace of God, music has so progressed and changed, it would be absurd if we had not tried to improve the keyboard, so that well-composed modern pieces should not be ruined, and a howl come out of them. . . . Some would like to say that one should not compose in every key, such as C♯, F♯ and G♯. But I say that if one does not do it, another will. . . . And why should I set limits for this person or that, and want to prohibit him from composing in this key? . . . The free arts want free geniuses.[6]

Buxtehude must certainly have been interested in this new temperament, and he later developed a friendship with Werckmeister, as discussed in chapter 4. In a 1985 article and in the first edition of this book I proposed a hypothesis that at Buxtehude's instigation the organs of St. Mary's had been retuned to Werckmeister III in 1683. I based my hypothesis on information in the accounts that the bellows treader had received pay for thirty and a half extra days of work while the organ builder Michel Briegel had "thoroughly tuned" (durchgestimmet) both organs *without* their reeds, which Buxtehude had presumably already retuned himself. This theory was widely accepted, but it rested on incomplete evidence: the St. Mary's account books then available under the custody of the German Democratic Republic extended only through 1685; the rest were presumed lost. The return of the later books from the Soviet Union in 1988, however, made new evidence available, which Ibo Ortgies mined for his dissertation "Die Praxis der Orgelstimmung in Norddeutschland" (2004). He found payments to bellows treaders for extra work of twenty-seven and a half days during tunings in 1688 (including repairs to both organs), fifty-seven days in 1701 (for a renovation of the small organ), 110 days in 1704 (when three new stops were added to the large organ), and 191 days in 1782.

The 1782 accounts are of particular interest, because that is the only organ repair for which an actual contract still exists; it is transcribed in its entirety in appendix 4, D9. The provision to tune the organ in equal temperament comes in paragraph 6; before that the organ builder, Jochim Christoph Kaltschmidt, agreed to polish the facade pipes, repair the bellows where necessary, take all the pipes out of the organ, clean them, replace them if necessary, and revoice them. In paragraph 8 the church is required to supply a bellows treader for the entire time and in addition a boy to hold the keys during the tuning. An inspection of the accounts for 1782 reveals that the bellows treader worked nearly every week from February 25 through December 17, but the key holder only the weeks of July 29, August 5, and September 16 through December 1 for a total of eighty-three and a half days for the large organ. It may have been common practice, then, to employ the bellows treader for the entire duration of a repair, and thus the days worked cannot be used as a gauge for the extent of a tuning if other work was being done as well. In 1683 the account suggests that the thirty and a half days of work was entirely devoted to tuning; still, in view of the great discrepancy with eighty-three and a half days in 1782, it appears that my hypothesis that the temperament was changed to Werckmeister III in 1683 can no longer stand.

Were the St. Mary's organs then tuned in quarter-comma mean tone during Buxtehude's time, or perhaps in some modification of it? We do not know. During the first part of the seventeenth century the tonal range of a number of organs in Hamburg was extended by the addition of subsemitones, split keys governing separate pipes to give both E♭ and D♯, G♯ and A♭, and occasionally A♯ and B♭;[7] these organs were all presumably tuned in quarter-comma mean tone. In Lübeck, Stellwagen had installed E♭/D♯ subsemitones in the Brustwerk of the organ in St. Aegidien Church in 1645–48, but St. Mary's never had them. Modifications of mean tone may have been in use in some organs, but in none of the theoretical literature are they described so precisely as quarter-comma mean tone or the various unequal circulating systems, beginning with Werckmeister and multiplying throughout the eighteenth century.[8] We find only vague descriptions, such as Praetorius's speaking of raising G♯ somewhat so that it could almost make a minor third as an A♭ with F, or Werckmeister's suggestion that those who want to stay with mean tone should just tune E♭ a bit lower.[9]

Harald Vogel believed that he had found a somewhat more precise description in the records of the inspection of the organ in the Liebfrauenkirche in Bremen by Heinrich Scheidemann and Jacob Praetorius in 1641, and from that he constructed a modified mean-tone temperament that yields a usable D♯ but still lacks a real A♭. Because Scheidemann also inspected the St. Mary's large organ that same year, following Stellwagen's renovation and just before Franz Tunder's arrival, I suggested in the first edition of this book that the St. Mary's large organ might have been tuned with this modification of mean tone at that time. Vogel's hypothesis, however, rests not on the actual report of Scheidemann and Praetorius, but on his interpretation of a quotation by the organ builder Siburg stating what he planned to do to resolve the dispute: "Joh. Siborch will try as much as possible to tune this fifth between A and D pure, to sharpen the thirds, and to distribute the beating fifth elsewhere."[10] Ortgies interprets this quotation differently; in fact, he rejects intentionally modified meantone on seventeenth-century North German organs altogether. For the purpose of comparing a modified-meantone temperament with an unequal circulating temperament such as Werckmeister III, table 3-1 gives the modified meantone temperament that Vogel constructed for the restoration of the 1650 Kröger organ in Langwarden, based partly on Michael Praetorius and partly on some existing pipe lengths in the organ. Its D♯ and A♭ are marginally usable, but it still has a wolf fifth of nearly one comma. Vogel has recorded three Buxtehude works on this organ.[11]

It is still tempting to propose that Stellwagen might have tuned the large organ in some modification of quarter-comma mean tone during his major rebuilding in 1637–41, perhaps because there was no room in the existing case to install subsemitones, and that adjustments to the temperament, including further modification of mean tone or even adoption of a circulating temperament, may have occurred during some of the major tunings of 1642, 1673, 1683, or 1704. In 1642, for example, following Tunder's arrival, Stellwagen spent nineteen days "newly" tuning the large organ. But temperament is never mentioned in the accounts, even in 1782. It is impossible to tell from them how long it would have taken just to tune the organ without making any changes, because we do not know what else was done at the same time. To the account of the 1673 renovation of the large organ, which took twenty-nine days, Buxtehude wrote a marginal note: "This renovation consists only in tuning and cleaning of the entire organ." But does that mean that all the pipes were removed for the cleaning, as they were in 1782? And those eighty-three and a half days in 1782 included revoicing all the pipes as well as tuning them to equal temperament. In 1678, Michel Briegel tuned all the mixtures in the large organ, as well as adjusting the reeds and soldering many pipes that had been eaten by rats, in eight days. And the twenty-seven and a half days spent tuning both organs *with* their reeds in 1688 also included many other repairs.

In short, the organs are gone. The account books have returned to Lübeck, but they do not tell us everything that we would like to know, and we will never be certain of the temperament of the St. Mary's organs during Buxtehude's long tenure. But the likelihood that they were in some form of mean tone, together with the presence of the short octave, raises serious questions as to whether a number of Buxtehude's compositions could in fact have been played on them in the form in which they have been transmitted by their manuscript sources. These questions will be addressed further in chapter 7.

Some time after the repairs of 1782, the organist Johann von Königslow described the pitch of the large organ as "hoch Chorton," probably in the range $a' = 475$–480 Hz. The accounts of St. Mary's further document the fact that in the seventeenth century the pitch of the organs was different from the normal performing pitch of the day (Kammerton). The church purchased a number of instruments for use with the organ, and on at least two occasions Buxtehude specifically mentioned that they were in tune with the organ: in 1679 three shawms and two flutes "adjusted to this organ," and in 1685 a reed for a newly purchased bass bombarde to bring it into tune with the organ.[12]

Buxtehude's tenure as organist in St. Mary's corresponds approximately to the years when Arp Schnitger flourished as an organ builder in Hamburg. In May 1687, the church paid Buxtehude's expenses (including French wine at every meal) for a four-day trip to Hamburg to test Schnitger's new organ in St. Nicholas's and to speak with him about the organs at St. Mary's. Buxtehude was very pleased with the instrument at St. Nicholas's and invited Schnitger to come to Lübeck. He came in 1689 to inspect both organs and made a written offer to the directors for their repair, but it was not accepted. Buxtehude complained at the meeting of the church directors in 1701 that the large organ "had not been repaired in fifty or sixty years and longer, was full of dust, and had many other defects that prevented it from giving its proper resonance, and thus was greatly in need of repair." In 1702 Schnitger was called to Lübeck again, and once again his offer was rejected; he did not even receive sufficient compensation for his travel costs (see appendix D8). Between these two fruitless visits he built a new organ in the Lübeck cathedral of forty-five stops with three manuals and pedal. The large organ at St. Mary's finally received a minor renovation in 1704 from Otto Dietrich Richborn, a former apprentice to Schnitger, with three new stops: Vox humana, Sexquialtera, and Dulcian 16'.

Buxtehude, the leading organist in northern Germany, must have been sorely disappointed that he could not have at his command an organ renovated by Schnitger, the leading organ builder of the day. But his complaint that the organs had not been repaired in fifty or sixty years was not true; during his entire tenure scarcely a year went by without at least one payment to an organ builder for working on one or both organs. Joachim Richborn performed the cleaning and tuning of the large organ in 1673. From 1678 to 1694 the organ builder Michel Briegel, Friedrich Stellwagen's son-in-law, usually worked on the organs; he performed the major tuning in 1683. Beginning in 1697 Johan Hantelman, a former journeyman for Schnitger who had settled in Lübeck and did most of the work for Schnitger's organ in the Lübeck Cathedral, appears in the St. Mary's accounts. Most of the repairs were minor and involved one to three days' work; Buxtehude's usual description was "corrected a few defects." Often these defects had been caused by rats eating the pipes; Buxtehude recorded numerous purchases of rat traps and rat poison for the organs and payments to the organ builder for soldering pipes. (Rats like to eat the lead acetate, or "sugar of lead," that is produced by the corrosion of lead pipes.[13]) Despite his complaints, Buxtehude, an organ expert, is hardly likely to have allowed his organs to fall into a state of disrepair; in fact, their routine maintenance was probably included among his duties as organist.

The missed opportunity with Schnitger illustrates a change that had come over the leadership of the church since its building and the installation of its magnificent sixteenth-century organ. Competition with the cathedral seems no longer to have been important, as the new Schnitger organ there demonstrated. At about the same time, the commercial guilds failed to come forward with their annual contribution for the Abendmusiken, and Buxtehude complained that the love of music in Lübeck was diminishing and growing cold. Indeed, appearance seems to have been more important to the church directors than sound. In 1704 the church finally paid Joachim Richborn 510 Lübeck marks to repair the large organ and polish its pipes; the following year it paid the painter Anton Wortmann 2,500 Lübeck marks to gild the organ facade and silver the wings of its newly carved angels.

Liturgy and Hymns

The services and liturgy in St. Mary's had been laid down in 1531 by Johann Bugenhagen, Martin Luther's delegate, in his *Lübecker Kirchenordnung*. Some details had changed since then, among them a shift in language from Low German to High German in the early seventeenth century, but the essentials remained the same. The most important services were the main morning service (*Haupt-Predigt*) and afternoon service on Sundays and feast days. The high feasts were Christmas, Easter, Pentecost—each celebrated for two days in Buxtehude's time—and Saint Michael's (29 September). The church also celebrated New Year's Day, Epiphany (6 January), the Purification of Mary (2 February), the Annunciation (25 March), the Ascension, the feast of Saint John the Baptist (24 June), and the Visitation of Mary (2 July). The core of these services was the sermon, preached from eight to nine o'clock in the morning on the gospel for the day by the head pastor and from three to four o'clock in the afternoon on the epistle by the superintendent. Each of these services began one hour before the sermon and lasted approximately three hours, according to the slightly later account of the cantor Caspar Ruetz, who was explaining why church musicians sometimes left the church during the sermon:

> There is another fact that must be mentioned which seems to work to the disadvantage of unanimous attendance of the entire church service: namely, that the time that is appointed for the public worhip lasts much too long in many places. . . . The cold region of the earth in which we live must also be taken into consideration, and a distinction should be made between winter and summer. . . . The mighty cold in winter

keeps many from the exact observation of all the hours that the church regulations prescribe. Whoever cannot withstand three hours in the morning and three hours in the
afternoon without damage to his health takes the liberty to come late and leave
early. . . . It is just these circumstances that cause those who work in the church services
sometimes to leave for an hour, if they are not needed then, and to come back toward
the time when their duty resumes.[14]

We can guess that Buxtehude, too, was not always present during the hour-long
sermon, even though there were coal stoves by both organs. It is still cold in
St. Mary's during the winter, despite electric heat under the floor, but the services
now usually last no longer than an hour. Nevertheless, the church makes blankets
available to those worshipers who brave the penetrating cold of a Lübeck winter.

The liturgy that surrounded the morning sermon was still called a mass by
Bugenhagen and took its structure from the Roman Catholic mass. The chants
of the Proper had been replaced by various German hymns, but the Ordinary
was still in place. On high feasts, the Kyrie, Gloria, Credo, and Sanctus were sung
in Latin; at other times, they might be replaced by their German hymn paraphrases. The Agnus Dei was sung as the hymn "Christe du Lamm Gottes." The
Communion service before the altar began with the Credo; during the distribution of Communion, hymns were sung or concerted music was performed.
Further details of later practice are found in the "Brief Guide (*Kurtze Anweisung*)
as to how the Church Service Will Be Conducted in the Lübeck Churches in the
Future," which was appended to the 1703 Lübeck hymnal discussed below and
excerpted in appendix 4, E6. The service began with the singing of "Komm
Heiliger Geist," and following the reading of the Athanasian Creed "Herr Gott
dich loben wir" (the German "Te Deum") was sung "with the playing of the
organ" (*mit Einschlagung der Orgel*). The organ intoned the Kyrie, and during the
Trinity season also played with the hymn "O adoranda Trinitas" (which is not
included in the 1703 hymnal). On feast days concerted music could also be performed following the reading of the epistle. Latin Prefaces were used only for
Easter, Pentecost, St. Michael's, and Christmas. The service ended with the
singing of a hymn.

The liturgy surrounding the afternoon sermon is less well documented. This
service began with the singing of "Komm heiliger Geist" and closed with
"Benedicamus Domino"; it included the reading of the epistle for the day,
numerous hymns, the singing of the Magnificat in German or Latin, and, on
feast days, concerted music both before and after the sermon, which began at
three o'clock. According to the 1703 "Anweisung," the Magnificat was to be in
German, and the German "Te Deum" was sung before the sermon during Lent;
further, on Judica (the fifth Sunday in Lent) and Palm Sunday special Passion
music was customarily performed in St. Mary's after the sermon. The organ was
played after the epistle and following the sermon, as an intonation to any concerted music or in its place "with preluding and playing" for two German hymns.

This service thus represented a combination of a preaching service with elements of Vespers, which it had replaced on Sunday and feast-day afternoons.

At the time of the Reformation, Bugenhagen had set up a regular schedule of daily Matins and Vespers to be sung in Latin by the schoolboys, but in Buxtehude's time only Vespers on Saturdays and the eves of feasts remained. Vespers consisted of Latin antiphons and psalms, responsory, hymns, and the Magnificat, together with collects and readings from the Bible. By the time of the 1703 "Anweisung," however, little Latin remained, and in St. Mary's Church—but not the others—a one hour sermon followed the end of Vespers. The "Anweisung" further specified that the organ played for the intonation of the German Magnificat and following the closing "Benedicamus Domino." In neighboring Mecklenburg, Latin was still in use for Saturday vespers in 1650, when a revised *Kirchen-Ordnung* was issued, an excerpt from which can be found in appendix 4, E1.

In addition to the regular services on Sundays and feast days, Lübeck sometimes celebrated special services of thanksgiving, particularly when the imperial forces in the Holy League won an important victory over the Ottoman empire, such as occurred in 1686, 1687, 1688, 1691, and 1697, ending with the celebration of the Treaty of Carlowitz in 1699. These services usually included a sermon, the singing of the "Te Deum," and the playing of trumpets and timpani from the tower while canons were fired from around the city wall. The coronation of Emperor Leopold's son Joseph I as king of the Romans in 1690 was celebrated in a similar way, as was a victory of the imperial army over the French and Bavarians in 1704. Following the death of Emperor Leopold I in 1705, however, the organ was silent for five Sundays, and during this month the biggest bell was rung for one hour each day. On the occasion of the dedication of the new Fredenhagen altar in St. Mary's on August 15, 1697, special music for three choirs with trumpets and timpani was performed before and after the morning sermon and during the Communion.[15]

Lübeck did not have an official hymnal until 1703, when the city council published the first edition of the *Lübeckisches Gesangbuch*, containing 303 hymns, with a listing of the lectionary and *de tempore* hymns for each Sunday and feast day of the church year. It represented a theologically motivated pruning of a much larger hymnal published a few years earlier, *Lübeckisch-Vollständiges Gesangbuch, anjetzo biß auf 974 Gesänge vermehret*,[16] with many seventeenth-century hymns. Neither the *Lübeckisches Gesangbuch* nor the *Lübeckisch-Vollständiges Gesangbuch* contains music. A source does exist, however, for most of the melodies used with the texts of the 1703 *Lübeckisches Gesangbuch*. In 1705 the cantor Jacob Pagendarm composed for the use of the choir simple four-part settings of most of these hymns. On May 23, 1705, Buxtehude recorded in the account book a payment of 60 Lübeck marks to the cantor Pagendarm "for writing the melodies, of which there are 303 altogether, into the four newly made hymnbooks (soprano, alto, tenor and bass), without the texts." Two "Aritmetici," probably teachers at St. Catherine's school, received 150 marks for entering the texts into all four partbooks. Three of these partbooks (SAT) are extant in the Lübeck archives. with texts and numbers corresponding almost exactly to those of the 1729 reprinting of the *Lübeckisches Gesangbuch* (the earliest edition presently available). The numbers do extend to 303, but twenty-two are missing, and these include some of the most familiar hymns in the *Lübeckisches Gesangbuch*, such as no. 66, "Allein Gott in der Höh sey Ehr" (the paraphrase of the Gloria); no. 79, "Wir glauben all an einen Gott" (the paraphrase of the Credo); no. 89, "Jesus Christus unser Heiland, der von uns"; and no. 91, "Gott sey gelobet und gebenedeiet," both familiar Communion hymns. But the very omission of these hymns that were so important to the liturgy gives a clue as to the purpose of this chorale book. Clearly the omitted hymns, which the congregation must have sung, were not sung by the *Cantorei* in four-part harmony. Perhaps these hymns were too important for the congregation not to sing all the verses, and when the *Cantorei* did sing hymns in harmony from these partbooks they sang alone, without the congregation, in an introductory or *alternatim* capacity. Or perhaps the missing hymns were accompanied by the organ instead.

Pagendarm wrote his chorale book so late in Buxtehude's life that it cannot be considered a source for his chorale settings. A soprano partbook from an earlier set, probably dating from Samuel Franck's cantorate (1663–79), returned to the Lübeck archives in 1998 from exile in Armenia.[17] This chorale book, with only 110 hymns, is much smaller than Pagendarm's, and it does not appear to be based on any known hymnal. Nearly all the chorales that Buxtehude used in his settings for organ or voices appear in both chorale books with virtually identical melodies, as listed in appendix 6. The rhythm often differs, however. Surprisingly, the older chorale book appears the more modern, with more frequent use of quarter notes and no lengthened anacruses to phrases in common time, which Pagendarm consistently employed.

Music for Feast Days

The texts for all the concerted music performed in St. Mary's during the feasts of the Christmas season 1682–83 are preserved in a printed text book, *Natalitia Sacra*, the only surviving document that illuminates the relationship between liturgy and music at St. Mary's during Buxtehude's time. The opening lines of all the texts in *Natalitia Sacra* are listed in appendix 4, E2. In the morning service for each of these feasts—first and second Christmas, New Year's Day and Epiphany—the Kyrie and the Gloria were performed in Latin in concerted style, with vocal soloists, capella, and instruments. On Christmas day the Credo and the Sanctus were performed with the same complement of performers as the Kyrie and the Gloria: eight vocal soloists, eight in the capella, and ten instruments. For the other three days, the incipit of the Latin Credo is given with no indication as to the performers, and the Sanctus is not mentioned. On these days probably only the Kyrie and Gloria—the Protestant *missa brevis*—were performed polyphonically. A note at the end of the text book gives the title of the work that would be performed before the morning sermon each day if there was time, referring to the fact that the set time for these services was the beginning of the sermon, not the beginning of the service as a whole.

The Communion music for these feasts was varied and required fewer performers than the settings of the Ordinary. On Christmas Day it was in German, beginning with the angel's greeting to the shepherds (Luke 2:10–12), scored for soprano and six instruments, followed by a four-line poetic response ("Biß willkommen du Edler Gast . . .") scored for two tenors and bass, and closing with the entire ensemble singing "Ehre sey Gott in der Höhe" (Luke 2:14). On the second day of Christmas it was the Latin antiphon "O admirabile commercium," set for two altos and four trombones. On New Year's Day the text was "Nun danket alle Gott," drawn from the Apocrypha (Ecclesiasticus 50:22–24), the same text that Buxtehude used in BuxWV 79, but here with different scoring: alto, tenor, bass, two violins, and two viole da gamba. "Bringet her dem Herren" (Psalm 29:1–4), for three basses and eight instruments, was the Communion music for Epiphany.

The afternoon services for the feasts in the 1682 text book contained four separate musical offerings, two before the sermon and two afterward. On each of the feast days, the first work was a motet for eight voices without instruments, two with Latin texts and two with German texts. The second work was often a multi-movement composition with varied scoring, never including capella. On Christmas Day, for example, it appears to have been a composite work scored for two sopranos, alto, tenor, bass, and twelve instruments: two violins, two violas, two clarini (trumpets), two cornetti, three trombones, and bassoon. It began and ended with a movement for the entire ensemble on a biblical text, "Uns ist ein Kind geboren," (Isaiah 9:6). In the middle, each of the vocalists sang one strophe of an aria, accompanied by two violins. The strophes were separated by varied ritornelli based on Christmas hymns, played by all twelve instruments. The Latin Magnificat usually followed the sermon, set in concerted style with vocal soloists, capella, and instruments. On Christmas Day it was performed *cum laudibus*, with interpolated hymns in German and Latin. On New Year's Day the Magnificat was replaced by the German "Te Deum," scored for five vocal soloists, five in the capella, and ten instruments. The final work in the afternoon was most often a large-scale sacred concerto; on Epiphany, however, it was a setting of "Laudate pueri" (Psalm 113) scored for alto, tenor, bass, twelve violins, and two violoni.

We might well ask who had composed all this music and who the performers were; unfortunately, the 1682 text book is completely silent on these important matters. Information at hand, however, enables us to make some educated guesses on these questions, and in so doing we can gain a more vivid picture of the musical life at St. Mary's in the year 1682.

Musicians

Fourteen musicians were on the regular payroll of St. Mary's. Heading the list was Dieterich Buxtehude, with an annual organist's salary of 709 Lübeck marks. In addition to this, he received another salary as Werkmeister of 180 Lübeck marks, plus an allowance for beef, wine, and clothing. His lodging in the Werkhaus was free, and he collected 55 Lübeck marks in annual rent on the house in which the organist had lived when the jobs of organist and Werkmeister were separate. He no doubt also received *Akzidentien* (additional payments) for commissioned compositions and teaching. His total salary was so much larger than what any of the other musicians earned that this alone would have cast him into prominence in Lübeck's capitalistic society. The cantor, Jacob Pagendarm, received only 80 Lübeck marks per year from the church, but this was not his chief source of income. His main position was that of a teacher in St. Catherine's school, for which he received a salary of 330 Lübeck marks plus free lodging. The cantor was third in command at the school, beneath the rector and sub-rector, an order established in Bugenhagen's *Kirchenordnung* for Lübeck. He was responsible for teaching Latin and religion to the second and third classes and music to the entire school. A university education in theology was the main pre-requisite for the position; a musical education was usually acquired on the side. Jacob Pagendarm (1646–1706) was born in Herford (Westphalia) and had studied at the universities of Helmstedt and Wittenberg. He had previously served as cantor in Osnabrück before coming to Lübeck in 1679[18] to succeed Samuel Franck (1633–79). Franck was Buxtehude's brother-in-law; both had married daughters of Franz Tunder.

Christoffer Knölcke, the trumpeter in the tower of St. Mary's, received an annual salary of 100 Lübeck marks. His main responsibility was that of a watchman and signaler, but on feast days he assembled a small group to play four-part chorales from the church tower.[19] He is not known to have participated in the music inside the church.

A total of ten instrumentalists were paid regularly to play from the organ and the choir loft at St. Mary's, including all seven municipal musicians. Of these, Johann Philipp Roth, the lutenist, and Hans Iwe, the sopranist and player of the violin and many other instruments, each received 30 Lübeck marks per year to perform from the organ. The other five—Hinrich Höppner, Peter Bruhns, Christoffer Panning, Jacob Hampe, and Peter Zachow—received 105 Lübeck marks among them—or 21 each—to play from the choir loft. Three other musicians also played from the choir loft: Daniel Grecke—a violinist who held the position of municipal drum player—and two unnamed members of the musicians' guild; they each received 12 Lübeck marks per year. The remaining members of the St. Mary's musical establishment were the player of the positive organ in the choir loft, who received 18 Lübeck marks per year; two regular organ blowers, who divided a salary of 30 Lübeck marks; and an organ blower for the positive, who received 6 Lübeck marks per year. The small disparity in salary between Daniel Grecke—an experienced professional musician—and the player of the positive, a boy who had only recently been hired and had to be examined by Buxtehude, is striking. If Grecke played only on feast days, however, whereas the boy had to appear every Sunday, then Grecke would have received about three times as much per service as the boy, which would then be commensurate with their experience.

The other musicians who performed regularly in St. Mary's were not paid; they were the choirboys from St. Catherine's school. The school had been founded as the city's Latin school in 1531; it was located very close to St. Mary's, in a former Franciscan monastery that had been dissolved with the Reformation. From the beginning, the cantor and his choir had been responsible for the choral music in St. Mary's. On ordinary Sundays the choir sang in unison; on feast days, figural music was performed. The motets at the beginning of the afternoon services in the feasts of the Christmas season 1682–83 and the capella parts in all the large concerted works were almost certainly performed by the St. Catherine's choirboys under the direction of the cantor. Some of the eight vocal soloists necessary for the works performed that season may also have come from the choir. The school was not well endowed with good singers that year, however. For the Abendmusiken, which had just ended the Sunday before Christmas, Buxtehude had had to hire a bass from Hamburg, because "the singers in the choir (*Cantorey*) of this school at the present time have been bad, and I could not use them." The announcement on the title of the 1682 text book that these works were to be performed "with sufficient vocal assistance" would seem to imply that outside singers were used at these services as well.

The ten instrumentalists regularly employed at St. Mary's would have been sufficient to perform most of the works listed in the 1682 text book, particularly if the musicians paid to perform from the organ joined with those whose responsibility was with the choir. The mass Ordinary on Christmas Day and both works following the afternoon sermon on New Year's Day called for exactly ten instruments. In the afternoon services of first and second Christmas and Epiphany, however, works were performed that required twelve to fourteen instruments. The cantata "Uns ist ein Kind geboren," for example, was scored for twelve instruments. It is possible to match known players with most of its instrumental parts: Iwe and Grecke could have played violin, Roth and Bruhns viola, Höppner and Zachow cornetto. Jacob Hampe was normally a violone player, but in this work the bass part was scored for dulcian; perhaps he played that as well. We do not know what instruments Christoffer Panning or the two from the musicians' guild played, but these musicians were all versatile; let us give them the three trombone parts. Two clarino parts remain, for which outside help would probably have been required, perhaps from Cristoffer Knölcke and one of his apprentices, or from the official Lübeck *Feldtrompeter*. There must have been a number of good trumpet players in Lübeck; in 1673 the church had purchased two special trumpets for the Abendmusiken, and three years later the purchase of mutes made it clear that the church owned six trumpets.

The church appears to have made funds available to pay the extra singers and instrumentalists who were required for these festival services at St. Mary's. Although no payments to individual musicians are recorded, in the first week of 1683 the cantor received a sum of 30 Lübeck marks that had been previously authorized by the church directors. A similar payment at the beginning of 1682 with the same authorization clarifies its purpose: to pay musicians. Since no such payments occurred at other times, this was probably the cantor's budget for the entire year. Still, Pagendarm seems to have been more fortunate in this respect than the later cantor Caspar Ruetz, who complained in 1752 that

> everything with a musical breath sings and plays in the Abendmusiken, because almost the whole citizenry participates, so that the music can be magnificent and richly scored. But when the holy feast of Christmas arrives, the solemn remembrance of the mystery of the incarnation of the Son of God, which the angels longed to behold, I have no more than eight municipal musicians and a couple of singers for the holiday music. If I want to perform richly scored and festive music appropriate to the feast, as I have often done, especially at the beginning of my tenure, the congregation won't contribute a shilling for it, but I must pay for everything out of my own pocket, which is a good way to play oneself to poverty.[20]

Musical Repertoire

We have a good idea of the musical repertoire of St. Mary's around 1682, for part of its music library still survives. In 1814, on the occasion of the Congress of Vienna, the imperial free city of Lübeck made a gift of the old St. Mary's music collection to Archduke Rudolf of Austria. Upon his death, it came to the library of the Gesellschaft der Musikfreunde in Vienna, where it remains. A list of the main titles included in this gift was kept in Lübeck, and on that basis the Lübeck librarian Carl Stiehl inspected and partially catalogued the collection in the late nineteenth century. A thorough examination of the partbooks in Vienna, based on archival documents now returned to Lübeck, reveals, however, that the 1814 list records only the first item in each set of bound partbooks, which could contain as many as six separate prints, so when these were unbound and rebound as separate items in Vienna, Stiehl did not know of their existence. The list of partbooks in the old St. Mary's choir library now given in appendix 5C is thus considerably larger than that of my first edition, which was based on Stiehl's published catalogue, the only source available at the time.[21]

The extant portion of the old choir library, comprising sixty-nine prints from 1546 to 1674 and one set of partbooks in manuscript, contains 2,144 works, or 2,010 different works with concordances eliminated. The most heavily represented composers are Andreas Hammerschmidt (131 works), Hieronymus Praetorius (122 works), and Hans Leo Hassler (98 works), but approximately one third of the compositions are by Italian composers, among whom Giovanni Rovetta (67 works), Simone Vesi (43 works), and Giovanni Gabrieli (33 works) figure most prominently; of the sixty-nine printed editions in the collection, two were published in Milan, six in Rome, and seventeen in Venice. Many of the parts for these works bear signs of use in the form of corrections, notes that a part has been copied or that a general bass for it can be found in a particular book, and changes to the text that enabled a work espousing Roman Catholic doctrine to be performed in Lutheran Lübeck. For example, Paolo Quagliati's motet "Ave sanctissima Maria" becomes "Jesu ex penetrali cordis," directing the petitions to Jesus as Redeemer rather than to Mary as intercessor. The choir library's copy of Rovetta's *Messa, e Salmi Concertati* of 1639 was apparently in too incomplete a state to be sent to Vienna; four of its original ten partbooks remain in Lübeck. Its setting of the Magnificat, for eight concerted voices (SSAATTBB), two violins, and continuo, shows many signs of use, attesting to the early introduction of Italian concerted vocal music into the Lübeck liturgy.

Two of the works surviving in the old choir library may have been performed in those festival services of 1682. The opening motet on Christmas afternoon of 1682, "Corde natus ex parentis ante mundi exordia, &c, *8 Vocum*" could have been the setting by Melchior Vulpius (ca. 1570–1615) contained in the first volume of Erhard Bodenschatz's *Florilegium Portense* and also in the manuscript partbooks. This is a polychoral work, scored for high and low choirs (SSAA / ATTB). Over one third of the extant library is devoted to polychoral motets; most of them appear in the early seventeenth-century anthologies of Schadaeus and Bodenschatz, but they extend to Rovetta's *Delli Salmi a otto voci* (1662) and Vesi's *Salmi a otto ariosi* (1663). The fact that all four of these festive afternoon services opened with an eight-voice motet attests to the continued popularity of this genre in Buxtehude's Lübeck. The setting of the Kyrie, Gloria, and Credo of the mass on New Year's morning, for "6 Strom. 6 Vocalst. 6 zur Capell," could have been Hammerschmidt's Mass XVI, published in 1663, for six voices (SSATTB), two violins, four trombones and continuo. This set of partbooks does not contain separate capella parts, but these would typically have been extracted by the cantor for the appropriate sections. A note by Jacob Pagendarm on the title page of Vox 12 states that he had bought these partbooks in 1673, while he was still cantor in Osnabruck.

The music from Lübeck presently in Vienna cannot comprise the entire music library that was available at St. Mary's in 1682, however. Hammerschmidt's *Musikalische Andachten*, part IV (1646), which had been purchased in 1652 and rebound in 1671, is not there, nor are the psalms of Heinrich Schütz and the sacred concertos of Samuel Capricornus purchased in 1660. And there must have been many more manuscripts; at that time, richly scored works such as were performed at those festival services were more likely to be disseminated in manuscript than in print.

The question naturally arises as to whether any of the works listed in the 1682 text book were by Buxtehude. Although not one of the combinations of text and scoring listed there corresponds to a known work of Buxtehude, there is a strong possibility that he was the composer of some of those works. It did not lie within his official duties either to compose vocal music or to direct its performance, yet Buxtehude left a large body of sacred vocal music: 114 extant works in the catalogue of his music. The apparent incongruity between Buxtehude's position as organist and this group of vocal works has led to considerable discussion among scholars as to the circumstances in which they might have been performed. Friedrich Blume, noting the nonliturgical character of most of Buxtehude's sacred music, wrote in 1940 that these works would most likely have been performed not during church services but in concerts. In 1957 he suggested "the possibility, if not the probability . . . that Buxtehude actually composed all these 'cantatas' not for Lübeck, but on commission from his friend and patron, the Stockholm court Kapellmeister Gustav Düben." Dietrich Kilian noted in his dissertation that many of these works were in fact appropriate for specific days in the church year and that the cantor could have performed them during church services. Martin Geck countered in his monograph that Buxtehude himself would have directed their performance and hypothesized a distinction in North German sacred music between *Kantorenmusik*—liturgical, choral, and traditional in style—and *Organistenmusik*—nonliturgical, written for ensembles of soloists, and modern in style. Friedhelm Krummacher disputed this strict division in his article on organ and vocal music in the works of North German organists. He challenged the assumption that they *regularly* directed vocal music, while granting that organists often did so during the distribution of Communion. Arnfried Edler discussed the problem further; he emphasized the lack of contemporary evidence for a sharp distinction in the type of music performed by cantors and by organists in North Germany, but he noted that there was ample evidence to document performances of vocal music both from the organ loft (*auf der Orgel*) and from the choir loft (*auf dem Chor*). The high social status that the North German organist enjoyed in his community gave him the *freedom*—not the responsibility—to compose and perform vocal music for the church service.

The account books of St. Mary's do indeed offer strong evidence that Buxtehude directed performances of concerted vocal music during church services. Visiting singers were occasionally paid by the church to perform from the organ: Johann Valentin Meder on the feast of the Visitation of Mary in 1674, a visiting singer from Kiel in 1675 who sang from both the organ and the choir loft, a singer named Longolius from the Gotha court in 1687, and an Italian singer for Pentecost 1693. An Italian castrato and a bass from Antwerp sang on Easter 1672 and an Italian singer on Ascension Day 1673, but the accounts do not specify where they performed. In 1678 the church purchased a 16' double regal; Buxtehude noted that the church directors had authorized its purchase at his request, "for the glory of God and for the encouragement of my music for feast days and my Abendmusik."

Presumably it was used as a continuo instrument on one of the balconies near the large organ. That these balconies were used for performances other than the Abendmusiken is documented by the fact that in the fourth week after New Year of 1670—not at the time of the Abendmusiken—boards were installed near the organ so that the musicians could get to the new balconies without damaging the organ pipes. In 1681 the church purchased twenty-two sets of parts from the widow of the late cantor, Samuel Franck; this music was designated "to be used both at the organ and in the choir." And the inventory of music to be sent to Vienna in 1814 is entitled "List of ancient music, which has been stored in the choir loft and at the large organ of St. Mary's Church."

Geck's examination of the texts and scoring of the works performed at the festival services of the 1682–83 Christmas season suggested that Buxtehude had composed and directed the music during Communion in the morning and the second composition before the sermon in the afternoon. The following types of texts appear in these positions:

Festival	Communion music	Afternoon II
Christmas 1	Bible + poetry (1 strophe)	Bible + poetry (5 strophes)
Christmas 2	Latin antiphon	Bible + poetry (1 strophe)
New Year's	Bible (Apocrypha)	poetry (5 strophes)
Epiphany	Bible (psalm verses)	Bible (complete psalm)

Texts of these types appear frequently in Buxtehude's preserved vocal works. His numerous concerto-aria cantatas are built on a combination of a biblical text and strophic poetry, his arias on strophic poetry alone. He used biblical texts in both German and Latin for his sacred concertos, and he left a significant body of works based on other Latin texts, both liturgical and nonliturgical. With respect to the scoring, the absence of the capella in all the works performed at these times is striking; all are scored for a solo singer or for an ensemble of up to five vocal soloists, as is the vast majority of Buxtehude's vocal music. The instrumental scoring of these works, however, was as rich as that of the works performed with capella.

If these works performed during Communion in the morning and directly before the sermon in the afternoon were not only composed by Buxtehude but were also directed by him from the large organ, then the instrumentalists responsible to the cantor, who normally performed from the choir loft above the rood screen at the east end of the church, would have had to move up to the balconies near the large organ at the west end in order to perform these works. In a church as large as St. Mary's this would have taken a considerable amount of time, and indeed it appears that the music for these services, particularly in the afternoon, was programmed so as to facilitate this movement of musicians. The afternoon services all began with a motet without instrumental accompaniment, except perhaps from the positive organ in the choir loft, and continued with a work that we have hypothetically ascribed to Buxtehude. During the entire first part of the service, then, the instrumentalists could have been in the balconies by the organ. Then came the hour-long sermon, during which—as we know from Caspar Ruetz—the musicians frequently left the church. All the concerted music with capella and instruments occurred after the sermon, giving the instrumentalists plenty of time to get to the choir loft. In the morning services, with the exception of Christmas Day, the situation was similar; the concerted Kyrie and Gloria were separated from the Communion music by the sermon. On Christmas Day, ten instrumentalists were needed by the cantor for the Credo and Sanctus following the sermon; among them were probably Iwe and Roth, who normally performed with Buxtehude. The six instrumentalists needed for the Communion music might have had to rush on that day.

The picture of musical life at St. Mary's thus emerges as one of friendly cooperation between the cantors Franck and later Pagendarm and the organist Buxtehude in the performance of vocal music, including their sharing of the instrumentalists responsible to them. The division of labor between them was probably not so sharply defined as Geck suggested; indeed, he himself pointed out that on Epiphany the last work of the afternoon service, normally a large-scale sacred concerto, was in this case a composition more akin to those of Buxtehude, perhaps because the choir was tired at the end of this demanding season. The music that the church owned, most of it purchased by the cantor, includes both liturgical and nonliturgical music, motets, small concertos, and large concertos with capella; it is by no means restricted to the traditional *Kantorenmusik* that Geck hypothesized. And the purchase in 1681 of the late cantor Franck's music collection for use both in the choir loft and at the organ suggests that Buxtehude might also have directed the performance of vocal works by other composers from the large organ.

Buxtehude's Responsibilities as Organist and Werkmeister

Very little concrete evidence survives concerning the nature of Buxtehude's specific duties as organist at St. Mary's; his contract is not extant, and the account books shed no light on his organ playing. Bugenhagen's *Kirchenordnung* required organists to play very few services:

> [The organists], together with their wives, can seek other suitable earnings, especially in teaching their art to others, because they play only on holidays and are free the whole week, apart from their being asked also to play the Benedictus, an antiphon, and the Benedicamus on Thursday mornings, further in the evening the hymn, the Magnificat, the antiphon, and the Benedicamus, also Saturday for Vespers.

By Buxtehude's time these had been reduced to the main morning and afternoon services on Sundays and feast days, and Vespers on Saturdays and the eves of feasts.

In Buxtehude's hands the *Praeludirung* to the hymns mentioned in the *Kurtze Anweisung* must have been quite elaborate; the ministers decided on December 10, 1701, to hang boards with the hymn numbers in the church, because "from the organ playing beforehand, the hymns can be recognized by only a few, and the new hymns, whose melodies are not known, by practically no one."[22] This was not actually done until 1704, following the introduction of the official hymnal. The phrase "with playing of the organ" (*mit Einschlagung der Orgel*) that appears several times in the *Kurtze Anweisung* could refer either to *alternatim* practice or to the accompaniment of certain hymns, although this did not become common practice in Lübeck until the mid-eighteenth century. The account of the life of the burgomaster Peter Hinrich Tesdorpf, a regular attendee of St. Mary's, states that he

> let his voice resound powerfully in the singing of hymns to the praise of the Lord. He took heartfelt pleasure in the noble sounds of the organ, which accompanied the singing of the Latin collects. He was particularly delighted with the playing of the cantor [*sic*] Buxtehude, who won in him an "admirer and true friend."

It was still the responsibility of the cantor and his choir to lead the congregational singing, however, and it was undoubtedly for this purpose that Pagendarm wrote his chorale book of 1705. *Alternatim* practice is documented in Lübeck as far back as the fifteenth century. The Mecklenburg *Kirchenordnung* of 1650 specifically calls for its use for the Magnificat in Saturday Vespers: "But where there are organs, the organist shall play one verse after the other."

The sketch of the Lübeck liturgy found in the *Kurze Anweisung* seems to offer scant opportunity for the performance of solo organ music; the services all begin and end with the singing of hymns, and when the organ is mentioned it is usually in connection with a hymn or an intonation to a sung portion of the liturgy. The only clearly independent organ music occurs at the close of Saturday Vespers, but it had to stop at three o'clock, calling therefore for a flexible improvisation. This requirement would appear to rule out the extended improvisations such as those known to have been performed during Saturday Vespers in Hamburg, but we do not know whether this requirement was only implemented in 1703, perhaps in response to overly long performances before that time, or codified the existing custom. Certainly extensive solo performances such as are represented by his *pedaliter* praeludia and chorale fantasias did not belong to Buxtehude's official duties as organist. But as was the case with his vocal music, he probably enjoyed considerable artistic freedom to display his art as an organist, whether during the church services at St. Mary's, following them, or in private concerts for the business community.

Continuo playing in ensemble music was an extremely important part of a North German organist's activity in the later seventeenth century. Nowhere is this more clearly demonstrated than in the description of the service that

Heinrich Scheidemann played to dedicate a new organ in Otterndorf/Hadeln in 1662. This famous visiting organist played only one free prelude during that service; his chief role was that of accompanist in three concertos for solo voice and two large concerted motets from Hammerschmidt's *Musicalische Andachten*, part IV (1646). It was in the accompaniment of Hammerschmidt's setting of Psalm 150, which was performed partly from the choir loft and partly from the organ, that the various stops of the new organ were demonstrated, "and the instruments with strings and pipes (such as violins, flutes, cornets, trombones and cymbals) were used as the text itself demanded." To be sure, it was only after the conclusion of the service that the real demonstration of the organ for the patrons and preachers began, and it continued for three hours.[23]

Buxtehude would not have played continuo for the vocal music directed by the cantor; a positiv organ in the choir loft had been purchased in 1664 from Michel Briegel for that purpose and an organist was regularly paid to play it. But Buxtehude was definitely involved in the performance of vocal and instrumental ensemble music from the large organ, most likely during the distribution of Communion. The practice of paying a municipal musician to play from the organ was established at St. Mary's long before the rise of baroque concerted style. From 1594, a violist was paid 20 Lübeck marks a year to play with the organist on all feasts and on some Sundays as well. During the latter part of Tunder's tenure, the musicians who played from the organ were the violin virtuoso Nathaniel Schnittelbach and the lutenist Joachim Baltzer. No independent instrumental ensemble music by Tunder survives, but the church purchased a collection of trio sonatas by Johann Heinrich Schmelzer in 1660 for his use. Buxtehude's lost sonatas of 1684 (BuxWV 274), scored for two to three violins, viola da gamba, and continuo, were designated as suitable for church or dinner music; they could have been performed with Iwe, Roth, and one or two extra violinists, probably Peter Bruhns and Daniel Grecke. The scoring of Buxtehude's published sonatas, opus 1 (1694?) and opus 2 (1696) suited the trio of Iwe, Roth, and Buxtehude perfectly; the fact that the continuo part was labeled "Cembalo" in the prints need not mean that Buxtehude did not play the part on the organ for church performances.

In addition to his activity as a performer, Buxtehude's responsibilities as organist undoubtedly included some routine maintenance of the organs. This practice can be traced back to the sixteenth century at St. Mary's; David Aebell's contract with the St. Mary's directors, dated 1564, requires of him extensive maintenance of the organs: "David Aebell intends to serve as an organist for his life time, and in addition to pay diligent attention to the organs and the works, and at his own expense to maintain them; however, David shall not be responsible for whatever damage rats or mice do to the bellows or other things."[24] One cannot help but wonder whether Buxtehude's contract contained a similar provision, in view of his frequent references in the account books to damage by rats. The extent of the organist's responsibility for the care of the organs may not have been so great in the seventeenth century, however; during the years 1645–59 the organ builder Friedrich Stellwagen maintained the organs in the five main churches of Lübeck under contract, and frequent payments for repairs to the St. Mary's organs were made to organ builders in later years. An organist was responsible for tuning the reeds of his organ every week, in Arp Schnitger's opinion, "for the organ builder has not yet been born who could make reeds that did not need to be tuned weekly."[25]

As Werkmeister, Buxtehude served as the administrator and treasurer of the church, a position of considerable responsibility and prestige. Frequent reference has already been made to the account books that he kept in this capacity. They were written on heavy paper in large format, normally 28 centimeters wide and 40.9 centimeters high. The financial transactions for one week typically were contained on facing pages, hence the name *Wochenbücher*. The receipts for the week were entered on the left or verso side; these consisted mainly of charges for burials and the ringing of funeral bells. In fact, until 1750 there were no separate burial books for the church; until then the account books served to keep the official death records. Rents for church properties and interest on investments provided another important source of income for the church, but these records were kept in separate books. Buxtehude's entries of expenses on the right or recto side of each opening provide a chronicle of the life of the church and reflect the varied nature of his duties as Werkmeister. He was responsible for the payment of salaries and the procurement of all sorts of supplies, from building materials for the constant repairs to the church to bread and wine for Communion. And it was his duty to oversee all the work that was done in the church and to pay the workers. Buxtehude kept the books faithfully from the day he took over, on 1 January 1669, until Saturday, 19 March 1707. His final illness must have overtaken him suddenly, because on the following Monday a new hand appeared in the account books, and Buxtehude's was gone forever. He died 9 May 1707.

Buxtehude's Predecessor: Franz Tunder

In his assumption of the duties of both organist and Werkmeister, as in many other respects, Buxtehude followed in the footsteps of his illustrious predecessor, Franz Tunder. Tunder was born in 1614 in Lübeck, the son of a bookseller of the same name. Mattheson's statement in the *Ehrenpforte* that Tunder had studied in Italy with Frescobaldi may be erroneous, but he certainly knew Italian music.[26] He served from 1632 to 1641 as court organist at Gottorf, seat of the dukes of Gottorf-Holstein and a flourishing center of musical culture. When he was appointed organist at St. Mary's in 1641, the Werkmeister was one Gerdt Black, who had served since 1628. Tunder assumed the duties of Werkmeister upon Black's retirement in 1647 but did not begin to collect the Werkmeister's salary until after Black's death in 1651. At that time he moved from the organ-ist's house on Hundestraße to the Werkmeister's apartment in the churchyard, but since he was still entitled to live in the organist's house, which was owned by the church, he collected rent on it, a prerogative which was passed on to Buxtehude. From Tunder's time until 1928, all but one of the St. Mary's organ-ists served also as Werkmeister.

Tunder's surviving compositions suggest that in all of his varied musical activi-ties, Buxtehude followed traditions that were already well established during Tunder's time. Tunder's improvised preludes to the congregational hymns may have been less elaborate than Buxtehude's, but his free organ works and espe-cially his chorale fantasias demonstrate a strong tradition of solo organ per-formance at St. Mary's. It was his organ recitals for the business community that had spawned the Lübeck Abendmusiken, and Buxtehude may have continued private recitals for the businessmen even after he had established the regular series of dramatic Abendmusiken. Tunder's vocal works, like Buxtehude's, are mainly nonliturgical and are scored for a small ensemble of vocal soloists and instrumentalists. We can assume that Tunder directed performances of these works from the large organ; the four smaller balconies nearest the organ were already in place at that time. In one important respect Tunder did not set a precedent for Buxtehude: He did not marry a daughter of his predecessor, Peter Hasse. Before returning to Lübeck, Tunder had already married Elisabeth Voight, daughter of the Gottorf court tailor, on 10 February 1640.

Buxtehude's Successor: Johann Christian Schieferdecker

By 1703, Dieterich Buxtehude had served for thirty-five years as organist of St. Mary's. He was about sixty-six years old, and he was no doubt concerned about the future of his three unmarried daughters: Anna Margreta, age twenty-eight; Anna Sophia, age twenty-five; and Dorothea Catrin, age twenty. He may also have been seeking an assistant to help him at the organ in his old age, and he began to look for a successor who would marry Anna Margreta. The first prospective candidates of whom we know were Johann Mattheson, age twenty-one, and George Frideric Handel, age eighteen, both of whom were employed at the Hamburg opera at the time. Mattheson relates the story in his entry on Handel in the *Ehrenpforte*:

> We travelled together on the 17th of August of that year 1703 to Lübeck, and in the coach we composed many double fugues, in our heads, not written down. The privy council president, Magnus von Wedderkopp, had invited me, in order to make me the future successor of the excellent organist Dietrich Buxtehude. So I took Händel along. There we played almost all the organs and harpsichords, and we arrived at a particular conclusion with respect to our playing, which I had realized elsewhere: namely, that he

wanted to play only the organ and I the harpsichord. We listened to that esteemed artist in his St. Mary's church with dignified attention. However, since he had proposed a marriage condition in the matter, for which neither of us expressed the slightest inclination, we took our leave, after being complemented and entertained. Johann Christian Schieferdecker later applied himself better to the goal, led the bride home after the death of the father Buxtehude, and received the fine position that Johann Paul Kuntzen so laudably fills at the present time.

Johann Christian Schieferdecker, born in 1679, was working at the Hamburg Opera as an accompanist and composer; he had come there from Leipzig in 1702 and then moved to Lübeck to serve as Buxtehude's assistant during his last year. Following Buxtehude's death, Schieferdecker was chosen organist and Werkmeister 23 June and married Anna Margreta Buxtehude on 5 September 1707. His experience as an opera composer must have made him well suited to continue the tradition of dramatic Abendmusiken that Buxtehude had established; he composed twenty-three such works, of which nineteen librettos survive, although their music is lost. Another series of lost works, *Geistliche Cantaten nach Ordnung der Sonn- und festtäglichen Evangelien,* suggests that his activity as a composer and director of vocal music for the church services was more regular than Buxtehude's had been. He served at St. Mary's until his death in 1732.

The Visit of Johann Sebastian Bach

Late in 1705, during the time that Buxtehude may still have been searching for a successor, Johann Sebastian Bach, at the age of twenty, made his famous trip from Arnstadt to visit Buxtehude in Lübeck. He most likely passed through the cities of Gotha, Mühlhausen, Duderstadt, Sesen, Braunschweig or Hannover, Lüneburg, and Mölln on his way to Lübeck, a distance of approximately 450 kilometers. Bach, too, may have been interested in obtaining the succession to Buxtehude's position, but there is no evidence that this was the case. The account of the trip in Bach's obituary states unambiguously that its purpose was to hear Buxtehude play the organ:

> In the art of the organ he took the works of Bruhns, Reinken, Buxtehude, and several good French organists as models. Here in Arnstadt he was once moved by an especially strong desire to hear as many good organists as possible, so he undertook a journey to Lübeck, indeed by foot, in order to listen to the famous Organist of St. Mary's Church there, Diedrich Buxtehude. He remained there, not without profit, for almost a quarter of a year, and then returned to Arnstadt.[27]

The proceedings of the Arnstadt consistory of 21 February 1706 support the position that the purpose of the trip was educational:

The Organist in the New Church, Bach, is interrogated as to where he has lately been for so long and from whom he obtained permission to go.

Bach: He has been in Lübeck in order to comprehend one thing and another about his art, but had asked permission beforehand from the Superintendent.

The Superintendent: He had asked for a leave of only four weeks, but had stayed away about four times as long.

Bach: Hoped that the organ playing had been so taken care of by the one he had engaged for the purpose that no complaint could be entered on that account.

The Consistory: Reprove him for having hitherto made many strange *variationes* in the *choral*, and mixed many foreign tones into it, so that the Congregation has been confused by it. . . .[28]

Bach's answer, "to comprehend one thing and another about his art," is rather vague, and we cannot expect that he would tell his present employer that he was in Lübeck seeking a new position. But had he been interested only in the job, he could have returned home as quickly as Handel and Mattheson did once they had learned of the marriage condition. Also, Schieferdecker may already have been the heir apparent at the time of Bach's visit, and Bach may already have been engaged to Maria Barbara. There seems little reason to believe that Bach was a serious candidate for Buxtehude's position.

The fact that Bach overextended his leave and remained in Lübeck for nearly three months offers a clear indication that he took the opportunity to learn all that he could from Buxtehude, and not just in the art of the organ. Bach appears to have timed his trip to arrive in Lübeck at the end of October 1705, just as the rehearsals for the Abendmusiken could be expected to begin. Whether the "ordinary" series of Abendmusiken took place that year is not known, but his time in Lübeck coincided with the performances of the "extraordinary" Abendmusiken, *Castrum doloris* and *Templum honoris*, on December 2 and 3. In an enterprise that ambitious, Buxtehude must have put every available musician to work, including Bach. Perhaps he was one of the twenty-five violinists who played in *Templum honoris*. This richly scored ceremonial music must have left a deep impression on him and may have come to mind when he himself had the opportunity to invoke civic pride with the composition of *Gott ist mein König* (BWV 71) for the inauguration of the Mühlhausen town council two years later. Buxtehude's influence can clearly be perceived in Bach's *per omnes versus* settings of *Christ lag in Todes Banden* (BWV 4), perhaps composed soon after his return to Arnstadt, and many years later *Jesu meine Freude* (BWV 227).

Bach was already familiar with Buxtehude's organ music before setting out from Arnstadt—and indeed even before he left Ohrdruf for Lüneburg in 1700—as shown by the recent discovery of the Weimar tablature, with his copy of Buxtehude's *Nun freut euch lieben Christen gmein*.[29] While he was in Lübeck, he must have made more copies of Buxtehude's music, which he himself studied and later made available to his circle of relatives, pupils and friends. At least thirty of Buxtehude's organ works have come down to us in manuscripts emanating from this circle, although it now appears that they cannot all be traced back to the Lübeck trip. These include more than two thirds of his free *pedaliter* organ works and half the free *manualiter* works. Bach's knowledge of organ building must also have been enhanced by his Lübeck experience. Two years later, as organist at St. Blasius, Mühlhausen, Bach drew up a list of recommendations for the renovation of the organ there, including the addition of a 32′ Subbaß to the pedal, modifications to the 16′ Posaune to achieve greater *Gravität*, and the addition of a 16′ Fagott for use in ensemble music and of a "perfect and beautiful" Sesquialtera. These particular recommendations may have been inspired by his recent acquaintance with the large organ at St. Mary's, Lübeck, whose Sesquialtera had been added only in 1704.

Bach's presence during those three months, at a time when Buxtehude perceived the love of noble music in Lübeck to be diminishing and growing cold, must certainly have brightened Buxtehude's old age. The Lübeck historian Ahasver von Brandt has written that

> Lübeck has never . . . held such a low position in the intellectual, religious, economic and political arena than around the year 1700. . . . The pilgrimage of the Arnstadt organist to Lübeck is almost the most significant event in the history of ideas in this entire, otherwise so empty period of Lübeck's history.[30]

Music historians would argue that Buxtehude's own accomplishments within the walls of St. Mary's Church during nearly forty years of an "otherwise so empty period of Lübeck's history" are of still greater significance.

Dieterich Buxtehude was buried in St. Mary's Church on 16 May 1707. As was customary for a church employee, the ringing of the bells occurred without charge to the family. His grave, near the steps to the choir loft above the rood screen, was destroyed in 1942, but a plaque in the rebuilt church perpetuates his memory. At the end of his account for the burial, the new Werkmeister Johann Christian Schieferdecker wrote: "*Requiem aeternam dona Ei Domine, sitque ejus memoria in pace, Amen.*"

Chapter Four

Beyond the Walls of Lübeck

Once settled in Lübeck, Buxtehude remained there, and he appears to have traveled little, apart from visits to Hamburg. His contacts with musical colleagues and his influence through his pupils covered a wide geographical range, however. We know that during his lifetime, Buxtehude's fame extended northward to Stockholm, northeastward along the Baltic coast as far as Narva, and southward to Nuremberg. For his own musical and intellectual stimulation—and also for entertainment—he himself turned westward to Hamburg.

Hamburg

Hamburg's fortunes had been ascending since the mid-sixteenth century; its population rose rapidly from twenty thousand in 1550 to nearly fifty thousand in 1620. Whereas Lübeck clung to the old Hanseatic guest laws, Hamburg rejected them, welcoming foreigners as both merchants and artisans. Cosmopolitan, progressive, and economically prosperous, seventeenth-century Hamburg supported an excellent musical establishment for the adornment of its church, school, and municipal functions. Two privately organized institutions flourished for a time as well: a collegium musicum and a public opera. William Carr, whose contemporary description of Lübeck appears in chapter 2, relates Hamburg's rich musical life to its prosperity:

> The Churches here are rich in revenues, and ornaments, as Images and Stately Organs wherein they much delight. They are great lovers of Musick; in so much that I have told 75 masters of severall sorts of Musick in one Church, besides those who were in the Organ-gallery. Their Organs are extraordinarily large. I measured the great pipes in the organs of St. Catharins and St. James's Churches, and found them to be 3 foot and 3 quarters in circumference and 32 foot long; in each of which organs there are two pipes 5 foot and 8 inches round. The wealth and trade of this citie increases dayly: they send one year with another 70 ships to Greenland, and have wonderfully engrossed that trade from England and Holland, and it is beleeved that small and great there are belonging to this Commonwealth five thousand sail of ships. After Amsterdam, Genoa, and Venice their bank is reckoned the chiefe in credit; but in trade they are accounted the third in Europe, and come next to London and Amsterdam. Hambourg is now become the Magazine of Germany and of the baltick and northern seas. They give great

priviledges to the Jewes, and to all strangers what soever, Especially the English Company of Merchant Adventurers, whom they allow a large building . . .[1]

Hamburg lies 60 kilometers southwest of Lübeck. A road connecting the two cities, passing through Oldesloe, had existed since the twelfth century, and another, more southerly route passed through Schönberg. Transportation services between Hamburg and Lübeck developed rapidly during the seventeenth century; beginning in 1660 two competing lines offered daily coach service to carry passengers, mail, and freight. During the light summer months the trip could be accomplished in one day; in the winter an overnight stop was usually necessary.[2] When the French physicist and mathematician Balthasar Monconys traveled from Hamburg to Lübeck in mid-October 1663, he left Hamburg in a private coach at noon and spent the night in Sandesneben. The following morning his party left at seven and arrived in Lübeck at one in the afternoon.[3] When Buxtehude went to visit Arp Schnitger on Monday, 2 May 1687, he stopped for lunch and changed coaches in Schönberg, arriving in Hamburg on the same day. His trips would not have been comfortable—the roads were unpaved and the coaches lacked springs—but they were not especially difficult.

Soon after his arrival in Lübeck, Buxtehude formed—or perhaps renewed—relationships with musicians in Hamburg. The leading personalities in Hamburg's musical life had changed considerably during the 1660s, while Buxtehude was working in Helsingør. The last two Sweelinck students among the organists had died, Johann Praetorius in 1660 and Scheidemann in 1663. Thomas Selle, cantor of the Johanneum, Hamburg's Latin school and gymnasium, had also died in 1663, followed in 1667 by the violinist Johann Schop and the poet Johann Rist. Johann Adam Reincken (1643–1722) had replaced his teacher Scheidemann as organist of St. Catherine's, and Christoph Bernhard (1628–92) had become cantor at the Johanneum. Matthias Weckmann (ca. 1619–74), organist at St. Jacobi since 1655, had advanced the appointment of his friend Bernhard; the two had worked together for Heinrich Schütz in Dresden from 1649 to 1655. As cantor of the Johanneum, Bernhard also enjoyed the title of *Director musices* for the city, bearing the responsibility for directing the concerted music in Hamburg's four principal churches—St. Peter's, St. Catherine's, St. Nicholas's, and St. Jacobi. For this purpose he had at his disposal the municipal musicians, a *Kantorei* consisting of eight paid solo singers, and the choir of the Johanneum. Georg Philipp Telemann and Carl Philipp Emanuel Bach occupied the same position in the eighteenth century.

Weckmann and Bernhard are best remembered in Hamburg for their activity in connection with the collegium musicum, an organization that Weckmann had founded in 1660. According to information from Mattheson's *Ehrenpforte*, the collegium met in the refectory of the cathedral and consisted of "fifty people, all of whom contributed to it. The best pieces were sent from Venice, Rome, Vienna, Munich, Dresden, etc.; indeed, this collegium attained such fame, that the greatest composers tried to attach their names to it." Kaspar Förster, Jr., sent his works, particularly his sonatas for two violins and gamba, to the collegium musicum, "for he knew well that there were famous people there, who were accustomed to appreciate such things more than a capricious court." When the candidates for the position of cantor sent their trial pieces to Hamburg in 1663, it was the collegium musicum that performed them. In a contemporary account, Johann Rist stated that

> one needs only to listen for two hours to the collegium musicum—which is specially held weekly in Hamburg by some students, businessmen, musicians and other praise-worthy amateurs of this noble art—and one must confess, half enchanted, that it would be difficult to find anything like it in Germany.[4]

The collegium performances, with their emphasis on new music, would certainly have attracted Buxtehude to Hamburg, and in all likelihood he participated in them himself from time to time, both as a performer and as a composer. It may have been there that he became acquainted with the new Roman style of sacred music, for which Bernhard was the most likely conduit. Bernhard had traveled to Rome himself in 1657, and the composers Vincenzo Albrici and Giuseppe Peranda had begun to introduce the Roman style to the Dresden court with the accession of the new elector Johann Georg II in 1656.[5]

Buxtehude came to know Christoph Bernhard—or at any rate an obscure piece of his music—no later than 1671, the year Buxtehude composed the two elegantly constructed counterpoints on the chorale "Mit Fried und Freud ich fahr dahin" (BuxWV 76-1) in memory of the Lübeck superintendent Meno Hanneken. Buxtehude undoubtedly modeled this piece on a similar work of invertible counterpoint by Bernhard, *Prudentia prudentiana*, which Bernhard had composed as a consolation to Rudolf Capell, his colleague at the Johanneum, and had published in 1669. The striking resemblance between these two works is discussed in chapter 6. Bernhard's well-known treatise on composition, "Tractatus compositionis augmentatus" (ca. 1660), contains an appendix on invertible counterpoint, but it was Bernhard's composition rather than his treatise that inspired Buxtehude.

Buxtehude's closest friend among the Hamburg musicians appears to have been Johann Adam Reincken, the famous organist who still held his position at St. Catherine's when J. S. Bach visited Hamburg in 1720. A painting by Johannes Voorhout executed in Hamburg in 1674 (frontispiece), housed at the Museum für Hamburgische Geschichte and now named *Musizierende Gesellschaft in Hamburg* in German, *Musical Party* in English (formerly *Häusliche Musikszene* and *Domestic Music Scene* respectively), documents the friendship between Buxtehude and Reincken. The central figure in a group of musicians, a man seated at the harpsichord, can be positively identified as Reincken by comparison with an existing portrait of him by Gottfried Kneller.[6] To his left a musician plays the viola da gamba. A man appearing to be younger than Reincken sits to the right of the harpsichord, his right hand cupped to his ear as he listens, his mouth open to sing. A sheet of paper floats beneath his right elbow, containing a canon for eight voices at the unison set to a Latin text from Psalm 133—"Behold, how good and how pleasant it is for brethren to dwell together in unity!"—followed by the inscription "In hon: dit: Buxtehude: et Joh: Adam Reink: fratr[um]." The handwriting of the canon shows marked similarity to that of Reincken. One would expect, then, that Buxtehude would also appear in this painting, but no known portrait of him exists for comparison. When Christoph Wolff identified the man to the right of the harpsichord as Buxtehude and the player of the viola da gamba as Johann Theile (1646–1724), it was assumed that Reincken was fifty-one at the time and Buxtehude thirty-seven, following the birth date of 1623 that Mattheson gives for Reincken in the *Ehrenpforte*; I followed his interpretation in the first edition of this book.[7] But with Ulf Grapenthin's recent redating of Reincken's birth to 1643, Buxtehude becomes the oldest member of the group, and thus these identifications must be reexamined.

Wolff's central argument for his identification of Buxtehude rests on a convention that the named persons in a group portrait will be placed in the center:

> The most important figure of the musical group next to the harpsichordist is doubtless the younger man in the listening posture with the music sheet. It is therefore tempting to see in him the 37-year-old Buxtehude. To judge from the symmetry of the composition, the musicians placed to the left and right of the central axis would represent the persons named on the canon sheet, that is Buxtehude and Reincken.[8]

In this case, however, Voorhout had to solve the compositional problem he had created by placing the harpsichord at the center of the painting: he would either have to keep the "brothers" central and separate them (Wolff's reading) or place them close together but off center. It now appears more likely that he adopted the latter course, because close observation reveals that although Reincken at the harpsichord and the gamba player slightly behind him are farther away from the viewer than the listener and the lutenist in front of the harpsichord, Voorhout painted them larger, with their heads on the same level. In this interpretation, the two dominant figures, reading from left to right, now correspond to Buxtehude and Reincken in the same order in which they are named on the sheet of paper. Further reinforcing this identification is the fact that if the listener is in fact Buxtehude, we would expect him to be looking at Reincken instead of gazing in the other direction; the gamba player, on the other hand, is looking toward Reincken as if to coordinate their music making. Finally, close examination of the left hand of the gamba player reveals that his second finger is placed on the second fret of the c-string and his first finger on the first fret of the a-string, creating the pitches d–b (b♭ in English), the initials of Buxtehude's name.[9] That Buxtehude is not known to have played the viola da gamba does not argue against this identification. Other famous keyboard players also played stringed instruments, notably Nicolaus Bruhns and Johann Sebastian Bach. Buxtehude left a magnificent body of music scored with viola da gamba, and his professional colleagues, the Lübeck municipal musicians, took pride in their ability to play numerous instruments.

In a recently published article, Heinrich Schwab argues that the painting is dominated by three pairs: Buxtehude and Reincken on the left, the amorous or dancing couple in the center middle ground, and the listener and the lutenist on the right. He interprets the last pair allegorically as "Auditus" and "Musica," representing the reception and performance of music. Wolff had noted that the woman playing the lute appears in another Voorhout painting, *The Artist and his Family*, also from 1674, in which she offers a vase of flowers to a baby sitting on its mother's lap; she cannot therefore have been a historical musician. In Schwab's reading, Theile does not appear in the painting at all. Wolff had brought Theile in as the composer of the canon because he was an expert in learned counterpoint and a known player of the viola da gamba, but Schwab points out that since Reincken's handwriting appears on the sheet of paper, he is the more likely composer of the canon. Also, as Hofkapellmeister to the Duke of Schleswig-Holstein at Gottorf, Theile enjoyed a higher social status than the city organists Buxtehude and Reincken, so it would be unusual for him to be in the painting but not named as the other two are. Schwab further demonstrates that in the position in which it is found in this painting, the sheet of music does not signify the composer, as Schmidt had supposed; in the many paintings where a composer is represented with a sheet or a roll of paper, he is always holding it. An allegorical interpretation of the man with the canon as "Auditus," also suggested by Wolff in addition to his identification with Buxtehude, has much to recommend it, particularly with respect to his lack of eye contact with Reincken. But if another historical person participated in the *Musical Party*, then Johann Philipp Förtsch (1652–1732) seems a more likely candidate than Theile. He had recently arrived in Hamburg; his presence as a tenor in the Kantorei is documented from summer 1674.[10] He also took a lively interest in learned counterpoint, and as a junior member of the "fraternity," only twenty-two at the time, he would not have needed to be named.

Although *Musical Party* cannot provide us with a definitive portrait of Buxtehude, Wolff's detailed analysis of it offers important insights into the lifestyle of Reincken and his circle in Hamburg, of which Buxtehude formed a part. Wolff sees Reincken as the one who commissioned the painting and first owned it. He is the dominant figure, with his head turned toward the viewer; he was a wealthy man and had commissioned other paintings. Reincken wears a Japanese silk brocade kimono, which was very fashionable at the time among the well-to-do in Holland, England, and North Germany; he was known to be not only wealthy but also pretentious. Mattheson noted this quality with disapproval in his entry on Reincken in the *Ehrenpforte*, referring to the engraved title page of Reincken's sonata collection *Hortus musicus*,[11] where he calls himself "Organi Hamburgensis ad D. Cathar. celebratissimi Directore" and introduces his initials into the pediments of the pillars. In the painting, the setting of ostentatious wealth projected by Reincken's costume is further accented by the clothing of the other figures. The middle ground and background contain allusions to physical love, in strong contrast to the platonic, brotherly love expressed by the canon in the foreground. Chief among these are the erotic gestures of the couple in the middle ground. Wolff suggests that this couple may even represent a reworking of the figures of Reincken and the lute player, the latter now cast in the role of prostitute. Such double portraiture was not uncommon, and Mattheson's obituary relates that Reincken was a "constant lover of women and of the Rats-Weinkeller," and that in his will he did not forget "the unknown ladies whom he had in his house until his death." Indeed, in offering grapes to Reincken at the harpsichord, the black page—another symbol of wealth—is inviting him to taste of sensual pleasure. Warm reds and oranges unite all three levels of the painting.

To find Buxtehude portrayed in such a setting must dispel any one-sided image we might have had of him as merely a pious church organist. His elegant clothing places him comfortably in this decidedly secular atmosphere, and his presence here reveals a pleasure-loving facet of his personality that was almost unknown before this painting came to light in 1975. He had given a hint, however, that pleasure was to be found in Lübeck as well as in Hamburg—in the text of the canon that he wrote for the young Meno Hanneken in 1670: "Let us divert ourselves today, let us drink to the health of my friend" (BuxWV 124).

The relationship between Buxtehude and Reincken signified by the canon in this painting is one of brotherly love and of intellectual and professional kinship. In the inscription they are named as brothers, and the words of the canon underscore this connection. With its Latin text and strong intellectual association, the canon represented not only the high level of their relationship but also their shared common interest in learned counterpoint, which Buxtehude was cultivating precisely at this time. In a 1980 article I suggested that a coterie of musicians active in Hamburg and Lübeck in the early 1670s, including Bernhard, Reincken, Buxtehude, Theile, and probably Weckmann, pursued studies of learned counterpoint together. I would now add Förtsch to this list.

At the time of his death, Reincken owned two manuscript counterpoint treatises, each containing a separate version of Sweelinck's *Compositions Regeln*, which are but poorly represented by Hermann Gehrmann's 1901 edition in Sweelinck's *Werken*. These manuscripts were presumed lost following the bombing of Hamburg in 1943, but they have recently returned to the Staats- und Universitätsbibliothek Hamburg, where Ulf Grapenthin has studied them and issued reports of their precise contents, with a new edition forthcoming. Reincken had himself written the earlier of the two, ND VI 5384, in 1670. It contains two treatises, the first entitled *Erste unterrichtung zur Compesition* [*sic*], seemingly assembled by Reincken himself, and the second, entitled *Arcana geheimnißen oder handtgriffe der wahren wißenschafft der Composition*, dealing with imitation and canon and corresponding to the third part of Sweelinck's *Compositions Regeln*, which was transmitted in the other manuscript, MD VI 5383. Gehrmann believed that Matthias Weckmann had copied the first two parts of 5383, which contain the *Compositions Regeln* and a treatise on invertible counterpoint that Theile is now known to have written; Grapenthin, however, argues that these two parts were copied considerably later, using an exemplar for the first part that Weckmann had once annotated. Reincken wrote the third part himself, dealing with invertible counterpoint at the octave and twelfth, as an appendix to part 2.

The Theile treatise in part 2 of 5383, unattributed there and with a head title "Kurtze doch deütliche Regulen von denen duppelten Contrapuncten," contains a "Canon Duplex à 4 per augmentationem" that is very similar to the canon that Buxtehude wrote into Johann Valentin Meder's autograph book in 1674 (BuxWV 123). Theile could have written this treatise any time from the mid-1670s to 1691,[12] the date of his contrapuntal masterpiece, *Musikalisches Kunstbuch*. In 1673 Theile had published in Lübeck a collection of six masses in *stile antico*, dedicating it to the twenty-four men who had paid its publication costs. These included Buxtehude and numerous other Lübeck musicians and businessmen, but from Hamburg only Reincken, although Christoph Bernhard wrote an open letter praising their old style of composition. The masses contain numerous examples of invertible counterpoint, but none that show the sophistication of Buxtehude's settings of "Mit Fried und Freud," from 1671, or his canon for Meder. Many years later, Theile claimed to have been a teacher of Buxtehude during this stay in Lübeck. When Johann Mattheson published Theile's obituary in 1725, which he based on handwritten information from Theile, he included the following statement:

> Next he went to Stettin, and there he instructed organists and musicians; he also did this in Lübeck, and was an *informator* of the well-known Buxtehude, of the organist Hasse, and of the municipal musician Zachau, among others.[13]

The friendship that Theile and Buxtehude enjoyed in Lübeck—and probably also in Hamburg—must have included many discussions of counterpoint, but Theile cannot have been Buxtehude's teacher.

The interest and enjoyment of learned counterpoint displayed by Buxtehude, Reincken, and Theile in the early 1670s continued into the next generations of German musicians, including Georg Österreich (1664–1735), Heinrich Bokemeyer (1679–1751), and Johann Gottfried Walther (1684–1748). For them, learned counterpoint was an arcane art, related to alchemy, as David Yearsley has shown in his article "Alchemy and Counterpoint in an Age of Reason." He does not make this claim for Reincken or Buxtehude, but Reincken offered a clue that he may have thought similarly when he described the third part of Sweelinck's *Compositions Regeln,* dealing with canon and invertible counterpoint, as "arcane secrets"[Arcana geheimnisse].[14] Michael Maier had brought alchemy and canon together in has *Atalanta fugiens* of 1612, and Theile's *Musikalisches Kunstbuch* shows similarities to it in the use of emblematic epigrams accompanying the canons. If Theile and Reincken were relating music to alchemy, then Buxtehude may have been as well, although he left no such clues. This is not to say that the composers were necessarily performing experiments in a laboratory; alchemy involved magical transformation, and it could take place chemically, spiritually, or musically. What is the inversion of a four-part counterpoint if not a transformation of a piece of music from one state to another? Whatever the depth of their involvement with alchemy, in the pre-Enlightenment world of the seventeenth century their experiments with learned counterpoint had a much deeper meaning than the mere intellectual satisfaction of creating and solving musical puzzles in their minds or on paper.

For Buxtehude and Reincken, the study of learned counterpoint formed a sideline to their main activity; their sense of professional kinship would have stemmed primarily from the fact that they held analogous prestigious positions as organists in Lübeck and Hamburg, respectively, where they cultivated the art of the organist at its highest level in North Germany. The following generation of organists would recognize their joint position at the pinnacle of the profession. Apart from his Lüneburg teacher Georg Böhm, they are the only two organists whom J. S. Bach is known to have sought out personally. Georg Dietrich Leiding made a trip to Hamburg and Lübeck in 1684, in Johann Gottfried Walther's words, "in order to profit from the two extraordinary famous organists, Messrs. Reincken and Buxtehude, [who were] there at that time."

Both Reincken and Buxtehude referred to themselves as "director of the organ" on the title pages of their sonata publications, and they both commanded large instruments. The organ that Reincken played at St. Catherine's in Hamburg contained fifty-eight stops on four manuals. The addition of the fourth manual, as well as that of a Principal 32′ and a Groß-Posaun 32′ in the pedal, had been accomplished in a renovation of 1671–74. The stated goal of the renovation had been that "our organ can be at least as good as, if not better than, the large organ at St. Mary's in Lübeck in the nature and sweetness of its stops."[15] This objective must have been achieved, for the new 32′ stops were the ones that Bach later admired and remembered.[16] It is noteworthy that although Reincken had assumed his position in 1663, it was only in 1669—shortly after Buxtehude's arrival in Lübeck—that this comparison with the Lübeck organ was set down in the contract for this work, which presupposes a visit by Reincken to Lübeck and perhaps a friendly rivalry with Buxtehude. If they had both been students of Scheidemann from 1654 to 1657, as we know Reincken was, it would have been natural for them to resume their relationship as soon as Buxtehude moved back to the area in 1668. The hypothesis I advanced in chapter 1 that

Buxtehude might also have studied with Scheidemann during these same years rests in part on his friendship with Reincken, demonstrated in *Musical Party*. In July of 1674, the year of this painting, two unknown organists were paid 300 Lübeck marks for testing the St. Catherine's organ;[17] could one of them have been Buxtehude?

In his obituary of Reincken in *Critica Musica* (1723), Mattheson relates that he

> always kept his organ uncommonly neat and well-tuned and was forever talking about it, because it really has a very beautiful sound. He also knew how to play it in such a particularly clear way, that—in the things that he had practiced—had no equal in his time.

The organ in St. Catherine's that Reincken, Bach, and probably Buxtehude played was destroyed by bombs during World War II, but pipes from twenty different stops survive, and a foundation has been established to finance its reconstruction.[18]

Two distinguished Hamburg composers are conspicuously absent from the *Musical Party*: Matthias Weckmann and Christoph Bernhard. Weckmann died on 24 February 1674, and just at that time the Elector Johann Georg II called Bernhard back to Dresden to supervise the education of his two grandsons. With Weckmann and Bernhard gone, the state of music in Hamburg declined rapidly, as Mattheson relates in the *Ehrenpforte*:

> In a word, Bernhard had to leave Hamburg in the year 1674, after he had directed and led the music there for ten years. At the time of his departure, he prophesied many changes, both in the sacred and the secular [realms], which were in some measure fulfilled. Among other things, he said that music had now bloomed in Hamburg for fourteen years—he was counting also the four years of the great collegium musicum before his time—but that now it would decline. That is indeed what happened. For although a couple of fine men distinguished themselves in their art, no one cared in general or at all for the common good of music, either in churches or in concerts; indeed, the concerts disappeared completely. Weckmann's funeral was the last event in Hamburg at which Bernhard was present.

After Weckmann's death, Reincken reigned supreme as Hamburg's leading organist until the arrival of Vincent Lübeck in 1702. Bernhard's successor, Joachim Gerstenbüttel, was a man of mediocre talent, unable to maintain the tradition of splendid church music that Selle established and Bernhard continued. In the resulting vacuum, the way was open for a new musical genre to emerge in Hamburg: opera.

With its busy harbor, teeming commerce, and cosmopolitan bourgeois population, Hamburg could consider itself a kind of Venice of the north, and in opening the first public opera house in Germany, Hamburg consciously modeled itself on Venice. The leading founder and first director of the Hamburg opera, the lawyer Gerhard Schott, had traveled widely and attended operas in many places.

Christian Albrecht, the duke of Schleswig-Holstein living in exile in Hamburg, worked closely with him, as did the senator Peter Lütkens and Reincken, the only musician among the founders. Together they financed the building of an opera house at the Gänsemarkt in the summer of 1677, and the opera opened officially on 2 January 1678 with the performance of a Singspiel, *Orontes*, with music most likely composed by Johann Theile, Christian Albrecht's Kapellmeister. A traveler's diary tells us, however, that an earlier opera had preceded *Orontes*. Recounting his visit to Hamburg 21 January 1678, Adam Ebert of Frankfurt/Oder wrote: "The *Opera* here had begun shortly before, at the end of the preceding year, with the piece 'Adam and Eva,' to recommend the introduction of opera to the clergy."[19] This would have been *Der erschaffene, gefallene und aufgerichtete Mensch*, by Johann Theile, which is often credited with having inaugurated the house. Although its music is lost, the libretto survives—in four different versions. The text is written in madrigalesque poetry with numerous strophic arias.

Given Buxtehude's friendship with Reincken and Theile, his presence in Hamburg in 1674 for the painting of *Musical Party*, and above all the fact that he presented his first dramatic Abendmusik, *Die Hochzeit des Lamms*, in December of 1678, it is very likely that he attended performances of Theile's operas in Hamburg. Buxtehude announced in 1684 that he had drawn on operatic style, "with many arias and ritornelli," for his five-part oratorio *Himmlische Seelenlust auf Erden*, which he most likely presented in the Abendmusiken of 1681 or 1683. Theile composed an opera on the same subject, *Die Geburth Christi*, which was performed in Hamburg in 1681; the author of its text was probably Hinrich Elmenhorst, the preacher at St. Catherine's Church. Elmenhorst, in his *Dramatologia Antiquo-Hodierna* (1688), referred to the works that Buxtehude performed in his Lübeck Abendmusiken as operas.

Several composers besides Theile were active in the early years of the Hamburg opera: Nicolaus Adam Strungk (1640–1700), Johann Wolfgang Franck (1644–ca. 1710) Johann Philipp Förtsch (1652–1732), and Johann Georg Conradi (ca. 1645–99). Buxtehude probably knew them all. Many librettos survive from these years, as catalogued by Hans Joachim Marx and Dorothea Schröder, with texts drawn from a wide variety of sources. A few from the early years besides Theile's were based on sacred subjects: *Die Wol und beständig-liebende Michal* and *Die Macchabaeische Mutter mit ihren sieben Söhnen* (both by Franck, 1679); *Esther, Die liebreiche, durch Tugend und Schönheit erhöhete* (Strungk, 1680); *Cain und Abel* (Förtsch, 1689). Subjects drawn from Greek and Roman history or mythology—often by way of Italian or French opera librettos—predominate, however. Recent history could also provide the subject matter; Franck's two *Cara Mustapha* operas of 1686 were based on the Turkish siege of Vienna in 1683. Very little music survives from these early years, however, most of it in the form of aria collections or arrangements.

Among the handful of remaining German opera scores from the seventeenth century are Franck's *Die Drey Töchter Cecrops* and Conradi's *Die schöne und getreue*

Ariadne. Franck first presented *Cecrops* in Ansbach—probably in 1686, according to Werner Braun—and only afterwards did he bring it to Hamburg, in a much-shortened version. Thus Conradi's *Ariadne* from 1691, with a libretto by Christian Heinrich Postel, is the oldest extant opera composed specifically for Hamburg. The much acclaimed revival of *Ariadne* by the Boston Early Music Festival in 2003 and the subsequent recording of this production have lifted seventeenth-century Hamburg opera from its former obscurity and revealed a work of remarkable beauty. During his short tenure as Kapellmeister of the Hamburg opera (1690–93), Conradi introduced French and Italian operas to Hamburg, and these in turn influenced his own musical style. Among *Ariadne*'s notable features that were derived from the French operatic stage is a 314-measure *Passacaille* in the penultimate scene of the opera, which could have inspired Buxtehude to conclude his Abendmusik *Templum honoris* with a passacaglia. Conradi also introduced the French *hautbois* to the Hamburg orchestra, which Buxtehude used only in *Templum honoris* and two late vocal works (BuxWV 50 and 120). The comic character Pamphilius, however, derives from the Venetian and earlier Hamburg traditions.

It is noteworthy that neither Buxtehude nor Reincken ever composed an opera for Hamburg. Buxtehude, of course, found ample outlet for his dramatic instincts in the Lübeck Abendmusiken, where he enjoyed complete artistic control. Reincken's failure to compose for the opera cannot be explained by his position as a church organist, since a preacher at his church, Hinrich Elmenhorst, wrote librettos for the opera. Also, both Strungk and Franck held the position of music director for the cathedral.

The friendship between Buxtehude and Reincken continued until at least 1685, the year in which Reincken married Anna Wagner. Buxtehude's printed music for the wedding survived in Hamburg until World War II and appeared in an exhibit, "Die Musik Hamburgs im Zeitalter Seb. Bachs" (The Music of Hamburg in the Age of Sebastian Bach), held in Hamburg in 1921. The catalog for this exhibit includes the following entry:

575. [Buxtehude, Dietrich]
    "... Johanne Adamo Reincken ... Verehligung mit ... Annen Wagners von Deo Beante." Lübeck, Moritz Schmalhertz, 25. Febr. 1685.
    Anfang: "Drei schöne Dinge sind."

Although Buxtehude's actual name did not appear on this print, the initials D. B. of the pseudonym "Deo Beante" and the fact that it was printed in Lübeck leave no doubt as to the composer. Wolff has identified this music with a work by Buxtehude beginning with the same text but transmitted in manuscript, BuxWV 19.

Buxtehude's *Drei schöne Dinge sind* (BuxWV 19) is a concerto-aria cantata, its first movement set to the text "There are three things which are pleasing to both God and men." (Sirach 25:1a). The remainder of the biblical verse—not set in the cantata—spells out what these are: "agreement between brothers, friendship

between neighbors, and a wife and husband who live in harmony." The five strophes of the following aria expound on these topics. Certainly this text, with its
celebration of both brotherhood and marriage, would have lent itself to the
occasion. The scope of the work also suggests that Buxtehude composed it for
the wedding of someone special to him; most of his other wedding pieces are
rather more modest. However, at least one of the manuscript sources, *Uu* 82:35,
can be shown to have been copied early in 1684; this manuscript is discussed in
chapter 10. If BuxWV 19 is the work printed for Reincken's wedding, it appears
that either Buxtehude used a work he had composed earlier—as he did for his
father's funeral—or that he composed it specifically for Reincken, but the wedding had been postponed. Another print celebrating Reincken's marriage was
displayed in the 1921 Hamburg exhibit:

> 238. Rogge, Heinrich, Organist in Rostock
> "...Johann Adam Reincken ... Anna Wagnerin ... Hochzeitlichen Ehren Tag..."
> Rostock, Jacob Riechel, zu finden in Hamburg, 15 Febr. 1685.
> Arie mit Ritornell: "Auf, auf ihr edlen Töchter."

J. C. M. van Riemsdijk reprinted this work in its entirety as an appendix to his
biographical study of Reincken. It consists of a ritornello, a thirteen-strophe aria
in two-part invertible counterpoint, and a "Canon quadruplex à 5." The text
of the canon, "Reincken Nahme bleibt ein Kern, unter allen Orgel-Herrn!"
(Reincken's name remains a kernel [or hard core] among all men of the organ)
rearranges the letters of Reincken's name to form the words "ein Kern." Klaus
Beckmann noted in his Reincken-Buxtehude study that two strophes of the aria
point to Buxtehude as the composer of the canon:

Herr Buxtehud', des Lübeck's Zierde	*Mr. Buxtehude, the glory of Lübeck,*
Weiss, was von ihm zu halten sey,	*knows how to consider him;*
Es legt ihm seine Pflicht-Begierde	*His offering to him lies*
Auch gerne diesen Ruhm mit bey;	*willingly beside this accolade.*
Ja, wer Herr Reinken recht wird kennen,	*Yes, he who knows Mr. Reinken properly*
Sagt, dass Er sey ein Kern zu nennen.	*says that he should be called a kernel.*
Verzeih' indessen dem Erkühnen,	*Meanwhile, forgive the presumption,*
Du vorgedachter Lübeck's Preiss!	*you aforesaid prize of Lübeck,*
Dass auch dein Beifall mir soll dienen	*that your ovation should also serve me*
zu Herren Reinken Preis-Beweiss:	*in demonstration of praise for Mr. Reinken;*
Ihr seyd beruhmt im Componiren,	*you [both] are famous in composition*
Auf Chören, Orgeln und Claviren	*for choirs, organs and [other] keyboards.*

Rogge (1654–1701) had in 1684 become the organist of St. Mary's Church in
Rostock, a port on the Baltic 113 kilometers northeast of Lübeck. Prior to that

he had studied with Reincken in Hamburg for five years.[20] Mattheson reports in the *Ehrenpforte* that Rogge

> had the reputation for having understood the foundations of musical composition well, as can be seen from his work.
>
> Nevertheless, it is said that he was more successful in making fantasies at the organ from his free imagination, *ex tempore*, as one says, than in composition. But the vocal and organ works that he has put to paper sound good and touch the heart as well as the ear.
>
> In addition to sacred concertos, he often composed wedding and funeral odes with added instrumental parts, if that was desired, had the words and music printed together on a sheet of paper, and let these examples be distributed to the listeners before the subsequent performance of the music.

Since Buxtehude made his own printed contribution to Reincken's wedding celebration and Rogge apologized to Buxtehude for including his canon with his own offering, it appears unlikely that Buxtehude composed this canon specifically for Reincken's wedding or would have chosen to present it to him in such an obscure manner. A much more suitable occasion for the composition and presentation of this canon would have been the gathering depicted in *Musical Party* in 1674. The canon is included in the second edition of the *Buxtehude-Werke-Verzeichnis* as BuxWV 124a, and a solution is given in chapter 6.

During the 1680s Buxtehude became friendly with another illustrious resident of Hamburg, Arp Schnitger (1648–1719), the leading North German organ builder of the day. Schnitger had established himself in Hamburg in 1682, and from 1682 to 1687 he built his masterpiece at St. Nicholas's Church there, an instrument with sixty-seven stops on four manuals and pedal. In May of 1687, Buxtehude traveled to Hamburg at the expense of his own church in order to inspect Schnitger's new organ, which he found very much to his liking. The following year Schnitger spent four weeks in Lübeck, during which time he took all his meals with Buxtehude. Buxtehude's failure to persuade St. Mary's to hire Schnitger to renovate the large organ is recounted in chapter 3. Reincken was apparently less impressed with Schnitger than was Buxtehude, and Reincken never called upon him to work on the St. Catherine's organ.

Buxtehude may have established some sort of business relationship with Schnitger, giving his endorsement for a fee just as celebrities do today. On at least two occasions, in 1695 and again in 1698, he recommended Schnitger as a builder for the new organ in the St. Jacobi Church of Stettin. Shortly after his second letter to Stettin, another citizen of Lübeck, Jochim Werner Langelotz, wrote to recommend Hans Hantelman, a former journeyman to Schnitger, for the work. He stated, "the reason that Mr. Buxtehude here does not want to suggest him is probably because it is his custom to receive money for all his recommendations."[21]

Hamburg was also the home of one of the great builders of stringed instruments at the time, Joachim Tielke. Although no evidence apart from his hypothetical identification in *Musical Party* suggests that Buxtehude himself played any bowed or plucked stringed instruments, his compositions demonstrate his great admiration for strings, in particular the bass viola da gamba, which was Tielke's particular specialty. Tielke worked in Hamburg from 1667 until his death in 1719 and was well known in musical circles there; it would be surprising if Buxtehude had not been acquainted with him.

One final connection between Buxtehude and the city of Hamburg is noteworthy: he chose a Hamburg printer for the publication of his sonatas for violin, viola da gamba, and harpsichord. All his known compositions for weddings show a Lübeck imprint, but for the printing of these two important collections of sonatas Buxtehude turned to Nicolaus Spieringk of Hamburg. Spieringk printed opus 1 at Buxtehude's own expense, probably in the year 1694. Opus 2 appeared in 1696 at Spierink's expense. He also published Johann Sigismund Kusser's *Arien aus der Oper: Erindo* (1695), Georg Bronner's *Geistliche Concerten* (1696), and Reinhard Keiser's *Gemüths-Ergötzung* (1698).[22]

In later years, Buxtehude appears to have traveled to Hamburg less often, if at all; when Mattheson and Handel journeyed to Lübeck to visit him in 1703, they were not previously acquainted with him. He must have kept in touch with the activities of the Hamburg opera, however, through his assistant Johann Christian Schieferdecker, who had worked as an accompanist at the opera before coming to Lübeck.

The city of Hamburg must have contributed enormously to the quality of Buxtehude's life during his Lübeck years, providing musical stimulation through the collegium musicum, the opera, and the musicians there who were his friends. In contrast, Buxtehude seems to have had little effect on the musical life of Hamburg; no reports exist of any performances of his music there during his lifetime. Buxtehude's influence was felt mainly to the north and to the east, in a striking analogy to the movement of salt and finished goods in Hanseatic trade. Apart from Lübeck, the city where his music was most performed and appreciated during his lifetime lay far to the northeast, across the Baltic Sea.

Stockholm

Commercial relations between Lübeck and Stockholm had always been strong. Stockholm had been settled in the mid-thirteenth century largely by German immigrants, and Lübeck merchants traditionally handled much of the trade between Stockholm, Lübeck, and Flanders; one of the important commercial guilds of Lübeck was known as the Stockholmfahrer. Since the Middle Ages, Stockholm had exported large quantities of copper, iron, and butter and imported cloth and salt. During the 1670s and 1680s, the musical establishment of the Swedish royal court in Stockholm imported large quantities of Dieterich

Buxtehude's music for voices and instruments. Under the direction of Gustav Düben, Kapellmeister to the king, this music was copied there, and the originals were then presumably returned to Lübeck. Although virtually all of these Lübeck originals have been lost, the Swedish copies survive, now at the university library in Uppsala. Düben thus became the most important figure in the preservation of Buxtehude's music. A database catalog of this extensive collection, edited by Erik Kjellberg and Kerala Snyder, has just become available on the Internet.[23]

Gustav Düben was born in Stockholm about 1629. His grandfather, Andreas Düben, had been organist at St. Thomas's Church in Leipzig. Gustav's father, also named Andreas, had studied with Sweelinck in Amsterdam from 1614 to 1620 and had then emigrated to Stockholm, where he served the Swedish royal court as organist from 1620 to 1640 and as Kapellmeister from 1640 until his death in 1662. From 1625 he also served as organist of the German church of St. Gertrude in Stockholm.

Gustav Düben studied in Germany from no later than 1645 until about 1648, first at his father's expense and later on a three-year stipend from the king. The exact location of his study is not known, but in his application to succeed his father as Kapellmeister he indicated that it had been in more than one place. He returned to Stockholm in 1648 and joined the Hofkapelle, became Kapellmeister to the king and organist of the German church in 1663, and held both positions until his death in 1690. Although it has been suggested that he made later trips to the continent, Gustav Düben's presence in Stockholm as a court musician is documented for the entire period 1648–90, and evidence for any trips outside Sweden after 1648 is totally lacking.

Buxtehude demonstrated his friendship with Düben by his dedication in 1680 of the cantata cycle *Membra Jesu Nostri* (BuxWV 75) "to a foremost man, Gustav Düben, most noble and honored friend, Director of Music to His Most Serene Majesty, the King of Sweden" (fig. 4-1). The fact that Buxtehude is the most heavily represented composer in Düben's collection is further testimony to a close relationship between the two men. Yet there appears to have been no time in their adulthood when their paths might have crossed. It is more than likely that Düben passed through Helsingør on his way to and/or from Germany during the 1640s. At that time he might have made the acquaintance of Johannes Buxtehude, another German organist—like his own father—who was working in Scandinavia. Johannes's son Dieterich was still a child then, only about eleven years old at the time of Gustav Düben's return to Stockholm in 1648.

Dieterich Buxtehude was well established as organist of St. Mary's Helsingør when Düben was appointed Kapellmeister in 1663. During the following four years Düben assembled nearly 40 percent of his collection of vocal music, yet compositions by Buxtehude are totally lacking from this early layer of the collection.[24] It appears that it was only upon Buxtehude's move to Lübeck in 1668 that Düben began to notice him, just as his copying activity otherwise was

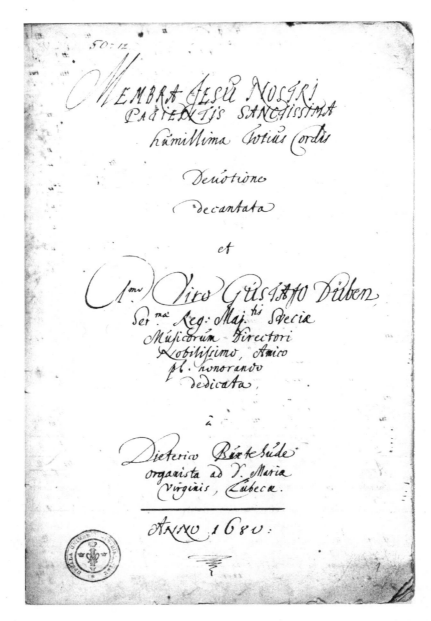

Figure 4-1. Buxtehude, *Membra Jesu nostri* (BuxWV 75). Autograph tablature dedicated to Gustav Düben (Uppsala Universitetsbibliotek, vokalmusik i handskrift 50:12, fol. 1r).

beginning to wane. Düben's earlier Buxtehude copies probably represent a continuation in the trade in music manuscripts between Lübeck and Stockholm that had begun in 1663, but the bulk of the Buxtehude works in the collection were copied during the 1680s, following the dedication of *Membra* to Düben. It is as if the friendship developed slowly during the 1670s and intensified during the last decade of Düben's life. And this friendship was probably carried on entirely by letters, not unlike the friendship between Johann Gottfried Walther and Heinrich Bokemeyer, which was sustained through sixteen years of correspondence, even though the two men never met. Walther referred to Bokemeyer with phrases such as "meinem liebwehrtesten Herrn und Freunde" (12 March 1731) and "allerliebster Freund" (3 August 1731); he designated himself as "einen alten *per literas* bekandten Freund" (3 August 1739).[25]

Although Gustav Düben may never have met Buxtehude, at least one of his sons apparently did. Anders Düben, the youngest son, born in 1673, served as a boy soprano at the court in 1686 and 1687; during that time he probably sang many of Buxtehude's soprano parts. He studied abroad on a royal stipend from 1692 to 1694, and his signed copy of a Buxtehude sonata (BuxWV 267) is dated 27 September 1692. His older brother, Gustav the younger, born in 1660, had studied lute in Paris at some time prior to 1684; he would have passed through Lübeck on his way. The two brothers served in turn as Kapellmeister, Gustav junior from 1690 and Anders from 1698. Anders must have been a versatile musician; among the instruments that he owned at the time of his death in 1738 were a harpsichord with four stops, six ivory concert flutes, a viola da gamba, and a large viol. It was he who donated his father's music collection to Uppsala University in 1732.

Buxtehude's ties to the Düben family are of inestimable historical significance, since their collection and preservation of his music account for about 80 percent of his vocal music and 95 percent of his instrumental chamber music. Beyond that, the Düben family made Stockholm second only to Lübeck as a center for performances of Buxtehude's music during the seventeenth century. With archives undisturbed by wars and a large number of performing parts in the Düben collection, Stockholm and Uppsala now offer the most information to be found anywhere concerning the performing practice of Buxtehude's ensemble music. Erik Kjellberg's dissertation on the Swedish court musicians provides a detailed investigation of the performing conditions at the court and the German church. The information that follows is drawn largely from his study.

The court musical establishment over which Gustav Düben presided varied from ten to sixteen members. From 1683 to 1687, during which time much of Buxtehude's music must have been performed, it was stable at fourteen members. These included two boy sopranos and at least two other singers, Johann Kessell, a bass, and David Duncker, whose vocal part is unknown. Andreas Schultz, known only as an unspecified instrumentalist, may have sung alto as well; he had replaced Carl Hintz, who was both an alto and a violinist, in 1674. If David

Duncker was a tenor, then the standard five-part vocal ensemble would have been present. Among the instrumentalists were three violinists (Pierre Verdier, Reiner Krampau, and Johan Rohman), two players of the viola da gamba (Johann Christoff Wolff and Conrad Bohn the younger), one violist (Petter Paul Hoppe), one lutenist (Hinrich Niewerth), and one organist (Christian Krahn). In addition, Johann Flemming, an unspecified musician, was with the Hofkapelle from 1681 to 1685, and Gustav Düben the younger, a lutenist, from 1685 to 1688. It can be presumed that most of the instrumentalists played more than one instrument; also, extra musicians were hired for special occasions.

The royal Swedish trumpet corps was organized separately; during this period it averaged twelve trumpeters and two timpanists. Their services were mainly of a military nature, but they were called on occasionally for art music as well. This would surely have been the case for the performance of *Klinget für Freude* (BuxWV 119), which Buxtehude—no doubt at Düben's request—composed for the marriage of King Charles XI of Sweden to Princess Ulrika Eleonore of Denmark in 1680. The actual wedding ceremony took place at Halmstad, north of Helsingborg, on 6 May, and Düben was apparently not in attendance. For the couple's entry into Stockholm the following November, however, Düben led "a beautiful ensemble of voices and instruments" from the top of a triumphal arch that had been erected on the north bridge leading to the royal castle.[26]

Düben's royal letter of appointment required him to "direct the appointed musicians both in the church and in other places which We shall desire."[27] The court's church services took place both in the castle church, located on the north side of the courtyard, and in the old dining room in the northwest corner of the main part of the castle Tre Kronor, the royal residence and seat of administration until it was destroyed by fire in 1697. Although the court was Calvinist, the order of worship issued in 1664 called for concerted music at the beginning and end of the preaching service; the mass was normally spoken, perhaps because there was no school choir to perform liturgical music. The castle church included an organ gallery, but no large organ was installed in it until 1696, one year before the fire. The court owned two positive organs, one in the castle church and one in the old dining room, where the preaching services for the royal family were held. A gallery for musicians was located on the wall of the old dining room, and an adjacent room was used for instrument storage. Since most of Buxtehude's works preserved in the Düben collection are sacred and nonliturgical, it can be presumed that they were performed at the preaching services held in the old dining room, which measured approximately 10 by 22 meters.

During his years as Kapellmeister, Düben also held the position of organist at the German Church of St. Gertrude in Stockholm. This congregation had been chartered in 1571 and still meets in its handsome seventeenth-century building in the oldest part of Stockholm. Incorporated with it was a German elementary school, committed to teaching reading, writing, and singing. The cantor from

1667 to 1691 was Johan Stockmann, and his letter of appointment specifies that he was to be "the absolute director of the choir" and that the organist was to be responsible to him.[28] Düben contested this division of power in 1683, finding it beneath his dignity as court Kapellmeister to be subservient to a cantor, but the matter was resolved only by the directive that when concerted music was to be performed, the organist and cantor should discuss it and be in agreement. Church music was ordinarily performed by the school choir under the direction of the cantor, but on special occasions members of Düben's Hofkapelle joined them. The five members of the Hofkapelle who performed at the German church in 1682 included two singers, two string players, and Andreas Schultz, the unspecified instrumentalist.

The organ in the German Church stood in a gallery under the tower at the back of the church. Paul Müller from Spandau had built the original instrument in 1608–9, and it enjoyed several expansions in later years. When Gustav Düben wrote down its specifications in 1684, it contained thirty-five stops on three manuals and pedal and was one of the largest organs in Sweden. The church sold the organ in 1779 to the parish of Övertorneå, on the Finnish border just below the Arctic Circle. This church installed the Hauptwerk and Oberwerk, which remain to this day, and sold the Rückpositiv to the neighboring village church in Hedenäset, which converted it to a self-contained positive organ. With these two instruments and the extensive German Church archives as the basis, the German Church organ of 1684 was reconstructed in 1997—built by Grönlunds Orgelbyggeri of Gammelstad and installed in the parish church of Norrfjärden, in cooperation with the School of Music in Piteå. Two years later the original organ in Övertorneå was restored.[29] The German Church in Stockholm now houses on its south wall the second replica of its former organ, inaugurated in 2004. It is tuned in quarter-comma meantone, with subsemitones for E♭/D♯.

Since almost no organ music of any kind survives in the Düben collection, it is impossible to know whether Düben played any of Buxtehude's organ music on the German Church organ. Düben definitely viewed his position as organist of the German Church as secondary to his post as court Kapellmeister. When asked in 1684 why he had sent a substitute instead of playing himself, he replied that his presence had been required at court. On an earlier occasion his substitute, Christian Krahn, had displeased the congregation, "because yesterday after the morning sermon he played again in his old manner, and made several big mistakes, so that the priest before the altar and other people in the church laughed at it".[30] Christian Krahn, born in Lübeck, served the court as organist from 1681 until his death in 1704. If he was Caspar Krahn's unnamed son, who was baptized at St. Peter's Church, Lübeck, on 31 May 1661, then he could have been a pupil of Buxtehude. If this was the case, it may not be entirely coincidental that the response of this congregation to his playing was not unlike that of the Arnstadt congregation when J. S. Bach returned from his trip to Lübeck.

Since Düben did not hold primary responsibility for the performance of concerted music at the German Church and viewed his duties to the church as secondary to his responsibilities at court, it appears that he must have assembled his extensive collection of vocal music more for performance at court than at the German Church. Kjellberg's demonstration that a considerable number of manuscripts in the Düben collection were copied from printed editions purchased by the German Church lends support to this view. Nevertheless, since the participation of members of the Hofkapelle in the music of the German Church is documented for precisely those years when Düben's acquisitions of Buxtehude's music were at their peak, there can be no doubt that his music was heard there as well as at the Swedish court.

Düben's responsibilities as Kapellmeister included the performance of dinner music at banquets, and it was perhaps on these occasions that Buxtehude's sonatas were performed. Unlike Buxtehude's vocal music, however, virtually all of which came into the collection before Gustav Düben's death in 1690, most of the instrumental ensemble music came into the collection after that date. This includes the sonatas opus 1 [1694] and opus 2 (1696) and two sonatas copied by Anders Düben (BuxWV 266 and 267). The presence of these works in the collection bears witness to a continuing interest in Buxtehude's music on the part of Gustav Düben's sons.

Colleagues in Other Cities

Buxtehude's reputation also spread to the south, to Halberstadt in Thuringia and to the free imperial city of Nürnberg, where he caught the attention of two of his most important contemporaries among German musicians, Andreas Werckmeister (1645–1706) and Johann Pachelbel (1653–1706).

Although Werckmeister earned his living as an organist throughout his life, he is known not as a performer or composer but as an expert on organ construction and a leading music theorist. In his first published treatise, the original *Orgel-Probe* of 1681, he proposed a system of unequal temperament that allowed music to be played in all major and minor keys. In all likelihood, a friendship by correspondence between the two men began at that time, on Buxtehude's initiative, but the first evidence of their friendship comes from the year 1702, when Buxtehude contributed two congratulatory poems to Werckmeister's composition treatise *Harmonologia Musica*:

Ad Dn. Authorem.	*To the author:*
Es sagen insgesamt von Ihm die klugen Geister:	*The intelligent minds all say of him:*
Mit höchsten Ruhm und Preiß, lobt dieses Werck den Meister.	*With the highest fame and glory, this work praises the master.*

Aliud.
Wer ein Kunst-Werck recht betrachtet,
Es nicht unerkannt verachtet,
Redet frey ohn' arge List,
Christlich, wie es billig ist;
Kömmt es denn auch auf die Proben,
Muß das Werck den Meister loben.
Er mein Freund! hat wol erwogen,
In dem Buch, und ausgezogen,
So der Kunst ersprießlich sey,
Treulich und ohn Heucheley,
Er ist auch Werckmeister worden,
Rühmlich in der Musen-Orden.

Another:
Whoever views a work of art properly,
does not disdain it anonymously,
speaks freely without arrant cunning,
in a Christian manner, as is right,
for when it comes to the test,
the work must praise the master.
He, my Friend, has considered well,
in the book, and excerpted,
what is useful to art,
honestly and unfeignedly,
he has also become workmaster,
praiseworthy in the order of muses.

Dieses wolte dem Herrn AUTHORI als
seinem Hochgeschätztem Freunde
glückwünschend zuruffen, sein
Ergebenster

[The undersigned] wanted to exclaim this to
congratulate the author, as his highly
treasured friend, his most devoted

Dieterich Buxtehude
Organ. an der Haupt-Kirchen zu
St. Marien in Lübeck.

Dieterich Buxtehude
Organist at the principal church of
St. Mary in Lübeck.

Buxtehude must have read Werckmeister's composition treatise with great interest, because it teaches the same techniques of invertible counterpoint and canonic writing that he himself had cultivated—along with Bernhard, Theile and Reincken—in the 1670s. Werckmeister gives examples of quadruple counterpoint against a chorale melody and proposes the use of double sets of parallel thirds as the key to all kinds of canons and double, triple, and quadruple counterpoint.[31] This is precisely the technique that Buxtehude had used in his canons for both Meder and Reincken.

In addition to the interests Werckmeister shared with Buxtehude in learned counterpoint, organ construction, and the expansion of tonal horizons, he also became a collector of Buxtehude's organ music. Werckmeister later passed these works on to his student Johann Gottfried Walther (1684–1748). In a letter to Heinrich Bokemeyer, dated 3 October 1729, Walther wrote:

> I must honestly confess that for my modest ability, in whatever it may consist, I must thank, besides God, in the beginning the late Werckmeister (for whose sake I travelled to Halberstadt in the year 1704, [and] who also honored me later with some letters and keyboard works by Buxtehude) and later the work of good composers in score.[32]

The manuscripts of Buxtehude works that Werckmeister gave to Walther consisted of both autographs and copies. In 1729, Walther owned over two hundred pieces by "the famous Buxtehude and Bach . . . The first I have for the most part from the late Mr. Werckmeister, and from Mr. Buxtehude's own hand in German tablature; the second I have received from the author himself."[33]

Walther's extensive collection of Buxtehude's organ works—discussed further in chapter 9—presently contains no autographs and consists entirely of chorale settings. Buxtehude's chorale settings are far less adventurous tonally than his free organ works; most of them can in fact be played in mean-tone temperament. It would have been surprising if Buxtehude had not sent to Werckmeister examples of his keyboard compositions that boldly broke the tonal barriers of mean tone, requiring a circulating temperament such as Werckmeister had devised. We must assume that Walther's extant copies of Buxtehude works are a selection from a larger collection owned by Werckmeister and that Walther's own collection has not survived in its complete form.

Johann Pachelbel, organist at the Church of St. Sebald in Nuremberg, demonstrated his respect for Buxtehude by dedicating his *Hexachordum Apollinis* of 1699 to him, together with Ferdinand Tobias Richter (1651–1711). Pachelbel prefaces this collection of six variation sets for organ or harpsichord with the following dedicatory flourish:

> To the Most Noble and Excellent Gentlemen, Mr. Ferdinand Tobias Richter, Most Worthy Court and Chamber Organist to His Roman Imperial Majesty, and Mr. Dietr. Buxtehude, Most Worthy Organist of the Principal Church of St. Mary in Lübeck and *Director musices*, Both World Famous Musicians: . . .
>
> You, most worthy gentlemen and my most honored patrons, will be able to give the best weight to this [the idea of the previous paragraph: that music is the crown of all the other arts]; your praiseworthy desire—with that of several other excellent virtuosos—to bring this noble art to the highest peak of perfection in this our time, when almost all other arts have climbed to the clouds, is known the world over; also your very own magnificent and never sufficiently praised enterprises, experiments and discoveries are evident to each and every admirer with the same astonished wonder. . . .
>
> I gladly confess that something weightier and more unusual [than the work at hand] should have been produced for you and other world famous virtuosos, to entertain your ears and spirits, which strive for accurate things, but since your good will, combined with the most perfect friendliness, is more than well known to me, I have confidently ventured to risk it herewith, and thereby to wish to make the most respectful entreaty in behalf of my now thirteen-year-old son, should the Almighty be so gracious as to allow him the prolongation of his future years of life, that he might then most humbly appear before you, and pay the appropriate respects, [and] that you would then most graciously be pleased to accept him favorably and allow but a few little drops of your richly flowing fountain of art to flow upon him. . . .

With one eye to the south and the other to the north, Pachelbel—himself a keyboard virtuoso and an eminent teacher—singled out Richter and Buxtehude as the two musicians with whom he would most like his oldest son Wilhelm Hieronymus (1686–1764) to study. Johann Pachelbel's reference to the friendliness of his dedicatees is too impersonal to indicate that he was acquainted with either of them, even through correspondence. His use twice of the word *virtuoso* suggests that it was primarily their fame as keyboard performers that impressed him, but it is noteworthy that both Richter and Buxtehude were heavily involved in the composition of dramatic music, Richter for Jesuit school plays and Buxtehude for the Lübeck Abendmusiken. In addressing Buxtehude as *Director musices*, Pachelbel is alluding to this aspect of his reputation. Having himself worked for a time in Vienna, Pachelbel's ties with that city must have been much closer than his contacts with North Germany, making his choice of Buxtehude all the more significant. Wilhelm Hieronymus Pachelbel is not known to have studied with either Richter or Buxtehude.

Buxtehude's Pupils

Numerous organists did study with Buxtehude, the most notable of whom were Johann Sebastian Bach—discussed in chapter 3—and Nicolaus Bruhns. Bruhns (1665–97) came to Lübeck at the age of sixteen to study violin and viola da gamba with his uncle, the municipal musician Peter Bruhns, and organ and composition with Buxtehude. Concerning his study with Buxtehude, Mattheson reports in the *Ehrenpforte* that

> In keyboard and in composition he endeavored in particular to imitate the famous Dieterich Buxtehude, Lübeck organist at St. Mary's Church; he brought this to such perfection that at his request [Buxtehude] recommended him to Copenhagen, where he remained for several years, and afterwards he was called as organist to the city church in Husum [in 1689].

Johann Lorentz was still organist at St. Nicholas's Church in Copenhagen, and it was most likely to him that Buxtehude sent his illustrious pupil for help in establishing himself as a musician in that city. Bruhns's surviving organ and vocal works are definitely cast in a Buxtehudian mold, and his untimely death did not prevent him from being one of the composers to whose organ works J. S. Bach devoted particular attention. Nicolaus Bruhns's younger brother Georg also studied in Lübeck, but he took his organ lessons with Bernhard Olffen, the organist at St. Aegidien.

Among the other known pupils of Buxtehude, three achieved significant careers as organists: Daniel Erich (1649?–1712), Georg Dietrich Leiding (1664–1710), and Friedrich Gottlieb Klingenberg (d. 1720). Erich was the son of a Lübeck lutenist and builder of stringed instruments; Buxtehude purchased a tenor viola for the church from the father in 1677. The son served as player of the positive organ in the choir loft at St. Mary's from 1675 to 1679 and then became organist at the parish church of Güstrow. Like his teacher, he was unsuccessful in his

attempt to convince his church to have Schnitger rebuild his organ, but he did
have the opportunity to play for the dedication of the new Schnitger organ in the
castle church at Dargun in 1700. A poem composed for that occasion reads in part:

So komm HERR ERICH dann,	*So come then, Mr. Erich,*
du Sohn des BUXTEHUDEN,	*you son of Buxtehude,*
In seiner schönen Kunst,	*in his beautiful art,*
die Er dir anvertraut,	*which he entrusted to you,*
Komm zeige deine Frucht	*come show your fruit*
von diesem Haupt der Musen,	*from this head of the muses*
In diesem Orgel-Werck,	*on this organ*
das hie ist auffgebaut.[34]	*which has been built here.*

Of the fruits of his study only four chorale preludes remain.

Georg Dietrich Leiding had studied with Jacob Bölsche in Braunschweig
before making his trip to Hamburg and Lübeck in 1684 to study with "the two
extraordinarily famous organists Reincken and Buxtehude." Walther reports
that Leiding's stay in Lübeck was cut short when Bölsch called him back to substitute for him during his illness. Bölsch died that same year, and Leiding succeeded to his positions at St. Ulrich's and St. Blasius's churches in Braunschweig.
He continued his composition lessons with Johann Theile, who had just become
Kapellmeister at the court in Wolfenbüttel. Among Leiding's five extant compositions for organ are three praeludia with virtuosic pedal parts, but as works
of a student of Buxtehude, Reincken, and particularly Theile these works show
remarkably little contrapuntal interest.

Friedrich Gottlieb Klingenberg, a native of Berlin, studied with Buxtehude
around 1689, before taking up the post of organist at St. Nicholas's in Berlin. In
1699, while Schnitger was building the new organ for St. Jacobi Church, Stettin,
the old organist died, the position of organist was upgraded, and Klingenberg
received it. Perhaps he, like Schnitger, had come on Buxtehude's recommendation; a director of the church, Johann Köhler, was an old friend of Buxtehude's
from Lübeck—Buxtehude addressed him as "mon tres honore Amy a Stettin"—
and it was he who had originally written to Buxtehude for his recommendation
of an organ builder.[35] Klingenberg took two full weeks to test the organ and later
complained that Schnitger's assistant, Johann Balthasar Held, was not maintaining it properly. He did not get along well with the cantor, either, and probably
had a difficult personality. As a composer he is known only for his vocal works.[36]

As a teacher, Klingenberg passed his legacy from Buxtehude on to his pupils.
He must have had a collection of Buxtehude organ works that served as the
exemplars for the copies that Gottfried Lindemann made in Stettin in 1713 and
1714, probably while studying with Klingenberg. Lindemann later went to
Sweden, and his copies of Buxtehude organ works are now at the university
library in Lund. Probably Klingenberg's most illustrious pupil was the writer

Martin Heinrich Fuhrmann, who studied with Klingenberg in Berlin. Fuhrmann must have attended a Buxtehude Abendmusik, for he describes Buxtehude's direction of a large orchestra—which is quoted in chapter 11—in his *Musicalischer-Trichter* (1706). He later wrote of the three great B's in German music: Buxtehude, Bach, and Bachelbel.[37]

We know the names of several other Buxtehude pupils. His influence extended to the easternmost reaches of the Baltic Sea with Lowies Busbetzky, organist in Narva from 1687 until his death in 1699. Two of his vocal works preserved in the Düben Collection, *Laudate Dominum* and *Erbarm dich mein*, were formerly attributed to Buxtehude, but Martin Geck established that Busbetzky is the correct composer and that he described himself as a pupil of Buxtehude.[38] Joachim Ruetz of Wismar, father of the later St. Mary's cantor Caspar Ruetz, was also a pupil of Buxtehude, probably during the years 1694–98, when he served as organist of St. Lorenz, outside the walls of Lübeck. Two keyboard players who went from Lübeck to Stockholm also may have been Buxtehude pupils: Christian Krahn, the Swedish court organist, and Johan Fanselow, who had been playing the positive in the choir loft and left for Stockholm in 1683. Moving in the opposite direction, Anders Düben probably studied with Buxtehude when he was in Lübeck in 1692. And a student from the town of Buxtehude, Andreas Hermannus Helberg, assisted with the music at St. Mary's from 1668 to 1672; he might also have been a pupil of Buxtehude.

Not all of the organists who learned from Buxtehude came to Lübeck or ever met him personally. Christoph Raupach studied Buxtehude's compositions as a young man, according to Mattheson's *Ehrenpforte*. Both Johann Sebastian Bach and Johann Gottfried Walther claimed that much of their musical education had come from the study of the scores of other composers, and this must have been the case for others as well. Neither Georg Böhm (1661–1733) nor Vincent Lübeck (1654–1740) is known to have studied directly with Buxtehude, but his influence on their music is unmistakable. And with Bruhns's early death, they were the members of the next generation who would carry the distinctive art of the North German organist at its highest level into the eighteenth century.

Buxtehude the Man

Our survey of Buxtehude's world now enables us to begin to assemble a picture of Buxtehude the man, a picture that can be completed only by the following studies of his music and the sources that transmit it.

The documents that survive to illuminate Buxtehude's life and personality are meager indeed. His preserved writings include seventeen business letters, at least six poems, and the dedications to his two published sonata collections—all listed in appendix 2—plus the entries in the St. Mary's account books. We are well informed concerning the births and deaths of the members of his family but know little else about them. For him, no baptismal record survives, no documentation concerning his whereabouts before the age of twenty-one, no contracts of employment, no personal correspondence, no will, no listing of his estate, his books, his music, his musical instruments.

From the information that does exist, however, a multifaceted personality emerges to match the broad stylistic range of the music that he composed. In addition to his varied activities as a musician—composer, keyboard player, conductor—he worked with both words and numbers as a poet and an accountant. He was both a dutiful employee—a "faithful servant of the church," as he wrote in his memorandum concerning the organist's house—and a bold entrepreneur in his management of the Abendmusiken. His choice of texts for his vocal music indicates deep Christian piety, while his portrait in *Musical Party* shows a man of the world. The same juxtaposition of the pious and the worldly appears in his canon for Meno Hanneken, Jr. (see fig. 6-1), headed by Buxtehude's personal motto "Non hominibus sed Deo"—not to men but to God—and set to a text celebrating pleasure. He was generous with his own funds in helping others and in offering hospitality, but he was also a skillful fundraiser and frequently sought and received reimbursement for money he had advanced for various purposes. He was cosmopolitan in his outlook but hardly adventurous in his travel.

Buxtehude had an excellent command of language. His poetry may not have achieved a place in literary history, but he obviously took great delight in writing it. Besides his known poems, we can imagine his authorship of a number of the anonymous texts in his vocal music, particularly the wedding arias. Growing up bilingual may have given him an early advantage in learning foreign languages; besides German and Danish, he knew Latin and Greek, French, Italian, and Swedish.

In his capacity as Werkmeister, Buxtehude kept the accounts of the church neatly and accurately, week after week, year after year, until his final illness. Nowhere does he act the role of dutiful employee more than here. His friend Johann Adam Reincken refused such work, finding it incompatible with his profession as a musician, but Reincken received an exceptionally high organist's salary, 1,200 Lübeck marks annually, considerably more than Buxtehude's combined salaries. We can be thankful that Buxtehude needed the extra salary, because in his entries relating to musical expenses he often conveyed much more information than was strictly necessary for an accountant to give. Numerous excerpts from these accounts appear in appendix 4, D7. Buxtehude even found a way to combine his activities as poet and accountant in a brief poem of thanks for a gift from the church, which he entered into the account book in 1669.

The interest in learned counterpoint that Buxtehude demonstrated in the 1670s offers only a very narrow glimpse into his intellectual world. We would like to know much more. Were his seven lost sonatas on the nature or quality of the planets based on the intervals and motives that Johannes Kepler assigned to each of the planets in *Harmonices mundi libri V* (1619)? Marcus Meibom's library contained this book. When Buxtehude walked by the astronomical clock in St. Mary's Church, did he stop to consider that it presented a pre-Copernican view of the universe?

Buxtehude appears to have taken his place comfortably in Lübeck's society. On the one hand he ranked as the most respected musician in the city and had frequent dealings with its political and financial leaders. On the other, he was a member of the fourth class of this society, and the obsequious phrases in his letters and dedications indicate that he knew his place. The words from the chorale "Aus meines Herzens Grunde" that he set in BuxWV 4 may have articulated his own feelings as well:

Drauf streck' ich aus mein' Hand,	*So I stretch out my hand,*
greif' an das Werk mit Freuden,	*and undertake with joy the work*
dazu mich Gott bescheiden	*to which God has destined me*
in mein'n Beruf und Stand.	*in my vocation and class.*

The few words that others wrote about him during his lifetime and shortly afterward add little to the picture of Buxtehude that is seen in the documentary sources. The first to take note of him was a Dane, Matthias Schacht, rector of the Latin school in Kerteminde, who wrote a manuscript treatise "Musicus Danicus eller Danske Sangmester" in 1687. Buxtehude's name appears in its "Bibliotheca musica" or list of authors of both theoretical and practical works. The complete entry reads "BUXTEHUDIUS edidit Modulationes funerales sub titulo freudenreicher hinfahrt in fol.," referring to BuxWV 76 without even giving the composer's first name. Hinrich Elmenhorst's mention of "the well known Lübeck musician . . . Diedericus Buxtehude" as director of the Lübeck Abendmusiken appeared in print the following year. Wolfgang Caspar Printz included him in a list of seventy-four "more recent and more famous composers and musicians of this century" in 1690. Buxtehude is one of the few who receives a brief comment beside his name: "an excellent organist and composer at St. Mary's Church in Lübeck." In his *Musicalischer Trichter* of 1706 Martin Fuhrmann described the precise conducting of "the incomparable Mr. Buxtehude" at Lübeck, and he praised Buxtehude's free organ works even over those of Frescobaldi. Fuhrmann's comments are quoted and discussed in chapters 11 and 7, respectively. The reports published in Lübeck in the 1697 guidebook and in the *Nova literaria* concerning Buxtehude's Abendmusiken are given in chapter 2.

The most prolific German writer on music of the early eighteenth century, Johann Mattheson, was personally acquainted with Buxtehude; Mattheson's account of his trip to Lübeck with Handel in 1703 will be recalled from chapter 3. One suspects that no great meeting of the minds took place on that occasion, for Mattheson did not accord Buxtehude an individual entry in the *Ehrenpforte*, despite his acknowledgment of Buxtehude's fame in the article on Nicolaus

Bruhns. It is from Mattheson's *Vollkommener Capellmeister*, however, that we learn
of Buxtehude's lost set of keyboard suites:

> Buxtehude (Dietrich), the similarly highly esteemed, former Lübeck organist, also put
> such works [as those of Froberger] to paper in his time, with a good reception—among
> others, the nature or quality of the planets, nicely depicted in seven keyboard suites. It
> is a shame that from this excellent artist few or none of the well-composed keyboard
> works—in which he endowed most of his power—have been published (II/4, §73).

The famous musical lexicographer Johann Gottfried Walther did not know
the dates of Buxtehude's birth and death, even though he had received copies
of his organ music directly from Buxtehude's friend Andreas Werckmeister. In
the course of the research for his *Musicalisches Lexicon,* Walther wrote to
Heinrich Bokemeyer, the cantor in Wolfenbüttel, asking him, among other
things, for Buxtehude's birth and death dates. The dictionary appeared in 1732
without this information, so Bokemeyer was apparently unable to supply it, even
though his collection of music also included works of Buxtehude. Walther's
complete entry reads:

> Buxtehude (Dietrich). Organist at the principal church of St. Mary's in Lübeck, a son
> of Johann Buxtehude, who had been organist for 32 years at the St. Olai Church in
> Helsingör in Denmark. He published two *opera* for violin, viola da gamba, and harpsi-
> chord, the latter work in the year 1696 in Hamburg. Of his many artful keyboard works,
> to my knowledge none have been published other than the chorale "Mit Fried und
> Freud ich fahr dahin, etc.," which he set upon the occasion of his father's death,
> together with an elegy.

It is not surprising, then, that there is no record of his having played the viola
da gamba.

Although he holds no place in Mattheson's "Triumphal Arch," Buxtehude was
honored, both in his own century and in the one that followed, in a manner that
was ultimately of far greater significance than any number of verbal accolades
might have been: by the copying of his music, the story of which unfolds in chapter 9. Much as we would like to know further details concerning Buxtehude's
life, they would be worth little if we did not have his music. And we do have his
music, not all of it by any means, but more, and in a greater variety of genres,
than survives from any of his North German contemporaries.

Part II

Buxtehude's Compositions

Chapter Five

Vocal Music

Although Buxtehude never held a position that required him to compose vocal music, more vocal works of his survive than keyboard or chamber works. The Buxtehude-Werke-Verzeichnis (BuxWV) lists 122 works for voices and instruments, seven of which might be subtracted from a list of discrete, complete authentic works. Two works survive only as fragments; BuxWV 16 breaks off after two and a half measures in its only source, and the print for BuxWV 121 has been missing since 1942. Pirro copied out the incipits of its vocal line, ritornello, and concluding gigue and published them in his book, but for the present this work must be considered lost. Two works, BuxWV 26 and 65, are parodies (of BuxWV 122 and 119, respectively), with only the texts changed. And the authenticity of three works included in the main list—BuxWV 1, 43, and 101—appears doubtful. *Membra Jesu*, however, listed as BuxWV 75, is a cycle comprising seven discrete works, and BuxWV 76 includes two works. With these adjustments, the total number of vocal works under consideration remains at 122. This number may be compared with 114 complete keyboard works—70 pedaliter and 44 manualiter—and 20 complete sonatas for strings.

Buxtehude's vocal works cover an extremely wide range of texts, scoring, genres, compositional styles, and length. Texts are found in four languages, and performing forces range from one voice with one instrument and continuo (BuxWV 64 and 98) to nine voices with fifteen instruments and continuo, divided into six choirs (BuxWV 113). A work may be as short and stylistically unified as BuxWV 105—a ten-measure strophic aria framed by a short sinfonia and ritornello—or as long and complex as BuxWV 34, a composite work of 310 measures composed of movements in separate genres, or BuxWV 41, a setting of three chorale strophes totaling 525 measures. The fact that Buxtehude composed his vocal music freely—quite apart from his official duties as organist—may help to explain its great variety.

Texts

German and Latin texts serve as the basis for the vast majority of Buxtehude's vocal works: eighty-six in German and thirty-three in Latin. Such a large number of works with Latin texts might appear somewhat unusual for a Protestant composer working in North Germany, but other Latin-texted works were frequently performed at St. Mary's, Lübeck. In fact, most of the printed works in the church's old music library (appendix 5C) had Latin texts, and a number of the works performed in the festival services of 1682–83 were in Latin. Gustav Düben's strong preference for Latin-texted works may explain the preservation of all but one of Buxtehude's Latin-texted works in the Düben Collection, but it does not account for their composition, with the possible exception of *Membra Jesu*, which Buxtehude dedicated to Düben. Two works with Swedish texts (BuxWV 8 and 40) may have been commissioned by Düben. One wedding aria (BuxWV 117) has an Italian text, as did the lost BuxWV 121. Buxtehude is not known to have composed any works with Danish texts; the single work that can definitely be ascribed to his Helsingør years (BuxWV 7) has a Latin text.

Whatever their language, nearly all the texts of Buxtehude's surviving works consist either of biblical prose or strophic poetry. Madrigalesque poetry—nonstrophic, with an irregular metrical and rhyme scheme—which is so often found in seventeenth-century opera and eighteenth-century German church music, is completely missing from Buxtehude's extant vocal music, although it does appear in the texts of the otherwise lost *Castrum doloris* and *Templum honoris*. Buxtehude set biblical and poetic texts both alone and in combination, the most common combination consisting of a short biblical text followed by a poem paraphrasing or expanding on it. The following discussion of Buxtehude's texts concentrates on their sources and ignores the distinction between works with homogeneous or heterogeneous texts; we will consider the relationships of mixed texts later, in light of their musical settings. The work of identifying the sources of these texts, begun by Philipp Spitta, continues and is not yet complete; the second edition (1985) of the Buxtehude-Werke-Verzeichnis summarizes the state of knowledge to date. Martin Geck's book considers the subject extensively, and its appendix contains a complete transcription of all but the secular and chorale texts.

Buxtehude's most important biblical source was the book of Psalms, from which he drew texts for twenty-five works. Unlike his predecessors Schütz or Rosenmüller, he did not often set complete psalms, but preferred instead to expand musically on a few verses. Only three complete psalm settings survive, BuxWV 17, 23 and 69—all in Latin, the second of which consists of only three verses. The other two are the familiar Sunday Vespers psalms "Dixit Dominus" (Psalm 109) and "Laudate pueri" (Psalm 112), both complete with Gloria Patri. The singing of the Latin Vespers psalms did not form a regular part of the Lübeck liturgy for Sundays and feast days, but a setting of the complete "Laudate pueri"—in a different scoring from BuxWV 69—was performed at St. Mary's at the afternoon service on Epiphany, 1683. Psalm texts have the advantage of being appropriate for almost any day in the church year. Most of those that Buxtehude chose express sentiments of praise or trust in God.

The sensual imagery in the Song of Solomon held great appeal for seventeenth-century composers, and Buxtehude was no exception. He used verses from it in four works (BuxWV 45, 50, 75/4, 75/6), and numerous phrases of the poetic text for BuxWV 70 are drawn from this book. Buxtehude followed a long church tradition in interpreting the love between man and woman described in the Song of Solomon allegorically as the love between Jesus and the soul. In BuxWV 50, the vignette of the lover lost from the bed, sought, and finally found, appears both in its original biblical form (Song of Solomon 3:1-4) and in poetic paraphrase. BuxWV 111 converts the story into a poetic dialogue between Christ and the faithful soul.

Of the remaining biblical texts, Buxtehude drew three from Isaiah (in BuxWV 31, 34, 75/2), three from the apocryphal book of Sirach (in BuxWV 19, 55, 79), and the rest from scattered verses throughout the Old and New Testaments. Fourteen works contain New Testament texts, of which six come from the Epistle or Gospel readings appointed for specific days in the church year: BuxWV 5 (John 3:16, Pentecost Monday); BuxWV 30 (Luke 2:10–11, Christmas); BuxWV 37 (Luke 2:29–32, Purification); BuxWV 48 (Romans 8:18, Fourth Sunday after Trinity); BuxWV 54 (Matthew 22:17b, 21b; Twenty-third Sunday after Trinity); BuxWV 97 (John 3:14–15, Trinity Sunday). The last of these is in Latin. Apart from psalm texts and the biblical verses chosen to introduce the poetry of *Membra Jesu*, most of Buxtehude's biblical texts are in German.

Among the six Latin prose devotional texts in Buxtehude's vocal works, three (BuxWV 2, 82, 92) are composed in whole or in part of combined biblical texts. *Quemadmodum desiderat cervus* (BuxWV 92) begins with a quotation from Psalm 41, 2–3 [Latin numbering] and later weaves Psalm 117:24 into its mainly non-biblical prose. The beginning of this text (through the words "ante faciem tuam") is drawn from the pseudo-Augustinian soliloquies and appears in a Latin devotional manual, *Precationes ex veteribus orthodoxis doctoribus*, compiled by a sixteenth-century Lutheran theologian, Andreas Musculus (1541–81). Heinrich Schütz drew extensively on this manual for the texts of his *Cantiones sacrae* (1625), and he set "Quemadmodum" (SWV 336) in part II of the *Kleine geistliche Konzerte* (1639). Schütz's text follows Musculus in its entirety; Buxtehude's does not, and must have been drawn from another source. Latin devotional manuals such as Musculus's *Precationes* and the *Paradisus animae christianae* by Jacob Merler, a Roman Catholic, circulated widely among Catholics and Protestants alike. The sources of three other Latin devotional texts (BuxWV 11, 83, 94) have not been identified, but in their ecstatic language and mixture of prose and poetry they resemble the texts set by Albrici and Peranda at the Dresden court, which Mary Frandsen discusses extensively in *Crossing Confessional Boundaries*.

Latin strophic poetry is found in seventeen of Buxtehude's works. Four of these poems are hymns from the Roman Catholic church associated with particular feasts: "Surrexit Christus hodie" (BuxWV 99), a nonliturgical Easter hymn; "O lux beata Trinitas" (BuxWV 89), an Ambrosian hymn associated with Trinity; "Pange lingua" (BuxWV 91) and "Lauda Sion Salvatorem" (BuxWV 68), the Vespers hymn and sequence for the feast of Corpus Christi. At least three of these hymns continued in use in Lübeck after the Reformation: "O lux beata Trinitas" and "Lauda Sion Salvatorem" appeared in Hermann Bonnus's *Hymni et Sequentiae* (1559), now lost, and "O lux beata Trinitas" and "Surrexit Christus hodie" in the *Lübeckisches vollständiges Gesangbuch* (1699). "O lux beata Trinitas," "Lauda Sion Salvatorem" and "Pange lingua" are all included in Musculus's *Precationes*. The feast of Corpus Christi was not celebrated in the Lutheran church, but texts proper to it were appropriate for Communion music at any time of the church year.

Two medieval poems that circulated under the name of Saint Bernard of Clairvaux, "Salve mundi salutare" and "Jesu dulcis memoria," enjoyed wide popularity during the seventeenth century, as evidenced both by printed editions in Latin and by numerous translations and paraphrases into other languages, among them the familiar hymns "O Sacred Head Now Wounded" and "Jesus, the Very Thought of Thee." Together they supply the texts for ten Buxtehude works. "Salve mundi salutare," also known as the "Rhythmica oratio," is a lengthy meditation on the passion of Christ actually written by Arnulf of Louvain (d. 1250). It is divided into seven parts, each devoted to one of the members of Christ's crucified body: feet, knees, hands, side, breast, heart, and head. Buxtehude selected three strophes from each part for the arias in *Membra Jesu* (BuxWV 75). Two other works, BuxWV 14 and BuxWV 6, have texts derived from the "Rhythmica oratio." The text of BuxWV 14, *Dein edles Herz*, comes from part 6, "To the Heart," of Johann Rist's free translation of the "Rhythmica oratio," first published in 1648 under the title *Der zu seinem allerheiligsten Leiden und Sterben hingeführter und an das Kreütz gehefteter Christus Jesus*. The second edition of this book, published in 1655, also contains translations of Rist's poems into Latin by Tobias Peterman. His translation of Rist's part 4, "To the Side" ("Ist dieser nicht des höchsten Sohn"), supplies the text for BuxWV 6, *An filius non est dei*. "Jesu dulcis memoria," also known as the "Jubilus Bernardi," is a fifty-strophe meditation on the name and person of Jesus. Buxtehude selected strophes from it for three works, BuxWV 56, 57, and 88.

German poetry is the single most important textual category for Buxtehude; it appears in seventy of the 122 works under consideration. These poems may be divided into two classes: those dating from the sixteenth century or earlier and those from the seventeenth century, to which all of the unidentified texts are assumed to belong. Among the seventeenth-century poems are seven texts relating to weddings, two to funerals, and one (BuxWV 96) to the glory of Lübeck; the rest are sacred songs, as are all the earlier poems. In terms of the poetic structure, there is little difference between the earlier and the later groups. Thematically, the seventeenth-century group tends to be far more personal and emotional, although the distinction often drawn between sixteenth-century *wir* hymns and seventeenth-century *ich* hymns is by no means absolute in this selection of poems. Buxtehude drew an important musical distinction between the two groups, however. With but a few exceptions, the sixteenth-century hymns were associated with melodies that he chose to use as cantus firmi in his compositions; the seventeenth-century texts he set freely, even though most of those that have been identified were accompanied by melodies in their sources. Although there is no real textual distinction between them, it will be useful to refer to those texts that Buxtehude used with their attendant melodies—all but five from the sixteenth century or earlier—specifically as chorales and those that he set freely—all but one from the seventeenth century—variously as poems, hymns, or sacred songs (*geistliche Lieder*).

Buxtehude used German chorale texts in twenty-two vocal works. He rarely used the same chorale twice, and no chorale author other than Martin Luther is represented more than once. Buxtehude set four Luther texts: "Erhalt uns, Herr, bei deinem Wort" (BuxWV 27), "Nun freut euch, lieben Christen gemein" (BuxWV 32), "Mit Fried und Freud ich fahr dahin" (BuxWV 76-1), and "Wär Gott nicht mit uns diese Zeit" (BuxWV 102). One pre-Reformation chorale, "In dulci jubilo" (BuxWV 52), and two chorale texts from the 1520s, "Durch Adams Fall ist ganz verderbt" (BuxWV 34) and "Verleih uns Frieden gnädiglich" (BuxWV 27), complete Buxtehude's selection of core Reformation chorales. "Verleih uns Frieden," a translation of the Latin antiphon "Da pacem Domine," is not actually a poetic text. Johann Walter added a second, irregular stanza to it in 1566:

Gib unserm Fürsten und aller Obrigkeit Fried	Give to our prince and to all in authority peace
und gut Regiment, daß wir unter ihnen ein	and good government, that under them we may
geruhig und stilles Leben führen mögen in	lead a calm and quiet life in all godliness and
aller Gottseligkeit und Ehrbarkeit. Amen.	honesty. Amen.

The *Lübeckisches Gesangbuch* appended both stanzas of "Verleih uns Frieden" to "Erhalt uns, Herr," as Buxtehude did in BuxWV 27, and it substituted "Rat" (council) for "Fürsten" (prince). Buxtehude set the second stanza in BuxWV 29 as well, and in both cases the word "König" (king) appears at this point. These works are preserved only by copies in the Düben Collection, however, and it is quite possible that Düben made this change in text to suit the Swedish political system; the instrumental parts seem to be modeled on the use of the one-syllable word "Rat." The majority of Buxtehude's chorale texts come from later in the sixteenth century or early in the seventeenth century. Among the most familiar are "Herzlich lieb hab ich dich, o Herr" (1570; BuxWV 41), "Wachet auf, ruft uns die Stimme" (1599; BuxWV 100), "Herzlich tut mich verlangen" (1611, BuxWV 42), and "Jesu, meine Freude" (1650, BuxWV 60). Johann Franck's "Jesu, meine Freude" quickly became attached to Johann Crüger's melody, published in 1653, and it is the youngest of Buxtehude's chorale texts.

The seventeenth century witnessed a veritable explosion in hymn writing, such that Philipp Wackernagel found it necessary to limit his collection of

German hymn texts to those written before 1600. It comes as no surprise, then, that fifty-two of Buxtehude's seventy German poetic texts come from the seventeenth century. His favored poets were Johann Rist, Ernst Christoph Homburg, and Johann Scheffler, also known as Johann Angelus Silesius. Paul Gerhardt (1607–76), the leading hymn writer of the time, is represented by only one poem in Buxtehude's works, "Wie soll ich dich empfangen" (BuxWV 109).

Johann Rist (1607–67), a Lutheran pastor in Wedel, outside of Hamburg, belonged to the circle of Bernhard, Weckmann, and the collegium musicum. Although Rist died just before Buxtehude's arrival in Lübeck, Buxtehude would have quickly become acquainted with his poetry through Bernhard and Weckmann if he had not known it already in Denmark. Buxtehude set four poems by Rist—five, if the Latin translation "An filius non est dei" is included—drawn from four different collections. He used two of these poems twice: "Du Lebensfürst, Herr Jesu Christ" (BuxWV 22 and 33) from the first part of the *Himmlische Lieder* (1641) and "O fröhliche Stunden, o herrliche Zeit" (BuxWV 84 and 85) from the *Neue musicalische Festandachten* of 1655. Both are strong poems recounting, respectively, Christ's triumphant ascension and resurrection, and Buxtehude undoubtedly intended these works for the feasts of Ascension and Easter. "O Gottes Stadt" (BuxWV 87), from the third part of the *Himmlische Lieder* (1642), voices a longing for heaven. Rist's passion hymn "Dein edles Herz" (BuxWV 14), discussed earlier, forms part of his poetic paraphrase of the "Rhythmica oratio." Rist published all five parts of the *Himmlische Lieder* with melodies by the violinist Johann Schop, leader of the Hamburg municipal musicians. The Hamburg cantor Thomas Selle supplied the melodies for the *Neue musicalische Festandachten*, and Rist's brother-in-law Heinrich Pape, a student of Jacob Praetorius, composed the original melodies for the passion cycle.

Ernst Christoph Homburg (1605–81), a court clerk in Naumburg, published 150 sacred songs in 1659, its two parts appearing together as one publication (DKL 1659–10). The composers of the melodies for the two parts were Werner Fabricius and Paul Becker, respectively. Buxtehude drew poems from part one for the texts of four works: *Jesu, komm, mein Trost und Lachen* (BuxWV 58); *Jesu, meines Lebens Leben* (BuxWV 62); *Kommst du, Licht der Heiden* (BuxWV 66); and *Liebster, meine Seele saget* (BuxWV 70). The recurring words "Jesus" and "come" in the first three titles represent a common Homburg theme of love and longing for Jesus; it occurs in the last poem as well, the imagery of which is drawn from the Song of Solomon.

Johann Scheffler (1624–77), later called Johann Angelus the Silesian, was a true mystic. Raised a Lutheran and trained as a physician, Scheffler was prompted by his study of medieval mystical writings to convert to Roman Catholicism in 1653, whereupon he changed his name from Scheffler to Angelus Silesius. He later became a priest in the Franciscan order. His "Sacred Shepherd Songs," *Heilige Seelen-Lust, Oder Geistliche Hirten-Lieder Der in ihren JESUM verliebten Psyche*, published in 1657 with melodies by Georg Joseph, provided texts for three Buxtehude works: *Jesu, meine Freud und Lust* (BuxWV 59); *Meine Seele, willtu ruhn* (BuxWV 74); and *Nun freut euch, ihr Frommen, mit mir* (BuxWV 80). Angelus describes the love between Jesus and the soul with sensuous imagery:

Nu freut euch ihr Hirten mit mir,	Rejoice, now, you shepherds, with me,
Ich habe den Bräutigam hier	I have the bridegroom here.
O glückliche Stunden!	O happy hours,
Nu hab ich gefunden,	Now I have found
Den ich gesuchet mit stether Begiehr.	the one for whom I have been searching with constant longing.
O Jesu, wie süsse bistu!	O Jesus, how sweet you are,
Was bringstu für selige Ruh	What blessed peace you bring me.
O Jesu mein Leben,	O Jesus, my life,
Was soll ich dir geben?	what shall I give you?
Süsser als Honigseim bistu mir nu.	You are sweeter than honey to me.
Du riechest so kräfftig und gut,	You smell so robust and good,
Erquickest Leib Leben und Blut;	you refresh body, life and blood;
Du klingest so schöne	You sound so beautiful,
Wie Engel-Gethöne	like the sounds of angels,
Setzest in jauchtzen den traurigen Muth.	you make the sad spirit rejoice.

The love of Jesus likewise permeates the other two poems by Angelus that Buxtehude set. A fourth text, "Jesulein, du tausendschön" (BuxWV 63), by an unidentified author, may have been inspired by an Angelus poem, "Ich liebe dich von Hertzen-Grund," from the same collection.

Heightened sensuous imagery, drawn in part from Angelus, pervades the poem by Heinrich Müller that Buxtehude employed in BuxWV 108:

Wie schmeckt es so lieblich und wohl,	How lovely and good it tastes,
wie bin ich so trunken und voll!	How intoxicated and full I am!
O selige Stunden, nun hab ich empfunden,	O blessed hours, now I have experienced
was mich erfreuen und sättigen soll.	what shall delight and satisfy me.
Wie hat mich mein Jesus erquickt	How my Jesus has refreshed me
und an seine Brüste gedrückt.	and pressed me to his breast.
Wie reichlich beschenket mit Wollust getränket,	How richly he has bestowed and intoxicated with desire,
wie lieblich bis in den Himmel entzückt.	how lovely, transported into heaven.
Wie hat mich die Wollust entzünd't,	How the desire has inflamed me,
wie hat mich die Liebe verwund't!	how the love has wounded me!
Kommt, schauet die Flammen, die schlagen zusammen,	Come, look at the flames which burn together

über das Herze, das Jesum empfundt.	*over the heart that has experienced Jesus.*
O, bin ich doch nun nicht mehr mein,	*O, now I am no longer my own,*
denn was ich bin, ist alles sein.	*for what I am is all his.*
Mein Lieben und Hassen hab ich ihm	*My love and hate I have given over to him.*
gelassen.	
Alles wirkt in mir sein kräftiger Wein.	*His powerful wine has taken effect in me.*
Kommt, jauchzet ihr Frommen mit mir;	*Come, rejoice, you pious with me;*
ich habe die Freudenquell' hier!	*I have the source of joy here.*
Kommt, lasset uns singen mit Spielen und	*Come, let us sing with play and dancing,*
Springen,	
lasset uns brennen in Liebesbegier.	*Let us burn in the desire of love.*

Heinrich Müller (1631–75), a Lübecker by birth, was archdeacon of St. Mary's Church in Rostock and a professor first of Greek and later of theology at the university there. This poem appears in his collection *Geistliche Seelen-Musik* of 1659, which also contains Angelus's "Nu freut euch ihr Hirten mit mir"—with "the shepherds" changed to "the pious," the form that Buxtehude used. Another text set by Buxtehude, Siegmund von Birken's "Klopfet an die Himmelspforte" (in BuxWV 112), was inspired by a meditation in Müller's *Geistliche Erquickstunden.*[1]

Buxtehude drew two texts from a collection assembled by Ahasverus Fritzsch (1629–1701) to accompany his treatise *Himmelslust und Welt-Unlust.* "Entreißt euch, meine Sinnen" (BuxWV 25) comes from the first edition of 1670; "Was mich auf dieser Welt betrübt" (BuxWV 105), from the second edition of 1679. Since Fritzsch mixed his own poems with those of other authors, usually without attribution, it is unknown whether he himself was the author of these texts. Fritzsch distinguished his collections thematically either as "Jesus songs" or "Heaven songs," the category to which these two texts belong. Most of Buxtehude's poetic texts could in fact be classed in one or the other of these categories. Often they merge, as in the aria "So komm doch, Jesu," to a text by an unidentified author, which Buxtehude himself inserted into the manuscript copy of BuxWV 51:

So komm doch, Jesu, komme bald,	*So do come, Jesus, come quickly*
uns gänzlich zu befreien,	*to free us completely;*
komm, unser Seelen Aufenthalt,	*come, abide in our souls*
uns ewig zu erfreuen.	*to cheer us forever.*
Komm, Jesu, komm und säume nicht,	*Come, Jesus, come, do not delay,*
laß uns in deines Himmels Licht	*let us in the light of your heaven*
dein ewiges Lob ausschreien	*proclaim your eternal praise.*

One other of Buxtehude's poets must be mentioned: the theologian Johann Wilhelm Petersen (1649–1727) lived in Lübeck from 1676 to 1677 and may have composed the libretto of *Die Hochzeit des Lamms*, as discussed in chapter 2. The one identified poem of Petersen's that Buxtehude set, "O wie selig sind, die zu dem Abendmahl des Lammes berufen sind" (BuxWV 90), is a Communion hymn, imbued with mystic-erotic imagery.

The remaining German poetic texts include twelve poems by identified authors, one that appears anonymously in a contemporary hymnal, and nineteen whose authors are unknown, including the parody texts BuxWV 26 and 65. This number does not include the three texts attributed to Buxtehude himself in earlier chapters: the *Klag-Lied* for the funeral of his father (BuxWV 76-2) and two wedding poems, BuxWV 119 and 120. Buxtehude's authorship may also be suspected for the other wedding texts and for some of the poems within the combined texts, many of which remain unidentified. The two parody texts appear to have been composed in Stockholm. A draft of the text for BuxWV 26, with many corrections, uses the same paper as Düben's intabulation of the work (both in *Uu* 50:15), and the text for BuxWV 65 is written in the same hand. Among the poetic texts by identified authors, the only one dating from the sixteenth century is the New Year hymn "Das neugeborne Kindelein" (BuxWV 13) by Cyriacus Schneegaß, first published in 1588. Although it appeared in most contemporary hymnals—but not in the *Lübeckisches Gesangbuch*—it was set to several different melodies concurrently, which may account for the fact that Buxtehude chose to set it freely, without a cantus firmus. No author in this group is represented by more than one poem, but two poems appear twice, one in a revision (BuxWV 46 and 47) and the other, "Wenn ich, Herr Jesu, habe dich" by Anna Sophia, countess of Hesse-Darmstadt, in two different settings (BuxWV 39 and 107).

If one eliminates from the corpus of Buxtehude's texts those intended for a specific occasion—wedding, funeral, secular—and the two in Swedish, over one hundred sacred texts in German or Latin remain. We can firmly identify a number of these with specific seasons of the church year:

Advent: BuxWV 51 and 109
Christmas: BuxWV 30 and 52
New Year: BuxWV 3 and 13
Purification: BuxWV 37
Passiontide: BuxWV 6, 14, 31, 62, 75
Easter: BuxWV 44, 84, 85, 99
Ascension: BuxWV 22, 32, 33
Pentecost: BuxWV 5
Trinity: BuxWV 48, 54, 89, 97
The end of the church year: BuxWV 100

The large majority of Buxtehude's texts, however—including the psalm texts, the "Jesus songs" and the "Heaven songs"—are not tied to any particular season and could have been used at almost any time during the church year. Furthermore, only one liturgical text appears among his works, the Kyrie and Gloria of the *Missa alla brevis* (BuxWV 114), which is discussed in chapter 6. In his wide-ranging choices of texts, Buxtehude demonstrated the freedom that he enjoyed to compose vocal music as he wished, not as the duty of a particular position.

Buxtehude and Pietism

The prominence of the poetry of Rist, Homburg, Angelus, Müller, Fritzsch, and especially Petersen—an avowed Pietist—among Buxtehude's texts raises the question as to whether Buxtehude himself was of the Pietist persuasion, even if his position prevented him politically from actively participating in the move-ment. The central thesis of Martin Geck's dissertation, whose title may be trans-lated as *Buxtehude's Vocal Music and Early Pietism*, is that Buxtehude belonged to the circle of those who sought to deepen their religious experience beyond that of traditional piety and that this experience, together with the musical ideal of the Pietist sacred song, provides the source of the lyricism in Buxtehude's vocal music and the best key to the understanding of this music.

The first difficulty with Geck's hypothesis stems from the fact that the Pietist movement, when broadly defined, included a program for church reform whose musical components would have excluded most of Buxtehude's known compo-sitions from performance within the church service. Theophil Großgebauer (1627–61), a deacon at St. Jacobi Church in Rostock and a professor of philos-ophy and theology at the university there, first enunciated this program in his tract *Wächterstimme aus dem verwüsteten Zion* of 1661. Strongly influenced by Calvinism, Großgebauer's complaints concerning the current state of Lutheran church music included the use of Latin texts, Italianate concerted style, artful organ music, and festive music performed during the distribution of Communion, all of which hindered true devotion. His description of the Italianate setting of biblical texts—"in which the biblical texts are torn apart and chopped up into little pieces through swift runs of the throat"—aptly describes the style that Buxtehude used in his sacred concertos. And Großgebauer's words concerning organists could be applied to at least three generations of North German organists: "There the organist sits, plays, and shows his art; in order that the art of one person be shown, the whole congregation of Jesus Christ is sup-posed to sit and hear the sound of pipes."

Music-loving orthodox Lutherans responded swiftly to Großgebauer's propos-als, and the controversy lasted for nearly a century. In 1665, Master Hector Mithobius, archdeacon of the church at Otterndorf/Hadeln, published his *Psalmodia Christiana*, the continuation of whose title may be translated:

You Christians, sing and play to the Lord, Ephesians 5, verse 19. That is basic instruc-tion for the conscience, [concerning] what it should think about Christian music, both vocal and instrumental. Directed against all old and new enemies of music, but especially the opinion of the late H. M. Theophil Großgebaur in his newly edited Wächterstimme chapter 11. Begun in a sermon with a regular exposition of the normal epistle for the 22nd Sunday after Trinity by the late Doctor Hector Mithobius etc. [his father, former pastor of the church, died 1655]; continued afterwards in two sermons, further executed with diligence and to the honor of God and also to the vindication of all musicians, cantors, organists, etc. With the approval of the full theological faculty at the world-famous Lutheran University at Wittenberg.

Mithobius reprinted the applicable chapter from Großgebauer's tract for easy reference. This is the publication that also contains the full description of Heinrich Scheidemann's dedication of the new organ at Otterndorf in 1662, discussed in chapter 3. The lower part of its frontispiece (fig. 5-1) depicts a small church with an organ—including Rückpositiv and pedal towers—in place of the altar; a lutenist and a violinist in the organ loft with the organist (as at Lübeck!); balconies to either side filled with more instrumentalists than singers; and a cantor conducting from the center of the church in the midst of the congregation, which is listening quietly. Ninety years later in Lübeck, Caspar Ruetz's publications were still defending concerted church music against Pietist attacks.

Under no circumstances could Buxtehude have supported Großgebauer's proposals for the reform of church music. It was not necessary to do this, however, in order to participate in the heightened spirituality that the Pietists also cultivated. One could be pious—as Buxtehude undoubtedly was—without being a Pietist. In her article on German Pietists and church music, Joyce Irwin distinguishes between the mystical piety of Heinrich Müller and the ecclesiastical reforms advocated by Großgebauer:

> Significantly, several of Müller's writings were found among J. S. Bach's books in the following century. His *Göttliche Liebes-Flamme, Geistliche Erquickstunden* and *Schlußkette und Kraft-Kern* are listed in the inventory of books in Bach's possession at the time of his death. If, as seems to be the case, we can distinguish within the broader term "Pietism" between a practical impulse toward ecclesiastical and pedagogical reform and a devotional impulse inclined to mysticism, both Bach's relation to Pietism and Pietism's relation to music become less paradoxical. The opposition to artistic music in church was centered in the reform movement, whereas Bach's affinity was limited to the devotional movement.[2]

Irwin's solution to the puzzle of Bach's relation to Pietism applies equally well to Buxtehude. The mysticism expressed so vividly in Müller's poetry had roots deep within Lutheran orthodoxy, and it is within the orthodox tradition that we can best understand the wide variety of texts Buxtehude selected for his vocal music. Buxtehude announced on the title page of the libretto of his Abendmusik *Die Hochzeit des Lamms* (fig. 2-5) his intent to provide "Inner Consolation of the Soul and Sweetest Joy to the Pious and Those who Heartily Long for the Future of their Bridegroom of the Soul." Such language, frequently characterized as

Figure 5-1. Hector Mithobius, *Psalmodia christiana* (Jena, 1665). Frontispiece (Berlin, Staatsbibliothek Preussischer Kulturbesitz, Musikabteilung).

Pietist, must have enjoyed wide acceptance in Lübeck for Buxtehude to have used it so prominently in a production whose financing depended on contributions from the business community and at a time when the superintendent, Samuel Pomarius, was carrying on a polemic against the Lübeck spiritualists.

Significantly, perhaps, the bride of Jesus in this text is not the individual soul but the church.

A further difficulty with viewing Buxtehude's vocal music through the lens of Pietism emerges in the comparison of Buxtehude's arias with the music of the sacred songs that the Pietists cultivated. Although Geck is undoubtedly correct in identifying the aria as the central genre among Buxtehude's vocal works and the sacred song as the ultimate source of this genre as Buxtehude used it, Buxtehude distinguished his arias from sacred songs by grafting onto this stock stylistic elements from a genre that was basically inimical to it, and that the Pietist reformers rejected: the sacred concerto. Buxtehude's lyricism manifests itself in the concerto as well as the aria, and its roots are more readily found in Italian bel canto style than in the German sacred song.

Text, Genre, and Style in Seventeenth-Century German Church Music

Buxtehude inherited well-established traditions regarding the musical settings of the texts that he chose. German composers of the seventeenth century typically transformed biblical prose into sacred concertos and strophic poetry into songs or arias. This close association of text and musical genre was affirmed by Martin Fuhrmann, the pupil of Buxtehude's pupil Friedrich Gottlieb Klingenberg, in his *Musicalischer-Trichter*, published in 1706. Fuhrmann includes definitions of both the concerto and the aria among the "Names of the most important vocal pieces":

> 5. Concerto is a piece for voices and instruments in which the vocalists and instrumentalists as it were fight or contend with one another. For a church concerto a composer must take nothing but biblical texts, and indeed, those that are well known, if they are to be understood by the congregation. . . .
> 6. Aria (Italian), Air (French) is not only a vocal but also an instrumental piece. If an aria is sung, rhyming-texts or verses are laid under the notes. . . .[3]

Concerto

Fuhrmann's metaphor of fighting in his definition of the concerto is derived from Michael Praetorius's etymology of the word in *Syntagma musicum* III (1619), and this attribute of the concerto still figures in Johann Mattheson's discussion of it in *Der vollkommene Capellmeister* (1739):

> The real aim of the concertos was and still is this: to make the words of the text intelligible and to bring about a full harmony with one or more voices yet with the aid of the thoroughbass. . . . [T]he name derives from *certare*, to fight, and which is to say that in such a concerto one or more select voices wages an artistic battle with the

organ, or between the voices themselves, whoever could make it most charming. (II/13, §70)

In their use of the metaphor of competition or fighting, all three writers point to an important stylistic characteristic found in most concertos: the tossing of musical motives from one performer to another. The genre of the sacred concerto, together with this aspect of its style, had been derived from the polychoral motets of the late sixteenth century, works still frequently performed in Germany and Denmark during the seventeenth century from the *Florilegium Portense* and similar collections. Giovanni Gabrieli had added vocal soloists and instrumentalists to the choirs of the polychoral motet, and this form of the sacred concerto, calling for large numbers of performers, became popular in Germany early in the seventeenth century through the works of Michael Praetorius, Heinrich Schütz, and Samuel Scheidt. Both Praetorius and Mattheson acknowledged the sacred concerto for a few solo voices as the invention of Lodovico Viadana, and it, too, was derived from the motet. The genre was represented in Germany early in the century by works of Schütz, Scheidt, and Johann Hermann Schein. Sacred concertos formed a major part of the music collection of St. Mary's, Helsingør, including concertos by Andreas Hammerschmidt for both few and many voices in his *Musicalische Andachten*, parts III and IV, respectively.

Seventeenth-century composers did not always draw a clear distinction in terminology between the concerto and the motet as separate genres. But Hammerschmidt discusses their differences in his preface to Part IV of his *Musicalische Andachten*, subtitled "Sacred Motets and Concertos":

> Now in my opinion, concertos are very praiseworthy, not only because the text can be better understood with a singer who pronounces it distinctly and correctly, but also because their charm usually evokes a remarkable devotion in listeners.
> And yet I have to grant that this charm is often lacking when one assigns poor singers to them and thinks that a well composed concerto will always sound good if it is only good in itself, while the singers are doing whatever they please. But this produces more a mockery than suitable music, and in this case full-voiced motets, in which these deficiencies are not so easily perceived, far surpass concertos and are by no means to be scorned.

In the index he distinguishes between works designated as concertos and those "cum & sine Fundamento." Hammerschmidt's motets, then, are full-voiced sacred choral works for which the continuo part is optional, as opposed to concertos, which contain sections for soloists requiring the support of the continuo. Indeed, the works designated "cum & sine Fundamento" can be performed a cappella.[4] Fuhrmann defines a motet as "a church harmony, four voices strong (sometimes more) without instruments, set according to Hammerschmidt's standard, in which the voices make fugues and concertize only a little or not at all." This understanding of the motet—modeled on that of the late sixteenth century—appears to have been in use in Lübeck as well; the term "Motetta" is used in the 1682 text book to designate works for six or eight voices without instruments. In this restricted sense of the term, Buxtehude is not known to have composed any motets. The term *motet*, or *motetto concertato*, however, was also used in a broader sense—particularly in France and Italy—to designate works that are essentially sacred concertos. Two of Buxtehude's concertos, BuxWV 82 and 113, are in fact designated "motetto" in the Uppsala manuscript copies. Nevertheless, my use of the term motet is confined to its more restricted sense.

The concerto shared with the motet its basic compositional procedure: The composer chose a text, usually prose, and divided it into short phrases. Each phrase of text successively generated a musical section of the piece, with musical motives associated with particular words or phrases. Both motets and sacred concertos are thus essentially through-composed, sometimes with the addition of a refrain. The concerto usually departs radically from the motet, however, in the relationship of these musical sections to each other, preferring strong stylistic contrast between sections to the homogeneity typical of the motet.

Although both Hammerschmidt and Mattheson stress the intelligibility of the text in the concerto, for Fuhrmann the contrapuntal texture typical of this genre usually prevents the words from being understood; it is for this reason that he advocates the choice of a text already known to the congregation.

> For if he takes an unknown text and works out such florid counterpoint, a listener will understand hardly a single line of the text, especially when the instruments are added as well, and all the vocal and instrumental parts are mixed up simultaneously. . . . [I]f it is not in imitative counterpoint, but all the voices are mostly singing the same text at the same time, they can be better understood, but then it is no artful concerto but rather a motet. The matter is different with a well-known text, which the congregation already knows halfway or completely by heart.

The texture found in most seventeenth-century concertos is not so thoroughly contrapuntal as Fuhrmann suggests, however. More often, the voices begin imitatively but then move together toward the end of the phrase, producing a blend of counterpoint and homophony that is so characteristic that it can be called concertato texture. Also characteristic of concertato texture is imitation between voices in which only the beginnings and ends of phrases overlap, in the manner of the choirs of a polychoral motet, whose basic texture, as Fuhrmann observes, is more homophonic than contrapuntal (see ex. 1-1). In addition, concertos frequently include sections for solo voice in declamatory style, whose texture is totally homophonic.

Fuhrmann's definition of the concerto includes one other characteristic: the frequent inclusion of a final contrapuntal section to the words "Amen" or "Alleluia." In this case he has no objection to the simultaneous concertizing of four or more vocalists and a half dozen instrumentalists, because "even a child understands these words."

Chorale

Chorale texts and melodies do not figure in Fuhrmann's discussion of the concerto, but Protestant composers—notably Praetorius, Scheidt, and Schein—had used them in their concertos from the beginning of their cultivation of the genre. Chorale texts thus form an important exception to the dictum that the text of a concerto is normally prose. Chorale concertos differ from those composed to biblical texts in one important respect: it is normally the chorale melody rather than the phrase of text that generates their musical motives. Friedhelm Krummacher's book *Die Choralbearbeitung in der protestantischen Figuralmusik zwischen Praetorius und Bach* provides an extensive and definitive survey of this literature.

A purely homophonic tradition of chorale setting existed alongside the more contrapuntal and complex genre of the chorale concerto. It manifested itself in two closely related genres, the four-part harmonization with the chorale melody in the soprano, sometimes known as the cantional setting, and the figured-bass setting, which in fact reduced a harmonization to its basic elements—chorale melody and bass—by substituting figures to the bass line for the alto and tenor voices. Both these genres of chorale settings were transmitted mainly by hymnals. Lukas Osiander's *Fünfzig geistliche Lieder und Psalmen* of 1586 was the first hymnal to offer harmonizations with the melody in the soprano. The four parts were intended for the choir, not the congregation, but the chorale melody was more easily heard in the soprano than in the tenor, where it had lain in all previous polyphonic chorale settings, and thus the congregation could more easily sing the melody along with the choir. The Lübeck cantor Jacob Pagendarm composed his chorale harmonizations in 1705 with exactly the same intention: for the use of his choir in their leadership of congregational singing. This type of chorale setting became the standard of Protestant hymnody.

Figured-bass settings of chorale melodies were intended primarily for use in the home. The title page of the 1664 edition of Johann Crüger's *Praxis pietatis melica*, the hymnal most widely used during the second half of the seventeenth century, announces that it is intended "for the encouragement of church as well as private worship." In ever-expanding new editions, it provided figured-bass settings of both old chorales and new hymns. Hymnals offering only new hymns—Johann Rist's collections, for example—used figured-bass settings almost exclusively. In the case of both the old and the new hymns, these settings were extremely simple: strictly strophic, the melodies mainly syllabic, the rhythm and phrase structure following closely the meter and lines of the poetry, eschewing all repetition of words or phrases of text, and with a sparsely figured bass line which could be—and sometimes had been—the vocal bass line of a simple harmonization. Pieces such as these were normally called sacred songs—"geistliche Lieder."

Aria

The word *aria* is the only vocal genre designation that Buxtehude is known to have used himself. He wrote it into the autograph manuscripts of seven works (BuxWV 85 and 119, and five times in BuxWV 75), and it appears frequently in the prints and copies of his works. He might have become acquainted with the term through Caspar Kittel's publication *Arien und Cantaten mit 1. 2. 3. und 4. Stimmen sambt beygefügtem Basso Continuo*[5] of 1638, the only secular work contained in the music collection of St. Mary's, Helsingør. Kittel's collection included not only strictly strophic arias but also strophic bass variations, using ornamentation in the style of Caccini. Both the strophic aria and the strophic bass variation were popular in Italy in the early seventeenth century. The form of the strophic bass variation gives the composer freedom to change the melody of each strophe to accommodate the new words while retaining the recurring harmonic progressions and phrase structure of strophic form. An instrumental ritornello frequently articulated the division between strophes. In Germany, the Italian term *aria* was used chiefly for secular songs with high artistic aspirations, such as the collections of Heinrich Albert (1604–51) and Adam Krieger (1634–66). Both Johann Rudolph Ahle and Wolfgang Carl Briegel published sacred arias with instrumental ritornelli in 1660.

The Meeting of Concerto and Aria

In their earlier manifestations, the concerto and the aria possessed distinct stylistic characteristics. With the exception of the chorale concerto, concertos were settings of prose texts; arias were settings of strophic poetry. Following these texts, rhythm and phrase structure tended to be irregular in the concerto, regular in the aria. Texture was more contrapuntal in the concerto, homophonic in the aria. In form, the concerto was normally through-composed, its sections contrasting with one another; the aria was strophic and highly unified. Single words received particular attention in the concerto, and rhetorical figures abounded; in the aria they were subsumed under an overriding "affect" or emotional mood. Instruments, when they were present, participated in the very essence of the concerto, which consisted of a friendly contest among the performers; in the aria, they were kept quite separate from the voices, serving in ritornelli to articulate the vocal strophes. The one stylistic trait that the concerto and the aria shared was the essential presence of the basso continuo. This most baroque of features served also to separate them from the genres of the Renaissance from which they had sprung, the motet and the song, respectively.

In the hands of Buxtehude and his contemporaries, however, these formerly separate genres began to borrow stylistic traits from one another. Fuhrmann alludes to this stylistic mixing in the continuation of his definition of the aria:

And with arias, the same reminder applies as was just given for concertos; namely, if a church aria is to be understood by the listeners, it must not be sung in imitative counterpoint by four or more singers at the same time with instruments playing as well. If this is to happen, the text must be made known to the congregation; if it is not, the singing language of the vocalists will be as understandable to the listeners as parrot language.

Not only did concerto-like contrapuntal texture and instrumental participation invade the aria, but aria-like features, and indeed arias themselves, invaded concertos. The last concerto in Christoph Bernhard's *Geistlicher Harmonien Erster Theil begreiffende Zwanzig deutsche Concerten,* published in 1665, contains within it a strophic bass aria interspersed amid concerto sections set to a biblical text.

In Buxtehude's works, the meeting of concerto and aria occurred in two distinct ways. On the one hand he juxtaposed these genres as separate movements within a larger work, retaining most of the stylistic features associated with each genre, including their different texts. On the other hand, he extended each single genre by bringing into one or more sections of a work stylistic attributes associated with the other genre. The first and last strophes of an aria, for example, could be set in the style of a concerto, or a section of a concerto could grow to resemble an aria. In the latter case, however, the aria it resembles is not the strophic German sacred aria but rather the more freely formed bel canto aria of the Italian secular cantata by composers such as Giacomo Carissimi and Marc Antonio Cesti. This stylistic mix occurred in Italian sacred music as well. It is also evident in the music of Kaspar Förster, through whom, along with Christoph Bernhard, Buxtehude may have become acquainted with the mid-century Italian style. The Hamburg collegium musicum performed Förster's works as well as those of Italian composers.

Composite Works

Those works that consist of independent movements in juxtaposed genres clearly belong to an emerging new genre that did not yet have a name. A generation later, in 1695, Erdmann Neumeister, then a theology student at Leipzig University who had just completed a master's degreee in literature, gave a series of poetry lectures in which he used the term *oratoria* to describe sacred texts to be set to music that alternated biblical verses with poetry:

> An *Oratoria* is a particularly beautiful form, and it is especially pleasing for sacred matters and church pieces. It basically consists of the alternation of biblical texts and arias. Sometimes some chorale settings are also added.[6]

Neumeister's words perfectly describe Buxtehude's composite works, most of which consist of the juxtaposition of a concerto set to a biblical text and an aria set to a strophic poetic text, with a few adding one or more chorales as well. To use Neumeister's term *oratoria* to refer to them, however, would only confuse the modern reader, because of the strong association of the term *oratorio* with lengthier sacred dramatic works. Neumeister was also the first to apply the term *cantata*, which had previously referred only to secular works, to German sacred music, but he restricted its use to works that alternated arias with recitative set to madrigalesque poetry, not biblical prose:

> So briefly the cantata is fashioned in this way, that one alternates *Stylum recitativum* and arias with one another. With a word: a cantata looks like an excerpt from an opera.[7]

Neumeister later combined the elements of these two literary genres to form the texts that J. S. Bach and his contemporaries most typically set in their concerted church works, which have been called "cantatas" only since the publication of the Bach Gesellschaft edition in the nineteenth century, but are now generally considered the prototypes of this term.

The combination of prose and poetry in a single piece of church music appears to have arisen in Rome during the late 1640s, particularly in the music of Bonifatio Gratiani (1604/5–1664), maestro di cappella at the Jesuit mother church Il Gesù. Albrici and Peranda brought the style to Dresden, where Albrici directed the performance of his own composition on a text also set by Gratiani, *O cor meum quo vagaris*, on December 30, 1660. It begins with a concerted setting of a prose text and ends with an aria of three strophes. In his 1652 publication, Gratiani had called his composition a motet, but the Dresden court diaries refer to Albrici's work as a concerto; there, as in Lübeck, the term *motet* usually meant a work is *stile antico*. Frandsen has coined the more precise term *concerto with aria* to describe works such as this, which abound in the Dresden repertoire.[8]

Before arriving in Dresden, Albrici had worked at Queen Christina's court in Stockholm from 1652 to 1654. He must have maintained his contacts with the court, because thirty-seven of his works are preserved in the Düben Collection. Perhaps he also introduced Gratiani's music to Stockholm, because Christian Geist, who worked there as a court musician from 1670 to 1679, also demonstrated his respect for Gratiani by parodying two of his motets and by cultivating a very Italianate style in general, as Lars Berglund has shown. Geist composed one concerto with aria, *Die mit Tränen säen*, in 1673, but in his copy of it (*S-Uu* vmhs 25:7) Gustav Düben designated it a "motetto." In his book *North German Church Music in the Age of Buxtehude*, Geoffrey Webber, following Düben and the Italian practice, applies the term *motet* to the entire repertoire of North German concerted music, without regard to structure. The term *motet* had a different and specific meaning in Lübeck, however, and it is doubtful that Buxtehude would have used it for any of his works, with the possible exception of *Benedicam Dominum* (BuxWV 113), which could be termed a "motetto concertato" in the grandest sense.

The works in which Buxtehude juxtaposed different genres form a distinctive group within his vocal oeuvre; indeed; by labeling five of the arias in his autograph tablature of the *Membra Jesu* cycle as such, he called attention to the composite nature of these works. In most of them, the aria functions as a commentary on the biblical text and is analogous to a sermon, personalizing it for the individual believer. In the early 1960s, Friedhelm Krummacher coined the term *concerto-aria cantata* for works such as these. The use of the word *cantata*, albeit anachronistically, for Buxtehude's composite works allows comfortably for the addition of chorales to the mix; chorales do not occur in the Dresden repertoire investigated by Frandsen. The term *cantata* also has the virtue of being widely understood as a vocal work made of independent movements in contrasting genres.

To apply the term *cantata* to all of Buxtehude's vocal works, however, as is too frequently done, removes from the term its distinctive meaning. Although a number of works in extended discrete genres demonstrate a strong resemblance to the cantata with respect to the relative independence and stylistic contrast of their sections, the distinction between a concerto composed to a biblical text and a formally closed aria to a strophic poem is an objective fact, whereas that between a dependent section and an independent movement in a work with a unified text requires a subjective judgment, which will vary with the judge. And Buxtehude himself designated as an aria BuxWV 85, a work that appears quite cantata-like. Works such as this are best understood in relation to similar ones with sections not quite so clearly differentiated, and in the discussion that follows they are considered as belonging on the far end of a continuum within an extended genre rather than to a separate new genre. Chorale settings are considered as a separate genre, however, although a strict system of classification would place them within the genre of the concerto. Their relationship to the hymn tradition, manifested by the use of four-part harmonizations as well as the chorale melodies, separates them distinctively from Buxtehude's other concertos. We will also consider separately two other genres, the ciaccona and the dialogue, since they are so designated in manuscript sources, although the works they include also belong to the genres of concerto, aria, and cantata.

Buxtehude's Works in Discrete Genres

Concertos

BuxWV 2, 5, 7, 11, 12, 15, 17, 18, 23, 31, 37, 44, 45, 49, 53, 64, 67, 71, 73, 79, 82, 83, 94, 95, 97, 98, 113

This group of twenty-seven works is almost equally divided between German and Latin texts. Most are biblical, with the addition of three Latin devotional texts. Their scoring covers the entire range found in Buxtehude's vocal music. More than half, however, are scored for one solo voice and instruments, of which nine are for soprano.

The two concertos for one voice, one instrument, and continuo—*Jubilate Domino* (BuxWV 64) for alto and viola da gamba and *Singet dem Herrn* (BuxWV 98) for soprano and violin—are among Buxtehude's most attractive and virtuosic vocal works. In each case the voice is paired with a stringed instrument in the same range, so that the concertizing soloists can compete within the same tonal territory. There is no question of the instrument's accompanying the singer in these two works: they are equal partners in the concerto. The range of the viola da gamba is much wider than that of the alto, however, and Buxtehude exploits it ostentatiously. Both works are set to psalm texts with themes of joy and praise and imagery of music.

Like most of Buxtehude's vocal works, *Jubilate Domino* begins with an instrumental sonata. This sonata offers an excellent example of the way in which concertato style can be realized even when the scoring is reduced to the bare minimum of one soloist with basso continuo. Concertato interchange between viola da gamba and continuo begins at m. 15 (ex. 5-1) with imitative entrances of a one-measure motive, followed by a sharing of the motive between gamba and continuo (m. 17), then entrances of the first half of the motive while the other part rests (m. 18), and finally a statement in parallel thirds as they move to a cadence in B minor. The rests and parallel motion are typical of concertato texture; the competitors in this metaphorical battle are friendly and polite, each one often pausing so that the other can be heard. In the following measures the gamba dominates the scene, however, concertizing with itself by means of abrupt shifts of range and concluding the sonata with another downward sweep and wide arpeggios.

Example 5-1. BuxWV 64, mm. 15–19.

The text, Psalm 97:4–6, is divided into three main sections—each a verse of the psalm—which correspond to three discrete sections of the piece, articulated by meter changes and full cadences in the tonic:

1) C, mm. 29–84
Jubilate Domino omnis terra.   *Make a joyful noise to the Lord all the earth.*
Cantate et exsultate et psallite.   *Sing and rejoice and sing praises.*

2) 6/8, mm. 85–130
Psallite Domino in cithara et voce   *Sing praises to the Lord with the lyre and the*
   psalmi.   *sound of psalms.*

3) C, mm. 131–67
In buccinis et voce tubae, jubilate in   *With trumpets and the sound of the horn,*
   conspectu regis Domini.   *make a joyful noise before the king, the Lord.*

Example 5-2. BuxWV 64, mm. 104–7.

The first section opens with identical solos for voice and gamba, each concertizing with the continuo, and yet aria-like as well because of the lyrical melodic line, much of it generated by increasingly lengthy melismas on the word *jubliate*. Aria style is especially prominent in the second section, mm. 85–130, composed of regular phrases in lilting 6/8 meter over a two-measure quasi-ostinato. Here Buxtehude demonstrates his ability to turn prose into poetry, transforming the psalm verse into dactylic meter by repeating words and omitting the preposition *in* (ex. 5-2). The gamba accompanies the voice in this passage, but elsewhere they engage in relaxed concertato interchange, with frequent rests in both parts. Concertato style and virtuosity dominate the final section, beginning with an improvisatory gamba solo that ascends to a″, above the frets, and ending with a breathless display of voice and gamba in parallel thirds.

If *Jubilate Domino* was performed during the distribution of communion, as it might have been, then this one piece could serve as an example of everything that Theophil Großgebauer found objectionable in church music: an incomprehensible Latin text, Italianate style, emphasis on instrumental writing, "biblical texts torn apart and chopped up into little pieces through swift runs of the throat," and the display of virtuosity—by composer, singer, gambist, and continuo player alike—whereby "one chases after the other in concertizing and some contend with one another over which can do it most skillfully." It would probably have been the display of virtuosity that would have offended Großgebauer the most had he been alive to hear this piece. Buxtehude might have composed a work such as this for the visiting Italian castrato who sang at St. Mary's on Easter of 1672 or for a touring gamba virtuoso.

Ich sprach in meinem Herzen (BuxWV 49), for soprano, three violins, dulcian, and continuo, offers an example of a more traditional concerto, less influenced by the aria, more concerned with the individual word. The metrical shifts in the music divide its text, on the popular *vanitas* topic from Ecclesiastes, into five sections:

1) C, mm. 22–36
Ich sprach in meinem Herzen: Wohlan, ich will wohl leben

I said to myself: Well, I want to live well

2) 3/2, mm. 37–111
und gute Tage haben! Aber siehe, das war auch eitel.

and enjoy myself! But behold, that was vanity.

3) C, mm. 112–35
Ich sprach zum Lachen: du bist toll,

I said to laughter: you are mad,

4) 3/2, mm. 136–66
und zur Freude: was machst du?

and to joy: what use is it?

Example 5-3. BuxWV 49, mm. 112–17.

5) C, mm. 167–214

Da dacht' ich in meinem Herzen,
 meinen Leib vom Wein zu ziehen
 und mein Herz zur Weisheit
 zu ziehen, daß ich ergreife, was Torheit
 ist, bis ich lernete, was den Menschen
 gut wäre, das sie tun sollen, solange sie
 unter dem Himmel leben.

I searched with my mind how to cheer my
 body with wine—my mind still
 guiding me with wisdom—and
 how to lay hold on folly, till I
 might see what was good for people
 to do under heaven during
 the few days of their life.

The first four sections are all in concertato style, with words and phrases of text generating musical motives and phrases that are then picked up by the instruments, either in block homophony or concertizing among themselves. The word *Lachen* in section 3 inspires a somewhat rare madrigalism (ex. 5-3). In section 4, a tempo change from Presto to Adagio marks the contrast in emotion between its two halves. Section 5 offers a good example of the declamatory style that Buxtehude frequently employed to set biblical texts, more lyrical than recitative and with a more rapidly moving bass, but without the instrumental interjections and frequent repetitions of concertato style (ex. 5-4).

If *Ich sprach in meinem Herzen* appears somewhat emotionally detached, quite the opposite is the case for *O dulcis Jesu* (BuxWV 83, track 2 on the CD accompanying this book), set to a Latin devotional text. In its Christocentric devotion, longing for the mystical union, and allusions to "Jesu dulcis memoria," this text closely resembles one set by Peranda and first performed at the Dresden court in 1664, *Jesu dulcis, Jesu pie*, although in its fluid mixture of prose and poetry it

Example 5-4. BuxWV 49, mm. 167–74.

is more similar to Albrici's *Tu es cor meum* from 1660. But whereas Albrici and Peranda typically set their concertos for a small ensemble of voices (here SAB and SSB respectively), Buxtehude set *O dulcis Jesu* for solo voice, allowing for a closer identification of this erotic text with a single lover-believer. The text can be roughly divided into seven sections, with timings given for CD track 2:

00:00   Sonata: C, mm. 1–19

01:27   1. C, mm. 20–65

> *O dulcis Jesu, o amor cordis mei,*   *O sweet Jesus, o love of my heart, I*
> *desidero te, cupio dissolvi et esse*   *desire you, I wish to die and be with you.*
> *tecum. Nil cupio praeter te, tu mihi*   *I wish nothing besides you, you are my*
> *gaudium, tu corona, tu gloria, tu*   *joy, my crown, my glory, my salvation.*
> *salus es. O bone Jesu, quam dulcis es.*   *O good Jesus, how swet you are.*

04:23   2. 3/4, mm. 66–124

> *O Jesu, mi dulcis,*   *O my sweet Jesus,*
> *te semper amabo,*   *I shall love you forever*
> *te semper cantabo,*   *I shall sing forever,*
> *cum ore laudabo.*   *with my mouth I shall praise.*

05:51   3. 3/8, mm. 125–63

> *Non mundi fallaces*   *Not the false honors of the world*
> *sectabor honores*   *shall I pursue,*
> *sed coeli veraces*   *but the truthful loves of heaven*
> *conquiram amores.*   *shall I seek.*

06:31   4. C and 3/4, mm. 164–86

> *Non minas satanae, non mortes*   *Neither the threats of Satan, nor*
> *perfidas timebit pectus, cum magno*   *treacherous deaths shall the soul fear,*
> *robore tuae fortis dexterae tutetur*   *with the great strength of your strong*
> *acriter,*   *right hand it will be defended vigorously,*
> *non semper dulcia cantabit*   *it will not always sing sweet songs.*
> *carmina.*

07:22   5. 3/2 and 3/4, mm. 187–248

> *O Jesu dulcis, ah suscipe me,*   *O sweet Jesus, ah accept me,*
> *te semper amavi, speravi in te.*   *I have always loved you and hoped in you.*

09:12   6. C, mm. 249–58

> *O Jesu dulcis, ah suscipe me, deficit*   *O sweet Jesus, ah, accept me, my spirit*
> *anima mea et languet pro te, veni,*   *is faltering and languishing for you,*
> *morior sine te,*   *come, I shall die without you.*

09:57   7. 3/2 mm. 259–92

> *ah suscipe me.*   *ah, accept me.*

Buxtehude's musical setting reflects this text closely, with its prose portions in recitative or concertato style and its poetic portions in arioso or aria style. The fluidity of his transitions between these styles matches the style of the language. Indeed, this piece offers a striking demonstration of the fact that these musical styles cannot be rigidly separated, but must be seen as part of a stylistic continuum stretching between recitative and aria. Section 4 provides a good example, beginning in prose but completing the thought with a dactylic line. True secco recitative, with its syllabic text setting, frequent repeated notes, and slow-moving bass line in common time, occurs rarely in Buxtehude's vocal music, but he uses it here for the prose section, switching to triple-time arioso when he reaches the line of poetry at m. 171 (ex. 5-5).

Example 5-5. BuxWV 83, mm. 164–74.

The prose of section 6 is also cast in recitative style, but the emotional mood has changed radically from the courage expressed in section 4 to rapture, and Buxtehude responds with a shift from bland diatonic harmony to affective chromatic harmony, including a Neapolitan sixth chord at m. 258 which, together with the rests and repetition of the word "ah," may suggest that the mystical union has been achieved (ex. 5-6).

Example 5-6. BuxWV 83, mm. 249–61.

Example 5-7. BuxWV 83, mm. 20–34.

Buxtehude's recitative style at the beginning of section 1 is much more lyrical, but it soon blends into concertato style as the vocal part becomes more repetitive and the instruments seize on its motives at m. 30 (ex. 5-7, mm. 30–34).

Aria style and concertato style merge in section 2, where Buxtehude uses triple meter and fairly regular phrases to reflect the dactylic meter of the poetry. His use of similar musical motives for the phrases "O Jesu mi dulcis" and "te semper cantabo" deemphasizes the individual words and emphasizes poetic line and continuity. A long note on "semper" and a long melisma on "cantabo" emphasize those individual words, however, and the instruments break in with frequent interjections. Section 3 is the most aria-like in this work, its completely regular phrases relentlessly following the poetic lines of the text (ex. 5-8).

Because of this work's similarity to an Italian secular cantata, we might be tempted to call *O dulcis Jesu* a cantata as well. But when this term is applied to German sacred music, it implies a work with independent movements, and these are not found here. None of the sections in aria style could be called true arias, least of all section 5, which constantly shifts between 3/2 and 3/4 meter, corresponding to its first and second lines. In its use of constantly varying musical styles to reflect each nuance of the text, *O dulcis Jesu* is in fact a quintessential concerto.

Instrumental participation is an extremely important element in Buxtehude's concertos, but it is not absolutely essential. Three concertos for three voices and continuo, BuxWV 2, 12, and 53, dispense with melody instruments altogether, the only works in Buxtehude's vocal oeuvre to do so other than the *Missa alla brevis*. *Cantate Domino* (BuxWV 12) demonstrates the strong stylistic contrast that can be achieved between the sections of a concerto even without the use of

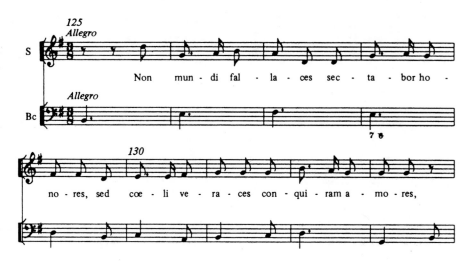

Example 5-8. BuxWV 83, mm. 125–33.

instruments. Its four verses from Psalm 95 plus the added Gloria Patri are divided into seven sections:

1. C, mm. 1–44, SSB

Cantate Domino canticum novum,	*Sing to the Lord a new song,*
Cantate domino omnis terra.	*sing to the Lord all the earth.*

2. 3/4, mm. 45–96, B

Cantate Domino et benedicite nomen eius!	*Sing to the Lord and bless his name!*
Annuntiate de die in diem salutare eius.	*Declare his salvation from day to day.*

3. 3/4, mm. 97–144, S1

Annuntiate inter gentes gloriam eius,	*Declare his glory among the nations,*

4. C, mm. 145–51, SSB

in omnibus populis mirabilia eius.	*his marvelous works among all the peoples.*

5. 3/4, mm. 152–204, S2

Quoniam magnus Dominus et laudabilis nimis, terribilis est super omnes deos.	*For great is the Lord and greatly to be praised; he is to be feared above all gods.*

6. 3/2, mm. 205–13, SSB

Gloria Patri et Filio et Spiritui Sancto,	*Glory be to the Father and to the Son and to the Holy Spirit,*

7. C, mm. 214–39, SSB

sicut erat in principio, et nunc et semper et in saecula saeculorum. Amen.	*as it was in the beginning, is now and ever shall be, world without end. Amen.*

This text contains neither the emotional nor the stylistic contrasts seen in *O dulcis Jesu,* and the contrasting musical styles of Buxtehude's setting could be said to reflect purely musical purposes. Sections 1 and 7 contain fugal expositions, the first examples of truly contrapuntal texture that we have seen in Buxtehude's concertos. The other two sections for three voices begin homophonically and then move into concertato texture, imitative at first but coming together for the end of the phrase (ex. 5-9).

Pure homophonic texture is found in the three sections in aria style, one for each soloist. Although *Cantate Domino* is through-composed, Buxtehude's arrangement of contrasting textures, number of voices, vocal registers, and musical styles indicates a clear formal plan that approaches symmetry.

Fürwahr, er trug unsere Krankheit (BuxWV 31) calls for five vocal soloists, five instruments, and optional cappella to reinforce the voices in the tutti sections.

Example 5-9. BuxWV 12, mm. 145–48.

It contains not a single change in meter; its sectional structure is articulated by shifts in scoring, instrumental postludes, and a complex scheme of repeated and varied-repeated sections. The text is drawn from Isaiah 53, the account of the suffering servant. The musical structure that Buxtehude imposed on this text may be sketched as follows:

1. mm. 1–25, B with instr.

Fürwahr, er trug unsere Krankheit und
lud auf sich unsere Schmerzen.

Surely, he has borne our griefs and
carried our sorrows.

2. mm. 26–38, SS

Wir aber hielten ihn für den, der geplaget
und von Gott geschlagen
und gemartert wäre.

Yet we esteemed him as one who was
afflicted, and smitten and
tormented by God.

3. mm. 39–63 = section 1.

Surely . . .

4. mm. 64–86, ATB + instr.

Wir aber hielten ihn für den, der
geplaget

Yet we esteemed him as one who
[was] afflicted,

5. mm. 87–97, tutti

Wir aber hielten ihn für den, der
geplaget

Yet we esteemed him as one who
[was] afflicted,

6. mm. 98–111, ATB + instr.

und von Gott geschlagen und
gemartert wäre.

and smitten and tormented
by God.

7. mm. 112–24, S1 with vle.

Aber er ist um unser Missetat willen
verwundet und um unser
Sünden willen geschlagen.

But he was wounded for our
transgressions, and he was
smitten for our sins.

8. mm. 125–35 = section 5

Yet we esteemed him . . .

9. mm. 136–76, various scoring

Die Straf' liegt auf ihm, auf daß wir
Frieden hätten, und durch seine
Wunden sind wir geheilet.

Upon him was the punishment, so
that we might have peace, and
with his wounds we are healed.

In the opening sinfonia (fig. 5-2), with its stark dynamic juxtapositions and abrupt rests, Buxtehude forecasts the dramatic intensity with which he will set this text. The two sections for solo voice carry the main burden of the text, the bass in concertato style with the full corpus of instruments and the soprano in a dramatic recitative (ex. 5-10) accompanied by the gambas, whose parts are marked "tremulo" in Buxtehude's autograph score. Buxtehude dramatically renders the response of the community to the suffering servant in ever-increasing intensity, from duet, to trio, to the entire ensemble, the latter in close imitative

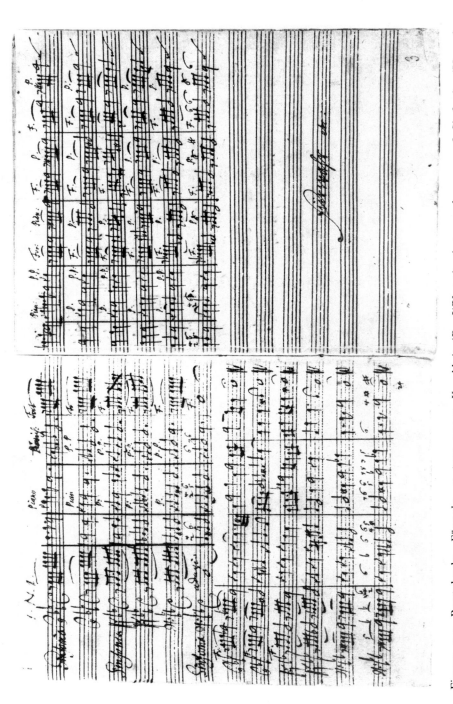

Figure 5-2. Buxtehude, *Fürwahr, er trug unsere Krankheit* (BuxWV 31). Autograph score of Sinfonia (Uppsala Universitetsbibliotek, vokalmusik i handskrift 6:9, pp. 2–3).

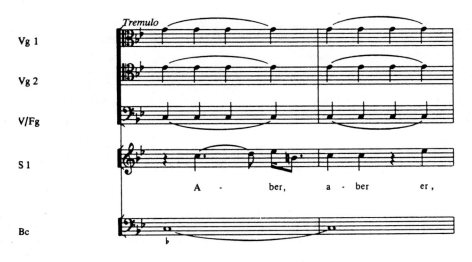

Example 5-10. BuxWV 31, mm. 112–16.

counterpoint. The same intense contrapuntal writing returns for the final phrase of text in section 9, as if to multiply the wounds, contrasting sharply with the block homophony that precedes it with the words "that we might have peace." In this work we may catch a glimpse of the dramatic power of the lost Abendmusiken.

With *Benedicam Dominum* (BuxWV 113), Buxtehude presents us with his most opulent scoring, six choirs of voices and instruments, presumably to be placed in the six balconies surrounding the large organ of St. Mary's so that Lübeck might briefly be transformed into a Venice of the north. Here indeed is a biblical text—from Psalm 33—chopped up into little bits and placed at the service of music:

1. C, mm. 1–26
Benedicam Dominum in omni tempore.   *I will bless the Lord at all times.*

2. 3/2, mm. 27–93
Semper laus eius in ore meo.   *His praise shall continually be in my mouth.*

3. C, mm. 94–118
In Domino laetabitur anima mea,   *My soul rejoices in the Lord,*

4. 3/2, mm. 119–28
anima mea.   *my soul.*

5. C, 3/2, mm. 129–91
Audiant mansueti et laetentur.   *Let the afflicted hear and be glad.*

6. C, mm. 198–260
Magnificate Dominum mecum et   *Magnify the Lord with me, and let us*
    exultemus nomen eius in id ipsum.   *exalt his name together.*

7. 6/4, mm. 261–97
Alleluia.   *Alleluia.*

This work provides textbook examples of concertato style on a large scale: the juxtaposition of soloists and tutti; the tossing of musical motives from one choir to another, sometimes associated with a single word, such as "laetabitur"; a shift into triple meter to set one joyful word, "laetentur"; the use of contrapuntal or concertato texture for soloists and homophony for the whole ensemble; and a stirring Alleluia section at the end. Ten other Buxtehude concertos end with an Amen or Alleluia section.

The examples of Buxtehude's concertos that we have discussed cannot be said to be typical, because each of these works is unique, but they are representative of the wide variety of scoring and styles found in these works. The penetration of aria style into the concerto that has been noted in three Latin-texted works can be found in German-texted works as well, notably BuxWV 71, 73, and 98. In the discussion that follows, it will become clear that the concerto exerted its stylistic influence on the other genres even more strongly.

Ciacconas

BuxWV 38, 57, 62, 69, 70, 92

Buxtehude composed each of these six works entirely over an ostinato bass, apart from the independent sinfonia that begins BuxWV 62. This genre cuts across the genres of concerto and aria; BuxWV 38, 57, 69, and 92 are also concertos, BuxWV 62 and 70 arias. BuxWV 62 is in fact designated "Aria" in its manuscript sources, while BuxWV 57, 69, 70 and 92 all bear the title "Ciaccona," in a variety of spellings. Both ciaccona-arias are set to poems by Ernst Christoph Homburg. The texts of the ciaccona-concertos are all different: part of a German psalm, an old Latin poem, a complete Latin psalm, and a Latin devotional text. The six ciacconas are scored for one, two, three, and four voices with instruments.

In all cases, the ostinato bass is maintained rigorously throughout the work, without variation or modulation. The separate continuo part for three of these works contains the ostinato only once, followed by the instruction to repeat it the requisite number of times. The ostinato for BuxWV 38 (g f♯ / e B / c d, all half notes) is the simplest and most closely related to the descending tetrachord often found in ciaccona basses. It is followed closely in this respect by BuxWV 62 (d c B♭ A / f e d a, all quarter notes) and BuxWV 92 (F f–e d d–c / B♭ A B♭ c, quarters and eighths). The bass patterns of BuxWV 57 and BuxWV 70 are somewhat more complex, although still only three measures long; the eight-measure ostinato of BuxWV 69 stretches the ability of the ear to perceive it. All begin on the tonic and end on the dominant, however, and they are equally divided between major and minor modes.

Since ostinato structure imposes a high degree of unity on a work, it seems a surprising choice for a concerto, which normally glories in its diversity. BuxWV 57 in particular, atypically set to a poetic text, requires examination to see what is concerto-like about it. The text of *Jesu dulcis memoria* (BuxWV 57) consists of seven selected strophes from the "Jubilus Bernardi" plus the Gloria Patri. Buxtehude chose not to articulate the strophic structure of the poetry, and although its meter is reflected in the musical rhythm, irregular musical phrases blur the line lengths and rhyme scheme. Concertato texture is found throughout, and the instruments participate in motivic interchange with the voices. Individual words are occasionally singled out for special treatment: "gaudia" and "canitur" with melismas, and "suspirantis" with multiple rests (ex. 5-11).

A comparison of BuxWV 57 with Buxtehude's setting of essentially the same text as an aria in BuxWV 56 helps to illuminate the differences between concerto and aria, even though both works stand near the borders of their genres. BuxWV 56 also uses concertato texture in the duet sections, but otherwise the texture is homophonic. Although it is through-composed, changes in meter and scoring articulate the strophes of poetry. The voices are often alone with the continuo, the instruments mainly playing interludes and ritornelli. The melodic

Example 5-11. BuxWV 57, mm. 91–93.

writing is much more lyrical; more regular phrasing and articulation between poetic lines keep the listener always aware of the fact that the text is poetry. The same can be said for the two ciaccona-arias, BuxWV 62 and BuxWV 70. The strict ostinato structure prevents changes of meter, but the individual strophes are strongly articulated by changes in scoring and instrumental interludes, and the phrasing emphasizes the poetic lines.

Buxtehude used an ostinato bass, both strictly and loosely, in portions of several other vocal works, most frequently in an Amen or Alleluia section at the end of a work, as occurs in BuxWV 3, 15, 89, and 96. It also appears prominently in his organ works and sonatas. Buxtehude's ostinato technique is discussed further in chapter 10.

Arias

BuxWV 6, 8, 9, 13, 14, 22, 25, 28, 56, 58, 59, 63, 66, 68, 72, 74, 76 (Klag-Lied), 80, 84, 85, 87, 88, 89, 90, 91, 93, 96, 99, 104, 105, 106, 107, 108, 109, 110, 115, 116, 117, 118, 119, 120

The aria is the central genre within Buxtehude's vocal oeuvre. If we add the twenty-seven cantatas that contain arias to the forty-one works listed here, the total accounts for well over half of Buxtehude's vocal works. This group of single arias includes one composed for a funeral and six for weddings. All texts are strophic, the great majority of them in German. Although the aria is often considered to be a genre for solo voice, only thirteen of these works are so scored, ten for soprano and three for alto, forming a considerably smaller portion of the total than is the case for the concerto. Half are scored for a small ensemble of two or three singers with instruments and seven for a larger ensemble, including BuxWV 110 for six singers and sixteen instruments.

A striking correspondence can be noted between Buxtehude's arias for solo voice and his use of pure strophic musical form: Of thirteen arias for solo voice and twelve in strophic form, nine belong to both categories. For Buxtehude, the genre at its minimum required one singer, two violins, continuo, and strophic form, as is found in BuxWV 8, 25, 105, 107, 117, and 120. It is significant that he did not further reduce the requirements of his aria genre to those of the sacred song by dispensing with the violins, as he did in three concertos.

Parts for violins are seldom found in the sacred-song repertoire. In 1666 and 1667, Johan Georg Ebeling, music director in Berlin, published a collection of Paul Gerhardt's hymns "with new melodies, suitable for use at worship in church and at home; with four voices and two violins besides the general bass." No violin parts appear in this elegant first edition in folio format, however, only the four vocal parts; the violin parts must have been published separately and thus cannot be considered essential to these songs. In subsequent editions of 1669

Example 5-12. BuxWV 105, Aria, mm. 1–11.

Example 5-12 (*continued*).

Example 5-13. Anonymous, *Was mich auf dieser Welt betrübt.*

and 1683, Ebeling reduced the scoring to melody and continuo. Johann Löhner likewise omitted violins from his *Poetischer Andacht-Klang* of 1679. In its foreword, he wrote: "I wanted to set these pieces with violins, as I did before in the songs printed in my *Geistlichen Sing-Stunde* of 1670; but because not everyone is an admirer of this, I have left them out." In making the violins an essential part of even his most modest arias, Buxtehude clearly had higher artistic aspirations than those of domestic devotional singing.

One of Buxtehude's simplest yet most attractive strophic arias, *Was mich auf dieser Welt betrübt* (BuxWV 105, ex. 5-12, CD track 1), may be compared with an anonymous musical setting of this text in Ahasverus Fritzsch's *Himmelslust und Welt-Unlust* of 1679 (ex. 5-13). The first strophe of the poem, possibly by Fritzsch himself, may be translated as follows:

Was mich auf dieser Welt betrübt,	*What troubles me in this world,*
das währet kurze Zeit.	*that lasts a short time.*
Was aber meine Seele liebt,	*But what my soul loves,*
das bleibt in Ewigkeit.	*that lasts forever.*
Drumb fahr, o Welt,	*So go away, o world,*
mit Ehr und Geld	*with your honor and money*
und deiner Wollust hin.	*and desire.*
In Kreuz und Spott	*In cross and derision*
kann mir mein Gott	*my God can for me*
erquicken Mut und Sinn.	*refresh courage and spirit.*

A number of similarities in the two melodies indicate that Buxtehude used the anonymous song as the model for his aria. Both settings are almost entirely syllabic, with regular phrases determined by the poetic lines. Both are in common time, in the same key of G major, and both use the familiar bar form, giving lines 3 and 4 the same music as lines 1 and 2. Buxtehude's melody for the first line of text is nearly identical to that of the song, as is his motive for the words "drumb fahr, o Welt" and its sequential repetition to the rhyming line "mit Ehr und Geld." This use of a musical motive to emphasize the rhyme scheme of the poem and to unify the composition separates the aria from the concerto, in which musical repetition and sequence normally occur in conjunction with text repetition. At line 8 Buxtehude departs from his model, which repeats the melody of lines 5 and 6 at the same pitch level. Buxtehude instead carries the sequence further upward to a melodic climax on e″ at the word "Kreuz" and then directs it downward toward the tonic cadence on the first beat of m. 9. Had Buxtehude ended his composition here, we would have only an improved version of a sacred song. Up to this point, both versions have an identical melodic range of a ninth, d′–e″, and no text repetition has occurred. Instead, Buxtehude repeats the last three lines, inverting the motive and pushing it upward to a second climax on g″. With this extra musical phrase and with the addition of an instrumental sinfonia and ritornello, Buxtehude transforms a song into an aria, as it is designated in its manuscript source.

A comparison of the bass line of Buxtehude's aria with that of the song reveals much greater differences than can be found in their melodies. The bass of the song can only be characterized as primitive. Three-quarters of its pitches fall on either tonic or dominant, and dissonances with the melody that would be acceptable if the bass note were held are instead emphasized by octave leaps or repeated notes, as in mm. 1, 6, and 10. Buxtehude's is a sophisticated continuo bass line, figured to yield richer harmony than is implied by the two voices. It provides rhythmic continuity by bridging the gaps between vocal phrases, and it participates imitatively in the "drumb fahr o Welt" motive. The bass line of the song is quite dispensable; the song would in fact be stronger without it. Buxtehude's continuo bass, like that of all arias, forms an essential part of the composition.

Buxtehude's setting of *Was mich auf dieser Welt betrübt* can be considered the prototype of all his arias, the genre distilled to its essence. Only two arias are reduced still further, BuxWV 8 and BuxWV 118, which contain no text repetition. Most of the others expand upon this prototype with more voices, more instruments, more interrelationship between voices and instruments, more text repetition, more melismatic melodies, more complex textures and, above all, numerous and varied expansions of strophic form. Even those arias that are totally through-composed find musical means to articulate the strophic form of the poetry. All but a handful of Buxtehude's arias contain a ritornello that both articulates the strophes and provides unity to the whole composition. The degree of complexity of these works can in no way be used as a gauge of their chronology; in fact, evidence from the manuscript of BuxWV 105 suggests that it was one of Buxtehude's later vocal works.

A key element in the expansion of Buxtehude's arias is the stylistic influence of the concerto. Even in BuxWV 105, the instrumental sinfonia and ritornello have concertato texture. Further influence of the concerto can be seen even in such a modest work as *O wie selig* (BuxWV 90), a strophic setting of Johann Wilhelm Petersen's poem for two voices and three instruments, labelled "Aria" and "Sub Communione" in its manuscript source. Apart from its sonata and ritornello, the texture of this work is completely homophonic; the tenor and bass sing in parallel thirds or sixths much of the time. But the style of the concerto intrudes upon this aria by means of instrumental interjections within the strophe and the singling out of the word "nichts" at the beginning of the last line for special treatment: a fourfold repetition, separated by rests and accompanied by the instruments. The limitations of strophic form emerge in the second strophe, where the last line becomes "All-, all-, all-, all-, alle Lust der Welt zu fliehen." Neither the instrumental interjections nor the word repetition, however, disturb the absolute regularity of the phrase structure in BuxWV 90. The two strophic arias for three voices, BuxWV 116 and BuxWV 119—the latter composed for the wedding of the King of Sweden—have concertato texture in the vocal portion without instrumental interjections.

Buxtehude's other arias in pure strophic form—BuxWV 76-2, 115, 116, 118, and 119—were all composed for weddings or funerals, and three of these contain significant amounts of contrapuntal writing. The soprano vocal part of the *Klag-Lied* (BuxWV 76-2) upon the death of his father is accompanied throughout by unnamed instruments—most likely violas—in a contrapuntal texture unusual for the aria but complementary to the chorale counterpoint "Mit Fried und Freud," which Buxtehude published with the *Klag-Lied*. The *Klag-Lied* is the only one of Buxtehude's strophic arias not to contain a sinfonia or ritornello. BuxWV 115, composed a year earlier, in 1673, contains a similar accompaniment and a fugal ritornello; BuxWV 118, from 1675, a fugal ritornello. This was the time during which Buxtehude was involved with Theile and Reincken in the cultivation of learned counterpoint. Fugal procedure is foreign to the nature of the aria, and when Buxtehude applied it to the aria he generally used it extrinsically, as in the introductory sinfonia (BuxWV 9, 14, 66) or in an Amen or Alleluia section grafted onto the end (BuxWV 9, 59, 108).

The rest of Buxtehude's arias may be divided formally, following Sørensen, into those that are through-composed (BuxWV 6, 13, 28, 56, 59, 66, 80, 84, 87, 89, 91, 99) and those that participate to some degree in strophic form, no two of which are alike. Since all these works represent an extension of the genre, they may also be viewed stylistically in order to determine whether their characteristics most resemble those of the pure strophic aria, the concerto, or the cantata. It comes as no surprise to discover that the most concerto-like of the arias are also through-composed. It is noteworthy, however, that most of the arias that resemble cantatas are found among those with partial strophic form. The cantata, with its ideal of diverse independent movements, and the strophic aria, the most unified of forms, would seem to be mutually exclusive genres. By making selected strophes—usually the outer ones—concerto-like while keeping others aria-like, Buxtehude succeeds in combining these genres. But the unifying force of the underlying strophic form, sometimes represented only by its ritornello, prevents the individual strophes from becoming truly independent movements, and thus these works remain hybrids and not true cantatas.

The absence of a ritornello in BuxWV 13, 87, 89, and 99 helps to define these through-composed arias as concerto-like. In setting only the first and last strophes of Johann Rist's poem "O Gottes Stadt" in BuxWV 87, Buxtehude also deemphasizes the strophic nature of the poetry; he does articulate the strophes clearly, however, with an instrumental interlude and a change of meter at m. 109 of the aria. The beginning of the first strophe is aria-like in its use of the same melody for lines 3–4 as for lines 1–2 and its restriction of the accompaniment to the continuo. Its use of supple sarabande rhythm, however, with its emphasis on the second beat of mm. 1 and 3 and hemiola in mm. 5–6 (ex. 5-14), may be

Example 5-14. BuxWV 87, Aria, mm. 1–7.

compared with the strict regularity of Buxtehude's setting of the same iambic meter in common time in BuxWV 105 (ex. 5-12).

The continuation of the first strophe includes concerto-like textual repetitions, instrumental interjections, and the singling out of the word "seufze" for special treatment in a long melisma broken up by rests. The second strophe begins in common time at m. 109 and continues for 173 measures, an enormous expansion over the eleven measures used to set a poetic strophe of nearly the same length in BuxWV 105. A return to triple meter in m. 132 helps to achieve overall unity in this work. Nevertheless, *O Gottes Stadt* is one of Buxtehude's most concerto-like arias, if indeed it can even be called an aria; it is not designated as such in either of its sources. A vast stylistic gulf separates this artistically composed work from Johann Schop's modest setting of the same text as a sacred song in the original publication of Rist's *Himmlische Lieder*.

Among the arias that can be related to strophic musical form, BuxWV 9 and BuxWV 58 approach pure strophic form most closely. The first five versus— Buxtehude's term for a separate musical section corresponding to a strophe—of *Bedenke Mensch das Ende* (BuxWV 9) are virtually identical to one another, each set in concertato texture for the three voices alone, followed by a ritornello. Versus 6 adds the instruments, partially colla parte, to the voices and concludes with a fugato Amen section, the latter a characteristic of the concerto. *Jesu, komm, mein Trost und Lachen* (BuxWV 58) consists of strict strophic bass variations, with the same bass used for both the vocal portions and the varied sinfonias that separate them in the manner of a ritornello. This compositional procedure approaches that of the ciaccona, and like the two ciaccona-arias (BuxWV 62 and BuxWV 70), *Jesu, komm* is set to a poem by Ernst Christoph Homburg. A true ciaccona bass, however, is independent of strophic structure and usually cuts across it. That strophic form and not an ostinato bass governs BuxWV 58 can be seen in the fact that the last measure of each sinfonia is repeated, nicely articulating each strophe but slightly undermining the regularity of the recurring bass line.

Strophic form can still be clearly perceived as the governing structure in several works where stylistic attributes of the concerto figure more prominently. *Schwinget euch himmelan* (BuxWV 96), the hymn to the glory of Lübeck whose text is partially quoted on page XXX, could be characterized as bistrophic in form. Each of its eight versus consists of one of two recurring musical settings, producing the form AAABABAB. The A sections are completely aria-like: scored for one or three voices and continuo, in homophonic texture, with regular phrases reflecting the poetic lines, and followed by a ritornello (ex. 5-15).

Example 5-15. BuxWV 96, versus 5, mm. 1–21.

Va - ter, ach Va -ter, dein hei - li -ges Wort _____ las - se uns se - lig-lich,

las - se uns se - lig- lich, las - se uns se - lig- lich leuch-ten hin-fort _____

_____ , las - se uns se - lig - lich leuch - ten hin - fort.

Example 5-15 (*continued*).

The B sections are more concerto-like, contrasting tutti portions in block homophony (ex. 5-16) with phrases for solo voices and with instrumental interjections. This aria, entirely in 6/4 meter, concludes with an Amen section over an ostinato bass. In *Mein Gemüt erfreuet sich* (BuxWV 72), Buxtehude inserts three contrasting sections into a setting of eleven strophes in the form AAAB-CAA′ADAA. In the case of each of the more concerto-like insertions, it is the text that prompts the departure from strophic form by naming musical instruments in strophes 4 and 5 and by an abrupt shift in mood with the words "Mensch, o Mensch" at the beginning of strophe 9.

Characteristic of the cantata-like arias is the differentiation of their versus from each other by means of changes in scoring and texture; all but one of these arias call for three or more voices with instruments. Normally their outer sections employ fuller scoring and more concerto-like style. The degree to which they depart from strophic form varies considerably. *Dein edles Herz* (BuxWV 14) consists mainly of strophic-bass variations. In BuxWV 85, Buxtehude's C-major setting for four voices of Rist's Easter poem "O fröhliche Stunden, o herrliche

Example 5-16. BuxWV 96, versus 6, mm. 1–8.

Zeit," the music of the first versus recurs only once, as versus 5, varied slightly by the addition of a fourth voice. But its uniform rhythm in 6/4 meter, fairly regular phrases, and alternation of vocal sections with instrumental ritornelli make it sound more strophic than it actually is. We can compared it in this respect with BuxWV 84, the through-composed and more concerto-like setting of essentially the same text in A major for soprano solo.

Elements of strophic form occur also in works that are still more cantata-like than those just discussed. Metrical differentiation between the inner and outer sections of *Du Lebensfürst, Herr Jesu Christ* (BuxWV 22) enhances its cantata-like character. This aria contains a distinct correspondence between versus 1 and

Example 5-16 (*continued*).

versus 5, and a ritornello joins versus 2 with versus 4, imparting an overall symmetrical structure to the work as a whole. In *Wie schmeckt es so lieblich und wohl*
(BuxWV 108), a setting of the sensuous poem by Heinrich Müller quoted earlier in this chapter, Buxtehude uses strophic form to help define a central complex within the work and set it apart from the outer sections. This central section
in 3/2 meter falls into three parts, each consisting of a strophe set freely for one
voice paired with a strophe set as a musical refrain for three voices and followed
by a ritornello. An opening concerto-like section and a separate fugal Alleluia
section provide the framing elements.

   The extremes of scoring in the cantata-like arias are met in BuxWV 80, for two
sopranos with two violins, and BuxWV 110, a polychoral work for a vocal choir
of six soloists, probably reinforced by capella, and two instrumental choirs.

In *Nun freut euch, ihr Frommen, mit mir* (BuxWV 80), Buxtehude employs the simplest of musical means to communicate the radiant joy of the pious soul's
encounter with Christ expressed in the Angelus Silesius poem, partially quoted
on page 143. Duets in the outer two versus frame the solos, one for each
soprano, of versus 2 and 3, in which a contrast in emotion is achieved by the use
of minor mode in versus 3. Although the vocal portions of this work are completely through-composed, the unifying 3/4 meter and ritornello, the lyrical
melodic style, and the underlying regular phrase structure attest to its derivation
from the strophic aria. Example 5-17 illustrates Buxtehude's use of harmony both
to heighten the emotional expression and to underline the phrase structure, by

Example 5-17. BuxWV 80, versus 2, mm. 22–36.

placing either a secondary dominant or a seventh chord on the first beat of alternate measures. The melisma at m. 32 has nothing to do with the word "nu"; it represents an outburst of pure lyricism. The solo-tutti contrast between inner and outer versus, which is only suggested in this work, manifests itself to the fullest in *Wie wird erneuet, wie wird erfreuet* (BuxWV 110), in which the tutti is composed of six voices, probably reinforced by capella, and sixteen instruments, including doublings.

The overall shape of Buxtehude's cantata-like arias approximates that of his concerto-aria cantatas, which we will discuss later. In both cases, more fully scored and more concerto-like outer sections frame a more lightly scored inner section in which the characteristics of the aria are more prominent. It was for concerto-like aria settings, "sung in imitative counterpoint by four or more singers at the same time with instruments playing as well," that Fuhrmann recommended that the texts be made known to the congregation, as they were in Lübeck at least for the Christmas season of 1682.

Chorale Settings

BuxWV 3, 10, 20, 21, 27, 32, 40, 41, 42, 52, 60, 78, 81, 100, 102, 103

The chorale setting for voices and instruments draws its characteristics from both the concerto and the aria—from the aria because of its strophic poetic text; from the concerto because of its association with that genre since the introduction of concerto style into Germany early in the seventeenth century. Unlike the aria, whose expansion to multistrophic forms approaching the cantata was a product of Buxtehude's generation, the separate strophes of chorales had been set in contrasting scoring and style since the time of Praetorius and Scheidt. All but one of Buxtehude's sixteen single chorale settings listed here include at least an indication for more than one strophe of the chorale; the degree of differentiation between strophes varies from pure strophic form to strong contrasts between separate versus in the manner of the cantata. The scoring of these works is somewhat more restricted than that seen in the concerto or aria, ranging from one voice with two violins to five voices with five instruments. Not included in this list is the setting of "Mit Fried und Freud" in BuxWV 76; as a work of learned counterpoint, it is discussed in chapter 6.

Buxtehude employed four distinct styles in his chorale settings, as well as mixtures between them: the chorale concerto and the chorale sinfonia, both inherited from earlier generations, and the chorale aria and the concertato chorale harmonization. This last category, which Sørensen calls the strophic or varied strophic chorale cantata and Krummacher calls the extended cantional setting, is a grafting of the instrumental interjections characteristic of the concerto onto the four-part chorale harmonizations found in the hymnals. It is Buxtehude's most characteristic form of chorale setting.

Half of Buxtehude's single chorale settings—BuxWV 10, 20, 27, 40, 52, 81, 102, 103—consist only of concertato harmonizations. The simplest of these is the Swedish chorale *Herren vår Gud* (BuxWV 40), whose source contains the direction to perform the second strophe to the same music as the first, although only the incipit of the second strophe is given. The rest contain settings of two to eight chorale strophes that vary only slightly from strophe to strophe. Like the hymnal harmonizations, most call for four voices—soprano, alto, tenor, and bass. Unlike the hymnal harmonizations, two violins, with or without a separate bass part for the violone, form an independent and essential part of the ensemble.

The degree to which the concertato style—represented chiefly by the instruments—breaks into Buxtehude's chorale harmonizations varies considerably. In *Walts Gott, mein Werk ich lasse* (BuxWV 103), the violins only articulate the division between each pair of lines (ex. 5-18), and no text repetition occurs. In *Befiehl dem Engel*, daß er komm (BuxWV 10), the instruments interrupt the chorale line itself, engaging in concertato interchange with the voices in conjunction with text repetition (ex. 5-19). The vocal parts are also much more ornamented here than in a simple chorale harmonization, and the two strophes of BuxWV 10 are set in different meters, in a considerable departure from pure strophic form. The most concerto-like of these settings is *In dulci jubilo* (BuxWV 52), in which the number of voices is cut back to three while the role of the instruments increases. In the fourth strophe, they play almost constantly, their obbligato part becoming an interlude when the voices pause. Aria-like, however, is the appearance of a ritornello in this work and in four others, as well as the predominantly homophonic texture of all these settings.

The stylistic disparity between Buxtehude's concertato chorale harmonizations and the hymnal harmonizations from which he derived them is made especially clear by the extensive Amen sections in concertato texture that close five of these eight works. Together with the essential instrumental parts, they give a definite signal that these works, simple as they are, belong to the world of art music rather than functional service music. The congregation could not possibly have sung along with these chorale settings; the instrumental interjections would have thoroughly confused them. Buxtehude's concertato harmonizations differ markedly in this respect from Johann Crüger's simple chorale harmonizations with obbligato but nonessential, ad libitum violin parts.[9] Buxtehude left no simple chorale harmonizations without instruments, just as he left no sacred songs. Jacob Pagendarm, the cantor, composed the chorale harmonizations for the new Lübeck hymnal in 1705, not Dieterich Buxtehude, the organist.

Three of Buxtehude's chorale settings, BuxWV 3, 32 and 42, can be classed as chorale concertos. The first of these, *All solch dein Güt wir preisen* (BuxWV 3), consists of only one strophe in a style close to that of the concertato harmonizations;

Example 5-18. BuxWV 103, mm. 6–11.

Example 5-19. BuxWV 10, mm. 16–20.

its text is the last strophe of the New Year hymn "Helft mir Gotts Güte preisen," and this setting is probably the last section of a lost larger work. The other two are true concertos, scored for soprano and two instruments. *Gen Himmel zu dem Vater mein* (BuxWV 32), with violin and viola da gamba, stands with the concertos *Jubilate Domino* and *Singet dem Herrn* as Buxtehude's vocal pieces with the most prominent instrumental parts. It ends with a section in triple counterpoint (ex. 5-20).

The remaining five chorale settings (BuxWV 21, 41, 60, 78, 100) tend toward the cantata in their differentiation of separate strophes by means of style and/or

Example 5-20. BuxWV 32, mm. 195–201.

Example 5-21. BuxWV 60, versus 5, mm. 1–6.

scoring. In *Jesu, meine Freude* (BuxWV 60), Buxtehude arranges the six versus in near symmetrical fashion, with concertato harmonizations for versus 1, 4 and 6, a concertato aria for bass and instruments for versus 3, and continuo arias for the two sopranos as versus 2 and 5. His transformation of the chorale melody into aria style is of particular interest. Even in versus 5, where its presence is somewhat obscure, the chorale still functions as the underlying melodic line (ex. 5-21).

Two of the complex chorale settings, BuxWV 21 and BuxWV 41, open with a chorale sinfonia. Praetorius describes the chorale sinfonia as "Style VII" (*Die VII. Art*) in his catalogue of chorale styles in *Syntagma musicum* III:

> when in one voice the chorale is sung by the human voice, [and] all the others, whether 2, 3, 4, 5 or more voices, perform their harmony, fantasies and fugues, etc. against the chorale only with instruments. . . .
> And in this style many wonderful pieces have now been composed by excellent and famous organists, who place the chorale sometimes in the soprano, sometimes in the tenor, alto or bass and compose beautiful and artful counterpoint upon it.

Buxtehude's own organ chorale settings rarely display the cantus firmus as plainly as his vocal chorale sinfonias, however. The chorale sinfonia differs from the chorale concerto for solo voice and instruments in that the voice does not participate in concertato interchange with the instruments but only holds the cantus firmus while the instruments concertize against it. The first versus of *Herzlich Lieb hab ich dich, o Herr* (BuxWV 41) consistently follows this procedure (ex. 5-22).

The following two versus of *Herzlich lieb* are set as chorale concertos, as are the first three versus of *Nimm von uns, Herr, du treuer Gott* (BuxWV 78), which uses

Example 5-22. BuxWV 41, versus 1, mm. 58–66.

Example 5-22 (*continued*).

the chorale melody "Vater unser in Himmelreich." In both works, Buxtehude endows the genre with great expressive power. Krummacher characterizes versus 2 and 3 of *Herzlich lieb* as "the most extensive settings of single chorale strophes in the history of the genre before Bach," and the work as a whole as the "high point of North German chorale settings altogether." Versus 3 (CD, track 3) offers particularly rich affective contrasts.

3. Ach Herr, laß dein' lieb Engelein	*Oh Lord, let thy dear little angel*
am letzten End die Seele mein	*carry my soul in the end*
in Abrahams Schoß tragen,	*to Abraham's bosom,*
den Leib in seinm Schlafkämmerlein	*while the body, in its bedchamber,*
gar sanft ohn einig Qual und Pein	*gently, without pain or suffering,*
ruhn bis am jüngsten Tage.	*rests until judgment day.*
Alsdann vom Tod erwecke mich,	*Then awaken me from death,*
daß meine Augen sehen dich	*so that my eyes behold you,*
in aller Freud, o Gottes Sohn,	*in all joy, O Son of God,*
mein Heiland und mein Gnadenthron,	*my savior and my throne of grace,*
Herr Jesu Christ,	*Lord Jesus Christ,*
erhöre mich, erhöre mich,	*hear me, hear me,*

Ich will dich preisen ewiglich.	*I will praise you forever.*
Amen.	*Amen.*

Beginning with tremolo strings accompanying the angel, Buxtehude then paints a hauntingly beautiful picture of the departed soul resting in Abraham's bosom, first with two slowly accumulating chords (m. 38, CD track 3, 01:50) and then with gentle rocking motion (m. 50, CD track 3, 02:14). For the joy of the awakend soul at the Last Judgment, two clarino trumpets replace the violins for just twenty measures (m. 78, CD track 3, 02:58). Buxtehude fills versus 2 and 3 with concertato contrasts between solo voices, instruments, and the tutti ensemble, in which the voices can be doubled by a capella (see chapter 11). Example 5-23 (CD track 3, 04:10) shows the crescendo in the last of a series of invocations to

Example 5-23. BuxWV 41, versus 3, mm. 136–45.

Example 5-23 *(continued)*.

Christ, beginning with a duet, the cantus firmus low in soprano 2; followed by all five soloists; and culminating with the tutti and an upward register shift in the cantus firmus at the prayer itself: "Erhöre mich."

Dialogues

BuxWV 36, 61, 111, 112

In view of Buxtehude's extensive cultivation of large dramatic forms in the Abendmusiken and the loss of the music for these oratorios, his few surviving works in a more modest dramatic genre, the dialogue, evoke particular interest.

Like the ciaccona, this genre cuts across the others; BuxWV 36 can also be called a concerto, BuxWV 61 and 111 arias, and BuxWV 112 a mixed cantata. BuxWV 111 and 112 are both designated "Dialogus" in their sources.

The least dramatic of these works is *Jesu, meiner Freuden Meister* (BuxWV 61), a funeral piece printed in 1677. Perhaps it does not even belong to the dialogue genre; the title page calls it only a "Trost-Lied." The text consists of twenty-five strophes of poetry, alternating in the beginning between the distressed soul and Jesus, later giving each several successive strophes. Buxtehude set this text as a bistrophic aria; the distressed soul is represented by soprano, alto, and tenor singing together in common time, while Jesus is a bass, singing in triple meter and accompanied almost throughout by four viols. Neither text nor music offers any dramatic progression.

The text of the other dialogue-aria, *Wo ist doch mein Freund geblieben* (BuxWV 111), is a poetic paraphrase of the story from the Song of Solomon of the lover lost from the bed. The title in the source reads "Dialogue between Christ and the faithful soul," and in this work the characters do interact, Jesus as a bass, the soul as a soprano. Although the poem is strophic, Buxtehude employs strophic musical form only at the beginning, while the soprano is alone and seeking the lover. As the lover is heard and then found, the aria becomes through-composed, enjoying greater tonal freedom, and duet style predominates. Perhaps the love duet in *Die Hochzeit des Lamms* resembled this music (ex. 5-24). Buxtehude's abandonment of strophic musical form in this work demonstrates his dramatic sense, but once the lovers have found one another there is no further development to the story.

In both BuxWV 36 and BuxWV 112, the musical claims of concerto and cantata, respectively, exert more influence than the dramatic ideals of the dialogue. The dialogue-concerto *Herr, ich lasse dich nicht* (BuxWV 36) recounts the story of Jacob wrestling with the angel in Genesis 32, with Jacob as a tenor and the angel as a bass. The work is set mainly in concertato style. Its most dramatic moment comes with an abrupt shift in meter, tempo, and key to recitative style when the angel refuses to answer Jacob's question regarding his name. Its dramatic power is undermined, however, by a varied repetition of this question and response complex followed by a repetition of the entire opening section. Dialogue structure is found only at the beginning of the cantata *Wo soll ich fliehen hin* (BuxWV 112), in which the conversation between the distressed soul (soprano) and Jesus (bass) is constructed by alternating chorale strophes for the soul, set strophically as a chorale sinfonia, with biblical verses for Jesus in lyrical recitative and concertato style. As in BuxWV 61, the static nature of strophic form hinders any sense of dramatic forward motion.

Although we can sense inherent music drama in BuxWV 36 and 111, none of these dialogues projects the dramatic power found in some other Buxtehude compositions, such as *Fürwahr, er trug unsere Krankheit* or the great organ praeludia. The dramatic style of the lost Abendmusiken remains a mystery.

Example 5-24. BuxWV 111, mm. 61–72.

Buxtehude's Cantatas

Concerto-Aria Cantatas

BuxWV 19, 24, 30, 33, 35, 39, 46, 47, 48,
50, 54, 55, 75 (cycle of seven cantatas), 77, 122

The concerto and the aria are by far the most important single genres among
Buxtehude's vocal compositions, and their combination to form the concerto-aria

cantata accounts for the largest number of works within Buxtehude's cantatas—twenty-one in all. With one exception, all are composed of a concerto set to a biblical text and an aria on a closely related poetic text. All but the seven cantatas of BuxWV 75 have German texts. The scoring of these works ranges fairly evenly from one voice to five, always with instruments.

We can see the normative pattern for Buxtehude's concerto-aria cantatas in *Membra Jesu nostri* (BuxWV 75), the cantata cycle that he dedicated to Gustav Düben in 1680. Following the introductory sonata, each cantata begins with a concerto on a short biblical text, normally scored for the maximum number of voices and instruments contained in that work: five voices and three instruments in all but the fifth and sixth cantatas, whose opening concertos call for only three voices, without instruments. An aria scored for fewer voices[10] follows; each cantata contains three selected strophes from successive sections of the poem "Salve mundi salutare," mostly set in strict strophic-variation form, articulated by a ritornello. The concerto usually returns to close the cantata, repeated exactly in the first five, with the addition of instruments in the sixth. In the seventh cantata, the third strophe of the aria is scored for the entire ensemble, and a concertato Amen section replaces the repetition of the opening movement.

In the case of *Membra*, it is clearly the poem that has generated the entire structure, both the seven-fold nature of the cycle and the choice of the biblical verses for the opening concertos. Most of them contain a reference to the part of the body to which that section of the poem is addressed, and that Buxtehude named in the title of each cantata. The sixth cantata, "Ad cor," contains the most expressive music in the entire cycle and truly functions as its heart. Buxtehude shifts the instrumental scoring for this one cantata from the two violins and violone used in the other cantatas to an ensemble of five viole da gamba. The biblical text is drawn from the Song of Solomon: "You have wounded my heart, my sister, my bride," and Buxtehude heightens its emotional impact by using the expressive figure of a descending sixth for the word "vulnerasti." When the viols accompany the voices in the return of the concerto they play repeated eighth notes in tremolo style, a device that Buxtehude reserved for especially expressive passages. He also directs the entire sonata of the second cantata to be played tremolo, and its half notes should probably all be performed as repeated eighths under one bow.

Although its individual cantatas are typical of the genre, as a cycle of cantatas *Membra* is unique among Buxtehude's works, and the question naturally arises as to whether he intended these cantatas to be performed together as a unit. It appears that Düben performed them separately, because the sets of parts that he extracted from Buxtehude's autograph tablature are written in different formats and on different papers. Furthermore, none of the title pages for the parts contains the inclusive cycle title *Membra*, although the last includes "No. 7." Düben's title for Number 6, "Ad Cor," is headed by the words "De Passione nostri Jesu Christi," and a note in another hand on the title page of Number 1 reads "for Easter or any time." Neither the number of works in this cycle nor its theme suggests performance in the

Abendmusiken, but since Buxtehude is known to have performed cyclical works separately in that context, he may have done so on other occasions as well. However, the presence of the Amen section at the end of Cantata 7 and the overall tonal scheme—ascending by fifths and then dropping abruptly to close in the initial key (c E♭ g d a e c)—suggest otherwise. The entire cycle may have been performed as the special Passion music following the afternoon sermon on Passion or Palm Sunday at St. Mary's. An analagous work, Joseph Haydn's orchestral *Seven Last Words of Our Savior on the Cross* (Hoboken XX/1 A), also consisting of seven similar parts, was commissioned for a Good Friday service in Spain.

In most of Buxtehude's concerto-aria cantatas, the biblical text of the concerto generates the structure; the aria comments on it. The concertos and arias within them are shorter and truer to the genre than his individual works in these genres; the concertos do not usually contain sections in aria style, and the arias stay close to strophic form. Occasionally, the individual strophes of the aria are separated from each other by sections of the concerto, producing an overall structure that is more sectional, and thus more concerto-like than cantata-like, as in BuxWV 33 and BuxWV 50. In another form of integration, a portion of the concerto returns as a refrain in the aria of BuxWV 77.

Ich suchte des Nachts (BuxWV 50), an unusual and perhaps late work within this group, offers an example of a concerto-like cantata. Its concerto text is the story from the Song of Solomon of the lover lost from the bed; the aria text, by an unknown poet, retells the story in poetry. Unlike in BuxWV 111, no attempt is made here to characterize the singers in dialogue fashion; BuxWV 50 is scored for tenor and bass, who relate the biblical account as a duet throughout. The tenor alone sings the aria. Its first two strophes have identical music in G minor, and they are placed just after the text that they paraphrase. The biblical account of the encounter with the watchmen follows, after which the tenor sings the paraphrasing third strophe, transposed into B♭ major at the beginning and continuing freely. With the final line "I am still more distressed," the aria ends in B♭ minor. The cantata concludes on a joyful note in an aria-like final section of the concerto to the biblical account of the finding of the lover. Paradoxically, this work is much more dramatic than Buxtehude's dialogue setting of the same story. Here he introduces oboes to imitate the watchmen's horns, and he skillfully manipulates an unusually wide-ranging tonal scheme to reflect the changing emotions and scenes. The aria provides a pause in the action to reflect an emotional state, just as in opera.

Other Two-Part Cantatas

BuxWV 29, 86

We can understand Buxtehude's other two-part cantatas as variants of the genres already discussed. *O Gott, wir danken deiner Güt* (BuxWV 86), a chorale-aria cantata, substitutes a concertato harmonization of a chorale for the opening concerto movement of a concerto-aria cantata. The opening movement is repeated following the more lightly scored strophic-bass aria, whose text expands on the theme of the sixteenth-century chorale. If we looked only at the words, we might consider *Frohlocket mit Händen* (BuxWV 29) a mixed cantata, because its text contains three distinct elements: a psalm verse, the second strophe of the chorale "Verleih uns Frieden gnädiglich," and between them a bit of poetry:

Gott, gib Fried in deinem Lande,	God, give peace in your land,
Glück und Heil zu allem Stande.	prosperity and safety to all estates.

This pair of lines is an early Lutheran prayer introduction; it is found in the Babst hymnal of 1545 immediately following "Verleih uns Frieden gnädiglich." Buxtehude's setting of this poetic text could hardly be called an aria; it continues as another section of the concerto in the same style as that which precedes it. The chorale setting, too, is not distinguished stylistically or by means of scoring from the concerto, apart from the presence of the cantus firmus. This work can be called a concerto-chorale cantata, and it is listed here because it contains two compositional elements, a free concerto and a chorale concerto. But this is a large and richly scored work, with five voices, strings, and trumpets, and the lack of any scoring differentiation between its movements—or sections—prevents it from sounding like a cantata. Stylistically, it belongs with the concertos.

Mixed Cantatas

BuxWV 4, 34, 51, [112]

Four of Buxtehude's vocal works, including the dialogue BuxWV 112, combine three genres: concerto, aria, and chorale setting. Each one combines these elements in a unique way, but we can consider all of them to be expanded versions of the pattern seen in the concerto-aria cantata: an opening and closing concerto of some sort, with a more lightly scored aria within. They are scored for from four to six voices with instruments, and all four are approximately three hundred measures in length.

Two of these cantatas open with a chorale sinfonia, in the manner of *Herzlich lieb*. In the case of *Wo soll ich fliehen hin* (BuxWV 112), the chorale setting is part of a chorale-concerto dialogue complex. The text of the strophic tenor aria that follows it relates to the final words of Jesus' statement: "Knock, and it shall be opened to you." The cantata ends with a three-part complex built on another chorale, "Herr Jesu Christ, du höchstes Gut," and consisting of a chorale sinfonia, a concertato harmonization, and an Amen section. With *Ihr lieben Christen, freut euch nun* (BuxWV 51) the chorale sinfonia introduces a concerto for the entire large ensemble to the text "Behold, the Lord comes with many thousands of saints." The central portion consists of a concerto section for bass (understood to be Jesus) with two muted trumpets to the text "Behold, I am coming soon" and the response in a single-strophe aria for alto, tenor, and bass with strings to the text "So do come, Jesus, come quickly," quoted on page 144. The urgency of this wish is underlined by the transformation of the opening chorale into triple meter in the closing complex, which is framed by Amen sections.

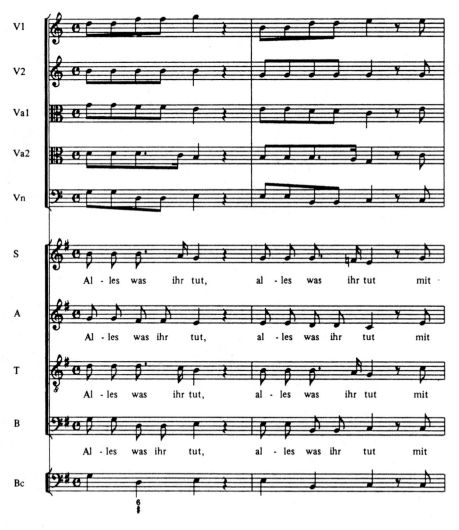

Example 5-25. BuxWV 4, Movement 2, mm. 1–3.

Example 5-25 (continued).

The opening and closing concerto complexes of BuxWV 4 and BuxWV 34 are
based on the Bible. *Gott hilf mir* (BuxWV 34) begins with a complex of four concerto sections: for bass with tremolo strings ("God, help me"); a tutti response
("Fear not"); an aria-like section for bass ("Israel, hope in the Lord") in which
Buxtehude once again turns prose into poetry; and an unusual setting of the
chorale "Durch Adams Fall ist ganz verderbt," in which the chorale melody is
heard only in the violins. The central aria ("Yes, Lord, I hope in you") is set

strophically for three voices, and a concluding tutti section expands on the earlier aria-like section of the bass.

The opening and closing concerto of *Alles was ihr tut* (BuxWV 4) proclaims the first portion of its biblical text ("Whatever you do, in words or deeds, do everything in the name of Jesus") in pure homophony (ex. 5-25) before moving into concertato texture for the second half of the movement. Its aria ("To you, Almighty, I dedicate my senses, powers, and desires") is set strophically for four voices in the style of the concertato-chorale harmonizations. Two strophes of the chorale "Aus meines Herzens Grunde" are also set as concertato harmonizations, but the normal four voices are reduced to soprano and continuo in the first strophe. *Alles was ihr tut* offers no visions of heaven, no intimacy with Jesus, no distressed souls. In a straightforward musical style, almost completely homophonic in texture, it addresses itself to the concerns of the ordinary citizen in the workaday world; its chorale concludes: "so I stretch out my hand, and undertake with joy the work to which God has destined me in my vocation and class." *Alles was ihr tut* also appears to have been Buxtehude's most popular vocal work; it is the only one included in all three of the principal manuscript collections that transmit Buxtehude's vocal music.

Music for Connoisseurs and Ordinary Citizens

Although Martin Fuhrmann was himself a connoisseur of music, he spoke for the ordinary citizen in his reiterated complaint that texts in concertato style could not be understood. Following his discussion of the intrusion of concertato style into the aria, his definition concludes:

> If the poem of an aria is unknown to him, the ordinary citizen likes best to hear it sung by a single singer (NB preferably a soprano, alto or tenor) with a pleasant and penetrating voice, accompanied from time to time by a few violins (for violas scream into the ears and snarl from a distance), because thus he can best understand an unfamiliar poem.

In his discussion of the concerto he refers similarly to the tastes of the ordinary man:

> If I may openly express my opinion concerning the concertos that all people love and praise, then the ordinary man prefers to hear a concerto in which each singer can be heard by himself for the most part—or occasionally only a pair of vocalists concertize, to whom the instrumentalists provide company—for then no one complains that he cannot understand the singers.

Lack of intelligibility was an important factor in Theophil Großgebauer's rejection of concerted church music, and his views found considerable public support. Fuhrmann, himself a practicing church musician, did not reject this music; he found concertos "artful," and he proposed the practical solution of distributing unfamiliar texts to the congregation if the style of their setting prevented the words from being clearly understood.

Much of Buxtehude's extant vocal music, particularly his concertos with Latin texts, probably held little appeal for the ordinary citizens of Lübeck. Precisely those qualities in these pieces that engage the knowledgeable listener—the skillful matching of voice and viol in *Jubilate Domino*, of text and style in *O dulcis Jesu*, the counterpoint of *Cantate Domino*—would have caused it to be incomprehensible to the average churchgoer. Even the masterpiece *Herzlich lieb hab ich dich, o Herr*, with its familiar German text and chorale melody, might have struck the ordinary citizen as being much too long.

We know, however, that Buxtehude composed music that did appeal to the citizens of Lübeck; had this not been the case, they would not have given their financial support to his Abendmusiken year after year. And among his extant compositions, two works provide the key to the style that the general public in Lübeck liked: *Alles was ihr tut* and *Schwinget euch himmelan* (Examples 5-15, 5-16, 5-25). The texts of these two works are so clearly directed toward the general citizenry of Lübeck that we must assume that their music was as well. Among the stylistic characteristics that these two works share are German texts, predominantly homophonic texture, and an emphasis on strophic musical form. Both works are simple, direct, and largely predictable. These characteristics pertain as well to most of Buxtehude's wedding arias commissioned by Lübeck citizens. In requesting wedding music to Italian texts, Joachim Carstens and Benedict Winkler singled themselves out as connoisseurs. Other connoisseurs among the Lübeck citzenry may have included Friderich Osnobrück, Berendt von Warle, and Rudolph Wedeman—the only three Lübeck businessmen who supported the publication of Theile's contrapuntal masses in 1673—and Johann Ritter, the recipient of Buxtehude's dedication—in Italian—of his sonatas in 1696.

If we use *Alles was ihr tut* and *Schwinget euch himmelan* as the standards, it becomes possible to identify other works within Buxtehude's extant vocal oeuvre that would have appealed to a wider public and thus might be somewhat representative of the music in the lost Abendmusiken. These include all the arias in pure or extended strophic form—among which, incidentally, none has a Latin text—and all the concertato chorale harmonizations. In this context, the concerto-aria cantata becomes a means of making the concerto more accessible to the general public. Just as its poetic text interprets and personalizes the biblical text for the individual believer, so the aria shortens the opening concerto, while its strophic form speaks directly to the average listener. All Buxtehude's cantatas—with the exception of the *Membra* cycle, which he dedicated to Gustav Düben, the ultimate connoisseur—have German texts, predominantly homophonic texture, and at least some elements of strophic form.

The audience for Buxtehude's Latin-texted works and more sophisticated concertos was probably quite small, and the greatest admirers of this music may have been the performers themselves, those versatile municipal musicians of Lübeck. In choosing to compose music that did not appeal directly to the widest possible public, Buxtehude once again demonstrated the freedom he enjoyed as an organist who composed vocal music by choice, not out of duty.

Questions of Authenticity

In 1961, Martin Geck published an article in *Die Musikforschung* questioning the authenticity of a number of vocal works attributed to Buxtehude. Many of the problems that he raised have since been resolved. The Lübeck tablature A 373, long believed lost, reappeared, and Georg Karstädt, in his monograph on this manuscript, demonstrated convincingly that all the works in it, including those with no composer ascription, are by Buxtehude. Geck identified Lowies Busbetzky as the composer of *Erbarm dich mein, o Herre Gott* and *Laudate Dominum omnes gentes*, which had been published as works of Buxtehude. Bruno Grusnick, who first published an anonymous *Magnificat* as a work of Buxtehude in 1931, later acknowledged that Buxtehude could no longer be considered the composer;[11] nonetheless it remains in print under his name in numerous editions. Karstädt's Buxtehude-Werke-Verzeichnis includes an appendix of doubtful and inauthentic works, including the *Magnificat*, and references to the literature concerning these pieces may be found there.

At the beginning of this chapter I suggested that BuxWV 1, 43, and 101 also be included in the list of works of questionable authenticity. *Accedite gentes, accurite populi* (BuxWV 1) has two sources in the Düben Collection, a set of parts and a tablature, both anonymous. The set of parts, *Uu* 38:1, contains only this work; the tablature, *Uu* 82:34, contains two others, Buxtehude's *Ecce nunc benedicite* (BuxWV 23) and *Laudate pueri* by Clemens Thieme. *Accedite gentes* has been attributed to Buxtehude by virtue of the fact that it is followed by *Ecce nunc benedicite* in the tablature. This rather short anthology of twelve folios may be compared with two similar tablatures in the Düben collection: *Uu* 83:69-73, sixteen folios in length, contains one work by Cesti, two attributed to Benedictus a Sancto Josepho, BuxWV 28, and one work by Johann Philipp Krieger, all attributed; *Uu* 82:37 (eight folios) contains the early and later versions of BuxWV 62, separated by a work of Pohle, all attributed. Most of the works contained in Düben's tablature collections are in fact attributed to composers, and the fact that *Accedite gentes* carries no ascription in either source suggests rather strongly that Düben did not know who the composer was. It could as easily be a work of Thieme or of a third composer as a work of Buxtehude.

Heut triumphieret Gottes Sohn (BuxWV 43) and *Wachet auf, ruft uns die Stimme* (BuxWV 101, in C) are both transmitted uniquely in the Österreich-Bokemeyer collection in scores to which Buxtehude's name was added only later. BuxWV 101, if authentic, would be the only chorale text firmly associated with a melody that Buxtehude set without its cantus firmus. Krummacher doubts its authenticity on the basis of its poverty of contrast and affect, its primitive compositional technique, and its simple harmony. This work may be compared with *Das neugeborne Kindelein* (BuxWV 13), in which Buxtehude chose not to use any of the available melodies as a cantus firmus. There he set the text in aria style, emphasizing its metrical and strophic structure with typically generous use of the instruments to articulate the form of the poetry. In BuxWV 101, the poetry is set as if it were prose, and the instruments do not receive the prominence that Buxtehude usually gives them. It seems unlikely that Buxtehude, who could make poetry out of prose, would have chosen to ignore both the chorale melody and the poetic nature of the text. *Heut triumphieret Gottes Sohn*, if authentic, would contain in its closing "Alleluia" Buxtehude's only fugal exposition consisting entirely of entrances of the subject in the tonic, and the harmonic blandness of the entire work is quite uncharacteristic of Buxtehude's vocal music.

We can add one new work to the list of doubtful works, a concerted Kyrie attributed to "J. Bocksdehude" in its tablature source in the Großfahner music collection near Gotha.[12] The manuscript was copied by Johann Christian Starckloff (1655–1722), cantor in Eschenbergen, and it is one of numerous copies in tablature in his collection, which favors the works of Johann Philipp Käfer (1672–ca. 1730), Liebhold (fl. early 18th ca.), and Christian Friedrich Witt (1660–1716). Since Johannes Buxtehude is not known to have composed any music, and the tonal plan of this piece seems in any event to be too advanced for his generation, the question must be raised as to whether Dieterich Buxtehude could be the composer.

The "Bocksdehude" Kyrie, scored for five voices (SSATB), two violins, and continuo, is in two sections, Kyrie (C, 34 measures) and Christe (3/4, 55 measures), with the instruction to repeat the Kyrie. The voices begin and end the Kyrie in block homophony and engage in imitation, often paired in parallel thirds, in the central portion. The two violins move relentlessly in sixteenth notes for the entire section, a procedure encountered nowhere in the works of Buxtehude. The Christe is constructed over a seven-measure ostinato bass, appearing twice in D minor at the beginning and end and once each in F major and A minor in the middle, with four-measure transitions between tonal areas. This is precisely the tonal plan that Buxtehude used in his D-minor passacaglia for organ (BuxWV 161). Here, however, unlike in Buxtehude's ostinato works, very little variation occurs; the parts are merely transposed and exchanged over the recurring ostinato. The style of this work, then, does not suggest that Dieterich Buxtehude composed it, although his passacaglia may have inspired the Christe. It could be a work of Johann Heinrich Buttstett (1666–1727), who is represented in Starckloff's collection by six works and whose name is sometimes confused with that of Buxtehude in manuscript sources of organ music.

Finally, the discussion begun in chapter 2 of the anonymous oratorio *Wacht! Euch zum Streit*—the so-called *Jüngstes Gericht* (BuxWV Anhang 3)—must be concluded. In her comprehensive study of *Wacht! Euch zum Streit*, Sara Ruhle affirms the kinship of its libretto with the Lübeck Abendmusiken but declines to ascribe the composition of the work to Buxtehude on the basis of the overall simplicity of its musical style. In her musical analysis, she finds that the settings of biblical texts in arioso style provide the most interesting music in the oratorio and that they "exhibit a degree of organization and invention that is worthy of the best concerted writing of Protestant church composers." Following Krummacher, she finds that the style of the chorale settings—all concertato harmonizations— resembles one of the styles cultivated by Buxtehude, but she would expect Buxtehude to have used a greater variety of styles in the chorale settings if he were the composer of this work. It is primarily the proliferation of strophic arias, however, that causes her to reject Buxtehude as the composer of *Wacht! Euch zum Streit*. She finds these arias dramatically weak, stagnating the pace and weakening the plot. Although their music fits the words well, effectively rendering the regular meter and strophic form of the texts, she correctly observes that the arias of Buxtehude's cantatas transcend the predictably regular style of the arias in *Wacht! Euch zum Streit*. Comparing the arias in *Wacht! Euch zum Streit* with the wealth of musical creativity she finds in Buxtehude's aria "Du Lebensfürst, Herr Jesu Christ" from the cantata BuxWV 33, she concludes that "such creativity, in particular rhythmic variety, sets this aria apart from the sing-song type of aria found in *Wacht! Euch zum Streit* and seems to exclude Buxtehude as a possible composer of *Wacht! Euch zum Streit*."

Buxtehude did, as Ruhle rightly observes, compose some strophic arias that demonstrate the regularity of rhythm and phrase characteristic of so many arias in *Wacht! Euch zum Streit*. Ruhle offers *Klinget für Freuden* (BuxWV 119) as an example of a Buxtehude aria in the style of *Wacht! Euch zum Streit*. The rhythm and phrase structure of "O gnadenreiches Leben" from BuxWV 30, *Was mich auf dieser Welt betrübt* (BuxWV 105, ex. 5-12), and *Schwinget euch himmelan* (BuxWV 96, ex. 5-15) are even more regular. In Buxtehude's cultivation of the genre, these three arias lie at one end of a continuum that moves to the extreme flexibility of works such as *O Gottes Stadt* (BuxWV 87, ex. 5-14). Although we cannot consider BuxWV 30, 96, and 105 typical of Buxtehude's arias, their very regularity embodies the principle that underlies all of his arias and from which he departs to varying degrees, but rarely to the extent of BuxWV 87.

Wacht! Euch zum Streit also contains some arias that are more flexible in their rhythm and phrasing. Their style more closely approximates that of the majority of Buxtehude's arias in the middle of his spectrum. Chief among these is "Süßer Jesu, Jesu du" from act III (ex. 5-26; number 53 in Maxton's edition).

Example 5-26. *Wacht! Euch zum Streit*, Act III, "Süßer Jesu," mm. 9–22.

The language of this text, with its sensuous imagery, recalls the poems of Johann Angelus Silesius and Heinrich Müller, although it is far beneath theirs in literary quality.

Süßer Jesu, Jesu du,	*Sweet Jesus, thou Jesus,*
Meine Ruh,	*My peace,*
Banquetieren, jubilieren	*Banqueting and singing praise*
kann ich immerfort von dir,	*I can do forever with thee,*
und so süß ist dein Genuß	*and so sweet is thy pleasure*
daß stets wächset die Begier.	*that desire grows steadily.*
Deiner Liebe, Liebe Wein,	*The wine of thy love*
flößet ein	*instills [in me]*
zuckersüße Himmelskräfte,	*sugar-sweet powers of heaven,*
daß ich alle Welt vergeß,	*so that I forget the whole world;*
deine Brust tröpft solche Lust	*thy breast drips such pleasure,*
welche ich noch nicht ermäß.	*as I have not yet measured.*

With the composer's setting of trochaic meter in 6/8 time, this aria is atypical of both Buxtehude's arias and those of *Wacht! Euch zum Streit,* both of which usually employ common time for trochaic meter. At the beginning of the aria, the composer alternates quarters and eighths for the stressed and unstressed syllables of the poetic meter. As it progresses, however, the first stressed syllable of the poetic line becomes part of the anacrusis in the musical phrase, as with "banquetieren" in mm. 14 and 15 and "jubilieren" in m. 19. The instrumental introduction and first vocal phrase also lead us to expect that this aria will consist of two-measure phrases. This expectation is rarely fulfilled, however, partly because the line lengths of the poem itself are irregular.

Few of the arias in *Wacht! Euch zum Streit* contain concertato instrumental interjections such as are found in "Süßer Jesu" and that occur frequently in Buxtehude's arias. This was also the case with the arias of the Hamburg opera; among the forty-one arias from Johann Wolffgang Franck's *Aeneas* (1680), all but two restrict the instrumental participation to ritornelli. As a practical matter, an aria whose vocal portion is accompanied only by continuo requires less rehearsal time than one with concertato instrumental interjections.

Wacht! Euch zum Streit is in fact almost totally devoid of concertato style, and this, combined with its abundance of arias in pure strophic form, is what makes it sound so unlike most of Buxtehude's vocal music. But the ordinary citizen, on whose financial support the Abendmusiken depended, did not care much for music in concertato style; it was too difficult to understand. Strophic form, on the other hand, is the most readily comprehensible of all musical forms. It is not dramatic, as three of Buxtehude's dialogues demonstrate, but it was and remains popular with the general public, particularly when performed by a solo singer, as Fuhrmann wrote, "with a pleasant and penetrating voice, accompanied from time to time by a few violins." Of forty-one solo arias in Franck's *Aeneas*, twenty-six are strophic. *Himmlische Seelenlust*, one of the Abendmusiken Buxtehude announced for publication in 1684, was to be "in opera style, with many arias and ritornelli." *Wacht! Euch zum Streit* contains thirty-four strophic arias, twenty-one for solo voice, each with a ritornello. Surely Buxtehude cannot be excluded as the composer of this work for writing in a style that appealed to the general public.

The chief musical elements of *Wacht! Euch zum Streit*—strophic arias, settings of biblical texts in lyrical recitative, and concertato chorale harmonizationas—are precisely those found in *Alles was ihr tut*, Buxtehude's cantata for the ordinary citizen. If the multiplication of these elements within a much larger work strikes the connoisseur of Buxtehude's music as lacking in variety or dramatic power, we must remember that the cultivation of larger dramatic forms in North Germany was in its infancy in the early 1680s, when *Wacht! Euch zum Streit* was composed, and that if it was an Abendmusik only one act of this work would have been performed on a given evening. A performance of this work on three successive evenings at the Westfield Center's "Scheidt to Buxtehude" conference in 1987 proved more dramatically satisfying than performances of all three acts in a single concert. If its modest scoring and restriction to three acts fall short of the expectations that later accounts of the Abendmusiken have created, we can recall Buxtehude's letter of February 1683 to his financial backers:

> Although in the most recent time [I] have not been able to present as complete a work as [I] wished and intended, on account of impediments which have occurred, nevertheless [I] have the most respectful confidence in my highly and widely honored gentlemen, that they will have kindly accepted the little that has been presented.

Buxtehude's confidence must have rested in his knowledge of his own ability to compose in the simple style that appealed to the ordinary citizen. I believe that *Wacht! Euch zum Streit* is the work that Buxtehude presented in his Abendmusiken of 1682.

Chapter Six

Works of Learned Counterpoint

Seventeenth-century composers worked with an acute consciousness of stylistic differentiation. Early in the century, Monteverdi had coined the term *seconda prattica* to identify the modern style of composition, which distinguished itself from sixteenth-century practice by its much freer treatment of dissonances, as codified by Gioseffo Zarlino in *Le Istitutioni harmoniche* (1558). Unlike the composers involved in previous stylistic revolutions, however, Monteverdi and his successors continued to cultivate the old style alongside the new.

Not only did seventeenth-century musicians compose in both styles, they also developed elaborate systems to categorize the music of their contemporaries according to style. Buxtehude would certainly have been familiar with the system that Christoph Bernhard expounded in his treatise *Tractatus compositionis augmentatus*. Bernhard, like Monteverdi, based his stylistic distinctions primarily on the use of consonances and dissonances. He divided counterpoint in general into two types: equal or simple counterpoint, also known as first species counterpoint, in which only consonances are used; and unequal or florid counterpoint, which employs both consonances and dissonances. Bernhard's division of florid counterpoint into two styles—severe or old style and luxuriant or modern style—corresponds exactly to Monteverdi's two practices. Bernhard divided the luxuriant or modern style again into two types, common and theatrical, with the theatrical style allowing more dissonances than the common style.

All of Buxtehude's vocal compositions discussed in chapter 5 belong to the luxuriant style, which Bernhard describes as well suited to move the emotions by virtue of its faster note values, greater variety of melodic intervals, and greater number of dissonance figures than are allowable in the old style. Bernhard based his distinction between the common and theatrical branches of the luxuriant style solely upon the treatment of dissonance. Common style is found mainly in church and chamber music. Theatrical style—which he also calls recitative or oratorio style—occurs mainly in the theater. Both classes of dissonances within the modern style can be found in Buxtehude's vocal music, although those of the common style naturally occur more frequently. *O dulcis Jesu* (BuxWV 83) offers several examples of dissonance figures that Bernhard allows only in the theatrical style. In example 5-7, *ellipsis*, or the absence of an expected consonance, occurs with the rest in m. 22; *mora*, or the upward resolution of a suspension, occurs in m. 25; and *transitus inversus*, in which the first part of a measure is dissonant, occurs at m. 29. In example 5-6, *abruptio*, in which a line breaks off instead of proceeding to the expected consonance, occurs from m. 250 to m. 251, and *extensio*, a prolonged dissonance, occurs at m. 253 on the word "languet"; the leap to the unprepared seventh at m. 260 has no justification within Bernhard's system. In his *Klag-Lied* for the funeral of his father (BuxWV 76-2), Buxtehude used dissonance figures from the common style to convey the affect of deep sorrow: suspensions (*syncopatio*), downward leaps of a minor sixth and diminished fifth (*saltus duriusulus*), and chromatic motion (*passus duriusculus*). Had Buxtehude himself been inclined to theorize about the styles that he cultivated, he might have divided his many works in the modern style into those for the connoisseur and those for the ordinary citizen.

The old style of composition, or *stile antico*, was definitely reserved for connoisseurs. As noted earlier, only three Lübeck businessmen supported the publication of Theile's *stile antico* masses in 1673; the remaining thirteen backers from Lübeck included professional musicians, teachers, and a theological student, Meno Hanneken, Jr. Bernhard describes the old style as having long note values, rare use of dissonance, and, following Monteverdi, as paying more attention to the harmony than to the words. He allows only four dissonance figures in this style: *transitus*, a passing tone or auxiliary on an even beat; *quasi-transitus*, the same figure on an odd beat; *syncopatio*, a suspension; and *quasi-syncopatio*, an untied suspension or prepared appogiatura. Three of Bernhard's own compositions in pure *stile antico* survive: *Missa à 5* and two funeral pieces, *Zur selbigen Zeit* (Hamburg, 1667) and *Prudentia prudentiana* (Hamburg, 1669).[1] The motet "in the contrapuntal style of Palestrina" that he composed in 1670 at the request of Heinrich Schütz for performance at his funeral is lost.

Among the contrapuntal techniques that seventeenth-century composers inherited from the sixteenth century were the devices of canon and invertible counterpoint. They incorporated these techniques into compositions in both the old style and the modern style. Occasionally, they also isolated them in compositions devoted solely to one or the other of these devices. Such canons and works in invertible counterpoint formed the most esoteric group within the music for connoisseurs, and the composition of such pieces functioned as a badge of membership in the fraternity of skilled composers. It is no accident that the friendship between Buxtehude and Reincken is documented by a canon in the painting *Musical Party*. We may also recall Handel and Mattheson's trip to visit Buxtehude in Lübeck, during which they passed the time in the coach by composing double fugues in their heads.

Compositions in *stile antico*, canons, and pieces in invertible counterpoint may be grouped together as works of learned counterpoint. A small amount of music by Buxtehude in each of these three categories survives.

Invertible Counterpoint

BuxWV 76-1

Buxtehude's most ambitious and successful work of learned counterpoint is his setting of the chorale "Mit Fried und Freud ich fahr dahin" in BuxWV 76. He composed it in 1671 for the funeral of the Lübeck superintendent Meno Hanneken, Sr., performed it again at the funeral of his father in 1674, and published it that year, together with the *Klag-Lied* that he composed on his father's death. Only a printed title page survives from 1671 as the last page of a collection of poems by Hanneken's friends and colleagues.[2] Buxtehude's title reads:

Simeons Abschied Bey Absterben Des Weyland Hoch-Ehrwürdigen und Hochgelahrten Herrn, Herrn MENONIS HANNEKENII, Der Heil: Schrift weitberühmbten Doctoris und der Stadt Lübeck hochansehnlichen SUPERINTENDENTEN Zu Bezeugung schuldiger Wohlmeinung gesetzet und in zween Contrapunctis abgesungen von Dieterico Buxtehude, Organisten an der Hauptkirchen zu St. Marien in Lübeck.	*Simeon's Farewell, upon the death of the late highly honored and very learned gentleman, Mr. Meno Hanneken, famed doctor of the holy scriptures and highly respected superintendent of the city of Lübeck, composed to declare his dutiful benevolence and performed in two counterpoints by Dieterico Buxtehude, organist at the principal church of St. Mary's in Lübeck.*

Hanneken had studied at the University of Wittenberg and had served as a professor of theology at the University of Marburg from 1626 to 1646 before assuming his post in Lübeck. His tenure as superintendent in Lübeck was marked by his strong defense of Lutheran orthodoxy. In choosing a chorale by Martin Luther as the cantus firmus of this work, Buxtehude honored Hanneken's orthodoxy; in setting it with intricate quadruple counterpoint, Buxtehude acknowledged Hanneken's erudition and at the same time demonstrated his own.

The published version of "Mit Fried und Freud" matches the 1671 title, consisting of two separate contrapuntal settings, titled Contrapunctus I and Contrapunctus II. In each of these the chorale melody appears in D Dorian, unadorned and in its normal rhythm, moving mainly in half notes, in the soprano voice. The three lower voices move mainly in quarter and eighth notes in a contrapuntal style that is occasionally loosely imitative. In the printed Evolutio to Contrapunctus I, the soprano moves down an octave plus a fourth to become the bass, the alto moves down a fourth to become the tenor, the tenor moves up a fifth to become the alto, and the bass moves up an octave plus a fifth to become the soprano. In the Evolutio to Contrapunctus II, the parts not only make the same exchanges as before, but they move in contrary motion as well. In each voice, the first and fifth degrees D and A of the contrapunctus become A and D, respectively, in contrary motion (ex. 6-1). These voice exchanges effect a tonal shift in each Evolutio to A Dorian, notated with a key signature of F♯ only in the second Evolutio. The entire work is printed in open score, with a successive strophe of Luther's hymn underlaid beneath each appearance of the chorale melody, including its inversion in the second Evolutio.

The first two movements of Bernhard's *Prudentia prudentiana*, published in 1669, are constructed identically to "Mit Fried und Freud" and appear to have served as a model for Buxtehude. Bernhard composed his counterpoints on the funeral hymn "Jam mesta quiesce querela" by Aurelius Prudentius. He dedicated the work to Rudolf Capell, his colleague at the Johanneum in Hamburg, as a consolation to him upon the recent deaths of his mother and wife. Bernhard's second counterpoint is more imitative than Buxtehude's, but the

Example 6-1a. BuxWV 76-1, Contrapunctus II, mm. 1–3.

Er ist das Heil und se - lig

Licht,   Für

Example 6-1b. BuxWV 76-1, Evolutio II, mm. 1–3.

voice exchanges and intervallic relationships of its Revolutio are the same as
Buxtehude's (ex. 6-2). The appearance of the two printed scores is also similar,
although Bernhard placed the hymn text under the cantus firmus of only the
counterpoints, not their inversions. Like Meno Hanneken, Rudolph Capell was
a learned man, a professor of rhetoric and Greek, and Bernhard's offering to
him of this esoteric contrapuntal work was probably a sign of their intellectual
kinship. Its third and fourth movements contain further complexities: a setting
that can be performed in retrograde inversion and a six-part setting with two
canonic voices. It is doubtful that this work of abstract counterpoint was performed at either funeral; its title page states only that the work had been "elab-
orated" (*elaborata*) by Bernhard.

Example 6-2a. Bernhard, *Prudentia,* Contrapunctus II, mm. 1–7.

Example 6-2b. Bernhard, *Prudentia,* Revolutio II, mm. 1–7.

Buxtehude's "Mit Fried und Freud," on the other hand, was performed at two funerals, and this shift from the abstract to the concrete is reflected in its musical quality, which far surpasses that of its model. Buxtehude most likely performed it on the organ; Johann Gottfried Walther considered it an organ piece in his *Lexicon* entry, although Heinrich Bokemeyer supplied it with continuo figures in his manuscript copy. With Bernhard's print in mind as a model, we can understand the text underlay beneath the cantus firmus as belonging to the intellectual foundation of the work rather than as an indication that the part is to be sung by a voice.

In publishing this most esoteric piece of counterpoint together with his *Klag-Lied* in the modern style, Buxtehude consciously juxtaposed the *stylus gravis* with the *stylus luxurians*, a work for the connoisseur with one for the ordinary citizen, a consonant work in the old Dorian mode with a dissonant one in modern E minor. More than that: as David Yearsley's allegorical interpretation has shown, he was also juxtaposing the heavenly music beyond death that his father was now enjoying with the earthly grief that the son was expressing with his affect-laden poem and song, the macrocosm with the microcosm, the eternal order of God with a "troubled and anxiety-wracked world."

Canon

BuxWV 123, 124, 124a

Following a well-established tradition among composers, Buxtehude entered his musical puzzles, the canons BuxWV 123 and 124, into the autograph books of two connoisseurs, the theological student Meno Hanneken, Jr., and the composer and singer Johann Valentin Meder. Although both autograph books are now lost, photographs of Buxtehude's entries survive.

Buxtehude composed his canon for Meno Hanneken, Jr. (BuxWV 124, fig. 6-1, ex. 6-3) in 1670. His dedication to Hanneken reads:

> In recognition of the happiness that I have had in your conversation, I offer you a little song which represents my esteem for you and will, without doubt, sometimes give you occasion to remember that I am, sir, your most humble servant, Dieteri. Buxtehude, organist of the church of St. Mary in Lübeck.

As Johann Philipp Förtsch wrote, it is easier to compose a canon than to solve one.[3] Buxtehude's directions call for entries at the upper fifth and upper octave, but these do not work well; my solution brings the other voices in at the upper octave and lower fifth. Michael Belotti has proposed an alternate solution with entries at the lower fifth and and upper fourth. He makes a perpetual canon of

Figure 6-1. Buxtehude, canon for Meno Hanneken, Jr. (BuxWV 124), 1670.

it (which the notation does not suggest) and succeeds in ending all three voices together, but at the expense of closing with the word "bouvons," and in a different key from that in which the canon began.

The musical entries in the autograph book belonging to Johann Valentin Meder[4] (1649–1719) indicate visits to Johann Pezel and Sebastian Knüpfer in Leipzig (1670), his brother Maternus in Meiningen (1671), Martin Radeck and Michael Zachaeus in Copenhagen (4 and 13 June 1674), and Buxtehude in Lübeck (25 June 1674). Meder sang from the organ at St. Mary's for the feast of the Visitation of Mary (2 July) that year. All the musicians except Radeck entered canons into Meder's autograph book; Radeck wrote a fugue in organ tablature. Maternus Meder noted that he was adding his canon "not so much out of a liking for this type of art as out of brotherhood." His is the simplest of the canons, for three voices at the unison. His brother, however, must have been a true connoisseur, for Buxtehude dedicated his canon

to a most outstanding man, Mr. Joh. Valentin Meder, who has always enjoyed music and literature of an uncommon character, [the undersigned] wished to place this canon here for his most honored patron, for the sake of a kind remembrance. Dietericus Buxtehude, organist in the eminent temple of Mary.

Example 6-3. BuxWV 124, Snyder solution.

Buxtehude's canon for Meder (BuxWV 123, fig. 6-2) is considerably more complex than his earlier one for Hanneken. The directions call for a second voice in augmentation and for four voices to sing simultaneously. This is achieved by bringing in the voice in augmentation at the lower fifth and doubling both voices with parallel thirds, below the written voice and above the one in augmentation (ex. 6-4).

Johann Theile's treatise on invertible counterpoint contains a similar canon,[5] as noted in chapter 4; he probably wrote it around 1691, in close conjunction with his *Musikalisches Kunstbuch*, which also contains an augmentation canon that is extended to four voices by the addition of parallel thirds. Precedents for making four parts out of two in this way can also be found in Bernhard's *Tractatus* (Das 69ste Capitel) and Athanasius Kircher's *Musurgia universalis* (Book VII, chapter 5).

A similar solution suggests itself for the canon (BuxWV 124a) that Heinrich Rogge printed with his music for Reincken's wedding and obliquely attributed to Buxtehude, as discussed in chapter 4. In this case, the voice in augmentation enters in contrary motion at the lower octave with the first repetition of the text, and each voice is doubled at the upper third (ex. 6-5). This solution does not

Figure 6-2. Buxtehude, canon for Johann Valentin Meder (BuxWV 123), 1674 (Paris, Bibliothèque Nationale, Fonds Pirro, Boîte 60).

Example 6-4. BuxWV 123, solution.

agree with the title of this canon, "Canon quadruplex à 5," as reprinted by J. C. M. van Riemsdijk; it neither has five voices nor can it be considered a quadruple canon. This source, however, is at best third-hand, since Rogge's print is now lost, and it is entirely possible that Rogge himself gave the title incorrectly.

Stile Antico

BuxWV 114

Buxtehude and his colleagues devoted particular attention to *stile antico* during the first few years of Buxtehude's tenure in Lübeck. Bernhard composed works

Example 6-5. BuxWV 124a, solution.

in *stile antico* between 1667 and 1670; Reincken copied an old-style composition treatise in 1670; Buxtehude's "Mit Fried und Freud" of 1671 follows *stile antico* in its treatment of dissonance; Theile published his masses "according to the old style of counterpoint" in 1673, with Bernhard praising their old style in his foreword, Buxtehude and Reincken backing him financially. It would be surprising if Buxtehude had *not* also composed a mass in *stile antico* at this time, and the manuscript of the *Missa alla brevis* (BuxWV 114) appears to have been copied by 1675.[6]

The authenticity of the *Missa alla brevis* has, however, been questioned by Martin Geck. Working from photocopies, he argued that the title and attribution to Buxtehude in the manuscript—written upside down at the end of the continuo part and titled "Missa a 4 alla brevis," suggest instead that Buxtehude composed a four-voice mass, now lost, and that this five-voice work is anonymous. An examination of the manuscript itself, however, together with those that surround it, resolves most of the questions in Buxtehude's favor. Although the upside-down title looks odd in facsimile—it is reproduced with the edition of the mass in volume IV of Buxtehude's *Werke*—it makes sense when seen on the manuscript itself (*Uu* 6:16), and there are others like it in the Düben collection, among them the parts for *O clemens, o mitis* (BuxWV 82; *Uu* 51:18). The manuscript of the mass bears Düben's ink catalogue number 504, and a survey of the manuscripts that Düben catalogued[7] with numbers from 400 to 525 shows that they are all either in quarto format or, as in *Uu* 6:16, in folio format folded to quarto size. When this is done, the continuo part at the bottom of the unfolded pile becomes the wrapper for the set of folded parts, and its bottom becomes the top. The title, which Düben himself added to the parts copied in another hand, is placed so that it can be read most easily. He erred in calling it a four-voice work, but Buxtehude is more likely to have composed a *stile antico* mass in five voices than four, since Bernhard's three masses and *stile antico* motet are all in five voices.

Buxtehude's mass is a *missa brevis*, consisting only of Kyrie and Gloria, the two movements normally used in a Lutheran Latin mass; its title, however, is *Missa alla brevis*, meaning that it was composed with the larger note values and longer measures, a breve in length, associated with the *stile antico*. As in many similar works, including Bernhard's *Missa à 5*, its continuo part is a basso seguente and is not essential to the performance of the work, whose texture normally employs the full five voices after their initial imitative entrances. The texture consists almost entirely of imitative counterpoint, interspersed with several very short sections of homophony in the Gloria. With but a few exceptions, Buxtehude limits himself to the four dissonance figures that Bernhard permits for the old style. One interesting exception occurs with the affective text "miserere nostri"[8] in the Gloria (ex. 6-6). Two of the dissonance figures that Bernhard classifies within the common modern style are found here: the *syncopatio catachrestica*, or irregular resolution of the suspension by a downward fifth in the soprano part at

Example 6-6. BuxWV 114, Gloria, mm. 97–108.

Example 6-6 (*continued*).

m. 99, and the *passus duriusculus*, or chromatic melodic line of the soprano and bass parts in mm. 104–6. Bernhard himself included a few isolated figures from the common modern style in two masses composed primarily in the old style, *Missa Christ unser Herr zum Jordan kam* and *Missa Durch Adams Fall.*

The strict contrapuntal techniques that Buxtehude displayed in "Mit Fried und Freud" and in the canons are employed more freely in the *Missa alla brevis.* The close entrances of the subject in the opening Kyrie make skillful use of canon, constantly varying the time interval of the second entrances. A countersubject in invertible counterpoint appears in both Kyries. A stretto beginning at m. 25 of the second Kyrie is followed by two simultaneous pairs of parallel thirds, although they are not canonic. The *Missa alla brevis* provides a link between Buxtehude's strict contrapuntal works and those in the modern style that employ contrapuntal techniques. Its two Kyries bear a striking resemblance to his canzonas and praeludia in their closely related subjects (ex. 6-7).

For Christoph Bernhard, the *stile antico* was the fundamental style of composition, the *stile moderno* an embellishment or extension of it that had developed from the practice of singers into a theory of composition. He more than any

Ky - ri - e e - lei - · · · · · ·

Example 6-7a. BuxWV 114, Kyrie I, alto, mm. 1–4.

Ky - ri - e _____ e - lei - · ·

Example 6-7b. BuxWV 114, Kyrie II, soprano, mm. 1–4.

other seems to have inspired Buxtehude to compose his works of learned counterpoint, and Buxtehude's interest in learned counterpoint for its own sake appears to have waned after Bernhard's departure from Hamburg in 1674. In composing these few works, however, Buxtehude had demonstrated his complete mastery of the fundamentals of the art of composition.

Chapter Seven

Keyboard Works

The art of the North German organist lay chiefly in improvisation. This fact is nowhere more clearly demonstrated than in the account of Matthias Weckmann's audition for the position of organist at the church of St. Jacobi, Hamburg, recorded by his pupil Johann Kortkamp:

> In the year 1655 the world famous organist and composer, a father of musicians, Matthias Weckmann, was chosen for the church of St. Jacobi and Gertrud and came to the position at St. Gertrud where his teacher, the most praiseworthy Jacobus Schultze [Praetorius] had been. The audition that this man endured had never before been heard. . . . When it came his turn to play, he fantasized on the full organ in the tone of the fugue that had been given him; it was supposed to be in the first tone, but it was mixed with the third tone, and was treated in a wonderful way. . . . Next he treated the sacred church hymn that had been given him: "An Waßerflüßen Babylon" with pedal and two manuals. In the Oberwerck he used the registration of the late Jacob Schultz, as was his custom at St. Peter's, namely Trommete 8, Zinke 8, Nassat 3, Gemshorn 2, Hohlfleute 4 foot; in the Rückpositiv, Prinzipal 8 and Oktave 4 foot for the soft middle part; in the pedal Posaune 16 foot, Prinzipal-Baß 24, Trommete 8 and 4 foot, Cornet 2 foot. All these stops, except Prinzipal 24, were on the Jacobi organ at that time. At the beginning he first played the chorale very plainly and simply, so that the ordinary man, as most of those in the church were, could understand it. Then he treated it fugally and led it through all transpositions, so that he even went through the semitones, and it was admirable, how skillfully he found the original tone again. After this he had to play a violin solo with Mr. Schop, so that his skill with the General-Bass could be heard. . . . He demonstrated that he had a good ear and good judgment, also that he was familiar with the delicate Italian style. Then he had to play a motet of the late Mr. Hieronymus Praetorius from the bass, in six voices, and afterwards vary it on two manuals. Finally, in conclusion, a merry fugue on the full organ.[1]

The "lustige Fuge" at the end might have been similar to Weckmann's Fantasia in D minor, which resembles a canzona, and although it too may have been improvised, it is the only part of the audition for which Kortkamp's report does not specify a given subject, chorale, or bass part as the starting point for improvisation.

Buxtehude's keyboard works include examples of all the genres in which Weckmann was required to play, with the exception of the continuo realization and the variation on the motet. Given the improvisatory nature of this art, it is surprising that so much of this music survives in written form. Buxtehude's twenty-six complete praeludia, all containing fugues, could be described as fantasies in the tone of the fugue. Of his forty-seven complete chorale settings, seven treat the chorale melody fugally, and twenty-seven chorale preludes are composed in a style requiring two manuals and pedal, with a soft middle part. Twelve canzonas, which might be described as "merry fugues," survive, as well as three large ostinato works, representing a genre not included in Weckmann's audition.

The vast majority of these works, catalogued as BuxWV 136–225, would appear to have been composed for the organ, even though the name of this instrument does not appear in a single source for these works. Most of them require the use of the pedal, which is made clear in the sources, in the case of the free works by the word *pedaliter* in the title or the designation *Pedal* at pedal entrances, in the case of the chorales by the frequent use of three staves for melody, middle parts, and pedal, an unusual practice for the time. In addition, many of the sources for the chorales include the manual designations *R[ückpositiv]* and *O[berwerk* or *Organo]*.

Nevertheless, both Ibo Ortgies and Siegbert Rampe have argued recently that Buxtehude did not write these pieces down with the intention of playing them on the organ, but rather to use them as models in the teaching of improvisation and composition, which was done not in the church but at a stringed keyboard instrument in the teacher's home. In Ortgies's words,

> The function of composed organ music in the highly professional realm lay by no means primarily in its performance but in its study for the development of the ability to improvise contrapuntally. Improvisation, contrapuntally correct and complex composing at the instrument, was the art of the organist, which found its learned counterpart in "the science of composition" in the study room. The science of composition created in its written-out works the necessary examples for the art of improvisation by professional organists.
>
> To the extent that individual compositions were not playable on the organ, they could be tried out on pedal clavichords and harpsichords. Such instruments could offer keyboard compasses that were not available on most organs, and stringed keyboard instruments were more flexible in their temperaments.[2]

Ortgies's conclusion rests mainly on his studies of temperament and his hypothesis that all North German organs, including those of St. Mary's, were tuned in quarter-comma mean tone during Buxtehude's lifetime; it is his solution to the problem posed by Buxtehude's many compositions that are not readily playable on a mean-tone organ without subsemitones and with a short octave in the bass. We can certainly imagine that Buxtehude wrote down his compositions in the comfort of the "kleine Schreib und *Studier* Stube" that the church had added on to the Werkhaus for him in 1675, that he had in his home a two-manual clavichord or harpsichord with a fully chromatic pedal, and that he had tuned it to Werckmeister III soon after the publication of the *Orgelprobe* in 1681.

Rampe's working hypothesis is similar: "the protestant organ music of the 17th and 18th centuries originated primarily for didactic purposes and in practice or instruction was played primarily on the clavichord or pedal clavichord."[3] He brings to the discussion an array of information concerning the education of organists in the seventeenth and eighteenth centuries, including the costs of tuition, the content and duration of study, fees charged for the copying of music, and references to the use of the pedal clavichord for teaching.[4] Joel Speerstra's recent study, *Bach and the Pedal Clavichord: An Organist's Guide* has added enormously to our knowledge of the history and pedagogical use of the pedal clavichord, and there can be no doubt that the clavichord, with or without pedals, was the primary teaching tool for organists. Martin Fuhrmann describes the clavichord as

> the first grammar of all keyboard players, and if they understand it well, they can not only play the above-mentioned six instruments [organ, positive, regal, harpsichord, clavicytherium, spinet], but they can also learn other instruments ten times sooner and play them better than one who is inexperienced at the keyboard.[5]

We should note, however, that the one extant contract for teaching by an organist that Rampe offers specifies that instruction will also be given on the organ: in 1787 Johann Christian Kittel agreed to teach Johann Christian Heinrich Rinck for one year, "for one hour each day the pure composition of music, both in playing on the clavier and the organ as well as in harmony."[6]

The sources for Buxtehude's free organ works do often reflect the fact that they had passed from teacher to student; this is particularly true of the Lund tablatures copied by Gottfried Lindemann, who had studied with Friedrich Gottlieb Klingenberg, who in turn had studied with Buxtehude (see chapter 9). And these works undoubtedly served as models to Buxtehude's students for their own improvisation and composition, much of which they would have worked out on a pedal clavichord. But these students were all preparing for careers as church organists, and we can scarcely imagine a teacher providing models to his organ students that could not be played on the organ; it must have been his organ playing that attracted them to him as a teacher in the first place. Surely Buxtehude's written-down praeludia, the summit of his art, must reflect the music that he played on the St. Mary's organs.

Buxtehude's chorale-based works also served as models for his students and other members of the next generation, as Lawrence Archbold has demonstrated for Daniel Erich and Georg Leiding, and Werner Breig for J. S. Bach and Johann Gottfried Walther.[7] But here the extant source transmission runs somewhat differently; we know from Walther, who copied most of the chorale-based works, that his exemplars had come from Werckmeister, who had in turn received the original autographs from Buxtehude, who was hardly his teacher, but rather his friend. And these works, particularly the chorale preludes and variation sets, must have been played on the organ during the liturgy, either as introductions or as *alternatim* verses to the congregational singing. Yet they too demonstrate the same problems with respect to mean-tone tuning and the short octave as do the praeludia, although not to the same degree. For example, nine chorale preludes in G major (BuxWV 182, 187, 191, 192, 197, 208, 209, 214, 215) employ the pitch class D♯ as part of a B-major secondary-dominant to an E minor chord; four of them use A♯ in the same way. These chords form such a characteristic part of Buxtehude's harmonic language that it is difficult to believe that their pitches were not available to him in some way on the organ that he regularly played.

Most of the works in question sound their best when played on a mean-tone organ equipped with subsemitones, as we can hear from Bine Bryndorf's recording on the newly reconstructed Düben organ in the German Church in Stockholm (Dacapo 6.220514) or from Hans Davidsson's performances on the North German organ in Örgryte Nya Kirka, Göteborg (Loft LRCD 1690–95), on the CD accompanying this book. But Buxtehude did not have subsemitones on the organs at St. Mary's, so if we are to continue to claim that he did in fact compose these works for the organ, then we must find a way to play them on a mean-tone organ without subsemitones.

The easiest solution assumes some kind of modified mean-tone tuning yielding a usable D♯ and A♭, and preferably an A♯ as well, which would cover all the *pedaliter* works with the exception of BuxWV 139, 141, 142, 146, 149, 150, 151, 156, and 159. For these we can consider a number of strategies, depending on the placement and importance of the offending notes. Often they go by so quickly that one hardly notices them, or their placement as the bass of a sixth chord renders them much less disturbing. A soft registration makes them much less noticeable, and many of the problematic notes occur in transitional passages in the praeludia, which are well suited to performance with just a principal and tremulant, as we can hear on CD track 5, 03:00. Transposition offers another possibility; it was a skill required of all organists at the time, and it can make a piece in the "transposed modes" [*modos fictos*] such as E major or F♯ minor—which may have been worked out on a well-tempered stringed keyboard instrument—playable on a mean-tone organ.

Even if the pitch problems are solved by modified mean-tone or well-tempered tuning, however, the problem of the short octave in all three manuals and pedal of the St. Mary's organs remains; many of Buxtehude's keyboard works contain low F♯ and G♯, a few even low C-sharps. This problem can only be resolved by acknowledging that the work concept was not so rigid a principle in Buxtehude's day as it later became. Since it is beyond dispute that Buxtehude's art lay in improvisation, we would not expect him to take his tablatures, written down in his study, to the organ with him, although we can expect that he would have carried in his head a good idea of the themes and organizational plans of the pieces he wished to play. At the organ he would have adapted them to the limitations of his instrument, whatever they were. But the *pedaliter* praeludia, where most of the problems occur, are tightly constructed works, and I do not mean to suggest that his performances of them at the organ strayed very far from the versions that have been transmitted to us.

If the organs of St. Mary's were in fact tuned in quarter-comma mean-tone from 1641 until 1782, as Ortgies contends, these same strategies can be applied, but to a much larger group of works, since only twenty-six of the *pedaliter* free works and chorale-based keyboard works fall within the normal E♭–G♯ mean-tone range. The various possibilities are discussed below in connection with individual pieces.

Buxtehude's *manualiter* keyboard works pose fewer problems with respect to tuning than do the *pedaliter* works, even though they could be played on the more easily tuned clavichord and harpsichord. These include four of the praeludia, all eleven canzonas, and a few of the chorale settings, as well as nineteen keyboard suites and six sets of variations on secular melodies.

Canzonas

BuxWV 166–76, 225

Apart from the few works of learned counterpoint discussed in chapter 6, Buxtehude's canzonas offer the only examples of works that are primarily contrapuntal in their design. Half of these twelve works are variation canzonas, belonging to a genre inherited from Frescobaldi and Froberger in which the subjects of several—usually three—successive fugues are variations of each other. The remaining canzonas contain only one fugue, normally quite simple. These works bear various titles in their sources—canzon, canzonetta, fuga—with no particular consistency. Most are nominally in four voices, although all four voices rarely sound simultaneously; BuxWV 167 and 175 are in three voices.

Lively subjects, mainly in eighth and sixteenth notes, are characteristic of all the canzonas. The majority of opening subjects are cast in a distinctly instrumental idiom: lengthy, breathless subjects in steady eighths or sixteenths, employing repeated notes and ornamental figuration to expand the melodic structure, making frequent use of sequence and disjunct intervals (ex. 7-1). The subject of BuxWV 225 in particular recalls the figuration idiomatic to the violin. Fugues of this type belong to the family of fugues that Stefan Kunze calls *Spielfugen*. The numerous ornamental and repeated notes found in these subjects often create dissonances against more slowly moving voices. These dissonances can frequently be identified with the figures of Bernhard's common luxuriant style, as Dietrich Kämper has noted. Five canzonas contain fugues in gigue rhythm, usually in the second or third position within the canzona; BuxWV 174 is a single gigue fugue.

Three canzonas—BuxWV 168, 169, 175—open with fugues whose subjects are more concise and more vocal in style than the others. These subjects, unlike

Example 7-1a. BuxWV 172, mm. 1–3.

Example 7-1b. BuxWV 225, mm. 1–3.

those of the *Spielfugen* and gigues, lend themselves to contrapuntal development. BuxWV 175, for example, is a counterfugue. Its subject (ex. 7-2a) has almost the same melodic structure as that of BuxWV 172 (ex. 7-1a), without the added ornamentation. An inversion of the tonal answer of the first fugue forms the subject of the second fugue (ex. 7-2b). The tonal answer of the second fugue—the original subject in contrary motion—can then serve in the third fugue as the answer in contrary motion to the subject of the first fugue while maintaining the same intervallic structure (ex. 7-2c). In a further exposition of the third fugue at m. 49, the subject of the second fugue is answered in contrary

Example 7-2a. BuxWV 175, mm. 1–3 (first fugue).

Example 7-2b. BuxWV 175, mm. 19–21 (second fugue).

Example 7-2c. BuxWV 175, mm. 39–41 (third fugue).

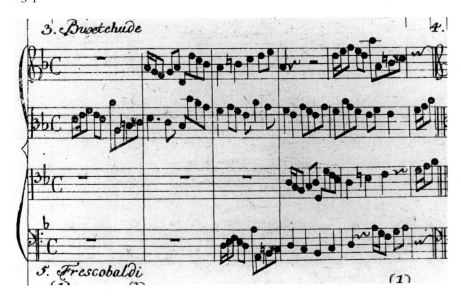

Figure 7-1. Friedrich Wilhelm Marpurg, *Abhandlung von der Fuge* (Berlin, 1753–54), Part I, plate XXXVI, figure 3: Buxtehude, Canzonetta in D Minor (BuxWV 168), mm. 66–70 (New Haven, Yale University Music Library).

motion by the answer of the first fugue. Each of the three voices in the third fugue has the subject and answer both rectus and in contrary motion in the course of four expositions; a fifth exposition occurs in stretto.

Friedrich Wilhelm Marpurg, a student of J. S. Bach, used a portion of BuxWV 168 as an illustration of a counterfugue in his treatise of 1753, *Abhandlung von der Fuge* (fig. 7-1). Marpurg emphasizes that this is an example of a simple fugue, not a double fugue, because only one theme is involved. Marpurg characterizes the imitation in contrary motion of BuxWV 168 as free, probably because the first three notes of the subject form a minor third, D–F, whereas the corresponding notes of the inverted answer form a major third, F–A. He further notes the stretto between the soprano and bass voices in the fifth measure of his illustration and the entrance in parallel thirds in the following measure.[8]

The fugue of Marpurg's example forms the third section of the variation canzona BuxWV 168, beginning at m. 66. A comparison of the subject and answer of this fugue with those of the first and second fugues of the canzona (ex. 7-3) shows that it is the answer in contrary motion, not the subject, of the third fugue that is related to the subject of the opening fugue. The subject of the second fugue retains the exact intervallic structure of the first subject while transforming its rhythm into 3/4 meter. The tonal answer appears before the subject, however, and the first three entrances are in stretto.

Example 7-3a. BuxWV 168, mm. 1–4 (first fugue).

Example 7-3b. BuxWV 168, mm. 30–33 (second fugue).

Fugal theory figures prominently in the writings of two of Buxtehude's Hamburg colleagues, Johann Adam Reincken and Christoph Bernhard. In his treatise of 1670,[9] Reincken mentions counterfugue, "Fuga Inversa," as he calls it, which can occur either with all the entries in contrary motion for a while (as in BuxWV 175, second fugue) or with some entries in direct imitation, others in contrary motion (as in the third fugues of BuxWV 168 and 175). For both Reincken and Bernhard, the most important issue in the composition of fugues concerns the subject and its answer. Although composers had used the tonal answer since the time of Josquin, it was not discussed as a part of fugal theory until the early seventeenth century in Italy and was first introduced to Germany by Marco Scacchi in his *Cribrum musicum* of 1643. Bernhard discusses fugal answers in his *Tractatus compositionis augmentatus* in the context of the modes. He considers a tonal answer to be in the corresponding plagal mode if the subject is in the authentic mode, and vice versa, producing a *consociation* of the two modes. This is the best type of answer to make the mode clear. He understands a real answer as being in the same mode, producing an *aequation* of the modes; it appears more often in stepwise motion than in leaps, more in the middle of a fugue than in the beginning.

Reincken's discussion of fugal answers also takes place within the context of the modes, but he is concerned that the ambitus of the mode not be exceeded by the subject and its answer combined. In his examples, all in the first (Dorian) mode, the opening fifth d′–a′ is answered by the fourth a′–d″ because the fifth a′–e″ would exceed the ambitus of the mode, d′–d″. This reasoning would not explain the tonal answer in the first fugue of BuxWV 168, however, whose subject fills an entire octave. Indeed, Reincken's own fugue subjects often extend to an octave or a ninth. The subjects of all but two of Buxtehude's canzonas have a range of at least an octave. Buxtehude uses mainly tonal answers in the canzonas, and his exceptions are covered by the explanations of both Bernhard and Reincken: real answers are justified if they proceed by step (as in BuxWV 166, m. 76, and BuxWV 225) or if they occur after the initial exposition (as in BuxWV 168, mm. 11, 17, 20; BuxWV 171, m. 11 and BuxWV 173, m. 14).

Reincken also speaks of double fugues, "two fugues together, commonly called Contrafugen," in which the knowledge of double counterpoint is essential.

> One can also develop two or more fugues together, however not continuously but singly, one after the other, and then a few times together and against one another, which is much more artful.[10]

According to Reincken's understanding, then, BuxWV 169 would not be considered a double fugue, because the countersubject that appears in its second section receives no exposition of its own. Buxtehude lends it particular prominence, however, by introducing it alone at m. 28 following a full tonic cadence (ex. 7-4). Its inclusion of a prominent rest is unique among Buxtehude's canzona themes, although rests occur frequently in the subjects of the fugues in the praeludia. Buxtehude employs stretto in BuxWV 168 and 175, as noted, and this too was a

Example 7-4. BuxWV 169, mm. 28–30.

contrapuntal device that interested Reincken. He gives several examples of "imi-tation in short" and emphasizes that it is not necessary for the imitation to be exact in this case.

Buxtehude does not usually employ these devices of contrary motion, counter-subject, and stretto in the more numerous *Spielfugen* and gigue fugues of his can-zonas. The contrapuntal fabric of these pieces is much more loosely woven; their texture often approaches homophony, with the voices that sound against the sub-ject doing little more than providing a chordal accompaniment or moving with the subject in parallel thirds, sixths, or tenths. With the exception of BuxWV 170, all the canzonas that begin with a *Spielfuge* continue to their conclusion in this loose contrapuntal vein. The third fugue of BuxWV 170 (CD track 4, 02:40), however, following a *Spielfuge* and a gigue fugue (CD track 4, 01:36), artfully juxtaposes two themes (ex. 7-5b), both derived from the original answer (ex. 7-5a). The counter-subject—the bass voice at m. 74—outlines the melodic structure in half notes; the subject—the alto voice at m. 74—decorates it in steady eighth notes. This is the only fugue in 3/2 meter within the canzonas; the others are all in common time, or compound meter for the gigues.

Three of the *Spielfugen* (in BuxWV 166, 176, and 225) dissolve into toccata-like free sections, a practice found already in the canzonas of Frescobaldi. The "Fuga" in B♭ (BuxWV 176) is the freest of all Buxtehude's canzonas. Its three fugues merge into each other without sharp sectional divisions, with the first two *Spielfugen* separated by a modulatory toccata section. The subject of the final gigue fugue is but loosely related to the opening subject, and it dissolves into a free ending over dominant and tonic pedal points.

Example 7-5a. BuxWV 170, mm. 3–4, answer in alto.

Example 7-5b. BuxWV 170, mm. 74–75.

Buxtehude's canzonas are all modest works in the modern style, hardly designed to dazzle an audience or to be useful within the liturgy at St. Mary's, and Kämper argues convincingly that these pieces were composed for instructional purposes. Indeed, the gigue portion of BuxWV 166 is found in the notebook (*B* 40268) begun in 1715 by Heinrich Nikolaus Gerber, father of the lexicographer, at the age of thirteen. The four canzonas now at Lund (BuxWV 167, 169, 170, 173), copied by Gottfried Lindemann, probably stem from his study with Friedrich Gottlieb Klingenberg in Stettin and Klingenberg's study with Buxtehude around 1689. Apart from BuxWV 168, 169, and 175, however, Buxtehude's canzonas give the impression of being more useful for instruction in performance than in composition. He employed his contrapuntal art to a much greater degree in his keyboard praeludia and ensemble sonatas than in his canzonas.

Ostinato Works

BuxWV 159–61

Philipp Spitta placed the Passacaglia in D minor (BuxWV 161) and the two ciacconas in C minor and E minor (BuxWV 159, 160) at the head of the first volume of his edition of Buxtehude's organ works, which appeared in 1875. He had been encouraged to publish them by his friend Johannes Brahms, to whom he had sent a copy of the first volume of his Bach biography in 1873. In it, Spitta had written of these three works that "for beauty and importance [they] take the precedence of all the works of the kind at the time, and are in the first rank of Buxtehude's compositions." Brahms, having recently completed his variations on a theme by Haydn (op. 56), which closes with a passacaglia, asked Spitta for copies of the Buxtehude works. On seeing the D-minor passacaglia, he hastily wrote to Spitta in January, 1874:

> Allow me a quick question: when I become acquainted with such a beautiful piece as the Ciaccona [sic] in D minor by Buxtehude, I can hardly resist sharing it with a publisher, simply for the purpose of creating joy for others. But first I must ask you whether you have anything against its publication.[11]

Spitta's opinion of these works was not overblown; both for depth of expression and for drawing on the potential of the organ, these pieces are unequaled among keyboard ostinato works of the seventeenth century.

Brahms was not alone in confusing a ciaccona with a passacaglia; Buxtehude's use of these terms does not demonstrate the distinctions that Alexander Silbiger has drawn between these genres in the works of Frescobaldi, apart from the fact that the 3/2 time signature of the passacaglia may indicate a slower tempo. All three are in the minor mode and in triple meter, with the ostinato extending for four measures. The E-minor ciaccona is built on a descending tetrachord, whereas the other two have bold, disjunct themes, but all three begin on the tonic and end on the dominant. The obvious distinction between Buxtehude's passacaglia and his two ciacconas—that the passacaglia keeps the ostinato intact in the pedal throughout the piece and modulates to two different keys, whereas the ciacconas treat the ostinato more freely but remain in the same key—bears no relation to works of other composers under these titles. Furthermore, Buxtehude's four vocal works with the title "Ciaccona" (BuxWV 57, 69, 70, 92) maintain the ostinato unchanged in the continuo part. Mattheson's attempted distinction in *Der Vollkommene Capellmeister*—whereby the ciaccona proceeds more slowly, prefers major keys and has a constant bass theme, whereas the passacaglia prefers minor keys, is never used in singing but only for dancing, and is restricted to no definite subject—clearly does not apply to Buxtehude's organ works. Johann Gottfried Walther came much closer to the mark in his *Praecepta der musicalischen Composition* (1708), in which he defined a passacaglia as a piece treated in the manner of a ciaccona.

Keyboard ostinato pieces were cultivated mainly in Italy and South Germany, not in the north, and Buxtehude must have been familiar with the southern repertoire in order to exploit this genre so successfully. No ciacconas or passacaglias are found among the keyboard works of Jacob Praetorius, Scheidemann, Tunder, Weckmann, or Reincken, or—with one possible exception—the members of the succeeding generation: Bruhns, Böhm, and Lübeck. Since the composers who were working with this genre—Frescobaldi and his followers, Kerll, Poglietti, Pachelbel—lived in areas where the pedal division of the organ was not so well developed as in the north, it is not surprising that their works are almost entirely *manualiter* and are often restricted to only two voices above the bass.

One northern keyboard ostinato piece may have been known to Buxtehude, a "Chiacona dell pas Egal" (passacaglia?) by Martin Radeck, organist of both Trinity Church and the Church of the Holy Spirit in Copenhagen. His entry in Meder's autograph book is dated just three weeks before Buxtehude's; Radeck may in fact have sent Meder on to Buxtehude. Radeck's Ciaccona in G major is preserved in a tablature of 1710, now at Lund (Litt. G. No. 29), which also contains BuxWV 236. Although the indication "tremulant" in three variations suggests that Radeck intended it for organ, this ciaccona, like its southern cousins, is basically a *manualiter* work and certainly does not exploit the forty-stop instrument with twelve pedal stops that Hans Christoph Fritzsche had built at Trinity Church in 1655. It contains a few novel effects, such as a "cuckoo" variation, a fugal variation, and one variation in A minor, but this modest work could hardly have served as an inspiration to Buxtehude.

Buxtehude's ostinato organ works all demand the use of the pedal, and all three are transmitted uniquely in the same manuscript, the "Andreas-Bach-Buch," discussed in chapter 9, which was copied by Johann Christoph Bach, elder brother of Johann Sebastian. The participation of the pedal is clearly indicated in each work. In the passacaglia, the word *pedaliter* is included with the title, and the pedal presumably carries the ostinato throughout the piece. Like most keyboard manuscripts of the day, the "Andreas-Bach-Buch" is written on two staves, with the participation of the pedal partly indicated by the word *Pedal* at its entrances and partly left to the discretion of the performer. This is the case with the two ciacconas, in which the ostinato is not confined to the bass part. Particularly idiomatic for the pedal, and so marked in the manuscript, are the sixteenth-note thirds, easily played with alternating feet, at m. 101 of the E-minor ciaccona.

In all three pieces, the pedal is used chiefly for the ostinato, thereby freeing both hands to carry on more complex variations above it than can occur in a *manualiter* work. In the D-minor passacaglia, for example, an eighth-note figure of a descending tetrachord circulates through three parts above the bass in variations 5–7, and in variation 8 a fourth part joins in the manuals with a new motive. The entire work is composed in four or five voices. The participation of the pedal not only thickens the texture but also widens the range without leaving a void in the middle. The climactic variations 24–26 exploit almost the entire range of the instrument. With the probable use of 16′ stops in the pedal and upper partials in the manuals, the extremes of pitch between right hand and pedal sound even wider than they appear on the page. The two ciacconas contain a greater variety of textures, varying from two to five voices.

Buxtehude's expressive use of harmony is particularly noteworthy in the E-minor ciaccona. Its opening measures contain dissonances that Bernhard allowed only in the theatrical style, an announcement that this work intends to plumb emotional depths unimagined in the playful canzonas. At variation 20, the descending tetrachord of the ostinato assumes the chromatic form. In variations 22 and 23 it reverses itself against a descending chromatic line in the soprano, the pedal drops out, and the parts converge inwardly to a point where all four voices occupy the range of only a fifth at the middle of the keyboard (ex. 7-6). Such intensity seeks relief, however, and the piece ends in a blaze of sixteenth-note figuration.

All three of these ostinato works contain a formal design that focuses beyond the individual cells of each variation and groups them into larger sections. Such a

Example 7-6. BuxWV 160, mm. 89–92 (variation 23).

plan emerges most clearly in the D-minor passacaglia, which is divided into four sections, each of seven variations, with the two inner sections in F major and A minor, the outer sections in D minor. This arrangement recalls Frescobaldi's "Cento Partite," but whereas Frescobaldi's somewhat haphazard sectional groupings produce a modal design, Buxtehude's sections in the passacaglia reflect a symmetrical and tonal plan. He achieves tonal variety in the C-minor ciaccona by means of transitions between sections in strict form and in the E-minor ciaccona with the section employing chromaticism. Within the larger sections, pairings of two variations, sometimes repeated exactly, sometimes varied, replace the indications to repeat each variation that are normally found in works of this sort. Buxtehude handles this procedure with great freedom, sometimes expanding the varied repetition to three variations, sometimes omitting the repetition altogether.

Praeludia

BuxWV 136–53, 155–58, 162–65

Buxtehude's praeludia—including a few works titled "Toccata" or "Praeambulum," but none titled "Praeludium und Fuga"—form the heart of his repertoire for organ, indeed of his works altogether. These were the pieces collected and copied during the eighteenth century by the circle of students, relatives, and friends of J. S. Bach, and theirs were the principal manuscripts of Buxtehude's works known to Spitta. Volume I of his edition contains seventeen praeludia, and although multitudes of Buxtehude's works have come to light since 1875, the pieces of this volume, particularly its fourteen *pedaliter* praeludia, remain the works by Buxtehude that are most admired, most performed, most recorded, and most discussed.

The essence of Buxtehude's praeludia lies in the juxtaposition of sections in a free, idiomatic keyboard style with sections in a structured, fugal style. As is the case with his vocal concertos, no two praeludia are alike. They may contain one, two, or three fugues, using a wide variety of styles and contrapuntal devices—or lack of them. The free sections, which invariably open them and which normally appear later in the piece, are composed in a dazzling array of textures and styles, from lengthy pedal points to fleeting sixteenth- and even thirty-second-note scales and arpeggios, from pure chordal homophony through various stages of its decoration to imitative counterpoint and fugato subsections, from tonal stability to daring harmonic excursions.

The relative weight that Buxtehude gives to the free and fugal sections varies greatly among the praeludia. In the Praeludium in E minor (BuxWV 142), he emphasizes the fugues. It is one of four praeludia to contain three fugues (the others are BuxWV 136, 141, and 150). Their subjects are related to each other as are those of the canzonas, but in a much subtler way. The first (ex. 7-7a) is a canzonalike *Spielfuge*, but unlike the canzona fugues, it is composed to be performed with pedal, and it maintains a full four-voice texture much of the time. The second fugue, in 3/2 meter, is perhaps the weightiest, the most contrapuntally elegant, and at the same time one of the most expressive fugues in all the praeludia. Sebastian de Brossard, author of a music dictionary first published in 1703, would undoubtedly have called it a *fuga pathetica*. We must assume that Buxtehude composed the second fugue's subject (ex. 7-7b) first and derived the subject of the first fugue from it. They share an opening leap of a fifth, an octave leap, and a chromatic progression, which forms the main substance of the second subject but is only hinted at in the first. The *saltus duriusculus* of a diminished fourth at the end of the second subject adds extra pathos. Chromaticism disappears completely from the subject of the third fugue (ex. 7-7c), a gigue in 12/8 meter. It emphasizes, instead, the octave leap and the diatonic descent of a fifth.

Buxtehude shows himself at the height of his contrapuntal powers in the masterful second fugue of BuxWV 142. The countersubject in its first two

Example 7-7a. BuxWV 142, mm. 17–18 (subject, first fugue).

Example 7-7b. BuxWV 142, mm. 52–54 (second fugue: subject in soprano, countersubject in alto).

Example 7-7c. BuxWV 142, mm. 114–15 (subject, third fugue).

expositions is a retrograde of the subject at the lower fifth, with the chromatic scale changed to a diatonic one (ex. 7-7b). A new countersubject in eighth notes appears with the third exposition, operating against the subject in both its direct form and in inversion. A stretto beginning at m. 75 alternates entrances of the subject with its inversion. The third fugue, in contrast, is as contrapuntally lax as the second was strict, dissolving into concertato texture after two expositions. The shift in texture emphasizes the powerful dance rhythm of this final section—perhaps a dance of death, given the pathos of the second fugue and the presence of Bernt Notke's *Totentanz* mural in St. Mary's.

The free sections of BuxWV 142 are modest in comparison with its fugues, exploring only two of the many stylistic possibilities encountered in the other praeludia. The opening section offers an example of figural decoration of a basically homophonic texture. As in virtually all of Buxtehude's praeludia, it begins with an opening flourish before settling on the tonic chord in m. 2. This opening section is more tightly knit than most; the opening figure of a sixteenth rest followed by an arpeggio appears in the upper three parts at various times throughout the section. Figural keyboard texture is similar to concertato texture in the tossing of motives between voices, but whereas the voices that do not have the motive often rest in concertato texture, they more often sustain a chord in figural texture. In the free section between the second and third fugues, the chordal structure is more in evidence, and the decoration, where it occurs, is more rhapsodic. Sections such as this often give rise to Buxtehude's most startling harmonies, but he is somewhat restrained here, allowing the main harmonic interest to reside in the second fugue.

The affect of sorrow conveyed by both BuxWV 142 and the ciaccona BuxWV 160 rests in part on their common E-minor tonality, which is also found in some of Buxtehude's most sorrowful vocal works, beginning with the *Klag-Lied* on the death of his father (BuxWV 76) and culminating in the sixth cantata, "Ad Cor," of *Membra* (BuxWV 75). Unlike the E-Phrygian mode of works such as BuxWV 152 and the "Te Deum" (BuxWV 218), E minor is a "modern" mode, and the D♯ of its dominant chord inevitably pushes it beyond the limits of traditional mean tone. If these organ works are to be played on a mean-tone organ, they must be transposed to D minor, and even then a few problems remain in the case of BuxWV 142, whose pitch-class range is the widest of all the praeludia, extending from E♭ to E♯, which becomes D♭ to D♯ when transposed. Clearly Buxtehude conceived this work for a circulating temperament.

The Praeludium in D major (BuxWV 139) contrasts strongly with the E-minor praeludium in the brightness of its D-major tonality, with its concurrent affect of joy and the lightness of its textures, and in the weight placed on its free sections. It has but one fugue (CD track 5, 01:13), whose contrapuntal texture is exceedingly thin. Its subject, consisting only of six repeated notes followed by a decorated descending third, articulated by rests, meshes in hocket fashion with a similar countersubject (ex. 7-8). When these voices are doubled at the third,

Example 7-8. BuxWV 139, mm. 21–24.

sixth, or tenth, a concertato effect is produced that is not at all typical of fugal texture and that recalls a similar interchange between manuals and pedal in mm. 13–16 of the opening free section. The spaces created by the articulation of the repeated notes and the lack of any significant melodic contour in the subject contribute further to the lightness of this fugue.

The two free sections that frame the fugue account for approximately two thirds of the measures in the D-major praeludium. The opening flourish, with its sparkling arpeggios, extends for six measures before arriving at a full tonic chord and the entrance of the pedal, which ushers in figural texture. The lengthy closing free section falls into four subsections. The first (mm. 62–69, CD track 5, 03:01), marked Adagio, introduces a startling shift in tempo, texture, and affect, a sudden mysterious darkness amid the brightness of its surroundings. Its dissonant suspensions recall the *durezze e ligature* of a Frescobaldi elevation toccata. The third subsection (mm. 87–94; CD track 5, 04:25) contains even more startling chords, this time with rhapsodic decoration, well exceeding the bounds of mean-tone temperament. If these sections are played in the manner of an elevation toccata, however, with just a principal and tremulant, not only is the structural contrast underlined, but the out-of-tune notes are scarcely heard as such. The extended sequential passage (mm. 70–86) between these two chordal subsections bears a striking resemblance to a similar section in Weckmann's Toccata in D minor[12] and depends for its effect on the contrasts between manuals and pedal achievable on the organ. Example 7-9 shows the strong textural and harmonic contrast of the second and third subsections. The final subsection (mm. 95–110) emphasizes the subdominant, a frequent occurrence toward the end of a Buxtehude praeludium. The subdominant chordal decoration and toccata-like passagework of mm. 95–103 combine with the tonic pedal point of the final seven measures to form a large-scale plagal cadence.

Buxtehude strikes an almost perfect balance between free and fugal writing in the Praeludium in D minor (BuxWV 140) and the Toccata in F major (BuxWV 157), two works that otherwise contrast rather sharply with one another. The D-minor praeludium is a weighty work with a five-part overall form, alternating three free sections with two fugues. The bold subject of its first fugue (mm. 20–44) is quintessentially Buxtehudian, combining three elements often found separately in his fugue subjects: octave leaps, rests, and repeated notes. The fugue is worked out in triple counterpoint with two simultaneous countersubjects that bridge the rests, providing continuity rather than the concertato effect

Example 7-9. BuxWV 139, mm. 85–91.

found in the fugue of the D-major praeludium. The subject of the second fugue (mm. 64–101), in 3/4 meter, maintains the intervallic structure of the first while dropping the rests and the repeated notes. The surrounding free sections contain rhapsodic chordal progressions, a fugato with two expositions in stretto, virtuosic pedal writing, and a quasi-ostinato passage in the subdominant.

The small F-major toccata (BuxWV 157) contains only two sections, one free and one fugal. Not only are they of approximately the same length but they also share motivic material to an unusual degree: repeated chords, pedal points, and figuration in the pedal. The balance between the sections is also reflected on a smaller scale within them by an unusually regular phrase structure. The work could not be more classic in its design; the first part of its fugue subject even shows an antecedent-consequent pattern, articulated by rests. All three expositions are completely periodic in their structure, with entrances every two measures.

Periodic fugal entrances occur in a number of Buxtehude's praeludia, including all those examined thus far, most notably the D-major praeludium. The regularity of this structure offers a contrast to the irregularity and unpredictability normally associated with the free sections. From a fugue with periodic entrances to a ciaccona is but a short step, and Buxtehude took that step in three praeludia, BuxWV 137 in C major and BuxWV 148, and BuxWV 149, both in G minor.

The C-major praeludium (BuxWV 137) is bold and virtuosic. Its opening flourish takes place with an extravagant pedal solo, answered by sweeping descending scales in thirty-second notes in the manuals (ex. 7-10). This pedal solo provides the motivic material for the subject of a *Spielfuge* (mm. 36–67) and

Example 7-10. BuxWV 137, mm. 6–11.

the three-measure ostinato bass of the closing ciaccona (mm. 75–99). Both the similarity of their themes and the presence of a second free section (mm. 68–74) between the fugue and the ciaccona make it clear that the ciaccona has taken the place of what might otherwise have been a second fugue. Snatches of imitation of the bass theme in the upper parts reinforce this perception. This praeludium offers an excellent example of a piece containing a few notes beyond the range of mean tone or the pedal compass that are either quite easily circumvented or that pass by nearly imperceptibly.

The ciaccona of BuxWV 148 also occurs as the last section of a praeludium, but in this case its role in the overall structure is not quite so clear. Its theme is derived from the development of the subject of the second fugue, which had occurred during its free ending, particularly in the pedal passage of mm. 104–6. The motive of ascending seconds separated by descending fourths had also appeared as the subject of the fugato in the opening free section (mm. 11–16). Following the first six statements of the ostinato in G minor, the ciaccona shifts to B♭ major for eight more variations, returning to G minor only for the last three measures of the piece. This move to the relative major resembles the move to the subdominant in many closing free sections, and the figuration of the upper parts is similar to that found in free sections. Furthermore, this ciaccona follows directly after two fugues that are separated by only a very short free section (mm. 52–57). Despite its periodicity, the ciaccona in BuxWV 148 appears to function more as a closing free section than as a closing fugue.

In BuxWV 149, the great G-minor praeludium, a ciaccona replaces the opening free section. In order to function in this way, it must be somewhat more unpredictable than ciacconas usually are, and Buxtehude achieves the desired irregularity with an extensive opening flourish of steady sixteenth notes, which eventually becomes the figuration over the ostinato. When the bass enters at m. 7, it is not apparent that it will be an ostinato until it is repeated. In addition to its unusual opening free section, this praeludium has other unique qualities. Its first fugue (mm. 21–56) is the only one within the praeludia in ricercar style, and it has a particularly sober effect by virtue of its juxtaposition with the sparkling opening section. The setting of the free section separating the two fugues (mm. 57–80, fig. 11-1), marked Allegro and in the style of a continuo realization, is also unique among the praeludia. Buxtehude derived the subject of the second fugue from that of the first in an unusual manner; by rearranging its key pitches as he changed the rhythm, he transformed a subject of no particular distinction into one both noble and tragic (ex. 7-11). This second fugue, a *fuga pathetica* marked Largo, ranks as one of his finest, and its turn toward B♭ minor at m. 126, beginning with an unprepared flatted seventh, is one of the most expressive moments in any of his fugues. This chord, heard as e♭, b♭, f♯′, c♯″, has a startling but by no means unpleasant effect in mean tone. The closing free section, beginning imperceptibly at m. 145 out of a subdominant entrance

Example 7-11. BuxWV 149, mm. 21–24, mm. 78–82.

of the fugue subject, contains a short ostinato passage on the subdominant, providing a closing link with the opening section. It is here that we run into problems with mean-tone tuning, due to the very prominent A-flats. Since G minor is a traditional mean-tone key, transposition offers no solution in this case. But most of his offending A-flats occur in the trill-like ornamentation, which occurs as oscillating thirds as well as seconds, and it is in a passage such as this that we can easily imagine Buxtehude adapting to the limitations of his organ without altering the structure of his composition.

Buxtehude's inclusion of a ciaccona within a praeludium is as isolated in the surviving North German organ repertoire as his composition of ciacconas alone. And yet Part II of Friedrich Erhard Niedt's *Musicalische Handleitung*, first published in Hamburg in 1706, includes a chapter "Concerning Praeludia and Ciacconas, and how these can be made from a simple General-Bass." The figured bass that he offers as an example contains sixteen measures in common time, ending on a half cadence. At this point, he advises the player to transform its first four measures into triple time and improvise a ciaccona over them, repeating the ostinato as many times as desired, and then to close with a slow "Final" in common time. "One could also introduce other meters here, such as 6/8 or the like, which would also please the listener; but to specify all this here would lead us too far astray." However, he instructs the player on how to begin the praeludium with a run from the discant to the bass, leading to the full chord. Niedt also advises that the note values of the continuo part that he gives do not have to be followed exactly, because "a praeludium must not be bound [to measures], but the more unconstrained and natural it is, the better it will sound." He then prints his full completed example, a simple *manualiter* piece with an opening free section, labelled "Praeludium," beginning with a three-measure opening flourish, a ciaccona of fourteen variations and a closing "Final." "This then would be the complete *Praeludium*, with its included *Chaconne*." Niedt thus uses the word *praeludium* to mean both the opening free section and the entire piece.

Niedt's use of a ciaccona rather than a fugue as the structured element of his praeludium, juxtaposed to the freedom of its opening section, is indeed notable in view of the preserved repertoire from the time in which he wrote. He explicitly intended his instructions for beginners, however, and a ciaccona is certainly more easily improvised than a fugue. The possible section in 6/8 meter could have been a gigue fugue, and perhaps he did not take the time to explain it because his beginning pupil was not yet ready to improvise fugues. Nevertheless, the prominence of the ciaccona within Niedt's discussion of the praeludium leads inevitably to the conclusion that the ciaccona must have been a more common element in the improvised praeludia of North German organists than the preserved written praeludia would lead us to believe.

Buxtehude's praeludia are unlike any of the written praeludia that preceded them, with respect both to the rich variety and exhuberance of their free sections and to the profiled nature of their fugues and ciacconas. The free sections of Scheidemann's *praeambula* are not at all virtuosic, nor are those of Jacob Praetorius. Tunder, by contrast, titled his few surviving compositions in this genre *praeludium* and began them all with an opening flourish. None of the fugues contained in these praeambula and praeludia are so distinctive as most of Buxtehude's. The North German composers of this generation devoted most of their compositional energy to chorale settings, but they made an important contribution to the praeludium by using the rich resources of the North German organ, particularly its pedal, to create praeludia that no longer functioned merely as introductions to parts of the church service but could stand on their own. Onto this northern root, Buxtehude grafted southern virtuosity and contrapuntal art based on thematic variation, which he had found in the toccatas, fantasias, and canzonas of Frescobaldi and Froberger.

Buxtehude's knowledge of Froberger's music almost certainly came through Matthias Weckmann. According to Mattheson's *Ehrenpforte* entry, a friendship between Weckmann and Froberger had begun when Froberger had visited the Dresden court, probably in 1649, and had continued through correspondence thereafter. Froberger had sent Weckmann "a suite in his own hand, wherein he set all the ornaments, so that Weckmann became quite well acquainted with the Frobergian manner of playing." Two Froberger dance movements are preserved in Weckmann's hand in the Hintze manuscript at Yale University. Weckmann's own Fantasia in D minor and Fugue in D minor demonstrate his command of thematic variation within a contrapuntal context.

Weckmann may have served as the conduit for Buxtehude's acquaintance with Frescobaldi's music as well, but Buxtehude could also have had access to it through Tunder. Mattheson believed that Tunder had studied in Italy with Frescobaldi. If this was the case, then it must have occurred before December 1632, when he was appointed Gottorf court organist at the age of eighteen. His predecessor at Gottorf, Johann Heckelauer, was also an organ builder, and he had built an organ in Florence in 1626. Nothing is known of Tunder's life before 1632, and it is conceivable that he did travel to Italy at a young age, either with Heckelauer or later. Alternatively, he could have been an indirect pupil of Frescobaldi by studying his printed music, or copies of it. Whether or not Buxtehude knew or studied with Tunder during his years of apprenticeship, he would have inherited Tunder's music collection upon assuming his post at St. Mary's and marrying his daughter; Tunder's only son was not an organist.

Frescobaldi's influence on Buxtehude's praeludia is acknowledged by Fuhrmann in his definitions of the praeludium and the toccata:

The names of the most important instrumental pieces are the following:

1. Praeludium (from praeludendo), Preslude (French) a playing before; or Praeambulum (from praeambulando) is a going before, when either an organist composes a Sinfonia ex tempore on his keyboard, during which the instrumentalists tune their violins, etc.; or when the instrumentalists at the beginning of a dinner music make

a praeludium among themselves on their viols, which happens at princely courts, and sounds quite good if the instrumentalists understand one another well.

2. Toccata (Italian voice) is also a praeludium on the keyboard, which an organist makes out of his head before he begins a fugue and works it through. The Italian Frescobaldi has set difficult and artful toccatas for the keyboard, and our German Buxtehude has also set some; but in my humble opinion there is a difference between them as between a copy and an original, and if one rubs the compositions of the Italian on the Buxtehudian touchstone, one can see what is chemical- and what is ducat-gold. *Ita hoc Germanus Italizat, imo multis parasangis praecurrit.* [Thus this German Italianizes; indeed he runs many miles ahead.][13]

The first part of Fuhrmann's definitions of praeludium indicates that the term was still in use for purely functional service music, such as the intonations that Buxtehude played before the Kyrie in the morning service and before the concerted music following the afternoon sermon. The second is somewhat reminiscent of Mattheson's account of the performance of a sonata by Kaspar Förster at the home of Christoph Bernhard, "in which each [instrumentalist] had eight measures to play his free improvisations, according to the *Stylo phantastico.*" Fuhrmann's observation in his toccata definition concerning the influence of Italian style on Buxtehude's praeludia has been echoed by more recent scholars, and his preference for the praeludia of Buxtehude over the toccatas of Frescobaldi is likewise reflected by the fact that Buxtehude's praeludia are more frequently performed than Frescobaldi's toccatas. Buxtehude borrowed many motives and styles of figuration from Frescobaldi, as Hedar has shown, but as tonal works, his praeludia sound much more modern than do the toccatas of Frescobaldi, which may account for Fuhrmann's preference.

Buxtehude's Praeludia as Examples of the *Stylus Phantasticus*

Among the styles of composition that Johann Mattheson describes in part I, chapter 10 of *Der vollkommene Capellmeister* (1739), the *stylus phantasticus* takes its place within the larger category of theatrical style. Following an eight-paragraph discussion of this style, which he understands as being almost completely improvisatory, he offers in §95 two short musical examples (fig. 7-2) "for the sake of those who at the present time lack examples of written-out compositions in this style (since our elders were more assiduous at this than contemporary composers)." He identifies the first example as "the beginning of a toccata by Froberger," but this incipit appears nowhere among Froberger's works, and all his extant toccatas begin with a sustained chord. Mattheson's example is in fact the first three measures of Buxtehude's Phrygian praeludium, BuxWV 152, as transmitted by the Lowell Mason Codex at Yale University (fig. 7-3). Mattheson begins his discussion in §88 by saying that "the fantastic name is otherwise very odious, but we have a manner of composing with this name that is well liked."

Figure 7-2. Johann Mattheson, *Der vollkommene Capellmeister* (Hamburg, 1739), part I, chapter 10, §95. The first example gives mm. 1–3 of Buxtehude's Praeludium (BuxWV 152).

A German-English dictionary published in Leipzig in 1716 translates the adjective "fantastisch" as "fantastick or fantastical" and more informatively the noun "Fantast" as "ein mensch von närrischen einbildungen, a fantastical fellow, a man that has strange fancies or fantastick conceits; that is troubled with freaks," which explains the odious connotation of the word. This manner of composing

Figure 7-3. Buxtehude, Praeludium (BuxWV 152), mm. 1–5, in the manuscript "E.B.—1688" (New Haven, Yale University Music Library, Lowell Mason Codex, p. 84).

takes its place principally in the orchestra and on the stage, not only for instruments but also for voices. It actually consists not as much in setting or composing with the pen as in a singing or playing that comes of free genius or, as is said, *ex tempore*. The Italians call this style *a mente non a penna*.

Mattheson also used the phrase *a mente non a penna* in the *Ehrenpforte* to describe the fugues that he and Handel composed in the coach on the way to visit Buxtehude in Lübeck in 1703. The concept of *contrapunto a mente* goes back at least as far as Zarlino's 1558 edition of *Le istitutioni harmoniche,* and is found as well in Giovanni Chiodino's *Arte prattica latina e volgare di far contrapunto a mente e a penna* (1610), which Johann Andreas Herbst translated into German in his *Arte prattica & poëtica* of 1653. Mattheson goes on to qualify his remark concerning extempore composition by adding that written or printed pieces also belong to this style, with titles such as *fantasia, capriccio, toccata,* and *ricercata* in Italian, Boutade and Vorspiel in German. In §91 he also qualifies the statement that this style is found principally in the theater,

but that does not prevent its being heard in the church and in chambers. . . . For what would the organists do if they could not fantasize their preludes and postludes out of their own minds? What would come out would be nothing but wooden, memorized, stiff things.

Keyboard instruments are best for the realization of the fantastic style, and Mattheson holds up Handel's accompaniments to his operas as a model example.

But singers execute it skillfully too, especially Italian singers, and he also mentions the lute, viola da gamba, and transverse flute as "tools" of this style. Italian composers in particular employ this style, which is especially enjoyed by connoisseurs. Sometimes they write it down, to spare singers and instrumentalists the trouble of improvising, but it is better if the composer only indicates the place—usually at the cadence—where such free ideas may enter.

"But what a shame that there are no rules at hand concerning this art of fantasy!" laments Mattheson in §92 before laying down his own rules in §93 and §94:

§93

For this style is the most free and unrestrained manner of composing, singing and playing that one can imagine, for one hits first upon this idea and then upon that one, since one is bound neither to words nor to melody, only to harmony, so that the singer or player can display his skill. All kinds of otherwise unusual progressions, hidden ornaments, ingenious turns and embellishments are brought forth without actual observation of the measure and the key, regardless of what is placed on the page, without a formal theme and ostinato, without theme and subject that are worked out; now swift, now hesitating, now in one voice, now in many voices, now for a while behind the beat, without measure of sound, but not without the intent to please, to overtake and to astonish. These are the essential marks of the fantastic style.

§94

In this manner of composing, one is bound only to the rules of harmony, and to no others. Whoever can bring forth the most artful decorations and the most unusual occurrences succeeds best. And if now and then a regular fast meter infiltrates, it lasts only a moment; if no others follow, then the meter takes a vacation. On account of its unrestrained character, themes and ostinatos cannot be completely excluded, but they cannot be joined directly to one another, much less can they be properly worked out: for those authors who work through formal fugues in their fantasias or toccatas have no proper concept of this noble style, to which nothing is so opposed as order and constraint. And why should a Toccata, boutade or caprice choose a certain key in which it must [also] close? may it not stop in whatever key it wishes? Indeed, must it not often be led from one key into another completely contrary and distant one when a regular song follows it? This condition is observed as little in writing out as the aforementioned, and yet it certainly belongs to the characteristics of the fantastic style.

It appears from his final remark that with respect both to the inclusion of formal fugues and to tonal closure Mattheson knew of many written fantasias and toccatas that did not conform to his ideal of the *stylus phantasticus*.

Mattheson drew both the concept of the *stylus phantasticus* and some of the language in his discussion from Athanasius Kircher's *Musurgia universalis*, published in 1650. But he introduced such significant changes into his own account of the style that Kircher's meaning is almost completely contradicted. Kircher's *stylus phantasticus* demonstrates the skill of the composer, chiefly through contrapuntal artifice; Mattheson's *stylus phantasticus* demonstrates the improvisatory skill of the performer and rejects formal fugues.

Kircher	Kircher	Mattheson (departures underlined)
The fantastic style is suitable for instruments. It is the most free and unrestrained method of composing; it is bound to nothing, neither to words nor to a melodic subject; it was instituted to display genius	Phantasticus stylus aptus instrumentis, est liberrima, & solutissima componendi methodus, nullis, nec verbis, nec subiecto harmonico adstrictus ad ostentandum ingenium,	§93. Denn dieser Styl ist die allerfreieste und ungebundenste Setz-<u>Sing- und Spiel</u>-Art, die man nur erdencken kan, . . . da man sich weder an Worte noch Melodie, obwol an Harmonie, bindet, nur damit <u>der Sänger oder Spieler</u> seine Fertigkeit sehen lasse;
and to teach the hidden design of harmony and the ingenious composition of harmonic phrases and fugues;	& abditam harmoniae rationem, ingeniosumque harmonicarum clausularum, fugarumque contextum fugarumque contextum	§94. <u>daher denn diejenigen Verfasser, welche in ihren Fantasien oder Toccaten förmliche Fugen durcharbeiten, keinen rechten Begriff von dem vorhabenden Styl hegen.</u>
it is divided into those [pieces] that are commonly called fantasias, ricercatas, toccatas, sonatas.	dividiturque in eas, quas *Phantasias, Ricercatas, Toccatas, Sonatas* vulgò vocant.	§88. Wiewol die so genannten: Fantasie, <u>Capriccie</u>, Toccatae, Ricercate &c. sie mögen geschrieben oder gedruckt seyn, allerdings hieher gehören.
For compositions of this type see the pieces in three voices composed by us in book V, fol. 243 and 311 and regard those adapted to the various instruments in book VI, fol. 466, 480, 487.	Cuiusmodi compositiones vide in libro V fol. 243. & 311. à nobis composita triphonia fol. 466. 480. 487. & libr. VI varijs instrumentis accomodatas considera.	

Kircher prints all five musical examples complete on the announced pages. The three-voice work of his own composition on page 243 is a vocal piece to the text "In lectulo per noctes quesivi" (Song of Solomon 3:1-2a); he introduces it as an example of counterpoint without a cantus firmus. The remaining examples are instrumental: the triphonia by Kircher on page 311; the *Phantasia supra Ut, re, mi, fa, sol, la* by Froberger as an example of harpsichord music on page 466; a sinfonia for four lutes by Lelio Colista on page 480; and a sinfonia for two violins and two violas by Gregorio Allegri on page 487. The five pieces have in common their lack of a cantus firmus and their use of imitative counterpoint. Kircher's introductory remarks concerning the Froberger piece are noteworthy, for they anticipate his discussion of *stylus phantasticus*:

Clavicymbala, Organa, Regalia & omnia polyplectra instrumenta musica . . . compositiones requirunt, quae quidem tales debent esse, vt ijs organoedus non tantum ingenium suum ostendat sed & ijs veluti praeambulis quibusdam auditorum animos praeparet, excitetq; ad symphoniaci concentus sequuturi apparatum; Vocant plerique huiusmode harmonicas compositiones praeludia, Itali Toccatas, Sonatas, Ricercatas cuiusmodi hic unam exhibemus, quam D. Io. Iacobus Frobergerus Organedus Caesareus celeberrimi olim Organedi Hieronymi Frescobaldi discipulus, supra Vt, re, mi, fa, sol, la exhibuet eo artificio adornatam, Vt siue perfectissimam compositionis methodum, fugarumq; ingeniosè se sectantium ordinem; siue insignem temporis mutationem, varietatemque spectes, nihil prorsus desiderari posse videatur: adeoque illam omnibus Organoedis, tanquam perfectissimum in hoc genere compositionis specimen, quod imitentur, proponendum duximus.

Harpsichords, organs, regals and all multiplucked musical instruments . . . require compositions, which indeed must be such, that with them the organist not only shows his own genius, but also with them as preambles as it were he prepares and excites the spirits of the listeners for the entertainment of the symphonic harmony that will follow. Many call harmonic compositions of this type praeludia, Italian toccatas, sonatas, ricercatas, of which manner we present one, which J. Jacob Froberger, imperial organist and formerly pupil of the most celebrated organist Hieronymus Frescobaldi made on ut, re, mi, fa, sol, la, prepared with such workmanship that whether you observe the most perfect method of composition and of fugues, the order of things following themselves cleverly, or the remarkable change of the time, it seems that nothing at all can be missing; and therefore we consider it to be set out before all organists as a most perfect example of composition of this kind, which they might imitate.

Kircher's *Musurgia* enjoyed wide circulation in Germany in its original Latin edition, and in 1662 it appeared in greatly abbreviated form in a German translation by Andreas Hirsch. He reduced Kircher's discussion of each of his ten styles—*Ecclesiasticus, Canonicus, Motecticus, Phantasticus, Madrigalescus, Melismaticus, Theatricus, Choraicus, Symphoniacus, and Dramaticus*—to a brief sentence, without any musical examples: "*Stylus phantasticus* pertains only to instruments, where the composer just displays his art and the elegance of his themes."[14] Kircher's musical examples for this style, however, had included one vocal piece. In his new book on the *stylus phantasticus*, Paul Collins devotes an entire chapter to Kircher, reprints excerpts from all of his musical examples, and gives a very useful summary of the scholarly commentary to date. One wonders, however, why "In lectulo meo" does not belong to the *stylus motecticus* or the instrumental ensemble pieces by Kircher, Colista, and Allegri to the *stylus symphoniacus*.

Because Froberger's hexachord fantasy is the only keyboard piece in Kircher's group of examples, it has received the most attention. It displays contrapuntal art to a high degree, consisting of seven different treatments of the hexachord subject in various meters and manifestations. Froberger was in Rome in 1648–49,[15] and Pieter Dirksen, noting the total absence of the term *stylus phantasticus* in any treatise composed by an Italian, has suggested that Froberger, rather than Kircher, may even have "invented" the concept.[16] If this is the case, then it would help to explain the incongruity of Kircher's other examples. Froberger's hexachord fantasy is in fact bound to a melodic subject—the hexachord—but it beautifully illustrates "the ingenious composition of harmonic phrases and fugues," and the logic behind the ordering of its seven sections lies somewhat hidden, or, as Kircher states in his introduction, "following themselves cleverly." A work composed in the Kircher/Froberger concept of the *stylus phantasticus*, then, should include a succession of sections incorporating imitative counterpoint and arranged in an unpredictable way. Froberger shared many secrets with Kircher, as his letter of 1649 attests, including the fact that he had taken the trouble to get someone else to copy a canonic psalm that he was sending, so that Kircher could pass it off as his own.[17]

Dirksen views Kircher's *stylus phantasticus* as a skill of composition, not extemporization, but in the seventeenth century composition was taught and practiced *a mente* as well as *a penna*. Given the history of *fantasia* as an art of contrapuntal improvisation, as Dirksen himself documents, is it not possible that Froberger had first improvised, or rather *fantasized*, this hexachord fantasy before writing it down? Could its origins in improvisation explain the fact that this style enjoys the greatest freedom? Could an origin in improvisation be the unwritten distinguishing characteristic of the *stylus phantasticus*, inherent in the hidden design of its harmony?

Although Froberger's hexachord fantasy could not have been further away from what Mattheson had in mind by the *stylus phantasticus*, Mattheson was perhaps following Kircher in choosing as an illustration a piece that he thought was by Froberger. But, unlike Kircher, he printed only three measures of it, so it is impossible to tell whether he considered the entire work an example of the *stylus phantasticus* or only its opening free section. BuxWV 152 consists of a figural opening free section, two fugues on varied subjects, and a short closing free section. Its Phrygian mode and the style of its first fugue, with a real answer at the lower fifth, make it sound archaic when compared with the Buxtehude praeludia we examined earlier, and it contains no displays of virtuosity or startling harmonies. Its two fugues are joined directly to one another, and they dominate the work as a whole. Would Mattheson have considered these two fugues "formal fugues"?

Mattheson devotes four chapters in part III of *Der vollkommene Capellmeister* to a discussion of fugues: simple fugues ("the most important, most used and most tolerable"), circle fugues (canons), invertible counterpoint, and double fugues. Like Bernhard and Reincken, he gives over the major portion of his discussion of simple fugues in chapter 20 to the matter of subjects and answers. Like his predecessors, Mattheson recommends that the range of the subject be confined to a fifth or a sixth, and he gives a practical reason for this restriction:

> No singer's voice will extend ordinarily in the same strength to two octaves; seldom to two sixths; but always to two fifths, nine to ten steps. And this is the surest way. I speak of fifths like this, because every voice must have the theme at least once as antecedent and once as consequent: hence the mentioned range is needed. (§127)

Reincken had not touched upon this aspect of fugue construction in his treatise, but Johann Gottfried Walther voiced the same requirement in his *Praecepta der musicalischen Composition* of 1708:

> These voices [*Dux* and *Comes*] are exchanged among one another until each voice (whether it is singing or playing) has had both the *Dux* and the *Comes* (especially if the fugue shall be long, and the *Ambitus* does not prevent it).[18]

Theile's fugues in the *Musikalisches Kunstbuch*—Fuga à 3, Praeludium à 4, and sections 2 and 6 of the Sonata à 5—all consist precisely of an entrance of subject and answer in each voice. Mattheson lays down no other formal requirements for a simple fugue other than the alternation of *dux* and *comes* in the first exposition. To be good, however, a fugue must also contain unexpected entries with suspensions and syncopations, the evasion of full cadences, and stretto. (§104)

Even though Buxtehude composed his fugues long before Mattheson wrote *Der vollkommene Capellmeister*, the majority of them follow Mattheson's conditions not only for formal fugues but for good fugues as well. Neither of the two fugues in BuxWV 152, however, contains entrances of the subject and answer in each of their four voices, and BuxWV 152 is unique among the multifugue praeludia in this respect. Its first fugue contains eleven entrances of the theme following the first exposition, but the tenor voice contains only subjects and the alto only answers. The same is true for the second fugue, in which four entrances follow the first exposition. Both of these fugues maintain contrapuntal texture throughout, however, a characteristic not always found in Buxtehude's praeludia fugues, a number of which dissolve into concertato or homophonic texture toward the end. The first fugue of BuxWV 152 also contains evaded cadences, unexpected entrances in the mediant and submediant, and a brief stretto.

Although Mattheson might not have considered the fugues of BuxWV 152 to be proper fugues, he still would have done far better to choose Buxtehude's Praeludium in F♯ minor (BuxWV 146) as an illustration of his concept of the *stylus phantasticus*. In this work, Buxtehude "gives the reins to his fancy," to use Spitta's words, and shifts the balance between free and fugal writing strongly in favor of the free sections. Its opening free section falls into two distinct subsections, "now swift, now hesitating," the first built around an opening flourish and a pedal point with sixteenth-note figuration throughout, the second in a chordal-sequential style based on quarter notes, ending with a rhapsodic cadence. The extensive final closing section begins hesitatingly with a chordal-rhapsodic passage (mm. 79–86) in which Buxtehude explores G♯ minor, the most distant harmonic realm found in any of his works. It then erupts into a virtuosic tour de force including an ostinato that is not at all "properly worked out," a two-measure pattern that appears in varied form, once in F♯ minor (mm. 94–95), twice in C♯ minor (mm. 99–102), and five times in diminution in B minor (mm. 114–18). Buxtehude's choice of F♯ minor for this piece demonstrates another aspect of the freedom inherent in its "fantastic" style. It is unplayable in this key on a mean-tone organ—even with subsemitones—but it works quite well, even if it loses some of its edge, when transposed to G minor, as Harald Vogel has demonstrated in his recording on the Langwarden organ, tuned in modified mean tone.

The second of the two fugues of the F♯-minor praeludium (mm. 50–78), marked Vivace, would have pleased Mattheson in not being "properly worked out"; its single complete exposition has the breathless quality of a fugato, and it soon dissolves into an extensive free ending, which includes at m. 67 a statement in A major of the quasi-ostinato that will reappear in the closing free section. The first fugue, marked Grave (mm. 30–49), must be considered a "formal fugue," however. The subject of this *fuga pathetica*, with its dotted rhythm and poignant leap of a diminished seventh, unfolds spaciously. Its two expositions contain the required entrances of subject and answer in each voice, together with a countersubject. Although it is quite short, this fugue is both "properly worked out" and memorable. So, too, and often to a considerably greater degree, are the fugues in most of Buxtehude's other praeludia. Even those whose contrapuntal texture dissolves at the end often contain entrances of subject and answer in each voice before this occurs, as in the single fugue of BuxWV 145 or the second fugue of BuxWV 155. We might even suspect that Mattheson might have been thinking of Buxtehude when he wrote that "those authors who work through formal fugues in their fantasies or toccatas have no proper concept of this noble style, to which nothing is so opposed as order and constraint."

Since Buxtehude lived in the generation between Kircher and Mattheson, one might expect that his own concept of the *stylus phantasticus*—if he thought of it by that name—or perhaps better, the style(s) suitable for praeludia, would fall somewhere between the contrary concepts articulated eighty-nine years apart by these two encyclopedists of music. Indeed, a blend of the ideas of Kircher and Mattheson illuminates Buxtehude's praeludia considerably. In them he demonstrated his genius both as a composer—undoubtedly an improvising composer—and as a performer. Fugues such as the second of the E-minor preludium (BuxWV 142) and the first of the D-minor preludium (BuxWV 140) recall his studies of learned counterpoint. In dazzling free sections such as those of the C-major praeludium (BuxWV 137) and the F♯-minor praeludium (BuxWV 146) the player "can display his skill."

Although Mattheson's concept of the *stylus phantasticus* does not adequately explain Buxtehude's praeludia as complete works, it brilliantly describes their free sections, in which textures shift constantly at the whim of the composer, fugatos and quasi-ostinatos are never "properly worked out," and the key often changes between the beginning and the end. Mattheson's remarks concerning the metrical freedom of the *stylus phantasticus*—that meter sometimes "takes a vacation," that a regular meter may occur within this style, but will not last long, that one sometimes plays behind the beat—are of utmost importance to modern performers of this music. So, too, his emphasis on the improvisatory nature of this style. Some of the simpler chordal sections in the praeludia—mm. 52–57 of BuxWV 148, for example—seem to cry out for improvised rhapsodic ornamentation such as Buxtehude wrote out elsewhere, perhaps to spare the player the trouble of improvising, more likely to teach a pupil how to do it. In this respect, we are reminded of Fuhrmann's definition of a toccata as "a praeludium on the keyboard, which an organist makes out of his head before he begins a fugue and works it through" and that in his Hamburg audition Weckmann "fantasized on the full organ in the tone of the fugue."

Mattheson can also be credited with recognizing that the *stylus phantasticus* properly belongs with theatrical style. The display of virtuosity, the sudden shifts of style, the rhetorical pauses of Buxtehude's praeludia are all highly dramatic. Their chordal-rhapsodic sections have more than once been characterized as "organ recitatives," and, like recitatives in vocal music, they often begin on a sixth chord in a new key. The free sections abound in dissonances that Bernhard allowed only in the theatrical style; the fugues generally do not. With respect to the theatrical style in general, Bernhard wrote:

> *Omnium rerum satietas* [one can have too much of a good thing]. Therefore one should see to it that one brings an aria into the recitative from time to time, like maxims at the close of periods. Therefore a poet should bring many songs into a theatrical work.[19]

The fugues of Buxtehude's praeludia serve a function analogous to the arias of an oratorio or opera. Like pieces in strophic form, they are tonally stable and reiterate a musical idea with a certain degree of predictability; they give the listener a melody that he or she can easily remember. And the role that Kircher assigned to preludes—to "prepare and excite the spirits of listeners" is similar to that of arias in dramatic music. The character of a Buxtehude fugue usually reflects the mode of the piece: the joyous, playful *Spielfuge* mostly in the major mode, the *fuga pathetica*, which Brossard defined as "appropriate for expressing a passion, especially sorrow," always in the minor. It comes as no surprise that Buxtehude, the composer and producer of the Lübeck Abendmusiken, should have composed and performed organ music of such a dramatic nature.

Finally, Mattheson can be credited with demonstrating that the *dispositio* of a well-ordered musical work follows the principles of classical rhetoric, even though it is unlikely that he would have applied the scheme that he lays out for an aria by Marcello in *Der Vollkommene Capellmeister* (II/14) to a work in his version of the *stylus phantasticus*. Sharon Gorman does so in her dissertation "Rhetoric and Affect in the Organ Praeludia of Dieterich Buxtehude," showing how the opening and closing free sections correspond to *Exordium* and *Peroratio*, the fugues to *Narratio* and *Confirmatio* in a forensic speech as described by Quintilian, and how this structure controls the use of figures. Speeches, too, were often improvised, but the orator relied not only on an underlying *dispositio* but also on images committed to memory, which Quintilian called *loci*. In the sixteenth century, Claudius Sebastiani joined this term with *fantasia* to describe musical images to be memorized for the purpose of contrapuntal improvisation.[20] These evolved into Chiodino's *loci communes musicales*, which Herbst translated into German, along with rules for composing invertible counterpoint *a mente*. With tools such as this, Buxtehude could carry the essence of his great praeludia in his memory and play a version that suited his instrument. It is striking that in his great G-minor praeludium (BuxWV 149), the problematic A-flats in the second fugue occur only after he has fulfilled the requirements of a "proper fugue" by providing an entrance of subject and answer in each voice, which would have flowed almost automatically once the subject was set.

Buxtehude's best opportunity to improvise such grand works may have come during privately arranged concerts for members of the business community along the lines of Tunder's stock-exchange concerts or as a postlude to the church services at St. Mary's. Five services in particular recommend themselves: the Vespers services that preceded the Abendmusiken. At the end of these services, those members of the audience who did not belong to St. Mary's parish and had not attended the Vespers service had to find their places in the church. During this time, we can imagine that Buxtehude took the opportunity to combine postlude and prelude with music that was both functional and artistic.

Chorale Settings

A specialty of the North German organist lay in the imaginative presentation of Lutheran chorales, and Buxtehude's forty-seven chorale settings make up the majority of his works for organ. The chorale thus assumes a much more significant role in his organ music than in his vocal music, and Buxtehude's choice of chorales within these two groups of works is markedly different as well. Whereas settings of chorales with melodies composed before 1550 form only about one third of the vocal chorale settings, they amount to over three quarters of the organ settings. This disparity suggests that Buxtehude's organ settings were more functional in nature, intended to complement the congregational singing of hymns that the ministers chose. For his vocal works, he enjoyed the freedom to choose more modern chorales.

Nearly all of the chorales from the early Reformation that Buxtehude set for organ may be found in both the *Geystliche Lieder* published by Valentin Babst in 1545—the last hymnal published with a foreword by Luther—and Hans Thomissøn's *Den danske Psalmebog* of 1569, the hymnal that was still in use during Buxtehude's youth in Helsingør. In only two instances—"Komm, Heiliger Geist, Herre Gott" and "Jesus Christus, unser Heiland, der den Tod überwand"—does *Den danske Psalmebog* employ a different melody from that of Babst, and Buxtehude used the traditional German melodies in his settings of these chorales. Most of the chorales that he set for organ, then, would have been familiar to him from the time of his youth.

The texts of virtually all the chorales that Buxtehude set for organ are contained in the *Lübeckisches Gesangbuch* of 1703 and their melodies in both Pagendarm's chorale book of 1705 and in the older chorale book from St. Mary's (here abbreviated MK13) described in chapter 3. The text for "Danket dem Herren" (BuxWV 181) is missing from the Lübeck hymnal, but its melody is found both in MK13 and in Pagendarm's setting of the similar text "Waß Lobes solln wir dir, o Vater, singen." Also, Pagendarm did not set "Ich dank dir schon durch deinen Sohn" (BuxWV 195), although the text is present in the hymnal. The Lübeck hymnal, like most hymnals to this day, arranged its hymns in the order of the church year and various topics of the faith. Appendix 6 lists all the chorales set by Buxtehude, together with their designated use in the Lübeck hymnal and information concerning their appearance in the Danish hymnal, MK13, and Pagendarm.

In the melodies for the chorales of the early Reformation, both MK13 and Pagendarm generally retained the original intervallic structure, as represented by Babst and the Danish hymnal, but brought them up to date by adding accidentals, making the rhythm more uniform and occasionally adding ornamental notes. Buxtehude's organ settings are often highly ornamented, but their melodic structure is normally quite close to these melodies, and in twenty-seven settings in the same key as well. In no instance do the Lübeck chorale books offer a different melody for a chorale that Buxtehude set, but in one case their melody varies significantly. Buxtehude's setting of "Ach Gott und Herr" (BuxWV 177) is based on a version of the melody in the minor mode dating from 1625 (Zahn 2050), whereas both MK13 and Pagendarm give a later version in the major mode (Zahn 2051). In only one organ setting—*Wär Gott nicht mit uns diese Zeit* (BuxWV 222)—does Buxtehude's melody correspond more closely to the version in the Danish hymnal than to that of Pagendarm; it is missing from MK13.

Unlike his free organ works, Buxtehude's chorale settings contain no genre designations in their titles, only the name of the chorale. They are easily divided, however, into three occasionally overlapping types: chorale preludes, chorale variations, and chorale fantasias. Most frequently encountered and most characteristically Buxtehudian are the chorale preludes, short pieces in which the chorale melody is stated just once in one voice, most often in the soprano. Cycles of such settings, or chorale variations, account for only six works. In the chorale fantasias, each phrase of the chorale is successively developed at considerable length in a number of voices.

Chorale Fantasias

BuxWV 188, 194, 195, 196, 203, 204, 210, 212, 218, 223

Kircher would probably not have accepted the chorale fantasia as belonging to the *stylus phantasticus* because of its adherence to a cantus firmus. But North German organists in the old Hanseatic cities—Scheidemann, Jacob Praetorius, Weckmann, Reincken, and Vincent Lübeck in Hamburg, Tunder and Buxtehude in Lübeck, Delphin Strungk in Braunschweig, Peter Morhard in Lüneburg—fused these two opposing principles to create a genre that flourished only briefly and was not named as such at the time. J. S. Bach participated in this tradition when he improvised for nearly half an hour at the organ of St. Catherine's Church in Hamburg in 1720 on the chorale "An Waßerflüßen Babylon," "in different ways, just as the better organists of Hamburg in the past had been used to do at the Saturday vespers," according to his obituary. This was the same chorale on which Weckmann had improvised during his audition at St. Jacobi in 1655, in which "he treated it fugally and led it through all transpositions, so that he even went through the semitones, and it was admirable, how skillfuly he found the original tone again." Reincken in turn had produced his own fantasia on this chorale, 327 measures in length, which he had composed in 1663 to demonstrate his ability to succeed Scheidemann as organist of St. Catherine's, a story recounted by Walther in his *Lexicon* entry on Scheidemann. Reincken's response to Bach's performance, "I thought that this art was dead, but I see that in you it still lives," can be understood as the epitaph of the genre in North Germany.

In treating each phrase of the chorale melody separately and in different voices, the chorale fantasia grew out of the organists' practice of playing and improvising on motets; recall that Weckmann was also required to do this in his audition. We can see this process in the most archaic of all Buxtehude's chorale settings, *Ich dank dir schon durch deinen Sohn* (BuxWV 195), which might be called a chorale ricercar on account of its long note values and totally contrapuntal style. Its first section, in alla breve notation, and its third section, in 3/2, develop the first and third phrases of the chorale canonically. The second and fourth sections, in common time, are both composed in invertible counterpoint: the second section in quadruple counterpoint and the fourth in triple counterpoint. Its only sectional contrasts lie in meter, contrapuntal procedure, and the presence or absence of countersubjects.

Most chorale fantasias resemble the praeludium in their strong sectional contrasts and the vocal concerto in their emphasis on opposing bodies of sound.

In the vocal concerto, these contrasting bodies of sound may be produced by a singer and a chorus, a singer and instruments, two singers, or even a singer and continuo. In the organ fantasia, they are achieved through the spatially separated divisions of the organ, or Werke, played by separate manuals and pedal. The Rückpositiv, in particular, hanging over the balcony of the organ loft or, as in the large organ at Lübeck, housed in a forward tower to either side of the organist, projects its sound into the church with a greater immediacy than do the other divisions. Weckmann's registration for his chorale improvisation employed the Rückpositiv for the "soft middle part," and used reeds for the contrasting parts in Oberwerk and Pedal. Such a registration might be suitable for the first thirteen measures of Buxtehude's grandest chorale fantasia, *Nun freut euch, lieben Christen gmein* (BuxWV 210), in which the first two phrases of the chorale appear in highly ornamented form, accompanied by three lower parts, divided between Oberwerk and Pedal. The accompaniment of the first phrase is in concertato style, however, with the part in the Oberwerk beginning with a competing flourish and interjecting punctuated chords at each pause in the soprano melody, so in this case the middle part cannot be too soft; the divisions must balance each other in strength while they contrast in quality, as between reeds and principals.

These first thirteen measures of *Nun freut euch, lieben Christen gmein* have worked through two of the seven phrases of the chorale and over one quarter of the notes it contains, and yet Buxtehude's composition will continue for another 245 measures. It is based on a hymn that Martin Luther had set to a fifteenth-century secular tune, given in example 7-12 in the MK 13 version.

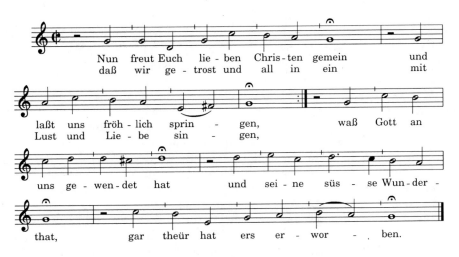

Example 7-12. "Nun freut euch, lieben Christen gmein," MK 13 melody.

Buxtehude's expansive setting of this melody falls into ten sections, each articulated by a change in texture, motivic material, and sometimes meter. In some sections, such as section II (mm. 13–44, phrase 3), IV (mm. 86–110, phrase 5) and VII (mm. 151–68, phrase 6), a complete phrase sounds clearly and recognizably in half notes. In others, the phrase is fragmented and repeated to such an extent that any association it might have had with its text is totally lost. In section III (mm. 45–85) the first four notes of phrase 4 are incorporated into a motive that, combined with a countermotive that is always above it, appears twenty-two times before completing the phrase in m. 68. The last four notes then appear by themselves four times, followed by a development of the last two notes in mm. 75–79.

Although passages such as section III of *Nun freut euch* or section IX (mm. 194–234, phrase 7), which is similarly constructed, may appear tedious on the page to the untrained eye, they come to life on an organ in which tonal and spatial contrasts between divisions can be achieved and at the hands of an organist who can realize the possibilities of the instrument through creative registration. Those twenty-two repetitions in section III depend for their execution on separate manuals because of the crossing of parts between the hands, and for their effect on contrasting tonal color between the divisions governed by those manuals. No other works by Buxtehude are so completely wedded to a particular type of instrument and acoustic as the chorale fantasias are to the North German multimanual organ resounding in a large Gothic church.

If the sense of the final phrase of the chorale as an entity is almost completely lost in section IX, it had been expressively laid out in the preceding section (mm. 169–93). Luther's hymn recounts the story of salvation obtained at a great price—the crucifixion of Christ. The last line of the first stanza alludes to this price, which will be spelled out in the eighth stanza of the hymn, and Buxtehude's initial setting of the associated melody phrase in section VIII clearly refers to this text in his use of a chromatic countermelody to phrase 7 of the chorale, which appears in half notes. A second, syncopated countermelody completes the triple counterpoint in which this section is composed. The "sweet wonderful deed" mentioned in the sixth line may also have suggested the composition of section VI (mm. 133–50) as a gigue fugue.

Buxtehude's *Nun freut euch lieben Christen gmein* contains all the elements that we expect to find in a North German chorale fantasia: a single exposition of the chorale melody in contrasting sections with various styles and in different voices; appearances of the chorale melody in long notes, ornamented monodic style, and fragmented; contrapuntal techniques, echoes, and dance rhythms; and great length. Pieter Dirksen has suggested that Buxtehude might have composed it as a *Meisterstück* to demonstrate his worthiness to succeed Franz Tunder at St. Mary's in 1668, just as Reincken had done with *An Wasserflüssen Babylons* in 1663, noting that it is exactly the same length as Tunder's longest chorale fantasia.[21] Dirksen has recently published a shorter, anonymous fantasia on this same chorale, which he tentatively attributes to a youthful Buxtehude. It is found in the Lüneburg manuscript KN 209 with an earlier reportoire of works by Scheidemann, Tunder, and Weckmann, but in the unusual key of A major. Its range bears the marks of transposition from G, however, so it may be a student exercise in transposition. Pending further information, I have listed it with the doubtful works in appendix 1.

Like his vocal concertos and praeludia, no two of Buxtehude's chorale fantasias are alike. Indeed, several works depart significantly from the model just examined. *Nun lob, mein Seel, den Herren* (BuxWV 212) foregoes the usual sectional contrast to concentrate exclusively on one of the frequently encountered devices of the chorale fantasia, echoes between manuals. But *Ich dank dir, lieber Herre* (BuxWV 194) contains no echoes at all. *Wie schön leuchtet der Morgenstern* (BuxWV 223) cycles through the chorale melody twice, which is unusual, the second time as a gigue fugue. Two works entitled *Magnificat primi toni* (BuxWV 203, 204) and the *Te Deum laudamus* (BuxWV 218) are not composed on chorale melodies at all and might better be called chant fantasias. They present problems with respect both to the establishment of a correct text and to their possible liturgical function.

Buxtehude's setting of the *Te Deum* (BuxWV 218; CD track 6) is based on the Latin chant, not on the German chorale version of it, which was sung more often in Lübeck. This chorale, "Herr Gott dich loben wir," is included in the *Lübeckisches Gesangbuch* and in both MK13 and Pagendarm's chorale book; it forms the basis for Tunder's setting under that title, which can properly be called a chorale fantasia. The first three phrases of the chorale melody (ex. 7-13) align perfectly with the upper voice in mm. 1–14 of Tunder's setting. I have not found a melody for the Latin "Te Deum" from post-Reformation Lübeck, but the Latin chant was used in Denmark; Niels Jespersøn's *Gradual* of 1573 contains it, together with a note that it was for use in market cities, of which Helsingør was one, so Buxtehude probably sang the Latin version as a schoolboy. It was also in use in Hamburg, and it is found as the first number in Franz Eler's *Cantica sacra* (Hamburg, 1588). Example 7-14 gives Eler's version of the four verses of the

Example 7-13. "Herr Gott dich loben wir," MK 13 and Pagendarm melody, mm. 1–13.

Te De - um lau - da - mus, te Do - mi - num con - fi - te - mur ...

Ple- ni sunt coe - li et ter - ra ma - ie - sta - tis glo - ri - ae tu - ae ...

Te mar - ty - rum can - di - da - tus lau - dat ex - er - ci - tus ...

Tu de - vic - to mor - tis a - cu - le - o,

a - pe - ru - i -sti cre - den - ti - bus reg - na coe - lo - rum ...

Example 7-14. "Te Deum," Eler melody, 4 verses.

chant that Buxtehude used in his *Te Deum*, which begins with a free forty-three-measure prelude. When Buxtehude introduces the chant into his organ setting at the beginning of versus 1 (CD track 8, 02:01), the long notes are in groups of six, corresponding to the six syllables of "Te Deum laudamus;" moreover, the chant for the second part of the verse, heard most clearly in the pedal at the end of this section (CD track 8, 05:02), also corresponds exactly to the syllables of "te Dominum confitemur." Buxtehude's version of the chant melody differs somewhat from Eler's and even more from Jespersøn's, but it resembles both versions far more closely than it does the chorale "Herr Gott dich loben wir."

Textual incipits of the four verses of Buxtehude's *Te Deum*, given in example 7-14, appear as sectional headings in the only complete extant source for this work (*B*, Mus. ms. Bach P 801): "Te Deum laudamus vers. 1" (p. 336): "Te Martyrum à 2 Clav: è ped": (p. 340); "Tu devicto cum et [or 3?] subjectis" (p. 342); and "Pleni sunt coeli et terra" (p. 346). In a second complete source, lost since World War II, the section headed "Pleni sunt coeli" also contained the indication "Secundus versus," according to Spitta. This section does not follow the first verse in P 801, however, but occurs last, and its position at the end of the piece not only disrupts the order of the verses as they appear in the chant (as in ex. 7-14) but also causes the work as a whole to end in G major rather than in the Phrygian mode on

E in which it begins. The chant verse "Tu devicto" does end on E, however, as does Buxtehude's setting of it, and his final cadence for this section offers a more suitable ending to the work as a whole. It certainly appears as if the original order of this work had been garbled in transmission; a third source provides only the first forty measures of the opening prelude and ends in A minor. Following the lead of performers, recent editors (Beckmann's revised edition [1995], Albrecht [1998], and Belotti in *Collected Works* [2007]) have placed Buxtehude's *Te Deum* in its liturgical and probably original order, with mm. 161–268 of the older editions inserted between their m. 94 and m. 95.

In the *Te Deum*, one of his grandest and certainly his longest keyboard work, Buxtehude combines stylistic characteristics of the chorale fantasia with those of the praeludium. The opening section resembles a three-part opening free section of a praeludium and sets the mode. A quasi-ostinato passage in the "Pleni sunt coeli" section (CD track 8, 05:25) is also reminiscent of the praeludium, but the variations above it draw motives from the chant. Echoes between Rückpositiv and Oberwerk later in this section (CD track 8, 08:59) are more characteristic of the chorale fantasia, as is the fragmentation of the chant into short motives. Once the chant has entered at the beginning of versus 1 it is present throughout the work, as is the case in the chorale fantasias. It appears in whole notes, as a fugue subject, fragmented, or complete and highly ornamented. Unlike the chorale fantasias, however, the *Te Deum* is based on a cantus firmus that consists only of reciting formulas. This cantus firmus can supply no association with a particular text, so it is necessary to identify the sections of the work with textual incipits. And unlike a chorale melody, a reciting formula conveys no sense of completion; it could go on forever, and thus it becomes possible for the sections of a work based upon it to become jumbled. But precisely by virtue of these qualities, this work conveys a much greater sense of the freedom and unpredictability characteristic of the *stylus phantasticus* than can be found in the fantasias based on German chorales. Buxtehude's *Te Deum* is perhaps the most sophisticated wedding between *stylus phantasticus* and cantus-firmus writing in the entire North German repertoire.

Buxtehude's *Te Deum* follows the Phrygian mode of the chant, and all its structural E cadences are either Phrygian (in which the sixth *f-d'* expands to an octave *e-e'*) or plagal (from an A-minor to an E-major chord). As such it is perfectly suited to mean-tone tuning, and the fifty-four-stop mean-tone organ at Örgryte Nya Kirka in Gothenburg, Sweden, reveals its glories to a degree greater than that of any other Buxtehude work that I have heard played on it.[22] A few D-sharps passed through Buxtehude's Phrygian filter, however, and for these the Örgryte organ's subsemitones are helpful. But these D-sharps are not structural, as they are in the E-minor praeludium BuxWV 142; they either pass by quickly, or they can be played as D-naturals. The *Te Deum* sounds at its best in mean tone.

The longer of the two works entitled *Magnificat primi toni* (BuxWV 203) resembles a praeludium in its juxtaposition of free sections and fugues, although its eight sections are shorter and its fugues less well developed than is the case in most of Buxtehude's praeludia. At first glance this work appears to be unrelated to the first Magnificat tone, given in example 7-15 from Eler's *Cantica sacra*. Closer examination, however, reveals that the eight sections of BuxWV 203 contain two complete statements of the entire formula. Example 7-16 shows Buxtehude's settings of the intonation in sections 1 and 5 and of the termination in sections 4 and 8. The motive F–G–A of the intonation also supplies the key of F major for the gigue fugue (section 5, mm. 76–91); it is uncharacteristic for a Buxtehude praeludium to include a fugue in a key other than that of the

Example 7-15. Magnificat, tone 1, Eler melody.

Example 7-16a. BuxWV 203, mm. 8–11 (intonation).

Example 7-16b. BuxWV 203, mm. 76–78 (intonation).

Example 7-16c. BuxWV 203, mm. 50–51 (termination).

Example 7-16d. BuxWV 203, mm. 138–41 (termination).

praeludium as a whole. The intermediate sections 2–3 and 6–7 contain motives associated with the words "Spiritus meus" in the chant. Sections 1–3 and 6–7 have their final cadence in A, 4 and 8 in D.

The shorter *Magnificat primi toni* (BuxWV 204) survives only in a late source outside of the main manuscript groups and in another copy derived from it. The head title "Magnificat 1ᵐⁱ Toni 9ⁿⁱ Toni et No 5 alla Duodecima. Dietrich Buxtehude" implies that three versets will follow, but there are in fact four. The second is headed "Noni Toni," the third "Versus Noni Toni," and the fourth "Vers. 5 alla Duodecima." The second section belongs to the first Magnificat tone, however, not the ninth, and it is catalogued in the Buxtehude-Werke-Verzeichnis as the second part of *Magnificat primi toni* (BuxWV 204). Together these two sections form a pair containing one statement of the Magnificat formula, the first with the intonation and ending on A, the second with the termination, ending on D. The two versets that follow do indeed belong to the ninth Magnificat tone, the *tonus peregrinus*, and they alone constitute the *Magnificat noni toni* in the Buxtehude-Werke-Verzeichnis (BuxWV 205) and in later editions, as opposed to the three parts seen in earlier editions. The ninth Magnificat tone can properly be called a chorale, for it appears with a prose translation of the Magnificat, "Meine Seele erhebt den Herren," in the Babst hymnal and with a Danish translation in the Danish hymnal. The indications "Versus" and "Versus 5" suggest that these two versets may have come from a once larger set. The first gives both halves of the ninth tone in long notes in the pedal, the second a fugue on the first three notes of the intonation, with a countersubject in invertible counterpoint at the twelfth, hence "Alla duodecima." Both are self contained and end on D, so BuxWV 205 is listed below with the chorale variations.

The Magnificat was sung in Lübeck at Saturday Vespers and the Sunday afternoon preaching service (only in German after 1703), and in neighboring Mecklenburg the organist played *alternatim* with the singing of the Magnificat (see appendix 4E, 6 and 1). A possible model for Lübeck practice comes from the *Natalitia sacra* of 1682, in which each two verses of the Magnificat sung polyphonically on Christmas afternoon were followed by interpolated *Laudes,* as can be seen in appendix 4E2; if organ *alternatim* playing were to follow this model it would call for six organ versets to be interpolated into the complete sung Magnificat. None of Buxtehude's surviving Magnificat settings supply six, but the two versets of BuxWV 205 or the two-part single verset of BuxWV 204 could supply models for the improvisation of others. Neither the cantus-firmus scheme nor the tonal plan of BuxWV 203 suggests that its eight sections were intended to be performed separately in *alternatim* performance, but it does divide neatly into two parts, which might work well as a framing device for a sung Magnificat in the first tone, perhaps as antiphon substitutes, and BuxWV 204 could be used in this way as well.

The "Te Deum" was sung in German in the morning service at least after 1703, and following the afternoon sermon, also in German, on New Year's Day 1683. The Latin "Te Deum" appears as the main musical event in the services of thanksgiving for victories against the Turks, for example in 1686 and 1699. Since the sections of Buxtehude's organ *Te Deum* (BuxWV 218) are labeled with text incipits, they may have been interpolated into a sung performance, with the unnamed praeludium and the opening verse played at the beginning.

Chorale Preludes

BuxWV 178, 180, 182, 183, 184, 185, 186, 187, 189, 190, 191, 192, 193, 197, 198, 199, 200, 201, 202, 206, 208, 209, 211, 214, 215, 217, 219, 220, 221, 222, 224

Single chorale settings in which the chorale melody appears complete in only one voice, usually without repetition, form the largest group within Buxtehude's keyboard works, and all but four of these thirty-one works are four-voice settings with the chorale in ornamented form in the soprano. Within this subgroup of twenty-seven works, although no two pieces are exactly alike—indeed, there are alternate settings of three chorales (BuxWV 191 and 192, 199 and 200, 208 and 209)—Buxtehude's approach to the chorale is so consistent that it is one of the most characteristic aspects of his compositional style.

A comparison of Buxtehude's two settings of *Nun bitten wir den Heiligen Geist* (BuxWV 208, 209; ex. 7-17) will demonstrate both the stylistic consistency and the rich variety within this group of works. Both correspond closely to the pre-Reformation melody (ex. 7-18). BuxWV 209 (CD track 6) is the simpler of the two settings. The three staves into which its source places its four voices correspond to three musical functions and three distinct layers of sound, to be realized by three separate divisions of the organ, governed by two manuals and pedal. The soprano voice in the right hand carries the chorale melody as a solo voice; the bass in the pedal supplies the harmonic foundation in the manner of a continuo bass; the two inner parts, written in the alto clef and played by the left hand, realize the harmony when the soprano is present and engage in imitation of the following chorale line during the interludes in which the soprano pauses, as if for breath. This top voice falls entirely within the range of the human soprano voice, and its ornamentation of the chorale is extremely vocal in character, beginning with none at all, allowing the opening notes of the chorale to be clearly perceived, becoming more intricate, and then pulling back to plain notes in a totally unpredictable fashion. The soprano line of BuxWV 208 (CD track 7) has a slightly wider range and is more heavily ornamented in

Example 7-17a. BuxWV 208, mm. 1–5.

Example 7-17b. BuxWV 209, mm. 1–7.

a somewhat more instrumental manner, but it never falls into any consistent, predictable pattern of figuration. The "Kyrieleis" at the end of the chorale here is nearly lost in the exuberance of a closing flourish that ends an octave higher than BuxWV 209. The functions of the parts are the same in both works, although the bass acts more like an organ pedal and less like a continuo in mm. 16 and 28 of BuxWV 208.

The ornamentation of these two works, particularly that of BuxWV 209, reflects the Italian manner of singing as taught, for example, by Christoph Bernhard in his short treatise "Von der Singe-Kunst oder Manier." He speaks of

Example 7-18. "Nun bitten wir den Heiligen Geist," MK 13 melody.

two manners of singing, one that remains with the notes, adding only a few passing notes, trills, and the like; the other, "cantar passagiato," varies the notes with diminutions and colaraturas. He advises employing the latter passagework sparingly, like salt and pepper, lest it become tiresome for the singer and tedious for the listener. Singing with the notes falls into two types, "cantar sodo," or plain singing, and "cantar d'affetto," which he describes in §26:

> *Cantar alla Napolitana* or *d'affetto* pertains only to singers, because only they have a text; nevertheless, instrumentalists can also make use of it to a degree, if they know how to use and moderate their instruments with joyful or doleful harmony appropriate to them.

According to Bernhard, the affects that music can best represent are joy, sadness, anger, and meekness. The use of *piano, cercar della nota* (searching for notes with a slight filling-in between them), anticipations, and a slower beat makes the music sound more melancholy.

Buxtehude's chorale preludes do indeed employ harmony as well as ornamentation to project the affect of the chorale text underlying them. *Durch Adams Fall ist ganz verderbt* (BuxWV 183) provides an example of a setting imbued with sorrow. This hymn of the early Reformation recounts the story of original sin through Adam, and although its later stanzas tell of redemption through Christ, it is the first stanza that dominates Buxtehude's setting. The Lübeck melody (ex. 7-19) differs little from that of the sixteenth-century hymnals, and it agrees

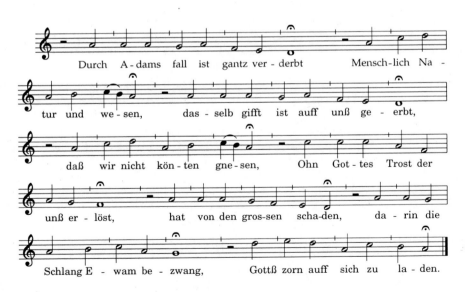

Example 7-19. "Durch Adams Fall ist ganz verderbt," MK 13 melody.

closely with the structural notes of Buxtehude's soprano line. The ornamentation of the chorale is almost entirely in the style of *cantar d'affetto*, with very little passagework. A descending chromatic line against the third phrase at mm. 14–15 and ascending chromatic lines at mm. 9–10 and 20–21 contribute greatly to the sorrowful affect. The function of the bass part at the beginning of this piece departs somewhat from Buxtehude's usual practice in these works: It does not perform any continuo function between m. 6 and m. 22; instead it drops out for five measures, then sounds two phrases of the cantus firmus and both versions of the chromatic countermelody. Its harmonic function in the first five measures is restricted to three descending fifths, intended perhaps as an illustration of the word *fall*. In the second half of the piece, however, it proceeds in a more typical manner.

Pure diatonic harmony and exuberant ornamentation convey the affect of joy in *Ein feste Burg ist unser Gott* (BuxWV 184), Buxtehude's chorale prelude on Luther's great Reformation hymn "A mighty fortress is our God." Amid its liberal ornamentation, we are reminded of the fact that in 1701 the ministers decided to hang boards with the hymn numbers in St. Mary's Church, because "from the organ playing beforehand, the hymns can be recognized by only a few." And yet here, too, the ornamentation always has a vocal quality about it, proceeding irregularly, pausing on the structural notes, with only two measures of the entire piece consisting only of sixteenth notes. It is this vocal quality in the soprano line that has caused these pieces to be described as "monodic."

Buxtehude never employs a completely instrumental style of ornamentation in a chorale prelude, but for the sake of comparison we can see it in the second of two variations on the chorale "Ach Gott und Herr" (BuxWV 177, ex. 7-20). The first phrase of the chorale melody consists of the descending tetrachord $d''-c''-b'-a'$, and in ornamenting it Buxtehude passes through the ranges of all four vocal parts, descending three octaves in as many measures and shifting register for the final structural note of the phrase. For the ascent from a' back to d'' in the second phrase he uses a division figure in sequential repetition. Figural ornamentation such as this can be found in Sweelinck's chorale settings—in his second and third variations on "Vater unser in Himmelreich," for example. He in turn had adopted this style from the English virginalists, and he passed it on to his pupils, particularly Samuel Scheidt.

In his monodic chorale preludes, Buxtehude follows the style of Scheidemann most closely, and it is in this respect that Scheidemann departs most significantly from his teacher, Sweelinck, as Breig has shown. Although Scheidemann's chorale settings also contain abundant use of figural ornamentation, some, such as his third variation on "Mensch, willt du leben seliglich," definitely employ the monodic style. Mattheson spoke of a "Scheidemannesque sweetness" (*Lieblichkeit*); in his biography of Weckmann in the *Ehrenpforte*, he wrote that during his study years in Hamburg under Jacob Praetorius, Weckmann also had had the opportunity to attend Vespers at St. Catherine's and hear Scheidemann,

Example 7-20. BuxWV 177 [versus 2], mm. 1–6.

which "gave him the inducement to moderate the Praetorian seriousness with Scheidemanesque sweetness." If Mattheson was referring to the vocal quality in Scheidemann's chorale settings, this Scheidemannesque sweetness is much more in evidence in Buxtehude's chorale settings than in Weckmann's.

As for Buxtehude's four chorale preludes that are not in the monodic style (BuxWV 198, 214, 215, 221), all present the cantus firmus in the soprano, three in unornamented form. In *Von Gott will ich nicht lassen* (BuxWV 221), Buxtehude carries figural patterns used to ornament the chorale through all four voices. With its consistent sixteenth-note motion and anacrusis of three sixteenths, it sounds very much like an allemande, specifically the *double* to the Allemande of *Auf meinen lieben Gott* (BuxWV 179).

Chorale Variations

BuxWV 177, 179, 181, 205, 207, 213

Chorale variations play the least important role in Buxtehude's keyboard music. Not only are they few in number, but the style in which most of them are composed is not distinctive. The majority of these variations consist of the plain chorale melody in one voice—most often soprano or bass—surrounded by figuration in the others, a style inherited from Sweelinck. Many are *manualiter* movements for two or three voices. Only one movement among them—versus 3 of *Nimm von uns, Herr, du treuer Gott* (BuxWV 207)—is in the monodic style. With one significant exception, these variation sets do not form convincing cycles, and they appear to have been composed either for *alternatim* performance or for teaching purposes.

The one set of variations that forms a convincing cycle is *Auf meinen lieben Gott* (BuxWV 179), composed in the form of a suite: [Allemande], Double, Sarabande, Courante, and Gigue. Buxtehude does not maintain the number of voices so consistently in this work as he does in his other chorale settings, and he may have intended it for harpsichord; all the movements are *manualiter*. It is transmitted in a large manuscript copied by Johann Gottfried Walther and consisting exclusively of chorale settings, however, the rest presumably intended for organ. The presence of dance rhythms does not necessarily exclude it from performance on the organ; the three largest chorale fantasias (BuxWV 188, 210, 223) all contain sections in gigue rhythm, as do a number of the praeludia and canzonas. A theological student visiting Lübeck in 1694 noted in his diary a discussion with theologians there on the question

> whether it is pleasing to God and at the same time useful to the pious soul if the organist expounds sacred hymns for morning, evening, prayer, penitence, lamenting and comfort, praise and thanksgiving, songs of life, death, and heaven in a dance-like manner, so that an upright Christian person becomes confused by such variations, wondering whether he is sitting in a house of God or in a dance hall.[23]

Suites and Secular Variations

As a variation suite based on a chorale melody, Buxtehude's *Auf meinen lieben Gott* appears to be unique, but the combination of variation technique with dance movements is exceedingly common. Galliards were often variations of pavanes in sixteenth-century dance music, and an allemande or other dance in duple meter was often followed by a strict proportional reworking in triple meter. Within suites of different dances, the opening measures of an allemande and courante often resemble one another, and one or more movements are often followed by a variation, or "double," in the same dance rhythm, as in BuxWV 179, 228, and 234. Variation also occurs often within dance movements; their usual binary form leads to improvised variation in the repetition of each strain, and sometimes the composer writes out the varied repetition, as Buxtehude did in the second sarabande of BuxWV 237. The theme of a set of variations is often a dance movement: Buxtehude's variation set BuxWV 245 is based on a courante, BuxWV 246 and 249 on sarabandes. Conversely, variation sets often contain individual variations cast in different dance rhythms. Reincken's variation set on "Schweiget mir vom Weiber Nehmen," for example, ends with variations 16–18 as courante, sarabande, and gigue, preceded by variation 14 as an allemande; Partite 9 and 19 of Buxtehude's *La Capricciosa* (BuxWV 250) are gigues, and Partita 25 a sarabande.

Buxtehude's suites and secular variation sets survive mainly in a few Scandinavian sources, and they came to light much later than his works in other genres; they have thus far elicited less interest on the part of performers and scholars than his other music. The edition of these works by Emilius Bangert, which first appeared in 1942 and has been reprinted by Kalmus, contains nineteen suites and six variation sets. Two of the suites, however, Bangert's number VIII in D minor and number XVI in G minor, appear as the first two suites in Nicolas-Antoine Lebègue's *Second Livre de Clavesin* (Paris, 1687), so they can no longer be considered works of Buxtehude, and they are catalogued as BuxWV Anhang 12 and 13 respectively. Two other suites not included in Bangert's edition (BuxWV 231 and 239) keep the total number of catalogued suites at nineteen, but two new ones have recently come to light.

The unique source for all the variation sets and all but six of the suites is the Ryge manuscript—discussed in chapter 9—which was long in private possession but is now located at the Royal Library in Copenhagen. The musical portion of this manuscript contains ninety pieces—each movement of a suite is separately titled—of which twenty-five are attributed to Buxtehude and the rest are unattributed. The number of attributions to Buxtehude may be increased to eighty-two, however, by virtue of the fact that the dance movements are definitely arranged in suites, and only the allemandes contain the composer's name, or, more frequently, initials. The initials "D. B. H." for Dieterich Buxte Hude are found in many other sources as well. Among the anonymous works, three variation sets from Pachelbel's *Hexachordum Apollinis*, which Pachelbel dedicated to Buxtehude in 1699, have been identified, as well as Reincken's variations on "Schweiget mir vom Weiber Nehmen" and a minuet by Lebègue. Among the works attributed to Buxtehude are the two suites by Lebègue.

The misattribution of the two Lebègue suites to Buxtehude casts some doubt on the accuracy of the other attributions to Buxtehude in the Ryge manuscript, apart from BuxWV 236 and 238, which have concordances in Uppsala. BuxWV 229, a suite in C major, bears a close resemblance in the opening of its Allemande and Courante to the corresponding movements of Lebègue's G-major suite from the *Second Livre de clavessin*. Gustafson suggests that Buxtehude composed this suite as a parody or homage to Lebègue after having copied out his suites in D minor and G minor and that the Ryge manuscript may be a direct copy from an autograph manuscript. Gustafson's extensive index of sevententh-century French harpsichord music enables him to state that none of the other pieces attributed to Buxtehude in the Ryge manuscript can be identifed as known works by seventeenth-century French harpsichordists. Beckmann, working independently, reports that the two Lebègue suites were copied not from Lebègue's first edition but from the pirated edition of Estienne Roger (Amsterdam, [1701]). He finds the style of BuxWV 229 to be more typical of Lebègue than of Buxtehude, and he banishes it to the appendix of his edition. Until further research clarifies this situation, we shall tentatively accept all the suites and variation sets catalogued in the main part of the Buxtehude-Werke-Verzeichnis as authentic.

Meanwhile, two new Buxtehude suites have come to light. A suite in A minor, its allemande attributed to "D. B. H.," appears in a manuscript copied around 1704 in Breitenberg, near Itzehoe, by the organist Johann Kruse.[24] And an Amsterdam publication from 1710, *VI Suittes, divers airs avec leurs variations et fugues pour le clavessin*, all anonymous in the print, contains as its second entry a suite in D minor whose sarabande is concordant with that of BuxWV 234 and whose courant is also found as a single anonymous movement in the Ryge manuscript (BuxWV Anhang 6).[25]

Suites

BuxWV 226–44, plus two BuxWV deest (1) and (2)

By the early eighteenth century, when all the sources for Buxtehude's suites were copied or published, the German suite had become regularized to consist of four movements—Allemande, Courante, Sarabande, and Gigue—in that order. Thirteen of Buxtehude's suites contain just these four movements, and four more add a second sarabande or double, as does his Suite in C major (BuxWV 226, CD tracks 9–12), which can serve to illustrate Fuhrmann's definitions of these dance types:

> 12. Allemande . . . is a German instrumental piece, it begins with an upbeat in duple meter, has two strains, and each is repeated twice immediately after one another. It is at the same time the proposition in a musical suite, from which the Corrente, Sarabande and Gique flow as parts.

The upbeat figure of three ascending sixteenths is quite typical for Buxtehude's allemandes, and he repeats it here in the dominant at the beginning of the second strain (CD track 9, 01:19). The courante that follows (CD track 10) uses another common upbeat figure of repeated notes in dotted rhythm, but it demonstrates its relationship to the preceding Allemande by bringing in the ascending fourth in the next measure. As in all of Buxtehude's suites (with the exception of *Auf meinen lieben Gott*), the sarabande and gigue do not bear any melodic resemblance to the allemande or courante.

13. *Corrente (Ital.) Courante (Gal.) a Currendo* from running, an instrumental piece, and it always starts with an upbeat in triple meter.

Fuhrmann uses the Italian term *corrente*, and although Buxtehude's sources use the French term, usually spelled "courent," all but one of his courantes are of the Italian type, in 3/4 meter with constant eighth-note motion, usually achieved by the use of *style brisé*.

14. Sarabande is an instrumental aria, usually eight measures and goes slowly in triple.

Each strain of the two sarabandes in BuxWV 226 (CD track 11) has exactly eight measures; these are normally the shortest dances in a Buxtehude suite. The second sarabande (CD track 11, 01:27) is a separate piece, not a *double* of the first. Fuhrmann's association of the sarabande with the aria recalls the fact that two of the "arias" that form the themes for Buxtehude's variation sets are in fact sarabandes. Fuhrmann does not mention an emphasis on the second beat so frequently encountered in eighteenth-century sarabandes, and it does not occur often Buxtehude's sarabandes.

15. Gique is an instrumental fugue, which goes in quick triplets.

Fuhrmann's "quick triplets" describe the Italian *giga*, most often notated in 12/8, as in BuxWV 226 (CD track 12). This gigue begins as a fugue, with an exposition in four voices and two more entrances in the first strain, but fugal procedure disappears altogether after three quick entrances of another subject in the second strain.

The two newly discovered suites display most of the stylistic characteristics seen in BuxWV 226, with the two most common upbeat patterns in their allemandes and courantes and Italian-style courantes and gigues. The A-minor sarabande emphasizes the second beat, as does the sarabande of *Auf meinen lieben* Gott (BuxWV 179). The gigue of the D-minor suite contains fugal expositions in both its strains, but fugal procedure is totally lacking in the A-minor gigue, which in this respect resembles that of BuxWV 240. Both new sources also contain known works by Reincken.

Weckmann and Reincken both composed keyboard suites; Weckmann owned copies of suites by Froberger, and Reincken chose to sit at his two-manual harpsichord as he posed for the painting of *A Musical Party*. If Buxtehude paid homage to Lebègue in BuxWV 229, as Gustafson suggests, both he and Reincken may have paid similar homage to Froberger. The openings of the Allemande and Courante of BuxWV 230, in C major, and of Reincken's Suite in G major bear a strong resemblance to one another and in turn to Froberger's F-major suite (Suite IV) from his volume of 1649, as can be seen in example 7-21. The courante begins as a variation of the allemande in all three suites.

Example 7-21a. Froberger, Suite IV, Allemande, mm. 1–2.

Example 7-21b. Froberger, Suite IV, Courante, mm. 1–2.

Example 7-21c. Reincken, Suite in G, Allemande, mm. 1–2.

Example 7-21d. Reincken, Suite in G, Courante, mm. 1–4.

Buxtehude's suites are comparable to his strophic arias in a number of ways. Both genres are quite simple and predictable, and Buxtehude's works in these genres generally lack the harmonic richness and dramatic intensity that characterizes so much of his other music. Indeed, not one of them exceeds the bounds of mean-tone tuning, if E♭ and B♭ are occasionally retuned to D♯ and A♯, which is easily done on a harpsichord. The suites belong to the realm of domestic music

Example 7-21e. BuxWV 230, Allemande, mm. 1–2.

Example 7-21f. BuxWV 230, Courante, mm. 1–2.

making, not to performances in church or public concerts, so they cannot have been intended to please a large audience of ordinary citizens. They do not appear to have been intended for connoisseurs either, however, but rather for musical amateurs or students. The manuscript sources that transmit these works seem to have been copied either for family use or during student days, and Buxtehude's suites are in fact technically much easier to play than most of his other keyboard music. Nonetheless, a skillful player can reveal subtleties in these works that do not leap to the eye from the page.

Variation Sets

BuxWV 245–50

Buxtehude drew mainly on well-known tunes for his six variation sets. "More Palatino" (BuxWV 247) is a student drinking song from the seventeenth century, and "La Capricciosa" (BuxWV 250) the widespread bergamasca melody. The sarabande that forms the basis of BuxWV 249 has been attributed to the French lutenist Germain Pinel (d. 1661), and it appears in seventeenth-century manuscripts from Belgium, the Netherlands, Denmark, England, and Germany, as Gustafson has shown. The most intriguing of Buxtehude's borrowed melodies, however, is the aria called "Rofilis" in BuxWV 248. Jean Baptiste Lully composed it in 1661 for his *Ballet de l'Impatience* (LWV 14); it opens the first entrée as a serenade sung to a lady named Iris (ex. 7-22). This tune, like Pinel's sarabande, circulated widely through keyboard manuscripts in the low countries,

Example 7-22. Lully, "Air pour Un Grand qui donne une Serenade a sa Maitresse," from *Ballet de l'Impatience.*

Germany, and Scandinavia. Gustav Düben included it under the title "Air de ballet" in a collection of dance movements for keyboard that he began in 1659, and it appears as "Bel[le] Iris" in two Dutch sources. The title "Rofilis," which bears only a remote resemblance to "Belle Iris," is found in two manuscripts apart from the Buxtehude source, one German and one Swedish. The other keyboard transcriptions are written both in Lully's original key of G minor and in D minor, the key that Buxtehude used.

Buxtehude composed only three variations to "Rofilis," but they enrich the tune considerably. A comparison of Buxtehude's first variation with Lully's air shows that not only has the unit of motion been changed from the quarter note to the eighth, but the harmonic rhythm has accelerated even more, particularly in m. 14. In his definition of the aria, Fuhrmann concentrated on the vocal form; concerning the instrumental form he wrote only that "if it is played, it must be taken in a slower meter." Buxtehude's setting must clearly be played to a slower beat than that to which Lully's air would be sung, particularly in view of the steady sixteenth-note motion of the second variation. This variation is also titled "Le double," and the rhythmic character of both variations is clearly that of the allemande. The third variation, notated in 6/8, prunes away the added ornamentation and quickens the motion to end the set as a gigue. This variation set is actually an abbreviated suite, although Buxtehude mutes the similarity to dance movements somewhat by not indicating a repeat of each eight-measure strain, as Lully did.

The bergamasca, or "La Capricciosa" (BuxWV 250), is also a dance, and Buxtehude includes the repeated strains of its binary structure in his thirty-two variations, his longest set. The bergamasca originally consisted only of a repeated I–IV–V–I harmonic scheme, which is still evident in Buxtehude's setting, although he modifies it often enough to sustain harmonic interest, particularly in Partita 12, a chromatic variation. In this set, Buxtehude presents an extremely varied vocabulary of variation techniques idiomatic to the keyboard—indeed, to the harpsichord. Here we find the consistent, instrumentally conceived figuration that he eschewed in his chorale preludes. Unlike the suites, these variations demand a considerable degree of virtuosity. We can imagine Buxtehude himself playing this piece in the parlor of one of Lübeck's patrician homes on the new harpsichord just purchased by one of his patrons, perhaps on a business trip to Antwerp. Since mainly amateurs in the family would play the harpsichord, it has only one manual; none of Buxtehude's solo harpsichord music requires more.

Although that patrician home was probably no more than two blocks away from St. Mary's Church, the stylistic distance between the suites and secular variation sets played in that parlor and the praeludia and chorale fantasias that Buxtehude performed on the large organ in St. Mary's is vast. The dance, with its regular rhythms and phrases, dominated the music played in the parlor and occasionally made its way into the organ loft as well. In the church, the dramatic and unpredictable *stylus phantasticus*, combined ingeniously with fugues and chorales, held sway.

Chapter Eight

Sonatas

Apart from the funeral music for his father, Buxtehude's only major printed works to appear during his lifetime were two collections of sonatas for violin, viola da gamba, and harpsichord published in the mid-1690s. Opus 1, printed by Nicolaus Spieringk of Hamburg at Buxtehude's expense, bears no publication date, but it is listed in the book fair catalogues of 1694. Opus 2, printed and published by Spieringk, appeared in 1696. Eight other sonatas for strings survive in manuscript in addition to the fourteen printed sonatas.

Although all Buxtehude's printed sonatas and two of his manuscript sonatas were edited by Carl Stiehl and published in *Denkmäler deutscher Tonkunst* in 1903, they lay virtually unnoticed on library shelves until the late 1970s. Within a very short space of time, however, they caught the attention of scholars and performers alike on both sides of the Atlantic. Doctoral dissertations by Eva Linfield and Christine Defant were begun and completed within months of one another. Through performances and recordings of selected sonatas, particularly by the Boston Museum Trio and Musica Antiqua Köln, these works became more widely known, and they now enjoy the secure place in the repertoire of seventeenth-century chamber music that they so richly deserve, as witnessed by the publication of the complete printed and manuscript sonatas in volume 14 of the Collected Works and their recording by the trio of John Holloway, Jaap ter Linden, and Lars Ulrik Mortensen on the Dacapo label.

Printed Sonatas

BuxWV 252–65

Buxtehude displays the same bold originality in his sonata publications as he does in his organ music. A comparison of Buxtehude's collections with Reincken's 1687 sonata publication, *Hortus musicus*, makes Buxtehude's lack of conventionality abundantly clear. Each of Buxtehude's prints consists of seven sonatas, not the usual grouping of six, as in *Hortus musicus*, or twelve, as in Rosenmüller's *Sonate* of 1682. Buxtehude chose groupings of seven elsewhere—the *Membra Jesu* cantatas (BuxWV 75), the lost keyboard suites on the nature and qualities of the planets, and the statements of the ostinato theme in each of the four sections of the D-minor passacaglia (BuxWV 161). In the case of *Membra* and the suites on the seven known planets, the subject itself already consisted of a group of seven. Buxtehude himself imposed the number seven on the sonata collections, however, and the arrangement of keys in the first set—F G a B♭ C d ·e—represents the extension of the *hexachordum molle* to seven notes, as in the *Heptachordum Danicum*, which he probably knew as a youth. The keys of the second set—c D E F g A B♭—also form a heptachord, although they do not appear in that order. The mode shift in five of these keys widens the tonal spectrum in both flatward and sharpward directions, far outside the old mean-tone keys.

In scoring his published sonatas for only one violin with viola da gamba and harpsichord, Buxtehude again displayed a degree of unconventionality, although this combination of instruments was by no means unique. Dietrich Becker, director of the Hamburg municipal musicians from 1674 to 1679, published a sonata collection in 1674 with this scoring,[1] and Philipp Heinrich Erlebach issued a similar print in 1694. Erlebach's title, however, notes that these sonatas may also be performed with two violins, however, a much more common scoring. Reincken's *Hortus musicus* calls for two violins, viola da gamba, and basso continuo. Apart from its solo sections, Reincken's gamba mainly stays in the bass range, often doubling the continuo. Buxtehude's texture is much more fluid: at times the gamba doubles the harpsichord continuo, or rather embellishes it, forming a texture of only two real voices; at other times the gamba is in the alto range, completely independent of the continuo, producing a true trio texture with the violin and harpsichord. Although designated "Cembalo," the harpsichord part is in fact a figured bass.

It is in the construction of the individual sonatas, however, that Buxtehude departs most significantly from Reincken. *Hortus musicus* consists of thirty numbered movements, grouped by key (a, B♭, C, d, e, A) into six five-movement works, each of which follows exactly the same plan: Sonata, Allemande, Courante, Sarabande, Gigue. Each opening sonata movement consists in turn of the same three parts: a slow section in concertato texture, a fast fugue, and a slow–fast solo section for the first violin, repeated note for note by the gamba at the lower octave. Only rarely does Reincken depart slightly from this plan, as in the A-major sonata, where he appends a short tutti to the end of the solo section. Buxtehude's sonatas, in contrast, vary from three to fourteen sections, and the only regular aspect of their overall construction is the alternation of slow and fast sections. As is the case with Buxtehude's vocal concertos and organ praeludia, no two of his sonatas are alike.

Buxtehude's printed sonatas contain the most abundant use of tempo indications found in any of his works. Fast movements bear the designations Vivace, Allegro, Presto, and Prestissimo; slow movements are marked Adagio, Lento, Grave, and Largo. With the exception of Vivace, these are precisely the terms that Reincken listed in his composition treatise of 1670. Reincken makes no distinction as to the degree of slowness for the latter four, but Prestissimo is faster than Presto, while Allegro is "merry or joyful." Fuhrmann's treatment of these terms more than thirty years later is nearly identical. Reincken's use of alternate terms before identical solo sections for violin and the viola da gamba in *Hortus musicus*—Largo and Adagio, Presto and Allegro in the A-minor sonata, for example—indicates that he considered the terms interchangeable. Buxtehude also used tempo markings interchangeably, as indicated by discrepancies between parts: Adagio and Lento in the final section of BuxWV 254, the tenth section of BuxWV 257 and the third section of BuxWV 262; Lento and Largo in the final section of BuxWV 257 and in the fourth section of BuxWV 261; Vivace and Allegro in the final section of BuxWV 255; Poco presto and Poco allegro in the eleventh section of BuxWV 257.

Buxtehude follows his chosen principle of alternation between fast and slow sections quite regularly in these sonatas. Only rarely do two designated sections of the same general tempo follow one another sequentially, as the Presto and Vivace sections do in BuxWV 258. The fast sections are generally more extended and written predominantly in sixteenth notes, the slow sections shorter and of an introductory, transitional, or cadential nature. Buxtehude employs the designation Andante in two sonatas, BuxWV 252 and 261, the only preserved use of this term in his entire oeuvre. Reincken does not mention it, and Fuhrmann groups it with the slow tempos. In both Buxtehude sonatas, however, it appears at the head of an extended section in sixteenth notes between two slow sections, suggesting by its placement that Buxtehude had at least a moderate tempo in mind. Seven sonatas contain sections in undesignated tempos, and one section in BuxWV 257 is marked "con discretione."

Just as the sections within the printed sonatas vary from three to fourteen in number, they also differ greatly in length, in the compositional techniques employed in them, and in their place on a continuum between totally dependent section and independent, tonally closed movement. The sonata in three sections (BuxWV 255) contains a closed ostinato movement of 113 measures and an open-ended Lento that merges into a final fugue. Some of the fourteen sections of BuxWV 257 combine to form larger sections, but none could be said to constitute a tonally closed movement. Its more structured sections include a fugue (Allegro, section 2) and a dance (Vivace, section 8); sections 4–7, amorphous in themselves, combine to form a larger aba'b' section built on contrast. The majority of the printed sonatas contain six or seven sections. Three of the six sections of BuxWV 253 could be considered independent movements: an extended section in invertible counterpoint in G major (section 2, Vivace), a dance in E minor (section 4, Allegro), and a final set of variations in G major, designated Arioso, which follows a transitional Largo.

Contrapuntal texture predominates in the sonatas overall, but fugue is not so essential a structural element in the sonatas as it is in the organ praeludia. One printed sonata (BuxWV 253) contains no fugue at all; four sonatas have two fugues and the rest, one. Every sonata fugue is a fast *Spielfuge*; we are struck by the total absence of slow, serious fugues such as occur in Buxtehude's organ praeludia or in Rosenmüller's 1682 sonatas. Each of these fugues contains an entrance of the subject and answer in all voices, but since most of the fugues are composed in only two real voices, this is usually achieved with four entrances of the theme. Once Buxtehude meets this basic requirement, he proceeds extremely freely, introducing episodic material that may or may not be related to the subject.

Once again, a comparison with Reincken's fugues in *Hortus musicus* brings Buxtehude's nonconformity into sharp relief. Each of Reincken's six sonata fugues is composed according to the same basic plan, beginning with two expositions in which each voice presents both subject and answer, always in the order violin I, violin II, viola da gamba. Two to four further expositions follow immediately, each of which is virtually identical to one of the first two. A countersubject is always present, but there are no episodes, entrances in keys other than tonic and dominant, or entrances in stretto. This technique comes close to the permutation fugue, seen for the first time in Sonata XV of Theile's *Musikalisches Kunstbuch*, dated 1691.[2] Although Mattheson refers specifically to keyboard fugues, he could almost have had these fugues in mind in the following passage from his discussion of simple fugues in *Der vollkommene Capellmeister*:

> One must even less restrict oneself to the practice of some organists, who first quite properly, without the slightest embellishment, perform the theme four times through on the entire keyboard in nothing but consonances and gentle thirds; then they begin again with the consequent just as circumspectly from its beginning; always producing the same tune; interposing nothing imitative or syncopating; but constantly only playing merely the concord, as if it were a thorough bass (III/20, §97).

When J. S. Bach arranged two of these sonatas for keyboard (BWV 965, 966), he retained the structure of all movements except the fugues, which he completely recomposed. He kept only the original subjects, providing a new, syncopated countersubject for the A-minor fugue and adding a great deal of episodic material. He did the same in his arrangement of the fugue from Reincken's B♭ sonata (BWV 954).

Buxtehude's sonatas include only one fugue structured similarly to a *Hortus musicus* fugue. It constitutes section 2 of BuxWV 264 and is scored atypically for three real voices. Its four expositions contain two entrances of subject and answer in each voice, always entering in the same order. It does contain an episode between the second and third expositions, however, in which a modulation from E to F♯ major occurs.

The fugue in section 2 of Buxtehude's A-minor sonata, op. 1, no. 3 (BuxWV 254), is more typical of his approach to fugal writing in the sonatas. Its subject is long and expansive: four measures of sixteenth notes spanning a diminished twelfth (ex. 8-1). It divides into three parts: a head motive (m. 22), a two-measure continuation, and a cadence on the dominant. Buxtehude introduces the head

Example 8-1. BuxWV 254, mm. 22–30.

motive unaccompanied by the harpsichord, and it quickly imprints itself on the memory with its insistent repetition of rhythm and tone. The rhythm is perceived as a series of dactyls, because the octave drop is heard as an eighth note rather than as two sixteenths, a perception reinforced by the rhythm of the countersubject (mm. 26–27). The compound melody of the cadential portion consists of descending scales of a sixth in the upper voice and an octave in the lower voice. With the adjustment of the tonal answer to end on the tonic, the scales are extended to a seventh and a ninth in the answer (mm. 29–30).

Following an entrance of the countersubject alone, the answer and subject appear in violin and gamba, respectively, and each voice has completed an entrance of subject and answer by m. 42. No further complete expositions will appear. An episode in concertato texture in mm. 42–45, not based on previous material, effects a modulation to C major, preparing for truncated entrances of the theme in C and G in mm. 46–49. One more entrance of the full subject appears in mm. 51–54, followed by a truncated answer, a reworking of the episodic material, and a truncated statement of the subject. The fugue lasts for forty-three measures.

BuxWV 254 is perhaps the most contrapuntally conceived of all Buxtehude's sonatas, and yet it contains only this one fugue among its seven sections. Two slow sections are composed in invertible counterpoint, the opening Adagio and section 3, Lento. The other two slow sections, Largo (section 5) and the final

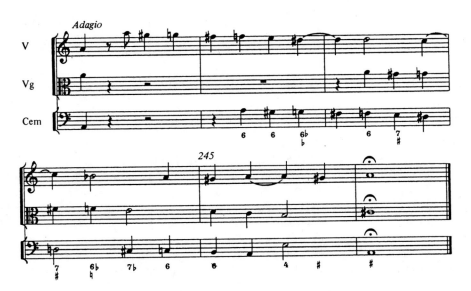

Example 8-2. BuxWV 254, mm. 241–46.

Example 8-3. BuxWV 254, mm. 82–92.

Lento or Adagio, are similar short, imitative sections based on a descending chromatic scale. The final section is particularly affective (ex. 8-2).

The fourth section, Vivace, could be said to contain an entrance of a subject and a real answer in each voice, but it does not really have the character of a fugue. It begins as if it would be a dance (mm. 82–84) and then proceeds to an eight-measure decorated descending melodic minor scale in steady eighth notes in the violin (mm. 85–92, ex. 8-3). The scale, but not the dance motive, is answered in the dominant by the gamba, accompanied by a countersubject consisting of syncopated parallel sixths. Although this theme dominates the section as a fugue subject would, its nature as a descending scale and the eight-measure periods that it forms lend it the character more of an ostinato theme than of a fugue subject. The dance motive at the beginning of each of its two parts further blunts whatever fugal character this section might have.

The descending scale, most prominent in its diatonic form in the central Vivace and in its chromatic form in the last two slow sections, unites all seven sections of BuxWV 254 motivically. It appears in numerous guises in the concertato Presto (section 6) and simultaneously in diatonic and chromatic form at the end of section 3, Lento (mm. 77–80). A descent from c″ to a′ begins the sonata, extended to the pentachord e″–a′ in the violin and the hexachord f′–a in the gamba at mm. 5–7. The dual scales at the end of the fugue subject and answer in section 2 extend the diatonic scale to an octave or a ninth. We can consider these first two sections discrete, closed movements, but following the introduction of the chromatic scale at the end of section 3, the sonata pushes relentlessly on to its conclusion without a full close.

Buxtehude's Sonata in G minor, op. 2, no. 3 (BuxWV 261; CD tracks 13–16), relies mainly on the ostinato for its structural underpinning. The first of its seven sections, Vivace (track 13), treats an ostinato bass freely; its fifth section, Andante (track 15), is a strict ciaccona over twenty-five repetitions of a four-measure bass pattern in the harpsichord. The opening free ostinato section begins as if it might be a fugue subject over a walking bass (ex. 8-4), and the gamba repeats this theme at its entrance in m. 7. Following the sixth appearance of the three-measure ostinato in G minor in the harpsichord, the gamba picks up its first measure and the violin imitates it at the fifth a measure later, continuing the fugal analogy (ex. 8-5; CD track 13, 00:52). The ostinato now begins anew in D minor, and at its fourth and fifth appearances the violin and gamba, respectively, repeat the theme with which the sonata opened, now in D minor. They have now each had an entrance of subject and answer, so to speak, and the ostinato breaks off. Following a modulation to B♭ major, the first of two free endings breaks in at m. 42 (CD track 13, 02:02), beginning canonically with a motive in persistent dactylic rhythm. The second free ending is a rhapsodic new section marked Lento.

Example 8-4. BuxWV 261, mm. 1–3.

Example 8-5. BuxWV 261, mm. 18–21.

    The fugue that follows as section 3, Allegro, of BuxWV 261 affirms its rela-
tionship to the preceding free ostinato, as can be seen in example 8-6 (CD track
14, 00:28). The head motive of the subject—in the gamba at m. 73—is somewhat reminiscent of the ostinato theme, as is the harpsichord line at m. 72. The
end of the countersubject—in the violin at m. 75—recalls the opening violin
theme. Following three expositions and two entrances in stretto, the fugue repeats
the beginning of the dactylic closing section to the Vivace at m. 87 and likewise
merges into a second free ending marked Lento, this time in simple chordal style.
    The ciaccona that forms the fifth section, Andante, of BuxWV 261 is built on an
ornamented version of the traditional descending tetrachord, whose tones arrive
on the third beat of each measure. The added pitches allow greater harmonic variety, including several Neapolitan sixth chords (ex. 8-7; CD track 15, 01:40). The
ostinato-fugue pair in the first half of this sonata is mirrored somewhat by the
ciaccona-gigue pairing in its second half. The gigue that forms section 7 (CD
track 16, 00:56) is the only named dance within the printed sonatas. Like the
gigues in most of Buxtehude's keyboard suites, but unlike those in Reincken's
Hortus musicus, the gigue at the end of BuxWV 261 is not a true fugue, although
it is consistently imitative. Motives in the gigue recall both the descending tetrachord of the ciaccona and the theme of the opening Vivace. The ciaccona-gigue

Example 8-6. BuxWV 261, mm. 72–76.

pair is separated by a short Grave (section 6), whose brief excursion to A♭ major is reminiscent of the Neapolitan chords in the previous section. Both ciaccona and gigue are tonally closed movements in G minor.

Unnamed dances occur in the printed sonatas with varying degrees of stylization. Most easily recognizable is the sarabande with double for violin solo that forms the second section of the C-major sonata, op. 1, no. 5 (BuxWV 256). The dance itself (mm. 40–71) falls into four eight-measure periods with the form AA′BC. The thoroughly consistent rhythm emphasizes the second beat at the beginning of each two-measure phrase. Although the tempo of the first statement is undesignated, the double (mm. 72–103) is marked Allegro. This tempo designation may not mark a change in the beat, however, but could rather describe the increased activity in the violin part to steady eighth notes. Two variations in

Example 8-7. BuxWV 261, mm. 145–49.

BuxWV 246, a C-major keyboard variation set—also based on a sarabande—are marked Allegro as well. The gigue that follows as section 4 of BuxWV 256, marked Allegro, is recognizable by its rhythm and mostly regular two-measure phrases. Its form, however—ABA'B'A"B"A'''—and tonal plan are considerably more complex than those of a normal gigue. A similar gigue with the form ABA is found as the fourth section, Allegro, of the G-major sonata, op. 1, no. 2 (BuxWV 253).

The foundation of Buxtehude's A-major sonata, op. 2, no. 5 (BuxWV 263), like that of BuxWV 261, rests on two sets of ostinato variations, one strict and one free, but in this case extensive solos for both violin and gamba endow the sonata with an air of improvisatory freedom. Following an opening fugue in gigue rhythm, sections 2 and 3 are devoted to the violin and section 4 to the gamba. In section 2, marked "Solo," the violin engages in rhapsodic figuration over a slowly descending bass line; section 3, Concitato, consists of eighteen variations over the descending tetrachord in A major. Monteverdi employed the term *concitato*, "agitated," to describe the style of rapid repeated notes that he used in compositions dealing with war. This section does indeed include many repeated notes, rapid ones in the violin part, slower ones in the bass. No tempo is given for either section, but the style indicates that they form a slow–fast pair. Section 4, marked Adagio, gives the gamba the opportunity to display its wide range as it descends from c♯" to E in the space of six measures. The remaining sections form a lengthy, freely treated ostinato complex, which shifts twice from F♯ minor to A major.

Buxtehude's Sonatas as Examples of the *Stylus Phantasticus*

The combination of the varied styles of the violin solo with an ostinato bass in BuxWV 263 brings to mind the sonata for two violins and viola da gamba by Kaspar Förster, which, according to Mattheson's account quoted in chapter 2, was performed at Christoph Bernhard's house in Hamburg in 1666. In it, "each had eight measures to play his free improvisations, according to the *stylus phantasticus.*" This sounds very much like an improvised ciaccona.

Several sonatas for two violins, viola da gamba, and continuo by Förster survive in manuscript, but unfortunately none contains a ciaccona or any indication that one was to be improvised. A trio sonata in F major titled "La Sidon" (*Uu* inst. 3:11) is of particular interest, however, because one of the violinists at the concert in Bernhard's house was Samuel Peter von Sidon. The sonata is in seven sections: [1] Allegro, a fugue; [2] Adagio, chordal, with ornamentation; [3] Presto or Allegro, imitative; [4–6] an Adagio–Allegro–Adagio complex for violin solo; [7] Allegro, an unnamed stylized gigue. The similarity to Buxtehude's sonatas in overall organization is striking. Furthermore, the second section may give an indication as to what Förster—and perhaps Buxtehude as well—meant by the *stylus phantasticus.* The texture of this nineteen-measure section is chordal throughout, but the first seven measures contain extensive ornamentation that passes from one instrument to another (ex. 8-8). The ornamentation ceases abruptly after the seventh measure, however, leaving the players themselves free to improvise, presumably on the same basis. A similar alternation in rhapsodic ornamentation is found at the beginning of the *Con discretione* section of Buxtehude's Sonata in D minor, op. 1, no. 6 (BuxWV 257; ex. 8-9), and an abrupt cessation in written ornamentation occurs in the Adagio of Buxtehude's A-major praeludium (BuxWV 151; ex. 8-10).

Free improvisation by a single performer—an organist, for example—is a relatively easy matter, but for a group of musicians playing a sonata it takes some planning. Förster's solution appears to have been one of agreed-upon alternation of improvisation, either for eight measures, presumably over an ostinato bass, or, in a shorter section, for as little as one measure. Buxtehude seems either to have composed certain sections of his sonatas to sound as if they were improvised, or to have written down the results of actual improvisations by his skilled colleagues among the municipal musicians.

The D-minor sonata (BuxWV 257)—the one that contains fourteen sections—is the most improvisatory in nature of all Buxtehude's printed sonatas. We have already mentioned the rhapsodic ornamentation of its *Con discretione* (section 3). Most evocative of the *stylus phantasticus*, however, in which "all kinds

Example 8-8. Förster, Sonata "La Sidon," mm. 28–35.

of otherwise unusual progressions . . . are brought forth . . . now swift, now hesitating," is the complex of sections 4–7 (mm. 53–80) and 9–10 (mm. 123–30),
which borders on the bizarre. Sections 4 and 6, each eight measures long, consist of the repeated oscillation of two chords decorated in the upper voices with
triplets, repeated notes, and octave leaps. The dynamics alternate between *forte*
and *piano* with each measure. These rapidly moving but harmonically static

Example 8-9. BuxWV 257, mm. 43–44.

Example 8-10. BuxWV 151, mm. 62–66.

sections alternate with the sustained and modulatory Adagio sections 5 and 7. Example 8-11 shows the end of section 4, all of section 5, and the beginning of section 6. Sections 9 and 10 repeat this alternation, substituting thirty-second notes for the triplets. Figure 8-1 reproduces a page of the original printed violin part for this sonata, beginning at the end of section 6, the last beat of m. 72. Section 7, Adagio, begins at the end of the first staff; section 8, 3/4 Vivace, in the middle of the second staff; section 9, in common time, at the beginning of the seventh staff; section 10, Lento, at the end of the ninth staff, and section 11, 6/8 Poco presto, on the tenth staff.

Even a sonata as "fantastic" as BuxWV 257, however, contains structured sections as well: section 2 is a fugue, and section 8 a dance in ABA form with perfectly regular phrases two and four measures in length, as can be seen in the second staff of figure 8-1. Marked Vivace, the dance is too fast to be a sarabande and lacks the upbeat of the courante; it must be a minuet. Mattheson describes the minuet in *Das Neu-Eröffnete Orchestre* as written in 3/4 but normally beat

Example 8-11. BuxWV 257, mm. 59–67.

almost as 3/8. Buxtehude's only named minuet, attached to the wedding aria *Deh credete il vostro vanto* (BuxWV 117), is in fact written in 3/8 (ex. 8-12). The head motive of the fugue subject of section 2 of BuxWV 257 (ex. 8-13a), a series of repeated octave leaps, gives a first hint of the octaves and repeated notes that will appear in sections 4, 6, and 9. Following its two expositions, the fugue continues with a considerable amount of free episodic material. The last entrance of the subject in the violin contains a notated ritard (ex. 8-13b), unique among Buxtehude's fugues.

Kircher included sonatas among the genres associated with the *stylus phantasticus,* so let us look once again at the instrumental ensemble pieces that he cites. Gregorio Allegri (1582–1652), *maestro di cappella* of the papal choir, is not known to have composed any instrumental music other than the *Symphonia* for

Figure 8-1. Buxtehude, *VII Suonate à doi* (Hamburg, [1694]), Sonata VI in D Minor (BuxWV 257), violin, mm. 72–139 (Uppsala Universitetsbibliotek).

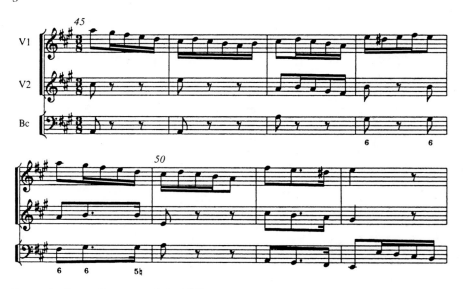

Example 8-12. "Menuetta" from BuxWV 117, mm. 45–52.

two violins, alto, and bass viola that Kircher prints in the *Musurgia*. It consists of four sections in different meters, each of them fugal to some degree, most clearly the first, in sprightly canzona style. The *Symphonia* for four lutes by Lelio Colista (1629–80) contains only one movement, also a fugue, but he left a large quantity of instrumental music, some of which calls for improvisation over bass patterns. In his *Itinerarium exstaticum* (1656), a book about astronomy, Kircher describes the performance of a piece for two violins and theorbo in which Colista took part that consisted of contrasting sections that evoked different affections in him.[3]

Mattheson did not include the sonata as one of the genres to which the *stylus phantasticus* applied, perhaps because by the time he was writing most sonatas were cast in the four-movement Corellian mold that had become standard. Buxtehude's sonatas are not at all like Corelli's. The freedom inherent in the *stylus phantasticus* underlies the overall plan of Buxtehude's sonatas as well as the rhapsodic style of some of their sections. Apart from the generally regular alternation of fast and slow sections, the content of those sections is unpredictable, as is their number. We can expect at least two orderly, structured sections, almost always among the fast sections, but we do not know what form they will take—a fugue? a variation set? a dance? Often these structured sections themselves contain surprises, such as the ostinato that becomes a fugue in the fifth section, Vivace, of BuxWV 262. But although the ordering of the sections in a

Example 8-13a. BuxWV 257, mm. 6–8.

Example 8-13b. BuxWV 257, mm. 37–42.

Buxtehude sonata gives the impression of being improvised, it has in fact been carefully planned, with the movements "following themselves cleverly," in Kircher's words, and motivic relationships between the sections tie them together in organic unity.

Buxtehude's sonatas stand together with his praeludia as his outstanding examples of the *stylus phantasticus*, and they share a number of traits, including their unpredictable arrangements of free and structured sections and the manner in which their fugues dissolve into free writing after they have completed the requisite number of entrances in each voice. Whether the sonatas originated in improvisation to the same degree as the praeludia is a question that we cannot answer until we know more about the practice, but if singers could compose fugues *a mente*, presumably string players could as well. The fact that the sonatas contain more ostinatos than the praeludia do may point in this direction.

Sonatas in Manuscript

BuxWV 266–73

Six complete sonatas for strings by Buxtehude and a seventh in fragmentary form survive in the Düben Collection at Uppsala; an eighth sonata ascribed to Buxtehude (BuxWV 268) is found in a peripheral source. Only the continuo part and the first two measures of the first violin part are extant for BuxWV 270, an F-major sonata in six sections for two violins and continuo. Its manuscript dates from the 1660s, demonstrating that Buxtehude was already composing sonatas while still in Helsingør. Of the complete Buxtehude sonatas in the Düben Collection, three are scored for two violins and viola da gamba (BuxWV 266, 269, 271), two for one violin and gamba (BuxWV 272, 273), and one for viola da gamba and violone (BuxWV 267), all with continuo.

The same book-fair catalogues of 1684 that list the lost Abendmusiken *Himmlische Seelenlust* and *Das allerschröcklichste* announce the forthcoming publication of "Sonaten à 2. & 3. Violini & Viola da gamba, cum continuo, zur Kirchen- u. Tafel-Music bequemlich, Lübeck, Samuel Otten u. Joh. Wiedemeyern" by Buxtehude. As is the case with the Abendmusiken, no evidence exists to indicate that the 1684 sonata collection ever actually appeared. Indeed, the fact that Buxtehude designated his 1694 collection "Opera prima" strongly suggests that it was his first collection to be published. The three sonatas for two violins, viola da gamba, and continuo may have been among those contemplated for publication in 1684, however. One of the manuscript sonatas for one violin and gamba, BuxWV 273, was taken into the 1694 printed collection in revised form; the revision is discussed in chapter 10.

Buxtehude's designation of the 1684 collection as "suitable for church- and dinner-music" indicates that he may have composed these sonatas for performance during services at St. Mary's. The two municipal musicians who played regularly with him at the organ until 1692, Hans Iwe and Johann Philip Roth, both played violin and viola da gamba, and other instrumentalists were paid from time to time for their performances from the organ, including Daniel Grecke in 1683; his principal instrument was the violin. The church paid for Franz Tunder's purchase in 1660 of trio sonatas by Johann Heinrich Schmelzer. His *Duodena Selectarum Sonatarum* of 1659 contains six sonatas for two violins, three sonatas for one violin and viola da gamba, and three sonatas for two violins and gamba, all with organ. Buxtehude specifically designated the harpsichord as the continuo instrument in his two printed collections, but the continuo part for BuxWV 273, the sonata taken into the 1694 collection, is labeled "Organo." Buxtehude probably performed all his sonatas both with the organ at St. Mary's and with the harpsichord in the homes of his Lübeck patrons.

Buxtehude demonstrates an approach to the overall organization of the six sonatas in the Düben collection similar to the one we have seen in the printed sonatas. The number of their sections varies from three in BuxWV 272 to nine in BuxWV 266 and 271. Four of the six contain two fugues, a much higher proportion than in the printed sonatas; all the fugues contain two expositions, except for BuxWV 273, which has three. BuxWV 272 contains no fugue; it consists of two strict ostinato settings, separated only by a ten-measure Adagio, and must be considered the most rigidly structured of all Buxtehude's sonatas. Sarabandes with doubles are found in BuxWV 267 and BuxWV 269. Four of these six manuscript sonatas contain solo sections, as opposed to only two of the fourteen printed sonatas, marking the greatest disparity between the two groups.

Several unique features may be observed in the manuscript sonatas that are not found in the published ones. BuxWV 273 contains a suite—Allemande, Courante, Sarabande, Gigue—that Buxtehude dropped when he revised this sonata for publication as op. 1, no. 4 (BuxWV 255). The inclusion of a second violin in three of Buxtehude's manuscript sonatas yields a fuller texture that is particularly noticeable in the fugues and chordal sections. It also heightens the contrast between the tutti sections and the solo sections that all three contain. The use of double stops in BuxWV 266 provides a polychoral effect at the beginning (ex. 8-14) and a rich, five-voice chordal close.

We can single out two particularly unusual sections from these manuscript sonatas: the ostinato that forms the sixth section of the G-major sonata, BuxWV 271, and the fugue that closes the F-major sonata, BuxWV 269. The Allegro of BuxWV 271 (mm. 49–125) is based alternately on two ostinato patterns in the continuo, one of eight measures, A, beginning with a descending tetrachord and ending on the dominant, and one of seven measures, B, which veers toward the submediant but likewise ends on the dominant. The first three variations in the first violin on the bass AAB are identical to the next three in the second violin. Both violins share variations 7-8 on the bass AB while the gamba doubles the continuo; all three instruments participate in the final variations 9 and 10 on the bass AB, with the gamba the most active. The fugue in mm. 186–253 of BuxWV 269 is also highly irregular. It begins with a ten-measure chordal introduction that sounds like a sarabande, the cadence of which begins the fugue subject (ex. 8-15). Following two expositions, the "sarabande" returns, a fourth higher, as an episode; subsequent chordal episodes separate an exposition on different degrees and stretto entrances, and the fugue concludes as a dance, with a petite reprise. Both these sections are highly structured, but it is not the

Example 8-14. BuxWV 266, mm. 1–9.

structure that we expect; the aesthetic of the *stylus phantasticus* appears to be at work.

The Sonata in D major for viola da gamba and violone (BuxWV 267) is notable for its unusual scoring. As might be expected, the viola da gamba remains in the alto and tenor range while the violone assumes a role somewhat similar to that of the gamba in the printed sonatas. The five sections of this sonata include a fugue that appears in two versions as sections 2 and 5. The fourth section is an engaging sarabande with three doubles, the first for gamba, the second for violone, and the third, marked Presto, for both instruments. In its fugal entrances and double, the violone—undoubtedly the 8′ instrument—is often independent of and above the continuo.

Two sonatas transmitted in peripheral sources are problematic: a solo sonata for viola da gamba and continuo (BuxWV 268) in a manuscript score at the Bodleian Library, Oxford, and a sonata, presumably originally scored for violin,

Example 8-15. BuxWV 269, mm. 187–201.

viola da gamba, and continuo that appears as an organ piece (BuxWV Anhang 5) in Yale's Lowell Mason Codex. Both sonatas raise serious questions concerning their authenticity as works of Buxtehude.

Apart from the introductory sonatas to the vocal works BuxWV 64 and 98, the sonata for viola da gamba and continuo in D (BuxWV 268) is the only extant sonata for a solo instrument attributed to Buxtehude. It consists of four through-composed sections, the first two undesignated as to tempo: [1] C (fast?), mm. 1–49; [2] 3/2 (slow?), mm. 50–92; [3] C, Allegro, 93–99; [4], Adagio, mm. 100–104. The overall layout is quite unbalanced; the individual sections consist mainly of figuration for gamba over a supporting bass and lack the stylistic contrast between sections that characterizes Buxtehude's other sonatas. Also lacking is any interchange between gamba and continuo such as we can observe in the sonata to *Jubilate Domino* (BuxWV 64), discussed in chapter 5. The manuscript collection in which this piece is found contains works by other Lübeck composers, however—four fantasias for two viole da gamba by Peter Grecke, a municipal musician from 1673 to 1678, and a sonata for viola da gamba and continuo by Davidt Adam Baudringer, possibly identical with David Arnold Baudringer, who was employed briefly in 1676 by St. Mary's as an extra instrumentalist at the large organ.

The D-minor sonata BuxWV Anhang 5 is titled "Sonata à 2 Clavir Pedal:" in the Lowell Mason Codex; an ascription to "Box de Hou" and a registration indication "Viol d Gamb:" between the two upper parts were added later, probably in the same hand. The two upper parts are written on separate staves while the pedal part appears in tablature below, a style of notation unique within this manuscript. The sonata consists of three sections, all undesignated as to tempo: [1] ₵ (fast), mm. 1–22; [2] C3/2 (slow?), mm. 23–47; [3] C (fast?), mm. 48–57. The piece bears no resemblance whatever to any organ work of Buxtehude, and Linfield has reconstructed it as a sonata for violin, viola da gamba, and continuo in the appendix to volume 14 of the Collected Works. Even in this form, however, the awkwardness of its composition cannot be overcome, and it is similar to Buxtehude's sonatas only to the extent that the gamba part performs divisions on the pedal part, now become continuo. Concordances to the sonata version, attributed to Johann Michael Nicolai (1629–85) and William Young (d. 1662), have recently come to light,[4] reinforcing the doubt of Buxtehude's authorship.

Both BuxWV 268 and Anhang 5 lack the firm structures that anchor Buxtehude's flights of fancy in his other complete sonatas and that can be detected as well from the continuo part of the early F-major sonata (BuxWV 270), in which the opening section appears to begin as a fugue and returns as the final section. Furthermore, with 104 measures and 57 measures, respectively, both of these problematic sonatas are considerably shorter than the shortest of the other sonatas, BuxWV 270, which contains 130 measures. Anhang 5 resembles a few of the introductory sonatas to Buxtehude's vocal music in total length but in no other respect.

Sonatas in Vocal Music

Buxtehude's most frequent use of the term *sonata* occurs not in his purely instrumental music but in connection with his vocal music. Eighty of his vocal works begin with a separate instrumental piece, ranging from eight to seventy-eight measures in length. Forty-six of these are called "Sonata," five "Sonatina" and twenty-one "Sinfonia"; the rest are undesignated. "Sonatina" should be a diminutive, but Buxtehude appears to have used it interchangeably with "Sonata." "Sinfonia," on the other hand, most often appears with shorter pieces; only once, in BuxWV 98, does it head a two-section piece with a tempo change, Adagio–Presto. The distinction is by no means clear-cut, however; "Sonata" is used in BuxWV 25 for a movement of only eleven measures, and it can be employed in a general sense for all of the introductory movements to Buxtehude's vocal works.

The large majority of Buxtehude's introductory sonatas are short, consisting of only one section and fewer than thirty measures. They are usually scored for the same instruments that will accompany the voices, most often two violins, with or without violone, or two violins, two violas, and violone, always with continuo. Only rarely do they employ motivic material from the vocal music that will follow; most often they are independent of it, although always in the same key. Most of the single-section sonatas are through-composed in trio or concertato texture, but pure chordal style and short fugues are also found. Of the few one-section sonatas that bear tempo markings, six are fast and two are slow. One in the latter category is the sonata of BuxWV 31, *Fürwahr, er trug unsere Krankheit*, whose autograph score is reproduced in figure 5-2. Its rapid dynamic shifts are exceptional but not unique among the introductory sonatas.

Of particular interest within the context of this chapter are the twenty-three introductory sonatas with more than one section. With few exceptions, they contain two or three sections that contrast with each other in both tempo and style. Tempo markings are not so consistently indicated as in the printed sonatas, but where they are present, they show the same alternation between fast and slow sections, and otherwise this tempo alternation is usually implicit. As in the strictly instrumental sonatas, the slow sections tend to be shorter and the fast sections more structured. A pattern frequently found contrasts one or more slow chordal sections with a fast fugal or imitative section. The sonata of *Ich halte es dafür* (BuxWV 48), for example, scored for violin, violetta, violone, and continuo, contains three sections: Adagio (mm. 1–5), chordal; Allegro (mm. 6–20), a three-voice fugue with two expositions; and a final undesignated section (mm. 21–29), chordal with repeated eighth notes in *tremolo*. The longest of the introductory sonatas, the opening movement of *Je höher du bist* (BuxWV 55), bears a strong resemblance to the strictly instrumental sonatas. Its first section is a stylized sarabande (mm. 1–42, ex. 8-16a) in the form AABBCC, with the repeated sections marked *piano*; a fugue follows with two expositions and countersubject (mm. 43–67, ex. 8-16b). The final section, marked Largo, is a chordal passage decorated in concertato style (mm. 69–78, ex. 8-16c). The seven sections of the sonata to "Ad cor: Vulnerasti cor meum," the sixth cantata of the *Membra Jesu* cycle, alternate slow chords with expositions of a fast fugue in a manner somewhat reminiscent of the fugue in BuxWV 269.

Example 8-16a. BuxWV 55, mm. 1–9.

Example 8-16b. BuxWV 55, mm. 47–50.

Example 8-16c. BuxWV 55, mm. 69–70.

The opening sonatas frequently reflect the affect of the texts that follow. No one could doubt that something both tragic and dramatic will follow the sinfonia of *Fürwahr, er trug unsere Krankheit* (BuxWV 31), with its C-minor tonality, slow *tremolo* chords and stark dynamic contrasts. The fast, bright sonatas of *Du Lebensfürst, Herr Jesu Christ* (BuxWV 22; Vivace, A major), *Jubilate Domino* (BuxWV 64, Allegro, D major) and *Mein Gemüt erfreuet sich* (BuxWV 72, Vivace, C major) likewise prepare the listener for the joyful texts of these works. The rapidly repeated chords in the sonata of *O fröhliche Stunden, o herrliche Zeit* (BuxWV 85) resemble the *stile concitato*, and the first strophe of the text indeed refers to victory in war; the key is C major. In its role as praeludium, the introductory sonata "prepares and excites the spirits of the listeners for the entertainment of the symphonic harmony that will follow,"[5] to use Kircher's words.

No discernible pattern emerges with respect to a relationship between the length and content of the introductory sonata and the genre of the vocal work as a whole. Although we might expect that a multimovement cantata would be preceded by a sonata in several sections, this is not always the case. *Alles was ihr tut* (BuxWV 4) begins with an Adagio–Presto sonata, which is repeated after the opening concerto, but the several movements of *Wo soll ich fliehen hin* (BuxWV 112) and *Ihr lieben Christen, freut euch nun* (BuxWV 51) follow single-section sonatas of fifteen and twenty measures, respectively. The multisection sonatas are distributed almost evenly among concertos, arias, and cantatas. A connoisseur of Buxtehude's music at St. Mary's Church in Lübeck who had received a printed copy of the text to a vocal work would have been able to form a reasonable expectation concerning the nature of that work—whether it would be a concerto, an aria, a chorale setting, or a cantata. Without a copy of the text, however, the opening sonata would have given him or her an idea of the basic affect of the vocal portions to follow but not a clue as to the form they would take.

It was certainly its freedom from the restraints imposed by the word that led Kircher to designate instrumental music as suitable for the *stylus phantasticus*, and Buxtehude demonstrates much greater freedom and fantasy in his instrumental music than in his vocal music. Among the several genres of instrumental music that Buxtehude cultivated, only the monodic chorale preludes and keyboard suites and variations have a structure that is at all predictable. We cannot predict the number or character of the individual variations, however, and the style of ornamentation in the chorale preludes, based on improvised vocal ornamentation, is highly unpredictable, leaving the suites as the only genre of Buxtehude's instrumental music in which the expectations aroused at the beginning of the piece are generally fulfilled. Among the instrumental genres, then, Buxtehude's suites seem to stand at the greatest distance from the freedom of the *stylus phantasticus*, and perhaps it was chiefly for this reason that he chose to eliminate the suite from his B♭-major sonata when he revised it for publication.

Part III

Studies Pertaining to Buxtehude's Music

Chapter Nine

The Sources of Buxtehude's Music

The esteem in which Buxtehude was held by members of his own and succeeding generations is reflected not so much by their words as by the painstaking copies that they made of his music. Through the study of the sources of his compositions, it becomes possible to trace the reception of his music both geographically and chronologically and to judge the relative importance of the various genres that he cultivated. An understanding of the sources is also an important if not indispensable aid to the performance of Buxtehude's music, with respect to both the actual notes that are to be played when editions differ and the manner of performance. This chapter gives a general account of the transmission of Buxtehude's music and a brief history of its most important sources. More information concerning these sources may be found in appendix 3; for detailed discussions see the critical reports of the Collected Works.

The Dissemination of Music in
Seventeenth-Century Germany

The major German composers of the first half of the seventeenth century published their music. Most of the works of Schütz, Michael Praetorius, Scheidt, and Schein appeared in print. Although publications of keyboard music appeared less frequently than those of vocal music, Scheidt's *Tabulatora nova* of 1624 stands out as a monument of the art of the German organist for which there is no counterpart in the second half of the century. During the later seventeenth century, the better composers turned away from publication in favor of manuscript dissemination of their music. This was the music collected and performed by the institutions with large and accomplished musical establishments: courts, the principal churches of large cities, and schools that cultivated music, such as St. Michael's in Lüneburg and St. Thomas's in Leipzig. Composers of music in a simpler style that more modest musical establishments could easily perform continued to publish their music in abundance; Andreas Hammerschmidt provides the most notable example. Krummacher has documented this entire development for the vocal music of the period in his dissertation *Die Überlieferung der Choralbearbeitungen.*

One reason for the reluctance of composers in the second half of the seventeenth century to publish their music lay in the fact that the more florid the music became and the more it employed smaller note values, the less easily it could be read when printed with movable type. Beamed groupings of eighth and sixteenth notes, which convey the placement of these notes with respect to the beat much more readily than single flagged notes, are easily written by hand but were difficult to print. With movable musical type, which German printers used well into the eighteenth century, each piece of type contained note head, stem, flag(s), and a small segment of each line of the staff, which was pieced together with its successive notes, sometimes in a rather bumpy fashion. Most seventeenth-century printed music contains no beams at all. The publisher of Rosenmüller's *Sonate* of 1682, an heir of Christoph Endter in Nuremberg, wrote in a foreword at the beginning of the *Violino Primo* part:

> With the advancement of the art [of music], the deficiencies of the music printed to date have finally become so great, that amateurs would rather copy their pieces with their own hands than submit to such irritation. Especially if a music lover wanted to play from such printed music he would pay a penalty, to tell the truth, because since in the runs the eighths, sixteenths and thirty-seconds cannot easily be recognized and distinguished from one another, it would almost be necessary to learn the piece by memory beforehand, if he wanted to play it correctly and not cause displeasure to delicate ears with false sounds.

Engraving on copper plates offered a fine solution to this problem—see the engraved example from Marpurg's *Abhandlung von der Fuge* (fig. 7-1)—but it was expensive and was not generally adopted in Germany until the eighteenth century. With the help of the Nürnberg organist Georg Caspar Wecker, Endter's heir printed Rosenmüller's sonatas in movable type with beams, and both volumes of Buxtehude's sonatas were similarly printed, as can be seen in figure 8-1. The technology was far from perfected, however, and these early beamed printed editions bear a distinct kinship to early examples of computer-printed music, in which beaming once again presented the most formidable problem. Mattheson used beamed movable type for the musical examples in *Der vollkommene Capellmeister*, and with reference to his "Beginning of a toccata by Froberger" (see fig. 7-2, actually BuxWV 152) he offers as an excuse for printing only three measures the fact that "because they are keyboard pieces, the notes entwined under and in one another cannot be properly represented with our printing."

Apart from his sonatas, only eight printed compositions for weddings and funerals by Buxtehude survived from his lifetime—all listed in appendix 3A—and four of these prints have been lost since 1942. They were usually published in a small issue by the family that had commissioned them, and many other similar works have probably disappeared. Buxtehude's funeral music for his father (BuxWV 76), a rather more ambitious work than the other occasional pieces, was published in 1674 by the Lübeck book dealer Ulrich Wettstein. Of the other three occasional prints presently extant, BuxWV 116 and 118 were printed in Lübeck by Gottfried Jäger's heirs in 1672 and 1675 and BuxWV 61 in Ratzeburg by Niclas Nissen in 1677. None of these four editions has beams.

Whether printed or in manuscript, ensemble music could be arranged either in score or in separate parts, depending on the use for which it was intended—a score to give an overview of the work, parts to serve the practical purpose of performing it. The commemorative nature of the four extant wedding and funeral prints is demonstrated by the fact that all are in score. The sonatas, like most printed music of the day, were issued in parts.

German organists employed another form of notation to gain an overview of an ensemble work as well as to write their keyboard music: the letter notation known as German organ tablature. The system consists of three parts: letters to indicate the pitch class; the use of upper case, lower case, and octave lines to designate the octave; and rhythm signs. The letters from *a* to *h* are used, with *b* designating B♭ and *h* B♮. Apart from B♭, the black notes on the keyboard are all indicated as sharps, with a downward hook on the letter, regardless of how they would have been notated in staff notation; E♭ always appears as D♯. Each pitch is notated as it is meant to sound; there are no key signatures in tablature. The Helmholtz pitch notation used in this book to distinguish octave levels derives from German organ tablature and is identical to it for the range covered. Instead of short lines for each letter—i.e. c′ for middle C—tablature uses long lines to group the notes of an entire measure; these lines thus clarify the meter as well as designating the octave. The potential for misreading or miswriting the octave lines is great, particularly when the melody skips between octaves within a measure. The rhythm signs consist of vertical strokes to represent each note and horizontal strokes to designate the note value: none for whole notes, one for half notes, up to five for thirty-second notes. Notes with identical values may be grouped together by joining their horizontal strokes, which serves a function similar to beaming. Rests are indicated by positioning the rhythm sign in place of a letter.

Example 9-1 offers an exact transcription of Gustav Düben's intabulation of the last five measures of *O dulcis Jesu* (BuxWV 83) and the first five measures of the sonata to *Kommst du, Licht der Heiden* (BuxWV 66) in the manuscript *Uu* 82:42 (fig. 9-1). Düben uses Gothic script letters for the pitches in the tablature and the title of BuxWV 66 and Latin letters for the text of BuxWV 83, the Italian scoring and tempo indications, and Buxtehude's initials. The difference is most apparent in the capital letter *H*: Gothic in the fourth and eighth letters of the continuo line to BuxWV 83 and Latin in the third of Buxtehude's initials [Dieterich Buxte Hude]. The accidentals appear in the transcription just as they do in the tablature, although they make no tonal sense for the B♭ major of BuxWV 66. Düben's indication of sharps is inconsistent; he sometimes crosses the hook, but usually he does not. Düben begins his new octaves with the pitch class H (B♮) rather than C, as can be seen in his use of double lines with the *h* in the voice at m. 288 of BuxWV 83. In Düben's hand, the signs for single half and quarter notes are quite stylized, and the sign for the quarter note resembles his lower-case *e*. Groups of half or quarter notes are indicated in the transcription with brackets.

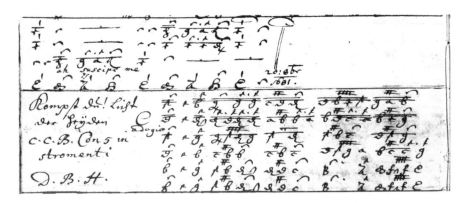

Figure 9-1. Tablature of Gustav Düben: Buxtehude, *O dulcis Jesu* (BuxWV 83), mm. 88–92; *Kommst du, Licht der Heiden* (BuxWV 66), Sonata, mm. 1–5 (Uppsala Universitetsbibliotek, vokalmusik i handskrift 82:42, fol. 17v).

Keyboard music was written in both tablature and staff notation. Tablature offered the advantage of keeping the contrapuntal lines separate and of requiring less space; staff notation is better suited to free textures in which the number of voices varies. No autographs of Buxtehude's keyboard music survive, but Johann Gottfried Walther owned pieces "from Mr. Buxtehude's own hand in German tablature," as he wrote to Heinrich Bokemeyer on 6 August 1729. Most of the copies of Buxtehude's organ music, however, are in staff notation. The use of a third staff for the pedal part of organ music did not become common until the nineteenth century, but Walther used three staves for many of his copies of Buxtehude's chorale preludes in order to separate the ornamented melodic line, the inner parts, and the pedal. Buxtehude's other organ music is notated in two staves, as in the Yale's Lowell Mason Codex (see fig. 7-3), and the Berlin manuscript 2681 (see fig. 11-1). Johann Friedrich Agricola modified this system somewhat by using red ink for the pedal part in his copy of some of Buxtehude's *pedaliter* praeludia (*Bc* U 26659). Michael Belotti's editions of Buxtehude's *pedaliter* works in *The Collected Works* employ the two-staff notation of the sources.

Buxtehude's Autograph Manuscripts

Caspar Ruetz, cantor of St. Mary's in Lübeck, wrote the following in 1753 concerning the music collection that he had inherited from his predecessors:

> I inherited a large pile of church music from my late father-in-law Sivers and grandfather-in-law Pagendarm. Of the pieces left by Pagendarm I have been able to use not a single

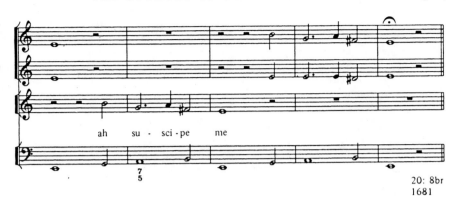

20: 8br
1681

Kompst du! Licht der Heÿden C.C.B. Con 5 in stromenti D.B.H.

Example 9-1. Transcription of figure 9-1 (BuxWV 83, mm. 288–92; BuxWV 66, Sonata, mm. 1–5).

one, and only a few from Sivers. They testify to the enormous diligence and industry of these upright men. Everything that these men wrote with so much trouble and work, or at great expense collected and had copied, has not the slightest value now, although no small amount of capital went into it. This mass of musical paper from many years ago has diminished by about half; much of it has gone into the stove in place of kindling, much has been used around the house, and much has been given to people who can use all sorts of scrap and paper in their shops. But I have tried to save most of the scores of the old pieces for the sake of their antiquity and in order to see what the taste and character of music from those times was like. I predict no better fate for my own music, and I am satisfied with that, because I am no better than my fathers. Recently I decided that I wanted to know how much all this old music, which takes up so much space in my house, might have cost. So I began to weigh it, and it came to 600 pounds, conservatively estimated. One book of music paper weighs at least a pound, so that is 600 books of paper. We shall reckon 6 shillings per book, although Sivers used the best paper, costing 8 to 10 shillings; that makes 3,600 shillings or 225 marks. A book contains 24 bifolios; figuring copying costs at 2 shillings per bifolio, that makes 3 marks per book paid to the copyist, or 1,800 marks for the 600 books. Added to the cost of the paper, 225 marks, that makes 2,025 marks. The cost for the use of the scores and postage we shall estimate at no more than 300 marks; that makes 2,325 marks. . . . Now if half of all the music of my predecessors is lost, and we add that, we get 4,650 marks. With that much capital one could really start something. But who will give anything for it, other than someone who needs scrap paper, for nothing is more useless than old music.[1]

We can assume that the same fate befell the manuscripts that Johann Christian Schieferdecker must have inherited from his father-in-law, for none of Buxtehude's autographs or performing materials survives in Lübeck. Only one major manuscript containing Buxtehude's music, the tablature A 373, remained in Lübeck until the twentieth century; following a postwar sojourn in the former East Berlin—its location at the time of the publication of the first edition of this book and volume 9 of the Collected Works—it is now back in Lübeck.

Seven autograph manuscripts of Buxtehude survive in the Düben Collection in Uppsala: the score of *Fürwahr, er trug unsere Krankheit* (BuxWV 31; *Uu* vokalmusik i handskrift 6:9, see fig. 5-2), the parts for *Herr, ich lasse dich* nicht (BuxWV 36, *Uu* 51:2) and the tablatures for *Membra Jesu* (BuxWV 75; *Uu* 50:12, see fig. 4-1), *Nimm von uns, Herr, du treuer Gott* (BuxWV 78; *Uu* 82:38), *Nun danket alle Gott* (BuxWV 79; *Uu* 82:39, fig. 9-2), *O Jesu mi dulcissime* (BuxWV 88 [fragment]; *Uu* 82:40), *O fröhliche Stunden, o herrliche Zeit* (BuxWV 85), and *Klinget für Freuden* (BuxWV 119), both in *Uu* 51:13a. In a study published in the *Svensk tidskrift* in 1966, Grusnick identified six of these manuscripts as autographs on the basis of comparisons with the canon BuxWV 124 and the few photographs of Buxtehude's letters that were then available. Peter Wollny has recently identified *Uu* vmhs 51:2 (*Herr, ich lasse dich nicht*) as an autograph.[2] The considerable amount of autograph material, principally the Wochenbücher, that has since come to light or reappeared has confirmed their judgment concerning these manuscripts. Grusnick also demonstrated that the parts for *Aperite mihi portas justitiae* (BuxWV 7; *Uu* 50:4, reproduced in *Werke*, vol. 7), are not written in Buxtehude's hand.

Figure 9-2 reproduces the first page of *Uu* 82:39, showing mm. 1–54 of *Nun danket alle Gott*. Buxtehude's tempo indications Allegro–Adagio–Allegro for the three-part sonata can be seen, as well as his direction for the entrance of the capella at m. 50. Buxtehude's tablature notation differs from Düben's with respect to the designation of the second octave above middle C; instead of Düben's more conventional double lines, Buxtehude uses a series of short, wavy strokes. Another characteristic of Buxtehude's tablature hand is his frequent use of a straight downward stroke rather than a hook to designate F♯; this can be seen in the third and fourth lines of the second system—presumably the violone

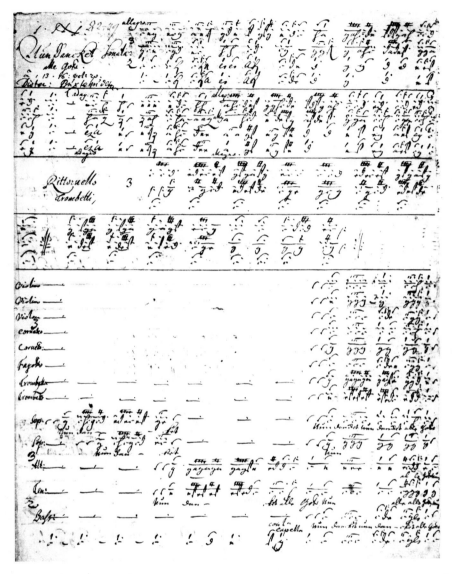

Figure 9-2. Buxtehude, *Nun danket alle Gott* (BuxWV 79), mm. 1–54. Autograph tablature (Uppsala Universitetsbibliotek, vokalmusik i handskrift 82:39, fol. 1r).

and continuo parts—in the Adagio section of the sonata. Buxtehude begins his new octaves with the pitch class C.

Buxtehude must have sent numerous autographs to Stockholm to serve as exemplars for the copies made there, and most of them were probably returned to him in Lübeck, only to be converted into scrap paper by subsequent generations. From the seven autograph manuscripts that remained in Stockholm, copies were made for three works—sets of parts for *Membra Jesu* and *Klinget für Freuden* and a tablature copy of *O fröhliche Stunden*. A comparison of Buxtehude's tablature of *Membra Jesu* with the parts that Düben extracted from it shows that Buxtehude left a number of details to Düben's discretion: the precise scoring of the first five cantatas, the continuo figuration, and the participation of vocal capella and ripieno instruments. In addition, Düben modified the ending of the concerto in the first cantata and added an extra viola part to the first and fourth cantatas.

The Düben Collection

Gustav Düben's close friendship with Buxtehude, discussed in chapter 4, accounts for the large number of Buxtehude's works in Düben's music collection. The collection—now in Uppsala—that he and his two sons assembled as Kapellmeisters of the Swedish royal court contains some 2,300 vocal and instrumental works in manuscript and twenty-five prints from the seventeenth and early eighteenth centuries. Buxtehude is the composer most heavily represented in the collection, and it in turn is by far the most important source for Buxtehude's music. Of the 122 vocal works considered in chapter 5, one hundred have sources in the Düben Collection, and the sources for eighty-four vocal works are found only there. For the sonatas, the Düben Collection contains the only complete copy of the prints and the only sources for all but the two problematic sonatas in manuscript. The libretto for Buxtehude's Abendmusik *Die Hochzeit des Lamms* forms part of the collection, as well as the parts for the oratorio *Wacht! Euch zum Streit*, transmitted anonymously but very likely by Buxtehude.

Düben's collection consists mainly of tablatures and part sets of vocal music, and his aim may have been to have a copy of each for every work in his collection. Forty-four of Buxtehude's vocal works are present in both tablature and parts. For the most part, Düben copied the tablatures himself into large volumes, which he undoubtedly used for reference purposes. A staff of assistants—probably court musicians—helped him with the copying of the part sets. Grusnick identified the hands of six different assistants, all of whom were involved in the copying of works by Buxtehude. In the case of three works—BuxWV 22, 62, and 91—for which I have collated the variants between tablature and parts, it can be shown that neither served as the exemplar for the other, but both derive from a missing source, probably one sent by Buxtehude from Lübeck and subsequently returned there. In each case the parts supply significantly more information concerning performance, such as continuo figures, articulation marks, and a more careful text underlay.

Gustav Düben's copying activity stopped in 1687, and he died in 1690. His youngest son Anders brought three Buxtehude sonatas and perhaps a few vocal works back with him from his study trip of 1692. The copy of the published sonatas of 1694 and 1696 that later became a part of the collection belonged at first to Jakob Boisman, a gambist for the Swedish court from 1702 until his death in 1729.

The contents of the manuscripts in the Düben Collection that contain works of Buxtehude are listed in appendix 3, B9. The study of these sources, particularly the part sets, reveals much information concerning the performance of this music: the number of voices and instruments that were involved, if and when they were doubled, and the types and number of continuo instruments. These matters are discussed in chapter 11. The *Düben Collection Database Catalogue*, edited by Erik Kjellberg and Kerala Snyder, was made public on the World Wide Web in 2006. In addition to basic information on the sources and works in the collection, it offers detailed descriptions of the individual parts and tablature volumes, inventories of watermarks and handwriting, and scanned copies of the manuscripts themselves.[3]

The Österreich-Bokemeyer Collection

This manuscript collection, assembled by Georg Österreich (1664–1735) and Heinrich Bokemeyer (1679–1751) and now housed at the Staatsbibliothek zu Berlin, contains over eighteen hundred vocal compositions by German and Italian composers and forms one of the most important sources for German Protestant music of the second half of the seventeenth century. Österreich studied composition with Johann Theile while working as a tenor at the court in Brunswick-Wolfenbüttel from 1686 to 1689 and then served as Kapellmeister to the Duke of Schleswig-Holstein at Gottorf castle in Schleswig from 1689 to 1702. His part of the collection includes works of Bernhard, Bruhns, Buxtehude, Capricornus, Förtsch, Knüpfer, Johann Philipp Krieger, Lübeck, Pohle, Rosenmüller, and Theile, among others. Peter Wollny has recently suggested that this was Österreich's private collection, never the property of the court, as was previously thought, and thus not copied exclusively during his Gottorf years.[4] He sold his collection in 1718 to Heinrich Bokemeyer (1679–1751), who augmented it with his own copies. Their collection also contains numerous theoretical treatises in copies by Österreich, Bokemeyer, and Bokemeyer's friend through correspondence, Johann Gottfried Walther. These include Bernhard's treatises on composition and singing and Theile's treatises on invertible counterpoint and his *Musikalisches Kunstbuch*. The collection later belonged to Johann Nikolaus Forkel and eventually came to the royal library in Berlin.

Österreich must have had ample opportunity to become acquainted with Buxtehude's music. He had worked as a singer in Hamburg during the mid-1680s, and Schleswig is only about 120 kilometers distant from Lübeck. It is surprising, then, that the entire collection contains only nine works by Buxtehude, including BuxWV 43 and 101, whose authenticity is questionable. Five manuscripts (containing BuxWV 17, 52, 80, 100, and 101) come from Österreich's collection; Bokemeyer added three (with BuxWV 43, 76-1, and 111), and the manuscript of BuxWV 4 is in a hand foreign to the collection. Eight of these manuscripts are bound together to form a convolute, *B* 2680; the ninth, containing BuxWV 111, remains alone as *B* 2679.

It is possible that Österreich's collection once contained more works by Buxtehude; Kümmerling suggests that the collection is presently only half its original size. Another North German collection of vocal music from the same period, however, had a similarly meager representation of works by Buxtehude. The inventory of the music collection at St. Michael's School in Lüneburg from the year 1696[5] shows only three works by Buxtehude out of nearly eleven hundred works listed. The presence of so few works by Buxtehude in these two large North German collections indicates that his vocal music was little known outside of Lübeck and Stockholm. Beyond the walls of Lübeck, Buxtehude's reputation was definitely that of an organist, not a composer of vocal music.

The Manuscripts of the Bach Circle

We must presume that Johann Sebastian Bach returned from his trip to Lübeck with copies of Buxtehude's works; his zeal for copying the music of other composers is well known. And yet the only manuscript of a Buxtehude work in his hand—the newly discovered Weimar copy of *Nun freut euch lieben Christen gmein* (BuxWV 210)—dates from several years before the Lübeck trip. This work was probably just one of numerous Buxtehude works that were already circulating in Thüringen well before Bach's first trip to North Germany in 1700. Regardless of Bach's own sources, however, at least thirty of Buxtehude's organ works are preserved in manuscripts emanating from Bach's circle of relatives, pupils, and friends. It seems clear that Bach transmitted his enthusiasm for Buxtehude's music to his associates and in some cases made his own copies available to them; they in turn disseminated Buxtehude's works along with those of Bach. Five centers of activity can be discerned: Ohrdruf, Berlin, Erfurt, Gräfenroda, and Apolda (Weimar).

Ohrdruf

Weimar, Herzogin Anna Amalia Bibliothek, Fol. 49/11 (BuxWV 210)
Berlin, Staatsbibliothek [*B*], Mus. ms. 40644 ("Möllersche Handschrift"; BuxWV 151, 165)
Leipzig, Städtische-Bibliotheken-Musikbibliothek [*LEm*], Sammlung Becker III.8.4 ("Andreas-Bach-Buch"; BuxWV 137, 150, 159, 160, 161, 174, 216)

The recent discovery by Michael Maul and Peter·Wollny of the Weimar tablature containing J. S. Bach's copy of a portion of Buxtehude's *Nun freut euch lieben Christen gmein* (BuxWV 210) marks an important development for both Bach and Buxtehude studies.[6] In this tablature, Bach follows the handwriting style of his older brother Johann Christoph, and thus Wollny dates it 1698–99, while Sebastian was still living in Ohrdruf. (In a slightly later tablature preserved with this one, a complete copy of Reincken's *An Wasserflüssen Babylon* dated 1700, Bach draws closer to the handwriting of his Lüneburg teacher, Georg Böhm.) The single leaf of tablature contains on its first side seven complete systems in its intact portion, with the first thirty-eight measures of *Nun freut euch*; below that in the torn portion are parts of two more systems. The second side contains mm. 54–83. A water stain, shared with the Reincken copy, blurs a part of the right edge.

That the thirteen- or fourteen-year-old Bach was copying—and presumably playing—such an ambitious work provides the best evidence yet found of the early development of his prodigious skills. Presumably his exemplar belonged to his brother and teacher Johann Christoph, who may have copied it from his teacher and friend, Johann Pachelbel. Pachelbel must have been well acquainted with Buxtehude's music, since he dedicated his *Hexachordum Appolinis* to Buxtehude in 1699. Bach's tablature provides the earliest evidence for the circulation of Buxtehude's distinctly North German chorale fantasias in central Germany and helps to explain Bach's decision to travel north for further study, first to Lüneburg and later to Lübeck. Bach's manuscript in turn became the exemplar for Johann Gottfried Walther's copy of this work, as discussed below.

Both the "Möllersche Handschrift" and the "Andreas-Bach-Buch" once belonged to the organist Johann Gottfried Möller (1774–1833), who was born in Ohrdruf. The first two are known to have belonged to the family of Johann Christoph Bach (1671–1721), organist in Ohrdruf, J. S. Bach's elder brother and the father of Andreas Bach, through the end of the eighteenth century. Hans-Joachim Schulze has identified Johann Christoph Bach as the principal scribe of both these manuscripts, the copying of which he dates between about 1705 and 1713.[7] Each of them contains an early autograph entry by J. S. Bach, BWV 535a in *B* 40644 and a Fantasia in C minor written in tablature in *LEm* III.8.4.[8] In addition to copies of numerous early Bach keyboard works, they both transmit a rich repertoire of North German keyboard music: works by Reincken, Böhm, Bruhns, Ritter, Heidorn, and Flor besides those by Buxtehude. A wide variety of genres is represented, including many suites, praeludia, and toccatas, but few chorale settings. Dances and other works presumably intended for harpsichord or clavichord predominate over *pedaliter* works for organ.

The works of Buxtehude transmitted by these manuscripts, especially the unica among them, are the most likely candidates for works that Sebastian brought back from Lübeck in 1706 and stand in rather sharp contrast to their repertoire as a whole. All but two of the Buxtehude works call expressly for pedal. Even more striking, four of his six complete works in the "Andreas-Bach-Buch" are ciacconas in whole or in part—his most significant keyboard works in this genre—for which this manuscript is the unique source. They stand beside only three other ostinato works in the manuscript, one by Pachelbel, one by J. C. F. Fischer and, most significantly, the Passacaglia and Fugue in C minor by J. S. Bach (BWV 582).

One other manuscript may belong to this group:

Pittsburgh, Carnegie Library [*Pc*], Call number rQM10 .B89 BuxWV 148 1695x (BuxWV 148)

This manuscript came to light in 1987 and also once belonged to Johann Gottfried Möller. Hans-Joachim Schulze initially identified Johann Christoph Bach as the principal scribe and the young Johann Sebastian as a possible second copyist, dating it about 1700, but both Wollny and Belotti have questioned this identification.[9] Wollny sees only one copyist and also questions the date; Belotti notes the resemblance of the handwriting to that of the Pachelbel school. In view of the correct first name on Bach's Weimar tablature, "Diet. Buxtehude," the Pittsburgh manuscript's incorrect ascription, "Praeludium. del Sig.[re] Daniel. Boxtehude. Org: Lubeci." casts further doubt on it as a Bach copy. The manuscript contains three leaves with one work, BuxWV 148, which shares with several works in the "Andreas-Bach-Buch" the fact that its final section is a ciaccona. This work was in circulation in central Germany possibly as early as 1675, in a lost tablature written by Johann Georg Grobe (see chapter 10), and definitely by 1688, in the Lowell Mason Codex, in which the work is similarly ascribed to "Sig: D Box de Hou. Org: Libec."

Berlin

Berlin, Staatsbibliothek [*B*], Mus. ms. 2681 (BuxWV 139, 140, 141, 142, 143, 145, 149, 153, 156, 163, 164, 168, 171, 176, 213)
Brussels, Bibliothèque du Conservatoire Royal de Musique [*Bc*], Ms. U-26659 (BuxWV 139, 140, 141, 142, 143, 145, 146, 149, 153, 156, 203)

Berlin was the principal center for the appreciation of the works of J. S. Bach during the later eighteenth century. C. P. E. Bach worked there from 1738 to 1768 as harpsichordist to Frederick the Great. Johann Friedrich Agricola (1720–74), composer and conductor at the court, had studied with J. S. Bach from 1738 to 1741 along with Johann Philipp Kirnberger (1721–83), who later served Princess Anna Amalia, the sister of Frederick the Great, and helped assemble her famous library. Agricola's and Kirnberger's passionate interest in what was by then "early music" was carried forward by Carl Friedrich Christian Fasch (1736–1800), second harpsichordist under C. P. E. Bach and founder of the Singakademie; Carl Friedrich Zelter (1758–1832), his pupil and successor as conductor of the Singakademie; and Georg Poelchau (1773–1836), director of the library of the Singakademie. Poelchau's own library, formed in part by purchases from the estates of C. P. E. Bach and Johann Nikolaus Forkel, provided an important early component of the music division of the royal library in Berlin.

Johann Friedrich Agricola copied most of the manuscript U-26659, now in Brussels, some time after he had moved to Berlin in 1741.[10] He devoted this manuscript exclusively to *pedaliter* organ works of Buxtehude and Bruhns, and it presents a marvelous selection of the Buxtehude organ works that are most appreciated and performed today, including the Praeludia in D major (BuxWV 139), E minor (BuxWV 142), F♯ minor (BuxWV 146) and G minor (BuxWV 149). Four other manuscripts derive from it, two of which belonged to Princess Anna Amalia's library.[11] I introduce it first not because it offers the best source for the works it transmits—it certainly does not—but because it best represents the enthusiasm for Buxtehude's music that Bach must have conveyed to his students, even if he himself did not supply the exemplars for the works it contains.

The notation of Agricola's manuscript suggests that he had three different exemplars. He probably copied the first piece, *Magnificat primi toni* (BuxWV 203), while he was still in Leipzig. It is the only Buxtehude work here based on a cantus firmus; it is on different paper from the rest of the manuscript, and it must have been joined to it later, since none of the derived manuscripts contains this work. Agricola wrote it on two staves using soprano and bass clefs; the use of pedals or manuals is indicated with the letters *p* and *m*. He also copied the central portion of the manuscript on two staves using the same clefs, but here he notated the pedal part in red ink. In the final portion, he used a G clef for the top staff of Buxtehude's F♯-minor praeludium (BuxWV 146) and Bruhns's Preludio in G major while continuing the pedal part in red ink; he wrote the last piece, Bruhns's *Nun komm, der Heiden Heiland*, with three staves, using the red ink to indicate Rückpositiv and Organo.

Belotti has now shown that Agricola copied the central portion of his manuscript (numbers 2-10 in the list of appendix 3, B2) from another that is now in Berlin, *B* 2681 (see fig. 11-1). Agricola once may have owned the Berlin manuscript, which later belonged to the library of Johann Nicolaus Forkel, Bach's first biographer, from whose estate Georg Poelchau purchased it in 1819.[12] Agricola copied these works in exactly the same order, but chose not to copy five *manualiter* works by Buxtehude and one by Buttstedt. One of these, BuxWV 164, also belongs to the Weimar branch of the Bach-circle transmission by virtue of a concordance in *B* Mus. Ms. 30194, probably copied by Bach's student Johann Martin Schubart.[13] The scribe of *B* 2681 remains unidentified, but Belotti has dated it about 1720 and suggests it originated around Erfurt. His close study of the numerous errors that it contains in comparison with concordant sources leads him to conclude that it is unlikely that it ever belonged to Johann Sebastian Bach and rather is the last of numerous redactions of a repertoire that was circulating in Thüringen before 1690. *B* 2681 was the principal source for Spitta's edition of the works that it contains.

Erfurt

New Haven, Yale University Music Library [NH]

LM 4838 (BuxWV 138)
LM 4983 ("Johann-Günther-Bach-Buch"; BuxWV 164, 172)

Erfurt had a rich organ tradition and many connections with the Bach family over the generations. Johann Sebastian's elder brother Johann Christoph was born there and studied there with Pachelbel. Another native son, Johann Christian Kittel (1732–1809), studied with Bach in Leipzig from 1748 to 1750 as one of his last pupils, later returning to Erfurt as organist. During his lifetime he assembled a very large music collection, which included many organ works of Bach and a few of Buxtehude. Johann Christian Heinrich Rinck (1770–1846) studied with Kittel in Erfurt from 1786 to 1789. He was the owner but according to Belotti not the principal copyist of LM 4838, whose contents derived from his studies with Kittel and which contains seven works of Bach in addition to a C-major praeludium by Buxtehude. Rinck's music library also included LM 4983, which was copied by another Johann Christoph Bach (1673–1727), cantor in nearby Gehren and second cousin to J. S. Bach.[14] This manuscript was later owned by his son, Johann Günther Bach, a municipal musician in Erfurt. J. G. Bach died there in 1756, the year in which Kittel was appointed organist of the Barfüßerkirche, so Kittel might have acquired the manuscript from Johann Günther Bach's estate and later passed it on to Rinck.[15] In addition to its two authentic Buxtehude works, LM 4983 includes a misattribution to Buxtehude: the chorale setting "Christ lag in Todesbanden" on page 53.[16] This same work appears ascribed to "N. V.," i.e., Nicolaus Vetter, in a copy by Johann Gottfried Walther (*B* 22541/3, p. 123), a more reliable attribution.

Rinck's music library was purchased in 1852 by Lowell Mason and brought to the United States. The famous codex "EB—1688" (the Lowell Mason Codex) also belonged to Rinck's collection, but he acquired it only in 1836, long after his study with Kittel. Its copies of Buxtehude works are quite independent of those from the Bach circle, and this important source is discussed separately below.

Gräfenroda

Lübeck, Bibliothek der Hansestadt [*LÜh*], Mus U 212 (BuxWV 218)
Berlin, Staatsbibliothek [*B*], Mus. ms. 30381 (BuxWV 145)

One of the early collectors of the works of Bach was Johann Peter Kellner (1705–72), cantor in the village of Gräfenroda, southwest of Arnstadt. Although he was not a pupil of J. S. Bach, Kellner was personally acquainted with him; his copies of Bach works begin about 1725.[17] Among Kellner's pupils was the organist Johannes Ringk (1717–78), who studied with him in Gräfenroda beginning about 1730. Two of Ringk's copies are dated that year, one containing Bach's wedding cantata *Weichet nur, betrübte Schatten* (BWV 202) and the other—the manuscript now in Lübeck—the beginning of Buxtehude's *Te Deum* (BuxWV 218). His other Buxtehude copy, contained in *B* 30381, dates from about the same time.[18] Ringk settled in Berlin about 1740 and was appointed organist of St. Mary's there in 1755. He was one of the organists whom Zelter remembered in 1829 as having played "almost nothing but works by the old Bach."[19] Perhaps Ringk played these works by Buxtehude as well.

Apolda/Weimar

Leipzig, Musikbibliothek der Stadt [*LEm*], Sammlung Seiffert, Ms. S4 (BuxWV 165)

One Buxtehude work, already present in Johann Christoph Bach's "Möllersche Handschrift," was also copied by Johann Gottlieb Preller (1727–86), one of the two main scribes of the Mempell-Preller collection, through which numerous works of J. S. Bach are transmitted. Preller came from Oberroßla, a small town near Apolda, where Johann Nicolaus Mempell served as cantor from 1740 until his death in 1747. According to Schulze, Mempell had probably been a pupil of Johann Peter Kellner in Gräfenroda; most of Mempell's copies derive from Kellner's exemplars. Preller, probably a pupil of Mempell, acquired his collection and complemented it with his own copies, which mainly derive not from Mempell's but from the Bach circle in Weimar; they probably date from the years 1743–49. According to Thomas Synofzik, Preller studied at the Gymnasium in Weimar from 1744 to 1751. Preller matriculated at the University of Jena in 1750 and served as cantor in Dortmund from 1753 until his death. There he enjoyed a reputation as a skillful keyboard player; he also composed, and his keyboard compositions were judged "too difficult for the left hand."[20]

Preller's copy of BuxWV 165 differs from that of Johann Christoph Bach by virtue of its lavish ornamentation and detailed fingerings. The ornamentation is reproduced in Seiffert's edition of the work; a sample of the fingering indications can be seen in example 11-6. Since the work exists in the earlier source without the ornamentation, and since Preller was known for his keyboard dexterity, it can be assumed that the ornaments, as well as the fingerings, are his own additions and do not reflect Buxtehude's practice, or even Bach's.

Taken together, these manuscripts from the Bach circle account for over two thirds of Buxtehude's free *pedaliter* organ works and half the free *manualiter* works. The narrow selection from Buxtehude's total oeuvre that these manuscripts offer is noteworthy. This group of manuscripts contains only five works based on a cantus firmus, but of these, three are on Latin chants—Magnificat, Te Deum, and a fragment of *O lux beata trinitas* (BuxWV 216). The short, monodic chorale preludes are totally absent, as are secular variation sets and suites. Also noteworthy is the fact that there are no concordances between the Ohrdruf and Berlin manuscripts. Perhaps the Ohrdruf exemplars became lost at an early stage—as the Weimar tablature did—and were not available to Bach's later pupils, for surely one of them would have copied the great ciacconas and passacaglia had they been available. The fact that there are no copies of Buxtehude's vocal music from the Bach circle does not necessarily mean that Bach himself was not interested in it, since Bach's own vocal music was not generally transmitted by these copyists.

The Manuscripts of Johann Gottfried Walther

Berlin Staatsbibliothek [*B*]:
    Mus. ms. 22541/1 (BuxWV 182, 189, 192, 197, 202, 211, 217)
    Mus. ms. 22541/2 (BuxWV 182, 189, 197, 202, 211, 217, 223)
    Mus. ms. 22541/3 (BuxWV 198, 199, 200, 208, 209, 224)
    Mus. ms. Bach P 801 (BuxWV 218)
    Mus. ms. Bach P 802 (BuxWV 188, 210)
The Hague, Gemeentemuseum [*DHgm*], 4.G.14 (BuxWV 178, 179, 180, 183, 184, 185, 186, 187, 190, 192, 201, 206, 207, 213, 214, 219, 220, 221, 222)

Johann Gottfried Walther (1684–1748) must of course be counted a member of the Bach circle; they were after all cousins. He deserves separate consideration, however, due to the extent of his collection and the fact that he appears to have acquired most of the exemplars for his copies of Buxtehude's music independently of, and in fact prior to, his association with Bach. According to his own account to Bokemeyer, quoted on page 127, he had received the Buxtehude works from Werckmeister following his visit to him in 1704. Werckmeister died in 1706, Walther moved to Weimar in 1707 to become organist at the church of St. Peter and St. Paul, and Bach arrived there in 1708 as court organist. Although Walther and Bach shared an interest in Buxtehude's music, their collections appear to have been quite different—Bach's mainly of free works, Walther's exclusively of chorale settings.

The manuscripts listed here fall into two categories. Walther participated in the copying of P 801 and 802 in collaboration with Johann Tobias Krebs (1690–1762), and they later belonged to the Krebs family; he copied the other manuscripts entirely himself. P 801 and 802 figure much more prominently in the transmission of Bach's keyboard music than of Buxtehude's. The three Buxtehude works included in them, however, are major works: the two large chorale fantasias *Gelobet seist du, Jesu Christ* and *Nun freut euch, lieben Christen gmein* and the *Te Deum*, all three copied by Walther. Bach's tablature of *Nun freut euch* served as the exemplar for Walther's copy, as demonstrated by the fact that their variants occur precisely at the points where an old water stain in the tablature makes the writing unclear. It must thus have been complete at the time Walther copied it, and this opens up the possibility that a Bach copy served as Walther's exemplars for its sister work, the chorale fantasia *Gelobet seist du Jesu Christ* (BuxWV 188), and the *Te Deum* as well. The *Te Deum* has already been mentioned as belonging to the manuscripts of the Bach circle by virtue of its association with Kellner.

Walther's other three Berlin manuscripts consist entirely of chorale settings, mostly of smaller proportions, arranged according to the church year: the first two for Advent and Christmas, the third for Easter, Pentecost, and Trinity. They contain numerous settings of the same chorales by various composers, and the two Christmas volumes share many concordances. The large volume at The Hague is similarly compiled of settings of the catechism chorales and those useful throughout the year. A comparable volume at Königsberg was probably destroyed during World War II; its readings are partially preserved in photographs at the Stadtbibliothek in Winterthur and through Spitta's edition, however.

Walther's manuscripts include information concerning performance—indications for manuals and pedal, ornamentation, and, above all, the notation of most of the Buxtehude works on three staves. The question naturally arises as to how much of this information came from his exemplars, which included Buxtehude autographs, and how much Walther added himself. The ornamentation in mm. 74–75 of *Wie schön leuchtet der Morgenstern* (BuxWV 223) was clearly added after he had already copied the piece, so it must be understood as an illustration of how Walther himself embellished slow, chordal passages. With respect to his various indications for manuals and pedals, it appears that if he did not copy his exemplars exactly, he reproduced their intent in the clearest possible manner for practical performance.

The large majority of the organ works that Walther copied are written with two staves, and Buxtehude's music represents the most striking exception to this common practice. The other pieces copied in three staves are mostly the works of other composers working in North Germany, principally Georg Böhm and Johann Nicolaus Hanff. One piece is notated in four staves—Georg Friedrich Kauffmann's *Gelobet seyst du, Jesu Christ* (B 22541/1, p. 128), as is its exemplar in Kauffmann's *Harmonische Seelen Lust* of 1733. Kauffmann included registrations in this printed edition, which Walther faithfully reproduced in his several copies from it. Two of the pieces for which Walther used three staves, however, are works from the *Orgelbüchlein* that J. S. Bach notated in two staves: "Das alte Jahr vergangen ist" (BWV 614) and "Herr Gott nun schleuß den Himmel auf" (BWV 617). Bach designated the first of these for two manuals and pedal in his autograph manuscript, and the running tenor voice of the second so overlaps the soprano and alto voices that it must be played with two manuals; the pedal is indicated. In both cases, Walther's three staves realize Bach's intention in a manner that is more easily read.

The Buxtehude works that Walther notated with three staves are all either chorale preludes of the "monodic" type or chorale fantasias, and in both types the soprano overlaps the inner voices at times. Tablature, which keeps the voices separate, is well suited to such music, as are three staves, with the alto and tenor parts on the middle staff. If we assume that all Walther's exemplars of Buxtehude's pieces were in tablature, then his use of three staves is the best possible adaptation of Buxtehude's original tablature to staff notation, both for ease of reading and to represent the differentiation of sound layers implicit in the music. The use of the letters *R* and *O* to indicate *Rückpositiv* and *Oberwerck* or *Organo* is then not really necessary and is usually found only when changes occur in the course of a chorale fantasia. The fact that Bach's tablature copy of *Nun freut euch* contains these indications and specifies "Org." at the beginning suggests that they may also have been present in Buxtehude's autographs, although Bach's copy must be at least two generations removed from the autograph. In the chorale fantasias, Walther did not use the third staff exclusively for the pedal, as he did in the chorale preludes. For the notation of the chorale prelude *Herr Christ, der einig Gottes Sohn* (BuxWV 192), Walther employed three staves in *DHgm* 4.G.14 and two staves *in B* 22541/1; only in the latter case did he use the indications *R, O,* and *ped.* to distinguish the voices.

Only fifteen of Buxtehude's forty-seven complete chorale settings for organ are transmitted by manuscripts not copied by Walther, and eight of these were in a manuscript at Plauen that appears to have derived from a Walther manuscript. The Plauen organ book was destroyed in World War II, but photographs of it exist at the Staatliches Institut für Musikforschung in Berlin. Clearly, Walther was as crucial a figure in the preservation of Buxtehude's organ chorale settings as Düben was for the vocal music.

Other Important Sources

The Lübeck Tablature A 373

Lübeck, Bibliothek der Hansestadt [*LUh*], Mus. A 373 (BuxWV 4, 5, 9, 16, 37, 39, 41, 45, 47, 48, 51, 59, 60, 67, 68, 74, 77, 79, 104, 110, 112)

Buxtehude, like Caspar Ruetz, might have used some of the music of his predecessors for kindling during the cold and dark Lübeck winters, and he too may have suspected that a similar fate awaited his own creations. Perhaps in the hope of saving some of his vocal works for posterity, he supervised the copying of a large tablature volume on paper of the same archival quality that he used for the accounts of St. Mary's, far heavier than the paper on which the autographs in Uppsala are written. He signed his name to six of the first nine works and helped to copy two of them, BuxWV 51 and 112. He also inserted a note within *Ihr lieben Christen, freut euch nun* (BuxWV 51) that the trumpet parts of this D-major piece needed to be copied in C. After fol. 40b, however, these autograph insertions cease, causing Spitta to suggest that Buxtehude had died at this point in the copying. The manuscript did survive in Lübeck until 1942, when it was taken away for safekeeping along with other important holdings from the Lübeck library and archives. Following the war, A 373 was long thought lost, but it reappeared at the Deutsche Staatsbibliothek in 1961 and returned to Lübeck in 1989.

The twenty complete works in A 373 provide a survey of the various genres and scorings that Buxtehude used in his vocal music, from the small sacred concerto *Herr, nun läßt du deinen Diener*, scored for tenor and two violins, to the cantata-like aria *Wie wird erneuet* for six voices and sixteen instruments. The *per omnes versus* chorale settings *Jesu, meine Freude* and *Herzlich lieb hab ich dich, O Herr* are here, as well as the popular *Alles was ihr tut* and two of the three other mixed cantatas. Nine works have concordances in the Düben Collection; the rest are unique to this manuscript.

The Codex "EB—1688"

New Haven, Yale University Music Library, "Lowell Mason Codex" (formerly catalogued LM 5056; now Music Deposit 4); BuxWV 136, 142, 144, 148, 152, 155, 158, 166, 175, Anh. 5)

This manuscript in Yale's Lowell Mason Collection provides the only extensive source of Buxtehude's organ music that survives from the seventeenth century. The volume is divided by repertoire and handwriting into two parts. The first 227 pages contain a seventeenth-century keyboard repertoire from northern Germany and Scandinavia (Buxtehude, N. Strungk, Heidorn, Martin Radeck), central Germany (Kindermann, Johann Krieger, Kuhnau), Vienna (Kerll, Poglietti), and Rome (Pasquini). A notice on page 228 dated 21 January 1779 declares that J. Becker had purchased the preceding at an auction in 1776 and has added what follows. Seven folios have been removed between the two parts. The second part contains nine keyboard works by Bach and Kirnberger, followed by fifty-one blank pages.

Three sorts of paper appear in this volume. Pages 1–124 are written on paper with a watermark of a large coat of arms that can be identified as that of Johann Georg III, elector of Saxony from 1680 to 1691. The watermark found on pages

125–228 and on the front endpaper depicts a smaller coat of arms with the word *Hainsbach* and the date 1686. This paper was probably produced at the paper mill in Niedereinsiedel, located near the Hainsbach estate, about 40 kilometers east of Dresden.[21] The copy of BuxWV 148 bridges the change from the first to the second paper. The second part of the manuscript consists entirely of paper with watermark small fleur de lis and countermark ICB, as yet unidentified. The three papers are of similar quality, although the first two have darkened slightly more than the third.

The volume is bound in brown leather, with the letters "EB" stamped in gold on the front cover and the numerals "1688" on the back. The binding has been rebacked, but the covers appear to date from the seventeenth century.[22] The surviving parts of the original spine, with its gold filigree design, have been glued onto the new spine, and they match it in width. The first part of the manuscript appears to have been copied before the volume was bound; writing has been trimmed off the bottoms of at least two pages (123 and 201), apparently by the binder, and notes frequently extend into the right margins of the verso sides. The second part was copied after the volume was bound, as evidenced by the fact that on two occasions the staff lines extend over the right edge of a recto side onto the edges of the remaining sheets in the volume.

It appears, then, that the first part of the Lowell Mason Codex was copied in Saxony, beginning some time after 1680 and ending by 1688, when the entire manuscript was bound. But of the composers most heavily represented in the first part—Buxtehude, Johann Krieger, Poglietti, and Nicolaus Adam Strungk—only Krieger had worked in Saxony before 1688. On 26 January 1688, however, Strungk was appointed vice Kapellmeister and chamber organist at the electoral court in Dresden. Strungk (1640–1700) may have known both Buxtehude and Poglietti personally. His study with Schnittelbach in Lübeck had occurred before Buxtehude arrived there, but Buxtehude surely visited Hamburg between 1678 and 1682, while Strungk was director of music at the cathedral and composing for the opera. Strungk had lived in Vienna from 1661 until 1665, during which time he could have become acquainted with Poglietti. Poglietti, the court organist there, could even have accompanied Strungk when he played the violin before Emperor Leopold I. Strungk had visited Vienna again before coming to Dresden, and although Poglietti was dead by then, Strungk could still have acquired copies of his music at that time, as well as works of Kerll, who had been active in Vienna since 1674. Strungk had even visited Rome, where he won the acclaim of Corelli, who traveled in the same musical circles as Pasquini. Strungk had accompanied Duke Ernst Augustus of Hanover to Venice in 1685–86 and composed a ricercar there in 1685; the titles to all his works in this manuscript are written in Italian.

Although Strungk appears to have been the guiding force behind the repertoire of the first part of the Lowell Mason Codex, he was not its copyist.[23] His role was rather to supply exemplars for the North German, Viennese, and Roman works to another organist working in Dresden, preferably one with the initials E. B. There was such a man: Emanuel Benisch, organist at the Frauenkirche and Sophienkirche from 1679 to 1695 and then at the Kreuzkirche from 1696 until his death in 1725. Benisch appears in fact to have been the only organist with the initials E. B. working in a Saxon city at this time.[24] In the first edition of this book, I presented the hypothesis that Benisch was the copyist of the Lowell Mason Codex, but had no time to verify it before the book went to press. Wolfram Steude later found an example of his handwriting in the Dresden archives that did so, and Belotti was able to use this information in later editions of his dissertation and in volume 15 of the Collected Works. I have since examined the Dresden materials[25] and can confirm Benisch as the scribe. Meanwhile, Belotti has tracked an earlier stage of Benisch's hand, suggesting that he may have had sources other than Strungk for the first five gatherings, leaving Strungk as the source only for the North German repertoire. It is unlikely, however, that Strungk would have spelled Buxtehude's name "D. Box de Hou," "D. Box de H." or "Box de Hude," as Benisch does; his exemplars probably had only Buxtehude's familiar initials "D. B. H."

Two of the works ascribed to Buxtehude in this manuscript are of doubtful authenticity. Belotti considers the Praeludium in F (BuxWV 144) more likely a student parody of Buxtehude's Praeludium in A Minor (BuxWV 153) and has placed it in the appendix to volume 15 of the Collected Works. The sonata arrangement (BuxWV Anhang 5) is discussed in chapter 8.

The Lindemann Manuscripts

Lund, Universitetsbibliotek [L], W.Lit. A 29 (BuxWV 42), N 1 (BuxWV 173), N 1b (BuxWV 154), N 2 (BuxWV 162), N 5 (BuxWV 142), N 6 (BuxWV 167), N 8 (BuxWV 170), N 9 (BuxWV 169), U 5 (BuxWV 149), U 6 (BuxWV 139)

The only sizable collection of Buxtehude's organ music to have survived in its original tablature notation is the group of manuscripts copied by Gottfried Lindemann in 1713–14 and preserved in the Lund University Library. Lindemann was the organist in Karlshamn, Sweden, from 1719 until his death in 1741. He had come from Stettin (now Sczcecin, Poland), and his copies dated there from 1713 to 1717 include a number of works by Friedrich Gottlieb Klingenberg, organist at St. Jacobi in Stettin and a former pupil of Buxtehude. Lindemann may thus have been a "grandpupil" of Buxtehude, and the exemplars for these manuscripts were most likely copies that Klingenberg had made in about 1689 during his study with Buxtehude. Belotti has discovered a second hand in the copying of BuxWV 142, which he discusses in the Critical Report to the Collected Works.

Since all the autographs of Buxtehude's organ music are lost, these manuscripts probably provide the best surviving example of Buxtehude's own notational style for this genre. It may thus be of some significance that only two are marked "pedaliter" or "manualiter," and none gives any indication as to where the pedals should or should not be used. The selection from Buxtehude's organ works made by Lindemann or Klingenberg contains only free works, and there are several unica among them. These manuscripts provide the principal sources for Hedar's edition of the works they contain. The one vocal work in the collection was owned by Lindemann but not copied by him. A smaller collection at Lund, formerly belonging to the Swedish organist Henrich Christoffer Engelhardt (born 1694), contains BuxWV 8 in parts, BuxWV 82 in score, and BuxWV 147 in tablature.

The Ryge and Ihre Manuscripts

Copenhagen, Det Kongelige Bibliotek [*Kk*], Mu 6806.1399, olim C II, 49
    (BuxWV 226–30, 232–38, 240–50)
Uppsala, Universitetsbibliotek [*Uu*], inst. mus. i hskr. Ihre 285 (BuxWV 231, 236, 238, 239)

The Ryge manuscript is the only major source for Buxtehude's strictly secular keyboard works. It is a handsomely bound volume that was passed down in the Ryge family from the eighteenth to the twentieth centuries. Its leather binding probably dates from the first decade of the eighteenth century. Reading in one direction, it contains the Ryge family history, begun in 1755 by the Danish author Andreas Nicolai Ryge (1724–67) and continuing to page 227. Reading in the other direction, it contains thirty-three keyboard pieces written in German organ tablature, filling eighty-three folios. The 124 pages in between are mostly blank. All of the writing appears to have been entered after the book had been bound. The scribe is unidentified, but it could have been Johann Christian Ryge (1688–1758), father of Andreas. J. C. Ryge was a pupil and later precentor at the Latin School of Our Lady in Copenhagen from 1701 to 1712; he then became cantor at the Latin school and cathedral in Roskilde. The musical contents of this manuscript, including its misattribution of two suites by Nicolas-Antoine Lebègue to Buxtehude, is discussed in chapter 7.

Suites of dances by various composers often formed the contents of the copy books of young musicians. The copy book of Thomas Ihre, now in Uppsala, offers an excellent example of such a book. Thomas Ihre (1659–1720), from Visby on the island of Gotland, began it on 12 December 1679 while he was a student at the university in Copenhagen. It contains four suites by Buxtehude, two of which also appear in the Ryge manuscript, in addition to suites by Froberger, Reincken, and Lorenz, and many anonymous dance movements. The Ryge manuscript is more neatly and uniformly written, but it could also be such a student copy book. If J. C. Ryge copied it toward the end of his own student days in Copenhagen, sufficient time would have elapsed to have allowed the works from the Pachelbel and Lebègue prints to have gone through several generations of manuscript copies in Copenhagen student circles and to have lost or changed their composer ascriptions.

The manuscripts and prints discussed here and inventoried in appendix 3 include all but two of Buxtehude's vocal works, one of the sonatas, three of the free organ works, and eleven of the chorale settings, nine of which were contained in the lost manuscripts of Königsberg or Plauen. The numerous other manuscripts that are listed in the Buxtehude-Werke-Verzeichnis are either peripheral—such as the copies of BuxWV 50 and 111 made by Nicolaus Knüppel, rector of Dömitz, in 1729—or derived from one of these principal sources.

If the concordances within Düben's and Walther's collections are disregarded, the great majority of Buxtehude's works were transmitted by only one source. The organ praeludia form a most striking exception to this rule, however; eight of them are found in two or three completely independent sources and several other derived sources. These include the praeludia in D major (BuxWV 139), E minor (BuxWV 142), and G minor (BuxWV 149), which must have been among Buxtehude's most popular works in the late seventeenth and eighteenth centuries and remain so today. Dieterich Buxtehude, organist in Lübeck, was and is known primarily for his praeludia.

Modern Editions of Buxtehude's Music

The comprehensive editing of Buxtehude's music began with Philipp Spitta's edition of the organ music, 1875–76. The fact that new editions of these same works continue to be published can be attributed to the appearance of new sources and the resulting difficulty in arriving at a definitive reading as well as to the enduring popularity of Buxtehude's organ music. The sources known to Spitta were primarily those of the Bach circle and Walther. Max Seiffert revised his edition in 1903–4, adding one free work and three chorale settings. With the discovery of other new sources, chief among them Yale's Lowell Mason Codex, Seiffert published a supplementary "Ergänzungsband" in 1939, which contained eleven newly discovered works and corrected readings for six works from his volume I. The Spitta-Seiffert editions were reissued in four volumes in 1952 with a new introduction by Walter Kraft, using the corrected readings from the "Ergänzungsband"; Kraft's edition has been reprinted in the United States by Kalmus and Dover.

Meanwhile, the Lund tablatures had come to light, and Joseph Hedar published a new edition of the then "complete" organ works in 1952, adding seven new free works and revising BuxWV 139, 142, and 149 with the Lindemann readings. Klaus Beckmann's edition of 1972 added BuxWV 138, 172, and 225 (in later printings) and attempted to emend errors in the sources and reconstruct

Buxtehude's original versions. In some cases, his solutions are highly convincing, particularly his rebarring of mm. 63–120 of the D-minor toccata (BuxWV 155). His critical report was published only with the "scholarly" edition, however, which soon went out of print. His revised edition of 1995–97 includes critical reports with each volume and takes recent research into consideration. Beckmann helped to compile the keyboard portion of the Buxtehude-Werke-Verzeichnis, and his was the first edition to contain all the organ works listed with their BuxWV numbers. Christoph Albrecht has since edited another complete edition of the organ works in five volumes, each with a short, critical report, but it went to press before Belotti's source-critical findings on the free organ works could be considered.

The editing of the vocal works and sonatas presents fewer problems, since these works are mainly transmitted by single or closely related sources from the seventeenth century. A collected edition of Buxtehude's works, *Dietrich Buxtehudes Werke*, was begun in Germany in 1925, but only eight volumes of vocal music appeared before its publisher, Ugrino Verlag, ceased operations in 1971. A new edition, *The Collected Works* published in New York by the Broude Trust, has thus far issued another volume of vocal works (vol. 9), the complete printed and manuscript sonatas (vol. 14), and the free *pedaliter* organ works (vol. 15), with the chorale-based organ works (vol. 16) and two further volumes of vocal music (vols. 10 and 11) in press.

As a direct consequence of their early popularity and the resulting multiplicity of sources, it is in the praeludia that the greatest differences among the various editions are to be found. Armed with an understanding of the sources on which these editions are based, however, the performer can make intelligent choices among these readings. All the major sources of the organ music, however, are at best third hand, and there can be no doubt that they contain numerous errors. When two independent sources agree on a disputed reading, however, we can be reasonably certain that it is correct. This is the case with the ending of the first fugue in the E-minor praeludium (BuxWV 142), in which the Lowell Mason Codex and Lindeman—and Hedar-Beckmann-Albrecht—agree

Example 9-2a. BuxWV 142, mm. 45–47, Spitta-Seiffert-Kraft reading.

Example 9-2b. BuxWV 142, mm. 45–47, Hedar-Beckmann-Albrecht reading.

against the Bach-circle manuscripts and Spitta-Seiffert-Kraft (ex. 9-2). Lacking the confirmation of Lindemann, Seiffert chose the Bach-circle reading of this passage over that of the Lowell Mason Codex in his corrected version for the "Ergänzungsband." Belotti in *The Collected Works* gives both readings, with that of the Berlin manuscript as a footnote. For the large G-minor praeludium (BuxWV 149), however, there are only two independent sources, Lindemann and the Bach circle, which differ as to whether the ostinato of the opening section should begin G-B♭-c (Lindemann) or G-G-c (Berlin MS, Agricola, and derived sources). Spitta-Seiffert-Kraft presented the Bach-circle reading (the only one they knew), while Hedar, Beckmann, and Belotti give the Lindemann version; Albrecht has reverted to the Bach-circle reading.

Another area of marked disparity among editions concerns the use of the pedal, which is discussed further in chapter 11. Knowing that most of these pieces were originally written first in tablature and then on two staves, and that pedal indications often vary considerably among sources or are entirely missing, frees the performer to make his or her own choices regarding the use of the pedal, as Buxtehude's contemporaries undoubtedly did. The Collected Works facilitates this choice by restoring the two-staff systems of the sources.

Chapter Ten

Toward a Chronology of Buxtehude's Music

It is fortunate that we do not need to know when Buxtehude's works were composed in order to enjoy them, for he left few clues concerning the chronology of his music. Only one autograph—the manuscript of *Membra*—is dated, and two of his prints even lack dates, although they can be quite easily supplied. Nevertheless, in our quest for knowledge about Buxtehude the composer, we want to know how his musical style developed. A study of the sources of his music does yield some information in this area, particularly the manuscripts of his vocal music, most of which were copied during his lifetime.

The Vocal Manuscripts and Prints

The ninety-five separate vocal manuscripts from the Düben Collection listed in appendix 3, B9, contain numerous dates, ranging from 1674 to 1687. None of these dates can be considered a date of composition, however, not even the date 1680 written on the *Membra* autograph, for this manuscript appears to be a fair copy and not the original composing manuscript. In manuscripts containing single works, a given date usually marks the copying date of the work in question. For works in the tablature volumes, a date entered at the completion of the copying of a work by Buxtehude or another composer may also apply approximately to undated works contained in the same volume if the manuscript is made up of only one type of paper and appears to have been copied consecutively. This is the case for *Uu* 82:35, for example, with dates of 23 July 1684 on fol. 14v, 14 August 1684 on fol. 17r and 1 December 1685 on fol. 28r. Manuscripts made up of two different sorts of paper may also have been copied consecutively. *Uu* 82:43, for example, comprises two gatherings, each of a different paper, the first containing the date 1683 on fol. 6r and the second 18 August 1683 on fol. 22v. The copying of Buxtehude's *Canite Jesu nostro*, dated 11 May 1683, spans the paper change from fol. 14v to fol. 15r. A more complex situation is encountered in *Uu* 84:29-42:1, also comprising two gatherings, each of a different paper, in which four leaves of a third paper (fols. 8–11) are inserted in the middle of the first gathering; the inserted leaves contain a date ten years later than the other dates in the manuscript. In table 10-1, those works that may be dated by proximity to other dated works are entered in parentheses.

Table 10-1. Copying dates for Buxtehude works in the Düben collection

Uu MS	Fol./Part	Date	Work
84:29–42:1	4v–5r	ANNO 1674	Geist, *Qui habitat*
	8v–10r	10 Feb. 1685	Anon., *O coeli sapientia*
	20v–22r		(BuxWV 69: *Laudate pueri*)
	22v–23r		(BuxWV 82: *O clemens, o mitis*)
	23v–25r	27 Aug. 1675	Geist, *O Jesu, dulcis dilectio*
51:7	Con.	June 1676	BuxWV 56: *Jesu dulcis memoria*
86:19–28	2r–3r	28 Sep. 1676	Geist, *Emendemus*
	9v–12r		(BuxWV 99: *Surrexit Christus hodie*)
50:12	title	ANNO 1680	BuxWV 75: *Membra Jesu* (fig. 4–1)
51:13	[Bc]	1680	BuxWV 119: *Klinget für Freuden*
83:69–73	8v–10r		(BuxWV 28: *Fallax mundus*)
	10v–14r	1 Feb. 1681	Krieger, *Exulta Jubila*
82:42	1r–3r		(BuxWV 93: *Salve desiderium*)
	2v–4r		(BuxWV 2: *Afferte Domino*)
	3v–6r	26 Feb. 1681	BuxWV 97: *Sicut Moses exaltavit*
	6v–8r	3 May 1681	BuxWV 32: *Gen Himmel zu dem Vater*
	8v–10r		(BuxWV 68: *Lauda Sion Salvatorem*)
	10v–13r		(BuxWV 106: *Welt, packe dich*)
	12v–15r		(BuxWV 46: *Ich habe Lust abzuscheiden*)
	15v–18r	20 Oct. 1681	BuxWV 83: *O dulcis Jesu* (fig. 9–1)
	17v–21r		(BuxWV 66: *Kommst du, Licht der Heiden*)
51:14	Org.	29 May 1682	BuxWV 68: *Lauda Sion Salvatorem*
51:6	Org.	4 Oct. 1682	BuxWV 49: *Ich sprach in meinem Herzen*
82:43	1v–2r		(BuxWV 98: *Singet dem Herrn*)
	2v–6r	1683	BuxWV 49: *Ich sprach in meinem Herzen*
	6v–8r		(BuxWV 44: *Ich bin die Auferstehung*)
	8v–13r		(BuxWV 33: *Gott fähret auf mit Jauchzen*)
	13v–16r	11 May 1683	BuxWV 11: *Canite Jesu nostro*
	15v–18r		(BuxWV 108: *Wie schmeckt es so lieblich*)
	19v–23r	18 Aug. 1683	BuxWV 48: *Ich halte es dafür*
	22v–26r		(BuxWV 52: *In dulci jubilo*)
83:41–45	2v–6r	7 Feb. 1684	BuxWV 91: *Pange lingua*
	6v–10r		(BuxWV 22: *Du Lebensfürst*)
82:35	1r–4r		(BuxWV 19: *Drei schöne Dinge*)
	9v–13r		(BuxWV 89: *O Lux beata Trinitas*)
	12v–15r	23 July 1684	BuxWV 55: *Je höher du bist*
	15v–17r	14 Aug. 1684	Pohle, *Amo te Deus meus*
	17v–19r		(BuxWV 109: *Wie soll ich dich empfangen*)
	19v–22r		(BuxWV 14: *Dein edles Herz*)

Table 10-1 (*continued*)

Uu MS	Fol./Part	Date	Work
	21v–25r		(BuxWV 94: *Salve Jesu*)
	24v–27r		(BuxWV 35: *Herr, auf dich traue ich*)
	26v–28r	1 Dec. 1685	BuxWV 30: *Fürchtet euch nicht*
85:1–18	4v–7r		(BuxWV 81: *Nun laßt uns Gott dem Herren*)
	6v–9r		(BuxWV 102: *Wär Gott nicht mit uns*)
	8v–12r		(BuxWV 72: *Mein Gemüt erfreuet sich*)
	12v–14r		(BuxWV 9: *Bedenke Mensch das Ende*)
	14v–18r		(BuxWV 60: *Jesu, meine Freude*)
	17v–23v		(BuxWV 24: *Eins bitte ich vom Herrn*)
	27v–31r		(BuxWV 87: *O Gottes Stadt*)
	30v–33r		(BuxWV 86: *O Gott wir danken deiner Güt*)
	33v–37r		(BuxWV 96: *Schwinget euch himmelan*)
	40v–43r		(BuxWV 103: *Walts Gott, mein Werk*)
	43v–45r	8 June 1687	BuxWV 40: *Herren vår Gud*
	44v–47r		(BuxWV 27: *Erhalt uns, Herr*)
	46v–50r		(BuxWV 18: *Domine, salvum fac regem*)
	49v–53r		(BuxWV 15: *Der Herr ist mit mir*)

We are immediately struck by the preponderance in table 10-1 of works copied during the 1680s. Two concordances between tablature and parts are also of interest: the tablature of BuxWV 68, *Lauda Sion Salvatorem*, appears to have been copied in 1681, whereas the parts are dated 1682; conversely, the parts of BuxWV 49, *Ich sprach in meinem Herzen*, are also dated 1682 and the tablature 1683.

We can gain further—although less precise—information concerning copy dates of Buxtehude works in the Düben Collection by studying the paper on which these works are written. Using the method developed by Theodor Gerardy, Jan Olof Rudén catalogued over two hundred variants of the foolscap design in watermarks of the Düben Collection and compared them with dated documents in the Stockholm archives written on the same sorts of paper. The large number of identical watermarks found both in the music manuscripts of the Düben Collection and in the official court documents in the archives indicates that Düben and his assistants were using paper supplied by the court, and the likelihood is great that the undated music manuscripts were copied at about the same time as the official court documents written on the same paper. We can encounter a range of up to five years in the use of a single type of paper, however, so the copy dates thus derived are even more approximate than those in table 10-1.

Twenty-two of Rudén's foolscap watermarks are found among the Buxtehude manuscripts, with dates ranging from 1675 to 1690. My own catalogue of watermarks in the Düben Collection includes over ninety other distinct watermarks found in the Uppsala manuscripts listed in appendix 3, B9; forty-seven are variants of the coat of arms of Amsterdam and fourteen of the Seven Provinces. In numerous instances identical watermarks within the Buxtehude manuscripts suggest the copying of several works at about the same time. Differing watermarks within part sets also help to distinguish a basic set of parts from duplicate parts copied later. These duplicate parts are listed following the symbols ". +" in appendix 3, B9. When the watermark table of the *Düben Collection Database Catalogue* is complete, it will be possible to compare watermarks throughout the collection, but it will still be necessary to examine the manuscripts themselves to determine whether a given watermark variant is identical to another.

Düben's ink catalogue numbers provide a further guide to the chronology of the early part of his collection, as Grusnick has shown. Running from 1 to 525, they include dated manuscripts from 1663 to 1676 in rough chronological sequence. The order of Düben's catalogue numbers appears to signify not the actual copying date but rather the presence of the manuscript in his collection. Five Buxtehude manuscripts have Düben ink numbers, four of which are listed in table 10-2. The fifth, no. 418, the set of parts for *Kommst du, Licht der Heiden* (*Uu* 6:15; BuxWV 66), appears to have been copied at least ten years after 1671, the date that its Düben catalogue number would suggest. The paper for the original part set, with watermark "Narr/7/IG," is unique in the Düben Collection, but Rudén found it in four archival documents dated 1681–83. The tablature of the work, listed in table 10-1, appears to have been copied in 1681.

Table 10-2. Buxtehude vocal works printed or copied before 1680

Source	Ink No.	Date	Work
Uu 50:4		(1662–68)	BuxWV 7: *Aperite mihi portas justitiae*
Uu 6:6	358	(1668)	BuxWV 23: *Ecce nunc benedicite*
Uu 6:13 (Bc)	416	(1671–74)	BuxWV 62: *Jesu, meines Lebens Leben* (ciaccona, earlier version)
Print		1672	BuxWV 116: *Auf! stimmet die Saiten*
Print		1673	BuxWV 115: *Auf, Saiten auf!*
Print		1674	BuxWV 76: *Fried- und Freudenreiche Hinfahrt*
Print		1675	BuxWV 118: *Gestreuet mit Blumen*
Uu 6:16	504	(1675)	BuxWV 114: *Missa alla brevis*
Uu 84:29-42:1		(1675)	BuxWV 69: *Laudate pueri* (ciaccona) BuxWV 82: *O clemens, o mitis*
Uu 6:5	506	(1675–76)	BuxWV 21: *Du Friedefürst* [SSB, G major]
Uu 83:1-20		(1675–76)	BuxWV 12: *Cantate Domino* BuxWV 53: *In te, Domine, speravi*
Uu 85:48-53		(1675–76)	BuxWV 70: *Liebster, meine Seele saget* (ciaccona) BuxWV 56: *Jesu dulcis memoria* [SS, E minor]
Uu 51:7		June 1676	BuxWV 56: *Jesu dulcis memoria*

Table 10-2 (*continued*)

Source	Ink No.	Date	Work
Uu 86:19-28		(1676)	BuxWV 99: *Surrexit Christus hodie*
Print		1677	BuxWV 61: *Jesu, meiner Freuden Meister*
Uu 6:11		(1679–82)	BuxWV 38: *Herr, wenn ich nur dich hab* (ciaccona)
Uu 50:17		(1679–82)	BuxWV 30: *Fürchtet euch nicht*

The data supplied by watermarks and Düben's catalogue numbers confirm the pattern seen in table 10-1, indicating that the large majority of Buxtehude's works in the Düben Collection were copied during the 1680s. We can nonetheless isolate a small group of works that appear to have been copied before 1680 and that may be added to the printed works of this period to form table 10-2. It is within these works that we might identify early characteristics of Buxtehude's compositional style. We can observe immediately that the proportion of Latin-texted works is much higher in this group than in Buxtehude's vocal music as a whole.

The dating of *Aperite mihi portas justitiae* (BuxWV 7) in the 1660s stems not from the physical evidence presented by its manuscript but from its dedication to the Swedish commissioner in Helsingør, who assumed that post in 1662, by Buxtehude as organist of St. Mary's Church there, the position that he relinquished early in 1668. The paper is unique within the Düben Collection and is not found in the Stockholm archives; the hand, however, is found in one other manuscript in the Düben Collection, *Uu* inst. 1:12, which transmits Buxtehude's fragmentary sonata BuxWV 270 and whose paper is found in Swedish documents from 1662 to 1667.

Aperite mihi is a pure sacred concerto made up of a succession of word-bound motives, unaffected by the influence of the aria we can find in many of Buxtehude's later sacred concertos. The motives for "ingressus in eas" and "confitebor Domino" are developed simultaneously in invertible counterpoint (mm. 22–58), whereas "benedictus qui venit" proceeds canonically (ex. 10-1). Clearly, Buxtehude's studies in learned counterpoint had already begun before his interaction with Bernhard, Reincken, and Theile in the early 1670s. Against these contrapuntal sections, Buxtehude juxtaposes a chordal refrain to the text "haec est dies, quam fecit Dominus," interrupting the phrase at an unnatural point with a rest, a rhetorical gesture that demonstrates a streak of nonconformity even at this early stage (ex. 10-2).

Grusnick dated the copying of *Uu* 6:6, the set of parts for *Ecce nunc benedicite* (BuxWV 23), by means of Düben's catalogue number 358 and the presence of its watermark, his "WZ 3," in fourteen manuscripts with catalogue numbers between 339 and 363. This work does demonstrate some stylistic characteristics

Example 10-1. BuxWV 7, mm. 183–85.

in common with *Aperite mihi*; it, too, is a pure sacred concerto, and both works rely heavily on parallel thirds, rhetorical use of rests and the repetition of modules, often in different keys. In both works, Buxtehude frequently employs imitation but not fugue. The "Alleluia" section at the end of *Ecce nunc benedicite* appears at first to be fugal, but each entrance of the "subject" is somewhat different.

The small group of works copied during the 1670s contains four of Buxtehude's six vocal ciacconas and three (BuxWV 12, 53, 114) of his four vocal

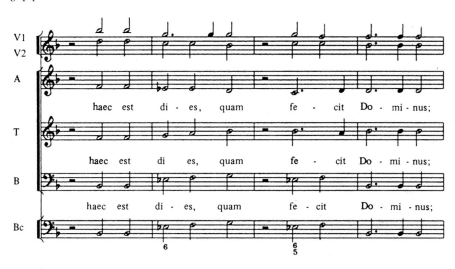

Example 10-2. BuxWV 7, mm. 78–81.

works without instruments other than continuo. The last three works are all strongly contrapuntal in their design. The *Missa alla brevis* belongs to the studies of learned counterpoint discussed in chapter 6; BuxWV 12 and 53 both begin with two-exposition fugues in which subject and answer appear in all voices. All three of the strophic wedding arias from this period have fugal ritornelli, and the arias of BuxWV 61, 76, and 115 have contrapuntal instrumental accompaniments. Only two chorale settings are present, both of which are also highly contrapuntal. Clearly the strong structures provided by counterpoint and ostinato constitute important elements of Buxtehude's compositional style during the 1670s. Only one cantata is present in this group, the concerto-aria cantata BuxWV 30 from the end of this period. The concerto-aria cantata becomes an important genre among Buxtehude's works copied during the 1680s, beginning with the seven *Membra* cantatas of 1680.

The large majority of the remaining manuscripts in the Düben Collection appear to have been copied between 1680 and 1687. It is in this group that Buxtehude's most characteristic vocal works appear—the concerto-aria cantatas, the cantata-like arias, and the concertato chorale harmonizations. At least two vocal works may date from Anders Düben's visit to Lübeck in 1692, however. *O wie selig sind* (BuxWV 90) and *Was mich auf dieser Welt betrübt* (BuxWV 105) are both written on the same paper—with the watermark "Freiberg/PR"—that Anders Düben used for his manuscript of the sonata BuxWV 267 (*Uu* inst.

13:24), signed and dated 27 September 1692. Johann Wilhelm Petersen's text for BuxWV 90 was not published until 1692, although Buxtehude probably knew Petersen and thus could have acquired it before its publication. Both vocal works are characterized by extreme simplicity; they are composed in the pure strophic form that Buxtehude usually reserved for occasional works or arias within cantatas. In the two wedding arias from the 1690s, BuxWV 117 and the lost BuxWV 121, both with Italian texts, instrumental dance movements replace the fugal ritornelli of the 1670s.

Only nineteen complete vocal works by Buxtehude are transmitted solely by sources other than the manuscripts of the Düben Collection or the published wedding and funeral music. Five of these are found in the Österreich-Bokemeyer Collection (three from Österreich's collection, two added by Bokemeyer); eleven are unique to the Lübeck tablature A 373; and three come down in peripheral sources. Österreich's three copies—BuxWV 80, 100, 101—could have been made during the 1690s. BuxWV 80, *Nun freut euch, ihr Frommen, mit mir*, displays a radiant simplicity similar to that of *Was mich auf dieser Welt betrübt*, although it is not in strophic form. Perhaps this simplicity marks one aspect of Buxtehude's style of the 1690s. The D-major *Wachet auf* (BuxWV 100) resembles *Nun freut euch, ihr Frommen* in its frequent use of an eighth-note trill motive for both vocal and instrumental ornamentation. The authenticity of the C-major *Wachet auf* (BuxWV 101), and of BuxWV 43, copied by Bokemeyer, are questionable, however, as discussed in chapter 5.

Buxtehude's ambitious production of the Abendmusiken *Castrum doloris* and *Templum honoris* in December 1705 indicates that he was still actively composing eighteen months before his death. The *hautbois* was just coming into general use in Germany at the turn of the eighteenth century, as witnessed by the appointment in 1702 of Alexander Fritz, an oboist, as one of the two instrumentalists to play regularly from the organ in St. Mary's Church. Buxtehude called for hautbois in *Templum honoris*, and they also appear in two extant works: the wedding aria *O fröhliche Stunden, o herrlicher Tag* (BuxWV 120) from September 1705, and *Ich suchte des Nachts in meinem Bette* (BuxWV 50), transmitted only by Nicolaus Knüppel's copy of 1729, now in Brussels. This dramatic cantata, discussed in chapter 5, is the only one of Buxtehude's vocal works to include a tonally closed movement in a key other than the tonic. Surely it provides an example of Buxtehude's most mature style.

Both Spitta and Karstädt dated the copying of the Lübeck tablature A 373 at the end of Buxtehude's life, and no evidence exists to contradict this assumption. Its repertoire is by no means entirely late, however, as demonstrated by nine concordances in the Düben Collection, all of which appear to have been copied during the 1680s. The eleven complete works unique to this manuscript are listed in table 10-3.

Table 10-3. Works unique to the Lübeck tablature A 373

BuxWV 5:	*Also hat Gott die Welt geliebet* (concerto)
BuxWV 41:	*Herzlich lieb hab ich dich, o Herr* (chorale cantata)
BuxWV 45:	*Ich bin eine Blume zu Saron* (concerto)
BuxWV 47:	*Ich habe Lust abzuscheiden* (concerto-aria cantata)
BuxWV 51:	*Ihr lieben Christen, freut euch nun* (mixed cantata)
BuxWV 59:	*Jesu, meine Freud und Lust* (aria)
BuxWV 67:	*Lauda anima mea* (concerto)
BuxWV 77:	*Nichts soll uns scheiden* (concerto-aria cantata)
BuxWV 104:	*Was frag' ich nach der Welt* (aria)
BuxWV 110:	*Wie wird erneuet* (aria, cantata-like)
BuxWV 112:	*Wo soll ich fliehen hin?* (dialogue-mixed cantata)

Herzlich lieb hab ich dich, o Herr (BuxWV 41) leaps out of this list immediately as a potential late work; for sheer length and expressive power it has no equal among Buxtehude's other vocal works. *Nichts soll uns scheiden* (BuxWV 77) stands out uniquely among Buxtehude's concerto-aria cantatas for the clarity of the tonal plan of its concerto. That two of Buxtehude's four mixed cantatas are unique to A 373 appears significant, but the mixed cantata is not necessarily a late genre; the other two were copied into the Düben Collection in the 1680s. Furthermore, both *Ihr lieben Christen* and *Wo soll ich fliehen hin*—as well as *Herzlich lieb*—begin with a chorale sinfonia, a somewhat archaic style of chorale setting that Buxtehude had already employed with great skill in the first versus of the G-major setting of *Du Friedefürst Herr Jesu Christ* (BuxWV 21), probably copied about 1675. *Ich habe Lust abzuscheiden* (BuxWV 47) is a thoroughgoing revision of a similar setting of the same text (BuxWV 46) copied into *Uu* 82:42 in 1681; both versions are discussed below. In short, A 373 does appear to have been copied later than the manuscripts of the Düben Collection, and it could date from the last years of Buxtehude's life, but no physical evidence presently substantiates the information gained from its repertoire.

The Instrumental Manuscripts and Prints

Buxtehude's sonatas, like his vocal music, were virtually all copied or printed during his lifetime, and we have already explored the relationship between the earlier sonata manuscripts and the later prints in chapter 8. Like all the manuscript copies discussed earlier, the dates of the printed editions cannot be equated with dates of composition; each is only a *terminus ante quem*, a date before which the piece must have been composed. Buxtehude's inclusion in his opus 1 of a manuscript sonata in revised form offers ample proof that other sonatas may have been composed earlier as well. The revision is discussed below.

Four of Buxtehude's keyboard suites—BuxWV 231, 236, 238, and 239—are found in Thomas Ihre's copy-book (*Uu* Ihre 285), the front page of which is dated 1679. This manuscript is a convolute, made up of seven different parts, in both tablature and staff notation, not entirely in Thomas Ihre's hand, and using at least nine different sorts of paper. The Buxtehude suites are found at the beginning of the second section, which is made up of two gatherings—one of seven sheets, the other of four—of paper with the watermark Amsterdam/LC, not found elsewhere among the Buxtehude manuscripts. Works by Reincken and Tunder fill out this section, which Ihre wrote in tablature. The manuscript contains no other written dates, but the paper from section 5, with works by Johann Lorentz, corresponds to archival sources from 1680 to 1682, and the paper of the final section could date from 1679. Thomas Ihre studied in Copenhagen from 1677 to 1680 and then moved on to Rostock and Uppsala; Copenhagen probably provided his best opportunity to acquire his exemplars for the works of both Buxtehude and Lorentz, and it is quite likely that he had copied this section by 1680. Ihre's manuscript contains two concordances with the Ryge manuscript, which also was probably copied in Copenhagen. Since the suites are so uniform in style, we can perhaps assume that they were all composed before 1680.

A chronology of Buxtehude's organ music is extremely difficult to establish, because none of it was printed and most of the extant manuscripts were copied after his death. The earliest known copy of a Buxtehude organ work was a tablature that contained the G-minor praeludium BuxWV 148 and bore the date 1675 somewhere within the manuscript, perhaps at the beginning of a copy-book that took several years to compile. It was already lost when Spitta prepared his edition in 1875, his source for which was "a manuscript belonging to A. G. Ritter in Magdeburg, kindly placed at the disposal of the editor. It was prepared in 1838 from a book written in 1675 by Georg Grobe in German tablature. At that time it was in the possession of the organist Hildebrand of Mühlhausen in Thüringen; following Hildebrand's death it was lost, together with the rest of his musical estate."[1] Ritter's copy is now lost as well.

The earliest extant source of Buxtehude's organ music is Yale's Lowell Mason Codex, which appears to have been both copied by and bound in 1688. The manuscript contains a number of dates within it, ranging from 1678 to 1686, including the date of 1684 for Buxtehude's D-minor toccata, BuxWV 155. These dates do not run in chronological sequence, and they appear to have been copied from the exemplars rather than indicating the date each piece was copied into this manuscript. This is particularly evident in the case of Strunck's pieces, whose dates seem to indicate dates of actual composition—e.g., "fatto il 4 Aug: 1683" for his *Capriccio della Chiave F* on page 183. Notes such as this suggest that the exemplars for the Strunck pieces were autographs, providing further evidence for the hypothesis that it was he who supplied most of the exemplars to the copyist Emanuel Benisch. If the date of 1684 marked the year in which Strunck made his own copy of Buxtehude's D-minor toccata, it probably means that he was still in contact with Buxtehude at this time even though he had left Hamburg and was back in Hannover. Strunck was in Venice in 1685 and in Vienna in 1686, according to notes accompanying other compositions in the Lowell Mason Codex. The year 1684 thus appears to be a reasonable *terminus ante quem* for the composition of all the Buxtehude pieces in the Lowell Mason Codex. These include seven praeludia, among them BuxWV 142.

Only one other dated manuscript of organ music survives from Buxtehude's lifetime, a tablature copy dated 25 June 1696 of the A-major praeludium, BuxWV 151. It forms the first item in a convolute formerly belonging to the Hamburg organist Heinrich Schmahl (d. 1892), later belonging to the royal library in Berlin as Ms. 40295, and now at the Jagiellonian library in Krakow. Its version of BuxWV 151 differs significantly from Johann Christoph Bach's later copy of the work in the "Möllersche Handschrift" (*B* 40644; see the facsimile and discussion in the Collected Works, vol. 15B). Johann Sebastian Bach's newly discovered copy of *Nun freut euch, lieben Christen gmein* (BuxWV 210) is the only known chorale-based keyboard work to have been copied during Buxtehude's lifetime.

Regarding the eighteenth-century manuscripts, it seems safe to say that those copied by Lindemann, now in Lund, contain works copied by Klingenberg during his study with Buxtehude around 1689, and thus composed before then. Belotti's hypothesis that the repertoire of *B* 2681 can also be dated before 1690 must be considered with caution, however. Even if all these works can be traced back to Pachelbel, he remained in contact with the Bach family, among others, after his move from Erfurt in 1690 and could have continued to transmit works that he acquired later, perhaps even beyond his dedication of *Hexachordum Appolinis* to Buxtehude in 1699.

Lacking the hard evidence that might have been supplied by more securely dated manuscripts of Buxtehude's organ music from his lifetime, attempts to construct its chronology have relied mainly on hypotheses related to the later manuscripts, tuning systems, circumstantial evidence, or musical style. Belotti's examination of the keyboard compasses of the organs that Buxtehude played yielded meager results; the Helsingør St. Mary's organ had the F♯ and G♯ in the pedal that his Lübeck organs lacked, but to assign all his organ works employing these pitches to the years before 1668 would be absurd, as Belotti freely acknowledges.

Buxtehude's Revisions as Guides to His Stylistic Development

Three authentic revisions exist in sources close to Buxtehude: the earlier and corrected versions of *Jesu meines Lebens Leben* (BuxWV 62); the revision of the manuscript sonata in B♭ (BuxWV 273) to become the printed sonata op. 1, no. 4

(BuxWV 255); and the two versions of *Ich habe Lust abzuscheiden*, BuxWV 46 in the Düben Collection and BuxWV 47 in the Lübeck tablature A 373.

Both versions of *Jesu, meines Lebens Leben* come down in two sources in the Düben Collection. The tablature *Uu* 82:37, in Düben's hand, contains the two versions, separated by a work of David Pohle. The title of the second version reads "aria Jesu meines Lebens Leben Corrigieret. D. B. H." The parts, *Uu* 6:13, contain a complete set for the corrected version and a discarded continuo part for the earlier version. This continuo part is written on paper used elsewhere in the Düben Collection with dates of 1672 and 1674; its Düben catalogue number, 416, suggests that it may have been in the collection in 1671; the remaining parts probably date from the 1680s. The paper of the tablature was used for another source in the Düben Collection dated 1680, four archival sources dated 1680, and two archival sources from 1684–85.

The principal difference between the two versions of BuxWV 62 lies in the addition of a seventeen-measure "Amen" section at the end, constructed over the same ostinato as the rest of the aria. The aria itself, in both versions, represents the most regularized setting of an ostinato bass that we find in Buxtehude's entire oeuvre. The text consists of five strophes of eight lines with the rhyme scheme *ababccdd*; the ostinato—quarter notes d c B♭ A / f e d a—occurs thirty-three times in the continuo without change. The first four strophes are contructed identically, with a pair of lines over each statement of the ostinato, one line per measure, except for the final line, which is extended by a quarter note to achieve a full cadence in D minor on the first beat of the next ostinato statement; the first three pairs of lines end on half cadences over A. Each strophe is separated by a four-measure instrumental interlude. Only with the final strophe does the pattern break, with one-measure instrumental interludes temporarily throwing off the strict two-measure periodicity. The added "Amen" section of the corrected version blurs the regularity of the ostinato still more by means of quasi-fugal entrances in the voices and instruments and irregular phrase lengths.

The ostinato variations that form the first section of the manuscript sonata BuxWV 273 are constructed much more artfully than the aria *Jesu, meines Lebens Leben*, but Buxtehude nevertheless blunts their regularity still further in his revision for the printed version. The ostinato pattern itself is three and one half measures long—a brilliant stroke in favor of irregularity. In the manuscript version it is introduced by the organ alone; in the published version, Buxtehude added a repeated-note figure, in two different metrical positions, to the violin part over the opening statement of the ostinato (ex. 10-3). He added this same figure at unexpected places throughout the first section, such that it begins to compete for attention with the ostinato itself. Its anapestic rhythm takes over the twenty-third variation (mm. 78–81) completely, and it insists on having the last word before the cadence in m. 112.

Buxtehude's most important change from manuscript to printed sonata was the elimination of the suite, perhaps to bring this sonata into conformity with the

Example 10-3. BuxWV 255, mm. 1–4.

others, perhaps to make it playable in church (although he does not mention this possibility in the title), or perhaps because he felt the predictable quality of the suite did not agree with the prevailing aesthetic of the *stylus phantasticus* that permeates the printed collection. The removal of the suite left only three sections, the second of which is a transitional Adagio in the manuscript sonata, its chordal texture decorated by repeated notes and enriched by double stops in the violin. It may have been to compensate for the loss of the suite that Buxtehude completely recomposed this second section for publication, retaining only the harmonic pattern from the first three measures of the earlier version (ex. 10-4a). Although the new Lento (ex. 10-4b) is only two measures longer, it conveys the impression of much greater substance by virtue of its concertato texture, eloquent lines, and greatly increased rhythmic vitality.

Example 10-4a. BuxWV 273, mm. 114–18.

Example 10-4b. BuxWV 255, mm. 114–18.

Buxtehude undertook his most comprehensive revisions with *Ich habe Lust abzuscheiden*, completely recomposing both the concerto and the aria of this concerto-aria cantata. The tablature of the Uppsala version (BuxWV 46; *Uu* 82:42) was copied in 1681, and the parts also in the 1680s. In this form it is quite typical of the majority of Buxtehude's concerto-aria cantatas. Its modest concerto, based on only a portion of a biblical verse (Philippians 1:23), contrasts block homophony for "My desire is to depart" with fugal treatment of "and be with Christ." All four versus of the aria are given to the singers alone and are articulated by instrumental ritornelli. The first two versus are in strophic form for the two sopranos; in the third, the bass continues freely, followed by a new ritornello; and the three singers perform the fourth versus in a somewhat more concertato style, still without the instruments. The sonata and opening concerto are then repeated to conclude the work. This rather clear contrast between concerto and aria is blurred in the Lübeck version (BuxWV 47; *LUh* A 373), which is presumably later. The opening concerto is shortened, and its fugue becomes less prominent because of an added homophonic accompaniment in each opening entrance (exx. 10-5a and 10-5b). The aria retains the same vocal scoring for each versus as the Uppsala version, but the instruments are added to versus 3 and 4, which are now composed completely in concertato style, including a section in triple time for the last line of versus 3. The repetition of the opening concerto thus becomes superfluous, and it is dropped in the Lübeck version.

Example 10-5a. BuxWV 46, Concerto, mm. 31–37.

In each of these three revisions, the changed or added sections do not fulfill the expectations of the listener as readily as the original version did. The strict metrical structure of the ostinato is somewhat obscured in the revisions of BuxWV 62 and BuxWV 255; the suite of BuxWV 273—the most predictable genre that Buxtehude cultivated—is dropped for BuxWV 255; the concerto

Example 10-5b. BuxWV 47, Concerto, mm. 21–28.

becomes more homophonic and the aria more concertato in BuxWV 47, and the concerto-aria cantata loses its traditional shape. These three revisions suggest that a growing desire to make his music less predictable—or perhaps a growing preference for the *stylus phantasticus*—formed an element in the development of Buxtehude's compositional style.

Ostinato and Fugal Technique

Although Buxtehude's vocal ciacconas appear to be concentrated in the 1670s, he was still composing variations over an ostinato at the very end of his life; *Templum honoris* closes with "Una Passagaglia con divers. Instrom. Vivace." Buxtehude's extant sets of ostinato variations include six vocal works (BuxWV 38, 57, 62, 69, 70 and 92); five sections within the manuscript sonatas (BuxWV 266, 271, 272 [2 sections] and 273); eight sections within the printed sonatas (BuxWV 252, 255, 261, 262, 263 [2 sections], 264 and 265); three complete organ works (BuxWV 159–161); and extended sections within three other organ works (BuxWV 137, 148, and 149), in addition to shorter, quasi-ostinato sections in a number of other works, notably in the sonatas, in "Amen" or "Alleluia" sections of vocal works and in free sections of the organ works. As suggested by the revision of his earliest datable example, *Jesu, meines Lebens Leben* (BuxWV 62), Buxtehude's ostinato settings appear to evolve from rather rigid structures to a much freer use of the technique.

The ciaccona that forms the final section of the G-minor praeludium BuxWV 148, perhaps composed as early as 1675, already takes a considerably freer approach to the ostinato than *Jesu meines Lebens Leben*. This ostinato also consists of eight quarter-notes—g f♯ g d / e♭ B♭ c d—and its two-measure periodicity is emphasized by regular alternation of the ostinato between pedal and manuals. After six statements of this pattern, however, the ostinato modulates to B♭ for eight statements, returning to the tonic of G minor only at the last possible moment, two measures before the end of the piece. Buxtehude used a variant of this procedure in the final sections of his A-major sonata, op. 2, no. 5 (BuxWV 263), twice beginning an ostinato on the sixth degree, F♯ minor, and moving to the tonic. Normally, however, Buxtehude's ostinatos remain in the tonic for all of their appearances. The D-minor passacaglia for organ (BuxWV 161), with its four perfectly balanced sections in D minor, F major, A minor, and D minor, is the most notable exception.

Two vocal ciacconas copied around 1675 both show considerable subtlety with respect to evading the regularity imposed by an ostinato. *Laudate pueri* (BuxWV 69) extends the ostinato to eight measures, challenging the ear to perceive it as a constantly returning bass melody. The first four psalm verses are fitted regularly into its eight-measure structure, and in verses 3 and 4 the caesura between the two halves of the psalm verse falls precisely on the F-major cadence midway through the D-minor ostinato (mm. 29 and 37). Variety is achieved with the placement of the instrumental interludes, however, and the verses do not routinely begin or end at a particular point in the ostinato; the fifth and sixth verses are combined into one statement. The expected cadence at the beginning of the ninth and eleventh statements (mm. 65 and 81) is evaded, and the Gloria Patri begins at m. 77 in the middle of a statement. The three-measure ostinato of *Liebster, meine Seele saget* appears to be constructed with the idea of avoiding regular phrases. A dominant cadence occurs at the beginning of the second measure, and the tonic cadence at the beginning of each statement is frequently evaded as the phrase heads for the dominant cadence beyond it; this occurs for the first time at m. 14. The irregular placement of lines, strophes, and interludes over this ostinato defies any attempt at prediction, and the piece ends with a quasi-fugal "Alleluia."

The sonatas contain a wide variety of ostinato treatments, as discussed in chapter 8; the same sonata may contain both a very free quasi-ostinato setting and a more regular one, perhaps as foils for one another, as in the G-minor sonata, op. 2, no. 3 (BuxWV 261; CD tracks 13–16). Even the more regular section 5 of this sonata evades the expected cadences at the beginning of each period by avoiding the first degree of the scale in the upper parts. The upper parts in both ostinato sections of the manuscript sonata in A minor (BuxWV 272), in contrast, regularly form a cadence at the beginning of each four-measure period. This sonata may have been composed at about the same time as the early version of *Jesu, meines Lebens Leben*, perhaps by 1670.

For variation within the ostinato bass itself, the two organ ciacconas (BuxWV 159, 160) are unequaled in the other genres. Together with the D-minor passacaglia (BuxWV 161), the melodic pattern of whose ostinato remains unaltered but is subjected to a broad tonal plan, these works offer Buxtehude's richest inventiveness in the treatment of the ostinato. They could well be very late works, which would help to explain their absence from any sources outside those of the Bach circle. The experience that Buxtehude had gained in composing variations over an ostinato in the continuo basses of his vocal and chamber music would then help to account for the special fluency with which he incorporated the pedal into a keyboard genre that had previously been mainly confined to the manuals.

Fugues figure even more prominently in Buxtehude's oeuvre than ostinato settings, and he appears to have arrived at his full command of the technique at a relatively early stage. The masterful second fugue of the E-minor praeludium (BuxWV 142; see ex. 7-7b), with its combination of contrapuntal complexity and harmonic richness, is present in the Lowell Mason Codex, which means that Buxtehude had probably composed it by 1684. The fugues of the G-minor praeludium BuxWV 148, possibly composed by 1675, already demonstrate a number of traits characteristic of Buxtehude's fugal writing. Both fugues have tonal answers and contain entrances of subject and answer in each voice, although the second exposition of the second fugue requires the shortened stretto entrances (mm. 80–86) for its full complement of entrances. The first fugue is a *fuga pathetica*, characterized by the leap of a diminished seventh, decorated with repeated notes in the North German style; the second dissolves into concertato texture after the stretto.

The principle of building a fugue with an entrance of subject and answer in each voice appears to have been well established in Buxtehude's mind by 1675, for the ritornello of the wedding aria *Gestreuet mit Blumen* (BuxWV 118), published in 1675, consists precisely of that: ten measures of subject and answer

Example 10-6. BuxWV 118, Ritornello.

alternating downward through the five voices, plus a five-measure concertato free ending (ex. 10-6). The first ten measures are completely periodic in their fugal entrances, and all the voices are nearly canonic, apart from the necessary adjustments for the tonal answers. Buxtehude's preoccupation with canon and invertible counterpoint during the early 1670s had given him the necessary technique for such composition, and his use of fugue even in an aria ritornello suggests that he was actively engaged with fugue at this time as well. The ritornello

Example 10-6 (*continued*).

of *Auf, Saiten, auf!* (BuxWV 115) from 1673 is also fugal, but its second exposition is only half complete.

A number of Buxtehude's fugues do not contain an entrance of subject and answer in each voice, but in most cases they are found within a canzona or praeludium along with another fugue that is complete. Such is the case, for example, with the D-minor praeludium (BuxWV 140), whose second fugue lacks an entrance of the subject in the alto voice. Where a complete fugue is totally lacking in a canzona or praeludium, however, we must suspect that it was composed earlier than 1675. The praeludium BuxWV 152—the work that Mattheson mistook for a toccata by Froberger—appears to be an early composition. Neither of its two fugues contains an entrance of subject and answer in all voices, and both use real answers, the first at the lower fifth. The Phrygian mode of this piece points further to an early origin, as does the fact that its unique source is the Lowell Mason Codex. The G-minor canzona (BuxWV 173) could also be a rather early work, although it does contain a tonal answer. It begins as a four-voice fugue, but the tenor voice drops out of the tablature early in the second exposition, leaving it incomplete. It is also possible that Buxtehude did not compose this work; Lindemann transmits it anonymously, albeit together with eight works that he ascribes to Buxtehude. The presence of subject and answer in each voice does not necessarily mean that a fugue was composed after 1675, of course. The first fugue of the Praeambulum in A minor (BuxWV 158) contains ample entrances of subject and answer, but its archaic qualities—real answer at lower fifth, paired canonic first exposition, metrically displaced final entrance (m. 53)—all point to an earlier origin.

All of the sonata fugues have subject and answer in each voice, as noted in Chapter 8, but since most are composed with only two real voices, this is usually accomplished with only four entrances. The smaller number of voices than the usual four of the organ fugues may also account for the fact that the sonata fugues are richer in episodes than the organ fugues; Buxtehude may have wished to extend the length of the sonata fugues without overburdening the individual voices with too many entrances. Since the presence of episodes is usually considered a progressive feature in fugal composition, we might otherwise be tempted to speculate that the sonata fugues had all been composed later than the organ fugues. The dissolution of contrapuntal texture into a concertato or homophonic free ending is common to both the organ fugues and the sonata fugues and is already present in the second fugue of BuxWV 148 and the ritornello of BuxWV 118, both from 1675, and the "Amen" fugue of *Afferte Domino gloriam honorem* (BuxWV 2), probably copied in 1680.

Since Buxtehude developed his contrapuntal skills so early in his career, his fugal technique does not provide very much help in establishing a chronology of his organ music. Due to the freedom inherent in the *stylus phantasticus*, his failure to complete a second fugal exposition or apply a countersubject consistently can more likely be attributed to his free choice than to lack of skill. And because he appears to have composed his canzonas in particular as teaching pieces, the simple three-voice fugues found in some of them more likely served as models for beginning students than as examples of his own contrapuntal development.

Harmony, Tonality, and Temperament

Buxtehude's expressive use of harmony constitutes one of the most engaging features of his compositional style, yet a comprehensive study of his harmonic practice still awaits an author. One of its most obvious characteristics—his liberal use of secondary dominants—is already evident in his G-major setting of the chorale *Du Friedefürst Herr Jesu Christ* (BuxWV 21; ex. 10-7), which was probably copied about 1675. In this case, the secondary dominants arise from chromatic motion induced by the text; the figure of the *passus duriusculus* emphasizes the urgency of the intercession sought with the text "dein Vater bitt." Often they have a purely harmonic function, such as the drive to the cadence at the end of versus 3 (ex. 10-8).

Buxtehude's sense of major-minor tonality was also well developed by 1675, as indicated by the ritornello to *Gestreuet mit Blumen* (BuxWV 118; ex. 10-6), whose original printed edition employs a modern key signature of four sharps for the key of E major. Many of the sources of Buxtehude's music lack modern key signatures, but since they probably derive from tablature exemplars, they reflect the practice of the copyists rather than that of the composer. The autograph score of *Fürwahr, er trug unsere Krankheit* (see fig. 5-2) has a Dorian two-flat signature for C minor, however; its date is unknown. Most of Buxtehude's music is functionally tonal, usually with a few faintly modal reminders that the work belongs to the seventeenth century, not the eighteenth. The broad, clear tonal plan of the D-minor passacaglia (BuxWV 161), with its extended modulations to the relative major and the dominant, is quite unusual within Buxtehude's oeuvre and helps to mark it as a late work.

The major-minor tonal system, with its transpositions to keys such as E major and F♯ minor, brought with it the breaking of the barriers imposed by the meantone tuning system, and Buxtehude stood at the forefront of this development. In the first edition of this book, I proposed a chronology of the organ works that was based on my hypothesis that the organs of St. Mary's Church were retuned to Werckmeister III in 1683. Other scholars followed this hypothesis with refined chronologies, notably Klaus Beckmann and Michael Belotti (in the first edition of his dissertation) for the free organ works, Pieter Dirksen and Matthias Schneider for the chorale fantasias.[2] With the return of the later account books to Lübeck and Ibo Orgies's subsequent research, however, this hypothesis can no longer stand, as recounted in chapter 3, and these chronologies must be revised. The most that we can now say in this respect is that the works that absolutely require a circulating temperament, such as the praeludia in E minor (BuxWV 142) and F♯ minor (BuxWV 146), must have been composed after the

Example 10-7. BuxWV 21, versus 2, mm. 30–39.

publication of the first edition of Werckmeister's *Orgel-Probe* in 1681, and that
Buxtehude probably worked out their written form as we have it at a pedal clavichord or harpsichord tuned in a circulating system.

Unlike the organ works, none of the harpsichord pieces requires a circulating
temperament. Thirteen can be played in traditional E♭–G♯ mean tone, and the
other twelve use only twelve pitch classes; even the A-major suite (BuxWV 243),
which uses a B♯, could theoretically be played on a harpsichord tuned in mean

Example 10-8. BuxWV 21, versus 3, mm. 76–79.

tone with its wolf located between G and B♯. It could also have been composed later; it is not contained in the 1679 Ihre manuscript. The lack of harmonic boldness in the harpsichord pieces as a group could indicate that Buxtehude composed them rather early, but it could also be related to the genre and to the performance of these pieces by amateurs.

The sonatas, in contrast, must have been originally composed for professionals, and only one, the A-minor manuscript sonata (BuxWV 272) with the two rigid ostinato settings, falls within the bounds of traditional mean tone. Although the performance of these sonatas did not depend on the tuning of the organ, it seems quite possible that Buxtehude composed them at approximately the same time as he was experimenting with wider possibilities in the organ works. As in the organ praeludia, the extreme pitch classes are found most often in the slow, transitional sections of the sonatas.

Buxtehude's vocal music employs pitch classes unavailable in mean tone at an earlier date and with much greater frequency than does his organ music. The "Klag-Lied" for the funeral of his father in 1674 uses both B♭ and A♯, and A-sharps appear in a number of other works copied in the 1670's, including BuxWV 12, 56, 99, and 21, which also contains an E♯ (ex. 10-7). The disparity in this respect between Tunder's organ and vocal works is even more striking.

The A-flats that rarely appear in Tunder's organ music are found with even greater frequency in his vocal music than in Buxtehude's; D-flats and A-sharps appear as well. The evidence for the performance of Tunder's and Buxtehude's vocal music from the large organ is so great that we must conclude that well before Buxtehude's arrival in Lübeck, Tunder had found a way to get around this problem, either through the retuning of one or two stops for continuo use on the large organ or through the use of other instruments.

A Sketch of Buxtehude's Stylistic Development

We can now combine the information assembled here to form a provisional sketch of Buxtehude's stylistic development. Only three works can be attributed with any certainty to his Helsingør years, the two vocal works BuxWV 7 and 23 and the sonata fragment BuxWV 270. To these we might add two organ works, the A-minor praeambulum BuxWV 158 and the Phrygian praeludium BuxWV 152. These few works suggest that before his arrival in Lübeck Buxtehude was a competent but not yet a distinctive composer; his appointment to that prestigious post may have been due chiefly to his flair as a performer.

Once Buxtehude settled in Lübeck, however, his compositional skills seem to have blossomed, perhaps partly as a result of the stimulation that he received from contact with his colleagues in Hamburg. During the early 1670s he was particularly interested in counterpoint, and his most concentrated essays in this style—"Mit Fried und Freud" (BuxWV 76-1) and the *Missa alla brevis* (BuxWV 114) date from this time. *Ich dank dir schon* (BuxWV 195) may have been composed then as well. The basso ostinato provided the structure for several vocal works, and he learned to treat it with increasing freedom and subtlety. Several works composed around 1675 demonstrate many characteristics of his mature style: fugues that contain entrances of subject and answer in all voices followed by free endings; varied and sophisticated treatment of chorale melodies; secure, fluent handling of all contrapuntal devices; a clear sense of major-minor tonality; and the abundant use of secondary dominants.

Buxtehude's first oratorio for the Lübeck Abendmusiken appears to have been *Die Hochzeit des Lamms* of 1678, and from this time onward he devoted a great deal of his compositional and organizational skills to the presentation of this annual concert series. In order to sustain the Abendmusiken on this enlarged scale, he had to compose music that would appeal to a large audience of ordinary citizens and inspire them to contribute money to support these productions. We first encounter evidence of a musical style directed toward the ordinary citizen in works copied during the 1680s, most notably *Alles was ihr tut* (BuxWV 4) and *Schwinget euch himmelan* (BuxWV 96). This style is characterized by German texts, a preference for homophonic over contrapuntal texture, an emphasis on aria and strophic form, and a distinctive style of chorale setting in which a simple harmonization is decorated by brief instrumental interjections in concertato style. At the same time, however, he was composing instrumental works that were increasingly directed toward the connoisseur. While he was ful-filling the expectations of ordinary citizens with some of his vocal works, he was surprising and delighting connoisseurs with music composed in a style that was totally unpredictable: the *stylus phantasticus*.

This divergence of styles, first noticed in the works copied in the 1680s, becomes even more pronounced in the works copied and published during the 1690s. A vast stylistic gulf separates vocal works such as *Was mich auf dieser Welt betrübt* (BuxWV 105), *O wie selig sind* (BuxWV 90), and *Nun freut euch, ihr Frommen, mit mir* (BuxWV 80) from the two collections of printed sonatas, in which the *stylus phantasticus* finds its most concentrated expression. Increasingly, the praeludia place their emphasis on the free sections rather than the fugues. Among the earlier praeludia that we find in the Lowell Mason Codex, the fugues far outbalance the free sections in all but the D-minor toccata (BuxWV 155). The Lindemann tablatures transmit one work, the praeludium in D major (BuxWV 139), with twice as many measures devoted to free sections as to its one fugue. Among the works that may be later, three stand out for their particularly extensive free sections: the praeludium in F♯ minor (BuxWV 146) and the toc-catas in F major (BuxWV 156) and G major (BuxWV 165).

Buxtehude may have later pulled back from the excesses of the *stylus phantas-ticus*, however. The clear tonal plan and balanced form of the D-minor pas-sacaglia stand out uniquely in Buxtehude's oeuvre and suggest that he may have adopted a more classic, balanced style late in life; similar traits can be seen in *Nichts soll uns scheiden* (BuxWV 77) and the revision of *Ich habe Lust abzuscheiden* (BuxWV 47) in the Lübeck tablature. His cultivation of dramatic music contin-ued unabated until the end of his life, as evidenced by the "extraordinary" Abendmusiken of 1705. His inclusion of recitative and his use of oboes and horns in these works show that his musical style was still developing at this late date. He also employed oboes to dramatic effect in *Ich suchte des Nachts* (BuxWV 50), which may be dated at the same time.

This rough sketch of Buxtehude's stylistic development relies mainly on his vocal and chamber music, almost all of which comes down in sources copied or printed during his lifetime. Several generations of commentators have failed to produce a convincing chronology of Buxtehude's organ works, and perhaps the time has come to acknowledge that the task is impossible. It is still worth noting the coincidence of the dates 1687, when Düben ceased his copying activity; 1688, the terminus ante quem for the works in the Lowell Mason Codex; and 1689, the end of Klingenberg's study with Buxtehude, by which time the exemplars for Lindemann's copies were presumably completed. Of Buxtehude's extant works, 85 percent of his vocal works can be securely dated before 1690, but only 20 percent of his organ works. It thus seems quite likely that he composed the organ music on which his reputation mainly rests throughout his long career.

Chapter Eleven

The Performance of Buxtehude's Music

> But as the Nature and Effects of *Musical Expression* do likewise relate to the
> *Performer,* and the different Instruments which are employ'd in the Practice
> of Music, so these in their Turn may be also considered.
>
> For, as *Musical Expression* in the *Composer,* is succeeding in the Attempt to
> express some particular Passion; so in the *Performer* it is to do a *Composition*
> Justice, by playing it in a *Taste* and *Stile* so exactly corresponding with the
> Intention of the Composer, as to preserve and illustrate *all* the Beauties of
> his Work.

Although Charles Avison was probably not thinking of the music of earlier composers when he published these lines in 1752,[1] we could find no better words to articulate the task of the modern performer of Buxtehude's music. Although about three hundred years separate us from the taste and style of Buxtehude's time, the sources of his music yield a considerable amount of information about his intentions regarding its performance. The chief issues to be explored in this chapter concern the type and number of voices or instruments, articulation, tempo, dynamics, and organ registration.

Choir and Soloists

The question of whether Buxtehude performed his larger vocal works with a choir of several voices to a part or with an ensemble of soloists is by no means so easily answered as it is often assumed to be. It is best approached through those works specifically designated for performance with capella. Johann Gottfried Walther defined capella as "that special or large choir that enters only occasionally for reinforcement and can be called *Chorus ascititius* [supplemental chorus], because it is taken from the other concertizing voices, and extracted." He defined the concertizing voices under the word *Concertante*: "This adjective is applied to all reciting voices, in order to distinguish them from those that sing only in the large choir, or *à Capella*." The distinction between concertizing soloists and supporting capella lies at the very roots of baroque style. Praetorius describes it most concisely in his explanation of the varying numerical designations, which are also found in the titles of Buxtehude's vocal works:

> When à 2.3.4.5.6.7. etc. is found at the head of a vocal concerto . . . it must be understood that the first number means the concertizing voices, the whole foundation of the concerto. The following numbers, however, designate the instrumental or capella voices, which are added only *per accidens, ornatus et plenioris concentus gratiâ* [accidentally, for the sake of a decorated and fuller harmony], as described above, and which can be completely left out if musicians are lacking.[2]

Martin Fuhrmann concurs that the capella can be omitted if necessary, "because [the parts] are already being sung by the concertizing soloists." It is clear from his discussion that the capella often consists of only one or two extra singers to a part, hardly a chorus in the modern sense.

Buxtehude used the word *capella* in two autograph manuscripts, *Uu* 82:39 and *Uu* 6:9, and in an autograph portion of a copy, *LÜh* A 373. In the first of these, the tablature for *Nun danket alle Gott* (BuxWV 79), he inserted the words "con la capella" just before the bass line of the first tutti entrance at m. 50 (see fig. 9-2). The top four voices had entered imitatively and in duet style without instrumental doubling, beginning at m. 43; at m. 50 the texture shifts to homophony, and the sopranos and bass are doubled by instruments (the scoring does not include instruments in the alto and tenor range). These two types of vocal writing alternate throughout the work, and presumably the capella is active in all similar homophonic tutti passages. The copy of BuxWV 79 in the Lübeck tablature A 373 includes the word *capella* in its side title: "Nun dancket alle Gott, der / à. 13: v. 18: / 2. Violini, Violon, / 2. Cornetti, Fagotto, / 2. Trombette, / 5. Voce con le Capella / di Diet: Buxteh." The designation of the composer is in Buxtehude's hand.[3] Both the arithmetic of the expression "for 13 or 18" and the placement of the word *capella* suggest that the five ad libitum parts double the five vocalists.[4] In contrast to Praetorius's description, Buxtehude's essential number of parts, thirteen in this case, always includes the instrumental parts. The basso continuo is never included in these enumerations.

Buxtehude's only preserved autograph score, *Uu* 6:9 (*Fürwahr, er trug unsere Krankheit*, BuxWV 31), may also serve as a model for his use of the capella. The only mention of the word *capella* is on the title page: "à 10: vel 15: doi Violini doi Viole de gamba con Violon o fagotto; doi Soprani Alto Tenore e Basso con le Capella." As in BuxWV 79, the vocal writing alternates between sections of one to three voices undoubled by instruments, often marked "Solo," and of all five voices, each doubled by an instrument in the same range, generally marked "Tutti." Two brief passages where all five singers are active without instrumental doubling at mm. 148 and 160 are marked "Solo." In this work the tutti passages are not all homophonic in texture, but it appears that the capella could be active wherever the instruments double the voices.

The side title for *Ihr lieben Christen, freut euch nun* (BuxWV 51) in the Lübeck tablature contains no indication for the participation of the capella. The numerical designation, written by the Lübeck copyist, is simply "à 13." Buxtehude inserted two autograph passages into this copy, however, the first beginning with the trio "So komm doch, Jesu" at m. 153 (fol. 8b) and extending through m. 212. With the second autograph insertion, beginning at m. 226, the tutti section "Ei lieber Herr, eil zum Gericht," Buxtehude has written "con Capella."[5] All five vocal parts are doubled by instruments, and the texture is completely homophonic.

One further work, BuxWV 54, includes the word *capella* on its title page, "Ist es Recht â 10 vel 20: 2 Soprani, Alto, Tenor, Basso, 2. Violini, 2. Viola, Violon con 5 Voci e 5 Strom. Capella" (*Uu* 51:11). Here the word *capella* seems to include doubling parts for both voices and instruments. Only the ten principal parts, plus the organ continuo, are preserved in this set of parts, however. The opening and closing concerto movements of this concerto-aria cantata alternate sections where the instruments double all five voices with other sections where voices and instruments interact independently; the capella doubling would presumably occur only at the tutti sections. The scoring is reduced for the aria: three voices accompanied only by continuo, with interludes and ritornello for two violins and violone. The viola parts contain the corresponding violin parts for the aria, marked "Violino complem[ento]." In this movement, the violin parts would thus be doubled, but the vocal capella would most likely not be active.

These four works, BuxWV 79, 31, 51, and 54, are all scored for five singers and various instruments. In each case the numerical designation does not include the capella among the essential performers. As stated in Walther's definition, the parts sung by the capella are contained within the parts for the principal singers, and they do not require separate lines in a score or tablature. Separate performing parts for the capella would normally have been copied, however, so it appears that Gustav Düben exercised the option to perform BuxWV 54 without capella in Stockholm. His court musicians included five singers at most; capella singers would have been available only when the court musicians performed with the choir of the German church or when extra singers were hired (see chapter 4).

Only one work by Buxtehude is preserved in which a supporting chorus is not optional: the six-choir concerto *Benedicam Dominum* (BuxWV 113), transmitted in the set of parts *Uu* 50:6. The numerical designation on the title page is simply "a 24"; all parts are essential. Two of its six choirs are vocal, "3. Chor: doi Soprani, Alto, Tenor è Basso" and "6. Chor: Soprano, Alto, Tenor è Basso." Although these choirs are not further distinguished on the title page, each of the parts for the third choir is marked "Concertato,"[6] whereas those of the sixth choir are not so marked. The singers in the third choir, all soloists, have exten-sive passages accompanied only by continuo and in a variety of textures. The singers of the sixth choir function chiefly as a capella, doubling the lower four voices of the concertato singers in tutti passages, and their music is almost entirely homophonic. When the sixth choir sings in concertato interchange with the third choir, as in mm. 95ff of the concerto, it is usually doubled by instru-ments, whereas the third choir often is not. The sixth choir is exposed without doubling only once, at m. 166, for the duration of three half notes.

Benedicam Dominum is the most lavishly scored of Buxtehude's extant works, the only one that approaches the large performing forces and variety of instru-mentation characteristic of the Abendmusiken. It is also the only preserved work whose scoring seems to have been intended specifically for the six balconies sur-rounding the organ at St. Mary's in Lübeck. Nearly forty singers and instru-mentalists participated in the Abendmusiken of 1679; if there were as many performers in *Benedicam Dominum,* whose Stockholm manuscript contains the date 1683, it could mean that the sixth chorus was sung with four voices to a part. This work, then, could serve to demonstrate the stylistic differences between Buxtehude's writing for an ensemble of soloists—the third chorus—and a choir that could include several on a part—the sixth chorus. They are the same distinctions noted in the works that specify capella, BuxWV 31, 51, 54 and 79: the capella sings where instruments double the voices and the texture is pri-marily homophonic.

Only one incomplete set of capella parts survives to document the actual prac-tice of doubling the vocal parts by an optional capella in Buxtehude's music. Three supplementary parts, marked "Cantus 1 in Ripieno," "Canto 2do in Ripieno," and "Alto in Ripieno," are preserved in the set of parts *Uu* 6:1 for "Surge amica mea," the fourth cantata of the *Membra Jesu* cycle (BuxWV 75-4). Gustav Düben copied both the principal parts in this set and the ripieno parts extracted from them, the latter presumably at a later date, since the paper is dif-ferent. Buxtehude's autograph tablature of the entire cycle (*Uu* 50:12), dedi-cated to Düben, makes no mention of capella, but he devoted little attention to scoring in this manuscript. Ripieno parts for tenor and bass may also have existed at one time, since the work is scored for five voices. The three extant parts include only the opening concerto, as would be expected, but they are inconsistent in the roles that they apportion to the capella. The alto part reflects the practice seen in BuxWV 79 and 113, whereby only those sections doubled by instruments are given to the capella; mm. 1–4, 39–41, and 49–54 are omit-ted. In contrast, the ripieno and concerted parts for Soprano 1 are identical. The soprano 2 ripieno part falls in between, including the undoubled line at m. 43 but omitting those at mm. 20 and 24.

The titles of three further works suggest performance with capella. BuxWV 3, like BuxWV 54, is designated "a 10 vel 20. 5 Voci e 5 Stromenti con 10 in Repieno" (*Uu* 50:1a). BuxWV 41, also scored for five voices and five instruments, is designated "a 10 vel 15" in the Lübeck tablature, with the optional five voices most likely designating a vocal capella that would double the voices when the instruments do. Example 5-23 shows a passage where this could occur, in mm. 143–45 of versus 3. At the head of BuxWV 4, the Lübeck copyist of A 373 left a blank following the numerical designation "â. 9: vel"; Buxtehude added the word *piu*, leaving it unclear how many supporting voices or instruments he wished.[7] The two other sources for BuxWV 4 give no indication of the participation of the capella. Both BuxWV 4 and BuxWV 41, however, contain extensive sections where the instruments double the voices, making these works similar to those in which capella is designated.

Of the works examined thus far, all but BuxWV 4 call for five concertato voices. In the passages where they are doubled by instruments, Buxtehude's normal practice is to double the two sopranos with violins, the alto and tenor with violas, and the bass with violone. Of the remaining works scored for five or six voices—BuxWV 18, 20, 24, 29, 34, 86, 96, 110, and 114—all but one contain homophonic sections in which the instruments double the voices. At the discretion of the conductor, the capella could easily have participated in those works even though it is not mentioned in the sources. The one work that contains no instrumental doubling is the *Missa alla brevis* (BuxWV 114), composed in *stile antico* for five voices accompanied only by basso continuo. Unlike the concerted works, in which the capella "enters only occasionally for reinforcement," this work was probably intended entirely for capella. Walther's definition of *Capella* includes a description of just such a work: "Accordingly one finds that skillful and experienced composers use only whole, half and quarter notes in *alla-breve* measures, but they apply them with great art and skill in a variety of ways; this serious style is then actually called *à* or *da Capella*."[8]

The above evidence suggests that the capella could have participated in all of Buxtehude's works for five or more voices; the case for the use of the capella in his works for four voices, however, is far less convincing. BuxWV 4 is the one work in this group with a source that hints at the presence of capella: "a 9 vel piu" in A 373. In the first concerted movement (II, "Alles was ihr tut"), the strings double the voices throughout with the exception of mm. 23–26. The four voices sing together homophonically in the following aria (III, "Dir, dir höchster") without instrumental doubling; the strings provide interludes and a ritornello. Instrumental doubling of the voices reappears in the last three phrases of the four-voice chorale setting (IV, mm. 110–21) and occurs throughout the final movement, a shortened version of the opening concerto. Violin II usually doubles the soprano, whereas violin I moves independently. If we assume that the capella enters whenever the instruments do, the resulting overall structure is very satisfying. The tuttis of the opening and closing vocal movements provide solid framing. The ensemble of soloists provides contrast in the aria, with its more personal text. And the chorale setting builds a crescendo from soprano solo to ensemble of soloists to tutti. This structure is still present without the participation of the capella, of course, and it appears that Düben's performance of this work in Stockholm was without capella. But the addition of a chorus enhances the dynamic contrasts between and within the movements of this cantata.

Only one other four-voice work, BuxWV 22, replicates the scoring and doubling of BuxWV 4. There the tutti sections of the opening and closing vocal movements seem to call for the participation of the capella. Other works are scored similarly, but instrumental doubling is either handled quite differently or totally avoided. In the final versus of BuxWV 14 and the final two versus of BuxWV 78, the violas and violone or bassoon double the lower voices at times, but the violins systematically avoid doubling the soprano. It is less likely that Buxtehude intended the capella to participate in these works, particularly since BuxWV 78 is preserved in autograph tablature (*Uu* 82:38) with its numerical designation simply "à 9." In the four remaining works scored for four voices and five strings—BuxWV 62, 85, 91, and 112—the instruments interact with the voices in concertato exchange and avoid doubling them. When they do come together in occasional tutti passages, the lower voices may be doubled, but not the soprano.

A large group of works—BuxWV 10, 15, 27, 40, 81, 102, and 103—are scored for four voices, SATB, two violins, and violone (BuxWV 102 lacks the violone). All but BuxWV 15 are multiverse concertato chorale harmonizations. In all these works, the vocal writing is for four voices throughout and is often—but by no means always—homophonic. The violin parts never double the voices; either they are separated in concertato interchange or they have independent parts above the soprano in the tutti sections. The violone and vocal bass parts often converge, but it is in the nature of both of these parts to double the basso continuo much of the time. It might be argued that these works are a capella throughout and that the vocal writing is so undemanding that the capella would have no need of instrumental doubling. Yet several of these works contain rather elaborate "Amen" sections that are definitely soloistic in nature. It is much more likely that Buxtehude intended this group of works for an ensemble of soloists without the capella.

Of the remaining works for four voices, three offer some possibility of the participation of the capella. The most convincing is BuxWV 23, whose title suggests the possibility of performance with capella: "Ecce nunc benedicite à 6 A.T.T.B. è 2 Violini Con 4 Ripien." (*Uu* 6:6). One of these four ripieno parts is present; it is labeled "Viole 1. Complem:" and it doubles the alto vocal part at all tutti sections. If two missing parts doubled the tenors, then both the instrumental and the textural prerequisites would be present for the participation of the capella. BuxWV 13 resembles the concertato chorale harmonizations somewhat, but it is scored for three violins instead of two, and the third violin systematically doubles the soprano in all tutti sections. These sections are all rather short, however, and capella doubling of only these portions would not produce a satisfying effect. *Schlagt, Künstler, die Pauken* (BuxWV 122 with sacred parody BuxWV 26) adds two trumpets and timpani to the ensemble of four voices (SSAB) and three strings. In the outer movements the violins do double the sopranos, but only when the trumpets and timpani are also playing. Again, capella doubling of just these passages would not be convincing. One final work, BuxWV 61, calls for four voices, but they never all sing together, and there is no instrumental doubling.

The conclusion seems inescapable that Buxtehude intended the majority of his works for four voices not for chorus but for an ensemble of soloists. In only three—BuxWV 4, 22, and 23—is the addition of capella convincing. In the remaining works, as in the portions of the works with capella that are not doubled by instruments, the style of the passages for four voices very much resembles his ensemble writing for two and three voices, all presumably for soloists. This conclusion is in complete accord with what we know about the working conditions at St. Mary's in Lübeck. Buxtehude was not the conductor of the choir at St. Catherine's school—that was the cantor's job—so he did not normally have a choir at his disposal. When he did, as in the Abendmusiken concerts, he was working with a large ensemble of vocal soloists and instrumentalists as well. The lost Abendmusik *Himmlische Seelenlust auf Erden*, for example, called for "6 voc. concert. nebst divers. Instr. u. Capell-St[immen]." Had Buxtehude worked as a cantor instead of as an organist, he would undoubtedly have left a very different corpus of vocal music, one in which both choral music and liturgical music played a much larger role.

Solo Voices

All of Buxtehude's vocal soloists, including the singers of his soprano parts, appear to have been men. The more usual singers of soprano parts—boys, castrati, and women—were not readily available to him. The choirboys were responsible to the cantor. There were no Italian castrati residing in Lübeck, although a visiting castrato did sing in St. Mary's on Easter Sunday of 1672, duly noted in the account book. Female sopranos were not permitted to perform in church. Male falsettists cultivated the soprano range to a much greater extent in the seventeenth century than they do today, however. Praetorius lists three types of singer in the soprano range: *Eunuchus* (castrato), *Falsetista*, and *Discantista* (boy soprano). The practice extended well into the eighteenth century; Walther's definition of "Cammer-Ton" includes the information that performance at this lower pitch was chiefly for the sake of adult *Sopranisten*, who do not command such a high range, and Johann Petri tells of a *Sopranist*—not a castrato—whose falsetto range extended to f‴.[9]

The principal singer of Buxtehude's soprano parts in Lübeck must have been Hans Iwe, the versatile municipal musician who assisted Buxtehude at the large organ from 1674 until his death in 1692. Iwe is most often listed in the pay records as a *Sopranist*, although he appears once as a *Violist*. In 1677, a second sopranist, Johann Albrecht Schop, was paid for the year. The participation of boy sopranos from St. Catherine's school in Lübeck cannot be ruled out, of course, and in Stockholm the soprano parts were regularly sung by boys. The range of Buxtehude's soprano parts is not particularly high; approximately half of both the first and second soprano parts extend only to g″. The highest pitch encountered is one b♮″ in BuxWV 80. Since this work would have been performed in Chorton at St. Mary's, this high note corresponds almost to c♯‴ at modern pitch of a′ = 440, still well below the top notes of Petri's sopranist.

Buxtehude's alto parts extend no higher than d″ (e″ in modern pitch), well within the reach of an adult male alto. The fact that vocal works were performed in Chorton at St. Mary's is most evident from Buxtehude's low bass parts, many of which extend down to written E or D; in one work (BuxWV 104) the bass part includes a C.

Instruments

The specific issues with respect to the performance of Buxtehude's instrumental music are similar to those concerning the voice: the nature of the instruments and the number of them that were used. As is the case with most of his contemporaries, we find the greater technical demands and variety in instrumental scoring not in Buxtehude's works for instruments alone but in his concerted works for voices and instruments. Only four vocal works (BuxWV 2, 12, 53, 114) are strictly speaking "vocal" in the sense that the voices are accompanied only by basso continuo; in all the others, instruments play a significant and sometimes an equal role.

Strings

The most important and the least problematic of the instruments in Buxtehude's inventory is the violin. The baroque violin had achieved its classic form by the time of Buxtehude's birth; in 1636 Mersenne characterized it as "the king of instruments." One of its greatest builders, Jacob Stainer, was an elder German-speaking contemporary of Buxtehude. And a few years after Buxtehude's death, Mattheson wrote that "among those [instruments] that are strung with gut and played with bows, the pleasing and penetrating violin stands out, which is suited to all things, whatever they may be called."[10] Indeed, all but one of Buxtehude's authentic instrumental works (BuxWV 267) and six of the vocal works with instruments (BuxWV 61, 64, 69, 75-6, 76-2, 116) call for at least one violin.

While the violin was in its ascendancy, another instrument "strung with gut and played with bows," the viola da gamba, was going out of favor. "It is a shame that [the Viol di Gamba] is now used so little," wrote Fuhrmann in 1706. "The French *Hautbois* have submerged it; for now one can hardly say to a professional musician, 'Sir, play me a sonata on the viola da gamba' (as was the case 20 or 30 years ago), but rather 'play me a march or a minuet on the oboe.' Thus times and instruments of music are changed, and men are changed with them."[11] Buxtehude, however, continued to be involved with the viola da gamba until at least 1696, the year of publication for his second set of sonatas for violin, viola da gamba, and harpsichord. And one of the great German builders of the viola da gamba, Joachim Tielke, was working in Hamburg from 1667 until his death in 1719. There can be no doubt that Buxtehude knew—and perhaps even played and composed for—Tielke's gambas. In fact, he may have been playing one in Voorhout's painting *Musical Party*.[12]

Buxtehude called on the viola da gamba for four different functions. In the sonatas and in three vocal works (BuxWV 5, 32, 64) it appears as a virtuoso solo instrument. There it is quite independent of the basso continuo, although it may at times double it in embellished form. In three vocal works (BuxWV 6, 39, 97) the viola da gamba serves as the bass in the instrumental ensemble, a function normally taken by the violone.[13] In three vocal works (BuxWV 31, 36, 115), the first of them preserved in an autograph score (*Uu* 6:9), Buxtehude uses viole da gamba for the middle parts in a five-part mixed instrumental ensemble. Finally, an ensemble made up entirely of parts labeled "viola da gamba" accompanies two other vocal works (BuxWV 69, 75-6).

The instrument required for the first two of the functions just described is undoubtedly the bass viola da gamba; the virtuoso parts exploit its entire range, while the bass parts concentrate on the lower part of its range. It is not entirely clear, however, whether the upper and middle parts in the ensembles, written in the soprano, alto, and tenor clefs, were to be played on the bass viola da gamba or on the tenor of the family, tuned a fourth higher. Niedt describes the viola da gamba as "a small tenor or bass fiddle, played between the legs, from whence its name comes."[14] For Speer, Mattheson, and Walther, however, the term *viola da gamba* is defined specifically as the bass instrument with the tuning D G c e a d'. "Whoever wants to play this instrument correctly," according to Speer, "must understand the bass, tenor, alto, mezzosoprano and even the soprano clef."[15] In only one work (BuxWV 75-6)—and then by only one tone—does one of these parts exceed the normal upper range of the bass viola da gamba, given by both Speer and Mattheson as d". The fact that every one of Tielke's surviving viole da gamba is a bass instrument would seem to indicate that this gamba was preferred in northern Germany during Buxtehude's time. Günther Hellwig catalogues seventy-one viole da gamba built between 1669 and 1717, of which one instrument has five strings and three or four have seven.

The account books of St. Mary's do not include purchases of violins or of viole da gamba, but in 1677 a payment of 6 Lübeck marks was made to Daniel Erich, a Lübeck instrument builder and father of Buxtehude's pupil of the same name, for a "Tenor Geige" that Buxtehude needed at the large organ. The church already owned two tenor violas, which had been built by Erich in 1660, and in 1696 the church owned two violins, four "Tenor Geigen," and two violones. According to Fuhrmann's definition, a *Tenor Geige* would be a viola da braccio, a member of the violin family; such an instrument is also pictured in plate XXI of Praetorius's *Theatrum Instrumentorum*. Buxtehude specified viole da braccio for the middle parts in the alto and tenor range of two works (BuxWV 66, 85), the second of which is preserved in an autograph tablature (*Uu* 51:13a). It also appears as the single middle part, in the mezzo-soprano clef, of BuxWV 58 and as an alternative to the viola da gamba for the middle parts of BuxWV 36. Far more common, however, is the simple designation "Viola," which is used for the middle parts of most of Buxtehude's works scored for a five-part instrumental ensemble and which can probably be understood to refer to the viola da braccio. Alto and tenor baroque violas were of different sizes but were both tuned in the same way as the modern viola, c g d' a'. Speer noted that the tenor viola da braccio rarely ascended to a' or used the fourth string, and Buxtehude's tenor viola parts usually conform to that range. The one tenor viola da braccio part with an autograph source (BuxWV 85), however, contains the repeated pitch a' in the opening sonata.

Buxtehude used one further term to designate the mid-range string parts, *violetta*. It is found for parts in the alto and tenor range in six works (BuxWV 22, 48, 59, 78, 82, 91), with the source for BuxWV 78 in autograph tablature (*Uu* 82:38). Fuhrmann equates the violetta with the *Alt-Geige*, which is used for complemento parts, and the viola da braccio with the *Tenor Geige*. Niedt defines a violetta as "a fiddle for the middle part; it can be done either on *braccien* or small viole di gamba." Walther quotes him, adding that the range of the discant viola da gamba is from c to a" and that of the alto viola da gamba, or violetta, from G to e". For Walther, then, an unmodified viola da gamba is a bass, and an alto [tenor] viola da gamba is a violetta. Only Sebastian Brossard is unequivocal: "Violetta. Diminutive of Viola, means properly small viol, which is to say our *Dessus de Viole*." Mattheson, on the other hand, equates the violetta with the viola da braccio:

> The filling Viola, Violetta, Viola da Braccio or Brazzo, is of larger structure and proportions than the violin, but is otherwise of the same nature, and is only tuned a fifth lower, namely a' d' g c. It serves for middle parts of all sorts, such as: Viola prima (as in voices, the high or true alto), Viola secunda (like the tenor), etc. And it is one of the most important elements in a harmonic *Concert*; for if the middle voices are lacking, the harmony is missing, and if they are played badly, everything else will be dissonant.

The question remains: What did Buxtehude mean by the term *violetta?* Autograph sources survive for three works scored with a five-part instrumental ensemble; in BuxWV 31 he specified viole da gamba for the middle parts; in BuxWV 85, viole da braccio; and in BuxWV 78, violette. The style and ranges of the alto and tenor parts, respectively, in these three works are quite similar, with the exception that viola da gamba 1 in BuxWV 31 has a section employing double stops. If he had meant the violetta parts to be played by viola da gamba *or* viola da braccio, he would probably have written exactly that, as he specified "Violon ô fagotto" for the bass instrument on the title page of BuxWV 31. It appears more likely that Buxtehude used the term *violetta* in its diminutive sense as a small viol—a tenor viol in most instances, perhaps a treble viol for BuxWV 82, which contains a part for violetta, written in the soprano clef, that exceeds the normal viola range, ascending to f″.

Whatever Buxtehude may have intended by the term *violetta*, it is quite clear both from the sets of parts preserved from Stockholm performances and from the statements of contemporary writers that the middle parts could be and were played by a variety of instruments. The parts for BuxWV 36, for example, specify on the title page that the tenor is to be accompanied by "tre viole de gambe." The three corresponding parts are labeled "Viola de gamba ô braccie 1" [alto clef], "Viola de gamba ô braccie 2" [tenor clef] and "Violon ô de gamba" [bass clef] on the upper right corner of each page. In addition, "Trombona 1" and "Trombona 2" appear as later additions on the upper left corners of the first two parts.

The bass instrument in Buxtehude's ensemble was most often the violone. In this function it plays with the other instruments, deriving its pitches from the basso continuo part and its rhythm from the other strings. When they are silent, it, too is silent; it is by no means another continuo part. The violone alone is named as the bass ensemble instrument in the sources for thirty-eight of Buxtehude's vocal works, and in another eight it is given with the *fagotto* (dulcian; see pp. 377–78) as an alternate instrument. The *fagotto* alone appears in this function in fourteen works, the viola da gamba in four. There is not a single instance of scoring for violoncello in any of Buxtehude's works. In Buxtehude's autograph manuscripts, the violone is specified in five works, the *fagotto* in one, and the alternatives of violone or *fagotto* and violone or viola da gamba in two. The violone serves a second function in the vocal music; in eleven sets of parts preserved from Stockholm performances, it is found doubling the continuo throughout the work. These parts are both figured and unfigured, and no other melody instrument serves in this way in these sources. Finally, the violone appears in one instrumental chamber work, a sonata for viola da gamba and violone (BuxWV 267). Clearly it is important to establish what sort of instrument Buxtehude wanted for these violone parts.

Two sizes of violone were in use in Germany during the seventeenth century. Praetorius pictures a "Violone, Groß Viol-de Gamba Bass" in plate VI and a "gar grosse Viol[o]n de Gamba Sub Bass" or "Groß Contra-Bas-Geig" in plate V of his *Theatrum Instrumentorum*. Jacob Stainer's 1669 price list also indicates two sizes of violone: He charged 12 taler for a "violin," 13 taler for a "violin de braccia," 15 taler for an "altviola," 20 taler for a "viola da gamba," 30 taler for a "violon," and 50 taler for an "octafviolon."[16] Fuhrmann also mentions two instruments:

"Violone, Bass-Geige. Violone Grosso, an Octav-Bass-Geige on which is found the 16-foot Contra-C." Speer, Niedt, and Walther give the tuning only for the 8′ instrument: GG C F A d g, with a range extending upward to d′ or e′. Brossard and Mattheson mention only the 16′ instrument.

St. Mary's Church purchased a violone in 1667 for the use of the cantor; this was probably the "großen Violon" for which strings were purchased in 1671. In 1672 the church bought a "große Octav-geige" for 30 Lübeck marks (10 rix-dollars) from Zacharias Cronenberg, one of the municipal musicians who played regularly at St. Mary's. He died that year, and Peter Grecke applied for his position, claiming that he could play "Clavier, violdegambe, Bassviolone, und violone." It is clear that both sizes of violone were known in Lübeck.

There can be no doubt that when Buxtehude called for the violone as the bass instrument in his ensemble, he had the 8′ instrument in mind. The other instruments used for this purpose—the *fagotto* and the viola da gamba—were both 8′ instruments, and it would make no sense to have an ensemble that skipped from the tenor to the contrabass range with no bass. The same can be said for the sonata, in which unwanted fourths below the continuo would occur if a 16′ violone were used. For the doubling of the continuo, however, a 16′ instrument may have been used. This possibility is discussed below.

Of all the members of Buxtehude's instrumentarium, the most unusual is the *Cymbalo*, which appears in only one work, BuxWV 110. Walther defines *Cimbal* as "a four-sided instrument with wire strings and double bridges, played with wooden sticks or hammers; otherwise called a *Hackebret*," a hammered dulcimer. Mersenne describes this instrument at some length under the name *Psalterium*. The instrument he depicts has thirteen double courses of strings tuned G, c–g′ diatonically and is less than two feet in length, to judge from the size of the tuning hammer and playing stick. But the psalterium "can be made of all sorts of sizes, for one can give a length of five or six feet to the thickest string, as one does to that of the greatest harpsichords, although one makes them only a foot long from each side, or thereabout, so that they may be carried." Its chief advantage over other instruments lies in the fact that

one learns to play it in the space of one or two hours. This makes it valued by those who have no more time to use in this exercise. Now these first strings are of brass and the others steel, which have a certain pungency and gaiety that is not found on the other instruments, as much because of the little leaps and spurts of the stick as because of the shortness and tension of the strings, which are capable of all sorts of songs, provided one places all the necessary strings on it. . . . One can receive some pleasure from this very cheaply and conveniently, since one can have it with all its science for a crown, and one can carry it in the pocket.[17]

The hammered dulcimer was apparently used mainly for dance music, but Fuhrmann implies its use in church: "Sambocca, a *Hackbrett*, a large one sounds good in *Capella* for filling out."

During the last decade of the seventeenth century, Pantaleon Hebenstreit, a musician and dancing teacher in Leipzig, modified the hammered dulcimer by greatly increasing it size. His virtuoso performance on the enlarged instrument before Louis XIV in 1705 caused the king to rename the instrument "pantaleon." Could Buxtehude have used this form of the hammered dulcimer in BuxWV 110? Buxtehude might have learned of it through his assistant, Johann Christian Schieferdecker, who had been a student in Leipzig during the 1690s.

The earliest description of the pantaleon comes from Johann Kuhnau, who wrote to Mattheson in 1717 that he had been infatuated with his *Pantalonischen Cimbal* for the past twelve years. It had a range of five octaves, extending diatonically from EE to G and then chromatically to e'''. Mattheson mentioned the instrument in 1713 in *Das Neu-Eröffnete Orchestre*, and in his 1718 reply to Kuhnau he wrote that he had become acquainted with it through "Monsr. Grünewald, the Darmstadt Capellmeister." Gottfried Grünewald, the vice Kapellmeister at Darmstadt from about 1713, gave a concert on the pantaleon in Hamburg in 1717. Both Kuhnau and Mattheson emphasize the great difficulty in tuning and particularly in playing the instrument—Kuhnau calls it *Herculeum laborem*—as well as the advantage that it offered over keyboard instruments in its ability to be played both loudly and softly.[18]

On his visit to Dresden in 1772, Charles Burney went to the home of Christlieb Binder, a former pupil of Hebenstreit, to see "the ruins of the famous *Pantaleone*. This instrument . . . is more than nine feet long, and had, when in order, 186 strings of catgut." Apparently unknown to Burney, Georg Noëlli, another former pupil of Hebenstreit, had been performing on the pantaleon in England. The following notice appeared in a Worcester newspaper in 1767:

> Mr. Noel will perform several Grand Overtures on the newly invented instrument, the Pantaleone. The instrument is eleven feet in length and has 276 strings of different magnitudes.[19]

Although the pantaleon was normally a solo instrument, Noëlli is pictured playing it as part of a small vocal and instrumental ensemble at a 1767 concert in Cambridge.[20]

The *Cymbalo* part in BuxWV 110 doubles the violone in the opening sinfonia and replaces it as the bass support for the violins and cornetts in the first and probably the final versus. It is an unfigured bass part with a range of sixteen notes from C to c',[21] only slightly larger than that of the instrument described by Mersenne. An ordinary hammered dulcimer seems to be all that was required for this part, not the much larger pantaleon, which would have fitted into a balcony in St. Mary's only with great difficulty.

Woodwinds

Late in September of 1679, Buxtehude recorded the purchase in Hamburg of three *Schallmeyen* and two *Quart-flöeten*, adjusted to the St. Mary's organ, which he intended to use in the upcoming Abendmusiken. These instruments would have been shawms and recorders. Buxtehude may have scored for woodwinds in other Abendmusiken; both *Himmlische Seelenlust auf Erden* of 1684 and *Templum honoris* of 1705 called for "diverse instruments." One work with diverse instruments survives, *Mein Gemüt erfreuet sich* (BuxWV 72), and it offers a glimpse of what such pieces from the lost Abendmusiken may have been like. The text mentions a number of musical instruments, and the scoring shifts with the mention of "Posaunen und Trompeten" (m. 62), "Dulcianen" (m. 69), "Flöten" (m. 71), and "Zinken" (m. 91). The two top instrumental lines in the tablature source for this work are marked "flauto" at m. 71, and these few measures, with a range of g′–g″, constitute the only surviving music that Buxtehude wrote for recorders. The flute parts contained in the part sets for four other works—BuxWV 24, 62, 66, and 73—can all be shown to be later additions in Stockholm and not part of the original scoring. No extant music by Buxtehude calls for shawms.

The French *hautbois* became popular in Germany at about the turn of the eighteenth century; Speer does not mention it, but three years later Niedt does, calling it "a French shawm," and Fuhrmann's remarks concerning its popularity will be recalled. Buxtehude's use of oboes in two works from 1705 is discussed in chapter 10. An extra oboe part, doubling the violin but transposed up one tone, was added in Stockholm to the part set for BuxWV 82. This is the only instance of a part for an instrument in Kammerton among the sources for Buxtehude's works.

Buxtehude called for *cornetti*, the "Zinken" of BuxWV 72, in seven vocal works (BuxWV 33, 44, 51, 72, 79, 110, 113). Two of the instruments on which this music may have been played can be seen at the St. Annen-Museum in Lübeck: curved cornetts from the seventeenth century, one of ivory, one of wood covered with leather. The watchman of St. Mary's still played the ivory cornetto from the tower during the early nineteenth century, and the other was acquired from the church. Speer gives fingerings for the cornett's normal range of a–c‴; Buxtehude exceeded it by one tone in BuxWV 51, where the cornetts double the violins in the tutti sections.

The wind instrument that appears most frequently in Buxtehude's works is the *fagotto*. At the mention of the word "Dulcianen" in BuxWV 72, the lower three instrumental lines are marked *fagotto*, and this early version of the bassoon, made of one piece of wood with eight finger holes and two keys, is the instrument that is now generally called the dulcian. Praetorius refers to the family as "Fagotten: Dolcianen," and they are pictured in plate X of *Theatrum Instrumentorum*; number 3, "Offen Chorist-Fagott C," is the bass instrument that

Buxtehude used. Speer called it a "Bass-Fagott" and gives its fingerings opposite page 240. Its range is C–f'. Fuhrmann distinguishes between *Fagotto seu Dolciano*, an 8' dulcian in Chorton, and *Bassone*, a French *Fagott* in Kammerton. Apart from giving it a brief obbligato appearance in BuxWV 72, Buxtehude uses the dulcian only as a bass in the instrumental ensemble. There seems to be no pattern to his choice of dulcian or violone for this function, apart from the fact that the dulcian more often supports a choir of cornetts or brass instruments (BuxWV 79, 113, 116).

In October of 1685, St. Mary's purchased "a splendid instrument, namely a *Quint* or *Bass Bombard*, . . . which we have long wanted for the adornment of our music here." A new brass reed was required to bring its pitch into conformity with the organ. This instrument, measuring 2.72 meters, is still in Lübeck, now at the St. Annen-Museum. Praetorius pictures it as the "Groß Doppel Quint-Pommer" in plate VI of the *Theatrum Instrumentorum*; in Fuhrmann's description, "it vigorously rumbles and bangs with a low 16-foot tone like a *Posaun-Bass* in the organ." This cannot be the bombarde that supports the third and fourth trumpets in BuxWV 113, because the manuscript source for that work contains the date 1683. Also, like the bombarde that serves as an alternative to the violone in BuxWV 27, the bombarde in BuxWV 113 is a true bass instrument, with a range of C–c', not a contrabass. The instrument to be used in these works would be the "Bas-Pommer" that Praetorius pictures in plate XI. The new *Quint* or *Bass Bombard* was probably used as a continuo instrument, and as such it is discussed below.

Brass Instruments and Timpani

Buxtehude took great pride in the 1673 purchase of "two trumpets for the embellishment of the Abendmusik, made in a special way, the likes of which have not been heard in the orchestra of any prince, where otherwise everything in noble music is advanced." The maker is not named in the account book, but he was obviously well skilled in the art of marketing. This purchase must have brought the total of the trumpets owned by the church to six, for in 1676 the local turner made mutes for the six trumpets belonging to the church. Three seventeenth-century trumpets by Nürnberg makers survive at the St. Annen-Museum in Lübeck—by Conrad Droschel (1640), Hans Hainlein (1640), and Michael Nagel (1654); two of these were acquired from St. Mary's.

Buxtehude's extant trumpet parts give no indication of what the special qualities of the new trumpets might have been. The designations *Tromba*, *Trombetta*, and *Clarino* are used interchangeably to indicate a natural trumpet in C Chorton. The insertion of a hollow wooden mute into the bell of the trumpet raised the pitch by a whole tone. The two extant works by Buxtehude scored for muted trumpets are both in D major. In BuxWV 116, a wedding aria from 1672, the muted trumpet and trombone parts are written in C, the voices and continuo in D. In BuxWV 51, all parts are written in D in the Lübeck tablature, but Buxtehude himself inserted a note that the *Clarini in Sordine* "must be copied in C."[22] Buxtehude's other works calling for trumpets are all in C major, and the trumpets are presumably unmuted. In two works, BuxWV 41 and 72, the trumpets appear only briefly, replacing the violins, and the range of each part is limited to only four notes; these trumpet parts may have been played by the violinists. The clarino range of the natural trumpet is fully exploited in the other works.

St. Mary's purchased two *discant Posaunen* in 1674 for the use of the cantor. Praetorius gives this name as an alternative for the alto trombone; he notes, however, as does Speer, that alto parts are playable on the ordinary tenor trombone. Speer gives extensive information on the slide positions for the tenor, alto, and quint (bass) trombones. Buxtehude's trombone parts encompass the alto, tenor, and bass ranges, and he never specifies the discant or alto version of the instrument for these parts. Four or five trombones are called for in BuxWV 113. *Trombona* 1., 2., and 3., written in the alto, tenor, and bass clefs, respectively, form the fifth choir. *Posauna*, in the bass clef, provides the bass for the first and second trumpets of the second choir, and *Trombona Grosse* is written as an alternative on the bombarde part in the same choir. The ranges of *Trombona 3*, *Posauna* and *Bombard ò Trombona Grosse* are nearly identical; all descend to C, the lowest note in Buxtehude's tonal realm. All these parts would most likely have been played on the bass trombone at 8' pitch. Buxtehude's use of muted trombones is unusual for the time; in addition to BuxWV 51 and 116, discussed above, they also appear in *Castrum doloris*.

Buxtehude calls for timpani in only one extant work, a wedding cantata from 1681 that is appropriately titled *Schlagt, Künstler, die Pauken* (BuxWV 122; sacred parody, BuxWV 26). The timpani are tuned in G and c, and they serve as the bass for the two trumpets, acting as the counterpart to the violone, which supports the two violins. The part is included in the tablature as well as the set of parts for this work (both in *Uu* 50:15); it is also counted in the number of essential parts ("à 10") and named on the title page. Trumpets and timpani also sounded together in *Templum honoris* in 1705. That year "two splendid copper kettledrums," were purchased by the church "for the honor of the Lord God, the enjoyment of the Christian congregation and the embellishment of noble music." This was probably a second set for the church; *Templum honoris* calls for two choirs of trumpets and timpani.

The pairing of trumpets and timpani was quite common in German music of the seventeenth century, and thus the question arises as to whether timpani parts might have been improvised in Buxtehude's other works scored with trumpets. In several of these works, however, other bass instruments support the trumpets: violone in BuxWV 29; dulcian in BuxWV 44; trombone and violone together in BuxWV 110; and trombone for the first and second trumpets and bombarde for the third and fourth trumpets in BuxWV 113. Two works with autograph sources, BuxWV 79 and BuxWV 119, contain ritornelli in which the trumpets are supported only by the basso continuo on the note c. BuxWV 116, transmitted in a print that was presumably approved by Buxtehude, contains an *Aufzug* in which the trumpets sound with no bass at all. In view of the specificity of the scoring for timpani in BuxWV 122 and the lack of it in other works with autograph or printed sources, it seems unlikely that Buxtehude intended additional timpani parts to be improvised.

Basso Continuo

The primary instrument for the realization of the basso continuo parts in Buxtehude's concerted works was undoubtedly the organ, and in most cases Buxtehude himself probably played the continuo part at the large organ. Had this not been the case, there would have been no necessity for the instruments purchased by the church to be in tune with the organ. Furthermore, continuo playing was one of the hallmarks of the art of the North German organist. Heinrich Scheidemann dedicated the organ at Otterndorf largely by playing continuo, and Niedt's introduction to his *Musicalische Handleitung* satirizes the organist who lacked this skill.[23] It is thus noteworthy that not one of the autograph manuscripts or contemporary printed sources for Buxtehude's works mentions the organ as the continuo instrument.

Buxtehude's works transmitted by autograph and printed sources fall into three categories: works that would have been performed at St. Mary's within a church service or Abendmusik, occasional works for weddings or funerals, and instrumental works. Buxtehude identified the continuo line as "Cont:" in the autograph manuscript for BuxWV 119 (*Uu* 51:13a, fol. 3r) and as "Continuo" in the printed sources for BuxWV 61, 116 and 118. These are all occasional works, and the funeral for which Buxtehude composed BuxWV 61 took place in Fehmarn, not Lübeck. In the other autograph manuscripts and in the "Klag-Lied" of BuxWV 76 the continuo line is unidentified. These are all works that would have been performed at St. Mary's, in services, in Abendmusiken, or, in the case of the "Klag-Lied," at the funeral of Buxtehude's father. This distinction might be understood to mean that the organ was taken for granted as the primary continuo instrument in St. Mary's and that the designation "continuo" for works that may have been performed elsewhere emphasized the fact that the choice of continuo instruments was open. The continuo parts for the sonatas of opus 1 and opus 2 are labeled "Cembalo."

Three of the church's instrument purchases suggest that the large organ was not the only continuo instrument used in Buxtehude's performances at

St. Mary's. In 1678 the church bought a *doppelt 16 füßiges Regal* at Buxtehude's request, "for the glory of God and the encouragement of my music for feasts and Abendmusik." An undated newspaper clipping in the library of the Fock Archive at the Schnitger-Zentrum, Golzwarden, depicts Walter Kraft, organist of St. Mary's from 1929 until his retirement in 1972, playing this instrument, which very much resembles the regal in plate IV of Praetorius's *Theatrum Instrumentorum*. It was apparently lost during World War II. Buxtehude probably used the regal to support singers in one of the balconies. The *große Octav-geige oder Violon* purchased in 1672 and the *Quint oder Bass Bombard* in 1685 were probably both 16' instruments, and they were very likely used to double the continuo line.

Martin Fuhrmann's *Musicalischer Trichter* provides important information concerning the use of 16' instruments for performances in churches. He defines *Violone Grosse* or *Octav-Bass-Geige* as an instrument that contains "the 16-foot contra-C," or CC, one octave below the lowest pitch found in Buxtehude's bass lines.

> This sort of a large fiddle ought rightly to be present in all churches, and it should always be played not only for concerted music, but also under the chorales. No one who has not heard it can believe what a penetrating and sweet resonance this big fiddle gives from afar on account of its 16-foot depth.

On the subject of the 16' *Bombardone*, Fuhrmann has even more to say:

> It is a magnificent instrument as a foundation (*pro fundamento*), and it is to be regretted that it has been brought into decline and that the 8-foot French *Bassons* are preferred in its place, which sound strong enough in a room, to be sure, but do not penetrate in a large church. For no 8-foot tone penetrates emphatically in a large congregation, because a human voice goes as deep; but a 16-foot tone, for example even a weak 16-foot Sub-Bass [an organ stop], penetrates through some thousand people, because it goes an octave beneath the depth of a human [voice]. One time I presented a richly-scored work of figural music in a large church, quaking and shaking full of people, in which for certain reasons the organ was not playing, and therefore about a dozen French bass fiddles were playing the foundation, which were doubled by about a half dozen French bassoonists. But the listeners heard best with wonder how powerfully, or rather how muted this extensive French foundation sounded from afar. Yes, I believe that had a single low *Bass-Bommert* with its 16-foot tone not emphatically penetrated, and made up for all the lack of foundation, that this beautiful music would have been completely without foundation.

Fuhrmann's remarks lead to the following conclusions with respect to the performance of the continuo in Buxtehude's vocal compositions. The continuo line at its written (8') pitch is basic to the work and must be clearly heard. The organ is normally sufficient for carrying this line; in its absence, bass (8') stringed and/or wind instruments can play it. In a large space, such as St. Mary's in Lübeck, this 8' line will not be heard without 16' support, either from 16' pedal stops or from 16' instruments such as the large violone or the bass bombarde. The choice of continuo instruments is thus determined by the acoustics of the room. In a small room, 16' doubling of the continuo line is not necessary and appears unwarranted. In a large space it should be used in addition to, but certainly not in place of, a strong 8' continuo line. The bass member of the instrumental ensemble, whether violone or dulcian, plays in addition to the continuo instruments.

Performance materials from Lübeck that might document these conclusions are unfortunately no longer extant. The part sets from Stockholm provide ample evidence of doubled, tripled, and even quadrupled continuo lines, but they give no concrete indication as to whether the doubling was at 8' or 16' pitch. In these part sets for Buxtehude's vocal music, the basic continuo part— that is, the part copied at the same time as the voices and instruments—is labeled *Organon, Continuo,* or nothing. Of the fifteen doubled continuo parts that specify violone, three are figured and the rest are not. The fact that here the instrument is mostly spelled "Violono," as opposed to the "Violon" usually found for the instrumental bass part, could indicate a different instrument, perhaps the larger violone at 16' pitch. The distinction is not absolutely consistent, however.[24] The doubling of the continuo line by the violone may have been prompted by the fact that the only organs at the Stockholm castle Tre Kronor were small positive organs, most likely without pedals.

The use of the theorbo as a continuo instrument is documented by the presence of theorbo parts for two works. In BuxWV 39 a figured continuo part in staff notation is labeled "Theorba" (*Uu* 67:24); BuxWV 30 has an unlabeled part in lute tablature (*Uu* 50:17). Example 11-1 shows the opening measures of each of the three movements of BuxWV 30 with the theorbo part transcribed into staff notation. The Stockholm Hofkapelle always contained one lutenist and sometimes two, and we can presume that a lute or more likely a theorbo would have been used as a continuo instrument in works other than these two for which it is specified. Other figured continuo parts are marked *Continuo* or are unlabeled; these extra parts could have been played by violone, dulcian, harpsichord, regal, organ, lute, or theorbo. Only one extra continuo part specifies organ (*Uu* 67:24). There is no discernible pattern in the number of voices or instruments or in the naming of the basic continuo part with respect to the presence or absence of extra continuo parts. The names of the separate continuo parts can be found in appendix 3, B9.

In the published sonatas, Buxtehude's designation of the figured-bass part as *Cembalo* rather than *Continuo* appears to preclude its doubling by a bass instrument. The viola da gamba does in fact double the harpsichord bass line some of the time, and where it performs divisions on the bass line, the presence of another bass instrument would muddy the texture. *Gen Himmel zu dem*

Example 11-1a. BuxWV 30, Sonata, mm. 1–11.

Vater mein (BuxWV 32), a vocal work with a texture very similar to that of the published sonatas, has two continuo parts, however, labeled *Organo* and *Continuo*, both figured. Here, too, the presence of a bass instrument doubling the continuo disturbs the textural balance, and the second continuo part might instead have been performed on lute or theorbo. Two manuscript sonatas specify organ for the continuo, BuxWV 269 and 273. The second of

Example 11-1b. BuxWV 30, Concerto, mm. 1–9.

these is an early version of the sonata op. 1, no. 4 (BuxWV 255), suggesting that Buxtehude may have performed other sonatas with organ continuo in St. Mary's. None of the Stockholm part sets for Buxtehude's instrumental music contains doubled continuo parts.

Example 11-1c. BuxWV 30, Aria, mm. 1–4.

Instrumental Doublings

Like the vocal parts, the vast majority of Buxtehude's instrumental parts appear to have been performed with one player to a part. Buxtehude departed from this practice on occasion, however, and on a scale far more dramatic than is the case with vocal performance. The occasion was most often the Abendmusiken, when the funds that he had solicited from the business community enabled him to engage a large number of players. *Templum honoris* of 1705 contained a "Sinfonia all' unisono â 25. Violin." Martin Fuhrmann's *Musicalischer Trichter*, published a year later, speaks of Buxtehude's practice with reference to the necessity of avoiding diminution and variation when there is more than one player to a part:

Whoever does not like this should hear sometime the incomparable Mr. Buxtehude perform at Lübeck. He puts not two or three violins on a part, but twenty and thirty and even more. But all these instrumentalists must not change a single note or dot, or bow otherwise than he has directed.

It may be that Fuhrmann was in the audience for that performance on 3 December 1705. Similar violin doubling occurs in a wedding aria (BuxWV 120) composed earlier that year for Anton Winckler, senior Bürgermeister of Lübeck, which begins with a "Sonatina forte con molti Violini all unisono."[25] Unison string writing can be found in arias composed by Keiser and Handel for the Hamburg opera at this time. Buxtehude's use of many violins on a part, however, dates back at least to 1678, the year of the first dramatic Abendmusik. *Die Hochzeit des Lamms* contained a passage where the soprano was accompanied by eleven violins. Whether they were in unison or divided is unknown.

Evidence exists for violin doubling on a more modest scale in several other works. Two works contain an indication in the title for optional doubling: "con due vel piu violini" in BuxWV 10 and "con tre vel piu violinis" in BuxWV 13. The part sets for three other works contain duplicate violin parts for the entire piece. For BuxWV 8 and 65 both violin parts are present; for BuxWV 30, only the first violin part. It is noteworthy that all five of these works are scored for two or three violins without violas. A number of works call for violin doubling only in certain movements. When the scoring in BuxWV 72 and 100 is reduced from four violins to two, the third and fourth violins double the first and second, respectively. In BuxWV 4, 24, 34, and 54, the viola players alternate between playing first and second viola and doubling first and second violin. The sinfonia of BuxWV 110 calls for "3 Violini doppo," but in the following movement cornetts double the violins. The doubling players were presumably the same. Violins are doubled by cornetts in BuxWV 51 as well. This piece also contains the only doubling of violas—by trombones—found in Buxtehude's extant works.

The words *ripieno* and *complemento* in the titles or parts of several works indicate various kinds of doubling. Where the viola players double the violins in BuxWV 24 and 54, the part is called *Violino complemento.* Where an actual viola part is labeled *complemento,* however, it is doubling the alto voice in the tutti sections, as in the parts for BuxWV 75-4 (*Uu* 6:1) and BuxWV 23 (*Uu* 6:6). The latter part set also includes the words "con 4 Ripien." on its title page. The word *ripieno* appears in the titles of BuxWV 3, 24, and 110, but without the parts present that would clarify its meaning; the flute, viola, and violone parts contained in the third layer of *Uu* 50:13 appear to belong to a different arrangement of BuxWV 24 rather than to a set of doubling parts. *Accedite gentes* (BuxWV 1) has not figured thus far in this discussion because of its doubtful authenticity. Its part set (*Uu* 38:1) does throw light on the meaning of *ripieno* in Düben's Stockholm, however, if not Buxtehude's Lübeck. The scoring information on the title page reads "a. 7. C.C.A.T.B. Con 2 violini e 2 ripieni si piace." The part set contains four extra parts, however, not two: Violino, Violetta, Brattio 1, and Brattio 2. They double portions of the top four voices, precisely those portions that would be appropriate for doubling by a vocal capella: mm. 12–22, 25–50, 97–105, 119–24 and 134–80. The complemento viola part for BuxWV 75-4 is identical in the vocal sections to the alto capella part, which is labelled *ripieno*; in the instrumental sections it functions as an extra "filler" part. It must be emphasized, however, that this part was added by Düben and was not contained in Buxtehude's original tablature.

Thus, we can identify two types of string doubling in Buxtehude's vocal music. The first consists of many violins to a part in works or movements scored for one to three violins without middle parts. It embodies a solidly documented performance practice by Buxtehude in Lübeck as well as by Düben in Stockholm. The second consists of the doubling of vocal parts by strings in tutti sections in a manner analogous to, and most likely combined with, the vocal capella. This practice is documented only for Stockholm, although the word *ripieno*, with which it is associated, appears with BuxWV 110 in the Lübeck tablature. Both kinds of parts may be labeled *complemento*. Notably absent from Buxtehude's extant music is the type of doubling associated with the string orchestra, in which each string part is played by more than one player.

Articulation

Perhaps no aspect of taste and style in performance has changed as much between Buxtehude's time and our own as articulation. In singing, string playing, and organ playing, a smoothly connected line has replaced the baroque ideal of the clear articulation of individual tones. The evolution of the violin bow from convex to concave reflects the concurrent shift in articulation. The flexible, convex bow of the seventeenth and eighteenth centuries favored a nonlegato stroke:

> While the modern bow and technique characteristically join one note to the next in a seamless continuum of individual strokes, the musical effect of a series of individual strokes with an early bow is analogous to a string of pearls each of which appears to be separated from, while actually just touching, its neighbors.[26]

Legato as a Special Effect

Buxtehude employed two methods of indicating a greater-than-normal connection between notes: the slur in vocal and instrumental parts and the written-out over-legato in keyboard music. In vocal lines, he used the slur exclusively to indicate a group of notes to be sung on one syllable, as ligatures had done in the old mensural music. The notes of a melisma, being sung on a vowel or diphthong, would naturally sound more connected than the notes of a syllabic line, articulated by consonants, but their connection was not normally so close as the modern legato. The famous castrato Pierfrancesco Tosi (ca. 1653–1732) clearly characterized a legato melisma as a special effect:

> Division, according to the general Opinion, is of two Kinds, the Mark'd, and the Gliding; which last, from its Slowness and Dragging, ought rather to be called a Passage or Grace, than a Division. In regard to the first the Master ought to teach the Scholar that light Motion of the Voice, in which the Notes that constitute the Division be all articulate in equal Proportion and moderately distinct, that they be not too much join'd, not too much mark'd. The second is performed in such a Manner that the first Note is a Guide to all that follow, closely united, gradual, and with such Evenness of Motion, that in Singing it imitates a certain Gliding, by the Masters called a Slur; the Effect of which is truly agreeable when used sparingly. The mark'd Divisions, being more frequently used than the others, require more Practice.[27]

The performer was left to decide when to invoke this special effect.

All vocal music thus contained a wide variety of articulations, from legato melismas used for special effects, through normal melismas that were moderately articulated, and through various degrees of sharp articulation caused by the different consonants. Since Buxtehude's vocal music is predominantly syllabic, its normal style of articulation would have been quite detached. And the human voice still served as the model for instrumental performance; as Mattheson wrote in Der vollkommene Capellmeister, "all musical instruments serve only to imitate the human voice." (II/3, §3)

The slur appears much less frequently in Buxtehude's string parts than in his vocal parts; in the string parts, it indicates that a group of notes is to be taken together with one bow stroke, an effect analogous to the melisma in vocal music. It occurs in two contexts: consistent groups of up to eight repeated notes, sometimes further marked tremolo, and isolated groups of two to four notes, normally conjunct, but occasionally disjunct or repeated. The first type occurs more frequently in the works for voices and instruments, and an example in Buxtehude's hand from the Sinfonia to BuxWV 31 may be seen in figure 5-2. An example of the second type from the sonata op. 1, no. 6, is shown in figure 8-1. The fact that repeated notes beneath the slur must be articulated in order to be heard at all demonstrates that the slur does not by itself indicate legato performance.

In the absence of slurs, the string player normally alternated bow strokes, using a downbow for notes that were metrically strong and an upbow for those that were metrically weak. Georg Muffat, in his Florilegium Secundum (1697), designated the strong notes "noble" (edle, nobiles) and the weak notes "bad" (schlechte, viles), and his abbreviations "n" and "v" for these Latin words may be the antecedents of the modern symbols for downbow and upbow (ex. 11-2).

Example 11-2. Georg Muffat, *Florilegium Secundum*, "Vorrede," Example Oo.

The metrically strong notes receive a slight extra accent from the added strength of the downbowing, but the change in bow strokes prevents their being slurred to the metrically weak notes. Fuhrmann's description quoted earlier of Buxtehude's conducting groups of twenty to thirty violins—"but all these instrumentalists must not . . . bow otherwise than he has directed"—indicates that Buxtehude, along with Lully and Corelli, was among the first to prescribe uniform bowing for string orchestras.

We can deduce that Buxtehude normally played his organ works in a detached style of articulation from the fact that he occasionally took the trouble to write out an exceptional passage in a more complicated notation that produced a legato, indeed an over-legato effect. The longer F-major toccata, BuxWV 156, offers a number of examples. Example 11-3a shows Buxtehude's notation of a passage that might have been written as in example 11-3b if normal, detached articulation had been his intention.

Keyboard Fingering

Lacking the consonants or the bow by which singers or string players achieve natural articulation, the keyboard player must devote more conscious effort to attaining a clear definition of individual tones. The various systems of paired fingerings that were in use in different parts of Europe from the sixteenth century into the eighteenth—surveyed in Ludger Lohmann's comprehensive study and shown in practical guides such as those by John Brock, Mark Lindley/Maria Boxall, and Harald Vogel[28]—tend to produce a clearer articulation than the modern technique whereby the thumb is passed under the third or fourth finger in scale passages. Girolamo Diruta laid out one such system in considerable detail in *Il Transilvano* of 1593. Like Georg Muffat, he identified metrically strong notes as "good" (*buona*) and weak ones as "bad" (*cattiva*), using the letters *B* and

Example 11-3a. BuxWV 156, m. 124, notation as in *B* 2681 and *Bc* U 26659.

Example 11-3b. BuxWV 156, m. 124, alternate notation.

C, respectively, and he assigned specific fingers of each hand to play the good and bad notes in ascending and descending scales. Of particular significance to articulation is the use of the same "good" finger on two successive notes if they are both metrically strong (ex. 11-4), which is analogous to Muffat's use of two successive downbows seen in example 11-2. Diruta was a pupil of Claudio Merulo, whose toccatas were the first to combine free and fugal sections, the ancestors of Buxtehude's praeludia.

Fingerings in the sources for a few of Sweelinck's works indicate that he used a system similar to Diruta's; in Sweelinck's practice, the third finger is generally the "good" finger of the right hand and the second the "good" finger of the left hand. The right hand ascends with the fingers *3 4 3 4* and descends *3 2 3 2*; the left hand ascends *2 1 2 1* and descends *2 3 2 3*. Using paired fingerings, the gap

Example 11-4. Diruta, *Il Transilvano*, fifth example.

in sound preceding the "good" note will normally be slightly longer than that preceding the "bad" note, creating an effect analogous to the downbow and upbow of the violin. The pairings are not applied absolutely uniformly, however, as can be seen in example 11-5; in all cases two other fingers may be added to the pair most frequently used, forming a group of four notes. Johann Lorentz's *Praeludium ex clave D* (see ex. 1-3) shows this system in use. According to examples given by Seiffert,[29] Scheidemann employed it as well, although no fingerings appear in the editions of his organ works prepared by Fock and Breig. We still find the Sweelinck fingering system in the "Applicatio" (BWV 994) that J. S. Bach wrote at the beginning of the notebook for his son Wilhelm Friedemann.

According to C. P. E. Bach, it was J. S. Bach who enlarged the role of the thumb in keyboard playing:

> My deceased father told me that in his youth he used to hear great men who employed their thumbs only when large stretches made it necessary. Because he lived at a time when a gradual but striking change in musical taste was taking place, he was obliged to devise a far more comprehensive fingering and especially to enlarge the role of the thumbs and use them as nature intended; for, among their other good services, they must be employed chiefly in the difficult tonalities.[30]

Example 11-5. Sweelinck, *Echo Fantasia* in C, mm. 115–22.

Since Buxtehude made use of those "difficult tonalities," and since those very pieces are the ones transmitted by the sources of the Bach circle, one suspects that Buxtehude might also have put his thumb to greater use and shared the technique with Bach, along with the works involved. The purpose of such a modification of technique would not have been to attain a legato line, however, but rather to facilitate movement of the fingers on the black keys. C. P. E. Bach still gives the Sweelinck fingering as one of three possibilities for the ascending C-major scale (his "Tab. I, Fig. 1").

Only two sources of Buxtehude's keyboard works contain fingerings, the Ryge manuscript and Johann Gottlieb Preller's copy of Buxtehude's G-major toccata (BuxWV 165). The Ryge manuscript contains a few fingerings in Partita 7 of *La Capricciosa* (BuxWV 250), all indicating the use of four fingers for four-note scale excerpts in both right and left hands. Preller's fingerings reflect his own practice and not Buxtehude's, as discussed in chapter 9. Two passages nonetheless command attention. The left hand of m. 35 is fingered so as to demand articulation at each quarter-note beat (ex. 11-6a). A modern organist would be tempted to use finger substitution at this point, a practice that began only gradually during the eighteenth century. And paired fingerings can still be seen in one of the few scale passages of this piece, m. 74 (ex. 11-6b).

Organ Pedaling

Most modern organists play the pedals using a technique consisting of a mixture of alternating toes of the two feet and the heel and toe of the same foot, a method

Example 11-6a. BuxWV 165, m. 35, Preller fingering.

Example 11-6b. BuxWV 165, m. 74, Preller fingering.

first advocated by Johann Christian Kittel in the preface to his *Vierstimmige Choräle mit Vorspielen*, published in 1803. Prior to this time, the two techniques had existed separately, with alternating toes generally deemed to be the simpler and more natural method. When using heel-and-toe technique, the left foot had normally been confined to the lower octave of the pedal board and the right foot to the upper. It is difficult to play with the heels on the short pedal boards of many early organs, however. Works with double pedal parts, such as Samuel Scheidt's *Modus ludendi pleno organo pedaliter à 6 Voc.*, versus 1 of Tunder's *Jesus Christus, unser Heiland*, and the five-voice portion of Reincken's chorale fantasia *An Wasserflüssen Babylon* nonetheless may require the use of heel-and-toe technique.

Buxtehude's organ works include double pedal only in isolated passages, such as the final four measures of *Lobt Gott, ihr Christen allzugleich* (BuxWV 202), mm. 79–80 of the *Te Deum* (BuxWV 218), and a few others noted by Belotti. The final six measures of the Praeludium in D (BuxWV 139) are clearly marked for double pedal in the manuscript *B* 2681, but Agricola's copy of this work (*Bc* U 26659) restricts the pedal part to the lowest line. In view of Buxtehude's scant use of double pedal, one might conclude that he himself preferred the pedaling technique of alternating toes. Most of the notes in Buxtehude's pedal parts do in fact fall most naturally under alternating toes.

In his study on the history of organ pedaling in Germany, Eduard Bruggaier concluded that Buxtehude's technique was based almost entirely on alternating toes. For only a few passages does Bruggaier recommend the use of the heel, and even in these instances alternate-toe pedaling is not only possible but in fact produces a clearer articulation, as can be seen from his examples 37–39, given here as example 11-7. In example 11-7c, the intervals are too widely spaced to achieve a legato through the use of the heels, as Bruggaier correctly observes. The articulation caused by the use of the same toe on successive notes produces an accent on the "good" notes of the measure, whereas the octave leap, a most comfortable interval for alternating feet, proceeds more smoothly to the "bad" notes, producing an effect analogous to the alternation of down-bow and upbow on the violin, or paired fingering. The same clear articulation, which emphasizes the metrical structure of the music, could be attained by using toes only in examples 11-7a and 11-7b, as well. Johann Tobias Kreb's copy of J. S. Bach's *In dir ist Freude* (BWV 615) in *B* P 801 gives a pedaling—using *s* (*sinister*) and *d* (*dexter*) for left and right—that produces a similar clear articulation (ex. 11-8).

Example 11-7a. BuxWV 145, mm. 102–3, Bruggaier pedaling.

Example 11-7b. BuxWV 188, mm. 96–97, Bruggaier pedaling.

Example 11-7c. BuxWV 156, mm. 54–55, Bruggaier pedaling.

Buxtehude's pedal voices—particularly in the free sections of the praeludia—can often be distinguished from the manual voices precisely because they are so idiomatically written for alternating feet. Some passages are ambiguous, however, and none more so than mm. 55–78 of the G-minor praeludium, BuxWV 149, reproduced from *B* 2681 in figure 11-1. This manuscript gives indications for the use of the pedal at m. 7, m. 46, m. 90, and m. 106 of the piece; Agricola's copy (*Bc* U 26659) uses red ink to mark the pedal voice for mm. 7–20, 31–39, 46–54, 68–78, 90–102, 106–48, 155, and 157–59; Lindemann's tablature (*L* W.Lit. U 5) lacks any mention of the pedal. Spitta, Seiffert, Kraft, and Beckmann (1971 edition) agree with Agricola in the contents of the pedal part that they place in the third staff; Beckmann's 1997 edition gives mm. 68–73 to the manuals alone. Hedar and Albrecht, however, gives mm. 55–67 to the pedal as well. If played with toes only, the bass line of mm. 55–78 receives an articulation that emphasizes the "good" notes, but it is difficult to execute at the specified Allegro tempo. The entire passage can also be played on the manuals, as *B* 2681 seems to suggest. Belotti's editions for *The Collected Works* restore the two-staff systems of the original sources, facilitating the decision between manualiter and pedaliter performance for the modern organist.

Example 11-8. J. S. Bach, *In dir ist Freude* (BWV 615), mm. 49–50, Krebs pedaling.

Figure 11-1. Buxtehude, Praeludium in G Minor (BuxWV 149), mm. 55–83, in an eighteenth-century manuscript copy (Berlin, Staatsbibliothek Preussischer Kulturbesitz, mus. ms. 2681, fol. 4ov).

Buxtehude's intentions with respect to the use of the pedal are generally clearer than they are in BuxWV 149, and since the range of possibilities for pedaling with only two toes is very much smaller than for fingering with ten fingers, the pedal line can often supply useful clues concerning the articulation of the manual parts; this is particularly true of fugues. The player of Buxtehude's keyboard music can also discover much useful information concerning articulation by studying his vocal and instrumental ensemble music. Buxtehude's arias supply countless examples of stressed syllables on "good" notes, and by singing them the keyboard player can learn of the rich variety in articulation available to the singer. The slurs in the string parts of the sonatas can likewise offer suggestions for the articulation of similar passages in keyboard music, and performances of the sonatas on original instruments can help to bring us closer to the taste and style of the seventeenth century, and perhaps to Buxtehude's intentions with respect to articulation. To play Buxtehude's keyboard music with old fingering and pedaling cannot be considered an end in itself, but it offers an excellent means to the end of recapturing the original "Beauties of his Work."

Tempo and Dynamics

Tempo and dynamic markings appear much more frequently in Buxtehude's vocal music and sonatas than they do in his organ music. The original manuscript copies of Buxtehude's organ works were intended for highly skilled professionals who were thoroughly familiar with the style of this music—a style that included a certain amount of freedom of interpretation—and who did not need specific instructions concerning its performance. As is the case with matters of articulation, however, we can discover some of Buxtehude's intentions regarding tempo and dynamics through the study of his vocal music and sonatas. The sonatas are particularly rich in tempo and dynamic markings, perhaps because Buxtehude could not assume that all the purchasers of this music would be familiar with its style.

Contrast in tempo forms an intrinsic part of those genres composed of contrasting sections: concertos, cantatas, praeludia, chorale fantasias, and sonatas. Where tempo markings are lacking in works such as these, a change in tempo is sometimes indicated by the notation and at other times must be supplied. Buxtehude's Helsingør concerto *Aperite mihi* (BuxWV 7) already contains the tempo markings Allegro, Adagio, and Presto; here, as in the other concertos, a change in tempo either relates closely to the text or, in the case of Adagio, closes a section. The sonatas contain the greatest variety of tempo designations, as discussed in chapter 8, but there does not appear to be a clear distinction between the various names for fast and slow tempos. The indication *con discretione* that appears in the praeludium BuxWV 141 and the sonata BuxWV 257 marks the *stylus phantasticus,* in which, according to Mattheson, "the meter takes a vacation." Indeed, one of the most important contrasts in the performance of these works comes between the metrical freedom appropriate to the free sections and the greater strictness of the fugues.

Dynamic markings range from a *fortissimo* in BuxWV 22 to *pianissimo* in a number of works. The sonata of BuxWV 31 (see fig. 5-2) offers one of Buxtehude's most specific records of the role of dynamics in the *stylus phantasticus.* The three-tiered progression from *forte* to *piano* to *pianissimo* very likely reflects his experience with the St. Mary's three-manual organ, and opportunities for similar dynamic effects may be found elsewhere. The D-minor sonata op. 1, no. 6 (BuxWV 257, see fig. 8-1) is also rich in dynamic contrast. Within the sonatas, changes in dynamics occur most frequently in dances, ostinato movements, and free sections; once, in BuxWV 266, *piano* and *forte* alternate in the free ending of a fugue, but never within a fugue itself.

Organ Registration

The manuscripts of Buxtehude's organ works offer some information concerning changes of manuals, but none whatever with regard to the stops to be drawn in the divisions governed by them. The designation "à 2 Clav:" or "à 2 Clav: et pedal" appears at the head of only a handful of chorale-based works, but it is implicit in Walther's use of three staves in his copies of many other chorale settings and in the appearance of the abbreviations "R" and "O" for Rückpositiv and Organo or Oberwerck in some of his copies. As discussed in chapter 9, it is not usually clear whether Walther found these indications in his exemplars or added them himself, but in no case are they unidiomatic to the style of the music. The North German tradition of performing chorale settings with two manuals and pedal goes back at least as far as Jacob Praetorius; the account of Matthias Weckmann's audition given in chapter 7 includes the registration for the beginning of a chorale fantasia that both Praetorius and Weckmann used:

Oberwerck: Trommete 8', Zincke 8', Hohlflöte 4', Nasat 3', Gemshorn 2'
Rückpositiv: Principal 8', Octava 4'
Pedal: Principal 24' [32'], Posaune 16', Trommete 8' and 4', Cornet 2'

All but Gemshorn 2' on the Oberwerck and Trommete 4' on the Pedal were available to Buxtehude on the large organ at St. Mary's. Davidsson uses a similar registration in his performance of the *Te Deum* (BuxWV 218) at m. 119 (CD track 8, 06:36).

The separate manuals could be used either simultaneously, in order to highlight a solo line and facilitate the crossing of parts, or successively, to produce an echo effect. Walther indicated a three-tiered echo in his copy of *Nun freut euch,* *lieben Christen gmein* (BuxWV 210) by the addition of *piano*, presumably for the Brustwerck, to the abbreviations for Rückpositiv and Organo in mm. 131–66. One would like to know whether this marking was present in his exemplar, Bach's Weimar tablature, but these measures are missing from the torn manuscript. In his discussion of organ registration in *Der Vollkommene Capellmeister*, Mattheson suggests a registration for a four-tiered echo, which was possible on the four-manual organs in Hamburg:

Werck: Principal 16', Octave 8', Octave 4', Octave 2', Rauschpfeiffe II, Mixtur
Rückpositiv: Principal 8', Quintadena 8', Octave 4', Quintflöte 1 1/2',
    Sesquialtera II
Brustwerck: Principal 8', Octave 4' Scharff
Oberwerck: Principal 8', Scharff
Pedal: Principal 32', Groß-Posaun 32', Principal 16', Posaun 16', Octave 8',
    Trommet 8', Octave 4', Schallmey 4', Mixtur, Rauschpfeiffe (III/24, §83).

A similar registration for the first three tiers would have been available to Buxtehude on the St. Mary's three-manual large organ; at no point do the sources for his music call for more than two echoes, but paired echoes, such as occur at mm. 220–29 of *Nun freut euch*, work well on four manuals. Davidsson uses them in his performance of BuxWV 139, mm. 70–86 (CD track 5, 03:34).

Mattheson divides organ registration into two types: plenum registration and the remaining, varied registrations, especially those for more than one manual and with softer, but carefully selected stops. The Praetorius-Weckmann registration belongs to the second type, and Mattheson gives a similar one as an example. To the plenum belong "Principals, Sorduns, Salicionals, Rausch-Pfeiffen, Octaves, Quints, Mixtures, Scharfs, Quintadenas, Zimbels, Nasats, Terzians, Sesquialteras, Super-Octaves, Posaunes in the Pedal, not the Manual" (III/24, §76). The first tier of Mattheson's echo registration, consisting of the *Werck* and the *Pedal*, provides an example of plenum registration. It is the basic organ sound, the descendant of the undivided medieval *Blockwerck*. Weckmann used it for his fantasy at the beginning of his audition, and Buxtehude undoubtedly used it for his praeludia, at least for their opening free sections. It remained the basic registration for the free organ works of J. S. Bach.

Buxtehude might have used a tiered registration not just for echo effects, such as are found frequently in the chorale fantasias, but also to delineate the sections of the free works. In their alternation of basically homophonic free sections with more contrapuntal fugues, Buxtehude's praeludia resemble his large vocal concertos, in which the capella participates in the more homophonic sections, where the instruments double the voices, and the vocal soloists carry the more contrapuntal sections alone. Lacking any information from the manuscripts of the free organ works, the organist might take a clue from Buxtehude's orchestration of his large ensemble works and play the fugues with a lighter registration than the plenum of the free sections. Harald Vogel's experience in performing Buxtehude's works on various North German organs of the seventeenth century led him to the conclusion that the fugues are best played with consort registration, and with the bass voice at the same pitch level as the other voices. Weckmann, however, played his "merry fugue" on the full organ. Certainly the freedom inherent in the *stylus phantasticus* must have extended to registration practice as well, and it seems unlikely that strict rules were in force for the performance of such varied and unpredictable music.

With respect to the registration to be used in continuo playing, Fuhrmann, Niedt, and Mattheson all agree that for the accompaniment of a solo voice or instrument the organist should draw just one stop: Gedackt 8. Niedt further recommends the addition of the 8' Principal for those passages in which the capella participates:

> Therefore it is best if an organist considers the following in his continuo playing: if only one or two voices sing or play, he needs only the 8-foot Gedackt in the manual, and no pedal whatever; if there are more voices to accompany, he can add the 16-foot Untersatz or Sub-Baß in the Pedal; however, if there is a tenor, alto, or soprano clef, which is called a *Bassetgen*, then he must leave the pedal out and play the notes only in the octave in which they are written. If, on the other hand, an entire chorus of eight to twelve or more voices enters (in this case the place is usually designated with the words Chor, tutti, ripieno, etc.), then he can draw the 8-foot Principal in the manual, and an 8-foot Octava may be added to the Sub-Baß in the Pedal. If a piece is scored with trumpets and timpani, a 16-foot Posaunen-Baß is added to the 8-foot Octava in the Pedal; however, the tones must not be held for a whole or a half measure, but one must only touch them.[31]

It is clear from the remainder of Niedt's discussion of continuo playing that the pedal never substitutes for the thoroughbass line in the left hand, but only reinforces it; in fast-moving passages, only the principal notes are played on the pedal. On the large organ in St. Mary's, the Gedackt 8 was located in the Brustwerck; Buxtehude may have used the regal purchased in 1678 as the extra continuo support for the capella.

Buxtehude's organ works are of course best performed on a large North German baroque organ with mechanical action, tuned in mean-tone or an unequal temperament, such as the Schnitger organ at St. Jacobi Church, Hamburg, or the North German organ in Örgryte Nya Kirka, Göteborg. But these works became part of the common repertoire by being played on organs with electropneumatic action tuned in equal temperament, using modern fingering techniques and heel-and-toe pedaling to achieve legato lines. In the time between the two editions of this book, it has become increasingly possible to play them with old fingering and pedaling techniques on organs with mechanical action, historical tunings, even with human-powered winding systems, and there are now many recordings of Buxtehude's music on period instruments, including the CD accompanying this book. As we play and hear these works performed in a taste and style closer to Buxtehude's intentions, they begin to reveal more of their secrets. Owen Jander reports from his experience as a calcant on the Fisk organ at Wellesley College that its flexible winding system produces special effects that Buxtehude appears to have built into his compositions. For performers of Buxtehude's music who still do not enjoy the privilege of playing on original instruments or on modern instruments built according to seventeenth-century principles, Barbara Owen's book on baroque organ registrations has good advice. If performers become sensitive to Buxtehude's taste and style and aware of his intentions, they can still do justice to his compositions and illustrate "all the Beauties of his Works" on almost any instrument.

Appendixes

Appendix 1

The Compositions of Dieterich Buxtehude

The list below is designed to aid the reader in identifying and locating the works of Buxtehude; more complete information on sources and editions may be found in the *Buxtehude-Werke-Verzeichnis*. Sources listed here are generally only those that appear in appendix 3; those sources not found in appendix 3 are given in parentheses for extant sources and brackets for lost sources. Single editions of the vocal works are listed only if the work has not yet appeared in the *Werke* or *Collected Works*. Older organ and harpsichord editions in common use that are lacking BuxWV numbers are given in addition to *Collected Works* listings. Works of questionable authenticity within the main list are so indicated with an asterisk.

Vocal Works

Bux WV	Title	Sources	Scoring	Edition	References
1	*Accedite gentes, accurite populi	Uu 38:1; Uu 82:34	SSATB; V V Bc	Dan	137, 206, 386–87
2	Afferte Domino gloriam honorem	Uu 6:4; Uu 82:42	SSB; Bc	W v,10	139, 156, 166, 339, 358, 371
3	All solch dein Güt' wir preisen	Uu 50:1a	SSATB; V V Va Va Vn Bc	BA, EM	145, 175, 187–88, 207, 367, 386
4	Alles was ihr tut	Uu 50:2; LÜh A373; B 2680	SATB; V V Va Va Vn Bc	CW ix,3	133, 201–4, 309, 322, 330, 362, 368–70, 386
5	Also hat Gott die Welt geliebet	LÜh A373	S; V V Vg Bc	W i,10	139, 145, 156, 330, 346, 372
6	An filius non est Dei	Uu 50:3	ATB; V V Vg Bc	W vii,49	140, 145, 175, 180, 372
7	Aperite mihi portas justitiae	Uu 50:4	ATB; V V Bc	W vii,62	27, 35, 138, 318, 341–44, 362, 396
8	Att du, Jesu, will mig höra	L Eng 712	S; V V Bc	Nor	138, 175, 179, 334, 386
9	Bedenke Mensch das Ende	Uu 85:1–18; LÜh A373	SSB; V V V Vn Bc	W v,14	175, 180–81, 339, 340
10	Befiehl dem Engel, daß er komm	Uu 50:5	SATB; V V Vn Bc	W viii,73	187–88, 190, 369, 386
11	Canite Jesu nostro	Uu 82:43	SSB; V V Vn Bc	W v,21	139, 156, 339
12	Cantate Domino	Uu 67:8; Uu 83:1–20	SSB; Bc	W v,29	156, 166–68, 341, 343–44, 361, 371
13	Das neugeborne Kindelein	Uu 50:7	SATB; V V V Vn/Fg Bc	W viii,121	145, 175, 180, 207, 369, 386

14	Dein edles Herz	SATB; V V Va Va Vn Bc	*Uu* 82:35	CW ix,35	140, 142, 145, 175, 180, 183, 339, 369
15	Der Herr ist mit mir	SATB; V V Vn Bc	*Uu* 85:1–18	W viii,85	156, 175, 340, 369
17	Dixit Dominus Domino meo	S; V V Va Sp/Vn Bc	*Uu* 50:8; *B* 2680	W ii,27	138, 156, 322
18	Domine, salvum fac regem	SSATB; V V Va Va Vn Bc	*Uu* 85:1–18	Dan	156, 340, 368
19	Drei schöne Dinge sind	SB; V V Vn/Fg Bc	*Uu* 50:9; *Uu* 82:35	W iii,10	117–18, 139, 198, 339
20	Du Friedefürst, Herr Jesu Christ [B♭]	SSATB; V V Vn Bc	*Uu* 50:10	BA;	187–88, 368
21	Du Friedefürst, Herr Jesu Christ [G]	SSB; V V Va Va/Fg Bc	*Uu* 6:5	W v,35	187, 191–92, 341, 346, 359–61
22	Du Lebensfürst, Herr Jesu Christ	SATB; V V Vt Vt Vn Bc	*Uu* 50:11; *Uu* 83:41–45	CW ix,61	142, 145, 175, 184, 309, 320, 339, 369–70, 373, 397
23	Ecce nunc benedicite	ATTB; V V Bc	*Uu* 6:6; *Uu* 82:34	W viii,105	138, 156, 206, 341–42, 362, 369–70, 386
24	Eins bitte ich vom Herrn	SSATB; V V Va Va Fg Bc	*Uu* 50:13; *Uu* 85:1–18	DdT xiv,15	198, 340, 368, 377, 386
25	Entreißt euch, meine Sinnen	S; V V Bc	*Uu* 6:7	W i,15	144, 175, 307
26	Erfreue dich, Erde! (parody of BuxWV 122)	SSAB; V V Va Va Vn Tr Tr Tm Bc	*Uu* 50:15	EM	137, 145, 369, 379
27	Erhalt uns, Herr, bei deinem Wort	SATB; V V Vn/Bom Bc	*Uu* 50:14; *Uu* 85:1–18	W viii,47	141, 187–88, 340, 369, 378
28	Fallax mundus ornat vultus	S; V V Bc	*Uu* 50:16; *Uu* 83:69–73	W i,17	175, 180, 206, 339

Bux WV	Title	Scoring	Sources	Edition	References
29	Frohlocket mit Händen	SSATB; V V V V Vn Tr Tr Bc	*Uu* 82:36	WH	141, 200–201, 368, 379
30	Fürchtet euch nicht	SB; V V Bc	*Uu* 50:17; *Uu* 82:35	W iii,18	139, 145, 198, 208, 340, 342, 344, 382–86
31	Fürwahr, er trug unsere Krankheit	SSATB; V V Vg Vg Vn/Fg Bc	*Uu* 6:9 AUT	BA, HE	139, 145, 156, 167–71, 307, 309, 318, 365–67, 372–74, 388, 397
32	Gen Himmel zu dem Vater mein	S; V Vg Bc	*Uu* 50:18; *Uu* 82:42	W i,23	141, 145, 187–88, 191, 339, 372
33	Gott fähret auf mit Jauchzen	SSB; V V Va/Tn Va/Tn Cn Cn Fg Tr Tr Bc	*Uu* 82:43	W v,44	142, 145, 198, 200, 208, 339, 377
34	Gott hilf mir	SSATBB; V V Va Va Vn Bc	*Uu* 50:19	DdT xiv,57	137, 139, 141, 201, 203, 368, 386
35	Herr, auf dich traue ich	S; V V Bc	*Uu* 51:1; *Uu* 82:35	W i,29	198, 340
36	Herr, ich lasse dich nicht	TB; V V Vg/Vb Vg/Vb Vn/Vg Bc	*Uu* 51:2 AUT	W iii,21	196–97, 318, 372–74
37	Herr, nun läßt du deinen Diener	T; V V Bc	*Uu* 51:3; *Uu* 85:76–88; *LÜh* A373	W ii,39	139, 145, 156, 330
38	Herr, wenn ich nur dich hab [con]	S; V V Bc	*Uu* 06:11	W i,35	173, 342, 354
39	Herr, wenn ich nur dich habe [con-ar]	S; V V Vn/Vg Bc	*Uu* 67:24; *LÜh* A373	W i,38	145, 198, 330, 372, 382
40	Herren vär Gud	SATB; V V Vn Bc	*Uu* 85:01–18	W viii,64	138, 187–88, 340, 369
41	Herzlich lieb hab ich dich, o Herr	SSATB; V V Va Va Vn/ Fg Tr Tr Bc	*LÜh* A373	BA 544	137, 141, 187, 191–96, 330, 346, 367–68, 379

			L Wen A29	Nor	
42	Herzlich tut mich verlangen	S; V V Bc			141, 187–88, 333
43	*Heut triumphieret Gottes Sohn	SSATB; V V Va Vn Tr Tr Bc	B 2680	BA, EM	137, 206–7, 322, 345
44	Ich bin die Auferstehung	B; V V Va Va Fg Cn Cn Tr Tr Bc	Uu 82:43	W ii,60	145, 156, 339, 377, 379
45	Ich bin eine Blume zu Saron	B; V V Vn Bc	LÜh A373	W ii,66	139, 156, 330, 346
46	Ich habe Lust abzuscheiden [earlier]	SSB; V V Vn/Fg Bc	Uu 51:04; Uu 82:42	W v,56	145, 198, 339, 346, 349, 351–52
47	Ich habe Lust abzuscheiden [revised]	SSB; V V Vn Bc	LÜh A373	W v,62	198, 330, 346, 349, 351, 353, 363
48	Ich halte es dafür	SB; V Vt Vn Bc	Uu 82:43; LÜh A373	W iii,30	139, 145, 198, 307, 330, 339, 373
49	Ich sprach in meinem Herzen	S; V V V Fg Bc	Uu 51:6; Uu 82:43	W i,47	156, 159–61, 339–40
50	Ich suchte des Nachts	TB; V V Vn Ob Ob Bc	(Bc 759)	W iii,41	117, 139, 198, 200, 335, 345, 363
51	Ihr lieben Christen, freut euch nun	SSATB; V V V Va Va Vn Cn Cn Fg Tr Tr Tn Tn Bc	LÜh A373	DdT xiv,107	144–45, 201–2, 309, 330–31, 346, 366–67, 377, 379, 386
52	In dulci jubilo	SSB; V V Bc	Uu 82:43; B 2680	W v,69	141, 145, 187–88, 322, 339
53	In te, Domine, speravi	SAB; Bc	Uu 83:01–20	W vii,8	156, 166, 341, 343–44, 371
54	Ist es recht	SSATB; V V Va Va Vn Bc	Uu 51:11	BA 1738	139, 145, 198, 366–67, 386

Bux WV	Title	Scoring	Sources	Edition	References
55	Je höher du bist	SSB; V Vn Bc	*Uu* 51:5; *Uu* 82:35	W v,76	139, 198, 307–9, 339
56	Jesu dulcis memoria [e]	SS; V V Fg Bc	*Uu* 51:7; *Uu* 85:48–53	W iii,51	140, 173, 175, 180, 339, 341, 361
57	Jesu dulcis memoria—Ciaccona [G]	ATB; V V Bc	*Uu* 51:8	W vii,72	140, 173–75, 239, 354
58	Jesu, komm, mein Trost und Lachen	ATB; V V Vb Vn Bc	*Uu* 6:12	W vii,81	142, 175, 181–82, 373
59	Jesu, meine Freud und Lust	A; V V Vt Vn Bc	*LÜh* A373	W ii,10	142, 175, 180, 330, 346, 373
60	Jesu, meine Freude	SSB; V V Fg Bc	*Uu* 85:1–18; *LÜh* A373	W v,87	141, 187, 191–92, 330, 340
61	Jesu, meiner Freuden Meister	SATB; Va Va Va Vn Bc	Print; MS: *Uu* 86:36		196–97, 314, 342, 344, 354, 370, 371, 380
62	Jesu, meines Lebens Leben [earlier version]	SATB; V V Va Va Vn Bc	*Uu* 6:13 (Bc); *Uu* 82:37	CW ix,249	142, 145, 173, 175, 181, 206, 320, 341,
62	Jesu, meines Lebens Leben [revised version]	SATB; V V Va Va Vn Bc	*Uu* 6:13; *Uu* 82:37	CW ix,91	348–49, 352, 354, 369, 377
63	Jesulein, du Tausendschön	ATB; V V Vn/Fg Bc	*Uu* 51:09	W vii,89	143, 175
64	Jubilate Domino	A; Vg Bc	*Uu* 51:12	W ii,19	137, 156–59, 191, 305–6, 309, 371–72
65	Klinget mit Freuden [parody of 119]	SSB; V V Tr Bc	*Uu* 06:14	W v,96	137, 145, 386
66	Kommst du, Licht der Heiden	SSB; V V Vb Vb Vn Bc	*Uu* 6:15; *Uu* 82:42	W vi,14	142, 175, 180, 315–17, 339, 341, 373, 377

67	Lauda anima mea	S; V V Vn Bc	LÜh A373	W i,57	156, 330, 346
68	Lauda Sion Salvatorem	SSB; V V Bc	Uu 51:14; Uu 82:42; LÜh A373	W vi,24	139, 175, 330, 339–40
69	Laudate pueri—Ciaccona	SS; Vg Vg Vg Vg Vg Vn Bc	Uu 6:17; Uu 84:29–42	W iii,59	138, 173, 239, 339, 341, 354, 371, 372
70	Liebster, meine Seele saget—Ciaccona	SS; V V Bc	Uu 85:48–53	W iii,65	139, 142, 173, 175, 181, 239, 341, 354
71	Lobe den Herren, meine Seele	T; V V V Va Va Vn Bc	Uu 85:76–88	W ii,44	156, 172
72	Mein Gemüt erfreuet sich	SAB; V V V V Fl Fl Tr Tr Tn Tn Cn Cn Cn Cn Fg Fg Fg Bc	Uu 85:1–18	W vii,10	53, 175, 183, 309, 340, 377–79, 386
73	Mein Herz ist bereit	B; V V V Vn Bc	Uu 51:15	W ii,74	156, 172, 377
74	Meine Seele, willtu ruhn	SSB; V V Vn Bc	Uu 51:16; LÜh A373	W vi,30	143, 175, 330
75	Membra Jesu			BA, EM	
	1. Ad pedes: Ecce super montes	SSATB; [V V Vn] Bc	Uu 50:12 AUT; Uu 6:2		121–22, 137, 140, 145, 153, 198–200, 284, 318, 339
	2. Ad genua: Ad ubera portabimini	SSATB; [V V Vn] Bc	Uu 50:12 AUT; Uu 6:3		199
	3. Ad manus: Quid sunt plagae istae	SSATB; [V V Vn] Bc	Uu 50:12 AUT; Uu 51:23		139, 371
	4. Ad latus: Surge amica mea	SSATB; [V V Vn] Bc	Uu 50:12 AUT; Uu 6:1		
	5. Ad pectus: Sicut modo geniti infantes	ATB; [V V Vn] Bc	Uu 50:12 AUT; Uu 6:18		139, 367, 386–87
	6. Ad cor: Vulnerasti cor meum	SSB; Vg Vg Vg Vg Vg Bc	Uu 50:12 AUT; Uu 46:25		139, 199, 243, 371–72
	7. Ad faciem: Illustra faciem tuam	SSATB; V V Vn Bc	Uu 50:12 AUT; Uu 51:10		200

Bux WV	Title	Scoring	Sources	Edition	References
76	Fried- und Freudenreiche Hinfahrt				
	1. Mit Fried und Freud	SB, 3 insts; or Org	Print; MS: B 2680	W ii,86;	3, 47, 133, 137, 314, 322, 341, 344
	2. Klag-Lied: Muß der Tod denn auch entbinden	S; [Va Va] Bc	Print; MS: Uu 164:9(inc)	CW xviA,111;	43, 109, 141, 187, 214–18, 362
				W ii,88	7, 145, 175, 180, 213, 243, 380
77	Nichts soll uns scheiden	SAB; V V Vn Bc	LÜh A373	W vii,20	198, 200, 330, 346, 363
78	Nimm von uns, Herr, du treuer Gott	SATB; V V Vt Vt Fg Bc	Uu 82:38 AUT	CW ix,109	187, 191–92, 318, 369, 373
79	Nun danket alle Gott	SSATB; V V Vn Cn Cn Fg Tr Tr Bc	Uu 82:39 AUT; LÜh A373	WH	92, 139, 156, 318–19, 330, 365–67, 377–78, 380
80	Nun freut euch, ihr Frommen, mit mir	SS; V V Bc	B 2680	W iii,69	143, 175, 180, 185–87, 322, 345, 363, 371
81	Nun laßt uns Gott dem Herren	SATB; V V Bc	Uu 51:17; Uu 85:1–18	W viii,9	187–88, 340, 369
82	O clemens, o mitis	S; V Vt Vt Vn Bc	Uu 51:18; Uu 84:29–42	W i,65	139, 151, 156, 224, 334, 339, 341, 373–74, 377
83	O dulcis Jesu	S; V V Bc	Uu 82:42	W i,71	139, 156, 161–66, 212–13, 315–17, 339
84	O fröhliche Stunden, o fröhliche Zeit	S; V V Va(B) Bc	Uu 85:76–88	W i,77	142, 145, 175, 180, 184
85	O fröhliche Stunden, o herrliche Zeit	SSAB; V V Vb Vn Bc	Uu 51:13a AUT; Uu 86:61	CW ix,151	142, 145, 153, 156, 175, 183, 309, 318, 369, 373

86	O Gott, wir danken deiner Güt'	SSATB; V V Vn Bc	Uu 85:1–18	EM, Han	200, 340, 368
87	O Gottes Stadt	S; V V Va Vn Bc	Uu 51:19; Uu 85:1–18	W i,84	142, 175, 180–81, 208, 340
88	O Jesu mi dulcissime	SSB; V V Vn Bc	Uu 82:40 AUT	W vi,39	140, 175, 318
89	O lux beata Trinitas	SS; V V V Vn/Fg Bc	Uu 51:20; Uu 82:35	W iii,76	139, 145, 175, 180, 339
90	O wie selig sind	TB; V V Vn Bc	Uu 51:21	W iii,83	43, 145, 175, 179, 344–45, 363
91	Pange lingua	SSAB; V V V Vt Vn Bc	Uu 51:22; Uu 83:41–45	CW ix,183	139, 175, 180, 320, 339, 369, 373
92	Quemadmodum desiderat cervus—Ciaccona	T; V V Bc	Uu 82:41	W ii,54	139, 173, 239, 354
93	Salve, desiderium	SSB; V V Vn/Fg Bc	Uu 51:24 Uu 82:42 (variant end)	W vi,46	175, 339
94	Salve Jesu	SS; V V Bc	Uu 51:25; Uu 82:35	W iii,86	139, 156, 340
95	Schaffe in mir, Gott	S; V V Vn Bc	Uu 85:76–88	W i,96	156
96	Schwinget euch himmelan	SSATB; V V V Vn Bc	Uu 70:8; Uu 85:1–18	BA	65, 140, 175, 182–85, 208, 340, 362, 368
97	Sicut Moses exaltavit serpentem	S; V V Vg Bc	Uu 51:26; Uu 82:42	W i,101	139, 145, 156, 339, 372
98	Singet dem Herrn	S; V Bc	Uu 51:27; Uu 82:43	W i,108	137, 156, 172, 191, 305, 307, 339
99	Surrexit Christus hodie	SSB; V V V Fg Bc	Uu 86:19–28	W vi,51	139, 145, 175, 180, 339, 342, 361
100	Wachet auf, ruft uns die Stimme [D]	SSB; V V V V/Va Fg Bc	B 2680	W vi,60	141, 145, 187, 191, 322, 345, 386

Bux WV	Title	Scoring	Sources	Edition	References
101	*Wachet auf, ruft uns die Stimme [C]	ATB; V V Bc	B 2680	W vii,100	137, 206–7, 322, 345
102	Wär Gott nicht mit uns diese Zeit	SATTB; V V Bc	Uu 85:01–18	W viii,22	141, 187–88, 340, 369
103	Walts Gott, mein Werk ich lasse	SATB; V V Va Bc	Uu 2:1; Uu 85:1–18	W viii,31	187–89, 340, 369
104	Was frag' ich nach der Welt	SAB; V V Vn Bc	LÜh A373	W vii,29	175, 330, 346, 371
105	Was mich auf dieser Welt betrübt	S; V V Bc	Uu 6:19	W i,113	137, 144, 175–81, 208, 344, 363
106	Welt, packe dich	SSB; V V Vn Bc	Uu 51:28; Uu 82:42	W vi,75	175, 339
107	Wenn ich, Herr Jesu, habe dich	A; V V Bc	Uu 6:20	W ii,25	145, 175
108	Wie schmeckt es so lieblich und wohl	SAB; V V Vn Bc	Uu 82:43	W vii,39	143, 175, 180, 185
109	Wie soll ich dich empfangen	SSB; V V Fg Bc	Uu 51:29; Uu 82:35	W vi,84	142, 145, 175, 339
110	Wie wird erneuet, wie wird erfreuet	SSATTB; V V V Va Va Vn Cn Cn Cn Tr Tr Tr Tn Tn Tn Cym Bc	LÜh A373	WH	175, 185, 187, 330, 346, 368, 375–77, 380, 386–87
111	Wo ist doch mein Freund geblieben?—Dialogus	SB; V V Fg Bc	B 2679; (Bc 758)	W iii,93	139, 196–98, 200, 322, 335
112	Wo soll ich fliehen hin?—Dialogus	SATB; V V Va Va Vn Bc	LÜh A373	CW ix,211	144, 196–97, 201, 309, 330–31, 346, 369

No.	Title	Scoring	Source	Edition	Pages
113	Benedicam Dominum	SSATB SATB; V V Vn Tr Tr Tr Tr Tn Bom Cn Cn Fg Tn Tn Tn Bc	Uu 50:6	W iv,23	137, 151, 155, 156, 172, 366–67, 377–80
114	Missa alla brevis	SSATB; Bc	Uu 6:16	W iv,12	146, 222, 224–27, 341, 343, 362, 368, 371
115	Auf, Saiten, auf!	S; V V Vg Vg Bc	[Print: *LÜh*]	BA	48, 175, 180, 341, 344, 358, 372
116	Auf! stimmet die Saiten	AAB; Tr Tr Tn Tn Fg Bc	Print: *Uu*; MS:*Uu* 6:10a	W vii,116	73, 175, 179–80, 314, 341, 371, 378–80
117	Deh credete il vostro vanto	S; V V Bc	[Print: *LÜh*]		138, 175, 298, 300, 345
118	Gestreuet mit Blumen	A; V V Va Va Fg Bc	Print: *Uu*		48, 175, 179–80, 314, 341, 355–59, 380
119	Klinget für Freuden	SSB; V V Vn Tr Tr Bc	*Uu* 51:13a AUT; *Uu* 51:13	W v,96	27, 124, 137, 145, 153, 175, 179–80, 208, 318, 339, 380
120	O fröhliche Stunden, o herrlicher Tag	S; V Ob Ob Bc	[Print: *LÜh*]	BA	54, 117, 145, 175, 345, 386
122	Schlagt, Künstler, die Pauken	SSAB; V V Va Va Vn Tr Tr Tm Bc	Uu 50:15	EM	137, 198, 369, 379–80

CANONS

No.	Title	Voices	Source	Pages
123	Canon duplex per Augmentationem	4 voices	(photo: *Pn*)	113, 218–19, 221–22
124	Divertisons nous aujourd'hui	3 voices	[*LÜh*]	43, 112, 218–20, 318
124a	Canon quadruplex	5 voices?	[print]	119, 218, 221–23

Bux WV	Title	Scoring	Sources	Edition	References
KEYBOARD WORKS					
136	Praeludium [C]	Organ ped	*NH* LM Codex	CW xvA,10; S Erg.#4; K ii,#20; H ii,#2	241, 331, 333
137	Praeludium [C]	Organ ped	*LEm* III.8.4.	CW xvA,3; S i,#4; K i,#4; H ii,#1	241, 245–46, 258, 323, 354
138	Praeludium [C]	Organ ped	*NH* LM4838	CW xvA, 17;	241, 326, 335
139	Praeludium [D]	Organ ped	*B* 2681; (*Kj* 40295); *L* Wen U6; *Bc* U26659	CW xvA,22; S i,#11; K i,#11; H ii,#11	84, 231, 241, 243–45, 324–25, 335, 363, 393, 398
140	Praeludium [d]	Organ ped	*B* 2681; *Bc* U26659	CW xvA,37; S i,#10; K i,#10; H ii,#19	241, 244, 258, 324, 358
141	Praeludium [E]	Organ ped	*B* 2681; *Bc* U26659	CW xvA,44; S i,#8; K i,#8; H ii,#14	231, 241, 324, 396
142	Praeludium [e]	Organ ped	*B* 2681; *Bc* U26659; *L* Wen N5; LM Codex	CW xvA,52; S i,#6 Erg. K i,#6; H ii,#9	84, 231, 241–43, 258, 267, 324–25, 331, 333, 335–37, 348, 355, 359
143	Praeludium [e]	Organ ped	*B* 2681; *Bc* U26659	CW xvA,62; S i,#13; K i,#13; H ii,#10	241, 324
144	*Praeludium [F]	Organ ped	*NH* LM5056	CW xvB,154; S Erg.#3; K ii,#19; H ii,#16	241, 331, 333
145	Praeludium [F]	Organ ped	*B* 2681; *Bc* U26659	CW xvA,83; S i,#15; K ii,#15; H ii,#15	241, 258, 324, 327, 393
146	Praeludium [f#]	Organ ped	*Bc* U26659	CW xvA,98; S i,#12; K i,#12; H ii,#13	84, 231, 241, 257–58, 324–25, 359, 363
147	Praeludium [G]	Organ ped	*L* Eng 216	CW xvA,107; H ii,#7	241, 324

148	Praeludium [g]	Organ ped	*NH* LM Codex; [Grobe tab]	CW xvA,128; S i,#5 Erg; K i,#5; H ii,#22	241, 245–47, 259, 324, 331–32, 347, 354–55, 358
149	Praeludium [g]	Organ ped	*B* 2681; *Bc* U26659; *L* Wen U5	CW xvA,111; S i,#14; K i,#14; H ii,#24	231, 241, 245, 247–48, 260, 324–25, 333, 335, 337, 354, 394–96
150	Praeludium [g]	Organ ped	*LEm* III.8.4.	CW xvA,120; S i,#7; K i,#7; H ii,#23	231, 241, 323
151	Praeludium [A]	Organ ped	(*Kj* 40295); *B* 40644	CW xvA,136; S Erg.#5; K ii,#21; H ii,#12a,b	231, 241, 295, 348
152	Praeludium [e Phrygian]	Organ ped	*NH* LM Codex	CW xvA,68; S Erg.#1; K ii,#17; H ii,#6	241, 243, 250–52, 256–57, 314, 323, 331, 358, 362
153	Praeludium [a]	Organ ped	*B* 2681; *Bc* U26659	CW xvA,142; S i,#9; K i,#9; H ii,#4	241, 324, 333
155	Toccata [d]	Organ ped	*NH* LM Codex	CW xvA,29; S Erg.#7; K ii,#30; H ii,#20	241, 258, 331, 336, 347, 362
156	Toccata [F]	Organ ped	*B* 2681; *Bc* U26659	CW xvA,73; S i,#20; K ii,#26; H ii,#17	231, 241, 324, 363, 389–90, 394
157	Toccata [F]	Organ ped	[Berlin, BHMK]	CW xvA,92; S i,#21; K ii,#27; H ii,#18	241, 244–45
158	Praeambulum [a]	Organ ped	*NH* LM Codex	CW xvA,149; S Erg.#2; K ii,#18; H ii,#5	241, 331, 358, 362
159	Giaccona [c]	Organ ped	*LEm* III.8.4; *B* 30069	CW xvA,161; S i,#2; K i,#2; H i,#3	231, 238–41, 323, 354–55
160	Giaccona [e]	Organ ped	*LEm* III.8.4.	CW xvA,168; S i,#3; K i,#3; H i,#2	238–41, 243, 323, 354–55
161	Passacaglia [d]	Organ ped	*LEm* III.8.4.	CW xvA,154; S i,#1; K i,#1; H i,#1	207, 238–41, 285, 323, 354–55, 359

Bux WV	Title	Scoring	Sources	Edition	References
162	Praeludium [G]	Kbd man	L Wen N2	H ii,#8	241, 333
163	Praeludium [g]	Kbd man	B 2681	S i,#16; K ii,#16; H ii,#25	241, 324
164	Toccata [G]	Kbd man	B 2681; NH LM4983	S i,#23; K ii,#29; H ii,#27	241, 324, 326
165	Toccata [G]	Kbd man	B 40644; LEm S4.	S i,#22; K ii,#28; H ii,#26	241, 323, 327, 363, 392
166	Canzona [C]	Kbd man	NH LM Codex	S i,#19; K ii,#24&32; H i,#4	232, 236–38, 331
167	Canzonetta [C]	Kbd man	L Wen N6	H i,#5	232, 238, 333
168	Canzona [d]	Kbd man	B 2681	S i,#25; K ii,#31; H i,#10	232, 234–36, 238, 324
169	Canzona [e]	Kbd man	L Wen N9	H i,#9	232, 236, 238, 333
170	Canzona [G]	Kbd man	L Wen N8	H i,#6	232, 237–38, 333
171	Canzonetta [G]	Kbd man	B 2681	S i,#24; K ii,#33; H i,#7	232–33, 236, 324
172	Canzonetta [G]	Kbd man	NH LM4983	BA 8223, EB 6662	232, 326, 335
173	Canzona [G]	Kbd man	L Wen N1	H i,#12	232, 236, 238, 333, 358
174	Fuga [C]	Kbd man	LEm III.8.4.	S i,#17; K ii,#22; H ii,#3	232, 323

175	Fuga [G]	Kbd man	NH LM5056	S Erg.#6; K ii,#25; H i,#8	232–33, 235–36, 238, 331
176	Fuga [B♭]	Kbd man	B 2681	S i,#18; K ii,#23; H i,#11	232, 237, 324
177	Ach Gott und Herr	Organ ped	[Plauen]	CW xviA,96; S Erg.#9; K ii,#34; H iii/1,#1	261, 274–76
178	Ach Herr, mich armen Sünder	Organ ped	DHgm 4.G.14	CW xviA,162; S ii/2,#1; K iv,#1; H iv,#1	270, 328
179	Auf meinen lieben Gott	Kbd man	DHgm 4.G.14	CW xviA,99; S ii/2,#31; K iv,#31; H iii/1,#7	275–76, 279, 328
180	Christ, unser Herr, zum Jordan kam	Organ ped	DHgm 4.G.14	CW xviA,165; S ii/2,#2; K iv,#2; H iv,#2	270, 328
181	Danket dem Herren	Organ ped	(B 30245)	CW xviA,104; S ii/1,#1; K iii,#1; H iii/1,#2	261, 276
182	Der Tag der ist so freudenreich	Organ ped	B 22541/1; B 22541/2	CW xviA,169; S ii/2,#3; K iv,#3; H iv,#3	231, 270, 328
183	Durch Adams Fall ist ganz verderbt	Organ ped	DHgm 4.G.14	CW xviA,174; S ii/2,#4; K iv,#4; H iv,#4	270, 273–74, 328
184	Ein feste Burg ist unser Gott	Organ ped	DHgm 4.G.14	CW xviA,178; S ii/2,#5; K iv,#5; H iv,#5	270, 274, 328
185	Erhalt uns, Herr, bei deinem Wort	Organ ped	DHgm 4.G.14	CW xviA,182; S ii/2,#7; K iv,#7; H iv,#6	270, 328
186	Es ist das Heil uns kommen her	Organ ped	DHgm 4.G.14	CW xviA,184; S ii/2,#8; K iv,#8; H iv,#7	270, 328
187	Es spricht der Unweisen Mund wohl	Organ ped	DHgm 4.G.14	CW xviA,187; S ii/2,#9; K iv,#9; H iv,#8	231, 270, 328

Bux WV	Title	Scoring	Sources	Edition	References
188	Gelobet seist du, Jesu Christ [fantasia]	Organ ped	B P802	CW xviA,33; S ii/1,#2; K iii,#2; H iii/2,#1	262, 276, 328–29, 394
189	Gelobet seist du, Jesu Christ [prelude]	Organ ped	B 22541/1; B 22541/2	CW xviA,190; S ii/2,#10; K iv,#10; H iv,#9	270, 328
190	Gott der Vater wohn uns bei	Organ ped	DHgm 4.G.14	CW xviA,192; S ii/2,#11; K iv,#11; H iv,#10	270, 328
191	Herr Christ, der einig Gottes Sohn	Organ ped	(B 30245)	CW xviA,195; S ii/2,#13; K iv,#13; H iv,#11b	231, 270–71
192	Herr Christ, der einig Gottes Sohn	Organ ped	B 22541/1; DHgm 4.G.14	CW xviA,198; S ii/2,#12; K iv,#12; H iv,#11a	231, 270–71, 328, 330
193	Herr Jesu Christ, ich weiß gar wohl	Organ ped	[KAu 15839]	CW xviA,201; S ii/2,#14; K iv,#14; H iv,#12	270
194	Ich dank dir, lieber Herre	Organ ped	[KAu 15839]	CW xviA,44; S ii/1,#3; K iii,#3; H iii/2,#2	262, 265
195	Ich dank dir schon durch deinen Sohn	Organ ped	[KAu 15839]	CW xviA,50; S ii/1,#4; K iii,#4; H iii/2,#3	261, 262, 362
196	Ich ruf zu dir, Herr Jesu Christ	Organ ped	[KAu 15839]	CW xviA,56; S ii/2,#15; K iv,#15; H iii/2,#4	262
197	In dulci jubilo	Organ ped	B 22541/1; B 22541/2	CW xviA,205; S ii/2,#17; K iv,#17; H iv,#14	231, 270, 328

198	Jesus Christus, unser Heiland, der den Tod überwand	Organ ped	*B* 22541/3	CW xviA,208; S ii/2,#16; K iv,#16; H iv,#13	270, 275, 328
199	Komm, Heiliger Geist, Herre Gott	Organ ped	*B* 22541/3	CW xviA,210; S ii/2,#18; K iv,#18; H iv,#15a	270–71, 328
200	Komm, Heiliger Geist, Herre Gott	Organ ped	*B* 22541/3	CW xviA,214; S ii/2,#19; K iv,#19; H iv,#15b	270–71, 328
201	Kommt her zu mir, spricht Gottes Sohn	Organ ped	*DHgm* 4.G.14	CW xviA,218; S ii/2,#20; K iv,#20; H iv,#16	270, 328
202	Lobt Gott, ihr Christen allzugleich	Organ ped	*B* 22541/1; *B* 22541/2	CW xviA,222; S ii/2,#21; K iv,#21; H iv,#17	270, 328, 393
203	Magnificat primi toni [fantasia]	Organ ped	*Bc* U26059	CW xviA,3; S ii/1,#5a; K iii,#5a; H iii/2,#5	262, 265, 267–69, 324–25
204	Magnificat primi toni [part 1] [part 2]	Organ ped	(*LEm* Becker III.8.26)	CW xviA,12; S ii/1,#5b; K iii,#5b; H iii/1,#3a CW xviA,14; S Erg.#10a; K ii,#35a; H iii/1,#3b/I	262, 265, 269–70
205	Magnificat noni toni	Organ ped	(*LEm* Becker III.8.26)	CW xviA,108; S Erg.#10bc; K ii,#35bc; H iii/1, #3b/II–III	269–70, 276
206	Mensch, willt du leben seliglich	Organ ped	*DHgm* 4.G.14	CW xviA,224; S ii/2,#22; K iv,#22; H iv,#18	270, 328

Bux WV	Title	Scoring	Sources	Edition	References
207	Nimm von uns, Herr, du treuer Gott [Vater unser in Himmelreich]	Organ ped	*DHgm* 4.G.14 (etc.)	CW xviA,116; S ii/1,#9a; K iii,#9a; H iii/1,#6	276, 328
208	Nun bitten wir den Heiligen Geist	Organ ped	*B* 22541/3	CW xviA,226; S ii/2,#24; K iv,#24; H iv,#19b	231, 270–72, 328
209	Nun bitten wir den Heiligen Geist	Organ ped	*B* 22541/3	CW xviA,229; S ii/2,#23; K iv,#23; H iv,#19a	231, 270–72, 328
210	Nun freut euch, lieben Christen gmein	Organ ped	*B* P802	CW 16A,61; S ii/1,#6; K iii,#6; H iii/2,#6	262–64, 276, 322–23, 328, 348, 398
211	Nun komm, der Heiden Heiland	Organ ped	*B* 22541/1; *B* 22541/2	CW xviA,232; S ii/2,#25; K iv,#25; H iv,#20	270, 328
212	Nun lob, mein Seel, den Herren [C major, echo]	Organ ped	[Plauen]	CW xviA,80; S Erg.#11; K ii,#36; H iii/1,#5	262, 265
213	Nun lob, meine Seel, den Herren [G major, 3 variations]	Organ ped	*B* 2681; *DHgm* 4.G.14	CW xviA,138; S ii/1,#7a; K iii,#7a; H iii/1,#4a	276, 324, 328
214	Nun lob, mein Seel, den Herren [G major, chorale prelude]	Organ ped	*DHgm* 4.G.14	CW xviA,154; S ii/1,#7b/I; K iii,#7b/I; H iii/1, #4b/I	231, 270, 275, 328
215	Nun lob, mein Seel, den Herren	Kbd man	[*KAu* 15839]	CW xviA,158; S ii/1, #7b/II;	215, 270, 275

	[G major, chorale prelude]			K iii, #7b/II; H iii/1, #4b/II	
217	Puer natus in Bethlehem	Organ ped	B 22541/1; B 22541/2	CW xviA,234; S ii/2,#26; K iv,#26; H iv,#21	270, 328
218	Te Deum laudamus	Organ ped	B P801; LÜh U212	CW xviA,16; S ii/1,#8; K iii,#8; H iii/2,#7	243, 262, 265–67, 270, 327–29, 393, 397
219	Vater unser im Himmelreich	Organ ped	DHgm 4.G.14	CW xviA,236; S ii/1,#9b; K iii,#9b; H iv,#22	270, 328
220	Von Gott will ich nicht lassen	Organ ped	DHgm 4.G.14	CW xviA,242; S ii/2,#27; K iv,#27; H iv,#23a	270, 328
221	Von Gott will ich nicht lassen	Organ ped	DHgm 4.G.14	CW xviA,244; S ii/2,#28; K iv,#28; H iv,#23b	270, 275, 328
222	Wär Gott nicht mit uns diese Zeit	Organ ped	DHgm 4.G.14	CW xviA,246; S ii/2,#29; K iv,#29; H iv,#24	261, 270, 328
223	Wie schön leuchtet der Morgenstern	Organ ped	B 22541/2	CW xviA,86; S ii/1,#10; K iii,#10; H iii/2,#8	262, 265, 276, 328–29
224	Wir danken dir, Herr Jesu Christ	Organ ped	B 22541/3	CW xviA,248; S ii/2,#30; K iv,#30; H iv,#25	270, 328
225	Canzonetta [a]	Kbd man	N 1136:2	BA 8223, EB 6662	232–33, 236–37, 335
226	Suite [C]	Kbd man	Kk 6806.1399	Ban #1	278–79, 334
227	Suite [C]	Kbd man	Kk 6806.1399	Ban #2	278, 334

Bux WV	Title	Scoring	Sources	Edition	References
228	Suite [C]	Kbd man	*Kk* 6806.1399	Ban #3	276, 278, 334
229	Suite [C]	Kbd man	*Kk* 6806.1399	Ban #4	277–79, 334
230	Suite [C]	Kbd man	*Kk* 6806.1399	Ban #5	278–79, 281, 334
231	Suite [C]	Kbd man	*Uu* Ihre 285	Lun #1	277–78, 334, 347
232	Suite [D]	Kbd man	*Kk* 6806.1399	Ban #9	278, 334
233	Suite [d, "d'Amour"]	Kbd man	*Kk* 6806.1399	Ban #6	278, 334
234	Suite [d]	Kbd man	*Kk* 6806.1399	Ban #7	276, 278, 334
235	Suite [e]	Kbd man	*Kk* 6806.1399	Ban #10	278, 334
236	Suite [e]	Kbd man	*Kk* 6806.1399; *Uu* I 285, etc.	Ban #11	239, 277–78, 334, 347
237	Suite [e]	Kbd man	*Kk* 6806.1399	Ban #12	277–78, 334
238	Suite [F]	Kbd man	*Kk* 6806.1399; *Uu* Ihre 285	Ban #13	277–78, 334, 347
239	Suite [F]	Kbd man	*Uu* Ihre 285	Lun #4	277–78, 334, 347
240	Suite [G]	Kbd man	*Kk* 6806.1399	Ban #17	278–79, 334
241	Suite [g]	Kbd man	*Kk* 6806.1399	Ban #14	278, 334
242	Suite [g]	Kbd man	*Kk* 6806.1399	Ban #15	278, 334
243	Suite [A]	Kbd man	*Kk* 6806.1399	Ban #19	278, 334, 360
244	Suite [a]	Kbd man	*Kk* 6806.1399	Ban #18	278, 334
245	Courant zimble [a; 8 variations]	Kbd man	*Kk* 6806.1399	Ban #23	277, 281, 334
246	Aria [C; + 10 variations]	Kbd man	*Kk* 6806.1399	Ban #20	277, 281, 294, 334
247	Aria: More Palatino [12 variations]	Kbd man	*Kk* 6806.1399	Ban #21	281, 334

248	[Aria] Rofilis [3 variations]	Kbd man	Kk 6806.1399	Ban #22	281–83, 334
249	Aria [a; 3 variations]	Kbd man	Kk 6806.1399	Ban #24	277, 281, 334
250	Aria: La Capricciosa [32 variations]	Kbd man	Kk 6806.1399	Ban #25	277, 281, 283, 334, 392

SONATAS

252	Opus 1, Sonata I [F]	V Vg Bc	Print: *Uu*	CW xiv,3	284, 286, 354
253	Opus 1, Sonata II [G]	V Vg Bc	Print: *Uu*	CW xiv,13	284, 286, 294
254	Opus 1, Sonata III [a]	V Vg Bc	Print: *Uu*	CW xiv,22	284, 286–91
255	Opus 1, Sonata IV [B♭]	V Vg Bc	Print: *Uu*	CW xiv,33	284, 286, 303, 349–52, 354, 384
256	Opus 1, Sonata V [C]	V Vg Bc	Print: *Uu*	CW xiv,44	284, 293–94
257	Opus 1, Sonata VI [d]	V Vg Bc	Print: *Uu*	CW xiv,55	284, 286, 295–99, 301, 388, 396–97
258	Opus 1, Sonata VII [e]	V Vg Bc	Print: *Uu*	CW xiv,65	284, 286
259	Opus 2, Sonata I [B♭]	V Vg Bc	Print: *Uu*	CW xiv,77	284
260	Opus 2, Sonata II [D]	V Vg Bc	Print: *Uu*	CW xiv,90	284
261	Opus 2, Sonata III [g]	V Vg Bc	Print: *Uu*	CW xiv,103	284, 286, 291–94, 354–55
262	Opus 2, Sonata IV [c]	V Vg Bc	Print: *Uu*	CW xiv,117	284, 286, 300, 354
263	Opus 2, Sonata V [A]	V Vg Bc	Print: *Uu*	CW xiv,127	284, 294–95, 354
264	Opus 2, Sonata VI [E]	V Vg Bc	Print: *Uu*	CW xiv,140	284, 287, 354
265	Opus 2, Sonata VII [F]	V Vg Bc	Print: *Uu*	CW xiv,151	284, 354
266	Sonata [C]	V V Vg Bc	*Uu* Inst 13:27	CW xiv,163	126, 302–4, 354, 397
267	Sonata [D]	Vg Vn Bc	*Uu* I 13:24	CW xiv,174	123, 126, 302, 304, 344, 371, 374

Bux WV	Title	Scoring	Sources	Edition	References
268	*Sonata [D]	Vg Bc	(Ob Sch.D.249)	CW xiv,184	302, 304–6
269	Sonata [F]	V V Vg Bc	Uu Inst 13:23	CW xiv,188	302–3, 305, 307, 383
271	Sonata [G]	V V Vg Bc	Uu Inst 13:28	CW xiv,201	302–3, 354
272	Sonata [a]	V Vg Bc	Uu Inst 13:26	CW xiv,213	302–3, 354–55, 361
273	Sonata [B♭, with Suite]	V Vg Bc	Uu Inst 13:25	CW xiv,223	302–3, 348–50, 352, 354, 383
deest	Suite [a]	Kbd man	(Breitenberg MS 692)	Ed. Küster	278
deest	Suite [d]	Kbd man	(Print, Pn)	Ed. Dirksen	278
FRAGMENTARY AND LOST WORKS					
16	Dies ist der Tag	S; V V Vn Bc	LÜh A373		137, 330
121	Opachi boschetti	S/T; V V Bc	[Print: LÜh]		53, 137–38, 345
125	Christum lieb haben ist viel besser	SSATB; 11 insts	(Lüneburg inv.)		
126	?Music for dedication of Fredenhagen altar	3 choirs	(Die Beglückte und Geschmückte Stadt Lübeck)		90
127	Pallidi salvete	4 voices, 6 insts	(Ansbach inv.)		
128	Die Hochzeit des Lamms		Libretto: Uu 6:8		see general index
129	Das allerschröcklichste und allererfreulichste	5 voices, insts	(1684 catalog)		62, 64, 68, 302
130	Himmlische Seelenlust auf Erden		(1684 catalog)		62, 64, 116, 211, 302, 370, 377
131	Der verlorene Sohn		(1689 letter)		65

		(Nova literaria)	
132	Jubilaeum—Hundertjähriges Gedicht		65
133	Abendmusiken of 1700 *23rd Sunday after Trinity:* I. Lob- und Dank-Lied wegen den behaltenen Frieden in der Nachbarschafft II. "Singet dem Herrn ein neues Lied" (Ps. 96:1–4; Ps. 100:4–5) III. "Allein Gott in der Höh sei Ehr" Chorale (4 strophes) *24th Sunday after Trinity:* I. Danck-Lied nach überstandener Kranckheit II. Selige Himmels-Freude III. "Erhalt mir Leib und Leben" Chorale (2 strophes)		65

Bux WV	Title	Scoring	Sources	Edition	References
	2nd Sunday of Advent I. "Wo der Herr nicht bey uns wäre" (Psalm 124) II. Welt-Verachtung/ Himmels-Betrachtung III. Es woll uns Gott genädig sein" Chorale (all strophes)				
	3rd Sunday of Advent I. "Jerusalem, du hochgebaute Stadt." Chorale (8 strophes) II. Winter-Lied III. "O Vater aller Frommen, geheiliget werd dein Nahm." Chorale				
	4th Sunday of Advent upon the wish of high patrons, the Jubilaeum or Hundertjähriges				

	Title	Scoring	Source	Edition	Pages
	Gedicht which was presented at the beginning of this year 1700 will be repeated				
134	Castrum doloris		Libretto:*LÜh*		see general index
135	Templum honoris		Libretto:*LÜh*		see general index
154	Praeludium [B-flat]	Organ ped	*L* Wen N1b	CW xvB,159	333
216	O Lux beata Trinitas	Kbd man	*LLim* III.8.4.		323, 328
251	7 Suites, "Die Natur oder Eigenschafft der Planeten"	[Kbd man]	(Mattheson, *Capellmeister*, II/4,873)	o.	79, 132, 134, 284–85
270	Sonata [F]	[V V] Bc	*Uu* Inst 1:12	CW xiv,261	302, 306, 342, 362
274	Sonaten ... zur Kirchen- und Tafel-Music bequemlich	[V V (V) Vg Bc]	1684 catalog		101
DOUBTFUL AND FALSELY ATTRIBUTED WORKS					
Anh.					
1	Magnificat anima mea, Domine	SSATB; V V Va Va Vn Bc	*Uu* 69:17; *Uu* 86:50	BA	206
2	Man singet mit Freuden vom Sieg	SSATB; V V Tr Tr Va/Tn Va/Tn Fg Bc	*B* 2680/5	HE	
3	Wacht! Euch zum Streit	SSATB; V V Va Va Bc	*Uu* Capsel 71	BA 543	68, 208–11
4	Natalitia sacra (see Appendix 4, F1)				

Bux WV	Title	Scoring	Sources	Edition	References
5	Sonata	Organ ped	*NH* LM Codex	CW xiv:265	305–6, 331, 333
6	Courante [d]	Kbd man	*Kk 6806.1399* Print *Pn*	Ban #27; ed. Dirksen	278
7	Courante [G]	Kbd man	*Kk 6806.1399*	Ban #27	
8	Simphonie [G]	Kbd man	*Kk 6806.1399*	Ban #28	
9	Erbarm dich mein, o Herre Gott (Lowies Busbetzky)	SATB; V V Vt Vn/Fg Bc	*Uu 82:32*	BA	206
10	Laudate Dominum omnes gentes (Lowies Busbetzky)	S; V V Vn/Fg Bc	*Uu 82:33*	BA	206
11	Erhalt uns Herr, bei deinem Wort (Pachelbel? Böhm?)	Kbd man	*DHgm 4.G.14 etc.*	S ii/2,#6; K iv/2,#6; H iv#26	
12	Suite [d] (Nicolas Lebègue)	Kbd man	*Kk 6806.1399*	Ban #8	277
13	Suite [g] (Nicolas Lebègue)	Kbd man	*Kk 6806.1399*	Ban #16	277
deest	Christ lag in Todesbanden	Organ ped	*NH LM4983; B 22541/3*		

(Nicolaus Vetter)

deest	Missa [Kyrie] J. Bocksdehude	SSATB; V V Bc	*Großfahner/Gotha*	Ed. Dirksen	
deest	Nun freut euch, lieben Christen g'mein	Organ ped	*Lr* K 209		264–65

Appendix 2

The Writings of Dieterich Buxtehude

A. Letters

1666, 28 September:
Unaddressed affidavit in Danish, signed Diderich Buxtehude
Copenhagen, Landsarkivet, Helsingør, Skt. Olai Korrespondancesager
facsimile and transcription in Friis, *Diderik Buxtehude*, planche VI

1666, 7 November:
To Jörgen Buhr, in Danish, signed D Buxtehude
Copenhagen, Landsarkivet, Helsingør, Skt. Olai Korrespondancesager
facsimile and transcription Friis, *Diderik Buxtehude*, planche VI

1667, 7 October:
To Jörgen Buhr, in Danish, signed D Buxtehude
Copenhagen, Landsarkivet, Helsingør, Skt. Olai Korrespondancesager
facsimile and transcription Friis, *Diderik Buxtehude*, planche VII

1671, 1 September
To burgomaster of Helsingør, in German, signed Dieterich Buxtehude
Copenhagen, Landsarkivet, Helsingør, Indkomne Breve til Magistraten
transcription appendix 4, B1

1683, 7 February:
To *Hispanischen Collecten* and *Dröge*, signed Dieterich Buxtehude
Lübeck, Archiv der Hansestadt, ASA Ecclesiastica, Lit. Vol. C Fasc. 5, Pak. 3765 Nr. 15116
facsimile and translation in chapter 2
transcription appendix 4, D1

1685, 16 February:
To *Hispanischen Collecten* and *Dröge*, signed Dieterich Buxtehude
Lübeck, Archiv der Hansestadt, ASA Ecclesiastica, Lit. Vol. C Fasc. 5, Pak. 3765 Nr. 15116
facsimile in Stahl, *Franz Tunder und Dietrich Buxtehude*, 63 and in *MGG* II, Tafel 19, Abb. 2
transcription appendix 4, D1

1686, 17 February:
To *Hispanischen Collecten* and *Dröge*, signed Dieterich Buxtehude
Lübeck, Archiv der Hansestadt, ASA Ecclesiastica, Lit. Vol. C Fasc. 5, Pak. 3765 Nr. 15116
transcription Hagedorn, 193–94

1687, 28 January:
To *Hispanischen Collecten* and *Dröge*, signed Dieterich Buxtehude
Lübeck, Archiv der Hansestadt, ASA Ecclesiastica, Lit. Vol. C Fasc. 5, Pak. 3765 Nr. 15116
transcription Hagedorn, 194–95
excerpt in appendix 4, D1

1689, 5 February:
To *Hispanischen Collecten* and *Dröge*, signed Dieterich Buxtehude
Lübeck, Archiv der Hansestadt, ASA Ecclesiastica, Lit. Vol. C Fasc. 5, Pak. 3765 Nr. 15116
facsimile Karstädt, *Abendmusiken*, Abb. 3; transcription Hagedorn, 196
excerpt in appendix 4, D1

1695, 19 August:
To Johan Köhler, Stettin, signed Dieter. Buxtehude
transcription Fock, *Arp Schnitger*, 171

1696, 22 February:
To *Hispanischen Collecten* and *Dröge*, signed Dieterich Buxtehude
Lübeck, Archiv der Hansestadt, ASA Ecclesiastica, Lit. Vol. C Fasc. 5, Pak. 3765 Nr. 15116
transcription appendix 4, D1

1697, 22 March:
To *Hispanischen Collecten* and *Dröge*, signed Dieterich Buxtehude
Lübeck, Archiv der Hansestadt, Dröge 172
transcription Spies, "Vier neuentdeckte Briefe"

1698, 3 March:
To church directors, St. Jacobi, Stettin, signed Dieterich Buxtehude
partial transcription Fock, 172–73

1698, 27 April:
To *Hispanischen Collecten* and *Dröge*, signed Dieterich Buxtehude
Lübeck, Archiv der Hansestadt, Dröge 172
transcription Spies, "Vier neuentdeckte Briefe"

1699, 12 April:
To *Hispanischen Collecten* and *Dröge*, signed Dieterich Buxtehude
Lübeck, Archiv der Hansestadt, Dröge 172
facsimile and transcription, Spies, "Vier neuentdeckte Briefe"
excerpt in appendix 4, D5

1701, 3 February:
To *Hispanischen Collecten* and *Dröge*, signed Dieterich Buxtehude
Lübeck, Archiv der Hansestadt, Dröge 172
facsimile and transcription, Spies, "Vier neuentdeckte Briefe"
excerpt in appendix 4, D5

Undated:
Memorandum concerning rental of organist's house
copy at Lübeck, Archiv der Hansestadt, ASA Ecclesiastica (Nachträge Winckler),
St. Marien, Vol. B, 7, 3
transcription appendix 4, D2

B. Poems

1669, poem of thanks for gift of 25 rixdollars, in account book
Lübeck, Archiv der Hansestadt, St. Marien, I [Bücher] 1a, 15: Wochenbuch
1662–1669, fol. 288r
transcription: appendix 4, D7

1673, dedicatory poem for Theile, St. Matthew Passion
Denkmäler deutscher Tonkunst, XVII, 109
original text and translation, Mackey, 317–18.

1674, [unattributed] "Klag-Lied" on death of father (BuxWV 76-2)
Werke II, 88

1680, [unattributed] text for *Klinget für Freuden, ihr lärmen Klarinen* (BuxWV 119)
Werke V, 96
excerpt with translation in chapter 1

1702, dedicatory poems for Werckmeister, *Harmonologia Musica*
original texts and translations in chapter 4

1705, [unattributed] text for *O fröhliche Stunden, o herrlicher Tag* (BuxWV 120)
partial text, appendix 4, E7

C. Dedications of Printed Works

[1694], *VII Sonate à doi . . . Opera prima*
Dedication to burgomasters and members of Lübeck city council
appendix 4, E3

1696, *VII. Suonate à due . . . Opera secunda*
Dedication in Italian to Johann Ritter
appendix 4, E4

Appendix 3

Principal Sources of the Works of Dieterich Buxtehude

For other sources, see *Buxtehude-Werke-Verzeichnis and Collected Works*

A. Prints of Music

Listed in chronological sequence; prints of librettos appear in the bibliography

Auff Das Hochansehnliche Hochzeit-Fest Des HochEdelgebohrnen, Gestrengen, Vesten, und Hochweisen Herrn, Herrn Henricus Kirchrink, Der Käyserl. Freyen und des Heil. Römischen Reichs- und Hansee-Stadt Lübeck hochverdienten Herrn Bürgermeistern, auff Brandenbaum und Reip. &c. Erbherren, und Der HochEdelgebohrnen, GroßEhr- und Tugendreichen Frauen, Frauen Agneta Kirchrings, gebohrnen von Stiten, Gehalten den 23. Tag des Herbstmonats; Setzte Seine schüldige Pflicht zu bezeugen nachfolgende Aria Dietericus Buxtehude, Organista an der Haupt-Kirchen zu St. Marien in Lübeck. Lübeck: Gedruckt durch Seel. Gottfried Jägers Erben [1672] [*Uu*]. (*Auf! stimmet die Saiten*, BuxWV 116); score: A1 A2 B; TrSor1 TrSor2 TnSor1 TnSor2 Fg; Con.

[*Als Tit: Herr Christoph Siricius JCtus und wolbestalter Secretarius allhie, Mit Tit: Jungfer Dorothea von Degingk, Des Tit: Hn: Caspar von Degingk, Hochansehnlichen Rahtsverwandten Eheleibliche Jungfer Tochter, Seinen Hochzeitlichen Ehrentag (war der 2. Juni dieses 1673sten Jahrs) beginge Setzte diese Aria, zu bezeugen seiner schuldigen Pflicht Dietericus Buxtehude, Organista an der Hauptkirchen zu St. Marien in Lübeck.* Lübeck: Jäger, 1673]; formerly at *LÜh*, missing since 1942. (*Auf, Saiten auf!*, BuxWV 115)

Fried- und Freudenreiche Hinfarth Des alten großgläubigen Simeons bey seeligen ableiben Des Weiland Wohl-Ehren Vesten Groß-Achtbaren und Kunstreichen Herrn Johannis Buxtehuden, In der Königlichen Stadt Helsingiör an der Kirchen S. Olai 32. Jahr gewesenen Organisten, Welcher im 72. Jahr seines Alters am 22. Januarii des 1674. Jahres alhier zu Lübeck mit Fried und Freude aus dieser angst und unruhevollen Welt abgeschieden, und von seinem Erlöser, (des Er längst mit verlangen erwartet) heimgeholet, und darauff den 29. ejusdem in der Haupt-Kirchen zu S. Marien daselbst Christlich beerdiget worden. Dem Seelig-verstorbenen, als seinem Hertzlich geliebten Vater zu schuldigen Ehren und Christlichen nachruhme in 2. Contrapuncten abgesungen von Dieterico Buxtehuden, Organisten an der Haupt-Kirchen zu St. Marien in Lübeck. "Lübeck: In Verlegung Ulrich Wettstein, Buchhändler in Lübeck, 1674" [*KA*]; facsimile ed. Max Seiffert; Lübeck: Ernst Robert, 1937. (*Mit Fried und Freud* and *Klag-Lied*, BuxWV 76,1-2); score: Contrapunctus: S; C3 C4 F4. Evolutio: B; C1 C3 C4. Klaglied: S; C3 C4; [Bc].

Das Edelste Ritterspiel Nemblich die Liebe Zu welchem Der Wohl Edeler, Fäster und Hochgelahrter Herr, Herr Achilles Daniel Leopoldi, Beider Rechten Doctor Mit Der WolEdlen, an Zier und Tugenden tapfren Jungfer, Jgf: Anna Margaretha, Des HochEdelen Vesten, Hochweisen und Hochgelahrten Herrn, Hn. Johannis Ritters Jcti, Und der Käyserl. Reichs-Stadt Lübeck, hochansehnlichen Bürgermeisters Eheleiblichen Jungfer Tochter, Am ersten Tage des Mertzmohnts dieses 1675 Jahres von Gott durch Priesterl. Hand eingeweihet, Besungen von Dieterico Buxtehuden, Organista an der Haupt Kirchen zu St. Marien. "Lübeck: Gedruckt durch Seel. Gottfried Jägers Erben" [1675] [*Uu*]. (*Gestreuet mit Blumen*, BuxWV 118); score: A; [V1 V2 Va1 Va2] Fg; Con.

Trost-Lied Hiebevor von dem Wittwer M.M.R. dem Hochwürdigen Hoch Edlen und Hochgelahrten Herrn, Herrn Sebastiano Nieman, der heiligen Schrifft hochbenannten Doctori, Hoff-Predigern und ihrer Hoch-Fürstl. Durchl. hochbetrauten General-Superintendenten zum Trost in gleichem Fall außgelieffert, Bey Beysetzung aber seiner seligen Ehe-Liebsten Margarita Rachelia Von den Herrn Cantoribus und Herrn Organisten auff Femern figuraliter abgesungen, Und auffs neu durch den welt- und weit-berühmten Herrn, Herrn Dieterich Buxtehuden, Organisten an S. Marien in Lübeck mit folgenden Stimmen gezieret. "Ratzeburg: gedruckt bey Niclas Nissen, 1677" [*Gs*]. (*Jesu meiner Freuden Meister*, BuxWV 61); score: S A T B; Va1(C1) Va2(C3) Va3(C3) Vn; Con.

VII Suonate à doi, Violino & Violadagamba, con Cembalo, di Dieterico Buxtehude, Organista della Chiesa della Beat. Virg. N.S. in Lubeca, Opera prima. "Stampata in Hamburgo per Nicolao Spiering, Alle spese dell' Autore & si vendano apresso Giavanno Widemeyer in Lubeca" [1694] [*Uu*]. (BuxWV 252–58); parts: V Vg; Cemb.

[*Trionfo festivo, per le gloriose Nozze del molto Illustre Signor, il Signor Gioachimo Lüdero Carstens, Secretario dignissimo dell' inclita imperiale Città di Lübeca sempre augusta, etc., con la molto illustre Signora, la Signora Anna Catharina Leopoldo, per Dieterico Buxtehude, Direttore dell' Organo del maestoso Tempio di S. Maria, in Lübeca.* "Nella Stamperia di Cristoforo Gottfrido Sagittario, l'anno 1695, 8 Luglio"]; formerly at *LÜh*; missing since 1942. (*Deh credete il vostro vanto*, BuxWV 117).

VII Suonate à due, Violino et Violadagamba con Cembalo, dà Dieterico Buxtehude, Direttore dell; organo del glorioso Tempio Santa Maria in Lubeca. Opera Secunda. "Stampata in Hamburgo alle Spese di Nicolo Spiring, & si vendano apresso Giavanno Widemeyer in Lubeca. M. DC. XCVI." [*Uu*] (BuxWV 259–65); parts: V Vg; Cemb.

[*Sonetto per honorar le felicissime Nozze degl; illustrissimi Sposi, Signor Dottor Benedetto Pietro Winkler, Figlio del magnifico Sign. Console regnante, e della Signora Margaretha de Hövelen, nata de Kerkring, posto in Musica da Dieterico Buxtehude, Direttore dell' Organo del venerando Tempio di S. Maria in Lubeca.* Lübeck: Christ. God. Sagittario, 14. mars 1698]; formerly at *LÜh*; missing since 1942. (*Opachi boschetti*, BuxWV 121).

[*Auff Hochansehnlichem Hochzeit-Fest des Magnifici, Hoch Edlen, Vest Hochgelahrt- und Hochweisen Herrn, Herrn Anthonii Winckler, J.U.D. und der Kayserl. Freyen auch des Heiligen Römischen Reichs- und HanSee-Stadt Lübeck Höchstverdienten ältisten Herrn Bürgermeistern, Mit der Hoch-Edel, Groß-Ehr- und Hoch-Tugendreichen Frauen, Frauen D. Elisabeth Niemanns Gebohrnen Fresin, Gehalten am 7. Tag Septembris des jetztlaufenden 1705. Jahrs, Wolte Zu Bezeugung schuldigster Pflicht mit nachfolgender Ariette gehorsamst aufwarten Dero ergebenster Diener Dieter. Buxtehude.* Lübeck, 1705]; formerly at *LÜh*; missing since 1942. (*O fröhliche Stunden, o herrlicher Tag*, BuxWV 120).

B. Manuscripts

1. Berlin, Staatsbibliothek zu Berlin, Preußischer Kulturbesitz, Musikabteilung [*B*]

Mus. ms. 2679: [Wo ist doch mein Freund geblieben] (BuxWV 111); score: [S B]; [V1 V2]; [Bc].

Mus. ms. 2680; convolute, scores:
#1: "Exemple 2 sonderbaren CONTRAPUNCTE . . . [Mit Fried und Freud] . . . Dieterico Buxtehuden" (BuxWV 76-1); Cpt. 1&2: [S]; C3 C4; [Bc]. Ev. 1&2: [B] (fig); C1 C3 C4.
#2: "[Heut triumphieret Gottes Sohn] d. buxtehude [red]" (BuxWV 43, unicum); [S1 S2 A T B]; [V1 V2 Va1 Va2 Vn]; [Tr1 Tr2]; [Bc].
#3: "Wachet auff rufft uns die Stimme . . . dietrich Buxtehude" (BuxWV 101, unicum); A T B; V1 V2; Con.
#4: "Wachet auff . . . Buxtehude" (BuxWV 100, unicum); S1 S2 B; V1 V2 V3 V4(C3) Fg; Org.
#5: "[In dulci jubilo] . . . Buxtehude" (BuxWV 52); [S1 S2 B]; [V1 V2 Vn]; [Bc].
#6: "[Nun freut euch ihr Frommen] . . . d. buxtehude" (BuxWV 80, unicum); S1 S2; [V1 V2]; [Bc].
#7: "[Dixit Dominus Domino meo] . . . Buxtehude [red] (BuxWV 17); [S]; [V1 V2 Va1 Va2 Vn]; [Bc].
#8: "Alles was ihr thut mit Worten od. mit Wercken. . . . Diedr. Buxtehude" (BuxWV 4); [S A T] B; V1 V2 Va1 Va2; Con.
Inventory: Kümmerling, 108; Collected Works, 9: 268.

Mus. ms. 2681, [crossed out: "Praeambula et Praeludia dell Sr: Buxtehuden"] "XV Präludien und Fugen, nebst dem Choral: Nun lob mein Seel, für die Orgel von *Dietrich Buxtehuden*, Organist zu Lübeck"; 2 staves:
#1: p. 1, "Praeludium. ex. E. moll. / Diet: Buxteh:" (BuxWV 142); pedal.
#2: p. 8, "Praelud: ex A: c. / Diet: Buxteh:" (BuxWV 153); pedal.
#3: p. 13, "Praeludium. ex. D. fis. / Diet: Buxteh:" (BuxWV 139); pedal.
#4: p. 18, "Praeludium ex. D. F. / Diet: Buxteh:" (BuxWV 140); pedal.
#5: p. 23, "Praeludium ex. E. gis. / Diet: Buxtehuden" (BuxWV 141); pedal.
#6: p. 29, "Canzonet. ex. G. ♮. / Diet. Buxtehuden" (BuxWV 171, unicum).
#7: p. 31, "Praeludium. ex. F: a: / Diet: Buxtehuden" (BuxWV 145); pedal.
#8: p. 38, "Fuga. ex. B: D: / Diet: Buxtehudern" (BuxWV 176, unicum).
#9: p, 43, "Praeludium. ex: E. G. / Diet: Buxtehuden" (BuxWV 143); pedal.
#10: p. 48, "Canzonet ex: D: F / Diet: Buxtehuden" (BuxWV 168).
#12: p. 58, "Praeludium: ex: G: B: / Diet: Buxtehuden" (BuxWV 163, unicum).
#13: p. 66, "Toccata. ex. F. a. / Diet Buxtehuden" (BuxWV 156); pedal.
#14: p. 72, "Toccata. ex. G: ♮ / Diet. Buxtehuden" (BuxWV 164).
#15: p. 75, "Praeludium. ex. G. B. / Diet: Buxteh:" (BuxWV 149); pedal.
#16: p. 82, "Nun lob mein Seel den Herren / Diet Buxtehuden" (BuxWV 213).
Other composer: "Diet. J.H. Buttstaed" (#11).
Inventory: Riedel, 198, 200, Collected Works, 15B: 20–21.

Mus. ms. 22541/1, "Praeludien und Fugen gesammlet von Zegert":
#2, p. 6: "Nun komm der Heyden Heyland. D.B." (BuxWV 211); 3 staves.

#7, p. 22: "Her Christ der einig Gottes Sohn. D.B." (BuxWV 192); 2 staves; pedal [added later]; R, O.

#21, p. 64: "Der Tag der ist so freüdenreich. D.B." (BuxWV 182); 3 staves.

#23, p. 69: "Puer natus in Bethlehem. D.B." (BuxWV 217); 3 staves.

#26, p. 72: "Gelobet seÿstu Jesu Christ. D.B." (BuxWV 189); 3 staves.

#37, p. 96: "In dulci jubilo. D.B." (BuxWV 197); 3 staves.

#40, p. 100: "Lobt Gott ihr Christen. D.B." (BuxWV 202); 3 staves.

Other composers: J. B. Bach, J. S. Bach, Böhm, Buttstedt, Fischer, Hanff, Heuschkel, Kauffmann, Keller, Kniller, Pachelbel, Vetter, Walther, Witte, Zachow.

Inventory: Klotz, NBA IV/2, KB 26–30.

Mus. ms. 22541/2, "Praeludien und Fugen gesammlet von Zegert":

#1, p. 1: "Wie schön leüchtet der Morgenstern. D.B." (BuxWV 223, unicum); 2 staves; pedal at end; ornaments added later.

#11, p. 25: "Nun komm der Heyden Heyland. D.B." (BuxWV 211); 3 staves.

#53, p. 100: "Gelobet seÿstu Jesu Christ. D. Buxtehude" (BuxWV 189); 3 staves.

#54, p. 101: "Lobt Gott ihr Christen allzugleich. D.B." (BuxWV 202); 3 staves.

#56, p. 103: "In dulci jubilo. D.B." (BuxWV 197); 3 staves.

#57, p. 104: "Der Tag der ist so freudenreich. D.B." (BuxWV 182); 3 staves.

#58, p. 106: "Puer natus in Bethlehem. D.B." (BuxWV 217); 3 staves.

Other composers: Alberti, J. B. Bach, J. S. Bach, Böhm, Buttstett, Fischer, Hanff, Heuschkel, Kauffmann, Keller, Kniller, Telemann, Pachelbel, Vetter, Walther, Witt, Zachow.

Inventory: Klotz, NBA IV/2, KB 30–33.

Mus. ms. 22541/3, "Praeludien und Fugen gesammlet von Zegert":

#24, p. 148: "Wir dancken dir Herr Jesu Christ, daß du gen Himmel. D.B." (BuxWV 224, unicum); 3 staves.

#33, p. 162: "Jesus Christus unser Heÿland. D.B." (BuxWV 198, unicum); 2 staves.

#36, p. 165: "Komm Heiliger Geist, Herre Gott. D.B." (BuxWV 199, unicum); 3 staves.

#37, p. 167: "Komm Heiliger Geist, Herre Gott. D.B." (BuxWV 200, unicum); 3 staves.

#47, p. 181: "Nun bitten wir den Heiligen Geist. D.B." (BuxWV 208, unicum); 3 staves.

#48, p. 182: "Nun bitten wir den Heiligen Geist. D.B." (BuxWV 209, unicum); 3 staves.

Other composers: J.B. Bach, J.S. Bach, Böhm, Buttstedt, Fischer, Heuschkel, Kauffmann, Pachelbel, D. Strunck, Telemann, Vetter, Walther, Zachow.

Inventory: Klotz, NBA IV/2, KB 33–35.

Mus. ms. 30381; convolute:

#3, p. 21; "Praeludium con Fuga ex F ♮. pedaliter. di Buxtehud. Scrips: Johannes Ringk" (BuxWV 145).

Other composers copied by Ringk: Böhm, Bruhns, Buttstedt, Pachelbel, Werckmeister.

Inventory: Kilian, NBA KB IV/5–6, 200–201.

Mus. ms. 40644 ("Möllersche Handschrift"):

#25, fol. 47r: "Praeludium a cis con Pedale di Buxdehude" (BuxWV 151); 2 staves.

#29, fol. 52v: "Toccata ex G ♮ Sig^{re} Diet Buxtehudee" (BuxWV 165); 2 staves through m.96, tablature to m. 103 (end).

Other composers: Albinoni, Joh. Andreas Bach, J. S. Bach, Böhm, Bruhns, Coberg, Dieupart, Edelmann, Fabricius, Flor, Heidorn, Lebègue, Lully, Mattheson, Pachelbel, Pez, Reincken, Ritter, Steffani, Zachow.

Inventory: Kilian, NBA IV/5-6, KB 100.

Mus. ms. Bach P 801:

#50, p. 333: "Te Deum Laudamus da Dieterich Buxtehude, Organista Lubec:" (BuxWV 218); 2-3 staves; pedal; R, O.

Other composers: J.S. Bach, Bustijn, Clerambault, d'Andrieu, d'Anglebert, Dieupart, Kauffmann, J.L. Krebs, Lebègue, Le Roux, Lübeck, Marcello, Marchand, Neufville, Nivers, Telemann.

Inventory: Klotz, NBA IV/2, KB 18–20; Zietz, 38–60.

Mus. ms. Bach P 802:

#3, p. 17: "Nun freut euch lieben Christen gemein, a 2 Clav: Diet: Buxteh:" (BuxWV 210); 3 staves; R, O.

#5, p. 57: "Gelobet seystu Jesu Christ. à 2 Clav: Diet: Buxtehude (BuxWV 188, unicum); 3 staves; pedal; R, O.

Other composers: Alberti, J.B. Bach, J.S. Bach, Böhm, Bruhns, Kauffmann, J.T. Krebs, Leiding, Lübeck, Pachelbel, Reincken, Vogler, Walther, Weckmann.

Inventory: Klotz, NBA IV/2, KB 21–25; Zietz, 15–37.

2. Brussels, Bibliothèque du Conservatoire Royal de Musique [Bc]

Litt U, No. 26659/ Wagener, "Dietrich Buxtehude, 11 Orgelstücke // Nicol. Bruhns, 2 Orgelstücke":

#1, p. 3: "Magnificat primi toni di Diter. Buxtehude" (BuxWV 203, unicum); 2 staves; pedal.

#2, p. 8: "Preludio da Dieterico Buxtehude" (BuxWV142); 2 staves; pedal red.

#3, p. 13: "Preludio" (BuxWV153); 2 staves; pedal red.

#4, p. 17: "Preludio da Diet: Buxtehude" (BuxWV139); 2 staves; pedal red.

#5, p. 21: "Preludio da Diet: Buxtehude" (BuxWV 140); 2 staves; pedal red.

#6, p. 24: "Preludio da Dietr: Buxtehude" (BuxWV 141); 2 staves; pedal red.

#7, p. 29: "Preludio di Diet: Buxtehude" (BuxWV 145); 2 staves; pedal red.

#8, p. 33: "Preludio da Dietr: Buxtehude" (BuxWV 143); 2 staves; pedal red.

#9, p. 37: "Toccata da Diet: Buxtehude" (BuxWV 156); 2 staves; pedal red.

#10, p. 42: "Preludio da Dieter: Buxtehude" (BuxWV 149); 2 staves; pedal red.

#11, p. 46: "Preludio di Dieter: Buxtehude" (BuxWV 146); 2 staves; pedal red.

#12, p. 51: "Preludio da Nicola Bruhns" (G major); 2 staves; pedal red.

#13, p. 57: "Nun komm der Heyden Heyland, von Nicol: Bruhns"; 3 staves: "Rückpositiv, Oberwerk, Pedal.

Inventory: Collected Works, 15B: 21–22.

3. Copenhagen, Det Kongelige Bibliotek [Kk]

Mu 6806.1399 / olim C II,49 (the Ryge manuscript), tablature:

#1, fol. [IIv]: "Allemanda di D.B.H."; #2–4: "Courant," "Saraband," "Gique" (BuxWV 235, unicum).

#5, fol. 3v: "Allemanda ex E di D.B.H."; #6–8: "Courent," "Saraband," "Gique" (BuxWV 236).

#9, fol. 5v: "Menue" (Lebègue, *Second Livre de Clavessin* [Paris, 1687 / Amsterdam, 1701], #5 from "Suitte en de la ré."

#10, fol. 6v: "Allemanda di D.B.H."; #11–13: "Courent," "Saraband, "Gique" (BuxWV Anh. 12; recte: Lebègue, [1687/1701], #1–4 from "Suitte en de la ré.")

#14, fol. 8v: "Courent zimble di D. Buxtehude" (BuxWV 245, unicum).

#15, fol. 10v: "Aria di D.B.H." (BuxWV 249, unicum).

#16, fol. 13v: "Allemanda d'Amour Suitte del Signore Dieterico Buxtehuden"; #17–20: "Courent," "Sarabande d'Amour," "Saraband," Gique" (BuxWV 233, unicum).

#21, fol. 15v: "Aria di D. Buxtehude" (BuxWV 246, unicum).

#22, fol. 22v: "Allemand di Dieter. Buxtehude"; #23–25: "Courent," "Saraband, "Gique" (BuxWV 227, unicum).

#26, fol. 25v: "Aria More Palatino di D.B.H." (BuxWV 247, unicum).

#27, fol. 31v: "Allemand di D.B.H."; #28–30: "Courent," "Saraband," "Gique" (BuxWV 240, unicum).

#31, fol. 33v: "Aria: Partite diverse una Aria d'Inventione detta La Capriciosa del Dieterico Buxtehude" (BuxWV 250, unicum).

#32, fol. 42v: "Simphonie" (BuxWV Anh. 8).

#33, fol. 43v: "Allemand di D.B.H."; #34–36: "Courent," "Saraband," "Gique" (BuxWV 238).

#37, fol. 45v: "Aria" (Pachelbel, *Hexachordum Apollinis* [1699], III).

#38, fol. 46v: "Allemand di D.B.H."; #39–42: "Courent," "Saraband," "Saraband," "Gique" (BuxWV 237, unicum).

#43, fol. 48v: "Aria" (Pachelbel [1699], II).

#44, fol. 51v: "Allemand di D.B.H. . . . Variatiò Le double"; #45–47: "Courent . . . Variatiò: Le Double," "Saraband," "Saraband" (BuxWV 234, unicum).

#48, fol. 53v: "Rofilis di D.B.H." (BuxWV 248, unicum).

#49, fol. 54v: "Aria" (Pachelbel [1699], I).

#50, fol. 56v: "Courent" (BuxWV Anh. 6; BuxWV deest, Suite in d).

#51, fol. 57v: "Allemand di D.B.H."; #52–54: "Courent," "Saraband," "Gique" (BuxWV 242, unicum).

#55, fol. 59v: "Aria" (Reinken, Die Meierin).

#56, fol. 65v: "Courent" (BuxWV Anh. 7).

#57, fol. 66v: "Allemand di D:B:H:"; #58–60: "Courent," "Saraband," "Gique" (BuxWV Anh. 13; recte: Lebègue [1687]/1701, #6,8,9,11 from "Suitte En g ré sol b").

#61, fol. 68v: "Allemand di D.B.H."; #62–64: "Courent," "Saraband," "Gique" (BuxWV 243, unicum).

#65, fol. 70v: "Allemand di D.B.H."; #66–67: "Courent," "Saraband" (BuxWV 229, unicum).

#68, fol. 72v: "Allemand di D.B.H."; #69–71: "Courent," "Saraband," "Gique" (BuxWV 230, unicum).

#72, fol. 74v: "Allemand ex A ♮ di D.B.H."; #73–75: "Courent," "Saraband," "Gique" (BuxWV 244, unicum).

#76, fol. 76v: "Allemand ex G ♮ di D.B.H."; #77–79: "Courent," "Saraband," "Gique" (BuxWV 241, unicum)

#80, fol. 78v: "Allemand ex C ♮ di D.B.H."; #81–84: "Courent," "Saraband," "Sarabande La Seconde," "Gique" (BuxWV 226, unicum).

#85, fol. 80v: "Allemand ex C ♮ di D.B.H."; #86–88: "Courent," "Saraband . . . Double," "Gique" (BuxWV 228, unicum).

#89, fol. 82v: "Allemanda D ♮ di D.B.H."; #90: "Courent" (BuxWV 232, unicum).

Inventory also in Gustafson II, 68–76; Beckmann, ed. Buxtehude, Sämtliche Suiten (EB 8078), 116–17.

4. The Hague, Gemeentemuseum [*DHgm*], 4.G.14:

#22, p. 40: "Nun lob mein Seel den Herren [versus 2]. D.B." (BuxWV 213, vs. 2); 2 staves.

#24, p. 42: [Nun lob, mein Seel]. "D.B." (BuxWV 214); 2 staves; pedal.

#25, p. 44: [Nun lob, mein Seel]. "D.B." (BuxWV 213, vs. 3); 2 staves.

#30, p. 70: "Gott der Vater wohn uns beÿ. D.B." (BuxWV 190); 3 staves.

#45, p. 96: "Mensch wiltu leben seeliglich. D.B." (BuxWV 206); 3 staves.

#47, p. 98: "Vater unser im Himmelreich. D.B." (BuxWV 207, vs. 1); 2 staves.

#49, p. 102: "Vater unser im Himmelreich. D.B." (BuxWV 207); 3 staves.

#51, p. 104: "Vater unser im Himmelreich. D.B." (BuxWV 219); 3 staves.

#59, p. 113: "Christ unser Herr zum Jordan. D.B." (BuxWV 180, unicum); 3 staves.

#77, p. 141: "Ach Herr mich armen Sünder. D.B." (BuxWV 178); 2-3 staves.

#84, p. 151: "Durch Adams Fall ist ganz verderbt. D.B." (BuxWV 183); 3 staves.

#88, p. 157: "Es ist das Heÿl uns kommen her. D.B." (BuxWV 186); 3 staves.

#103, p. 179: "Kommt her zu mir spricht Gottes Sohn. D.B." (BuxWV 201); 3 staves.

#114, p. 197: "Herr Christ der einig Gottes Sohn. D.B." (BuxWV 192); 3 staves.

#116, p. 199: "Von Gott will ich nicht laßen. D.B." (BuxWV 221); 2 staves.

#117, p. 200: [Von Gott will ich nicht lassen]. "D.B." (BuxWV 220); 2 staves; R, O.

#172, p. 295: "Es spricht der Unweisen Mund wohl. D.B." (BuxWV 187); 3 staves.

#178, p. 305: "Eine feste Burg ist unser Gott. D.B." (BuxWV 184, unicum); 3 staves.

#181, p. 311: "Wär Gott nicht mit uns diese Zeit. D.B." (BuxWV 222); 3 staves.

#186, p. 318: "Erhalt uns Herr beÿ deinem Wort. D.B." (BuxWV 185); 3 staves.

#206, p. 356: "Auf meinen lieben Gott. D.B." (BuxWV 179, unicum); 2 staves.

Other composers: Alberti, Armsdorff, J. B. Bach, J. M. Bach, J. S. Bach, Böhm, Buttstedt, Erich, Hanff, Kauffmann, Kellner, J. T. Krebs, Leiding, Pachelbel, Scheidemantel, N. A. Strunck, Telemann, Vetter, Walther, Zachow.

Inventory: Klotz, NBA IV/3, KB 19–28.

5. Leipzig, Städtische Bibliotheken – Musikbibliothek [*LEm*]

Sammlung Becker, Ms. III.8.4 ("Andreas-Bach-Buch")

#9, fol. 33v: "Ciaccone di Diet: Buxtehude" (BuxWV 159); 2 staves; pedal.

#23, fol. 8r/53a: "Praeludium. con ped. di Sig^re Diet Buxtehude" (BuxWV 150, unicum); 2 staves; pedal.

#26, fol. 61v: "Fuga di D.B.H." (BuxWV 174, unicum); 2 staves.

#42, fol. 91r: "Ciacona di Dit. Buxtehude" (BuxWV 160, unicum); 2 staves; pedal.

#51, fol. 107v: "Passacalia Pedaliter di Diet. Buxtehude" (Buxwv 161, unicum); 2 staves.

#53, fol. 110r: "O Lux beata Trinitas col Pedali da D:^co Buxtehude" (BuxWV 216 [fragment], unicum); 2 staves.

#55, fol. 111v: "Praeludium in C Pedaliter di D Buxtehude" (BuxWV 137, unicum); 2 staves. Other composers: J. S. Bach, Böhm, Buttstedt, Fischer, Küchenthal, Kuhnau, Marais, Marchand, Pachelbel, Pestel, Polaroli, Reincken, Ritter, Telemann, Witt.

Inventory: Kilian, NBA IV/5–6, KB 125.

Sammlung Becker, Ms. III.8,26

p. 25: Magnificat 1mi Toni 9ni Toni & No 5. alla Duodecema. di Dietrich Buxtehude Organ. in Lübeck (BuxWV 204).

p. 27: "Versus Noni Toni".

MS S4: "Toccata in G dur . . . Sign: Buxtehude G. Preller" (BuxWV 165); 2 staves.

6. Lübeck, Bibliothek der Hansestadt [*LÜh*]

Mus. A 373; tablature:
Italics indicate autograph insertions.

#1, fol. 1a: "I.N.I. Alles waß ihr thut mit Worten oder mit Wercken â 9: vel *piu. di Dieterico Buxtehude*" (BuxWV 4); [S A T] B; V1 V2 [Va1 Va2 Vn]; [Bc].

#2, fol. 5b: "Ihr lieben Christen freut euch â 13" (BuxWV 51, unicum); S1 S2 A T B; V+Cn1 V+Cn2 V+Cn3 Va+Tn1 Va+Tn2 Vn+Tn3 Fg; TrSor1 TrSor2; Con.

#3, fol. 11b: "Nun dancket alle Gott, der â 13: v. 18: . . . con le Capella *di Diet. Buxteh.* (BuxWV 79); [S1 S2 A T B]; V1 V2 Vn; Cn1 Cn2 Fg; Tr1 Tr2; [Bc].

#4, fol. 15b: "Wo soll ich fliehen hin. Dialogus â 9:" (BuxWV 112, unicum); S A T B; V1 V2 Va1 Va2 Vn; Con.

#5, fol. 19b: "Wie wird ernewet wie wird erfrewet à 16 . . . con Repieno. *di Diet: Buxtehude* (BuxWV 110, unicum); S1 S2 A T1 T2 B; V+Cn1 V+Cn2 V+Cn3 Cym; Tr1 Tr2 Tr3 Tn+Va1 Tn+Va2 Tn3+Vn; Org.

#6, fol. 26b: "Bedencke Mensch daß Ende â 7"(BuxWV 9); S1 S2 B; V1 V2 V3 Vn; [Bc].

#7, fol. 30a: "Hertzlich lieb hab' ich dich o Herr a. 10. vel 15. . . . *di Dieter. Buxteh.*" (BuxWV 41, unicum); S1 S2 A T B; V&Cl1 V&Cl2 [Va1 Va2 Vn]; Org.

#8, fol. 38b: "Lauda Sion Salvatorem . . . *di Dieter. Buxteh.*" (BuxWV 68); S1 S2 B; V1 V2; [Bc].

#9, fol. 40b: "*Nichts soll uns scheiden von der Liebe Gottes, à. 6. 3. Voci e 3. Strum. di Dieter. Buxteh.*" (BuxWV 77, unicum); S A B; [V1 V2 Vn]; [Bc].

#10, fol. 43b: "Ich habe Lust abzuscheiden â 6." (BuxWV 47, unicum); S1 S2 B; V1 V2 Vn; [Bc].

#11, fol. 47b: "Jesu meine Freude â 6." (BuxWV 60); S1 S2 B; V1 V2 Fg; [Bc].

#12, fol. 51b: "Was frag ich nach der Welt â 6. . . . di Dieterico Buxtehude" (BuxWV 104, unicum); S A B; V1 V2 Vn; [Bc].

#13, fol. 56b: "Meine Seele wiltu ruhn â 6." (BuxWV 74); S1 S2 B; V1 V2 Vn; [Bc].

#14, fol. 60b: "Herr, wenn ich nur dich habe â 4." (BuxWV 39); S; V1 V2 Vn; [Bc].

#15, fol. 65b: "Ich halte es dafür a.5." (BuxWV 48); S B; V Vt Vn; [Bc].

#16, fol. 70b: "Ich bin eine Bluhme zu Saron, â 4" (BuxWV 45, unicum); B; V1 V2 Vn; [Bc].

#17, fol. 74b: "Herr nun läst du deinen Diener im friede fahren â 3." (BuxWV 37); T; V1 V2; [Bc].

#18, fol. 77a: "Also hat Gott die Welt geliebet â 4." (BuxWV 5, unicum); S; V1 V2 Vg; [Bc].

#19, fol. 79b: "Lauda anima mea Dominum â 4." (BuxWV 67, unicum); S; V1 V2 Vn; [Bc].

#20, fol. 82b: "Jesu meine freud und Lust â 5." (BuxWV 59, unicum); A; V1 V2 Vt Vn; [Bc].

#21, fol. 86b: "Dis ist der Tag den der Herr gemacht hat â 4." [Fragment, crossed out] (BuxWV 16, unicum); V1 V2 Vn; [Bc].

Inventory also in Collected Works, 9: 266.
Extensive discussion in Karstädt, *Lübecker Kantatenband*.

Mus. U 212: "Gique et De Deum laudamur à 2 Clav: et Ped; di Bustehude Johannes Ringk 1730"
#1, fol. 1v: "Presto" [Muffat]
#2, fol. 2r: "Te Deum laudamur. à 2. Clav: et Ped: di D Bustehude" (BuxWV 218, mm. 1-40); 2 staves, ped.

7. Lund, Universitetsbibliotek [L], Sammlung Wenster

W.Lit. A 29: "Hertzlich thut mich verlangen / 2 Violini. Soprano con Organo di Buxtehude" (BuxWV 42, unicum); parts: S; V1 V2; Org.

W.Lit. N 1: "Cantzon ex: G: ♭. G. Lindemann Anno 1713 d: 6 April" (BuxWV 173, unicum); tab.

W.Lit. N 1b: "Praeludium di. Dieter. Buxtehude" (BuxWV 154 [fragment], unicum); tab.

W.Lit. N 2: "Praeludium. manualit: ex: G: ♮ di. Diet: Buxtehude. G: Lindemann." (BuxWV 162, unicum); tab.

W.Lit. N 5: "Praeludium ex: E: ♭. di. D.B.H. Pedalieter. G. Lindemann Ao: 1714 d: 17 Maÿ" (BuxWV 142); tab.

W.Lit. N 6: "Cantzon[et] ex: C: ♮ di. D. Buxthehude G: Lindemann Ao: 1713. d: 5. Martÿ" (BuxWV 167, unicum); tab.

W.Lit. N 8: "Cantzon. ex G ♮ di. Diet: Buxtehude. G: Lindemann." (BuxWV 170, unicum); tab.

W.Lit. N 9: "Cantzon ex E. ♭. di: Diet: Buxtehude. G: Lindemann . . . 1714. 31. Jan:" (BuxWV 169); tab.

W.Lit. U 5: "Praeludium ex: G: ♭. di. Diete: Buxthehude. G: Lindemann Ao: 1714 d: 15. Maÿ" (BuxWV 149); tab.

W.Lit. U 6: "Praeludium ex: D: ♮ di. Diet: Buxtehude . . . 1714 d: 3 Janu:" (BuxWV 139); tab.

8. New Haven, Yale University, Music Library [NH]

LM 4838
#10, p. 65: "Praeludium ex C ♮ di Diet: Buxtehude" (BuxWV 138, unicum); 2 staves; pedal.
Other composers: Bach, Sechter
Inventory: Kilian, NBA IV/5–6, KB, 146.

LM 4983
#1, p. 1: "Immanuel! Toccata di Sigre Dieter. Buxtehude G ♮" (BuxWV 164); 2 staves;
#5, p. 6: "Canzonetta Diet. Buxtehude" (BuxWV 172, unicum); 2 staves.
Other composers: Bach, Fischer, Pachelbel, N. Vetter
Inventory: Kobayashi, 170. The manuscript is presently out of order but is easily restored to its original order by placing Kobayashi's first three entries between pages 12 and 13 below.

Lowell Mason Codex ("EB—1688;" olim LM 5056)
#53, p. 81: "Sonata a 2 Clavier/Pedal: Box de Hou" (BuxWV Anh. 5, unicum); 2 staves plus tablature for pedal line.
#54, p. 84: "Praeludium D. Box de Hude. Org: Libeck Ped:" (BuxWV152, unicum); 2 staves.

#55, p. 88: "Praeambulum di Sig. D. Box de H. Ped:" (BuxWV 158, unicum); 2 staves.

#56, p. 92: "Praeludium del Sig. D. Box de H" (BuxWV142); 2 staves.

#57, p. 100: "Canzon Sig. D. Box de H." (BuxWV 166); 2 staves.

#66, p. 117: "Fuga Sig: Box de Hude" (BuxWV 175, unicum); 2 staves.

#67, p. 120: "Praeludium Sig: D Box de Hou. Org: Libec" (BuxWV 148); 2 staves; pedal.

#71, p. 134: "Praeludium Sig: Box de Hude à Libeck" (BuxWV 144, unicum); 2 staves, pedal.

#72, p. 137: "Praeludium Sigre. Box de Hude ex G ♮" (BuxWV 136, unicum); 2 staves; pedal.

#73, p. 142: "Toccata Sig^r. Box de Hude ex D ped: 1684" (BuxWV 155, unicum); 2 staves.

Other composers: (part 1) Böhme, Bölsche, Heidorn, Kerll, Kindermann, J. Krieger, Kuhnau, Pachelbel, Pasquini, Poglietti, Radeck, N.A. Strungk, Weisthoma; (part 2) J. S. Bach, Kirnberger.

Inventories: (part 1) Riedel, 106–111; (part 2) Kilian, NBA IV/56, KB 151.

9. Uppsala, Universitetsbibliotek [Uu]

Instrumentalmusik i handskrift:

1:12 "Sonata a doi Violini D.B.H." (BuxWV 270, unicum fragment); [Bc]

13:23 "Sonata due Violini è Violada gamba di Sig^n D.B.H." (BuxWV 269, unicum); parts: V1 V2 Vg; Org.

13:24 "Sonata à 2 1 Violon 1 Viol di gamb . . . di Dietrich Buxtehude Andreas Dubenn d. 27 Septembris Anno 1692" (BuxWV 267, unicum); parts: Vg Vn; Con.

13:25 "Sonata a 2 ex B con le Suite . . . Dieter: Buxtehude" (BuxWV 273,); parts: V Vg; Org.

13:26 "Sonata a 2 Violino è violadagamba di Dieter Buxtehude" (BuxWV 272, unicum); parts: V Vg; Con.

13:27 "Sonata â 3 2 Violini 1 Violdigamba: di Dieterich Buxtehude." (BuxWV 266, unicum); parts: V1 V2 Vg; Con.

13:28 "Sonata ex G ♮ a 3. doi Violini e violdagamba di Dit: Buxtehude" (BuxWV 271, unicum); parts: V1 V2 Vg; [Bc].

Ihre 285 (convolute):

p. 17: "1 Allem: ex Clav C . . . 2 Courant . . . 3 Saraband . . . D.B.H." (BuxWV 231, unicum); tab.

p. 22: "4 Allemand . . . 5 Courant . . . 6 Sarab: . . . 7 Gique . . . D.B.H." (BuxWV 238); tab.

p. 30: "8 Allemande . . . 9 Courant . . . 10 Saraband 11 Gique . . . D.B.H." (BuxWV 236); tab.

p. 38: "12 Allemand ex clave F . . . 13 Courant . . . 14 Sarab: . . . 15 Gique . . . D.B.H." (BuxWV 239, unicum); tab.

Other composers: Anonymous, Froberger, Lorentz, Reincken, Tunder.

Vokalmusik i handskrift:

6:1 "Ad Latus: Surge amica mea et veni . . . D.B.H." (BuxWV 75-4); parts: S1 S2 A T B; V1 V2 Va(F4); Con. + S1rip S2rip Arip; Va3com(C1); Vn(Bc,nf) [Bc](inc).

6:2 "Ad Pedes: Ecce Super montes pedes . . . Sig. D.B.H." (BuxWV 75-1); parts: S1 S2 A T B: V1 V2 Va(F4); Con. + Va3[com](C1); Vn(Bc,nf) Con.

6:3 "No 2 Ad Genua Christi: Ad ubera portabimini" . . . Sig. D.B.H." (BuxWV 75-2); parts: S1 S2 A T B; V1 V2 Va(F4); Con. + Vn(Bc,fig) Con.

6:4 "Afferte Domino gloriam honorem . . . D.B.H." (BuxWV 2); parts: S1 S2 B; Org.

6:5 "Du Frieden-Fürst Herr Jesu Christ . . . Dieterico Buxtehude" (BuxWV 21, unicum); parts: S1 S2 B; [V1] V2 Va1 Va2 Va3/Fg; [Bc].

6:6 "Ecce nunc benedicite . . . Sig: Dit. Buxteh." (BuxWV 23); parts: A T1 T2 B; V1 V2; Con. + Va1com; [Bc](nf).

6:7 "Aria. Entreist Euch meine Sinnen und steiget welcken ab . . . Sig. D.B.H." (BuxWV 25, unicum); parts: S; V1 V2; Con. + [Bc](nf).

6:9, AUTOGRAPH: "Fürwahr er trug unsere Kranckheit . . . Dieterico Buxtehude" (BuxWV 31, unicum); score: S1 S2 A T B; V1 V2 Vg1 Vg2 Vn/Fg; [Bc].

6:10a "Aria . . . Diet. Buxtehude" (*Auff Stimmet die Saiten* [BuxWV 116]; no text); tablature: A1 A2 B; Tr1 Tr2 Tn1 Tn2 Fg; [Bc].

6:11 "Herr wan Ich nur dich hab . . . Dit: Buxtehude" (BuxWV 38); parts: S; [V1] V2; Con.; tablature: S; V1 V2; [Bc].

6:12 "Jesu kom mein Trost und Lachen . . . Dit: Buxteh:" (BuxWV 58, unicum); parts: A T B; V1 V2 Vb(C2) Vn; [Bc].

6:13 "Aria ex D. Jesu meines Lebenß Leben . . . Diet: Buxtehude." (BuxWV 62, revised version); parts: S A T B; V1 V2 Va1 Va2 Vn; Con. + Fl(V1); [Bc], Con with crossed-out Con from earlier version.

6:14 "Aria In festo Circumcisionis . . . D.B.H." (*Klinget mit Freuden, ihr klaren Klarinen* [BuxWV 65]; sacred parody of BuxWV 119); parts: S1 S2 B; V1 V2; Tr1 Tr2; [Bc]. + S1; V1 V2; Vn(Bc,nf); tab: S1 S2 B; [V1 V2]; [Tr1 Tr2]; [Bc].

6:15 "Kompstu, kompstu, Licht der Heÿden . . . Dieterich Buxtehude" (BuxWV 66); parts: S1 S2 B; V1 V2 Vb1 Vb2 Vn; [Bc]. + Fl(V1)(inc).

6:16 "Missa a 4 [*sic*] alla brevis di Diterico Buxtehude" (BuxWV 114, unicum); parts: [S1 S2 A T B]; [Bc].

6:17 "Chiccona: Laudate pueri Dominum . . . Dieterico Buxtehude" (BuxWV 69); parts: S1 S2; Vg1(C1) Vg2(C3) Vg3(C3) Vg4(C4) Vg5(C4) Vn; [Bc](nf).

6:18 "Ad Pectus J. Christ: Sicut modo geniti infantes . . . D.B.H." (BuxWV 75-5); parts: A T B; V1 V2 Vg; Con. + Con [Bc].

6:19 "Aria: Was mich auf dieser Welt betrübt . . . D. Buxtehude" (BuxWV 105, unicum); parts: S; V1 V2; Con.

6:20 "Aria ex. E. Wenn ich Herr Jesu habe dich . . . D.B.H." (BuxWV 107, unicum); parts: A; [V1] V2 Con. + [Bc].

38:1 "Accedite Gentes, accurrite populi" (BuxWV 1, but anonymous); parts: S1 S2 A T B; V1 V2; Con. + V[rip] Vt[rip](G2) Vb1[rip] Vb2[rip]; [Bc] [Bc]

46:25 "De Passione nostri Jesu Christi Ad Cor Christi. Vulnerasti Cor meum soror mea . . . Sig: D.B.H." (BuxWV 75-6); parts: S1 S2 B; Vg1(C1) Vg2(C3) Vg3(C4) Vg4(F4) Vg5(F4); Con. + [Bc].

50:1a "All solch dein Gütt wir preisen . . . D. Buxtehude" (BuxWV 3); parts: S1 S2 A T B; V1 V2 Va1 Va2 Vn; Org. + Vn(Bc,fig) Con.; tab: [S1 S2 A T B]; [V1 V2 Va1 Va2 Vn]; [Bc].

50:2 "Alles was ihr thut, dass thut im Nahmen Jesu . . . D.B.H." (BuxWV 4); parts: S A T B; V1 V2 Va&V[com]1 Va&V[com]2; [Bc]. + Vn(Bc,nf) [Vn](Bc,nf) [Bc].

50:3 "An Filius non est Dei . . . Dieterico Buxtehude" (BuxWV 6, unicum); parts: A T B; V1 V2 Vg; Org.

50:4 "Aperite mihi portas iustitiae . . . Dietericus Buxtehude" (BuxWV 7, unicum); parts: A T B; V1 V2; Con.

50:5 "Befiehl dem Engel FIGURALITER . . . D. Buxtehude" (BuxWV 10, unicum); parts: S A T B; V1 V2 Vn; Org.

50:6 "Motetto. Benedicam Dominum im omni tempore . . . Dieteric Buxtehude" (BuxWV 113, unicum); parts: S1cto S2cto Acto Tcto Bcto; SATB [capella]; V1 V2 Vn; Cn1 Cn2 Fg; Tr1 Tr2 Tr3 Tr4 Po Bom/TnG; Tn1(C3) Tn2(C4) Tn3(F4); [Bc].

50:7 "Das neue gebohrne Kindelein . . . Dieter. Buxtehude" (BuxWV 13, unicum); parts: S A T B; V1 V2 V3 Vn/Fg; Org.

50:8 "Dixit Dominus Domino meo . . . D.B.H." (BuxWV 17); parts: S; V1 V2 Va1 Va2 Sp/Vn(fig); Org. + Vn(Bc,fig).

50:9 "Dreÿ schöne Dinge sind . . . Sigⁿ: D.B.H." (BuxWV 19); parts: S B; V1 V2 Vn/Fg; Con. + Vn(Bc,nf).

50:10 "Du Frieden-Furst Herr Jesu Christ FIGURALITER . . . D: Buxtehude" (BuxWV 20, unicum); parts: S1 S2 A T B; V1 V2 Vn; [Bc].

50:11 "Auff Himmelfahrt Christi. Du Lebenß-fürst Herr Jesu Christ . . . D.B.H." (BuxWV 22); parts: S A T B; V1 V2 Vt1 Vt2 Vn; Org. + [S1] [A](inc); Con.

50:12, AUTOGRAPH: "MEMBRA JESU NOSTRI PATIENTIS SANCTISSIMA . . . Dieterico Buxtehude . . . 1680" (BuxWV 75); tab: S1 S2 A T B; V1 V2 Vn; Vg1 Vg2 Vg3 Vg4 Vg5; [Bc].

50:13 "Eins bitte ich vom Herren . . . Dieter: Buxtehude" (BuxWV 24); parts (1): S1 S2 A T; V1 V2 Vcom&Va1 Vcom&Va2 Fg; Org.; parts (2, Swedish [Ett beder iag af Herren]): S1 S2 A T B; parts (3): B; + S1/2 [Aria]; Va2; Fl1(V1) Fl2(V2); Vn(Bc,nf).

50:14 "Erhalt unß Herr beÿ deinen Wort. figuraliter . . . D.B.H." (BuxWV 27); parts: S A T B; V1 V2 Vn/Bom; Con.

50:15 "Schlacht, Künstler! die Pauken / Erfreue dich Erde; du Himmel Erschall! . . . D.B.H." (BuxWV 26, 122); parts (1, "Schlagt . . . [BuxWV 122]) : SSAB;V& Va1V&Va2 Vn; Tr1Tr2Tm;Org.;parts(2,"Erfreue . . . " [BuxWV 26]): S1 S2 AB; + Tr1 Tr2; tab. ("Erfreue . . . "): S1 S2 A B; V&Va1 V&Va2 Vn; Tr1 Tr2 Tm; [Bc].

50:16 "Fallax mundus ornat vultus / Dolus latet sed occultus . . . Dit: Buxteh:" (BuxWV 28); parts: S; V1 V2; [Bc]. + [Bc] [Bc](nf).

50:17 Furchtet euch nicht Sihe ich verkundige Euch große freude . . . Dit: Buxtehude." (BuxWV 30); parts (1): S B pro libitu; V1 V2; Org; parts (2, Swedish [Frukten Eder Ey], concerto only): S B; + S; [V1]; [Bc] [Bc] [Th](tab).

50:18 "In Festo Ascensionis Christi: Gen Himmel zu dem Vatter mein . . . D.B.H." (BuxWV 32); parts: S; V Vg(C3-F4); Org. + Con

50:19 "Gott hilff mir denn daß Waßer geht mir biß an die Seele . . . Dieter: Buxtehude" (BuxWV 34, unicum); parts: S1 S2 A T B1 B2; V1 V2 Va1 Va2 Vn; Org.

51:1 "Herr auff dich traue ich. . . . Dieter: Buxtehude" (BuxWV 35); parts: S; V1 V2; [Bc].

51:2 AUTOGRAPH: "Herr ich lase dich nicht du segnest mich denn . . . Dieterico Buxtehude m.p." (BuxWV 36, unicum); parts: T B; V1 V2 Vg/Vb/Tn1 Vg/Vb/Tn2 Vn/Vg; Org.

51:3 "Herr nun läst du deinen Diener . . . Dieter: Buxtehude" (BuxWV 37); parts: T; V1 V2; Con. + T (Swedish); Con(inc).

51:4 "Ich habe Lust abzuscheiden . . . Dieterico Buxtehude" (BuxWV 46); parts: S1 S2 B; V1 V2 Vn/Fg; Org. + Vn(Bc,nf).

51:5 "Je höher du bist Je mehr demutige . . . D.B.H." (BuxWV 55); parts: S S B; V1 V2 Vn; Con. + Con(nf).

51:6 "Ich sprach in meinem Hertzen, wohlan Ich will woll Leben . . . Diterico Buxtehude" (BuxWV 49); parts: S; V1 V2 V3 Fg; Org ("1682 4 October").

51:7 "Jesu dulcis Memoria . . . Dieterico Buxtehude Anno 1676 in Junio" (BuxWV 56); parts: S1 S2; V1 V2 Fg; Con.

51:8 "Chiaccona: Jesu dulcis memoria . . . Dieter: Buxtehude" (BuxWV 57, unicum); parts: A T B; V1 V2; Con(nf).

51:9 "Jesulein du Tausendschön . . . Dietri. Buxteh:" (BuxWV 63, unicum); parts: A T B; V1 V2 Vn/Fg; Org.

51:10 "No. 7. Ad Faciem Jesu Nostri / Illustra faciem tuam Super Servum tuum . . . Dit: Buxtehude." (BuxWV 75-7); parts: S1 S2 A T B; V1 V2 Vg; Con. + Con.

51:11 "Ist es Recht . . . Dieter: Buxtehude" (BuxWV 54, unicum); parts: S1 S2 A T B; V1 V2 Va&Vcom1 Va2&Vcom2 Vn; Org.

51:12 "Jubilate Domino . . . D.B.H." (BuxWV 64, unicum); parts: A; Vg(C1-F4); Con.

51:13 "Aria a 3 Voci . . . Sopra la Nozze di Sua Maesta Il Re di Svetia. 1680. D.B." (BuxWV 119); parts: S S B; [Bc].

51:13a, AUTOGRAPH: tablature
#1, fol. 1r: "Sonata . . . Aria. O fröhliche Stunden . . . Dieter: Buxtehude m.p." (BuxWV 85); S1 S2 A B; V1 V2 Vb1 Vb2 Vn.
#2, fol. 3r: "Aria Sopra la Nozze di Sua Maesta il Re di Svecia [Klinget für Freuden] . . . Dieter: Buxtehude m.p." (BuxWV 119); S S B; V1 V2 Vn; Tr1 Tr2; Con.

51:14 "Lauda Sion Salvatorem . . . Dietr: Buxdehude Anno 1682 d 29 May" (BuxWV 68); parts: S1 S2 B; V1 V2; Org. + [Bc](nf) [Bc](nf).

51:15 "LVII. Psalm Davids: Mein Hertz ist bereit . . . Dieter: Buxtehude" (BuxWV 73, unicum); parts: B; V1 V2 V3 Vn; Org. + Fl1(V1) Fl3(V3); [Bc].

51:16 "Meine Seele Wiltu ruhn . . . Dieter: Buxtehude" (BuxWV 74); parts: S1 S2 B; V1 V2 Vn/Fg; Org.

51:17 "Nun last unß Gott den Herren figuraliter / Nu låt oß Gudh wår Herra . . . D.B.H." (BuxWV 81); parts: S A T B (Swedish); V1 V2; Con. + Vn(Bc,nf) Con`

51:18 "Motetto a cinq: voc: O Clemens o mitis o Coelestis pater. . . . Dieterico Buxtehude." (BuxWV 82); parts: S; V Vt[1](C1) Vt2(C3) Va4(F4); Con. + Ob(V); Con.

51:19 "O Gottes Stadt . . . Diete Buxtehude" (BuxWV 87); parts: S; V1 V2 Va Vn; Org.

51:20 "O Lux Beat Trinitas . . . D.B.H." (BuxWV 89); parts: S1 S2; V1 V2 V3 Vn/Fg; Con.

51:21 "Sub Communione. Aria. O Wie selig sind die zu Abendmahl . . . Dieterico Buxtehud" (BuxWV 90); parts: [T] B; V1 V2 Vn; tab: T B; V1 V2; [Bc].

51:22 "De Augustissimo Sacramento / Pange lingua gloriosi Corporis mūsterium . . . Diter: Buxtehude." (BuxWV 91); parts: S1 S2 A B; V1 V2 Vt1 Vt2 Vn; Con.

51:23 "Ad Manus Jesu Christi: Quid sunt plagae istae in medio . . . . D. BuxteHude" (BuxWV 75-3); parts: S1 S2 A T B; V1 V2 Va(F4); Con. + Va3(c1); Con Con.

51:24 "Salve Desiderium . . . D.B.H." (BuxWV 93); parts: S1 S2 B; V1 V2 Vn/Fg; Org. + [Bc].

51:25 "Salve Jesu . . . Dieter: Buxtehude" (BuxWV 94); parts: S1 S2; V1 V2; Con.

51:26 "Sicut Moses exaltavit serpentem in deserto. ita. . . . D. Buxtehude" (BuxWV 97); parts: S; V1 V2 Vg; Org. + Vn(Bc,nf).

51:27 "Singet dem Hern Ein neues Liedt . . . D.B.H." (BuxWV 98); parts: S; V; Org(inc).

51:28 "Welt-Valet. Aria Welt Packe dich, Ich sehne mich Nur nach dem Himmel . . . Diterico Buxtehude" (BuxWV 106); parts: S1 S2 B; V1 V2 Vn; Org. + Vn(Bc,nf).

51:29 "Aria. Wie soll ich dich empfangen und wie begegne ich dir . . . Diet: Buxtehude" (BuxWV 109); parts: S1 S2 B; V1 V2 Fg; Org.

67:8 "Cantate Domino" (BuxWV 12); parts: S1 S2 B; Org.

67:24 "Herr, Wenn ich nur dich Habe" (BuxWV 39); parts (1): S; V1 V2 Vn; Org. + Org; parts (2): S; V1 V2 Vg; Org. + Vn(Bc,nf); Th(Bc).

70:8 "Aria [Schwinget euch himmel an] . . . D.B.H." (BuxWV 96); parts: S1 S2 A T B; V1 V2 V3; Org. + Vn(Bc,nf).

71: "Actus 1^{mus} [+ 2^{dus}, 3^{tius}] Wacht euch zum Streit" (BuxWV Anh. 3, unicum); parts: S1 S2 A T B; V1 V2 Va1 Va2 Con.

82:34, tablature
   #1, fol. 2r: "Accedite gentes" (BuxWV 1, but anonymous); S1 S2 A T B; V1 V2; [Bc].
   #2, fol. 4v: "Ecce nunc benedicite Domino . . . D.B." (BuxWV 23); A T T B; V1 V2; [Bc].
   #3, fol. 7v: "Laudate Pueeri Dominum . . . C.T." [Clemens Thieme]
   Inventory: Grusnick, "Dübensammlung" 1966, p. 134.

82:35, tablature
   #1, fol. 1r: "Sonatina [Drei schöne Dinge sind] D.B.H." (BuxWV 19); S B; [V1 V2 Vn]; [Bc].
   #4, fol. 9v: "O lux Beata Trinitas . . . D.B.H." (BuxWV 89); S1 S2; V1 V2 V3 Fg; [Bc].
   #5, fol. 12v: "Je höher du bist ie mehr demutige dich . . . D.B. Hude" (BuxWV 55); S1 S2 B; [V1 V2 Vn]; [Bc]. 1684, 23 July.
   #7, fol. 17v: "Aria. Wie soll Ich dich mein Jesu empfangen . . . D.B. Hude" (BuxWV 109); S1 S2 B; [V1 V2 Vn]; [Bc].
   #8, fol. 19v: "Dein Edle Hertz . . . D.B.H." (BuxWV 14, unicum); S A T B; [V1 V2 Va1 Va2 Vn]; [Bc].
   #9, fol. 21v: "Salve Jesu Patris . . . Dit: Buxteh:" (BuxWV 94); S1 S2; V1 V2; [Bc].
   #10, fol. 24v: "Herr auf dich traue Ich . . . D.B.H." (BuxWV 35); S; V1 V2; [Bc].
   #11, fol. 26v: "Furchtet Euch Nicht . . . D.B.H." (BuxWV 30); S B; [V1 V2]; [Bc]. 1685 1 December.
   Other composers: J. P. Krieger, Peranda, Pohle.
   Inventory: Collected Works, IX.

82:36 "I.N.I. Frohlocket mit Händen . . . D.B.H." (BuxWV 29, unicum); tab: S1 S2 A T B; V1 V2 V3 V4 Vn; Tr1 Tr2; Con.

82:37, tablature
   #1, fol. 1v: "Jesu meines Lebenß Leben . . . D.B." (BuxWV 62, earlier version); S A T B; [V1 V2 Va1 Va2 Vn]; [Bc].
   #2, fol. 3v: "Der Engel des Hern . . . S.P." [D. Pohle]
   #3, fol. 6v: "aria Jesu meines Lebens Leben. Corrigieret . . . D.B.H." (BuxWV 62, revised version); [S A T B]; [V1 V2 Va1 Va2]; [Bc].
   Inventory: Grusnick,"Dübensammlung" 1966, p. 142.

82:38, AUTOGRAPH: "Nimm von uns Herr du getreurer Gott . . . Dieter: Buxtehude m.p." (BuxWV 78, unicum); tab: S A T B; V1 V2 Vt1 Vt2 Fg; [Bc].

82:39, AUTOGRAPH: "I.N.I. Nun Dancket alle Gott . . . Dieter: Buxtehude m.p." (BuxWV 79); tab: S1 S2 A T B; V1 V2 Vn; Cn1 Cn2 Fg; Tr1 Tr2; [Bc]; 1 part: Vn.

82:40, AUTOGRAPH: "O Jesu mi dulcissime . . . Dieter. Buxtehude m.p." (BuxWV 88, unicum fragment); tab: S S B; V1 V2 Vn; [Bc].

82:41, "Chiaccona, Quemadmodum desiderat cervus . . . D.B.H." (BuxWV 92, unicum); score: T; V1 V2; Con.

82:42, tablature

#1, fol. 1r: "Salve desiderium . . . D.B.H." (BuxWV 93); S1 S2 B; [V1 V2 Vn;] [Bc].

#2, fol. 2v: "Afferte Domino Gloriam . . . Dit: Buxtehude" (BuxWV 2); S1 S2 B; [Bc].

#3, fol. 3v: "Sicut Moses . . . Dit: Buxteh:" (BuxWV 97); S; V1 V2 Vg; [Bc]. "1681 den 26 Feb:"

#4, fol. 6v: "Gen Himmel zu den Vater . . . B.B.H. (BuxWV 32); [S]; V Vg; [Bc]. "1681. 3 Maÿ scripsi."

#5, fol. 8v: "Lauda Sion Salvatorem . . . D.B.H." (BuxWV 68); S1 [S2 B]; [V1 V2]; [Bc].

#6, fol. 10v: "Weldt Packe dich, Ich sohne . . . D.B.B." (BuxWV 106); S1 S2 B; V1 V2 Vn; [Bc].

#7, fol. 12v: "Ich habe Lust abzuscheiden . . . D.B.H." (BuxWV 46); S1 S2 B; [V1 V2 Vn]; [Bc].

#8, fol. 15v: "O dulcis Jesu amor Cordis mei . . . D.B.B. (BuxWV 83, unicum); S; V1 V2; [Bc]. "20: 8tr 1681."

#9, fol. 17v: "Kompst du! Licht der Heÿden . . . D.B.H." (BuxWV 66); S1 S2 B; [V1 V2 Va1 Va2 Vn]; [Bc].

#10, fol. 20v: "Nur in meines Jesu wunden . . . David Poh."

82:43, tablature

#1, fol. 1r: "Singet dem Herrn . . . D.B.H." (BuxWV 98); S; V; [Bc].

#2, fol. 2v: "Ich Sprach in meinem Hertzen wolan . . . D.B.H." (BuxWV 49); S; V1 V2 V3; [Bc]. "1683"

#3, fol. 6v: "Ich bin die auffErstehung und das Leben . . . D.B.H." (BuxWV 44, unicum); B; V1 V2 Va1 Va2 Fg; Cn1 Cn2; Tr1 Tr2; [Bc].

#4, fol. 8v: "Gott fähret auf . . . D.B.H." (BuxWV 33, unicum); S1 S2 B; V1 V2 Va[/Tn]1 Va[/Tn]2 Fg; Cn1 Cn2; Tr1 Tr2; [Bc].

#5, fol. 13v: "Canite Jesu nostro . . . Dit: Buxteh:" (BuxWV 11, unicum); S1 S2 B; V1 V2 [Vn]; [Bc]. "1683 11 May"

#6, fol. 15v: "Wie schmecket eß so lieblich undt wohl . . . D.B.H." (BuxWV 108, unicum); S A B; [V1 V2 Vn]; [Bc].

#7, fol. 18v: "Ich halt Es darfur daß . . . D.B.H." (BuxWV 48); S B; [V Va Vn]; [Bc]. "1683 18 Aug"

#8, fol. 22v: "In dulci Jubilo . . . D.B.H." (BuxWV 52); S1 S2 B; V1 V2; [Bc].

83:1–20, tablature

#16, fol. 28v: "Cantate Domino Canticum . . . Ditrich. Buxtehud." (BuxWV 12); S1 S2 B; [Bc].

#19, fol. 34v: "In te Domine Speravi. . . . D.B.H." (BuxWV 53, unicum); S A B; [Bc].

Other composers: Capponi, Carissimi, [Cossoni], Della Porta, Fabri, Foggia, Förster, Gratiani, J. P. Krieger, Mazzochi, Rovetta, Ruggieri, Tarditi.

Inventory: Grusnick, "Dübensammlung" 1966, pp. 159–60.

83:41–45, tablature

#42, fol. 2v: "Sonata. Pange lingua . . . D.B.H." (BuxWV 91); S1 S2 A B; [V1 V2 Va1 Va2 Vn]; [Bc]; End: "7 Feb: 1684."

#43, fol. 6v: "Du Lebenß furst herr Jesu Christ . . . D.B.H." (BuxWV 22); S A T B; [V1 V2 Va1 Va2 Vn]; [Bc].

Other composer: Capricornus

Inventory: Collected Works, IX.

83:69–73, tablature

#72, fol. 8v: "Fallax mundus ornat . . . Dit: Buxteh:" (BuxWV 28); S; V1 V2; [Bc].
Date at end of manuscript: "1681 1 Februar"
Other composers: Benedictus a Sancto Josepho, R. Cesti, J.P. Krieger, [Rosenmüller].
Inventory: Grusnick, "Dübensammlung" 1966, p. 164.

84:29–42:1, tablature

#38, fol. 20v: "Laudate pueri . . . Dit: Buxteh:" (BuxWV 69); S1 S2; Vg1 Vg2 Vg3 Vg4 Vg5 [Vn]; [Bc].
#39, fol. 22v: "O Clemens, o mitis o Coelestis Pater . . . . Dit: Buxteh:" (BuxWV 82); S; [V1 V2 Va Vn]; [Bc].
Dates within manuscript: fol. 5r: "ANNO 1674"; fol. 9v: "1685 10 Febr."; fol. 14v: "1675 27 Aug:"
Other composers: Anonymous, Capricornus, Geist, Gratiani.
Inventory: Grusnick, "Dübensammlung" 1966, p. 157.

85:1–18, tablature

#3, fol. 4v: "Nun Last unß Gott den Herren . . . D.B.H." (BuxWV 81); S A T B (both German and Swedish); V1 V2; [Bc].
#4, fol. 6v: "Wär Gott nicht mit unß diese Zeit" (BuxWV 102, unicum); S A T B; V1 V2; [Bc].
#5, fol. 8v: "Mein gemuhte erfreuet sich . . . D.B.H." (BuxWV 72, unicum); S A B; V&Fl&Cn&Tr1 V&Fl&Cn&Tr2 V3&Cn3&Fg1&Tn1 V4&Cn4&Fg2&Tn2 Fg3&Tn3; [Bc].
#6, fol. 12v: "Aria Bedencke Mensch . . . D.B.H." (BuxWV 9); S1 S2 B; V1 V2 V3 Vn; [Bc].
#7, fol. 14v: "Jesu Meine Freude . . . D.B." (BuxWV 60); S1 S2 B; V1 V2 Fg; [Bc].
#8, fol. 17v: "Einß bitt ich vom Herrn . . . D.B.H." (BuxWV 24); S1 S2 A [T B]; [V1 V2 Va1 Va2 Fg]; [Bc].
#9, fol. 27v: "O Gottes Stadt . . . Diete Buxteh:" (BuxWV 87); S; V1 V2 Va Vn; Con.
#10, fol. 30v: "O Gott wir danken deiner Gut . . . D.B.H." (BuxWV 86, unicum); S1 S2 A T B; [V1 V2 Vn]; [Bc].
#11, fol. 33v: "Aria. Schwinget euch Himmel an . . . D.B.H." (BuxWV 96); S1 S2 A T B; [V1 V2 V3 Vn]; [Bc].
#13, fol. 40v: "Walts Gott . . . D.B.H." (BuxWV 103); S A T B; [V1 V2 Va(A)]; [Bc].
#14, fol. 43v: "Herren wår Gudh . . . D.B.B." (BuxWV 40, unicum); S A T B (Swedish); V1 V2 Vn; [Bc]. "1687 d. 8ten Junÿ"
#15, fol. 44v: "Erhalt unß Herr beÿ deinem wort . . . D.B.H." (BuxWV 27); S A T B; [V1 V2]; [Bc].
#16, fol. 46v: "Domine Salvum fac Regem et exaudi . . . D.B.H." (BuxWV 18, unicum); [S1 S2 A T B]; [V1 V2 Va1 Va2 Vn]; [Bc].
#17, fol. 49v" "Der Herr is mit mir darumb . . . D.B.H." (BuxWV 15, unicum); S A T B; V1 V2 Vn; [Bc].
Other composers: Förster, Kress, J. P. Krieger, Pohle.

85:48–53, tablature

#48a, fol. 1v: "Liebster meine Seehle Saget . . . Dit: Buxteh:" (BuxWV 70); S1 S2; V1 V2; [Bc].
#50, fol. 4v: "Jesu dulcis memoria . . . D.B.H." (BuxWV 56); S1 S2; [V1 V2 Vn]; [Bc].
Other composers: Albrici, Bart, Geist, Pfleger, [J.] Weckmann.
Inventory: Grusnick, "Dübensammlung" 1966, pp. 169-70.

85:76–88, tablature

    #78, fol. 5v: "Schaffe in mir gott Ein rein Hertz. . . . Dit: Buxteh:" (BuxWV 95, unicum); S; [V1 V2 Vn]; [Bc].

    #79, fol. 7v: "103 Ψsalm Lobe den Hern meine Seele . . . Diter: Buxtehude" (BuxWV 71); T; [V1 V2 V3 Va1 Va2(T)]; [Bc].

    #82, fol. 11v: "Låffwa Hern min Siehl . . . D.B.H." (BuxWV 71); T (Swedish); [V1 V2 V3 Va1 Va2 Vn]; [Bc].

    #84, fol. 15v: "Herr Nun Låßest du deinen Diener . . . Dit: Buxtehude" (BuxWV 37); T; V1 V2; [Bc].

    #87, fol. 21v: "O fröliche Stunden . . . D.B.H." (BuxWV 84, unicum); S; V1 V2 Va(B); [Bc].

    Other composers: Erben, Fischer, Geist, Ritter, Theile.

86:19–28, tablature

    #23, fol. 9v "Surrexit Christus hodie Humano pro. . . . Diterich Buxteh:" (BuxWV 99, unicum); S1 S2 B; V1 V2 V3 Fg; [Bc].

    Dates in manuscript: fol. 2v: "1676 d 28. September"

    Other composers: Albrici, Anonymous, [Bernhard], Capricornus, Geist, Kreichel.

    Inventory: Grusnick, "Dübensammlung" 1966, p. 171.

86:36 "Aria Anima [Jesu meiner freuden meister]" (BuxWV 61); tab: S A T B; [V Va1 Va2 Vn]; [Bc].

86:61 "Sonata . . . Aria O fröhliche" (BuxWV 85); Tab: S1 S2 A B; V1 V2 [Va1 Va2 Vn]; [bc].

164:9 "Klag Lied" (BuxWV 76-2); parts: Vb2 [Bc].

Appendix 4

Selected Texts from Archival Documents and Early Printed Sources

A. Bad Oldesloe, Archiv der St. Peter-Pauls Kirche

1. Rechnungsbuch III (1610–1628) [*Nr. 111*]

1624, fol. 93v [Lübeck marks/shillings/pence]:
  Diderich Buxstehude, 7 puls   3/8/-

2. Rechnungsbuch IV (1629–1651) [*Nr. 112*]

1631, pp. 33–34:
  dem Orgelisten tho bestedigung sines Ambts geben 6/-/-
  Johannes dem Scholmeister sin Solarium ef ostern wegen des Seyers geben 6/-/-
  dem Scholmeister sin solarium vor den Seiger zustellen, auf Michaelis geben 6/-/-

1632, p. 39:
  der Orgelistken tho behoeff ihres Züges weg tho Vören gegeven 3/-/-

1636, p. 68:
  Einnamb fur bestettung der stule, und stande:
    Catrin Buxtehuden hatt Ihres verstorbenen Mannes standt, hinter der Jungkhers
  stulte am Piler gelegen dafur 3/-/-

B. Copenhagen, Landsarkivet for Sjælland, Lolland-Falster og Bornholm

1. Helsingør, Indkomne Breve til Magistraten 1660–1700

1671, 1 September:
  WohlEhrenvester Hochweiser Vollvürnehmer insonders hochgeEhrter H:
  Bürgermeister

Negst freundtlichen gruß, thue Ihr Hochweisheit unterdienstlich ersuchen demnach hier in Lübeck für lengst ein Mensch deren Nahm Margreta Fechters, gebürtig aus Helsingiör, Ihr Vater Clauß Fechter bestalter organisten an der dänischen Kirchen daselbst gewese: angelanget, und alszu bald in großeste Kranckheit und Ehlend gerahten. So das Sie nichts gehabt womit daß Leben könte conserviret werden, Mir aber immittelst umb hülffe ersucht welches ich aus Christlicher Liebe, ihr Zeit nach Zeit, mit bahrem gelde beygesprungen, so das es bis dato* [*d. 28 decemb: Ao: 70:] fünffzig RDr: geworden, laut ihr aufgegebene und mit eigener Handt untergeschriebene *obligation*, welche Ihr Hoch: hiemit übersenden, in der hohen Zuversicht, Ihr Hoch: ohnbeschwert wollen geruhen bey denen Vormünden dieses Menschens, alß Jost Hinrichsen und Jürgen Holmes, zu meiner Zehlung großg: wieder verhelfften, werde in allen begebenheiten Ihr HochWz: zu denen mich schuldiger massen verbunden, und *recommendire*, negst diese Sache, mich in ihre Hohe Gunst,

Verbleibe
Ihr HochWeißlichen
dienstgebener
Dieterich Buxtehude *m.p.*

P.S. mit angehengte bitte
Ihr Hochwz: wollen
mit ein kleines antwort
ohnbeschwert bewürdingen.

Lübeck, d: 1 Septemb:
Anno 1671.

2. Helsingør, Laerde Skole Regnskabs Protokol 1674–1696

1674, fol. 93r [ordinary dollars/marks/shillings]:
8 7bris [September] Hammerschmids Kirch undt taffle music   3/-/-
for dem at indbind, 9 partex à 6ß er   -/3/6

1675, fol. 94r:
for nogle schreffven Music Stücher aff H. Niels KieldßÖns 3/-/-
9 7bi: 9 böger at schriffve Music stöcher udi i hver een 1/2 bog papier à 1 M. bogen er 1/-/8.

3. Helsingør rådstud, Alm. regnskabsvaesen A. Kaemnerregnskaber

#411 (1639–1648)

1641–42, fol. 21r:
Organistenn Clauß Feitter . . . 125 Dlr

1645–46, fol. 17v:
Organisten giffvet Aarlige . . . 125 Dlr

1648–49, fol. 21v:
Organisten Hanss Buxtehude giffves Aarlig for Nÿtt Aars Daug i fire Terminer, hver Termin – 25 Curandtdaler, Er 125 Dlr.

#412 (1649–1652)

1649–50, fol. 26v:
Hanß Orgemester . . . 125 Dlr.M:

1650–51, 1651–52, 1652–53:
Organis[s]ten Han[n]s[s] Jensen [Jennssen]. . . 125 Dr.

#413 (1661–1665)

1662, Lille Kemner Regenschab:
Orginisten Hans Buxstehued . . . 50 Sleted:

1662, fol. 35r:
Organisten Hans Buxtehude . . . 75 Dr

1663, 1664, 1665:
Organisten Hans Buxstehude [Buxstehoed, Buchstehude] . . . 125 Dr:

#414 (1668–1673)

1668, 1669, 1670:
Organisten Hanß Buxtehudes [Buxstehuude] Aarlig Lohnn 125 Dr.

1671
Organisten Hanß Buxstehuude Er dette Aar giffven penge 100 Dr. Resten hafe den minder Kemner gifven til den unge Orgenist penge 36 Dr.

1671, Liden Kemners Regenschab:
betalt till Esias Organist 36/2/-

1672–73:
Organisten Hans Buxstehud och Esaias Hasse dereß Aarslön 125 Dr

1673:
Organisten Esaias Haße, Aarlig 125 Dr:

4. Helsingør, Rådstueprotokol 1666–1675

1671, 25 May, fol. 225:
[Agreement on retirement of Johannes Buxtehude.]

5. Helsingør Skt. Mariae kirke Regnskabsprotokol 1659–1760

1659, fols. 2v–3r:
Musicalische böger ere vorhaanden som folger
[Inventory of music; see appendix 6A]

1660, fol. 24v:
5 Octob: Geffved til Discretion, som Manerligt er, til tvende Orgamester dend Ene fra LandsCrone oc dend anden fra Helsingborg, som slog dereß proba 10 Rt: – 15 Dr.

1661, fol. 34v:
Organisten Et Aarß Lön   200 dr:

1662, fol. 46v:
>   Dirch Organist Ett Aar Lön   200 Dr:
>   For 1 Aarß Huußleÿe   20 Dr:

1662, fol. 47r:
>   Noch betalt paa 4. Terminer till M Hanß Christofferßen Orgelbauwer evter accord for orgelwercket at forferdige, evter hans Quittering – 393 Dr:
>   Noch till tvende organister, som haffr: besichtet orgelwercket, epter at det war ferdigt, foræret som sedwanligt er – 10 RDr: – 15 Dr:

6. Helsingør, Skt. Olai Kirke, Døde

1671, 27 December:
>   bleff begraffved udi Boghused, 2 Aln fra absconseled Heile Hans Organistis, Haffde Jorden och Alle Klocherne fri, effter W.W. Hrr. B. och Raads Zeddel.

7. Helsingør, Skt. Olai Kirke, Fødte

1645, 17 January, fol 72v:
>   Fredagen efter Dominica 1. p. Epiphanis
>   Hans Buxtehude, Organist |
>   } Peiter
>   Helle, Jespers Daater |

8. Helsingør, Skt. Olai Korrespondancesager 1616–1823

1648, 27 January:
>   Salut:
>   EhrenVeste, GroßAchtbahre Wollgelährte Unnd Wollweiße, Großgünstige Herrn Patronen und Hochgeëhrte beforderer, Eß ist E: GroßA: Wolgl: Wollw: mehrintheils und gnucksamb bewüst, wie das die Orgell in unsere dänische Kirche, ëhe und bevohr ich die Unterhänden Vertraut blieff, Unfertigh wahr, auch anitzo noch, selbiges groß Jammer, Insonderheit, Weilln es die Vornehmeste Kirspiell: und Heüpt Kirche alhie in hießiger Statt ist, dhazu auch Viell durchreisent frembder Nationen gibt, das ein solch Werck so elendigh stehen soll, zwar woll auswendigh ein frewdiges Und gutes ansähend habe, Aber dha, Zum ersten, das Rüg-*posetive* gantz nieder und stum liegt, Zum andern, daß Oberwerck inwendigh ein geringh ding bißer sich befindet, und /:weis Gott:/ eine guete *renovation* bedürftig, jha dhanach eilen und seufftzen thuet, wie der Hirsche nachm frischen Waßer, zum dritten, auch nodtwendigh, das dha mochte bleÿ überm Bälghauße gelegt: damit die Bälgen desto bißer fürm Regenn Und Schne Vorsehen, werden.
>   Weilln Großgünstige Hochgeëhrte Herrn Unnd Patronen itzo guete Zeit dhazu, und die Orgell /:wegen dießes trawrens:/ still stehet, hirein ihrern selbst eigen gueten Willen nach, mittel suchen und gebrauchenn wollenn.
>   Alß wolle ich E: GroßA: Wollgl: Wollw: wie meine Großgünstige Herrn Patronen und Hochgeëhrte beforderer hiemit gantz freündtfleißig und diemüetigh – Jha Lauter umb Gottes Willen gebeten haben, Sie wegenn Ihrer Hohe Authoriteten

Vorhingedachte inwendige, schwache und sehr kranke, Jha heülende Orgel noch einmaligh auff die füsse Verhelfen: und über sie erbarmen wollenn.

Solches gereichet Gott dem Allmächtigen zu ëhren, E: GroßA: Wollgl: Wollw: zu einen Weitberümbten gueten Nahmens, Wie auch dießer Unßere Groß und Vorneheme dänische Bürgerschafft und gemäine zum Wollgefallen, Verhoffend E. GroßAcht: Wollg: Wollw: ihrern gueten Willen hiereinn sëhen und spüren laßenn werdenn, Mit Angehengter Hoch: und freundtfleissiger bitte, gerne sehen und Wünschen mochte, das die Hochgeehrte Herrn so lange Zeit abrechen: und auff die Orgel tretten wollen, damit sie selber können sehen und erfahren, wie dhan es mit dem Werck erschaffen ist, Unnd an mir nicht erzürnen wollen, wie das ich so kühen drist E: GroßAcht: Wollgl: Wollw: mit dießes mein gahr einfältiges schreibent, Anhaltend, übereilen, beschweren und itzo auffhalten thue, Unnd Wan E: GroßAcht: Wollg: Wollw: ein guetes gewünschetes Antwort Zu erwartenn habe.

Helsingör denn 27 Januarij

Anno 1648
E: GroßAcht: Wollgl: Wollw:
Stets bereitwilliger gehor-
samber und pflichtschüldiger
diener so lange ich lebe,
Hans Buxtehude *m.p.*
Organist

1666, 9 October [note on another document]:
Nerverender Hans Mortensen er Calcant til Vaaris orgel udi Sanct Olai Kircke,
H. Buxtehude *m.p.*

org:

1667, 14 September:
[Receipt in Danish signed by] H. Buxtehude *m.p.*, org:

C. Copenhagen, Riksarkiv

1. Danske Kancelli C6 Sjællandske Registre

1668, 16 March, fol. 151r:
[appointment of Johann Radeck to succeed Dieterich Buxtehude]
G[ör] A[lle] V[itterligt]: At vi efter Underdannigste ansögning oc begiering Naadigst hafver beschicket oc forordnet Johan Radeck til at vere Organist til dend Tydske Kircke udi vor Kiöbsted helsingör udi forige /:om til Lübeck käldede:/ organistes sted.

1671, 17 January, fol. 377v:
[Appointment of Esaias Hasse to succeed Johannes Buxtehude.]

2. Forsvarets Arkiv, 3. Dept.
Kommandanten i København, Garnisonsjournal, 1666/4

1666, 12 February, p. 126:
Eodem ein Und aus Passiret
Oster Pfordt
Von Helsingnör
Corneliuß von der Welt |
} Log: im Judl: Wepn
Diederich Buxdhue |

3. Københavns Universitet Konsistorium,
Acta Consistorii 1626–1634

1633, 6 March, fol 477v:
[Two organists audition for position at Our Lady's church; the one from Helsingborg is chosen.]

D. Lübeck, Archiv der Hansestadt

1. ASA Ecclesiastica, Lit. Vol. C Fasc. 5, Pak. 3765 Nr. 15116
[Letters from Dieterich Buxtehude]

1683, 7 February:
Denen WollEhrenvesten, Großachtbarn und Wollfürnehmen sämptlichen Herren Eltesten und Directeurs der Hispanischen Collecten, auch Vorsteherrn eines Ehrsamen Kauffmans Dröge hieselbst. Meinen HochgeEhrten Herren und wehrten Gönnern:

Wollehrenveste, Großachtbahre und Wollfürnehmen sonders Hochgeehrte Herren und wehrte Gönner.
Denenselben sage nochmals gar dienstlichen danck, für die vorm Jahr mir gereichte ansehnliche *assistentz*, zu erstattung der auff die damalige Abend-Music verwandte Unkosten. Ob nun Zwar in negster Zeit nicht ein so vollenkommenes Werck, alß woll gewünscht und vorgehabt habe, wegen vorgefallener *impedimenten praesentiren* können. So trage doch das gantz dienstlich vertrauwen zu meiner allerseits hochgeehrte Herren, Sie werden daß wenige so dar gestellet, geneigt auffgenommen haben, und zu mehrer ermunterung zu einer künfftig völligern und größern Arbeit, mir Ihre Gewogenheit, rühmlich, angefangenen maßen, ferner bezeigen, in Vorführung, daß solches mich nicht allein zu begierlicher ambts arbeit, sondern auch zu *particulirer* dienstleistung gegen Meine HochgeEhrte Herren sambt und sonders anfrischen werde, der negst empfehlung Göttl: Gnaden obhüet bin und bleibe

Meiner HochgeEhrten Herren
Dienstfertigster
Dieterich Buxtehude m.p.

Lübeck
d. 7: Februarij
Ao 1683

1685, 16 February
  Denen WollEhrenvesten, Vorachtbarn und Wollführnehmen sämbtlichen Herren
  Ältesten und Vorwesern der Hispanischen Collecten und der Dröge allhier, Meinen
  anders großgünstigen und HochgeEhrten Herren
                                    Dienstfreundlich:

  Wollehrenveste, Vorachtbare und Wollführ sonders Großgünstige und
hochgeehrte Herren,
  Daß die selbe meine bißherige schlechte Arbeit in denen gewöhnlichen Abend
Musiquen Ihnen gefallen laßen und solches mit einem ansehnlichen *honorario* zu
erkennen gegeben, deßfals bei jeder Zeit hocherfrewet und sage billig schuldigen
danck. Alß den nun in den negst abgewichenen 1684sten Jahr mein Pfündlein in
selbigen Wercke, durch Gottes Gnad auch dero Gestald angelegt, daß hoffentlich
meine HochgeEhrte Herren einiger maßen vergnügt seyn werden /: wie woll es
wegen ermangelnder *Vocal*-Hülffe nicht allerdings meinem Vorsatz gleich gewesen
:/ so habe zuforderst für die geneigte anhörung fleisigt zu danken, und dan
sothane *Musique,* wie auch meiner Person zu ferner beforderung und aller·
gewogenheit hiemit *recommendiren* wollen bleibende
                              Meiner großgünstigen und
                              hochgeEhrten Herren
                              Dienstbereitwilligster
                              Dieterich Buxtehude *m.p.*
Lübeck d. 16: Febru:
Ao 1685

1687, 28 January:
  Desfals sage dienstlichsten Danck, und gleich wie Sie die sonderbahre Begierde zu
solchem löblichen und sonst nirgends wo gebräuchlichem Werck, da durch bezeuget
haben: ... Ich mag aber nicht ümbhin, meinen Hochgeehrten Herren und
Gönnern dienstlich vorzutragen, daß leider von jahren zu jahren die von alters her
beliebte *Collecte* sich immer vermindere, und insonderheit diß Jahr sich dero Gestalt
vermindert habe, daß auch nicht einmal die *adjutanten* davon bezahlen können: Muß
derowegen tringender noth halber zu meine Großgönstige und Hochgeehrte
Herren und Gönnern, alß *p.t.* Vorwesere der *Commercijrenden* Zunfften von welchen
diese Abend*musique* anfangs begehret worden, meine Zuflucht nehmen ...

1689, 5 February:
  Wann abermahl euserster müchligkeit und ungespahreten Fleises nach, meine jüngst
praesentirete Abend *Music* vom Verlohrnem Sohn, durch Gottes Gnade, zu Ende
geleget, daß ich nicht zweiffele, Meine HochgeEhrte Herren, und wehrte Gönner, mit
mir deßfals in geneigter Zufriedenheit stehen werden: ...

1696, 22 February
  Denen WohlEdlen, Großachtbahren und Wohlfürnehmen Herrn Ältisten der
Hispanischen Collecten und der Dröge, Meinen insonders HochzuEhrende Herren,
  WohlEdle, Großachtbahre, insonders Großgünstige HochgeEhrte Herren,
  Weilen ich noch zur Zeit an Dieselbe den behörigen Danck wegen einverleibter
gewöhnlichen *Discretion* meiner vorm Jahr zu rück gelegten Abend-*Musicque*, nicht
abgestattet, so verrichte dasselbige hiemit, und verbinde mich zu Meiner
HochzuEhrenden Herren stets angenehmen diensten, da benebend ersuchend dieselbe

ferner geruhen wollen, wegen der jüngsthin aberwertig *praesentirten Abend-Music* mit dero wohlvermögen *e communi Cassa* weiter beÿ zu treten und dero *Affection* allemahl *recommendiret* seyn zu laßen, der ich zu anwünschen vielen glücklichen Zeiten, auch glücklicher Obhut

Verharre
Ewrer WohlEdlen großachtbahre Gunsten
stets Verbundener
Dieterich Buxtehude *m.p.ia*

Lübeck, d. 22 Februarij.
Ao. 1696

2. ASA Ecclesiastica (Nachträge Winckler), St. Marien, Vol. B, 7, 3: [Acta die große Orgel betreffend]

Page 5 [Copy by Hermann Jimmerthal of a stoplist for the large organ written by J. von Königslow, organist at St. Mary's 1773–1833]:

> Das ganze Werk ist von vortrefflichem Metall und Holz, stimmt in der gleich-schwebenden Temperatur und zwar hoch-Chorton.

Pages 7–8 [Copy by Johann Kuntzen, organist at St. Mary's 1732–57, of an undated memorandum written by Buxtehude concerning the organist's house]:

> In der Kirche St. Marien grossen Rentebuch fol: 90 stehet:
>
> Ein Hauß in der Hundestrssen belegen. In diesem Hause der Kirchen gehörig, hat vor diesen der Organist freÿ gewohnet, weil aber der itzige Organist auch zugleich Werckmeister ist, und also auf dem Werkhause wohnet, ist dieses Hauß an Johann Hasse Goldschmidt verhäuret jährlich um 55 MLüb. Dieser findet sich im vorigen Rente-Buch nicht geschrieben. Ursach dessen ist, weil die Herren Vorsteher, dem Organisten für seine Aufwartung und geringen Organisten Gagie haben behalten, und einheben lassen, darum denn mein seel. Antecessor Franz Tunder solches genossen, nie zur Rechnung gebracht, noch von denen Herren Vorstehern begehret worden, um daß Sie zweifelsohne höchstgeneigt und vernunfftig erwogen, daß für vollen gedoppelten Arbeit völlig gedoppelter Lohn gebühret. Zumahlen die dienste ohn Manquement, so gut verwaltet werden als vorhin von zweÿen unterschiedenen Subjectis ist geschehen. Was nun die H. Vorsteher einmal gr[oß]g[ünstig]l[ich] beliebet, und beygelegt haben, wird verhoffentlich mir als einen getreuen Kirchendiener nicht entzogen werden.
>
> Dietrich Buxtehude

3. ASA Interna, Musik 3: Ratsmusikanten: [Personalien bis 1700]

[typescript transcription at Musikwissenschaftliches Institut der Christian-Albrechts-Universität zu Kiel]

4: 1652, 23/27 November [Letter from *Hinrich Höppner* to Lübeck City Council]:

> Demnach ich von Jugendt an, zu der Music für Allen Andern Freyen Künsten Lust und Liebe getragen, So haben meine Liebe Eltern solcher meiner Natürlichen

inclination auch nicht wiederstrebet, undt dahero mich bey dieser Stadt langk Jahr
wollbedienten Cornettisten und der Music Wollerfahrnen Hanß Fresen in die Lehre
gethan, bey welchem ich mich auch so lange auffgehalten, biß er mich, anderer
Orter ohnverweißlich in Musicis auffzuwarten, düchtig erachtet, worauff Ich für
etlichen Jahren mich in andere Orter undt Stedte begeben, Woselbsten Ich daßelbe,
Waß ich Alhie erlernet, mir zu nutzen machen, undt ferner excotiren könte, und ob
ich zwar in Konigl. und Fürstl. Höffen auffwartung undt Bestallungk haben können,
habe ich doch, Weil meine Natur zum Hoffe und wüsten Laben gantz nicht geneigt,
undt daß ich daselbsten, vieleicht weniger als in Stedten erlernen möchte, mich
dahin zu begeben, biß hero bedencken getragen, und Lieber mich in Stedten,
absonderlich zum Strallsundt bey einem Berühmten Cornetisten undt Musico,
deßen Stelle ich wegen ihm zugestoßner Beineschwachheit in Musicis eine zeithero
verwaltet, auffhalten wollen.

7: 1653, 14. April/11 June [Letter from *Hinrich Höppner* to Lübeck City Council]:
 Ew. Edl. Herl. und Hochw. Gunstl. alhie weitleufftig zu erinnern, waß massen
denenselben ich meine wenige Persohn in die durch des Seel. Peter
Roggenbucken, und Sel. Hanß Freesen erledigte Musicanten stellen für andern zu
befodern, unterdienstlich offeriret und recommendiret habe, erachte ich ohn notig
zu sein; Weill aber Gott und das glück Andern solche Stellen gegönnet, und
dieselbe auch zwar hinwider ersetzet sein, jetzo aber nach dem unwandelbahren
willen Gotteß Peter Hohman eines hochw. Raths Trummenschläger auß diesem
zeitlichen leben abgefordert, daß also abermahl eine stelle erledigt, und dadurch
mir zur beforderung einige hoffnung abermahl gemachet worden, gestaltsamb ich
durch Gotteß gnade so viel erlernet habe, daß so woll mit dem Cornet, alß Posaune
und Violin ich gleich andern, die vieleicht sich angeben möchten, und zugleich
solcher instrumentorum Musicorum auff erforderten fall nicht mechtig sein, priva-
tim und publice auffzuwarten, mich woll getrawen darff. Diesem nach habe ich
nötig erachtet, daß E. Edl. Herl. und Hochw. Gunstl. ich meine Persohn nun zum
drittenmahl supplicando offerirte . . .

10: 1668, 24/25 July [Letter from *Johann Philip Roth* to Lübeck City Council]:
 Nachdeme für kurzer Zeit, wie bei hisiger weltbeprisenen Kaiserl. Freien Reichs
Stadt eines HochEdelen Rates Lautenisten und Musici Stelle vacirete, ich in
Erfarung gelanget, so habe alhie meine Persohn geziemend ich prasentiren sollen,
und auf ihrer Wolweisen Gunstl. der Herren Wein-Herren gelibiges Wollen mich
auch bereit hören lassen.
 Wan nun in Weiland Seiner Hochfürstl. Dhlkeit zu Brunswig Lünäburg, Herzogen
Augustus Meines Gnädigst-gewesenen Fürsten und Herren dihnsten für Lauteniste
und Musicus /: nach deme neben der französischen und deutschen Laute, die Viole
di Gambo, Violine, Pandor zusamt andern mehren instrumenten ich übe :/ eine 23
Jahre aufgewartet; itzo aber nach Seiner Hochfürstl. Dhlkeit Christseligster
Gedächtnisse dotes-Abgehen, der Capelle zu Wolfenbüttel ausgehoben, Als gelanget
an ihrer Herligkeiten Hoch- und Wolweise Gunst, Meine Hoch- und Vihlgebitende
Herren Beforderer dises mein dihnstgeziemend-erbitliches Gesuche, mit hisiger
vacirenden Lautenisten-Stelle mich zubeschenken. . . .

12: 1669, 25 November /3 December [Letter from *Peter Zachow* to Lübeck City Council]:
 Ew. WohlEdl. herrl. und hochgelgsten, werden sich höchst geneigt zu erinnern
wißen, waßmaßen ich seit hero zu unterschiedenen mahlen, umb eine Raths

Musicanten Verlehnung, supplicando unterdienstlich angehalten, mir aber allezeit andere seynd vorgezogen worden. Wann nun großgönstige hochgebietende herren, ich itzo vernehme, daß abermahl eine, von des Raths Musicanten Verlehnung vaciret, und ich durch Gottes gnade auf allen Instrumenten: Principaliter aber auf das Cornettin, Zingk und Posaune, dergestalt (ohn üppigen Ruhm zu melden) meine Kunst gefaßet und gelernet, daß keinen, in gewißer maße, von hiesigen Musicis etwas werde nachgeben; und also gerne wolte, daß E. E. und hochw. Rath großgünstig belieben möchte, dahin order zu stellen, daß, (weil ich wenig favoriten, nescio quare! unter hiesigen Musicos finde, und sie also Sinistre judicando mir mein dessem zu verhindern sich bemühen dürfften) mir vorhero möchte zugelaßen und vergönnet werden, mich auff der orgel zu St. Marien alß künfftigen Sontag, geliebtes Gott hören zuelaßen. . . .

13[a]: 1672, 5 February [Letter from *Hans Iwe* to Lübeck City Council]:

WolEdl. herl. mittelst diesem unterdienstlich anzulangen, magk Ich nicht umbhin; Nachdem Ich vernommen, daß Zacharias Crohnenberg diese Weldt gesegnet, und dadurch unter Eines Hochw. Rahts bestelleten *Musicanten* die Bassisten stelle erlediget; Bey welcher occasion meine wenigkeit zu gehorsambsten diensten zu offeriren kürtzlich /: iedoch ohne ienigen ruhm :/ dieses anzuführen nicht unterlaßen mögen, daß Ich nemblich anfangs bey Hinrich Höpfener Eines Hochw. Rahts Musicanten alhie die Music auff allerhand instrumenten gelernet, auch nachgehents mit dem sehl. Schnittelbach auff Hochzeiten und sonsten gesungen, vor dem Sehl. Cronenberg mannigmahl mit der BasVioline auffgewartet, und sonsten durch Gottes gnade die Kunst der gestalt fleißigk geübet, daß Ich mich nicht schewe auff der Violine, Viol de Gambe, Violone, auch auff allerhand blaß instrumenten, Cornetto, Fagotte, Posaune, Quart Posaune und Flöten, gebührendt höhren zu laßen, auch da nötigk des Claviers und der Vocal music mich zu bedienen verstehe. . . .

13[b]: 1672, 21 February [Letter from Adam Hampe to Lübeck City Council in behalf of his brother, *Jacob Hampe*]:

Demnach durch Tödtlichen Hintrit Sehl. Zacharias Kronenberg die stelle eines Bassisten unter dehro bestaldte Musicanten eröfnet, und Ew. wollEdl. Herl. und Hochgel. Gunstl. dieselbe hinwiederumb zuvorgeben ohne Zweifel baldest möchten gesinnet sein, So habe unter andern fur meinen bruder Jacob Hampe mich gehorsambst mit angegeben, und deßen Persohn zu selbiger aufs fleissigste recommendiren wollen, und solches umb so viel getrawter, weil derselbe nicht allein bei Sehl. Zacharias Kronenberg eine guete Zeit von Jahren seine Music erlernet, von demselben auch vorhin so wol, alß in seinem letzten verschiedentlich ein solches guetes Zeugnis gehabt, daß er für andere zu seiner nachlassenden stelle geschickt und Capabel sein wurde, absonderlich da derselbe nunmehro biß in die 18. Jahr in Dennemarcken, Norwegen, Hollandt, Engellandt und anderen vielen Öhrten im Römischen Reich sich weiter versuchet, seiner Kunst nach gesetzet, und zu solcher perfection nunmehro bei seinem Mänlichen 36. Jahren Gottlob gedieen, daß er keinen Scheu tragen darff, sich bei allen und jeden Competitoren zu sistiren, und hören zulaßen . . .

13[c]: 1672, 24 February [Letter from *Peter Grecke* to Lübeck City Council]:

Allermaßen auch ich, ob ich gleich, auf dem Clavier, violdegambe, Bassviolone, und violone, alß die heute zu tage allenthalben mehrest beliebeten instrumenten, mich sonderlich gegeben, dennoch keinen schew trage, so offt und vielmahl es erfordert wirdt, auff Posaunen, QuartPosaunen, Cornetten und flöten, alles das jenige auch zu praestiren, was andere thun können und werden. Wie ich dann nicht allein schon vor Sieben Jahren alhie auf den Chören in allen Kirchen, auf allerhandt Blase instrumenten, mich, nebenste Eines Hochw. Raths Musicanten gebrauchen laßen. Sondern auch bereits außer Landes unterschiedliche discipulos, auf dergleichen instrumenten, sowohl alß andern, unterwiesen habe.

14: 1673, 28 October [Letter from *Hans Iwe* to Lübeck City Council]:
Wann dan nun durch tödtlichen hintrit Sehl. Elias Baudringen, dem ich sonst sein leben auff noch viele Jahre, wen eß dem lieben Gott hette gefallen mögen, gerne gegönnet hette, Eineß hoch. Rahtß Pauckenschlägerdienst vacant worden.
So habe geziemenden gehorsambs mich unterdienstlichst hiemit dazu anzugeben nicht unterlaßen wollen. E. Edl. hoch- und wolw. herl. und gstl. unterdienstlichsten fleißes ersuchend und bittend, sie wollen großgönstig geruhen, weil diese vacantz auff die mir ertheilte exspectantz die erste ist, ich auch ein paar eigener Paucken habe und dieselbe nach den noten zuschlagen mich mit fleiß geübt und also ohn ruhm zumelden woll schlagen kan, mich mit selber vacantz für andern wieder zubegönstigen und nicht zu zweifflen, ich werde, Gott den Allerhöchsten zue Ehren, und Einem hochw. Raht zu hochgeneigtem Wollgefallen, mit meiner Instrumental und vocal-music in Kirchen, und sonsten mich dabey dergestalt fleißig und zubezeigen nicht ermangeln . . .

22: 1692, 15 February [Letter from *Adam Hampe* to the Lübeck City Council]:
Ew. HochEdl. Herl. ruhet zweiffels ohne in hochgeneigten andencken, Waß gestalt Hanß Ive ohnlengst dieses Zeitliche gesegnet, und durch deßen absterben, eines Raths Musicanten stelle vacant und erlediget worden. Wan ich nun von der Music Profession mache, und durch Gott beystand und vermittels meines Fleißes es so weit gebracht daß ich bißher in wehrender Kranckheit, des Seel. Iven deßen stelle auff der Orgell in St. Marien Kirche die auffwartunge solcher gestalt verrichtet, daß ich ver- hoffe es werde der H. Buxtehude, und andere die mich gehöret, mir ein gut Zeugnüß von meiner erlernten Kunst geben können, So wünsche darbey nichtes mehr alß daß ich die Ehre, und daß glück haben möge, meine Erlernete Kunst zu Ew. HochEdl. Herl. Dienste alhier in meinen Vaterlande zu exerciren und damit auff zuwarten. . .

4. Bürger—Annahmebuch 1633–1801, Cameraria 1338

1668, 23 July:
Dietrich Buxtehude Werckmeister zu S. Marien mit ein Harnisch, 7 Rth
Anelinck Hansen
Bastian Spangberch

5. Dröge, 172 [Letters from Dieterich Buxtehude]

1699, 12 April:
Daß in einigen Jahren her, annoch die gewöhnlichen, auch von Dero Hochlöblichen Vorfahren aus E E Hochw Rath, und der Ehrliebenden Burger- und Kauffmanschafft, hieselbst angeordneten *Serenaden*, oder Abend-*Musicen*, in der Kirchen S. *Marien*, bis *dato* beybehalten worden, solches habe ich meines Ohrtes nebst viel andern *Music*- Libenden, negst Gott dem Allerhöchsten, Deroselben hohen *assistenz*, und *liberalitet*, alß welche darzu ein Merckliches (ansehnliches) *contribuiret* hat, billig zu dancken . . .

[addendum on separate sheet] N.B.
Zur dienst[lichen] Nachricht berichte daß meine *Musicalische Collecte* für dießes-
mahl gewesen 182 MLüb
    die darzu erforderte Unkosten aber: 206 MLüb
    Ist also mehr außgegeben als m[in]dest[ens]: 24 MLüb

1701, 3 February:
Wan nun aber HochzuEhrende Herren mein Zustandt sowohl alß der übrigen
welche mir in neuligsten Abendt-*Musiquen assistence* geleistet haben, täglich
schlechter wirdt, und leider mehr nicht, so sehr allhie alß die Liebe zu der Edlen
Music abnimmt und erkaltet, daher bey so gestalten Sachen noch manniger in
seinem Alter dabey *cripiren* muß, alß gelanget an Meinen HochzuEhrenden Herren
mein dienstschuldiges Bitten, Sie wollen hochgeneigt geruhen, die von Ihren
Löblichen Herren *Antecessoribus* mir vormahls Jährlich zugelegte 20 Rthr fernerweit
großg[ünstig] genießen zu lassen, damit solcher Gestalt das jenige was sonsten von
der Lieben Bürgerschafft *en particulier* zu hoffen gehabt dadurch möge verbessert . . .

6. St. Jakobi, Traubuch 1665–1725

[p. 247] 1713, Dom: 6. p. Trinitat.
Johan Nicolaus Herman ein Gewurz Cramer
u. Anna Sophia Buxtehuden in der großen burg straße in s. Hause

7. St. Marien, I [Bücher] 1a [allgemeine Wochenbücher]

[I wish to acknowledge the assistance of Ibo Ortgies in compiling the additions to this
section. Entries are for expenses (Ausgabe) unless otherwise noted as "Empfangen."]

12: Wochenbuch 1632–1646

1641, 14. Woche nach Ostern [25. Juli], fol. 333r:
Dingstedach Henricus Scheideman Orgeliste zu St. Cathrinen in Hamburgk, so auf
der Herren Vorsteher Begehren heruber gekommen, die große örgell alhie zu St.
Marÿen zu beschlagen, da fur ihme ist vorehret 50 Reichsthaler thun: 150/-/-

1642, 7. Woche nach Michaelis [13. November], fol. 369r:
Sonnabentt Friderich Stelwagen dem Örgelbuwer so die große Örgell von Neuwen
durchgestimmet und daran vorbeßert, auf Befehl der Herren Vorsteher zugestelt 10
Reichsthaler thun: 30/-/-

14: Wochenbuch 1654–1661

1659, 12. Woche nach Michaelis [18. December], f. 240r:
Montag, . . . Noch haben meine H: Vorsteher, auf *suppliciren* Jochim Baltzers deß
Lautanisten, demselben verordnet daß ihm Jährlich 10. RD: zu seiten gelt, deßglei-
chen Nathanaael Schnittelbachen auch 10. RD: sollen gegeben werden, zu dem ende,
daß, weil deß Lautanisten gebühr ist auf die Orgel alle Festtage zu gehen, er solches
desto fleißiger hinführo soll verrichten, und Schnittelbach ebenmäßig solcheß zu thun
soll schuldig sein, wie der H: Schluß, im Memorial fol: 10 : Punkt 29: 30: und 31.
enthalten, meldet: Ihnen für dießmal zugestellet, einem jed[en] 10 RD: sind: 60/-/-

1660, 13. Woche nach Michaelis [23. December], fol. 288r:
    Freitag . . . Auf Suppliciren des Cantoris Ao: 1659. . . hat der Cantor deß Capell
M. Heinrich Schützen Psalmen a 8 und mehr stimmen gekaufft . . . Noch hab ich
[i.e. Tunder] von Michel Volcken, deß Johan. Heinrich Schmeltzers Kaiserl:
Violinisten Sonaten â 3 gekaufft für   3/-/-
    Noch von August Johan Behren, laut Rechnunge entfange deß Capricorni
Messen und Psalmen, mit vielen stimmen und Repien, noch dessen Concerten, 1.
2. Theil: noch deßen Jubilum Bernhardi, mit vielen stimmen und Ripien, kosten
16/-/-

15: Wochenbuch 1662–1669

1664, 5. Woche nach Michaelis [30. October], fol. 107r:
    Eß haben meine H: Vorsteher ingesampt, den 12, *Januar.* dieseß jahreß aufm
Werckhause beisammen, auf *Samuelis* Francken deß ietzigen *Cantoris Suggestion* gewil-
liget, daß ein *Positiv,* zu Behuefs der ietzigen Ahrt *Music,* aufs Chor solte gemachet
werden, davon im *Memorial fol.* 41: auch fol: 20: schon der H: Vorsteher schluß mit
mehren zuersehen. Solches ist kurtz für abgewichenen Ostern zu Lüneburg bey dem
da verhandenen Orgelmacher, nahmenß Michel Beriegel, weil ietzo hie keiner verhanden, bestellet, der eß den auf seinen Kosten herübergebracht für 3. Wochen, hat
eß auch in etzlichen *Registern* in die *Orgel* eingerichtet, daß eß am vergangenen
Sontage für 8 Tagen, wahr der 23.*Octob.* da unsere L: Obrigkeit wegen deß getroffe-
nen friedenß mit dem Turcken, eine Dancksagung thun laßen, zum ersten mahl in
der *Music* gebraucht, . . . Für solches Positieff nachdem eß der Orgelmacher nun
diese Tage vollends verfertiget, ihm gezahlet, wie er von anfang davor gefodert, laut
seiner *Quitung* den 1. *Nov:* datiret 300/-/-

1667, 11. Woche nach Michaelis [8. December], fol. 237r:
    Dingstag, . . . Noch haben die H. H. Vorsteher in der Verwichenen Woche einen
fremden *Organisten* von Hamburg, mit Namen Johan Schade, laßen herüberkom-
men, welcher sich am vergangenen Sonntag als den 8. Decembr: hat hören lassen,
weil er Ihnen aber und der Orgell nicht angestanden, als ist er mit einem *viatico*
bestehend in 3 ducaten wieder dimittiret, welche der Kirche hiemit berechnet werden sind   18/-/-

1668, 6. Woche nach Neujahr [2. Februar], fol. 244r:
    Sonnabend, . . .Noch auf befehl der H. Vorstehern einem frembden *Musico* und
Organisten nahmens *Johannes Stanislaus Boronski* von Schönenberg aus Pohlen
welcher sich dieser tagen hören laßen. Zum *viatico* geben müß 4 Rthl: welche alhie
berechnet sind   12/-/-

1669, 14. Woche nach Neujahr [28. März], fol. 288r:
    Woledler Hoch und Großachtbarer, sonders hochgewoegene *Patronen,* wegen der
empfangenen gelder und *Honorabilen* Geschenck an gelde 25 Rthr: bedanke ich mich
von Hertzen, alleß selbst erwünschende wolergehen nebenst folgende erklärung:
Cum titulo!
    Die lieben freundes gaben, die mir geschencket seyn,
    die bleiben unvergraben, es bleibet stetig hangen
    im frischen angedenck; Ihr solt widrum empfangen
    den stets begehrter dienst, und ungefärbten schein
                    von Diderich Buxtehude *m.p.*   75/-/-

1669, 14. Woche nach Ostern [11. Juli] Empfangen, fol. 301v:
>   Montag hab mit bewilligung meiner Herren Vorstehere ich mein kleines Tochter Helena Buxtehude mit einem Kinderleuten in der Kirchen gemaurts begräbnus, für dem Thore, bestetigen laßen, solches haben meine H. Vorstehere wie meinen *Antecessoribus* so wol von *Organisten* alß Werckmeistern wiederfahren, auch mir freÿ gegeben, daß Arbeits Lohn dem Volcke habe ich gezahlt -/-/-

16: Wochenbuch 1670–1677

1670, 4. Woche nach Neujahr [23. Januar], fol. 4r:
>   Dienstag, . . . Noch hat Asmus Teuffel auf den newen Chören Bänke, Pulpetten und gantz umb, den tritt ein Fues höher gemacht . . . 12/-/-
>   Noch hat er auf der großen *Orgel* etzliche Bretter gehobelt, so einwendig für das Pfeiffenwerck sind vorgeschlagen, auf das wan die *Musici* nach den neuen Chören hin gehen, nicht die Pfeiffen anstoßen und beschädigen sollen, ihm geben 1/8/-

1671, 15. Woche nach Neujahr [9. April], fol. 64r:
>   Sonnabend, . . . Noch dem *Cantor* zu der großen *Violon* die aufm Chor gebraucht wirdt, eine Seide gekauft vor -/14/-

1671, 9. Woche nach Ostern [18. Juni], fol. 75r:
>   Freitag, . . . Noch Andreae Hammerschmidts Vierdter Theil Musicalischer andachten in folio, so sehr durch täglich gebrauch zerrissen, auf des *Cantoris* begehrend von newem einbinden laßen, welche 10 Bücher an Zahl sind darvor gegeben -/8/-

1671, 13. Woche nach Michaelis [24. December], fol. 101r:
>   Montag, . . . Noch auf des *Cantoris* begehrend eine Seide zu der Violon, so er aufm Chor gebrauchet, gekaufft, kostet -/6/-

1672, 2. Woche nach Neujahr [7. Januar], fol 103r:
>   Mittwoch, . . . Noch Zacharias Cronenberg für eine große Octav geige oder Violon, so die H: Vorsteherr auf meine ansuchung an die Kirche gekaufft zahlt 10 Rthr: . . . 30/-/-

1672, Ostern [7. April], fol. 112r:
>   Mittwoch, auf der Herrn Vorsteherr Befehl sindt zweenen Sängeren, als einen *Castraten Natione Italo* und einem *Bassisten Antwerpiensi*, welche sich in den Ostern Feier tagen zu St. Marien haben hören laßen, von wegen der Kirchen verehret worden 9 Rthr:, von welchen 5 Rthr: in der Herberge vor ihnen gezalt, die übrigen 4 Rthr: ihnen als ein *discretion* geschencket thut 27/-/-

1672, 2d Woche nach Ostern [14. April], fol. 112r:
>   Mittwoch auf der Hn. Vorsteherr Befehl einem *Studioso* Nahmens Andreas *Hermannus Helberg, Buxtehudensis*, so ins Vierte jahr alhier sich hat aufgehalten, und der Music zu St. Marien alzeit beigewohnet, eine *discretion* wegen der Kirchen zugestellet, thut 18/-/-

1673, 10. Woche nach Neujahr [2. März], fol. 150r:
>   Freÿtag sind unsere Leute mit dem abfegen biß an die große *orgel* gekommen, da sich der Orgelmacher in einem Korb hin auffwinden laßen, und die an der Seite beide stehenden Pfeiffen, so gantz stum gewesen, wiederumb zu ihrer thonung

gebracht und andere defecten in der *orgel* ersetzet, Ihm deswegen gegeben 3 Ml:
Cathrin der Belgentretterinen, für das sie den gantzen Tag mit auffgewartet geben 5
ß: 3/5/-

1673, 7. Woche nach Ostern [11.Mai], fol. 157r:
    Montag, auf befehl Ihr *Magnificentz* H. Rodde, einen *Italienischen* Sänger, welcher
sich bey der *Musick* diesen Himmelfahrt Christi hat gebrauchen laßen, wegen der
Kirchen gegeben 2 Rthr: 6/-/-

1673, 5. Woche nach Michaelis [26. October], fol. 174r:
    Donnerstag nachdem die große Orgel mit consens der sämtlichen H. Vorsteherr, laut
memorial fol. 67, durch Joachim Richborn, Orgelmachern, so alhier zu St. Jacob gearbeitet, *renovieret.* [Margin note: diese renovierung bestehet nur in Durchstimmung und
Sauberung der gantzen Orgel.] Ihm deswegen laut Quitung, zahlt 50 Rthr: 150/-/-
    Noch Trine, der Belgentreterin so ihm 29 Tage aufgewartet à Tag 10 sch: geben:
thut 18/2/-

1673, 9. Woche nach Michaelis [23. November], fol. 177r:
    Montag habe mit vorwissen und willen H. *Matthaei Rodden* Jun. zur Zier der Abendt
Music zweene auff eine Sonderbahre Ahrt gerichtete Trompeten machen laßen, dergleichen man bishero in keine fürstliche *Capelln,* /: da sonst alle Dinge in der edlen *Music*
vorgebracht werden :/ nicht vernommen, für selbe nebst unkosten zahlt: 15/-/-

1674, 1. Woche nach Ostern [19. April], fol. 194r:
    Sonnabend, . . . Noch haben *Ihr Magnificentz H: Rodde* auff ersuchen des *Cantoris
Samueli Francken* vergünstiget, daß er 2 *discant Posaunen* zu Zier der *Music* hat mögen
machen laßen, darvor zahlt 15/-/-

1674, 11. Woche nach Ostern [28. Juni], fol 201r:
    Freitag, . . . Noch einem frembden *Vocalisten, Johan Valentin Meder* auß Thüringen,
umb daß er am Tage *Visitationis Mariae* [2. Juli] beÿ anwesenheit des H: Engelschen
Residenten von Hamburg, auf unser *orgel* mit aufgewartet, auf befehl Ihro *Magnif: H:
Rodden,* gegeben 3/-/-

1675, 1st Woche nach Ostern [4. April], fol. 233v:
    Freÿtag wart mein kleines Töchterken Anna Sophia Buxtehudin mit einer
Kinderleuten in der Kirchen, in der für der Chortreppen belegene gemaurte
Begrebnus bestetiget, solches haben meine HHr: Vorsteherr, wie meinen
Antecessoribus, so wol von *Organisten* alß Werckmeistern wiederfahren, auch mir freÿ
gegeben, das Ungeldt dem Volcke habe ich gezahlet: -/-/-

1675, 8. Woche nach Ostern [23. Mai], fol. 241r:
    Sonnabend, Haben meine HochgeEhrte H: Vorsteher, auff mein Dieterich
Buxtehuden unterdienstlich ersuchen, laut *Memorial* fol: 75: großg: vergünnet eine
kleine Schreib und *Studier* Stube aufm Werckhauße, nach dem Kirchoff über der trep-
pen, auffzurichten, Und ist diese Woche damit ein anfang gemacht worden . . .

1676, 6. Woche nach Michaelis [5. November], fol. 307r:
    Sonnabend, . . . Noch habe zu den 6 *Trompeten* der Kirchen gehörig, 6 Sordinen
machen lassen, dem dreckschler fürs Stück geben 8 sch.: 3/-/-
    Vor 6 Stiekplaten auff der *Orgel* zu gebrauchen, à Stück zahlt 2 sch: ist: -/12/-

1677, 17. Woche nach Ostern [5. August], fol. 342r:

> Montag, Nachdem Ao. 1675. . . ein frembder Sänger von Kiel sich allhier zu *St. Marien*, in der Fasten und Osterfeÿer, hat gebrauchen laßen, und die *Music* so wohl auff der Orgel als aufm Chor beigewohnet, haben Ihro *Magnificentz H. Consul Rodde*, der Kirchen wegen Ihm 8 Rthr. verehret, welchen verschus, Hochgedacht Ihr Magnif. wieder entrichtet: thut: 24/-/-

1677, 19. Woche nach Ostern [19. August], fol. 343r:

> Dienstag, Von Daniel Erick Violmacher allhier eine *Tenor* Geige, welche auff der großen *Orgel* hochnötig habe, gekaufft vor 6/-/-

17: Wochenbuch 1678–1685

1678, 3. Woche nach Neujahr [13. Januar], fol. 4r:

> Laut *Protocolli* fol. 81 haben meine Hochgeehrten H. Vorsteher, auff mein bittliches ersuchen, zur Ehre Gottes und zur beforderung meiner Fästtaglichen- und Abend *Music*, ein Doppelt 16 füßiges *Regal* der Kirchen zum besten für 16 Rthr. gekaufft, sind: 48/-/-.

1678, 6. Woche nach Michaelis [3. November], fol. 37r:

> Sonntag, Laut *Memorial* fol: 82: dem *Cantore* Samueli Francken die 75 MLüb. 10 sch. wegen einiger gedruckten *Musicalien*, so er zum Gebrauch der St. Marien Kirchen gekauft, welche dem *Musicalischen Inventario* einverleibet sollen, entrichtet: sind: 75/10/-

1679 1. Woche nach Michaelis [28. September], fol. 81r:

> Montag, . . . Noch habe mit *Consens* der Herrn Vorsteherr dreÿ Schallmeÿen und 2 Quart-flöeten, so nach dieser *Orgel* eingerichtet, von Hamburg bringen lassen, welche /: geliebts Gott :/ in bevorstehender Abend-Music gebraucht werden sollen, vor die Schallmeien bezahlt 8 Rthr: die flöten 1 Rthr: sind: 27/-/-

1680, 7. Woche nach Neujahr [8. Februar], fol. 99r:

> Sonnabend, Führe hiermit ein die 100 MLüb welche meine Großgünstige Hochgeehrte H. Vorsteherr laut *Memor:* fol:85:b: auff die jüngst gehaltene Abend-*Music*, in ansehung des weitlauffigen Wercks und der großen mühe, so im *Componieren* und Schreiben auff die 400 bogen sich verstrecket, wie auch denen vielen gehülffen an *Instrumentisten* und Sängern, beÿ nahe in die 40 Persohnen, und waß dergleichen Unkosten mehr gewesen, aber schlecht von der Bürgerschaft *recompensiert* worden, alß eine ergetzligkeit und Hülffe der Kirchen wegen verEhret worden so mit schuldigster danckbarkeit allhie berechne: 100/-/-

1681, 22. Woche nach Ostern [28. August], fol. 176r:

> Dingstag, Auff Guthachten und bewilligung der p.t. Herrn Vorsteher, von des sel: *Cantore* Samuel Francken hingelassener Wittwen 22. *Musicalische Parteÿen* /: laut Specification :/ in der Kirchen, so wohl auff der Orgel alß auff dem Chor zu gebrauchen, entrichtet: 60/-/-

1682, 1. Woche nach Neujahr [1. Januar], fol. 192r:

> Montag, dem *Cantori* Pagendarm die von denen H. VorsteH: *ordinirte* 10 Rthr: Musicanten geldt laut *memorial* fol. 70 et 84 zugestellet: 30/-/-

1682, 4. Woche nach Neujahr [22. Januar], fol. 194r:
>Freitag, . . . Noch dem *Cantori* allhier, wegen eines Knabens, welchen Er seit *Johanni* Ao: 1681 zu dem *Positiv* aufm Chor gebraucht, die im *Memorial* fol: 88 benandte 9 Ml. entrichtet, und soll auff befehl der H: Vorsteherr derselbige erstlich vom dem *Organisten* zu *St. Marien examiniert,* und dan von Wohlgedachten H: Vorsteherrn angenommen werden . . .   9/-/-

1683, 1st Woche nach Neujahr [1. Januar], fol. 239r:
>Dingstag, dem *Cantori* Pagendarm die von denen H. Vorstehern *ordinirte* 10 Rthr, laut *memorial* fol: 70:, entrichtet: 30/-/-

1683, 2. Woche nach Neujahr [7. Januar], fol. 240r:
>Freitag, Demnach auch mit G.G. *Consens* Meiner HochgeEhrten H: Vorstehern, zu der jüngst *Praesentirten* Abend Music, einen Bassisten, nahmens *Jean Carl Quelmaltz,* von Hamburg verschrieben müßen, umb daß beÿ dießer Schulen in der *Cantoreÿ* ietziger Zeit schlechte Sänger gewesen, so nicht gebrauchen können, alß habe solche angewandte Unkosten, vor defrairung in der Herberge, wie auch zu *contentirung* mit einer *Discretion* an vorgedachten *Bassisten* gezalet 23 Rthr: weil solche beÿ ietzigen schlechten Zeiten und sehr geringen wieder vergeltung von der Bürgerschaft meinem Vermögen großen Schaden verursacht, alß sind die H.H. Vorsteher so gütig gewesen, und mit 10 Rtlr. der Kirchen wegen mir hierein zu Hülffe gekommen welches mit schuldigen danck hiemit wird angenommen und zur Rechnunge geführet, thut: 30/-/-

1683, 8. Woche nach Neujahr [18. Februar], fol. 245r:
>Sonnabend, mit *Consens* Meiner HochgeEhrten H. Vorsteherr, laut *memorial* fol: 91: hat der Orgelmacher Michel Briegel mit der kleinen Orgel durch zu stimmen den anfang gemacht, und 4 1/2 tagl: daran gearbeitet, à 3 MLüb. thut: 13/8/-
>Noch den *Calcanten* 4 1/2 tagl: à 6 sch. ist: 1/11/-
>Noch dem Wachtmeister mit seinen Leuten wegen der auffwartung in der Kirchen unter der jüngst hie gehaltenen Abend-*Music,* auch im Weinachten mit beliebung der H. Vorsteherr gegeben: 6/-/-

1683, 1. Woche nach Ostern [8. April], fol. 253r:
>Dienstag, . . . Noch Johan *Fanselow* dem *Regalisten* alhier aufm Chor, so heute sein abscheid genommen, und nach Stockholm gereiset, sein Quartal von Neuen Jahr biß diesen Ostern, gegeben, ist: 4/8/-
>Laut Memorial fol: Daniel Grecken einen *Discantisten,* so im vergang. Jahre bey mir in der *Music* so wol am festagen alß sonsten, auffgewartet, die 2 Rthr entrichtet, sind: 6/-/-

1683, 7. Woche nach Michaelis [11. November], fol. 279r:
>Sonnabend, . . . Noch Meister Briegel dem Orgelmacher, so mit *Consens* der H. Vorsteher, laut *Protocolli* fol: 87:91: die beide Orgeln ohne die Röhr wercke gantz durch gestimmet, und hat Er an der großen Orgel 18 1/2 tagl:, an der kleinen 13 tagl. gearbeitet sind 31 1/2 tagl: à 3 MLüb. thut so bezahlet: 94/8/-
>Noch denen *Calcanten* so ihm täglich auffgewartet, zahlt 30 1/2 tag à 7 sch. thut: 13/5/6

1683, 13. Woche nach Michaelis [23. December], fol. 284r:
>Sonnabend, dem Wachtmeister so mit seinen Leuten so wohl in der Abend *Musica* alß auch in Weinachtfest in der Kirchen gute Auffsicht gethan, gegeben: 6/-/-

1684, 1. Woche nach Neujahr [1. Januar], fol. 287r:
Mittwoch dem *Cantori* Pagendarm, die zu dem *Musicanten ordinirte* 10 Rthr: laut *Protocolli*, fol: 70: entrichtet, sind: 30/-/-
Noch Meister Briegeln, dem Orgelmacher, vor das *Positiv* aufm Chore so sehr *imperfect* und unrein gewesen, zu *Renoviren* und gantz durch zu stimmen zahlt, 6 tagl: à 3 Ml. thut: 18/-/-

1684, 4. Woche nach Neujahr [20. Januar], fol. 288r:
Weiln mit *Consens* Meiner HochgeEhrten HH: Vorsteherr beÿ verwichener *AbendMusic*, auß mangel dűchtiger Sänger in hießiger Schulen vom Kiel einen *Bassisten* und *Tenoristen* kommen laßen, denen der Eine durch Hanß Braschen *Liberalität* mit Tisch und *Logement* versehen worden, der Andre aber von der Kirchen *defrairet* worden sol. Alß habe der 7 Wochen wegen in sein *Quartier* bezahlet 12 Rtlr: im übrigen aber Ihnen beÿderseits *pro descretione* vor geleiste Hülffe von meinem *Colligirten* gahr schlechten Newjahr gegeben 14 Rtlr: berechne demnoch nur hieselbst wie vorerwehnt, die von denen HH. Vorstehern *Consentirte* 12 Rtlr: sind: 36/-/-

1684, 14. Woche nach Michaelis [28. December], fol 329r:
Noch dem Wachtmeister, so mit seinen Hinterhabenden Leüten, in dieser jüngst *praesentirten* Abend-*Musica*, als auch in Weihnachten in der Kirchen gute Auffsicht gethan geben: 6/-/-

1685, 6. Woche nach Neujahr [1. Februar], fol. 335r:
Sonnabend, ... Noch ward die grosse *Orgel* so sehr unbestendig, unrein und falsch, von einem durchreisenden Orgelmacher auß Lüneburg nahmens Baltzer Heldt in etwas *Corrigiret* und durch gestimmet, daran er 5 tage gearbeitet, Ihm davor geben müssen: 12/-/-
Noch der *Calcantinnen*, vor die Belgen in 4 tagen zu treten geben: 1/4/-

1685, 4. Woche nach Michaelis [23. October], fol. 362r:
Sonnabend, Alldieweil ietziger Zeit ein frembder Musicus nahmens Hinrich Ditmer, und derselbe ein vortreffliches *Instrument* als nemblich ein *Quint* oder *Bass Bombard* beÿ sich geführet, auch solches abstehen wollen, Welches vorlengsten schon zu auszierung hiesiger Music begehrt und gesucht worden, Alß haben die Herren Vorsteherr auff anhalten des *Cantoris* Pagendarm entleihen großg. *Consentiret* den selben *Bombard* vor unserer Kirchen zu kauffen, welcher denn vor 25 Rthr: gekaufft und bey behalten worden, thut so Ihm bezahlt: 75/-/-
Noch vor ein newes Messings *Es* oder Rohr an dem *Bombard* umb selben Orgelmässig zu bringen zahlt: 2/-/-

18: Wochenbuch 1686–1695

1686, 2. Woche nach Neujahr [3. Januar], fol. 2r:
Freÿtag. ... Demnach auch unle[n]gsten ein Berühmter Orgellmacher von *Dresden* hieselbst durch reisete, nahmens Johan Nette, welcher unsere große *Orgel* besehen und ausgehöret, dabej aber anzeigete, daß nebst anderen vielen *Fauten* auch unterschiedliche Mängel an denn Schnarrwercken vorhanden, denen beÿ zeiten müste vorgebeuget werden, daferne Sie nach diesem nicht schlimmer und zu *repariren* alßdan mehr kosten sollten, derowegen habe solches /: weill es vorhin schon von meinen hochgeehrten Herren Vorsteherrn insgesampt auf solchen fall ist

beliebet worden, laut *Protoc. fol.* 93:/ des Herren Burgermeister *Ritters Magnificentz* gebührendermassen *referiret*, und auf dero Befehl mit vorgedachten *Orgel*macher *accordiret*, daß Er die Schnarwercke sämptlich durch gehen, *examiniren* und *corrigiren* möchte, allermassen er auch solches mit großem fleiß und *curieusität* verrichtet, dabeÿ Er dan allerleÿ Arbeit gehabt, neue Zungen verfertiget und dergleichen mehr, welches in die 3te Woche gewehret, dafür Ihm der Kirchen wegen zahlen und zustellen müssen: 36/-/-

Noch der *Calcantinn*en so Ihm 10 Tage aufgewartet und die Belgen getreten zahlt: a taglohn 7 ß: thut: 4/6/-

1686, 25. Woche nach Ostern [19. September], fol. 24r:

Sontag, Heute hat man wegen Eroberung der so höchst *importanten* Vestung Ofen, so jeder Zeit die Königl HaubtStadt in Ungarn gewesen, auch von denen Christen seidt deßen Sie in der Türcken Gewaldt gekommen und behalten geblieben, Sechsmahl belägert, ietzo aber in der Siebenden Belagerung und Bluhtigen Bestörmung gewaltig erobert word[en], allhier ein Danckfest gehalten, Wo beÿ man nach verichteter Dancksagung von denen Cantzelen das *Tè Deum Laudamus* gesungen, und andere *Solenniteten* mit Spielen, *Musici*ren, Stücken lösen und Freuden Feür das Fest *celebriret* hat, Welchen Sieg der Christlichen Waffen Gott der Höchste in Gnaden ferner gesegnen wolle, damit wir mannigen *Triumph* über den Feindt des Christlichen Nahmens erhalten, und demselben dafür zu dancken Uhrsache haben mögen. Inzwischen alhier zu Rechnung führe, was deswegen verunkostiget, alß wegen des Geleute wie am hohen Festen gebräuchlich 2 Ml 4 ß und denen Brüdern vor das *Paucken* und Abblasen vom Thurm 9 Ml thut: 11/4/-

1687, 1. Woche nach Neujahr [2. Januar], fol. 36r:

Sonnabend, . . .Mit consens meiner Hochgeehrten Herren Vorsteherr, einem Vocalisten, nahmens *Longolio* auß der fürstl. Goteschen *Cappelle* so sich auff der *Orgel* etzliche mahlen wacker hat hören laßen, zu 2. Stübg. ReinschWein à 3 Ml berechnet: thut: 6/-/-

1687, 6. Woche nach Ostern [1. Mai], fol. 47r:

Sonnabend, Mit *consens* Meiner HochgeEhrten Herren *Vorsteherr*, bin am vergangenem Montag nach Hamburg gefahren, umb daselbst, wegen unserer beiden *Orgeln*, so eine Haubt *Renovation* höchst bedörffen, mit dem *Orgel*macher Arp Schnitker zu reden, auch zu gleich seine in St. *Nicolai* Kirchen, *Costi* gantz new gemachte große *Orgel* zu besehen und zu hören, Welches Werck mit gutem *Success* und jeder männiglichen Vergnügen verfertiget worden, auch selbsten als mit gutem *Contentement* befunden und *probiret* habe, welches ebenmässig zu hiesiger *correction* unserer *Orgeln* wohl wünschen möchte. Und ist dabeÿ verunkostet wie folgt,

Für die Fuhr hin und her à 4 Ml 8 ß: nebst Schreibgeldt ins Posthauß hin und her zu ieder Zeit, 3ß. thut 9/6/-

Denen Litzen Brüdern für Ab- und austragung, à 6ß. thut 3 mahl 1/2/-

Dem Fuhrman Trinkgeldt hin und her: -/2/-

Für eine MahlZeit zu Schöneberg: -/10/-

Für 4 Tage in Hamburg zu Zehren, à Mahlzeit 12 ß: thut 6/-/-

Extra alle Mahlzeit ein halb Planck fransch Wein a 1-1/2 ß: thut -/12/-

Denn Magten Trinckgeldt: -/6/-

Im Wegfahren vom Hamburg zum newen Raelstaet 5 ß: zum Schöneberg 2 ß: thut: -/7/-

1688, 16. Woche nach Ostern [29. Juli], fol. 83r:

> *Freÿtag*, . . .Weiln auch mit *Consens* Meiner hochgeehrten Herrn *Vorsteherr* in der 10: Woche nach Newjahr ein *Orgel*macher *subarhiret*, daß Er unsere *Orgeln* einiger massen *corrigiren* solte, und aber derselbe unverrichteter Sache davon gezogen, alß habe einen anderen Nahmens Johan R*a*tz*e*l von Dreßden, beÿ seiner durch Reise dahin vermacht, solche *correctur* über sich zu nehmen. Wann Er dann in 28 Tagen unsere beÿde *Orgeln*, sowoll Pfeiff= und Schnarrwerck durchgestimmet, viele neue Zungen in denn Schnarrwercken gemacht, theils Mundstücke in der grossen *Trommet* von 16: fueßthon in der grossen *Orgel* mit *Pargament* gefüttert, viele Pfeiffen, so von dem Ungeziffer zerbissen gelötet, die Belgen geleimet, und sonsten was in der kurtzen Zeit, weiln Er nicht länger bleiben wollen, hat können geschehen, verbessert, So habe Ihm täglich *pro Labore*, 2 Mk geben müssen, thut 56 Mk: für den Tisch, welchen auß Liebe zu denen *Orgeln*, in währender Zeit Ihm gegeben, verlange nichts; Wündsche nur daß diese Arbeidt, bis eins die Haubt *renovation* soll vorgenommen werden, beständig bleiben möchte. Berechne also nebst 2 Mk Trinckg[eldt] so Ihm zugegeben: 58/-/-
>
> Noch der *Calcantinnen so des Tages von 3: à 4: Uhr an des Morgens, bis 8 Uhr des Abends *continuir*lich beÿ denen Belgen hat seÿn müßen, geben für 27 1/2 taglohn a 7 ß: thut: 12/6/-

1689, 2. Woche nach Ostern [7. April], fol. 106r:

> Mit Consens meiner HochgeEhrten Herrn Vorsteher habe dem Hamburgischen Orgelmacher Mr. Arp Schnitgern, umb unser Große Orgel zu besichtigen, verschrieben, welcher auch herüber zu kommen, die märcklichsten Mängel und *defectus* darinn *observiret*, und darauff denen Herrn Vorstehern die *Relation* davon schriftlich übergeben, etc: für solche seine Mühe und Reise ist ihm von der Kirchen bezahlt 8 Rthr sind 24/-/-

1690, 8. Woche nach Neujahr [16. Februar], fol. 133r:

> *Donnerstag*, Auff E: Hochw: Raths Verordnung, ward wegen der am Stund 16: Januarÿ zu Regenspurg wohlbrachten Wahl und Kröhnung Eines Römischen Königs, alß unsers glorwürdigsten Käÿsers *Leopoldi* H: Sohn, *Josephi*, ein *Solennes* Danckfest vom 7: bis 11: Uhr morgens *cellebriret* und gehalten, und ist folgender *Text* auß dem *Gen*: 49, *Cap*: 22: Joseph wird wachsen, Er wird wachsen wie an einer Quelle, u. s. w. biß v. 24: aus ihnen sind kommen Hirten und Steine Israel, dar zu erwehlet und von unserm H: *Superintend. Doct*: Pfeiffern rühmligst erklärt worden. Nach geendigter Predigt, haben die auß der Brüderschafft unter dreÿmahliger Lösung der *Canonen* Eine *Ritornello* mit *Trompetten* und *Paucken* aufm Thurm da zwischen *Præsentiret*, darfür unserm Thurman, weiln Er ietzo mehr Leute alß vor hin darbeÿ gehabt, gefordert 12 Ml: welche Ihm der Kirchen wegen entrichtet 12/-/-

1691, 12. Woche nach Michaelis [20. December], Fol. 199r:

> *Sonnabend*, . . .Noch *Michel* Briegel dem *Orgel*macher für etzliche *Defecta* an denn *Trommeten* und sonsten, in der großen *Orgel* zu *corrigiren*, gegeben: 2/8/-

1692, 12. Woche nach Michaelis [18. December], fol. 234r:

> *Mittwoch*, . . . Noch dem Wachtmeister, für daß er mit seinen Leuten unter *præsentir*ung der Abend *Music*, so in diesem Jahre wegen der Traur Fall [death of Buxtehude's daughter, buried 16. Nov.] in meinem Hauße, nur 4 mahl geschehen, in der Kirchen herumb gegangen, geben: 5/-/-

1693, 6. Woche nach Neujahr [5. Februar], fol. 238r

    Sonnabend, Von einem frembden Mann etwas *preparirtes* Schlangengifft gekaufft, welches wegen des vielen Ungezieffers so auff denn beiden *Orgeln* sich zwischen denen Pfeiffen häuffig finden hinstrewen laßen, darfür zahlt: 1/8/-

1693, 8. Woche nach Ostern [4. Juni], fol. 249r

    Mittwoch, Auff Befehl des H[errn] Burgermeister Ritters Magnif[izenz] einem frembden Vocalisten natione italo, welcher dem lieben Gott zu Ehren, in diesem Pfingstfest auff der großen Orgel, sich hat hören laßen, der Kirchen wegen verEhrt6/-/-

1694, 3. Woche nach Neujahr [14. Januar], fol. 273r

    Sonnabend, . . . Michel Briegelen dem hiesigen *Orgel*macher für etliche *Defecten* in der großen *Orgel* zu *corrigiren,* auch unterschiedene abgebrochene Pfeiffen in denn Röhrwercken wiederumb zu löten, gegeben: 2/2/-

1694, 13. Woche nach Neujahr [25. März], fol. 278r:

    Freÿtag, . . . Marten Hundv[ogt] für die beid[en] feürherde auff denn *Orgeln* zu *repariren* gegeben 1. tagl[ohn] ist: -/10/-

19: Wochenbuch 1696–1704

1696, 2. Woche nach Neujahr [5. Januar], fol. 1r:

    Montag, Otto Berens dem *Violisten* aufm Chor, für daß Er die der Kirchen gehörige 2 *Violinen,* 4 *Tenor* Geigen und 2: *Violons,* im vergangenen Jahre mit Seiden versehen und unterhalten gegeben: 3/-/-

1696, 3. Woche nach Michaelis [18. October], fol. 32r:

    Mittwoch, . . . Dem *Orgel*macher gesellen, für die *Mixturen* im *Pedal* in der großen *Orgel,* durch zu stimmen, und etzliche *Claves* in denn beÿden *Posaun*en zu *corrigiren,* gegeben 1 taglohn ist: 1/8/-

    Dem *Calcanten* gegeben: -/6/-

1697, 20. Woche nach Ostern [15 August], Empfangen, fol. 54b-v:

    Montag, Nachdem nun vom 1696: Jahre her, wie in der 18: Wochen nach Ostern anfänglich zu ersehen, zu auffricht- und verfertigung des neuen Altars, in unserer Kirchen *St. Marien* gearbeitet, und solches Werck numehro, durch Gottes Gnade zum Stande gebracht worden, alß ward gestriges Tages, im Nahmen *Gottes,* dieser newer Altar, in großer Versamblung der Christlichen Gemeine, durchs Gebeth und Ausspendung des hochheiligen *Sacraments* im Heil. Nachtmahl, *consecriret,* und damit zum dienste Gottes und dieser Kirchen, feÿerligst gewidmet, wobeÿ dan des Morgens, Vor- und nach der Predigt, unter der *Communion,* eine starcke *Music per Choros,* mit Paucken und Trompeten gemacht, in allen 3. Predigten, aber, die *specialiter* darauff gerichtet wären, so woll dem allmächtigen *Gott,* alß auch dem milden Gäber, gebührend dafür gedancket würde, mit Anwunschung alles Gutens und vielen Seegens, so der Barmhertziger Gott, in gnaden erfören und bestetigen wolle, umb *Jesu Christi* willen! In zwischen zur Nachricht dienet, daß der milde Stiffter und Geber deßen, nemblich, der HochEdel-Vest und Wollweiser Herr, H: *Thomas Friedenhagen,* dieser Stadt Rathsverwandter und Mitvorsteher unserer Kirchen, dem lieben Gott zu Ehren, dieser Kirchen zum schönen Zierrath, Ihm selbst aber, zu unsterblichen

Ruhm, alle dazu erforderte Kosten, freÿwilligst daran *spendiret*, und solches Werck durch einen Brabander, nahmens *Sig: Thomas Quilini*, meisten theils dorten hat machen, und nicht sonder Gefahr zu Schiffe anhero bringen laßen, theils aber, ist hier noch dazu ausgearbeitet worden wo zu Meister Hinrich Beÿer, das Gemaur aufgeführet hat; wie vieles in allen zustehen kommen, ist bis *dato* noch unbekandt, es sÿnd aber 34500 Steine, 27 Mund Kalck, und [space] S# [Schiffspfund = ca. 150 kg] Eisen, darin vermauret, von dem alten Messings *Gallerie* so 5: S# 18: L# [Liespfund = ca. 7.5 kg] 3: # [Pfund = 484 gr] gewogen, X [marginal insert: und *S*: Wohlm. von der Kirchen laut Rech{nung} in der 7. Woche nach *Michaeli*: erhandelt hat,] das neuw umbgegossen, und gemacht worden. *etc.* Schließlich so wunsche, nebst schuldigster Dancksagung, für dieses vortrefflich Geschenck und Gedächtnis, wie auch für alle andern dieser lieben Stad und Kirchen, rühmligst erzeigte vielfeltige Wollthaten, nochmalen von Grund der Seelen, daß der Barmhertzige *Gott* und Vater Alle dabeÿ gethane Wünsche, in Gnaden erfüllen, und es bis an den lieben jüngsten Tag, unversehrt erhalten, insonderheit aber allergnädigst wolle verleihen, daß ein jeglicher der *Communicanten*, das hochheilige Nachtmahl würdiglich, dabeÿ empfangen, und Ewig sehlig werden möge. Das *Gott* gebe umb Jesu Christi willen, Amen!

1697, 3. Woche nach Michael: [17. October], fol. 62r:
    Sontag hat man alhier, auff Verordnung eines HochEd: Raths wegen der von Gott verliehenen Großen und herrlichen *Victoria* wieder den Christen feindt in Hungarn, dergleichen in diesem *Seculo* nicht geschehen, ein *solennes* Danckfest gehalten, da dann Sonnabends vorher, vom 1/4 vor 12: biß 1/4: Nach 1. Uhr alle Glocken geleutet, heute aber in denen Kirchen, beÿ guter *Music* ein Lob- und Danckpredig gehalten, das Herr Gott dich Loben wir gesungen, unter *Trompeten* und *Paucken* Schall von unserm Thurm, dreÿ mahl die Stücke rings um die Stadt loß gebrandt und alßo geendiget und beschlossen, *sit nomen Domini sit benedictum*! denen auß der Brüderschafft, so aufm Thurm die *Trompeten* geblaßen, ihr gewöhnliches gegeben – ist: 12/-/-

1697, 7. Woche nach Michaelis [14. November], fol. 64r:
    Mittwoch, Johan Hantelman, dem hiesigen *Orgelmacher*, für etzliche *defecten* in der großen *orgel* zu *corrigiren*, und das *Positiv* aufm Singechor ein wenig durch zustimmen, zahlt, 3 1/2 taglohn a 1 Mk 8 ß ist: 5/4/-
    Noch dem *Calcanten* 2 taglohn a 6 ß gegeben ist: -/12/-

1699, 5. Woche nach Ostern, fol. 117r:
    Sontag, Hat man allhier auff Verordnung eines HochEdl. Raths wegen den im negstverwichenen Jahre, mit I. Käyserl. Maÿt und den Türcken geschlossenen Frieden, ein solennes Danckfest celebriert und gehalten, da dann in denn Kirchen das *Te Deum laudamus* gesungen, unter der Trompeten und Paucken Schall von unsrem Thurm, dreÿmahl die Stücke rings umb die Stadt los gebrandt und also geendiget, *Deo ter opt. max. sit gloria et honor in sempiterna secula*. Denen aus der Brüderschafft alter gewonheit nach, ihre Gebühr entrichtet, ist: 12/-/-
    Das Nothhelffer Geldt wegen der Pulßglocken ausgegeben, ist: 2/4/-

1700, 1. Woche nach Neujahr [1. Januar], fol. 143r:
    Montag, . . . Alß auch für dießmahl[en] durch Gottes Gnade, die von alters her üblich gewesene Abend Musicen dieser Kirchen gehalten, absonderlich aber auff Begehren E: E: Hochw[eisen] Raths Ein Glückwünschungs Gedicht für die Wohlfahrt der Stadt Lübeck im Druck heraus gegeben, und beÿ volckreicher

Versamblung in einer Vollstendigen Musica öffentlich von mir præsentiret worden,
so hat deswegen, umb allen tumult zu verhüten in und für der Kirchen, die
Rathswacht auffwarten müssen, dafür Ihnen wie gebräuchlich gegeben: 6/-/-
Noch haben Meine Hochgeehrte H. Vorsteherr, wie dieselbe im vergangenen Jahre
d 19: Decembr aufm Werckhause waren, unsers Thurmans Sohn, Christoff Knölck, so
nach des Sehl. Hans Iwen Tode in 8: Jahren auff der Orgel mit der Violin die
Auffwartung gethan, für die 3. letzeren Jahren, à 30 Mk geben lassen – seindt: 90/-/-

1701, 27. Woche nach Ostern [25. Sept], fol. 209r:
Montag, Mit unterdienstl. gehorsamsten Danck führe alhie ein, die ienigen 100:
Ml. welche meine Hochgebietende Herren Vorsteher gg. belieben wollen mir beÿ zu
legen, wie zu sehen im *memorial* fol. 158. 100/-/-

1701, 7. Woche nach Michaelis [13. November], fol. 214r:
Freÿtag, Weil die kleine *Orgel* seiter *Anno* 1654 keine *renovation* gehabt, also die
höchste Nothdurfft erfordert solche vorzunehmen, So haben Meine Hochgeehrte
Herren Vorstehere auff unterdienstlichs Anhalten in deren *renovation etc. consentiret*,
worauff den von dem allhie wohnenden *Orgel*macher Meister Hans Hantelman den
20: *Julÿ* Jüngsthie der Anfang gemacht, und den 24: *September* damit geendiget worden, kostet also diese *reparation* wie in *specie* hernach folget
Dem *Orgel*macher für 9: Wochen und 3: tage sind 57: taglohn, a 2 Ml 8ß: 142/8/-
Dem Gesellen für 57: taglohn, a. 1 Ml 8 ß: 85/8/-
                                                                            228/-/-

Dem *Calcanten* 57: taglohn, a 6: ß: 21/6/-

1702, 24. Woche nach Ostern [24. September], fol. 249r:
Montag, . . . Noch Alexander Fritz dem Houtboisten auff der Orgel sein Jahrgeldt
gegb. ist: 30/-/-

1703, 10. Woche nach Neujahr [11. März], fol. 266r:
Montag, . . .Auff gut Befinden der Herren Vorsteher nach Barkentien geweßen
und daselbst die *Orgel* in sonderheit die ohnlengst darein gemachte, neue Stimmen
zu *examinieren*, weil der Meister Christian Kreÿnaw davon sich dadurch *recommendiren*
wollen, zur vorhabenden *renovation* unserer großen *Orgel*, und weil mir darzu ein
Wagen von Ew: Hoch: Raths Marschall verschaffet worden, so ist dabeÿ nur verunkostet: 1/8/-

1704, 1. Woche nach Ostern [23: Martii] fol. 303r:
Sonnabend, Nachdem E: HochEd[len] Hochw: Rath zu heilsamer Ordnung und
verbesserung hiesiger Kirchen, ein wolleingerichtetes GesangBuch außfertigen und
zur übung des öffentlichen *Gottes* Dienstes, d. 1: Januarij dieses Jahres *introduciren*
lassen, haben die h.g. Herren Vorsteher umb besserer auffmerckung und vernehm-
lichkeit, hochlöblichst verordnet, daß 6: Taffeln mit denen 208: darzu gehörigen
numeris sollten gemacht werden, umb hin und wieder an denn Pfeilern zu hangen,
für solche anzustreichen Frantz Christoff Haberman, dem Mahler, laut
Rechnung[en] 36: Ml zahlt gleich wie zu *St: Jacobi*, mit 27:Ml. 27/-/-

1704, 4. Woche nach Ostern [13. April], fol. 304r:
Dingstag, Die, laut *Memorial fol:* 161 den 17: *Punct*, Arp Schnitker dem *Orgel*macher
in Hamburg, zugelegte 10: Reichsthaler per *Wexel* übergesandt, seind: 30/-/-

[Comment in left margin]: *Vide Anno* 1705 In der 4: Woche nach *Michaelis* wegen diesen *punct.*

1704, 24. Woche nach Ostern [31.August], fol. 318r:
   Sonnabendt, . . . Otto Diederich Richborn dem *Orgel*macher, laut *Contract*, den ersten Termien bezahlet: ist: 150/-/-

1704, 26. Woche nach Ostern [14. September] fol. 319r:
   Sontag, Weil dann auch der grosse Gott, ohnlängsten Ihro Kaÿserl: Maÿtt.: und dero hohen *Allirten* Waffen dermassen *Secundiret* und gesegnet, daß Sie am 13: Aug: *nuperi*, beÿ Höchstätt kegen die Französische und Beÿersche *Armeen* einen so herrlichen *Completen* Sieg erhalte, dergleichen beÿ Menschen Gedencken nicht erhöret. Alß hat E: HochW: Rath nach dem *Exempel* anderer *Potenzen* und *Respubliquen*, alhie auch desfals dem Lieben Gott zu Ehren ein *Solennes* Danckfest angeordnet, da dann beÿm Gottes dienst eine völlige *Music* gemacht, und beÿ dreÿmahliger Lösen der *Canonen* umb die Stadt, auff dem Thurm die *Paucken* und *Trompeten* sich tapffer haben hören lassen müssen, wofür denen aus der Brüderschafft *Musicanten* ihr gewöhnliches *Compitent* gezalet mit: 12/-/-

1704, 7. Woche nach Michaelis [9. November], fol. 327r:
   Mittwoch, demnach durch Gottes Gnade, dem Orgelmacher Otto Dietrich Richborn, die vorgehabte *renovation* hiesiger großen Orgel, mit denen im *Contract* erwehnten dreÿen neuen Stimmen, genand *Vox humana, Sexquialtera* und *Dulcian* a 16 fues thon Zimblich wollgerathen, und solche weil nunmehro von Ihm verfertiget worden, Alß habe auff gg. Befehl Meiner Hochgeehrten *Herren Vorsteherr*, Ihm noch das rückständige *quantum* der *accordirten Summa* bezahlet mit: 300/-/-
   Noch mit *Consens* vor hochgedachten *Herren Vorsteherr*, für die *Polirung* der fordersten Pfeiffen, so nachgehends aller erst *extra Contractum resolviret* worden, *pro discretione* geben müssen   60/-/-

20: Wochenbuch 1705–1711

1705, Neujahrs Woche [1. Januar], fol. 1r:
   Freÿtag, . . . Noch dem Wachtmeister für da er unter praesentirung des im nestverwichenen Jahren gehaltenen Abend-Music, mit seinen Leuten in der Kirchen herumb gegangen, hat aber wenig geholfen, geben   6/-/-

1705, 6. Woche nach Ostern [17. May], fol. 18r:
   Sonnabend, wie die Herren Vorsteher am negst verwichenen Montage, aufm Werckhause bey abgelegter Kirchen Rechnung zusammen wahren, haben dieselbe ggl. consentiret, dem Cantori Pagendarm, für die Melodeyen derer 303 zusammen synd, in denn 4. neugemachten Gesangbüchern con canto, Alto, Tenor et Basso, ohne die Texte ein Zuschreiben pro Labore zu geben   60/-/-
   Noch Christian Partike et Wolter Möllraht, beiden Aritmetici, für den Text unter denn 303: Gesängen in quadruplo zu legen, laut Quittung zahlet   150/-/-
   Noch haben Meine HochgeEhrte Herren Vorsteher, dem Lieben Gott zu Ehren, der Christlichen Gemeine zu Ergetzlichkeit, und der Edlen Music zur Ziere, 2. fürtreffliche kupferne HeerPaucken an die Kirche gekaufft   5/-/-

1705, 9. Woche nach Ostern [7. Juni], fol. 20r:

Sonnabend, Ist im Nahmen Gottes, auf Befehl der Herren Vorsteher, wegen Staffierung unser großen Orgel am verwichenen Montag, mit aufführung einer Stellung der Anfang gemacht, der Liebe Gott wolle gnädigt verleihen daß es ohne den geringsten Schaden zum glücklichen und erwünschten Ende möge vollenbracht werden, daran haben gearbeitet. Erstlich 1: Maurgesell 4-1/2 tagl à 20:ß nebst 3:ß: ist   5/13/-

1705, 16. Woche nach Ostern [26. July], fol 27r:

Demnoch aus Göttlicher Verhängnis am jüngstverwichenen 5. May, Ihro. Röm. Kayserl: Maÿtt. Divus Leopoldus 1. Glorwürdigsten Andenckens weÿland unser Allergnädigste Kayser, König und Herr zu aller grösten Leidenwesen des gantzen Röm. Reichs, aller dero Königreichen, Herrschaften und Ländern, Vasallen und Unterthanen, dieses Zeitliche verlassen: und darumb überall, absonderlich in dieser benachbarten Fürstenthümern auff eine gewisse Zeit, die tiefe Trauer angeleget worden. Welchem rühml Exemplo auch die 3: Städte, Lübeck, Hamburg, und Bremen, gerne gefolget. Alß hat E.E. HochW. Rath alhier am 8. July deswegen folgendes *decretiret.*

Wegen fernerer Verfolg des *Ceremoniels* in denen Kirchen, und Celebrirung der *Exequien* des abgelegten Kaysers *Leopoldi* 1. Glorwürdigsten Andenckens, hat ein HochW. Rath *decretiret* und verordnet, daß nach dem 4: nacheinander folgende Sontag und die dazu gehörige gantze Wochen über, mit dem bißhero angefangenen Geleute *continuiret* worden, an dem 5ten Sontage, darauf /:welcher seyn wird, der 6te *post Trinitatis* oder 19: tag deß itzlaufenden Monaths Julÿ:/ alß dann in denen Haupt Predigten in allen Kirchen, so woll in der Stadt als auch dem Lande, die gewöhnliche *Textus* zwar beÿbehalten, auff höchstgedachter Ihr. Käÿserl. Maÿtt. *Leopoldi* Absterben aber *dirigiret* dabeÿ die gehörige *Condolenzen* oder *Parentationes* verrichtet, und mit Glückwünschungen wegen angetretenen Regierung der jetzige Käÿserl: Maÿtt: *Josephi* 1. geendiget werden sollen. Unter wehrenden Gottes Dienst sollen den Tag über, wie bißhero, die *Orgeln* auch nicht gerühret, sondern an deren staat, in denen Haubtkirchen eine liebliche Trauer *Music* gehalten; ferner nach geEndigtem GottesDienst, von 10. biß 11. Uhr, mit denen Sing= oder Spielglocken die beÿ denen Vornehmsten Leichen alhier Gebrauchliche Trauer Lieder durch den Küster zu St. *Marien intoniret,* darauf von 11. biß 12. mit dem gewöhnlichen Geläute verfolgen, auch nach Mittag von 4. biß 5. wieder eine Stunde geläutet, und endlich von 5. biß 6. Uhr mit schlagung des Glockenspiels diese Trauer *Ceremonien* geschlossen: Solche diese Verfügung aber dem H: *Superintendenti* von dem *Proto Notario* Joack: Lüts: Carstens *intimiret,* auch dem *Cantori* und Werkmeistern, Imgleichen dem Küster zu St. *Marien, respective* angedeutet worden, *Ita decretum in Senatu,* den 8: Julÿ: *Anno* 1705.

Welchem den in allem also *punctuellement* nachgekommen, und damit Eins Theils der tödtl. Hintrit unsers so allergnädigste Holdseligsten Sanftmütigen frommen u. unvergleichlichen *Monarchens,* so Ein besonderer Großer Liebhaber der Edlen *Music,* und darin nicht weniger, alß in allen anderen Wissenschaften u. Tugenden höchst *qualifi*ciert gewesene gebührend *condoliret,* andern Theils aber, derjetzo Regierende Käÿserl. Maÿtt: *Josepho* 1. wegen angetretener Newen *Regiment,* alle hohe *prosperiteten* und Glückseligkeiten sÿend angewünschet worden, *quod DEUS bene vertat!* und weil von dieser Kirchen St. *Marien* auch tägl. die grosse PulßGlocke eine Stunde geläutet, wo von auff jeder Stunde 2 Ml Unkosten so die Kirche biß auff ferner Verordnung verschossen, thut also für 30: Tage   60/-/-

1705, 4. Woche nach Michaelis [25. October], Empfang, fol. 36v:
Freÿtag, . . .Wie im negstverwichenen 1704ten Jahre in der 4. Woche nach Ostern zu ersehen, sind dem *Orgel*macher Arp Schnitker nach Hamburg, wegen gehabter Mühe und *capitelirung* der *renovation* unser großen *Orgel, pro discretione* 10: Reichsthaler in 2. mahlen übergemacht, alldieweil derselbe aber damit nicht friedlich seÿn und annehmen wollen, als habe auff Befehl Meiner hochgeehrten *Herren* Vorsteherr wie im *Memorial* Buche fol: 163; den 10. Punct davon mehr Nachricht ist, alhie der Kirchen wieder in Rechnung bringen, sind: 30/-/-

1705, 6.Woche nach Michaelis [8. November], fol. 39r:
Mit consens des H. Hübens, habe auff die, an der Kirchen gekauffte große Paucken, durch Casper Schririer dem Ziebenmacher, 2. neue felle, weil die alte rund umbher entzwey gesprungen, wieder drauf machen und spannen lassen, Ihm darfür geben müssen: 12/-/-

1705, 9. Woche nach Michaelis [29. November], fol. 41r:
Mittwochen und Donnerstag [2.-3. December], Nachmittag, von 4. biß 6 Uhren ward mit Consens und Vorbewust E.E.HochW. Raths und meiner HochgeEhrten Herren Vorstehern die extra ordinaire Abend-Music, als das Castrum Doloris so dero in Gott ruhenden Römisch: Kayserl. Maytt. Leopoldo 1. zum Glorwürdigsten Andencken auff dero Hohen Nahmens-Tag gewidmet, dan auch Templum Honoris dero jetzund Regierenden Kayserl: Maytt: zu unsterblichen Ehren und congratula-tion, im Nahmen der gantzen Stadt verfertiget habe, allhier in der Kirchen so wie es im druck herausgekommen, öffentlich praesentiret wo bey dan mit Vergünstigung des H: Consulis Magnif: und Herren Vorstehern verunkostiget, wie folget, so hiezu auff der Orgel und denen Chören an Wax und Talglichtern bey diesen Actibus ver-braucht, zahlet für 4½ # Wax= à1Ml und 4# Talglicht à5ß: ist 5/12/-
Und weil E: HochW: Rath 2. Corperals mit 18: Gemeinen für denn Kirchthürren positiren lassen, umb allen Muhtwillen und Unlust zu verhütten, der sich bey dem grossen Zulauff durch Neuligkeit dermaßen leicht begeben können, so haben diesel-ben zu discretion von der Kirchen genossen 6/-/-

1706, 4. Woche nach Michaelis [24. October], fol. 88r:
Dingstag, . . . Wegen des vielen Ungeziefers auff denn beiden Orgeln Gifft kauffen müssen für -/4/-

1707, 4. Woche nach Ostern [15. Maji] Empfang, fol. 110v:
Montag, ward Sehl. Dieterich Buxtehude, in die 40 Jahre gewesener *Organiste* und Werckmeister dieser Kirchen, mit einem Stundel. und Zutracht mit der Pulß, in das vor der Chortreppen *sub No:* 242 belegene groß Kirchengrab gesetzt; Er hatte alles alten Herkommen nach von der Kirchen frey, (welches die sämmtlichen Erben mit schuldigsten Dancke erkennen) das ungl. ward aus dem Trauerhauße entrichtet. *Requiem aeternam dona Ei Domine, sitque ejus memoria in pace, Amen.*

27: Wochenbuch 1773–1788

1782, Woche des 16. December,
d. 18. . . . Dem Orgelbauer *Jochim Christoph Kaltschmidt*, die ihm, laut *Contract* & *Protocolli* zugestandenen 900/-/-

8. St. Marien I [Bücher] 4 [Diverses], 13: Vorsteher-Protokoll 1650–1743

Anno 1676 Adij 18 Januarÿ, fol. 75v:

2/ deß man *per supplicam* zu [illegible] daß ein jeder welcher kunfftig zu E:E:Rathes *Musicanten* bestellet u: angenommen wirdt muß schuldig sein, die 5 Abendt *Musicen* auff der Örgel ohne einigen entgelt u: deß organisten unkostung mit beÿ zuwohnen.

Anno 1701 d. 1. Marti, fol. 157v:

4/ Hat der Werckmeister erinnert,. weil die große Orgell in 50: od: 60 Jahre und lengere nicht repariret, dieselbe aber voller staub wehre, und viel andere Mängell hette, dadurch selbige ihren gebührenden *resonans* nicht geben könte, und also die *reparation* groß nötig thete, so ist beliebet, daß dieselbe solle wiederumb *repariret* werden iedoch das der Werckmeister an einen tuchtigen Orgell bauwer schreiben, und einen überschlag machen solte, waß zu dießer werck erfodert, oder die *reparirung* an gelde sich belauffen solte, und davon dehnen Hr: Vorstehern einen aufsatz zu übergeben.

1702, 6. April, fol. 158v:

4/ Die grosse *Orgell* zu *repariren*, ist laud *protocoll* von vorigen Jahr beliebet, dabeÿ bleibet es, doch daß der Werckmeister dem *Orgell*bauwer von Hamburg mit ehrsten anhero zu kommen verschreibet, und sich desfolgs mit dehnen Herren Vorstehern bereden soll.

[marginal note] vide: fol. 159: den 3. punct.

1703, 1. Marti, fol. 159v:

3/ Dem Orgelbauwer Arp Schniddeker von Hamburg, weil er vergangen Jahr aufhero zu kommen verlanget worden, und nun die arbeit wegen die *Orgell* zu *repariren* nicht bekompt, soll ihm vor seine Reisekosten 6 rD gegeben werden.

[marginal note] vide fol: 161: d. 17. Punct.

1704, 7. April, fol. 161v:

17/ Der Orgell Bauwer Arp Schniddeker bescheint sich, daß er nur wegen seiner Reise Unkosten 6 Rd bekommen, aber mehr außgegeben, alß ist beliebet, daß ihm annach sollen 4 Rd zugegeben werden, kunfftig aber nichts mehr.

[marginal note]: Hats nichts annehmen wollen.

Anno 1706 d. 4 Maÿ, fol. 165r:

18/ ferner ist der Werckmeister Diederich Buxtehude seine an die sampliche H. Vorsteher übergegebene *Supplicatum* verlasen, darinnen er verlanget, daß die H. Vorsteher eine von seinen Töchtern nach seinem Tode mit seinen dienste Begünstigen wollen, wozu er ein gutes *Subjectum* im vorschlage hette. Darauff ist beliebet worden, wan sich künfftig würde ein gutes *Subjectum* angeben, so die H. Vorsteher anständig, und derjenige einen von seinen Tochtern heÿrathen würde, so würde derselbe auch ein gütlich *resolution* zu gewarten haben.

9. St. Marien III [Schriften], Orgel, 2: Die grosse vormalige von 1518

Reparatur durch Jochim Christoph Kaltschmidt

Kund und zu wissen sey hiemit, daß, nachdem die sämmtlichen S.T. Herren Ober- und Vorstehere der hiesigen St. Marien-Kirche beschloßen, die große Orgel in gedachter Kirchen, welche voller Staub und Unreinligkeit, und überhaupt sehr fehlerhaft geworden, durch eine gänzlichen *Reparation* in untadelhaften Stande setzen zu laßen; Auf *Ordre* und im Namen der S.T. Herren Ober- und Vorstehere, zwischen dem Organisten und Werckmeister dieser Kirchen Johann Wilhelm Cornelius von Königslöw an einnem, und dem Orgelbauer Jochim Christoph Kaltschmidt am andern Theil, wegen ermeldten Orgel, nachfolgende Reparations-Contract geschloßen worden.

1.

Es verspricht gedachter Orgelbauer Jochim Christoph Kaltschmidt die Pfeiffen so im Gesichte stehen, auf neu zu poliren.

2.

Die Bälge, wo sie schadhaft, zu bessern und gut zu beleimen.

3.

Die Beutels in den Windladen, welche mehrentheils entzwey sind, sorgfältig zu bessern, die schadhaften zu verwerffen und neue davor zu machen, so daß die Windladen nicht windleck bleiben.

4.

Das ganze Orgelwerk auseinander zu nehmen, die Staub und alles unreine auszukehren, die Pfeiffen beim heraus nehmen sorgfältig untersuchen, ob auch etwas daran fehle, die Fehler abzuhelfen, und wenn sie nicht zu gebrauchen sind, an deren Stelle neue zu machen.

5.

Wenn denn alle Pfeiffen in der ganzen Orgel, besonders in den Rohr- und Schnarrwerken, daß sie gleichlauten und proportionirlich intoniren, die Mundstücke, Stiefeln, Krük, Blätter, Federn &c so wie alles Übrige, in untadelhaften Stand gesetzet worden; so verspricht Herr. Kaltschmidt.

6.

Dieses schöne Orgelwerck in einer reinen und gleich schwebenden *Temperatur* eingestimmt abzuliefern.

7.

Alle Zuthaten, als: Metall, Holz, Leder, Drath &c schafft er sich selber aus seinen eigenen Mitteln an, wie es solches nach seinem Anschlag selbst zu liefern übernommen. Dagegen wird ihm

8.

Von der Kirchen ein Bälgertreter zur Handreichung, beim Stimmen ein Bursche zum Anhalten, und die erforderlichen Kohlen gegeben. Auch werden die Stellagen, und wenn Leute zum heben und winden nöthig seyn sollten, von der Kirchen besorgt.

9.

Für diese wichtige *Reparatur* empfängt Herr Kaltschmidt wenn das Werk zuvörderst bei der Ablieferung gewissenhaft und unpartheyisch von mir untersucht und untadelhaft befunden worden: die verlangte Summa von 750 Ml schreibe sieben hundert und funfzig MarkLübsch. Wann nun diese *Reparation* vollendet ist, so übernimmt Herr Kaltschmidt

10.

Da die bey den Orgelwerke gewöhnlich alle 2 Jahr, gründlich durchgestimmt, und die vorfallenden Mängel an die Pfeiffen abgeholfen werden, für welche Durchstimmung der großen Orgel, jedes mal 72 Ml und für die klein jedes mal 36 Ml Lübsch bezahlet werden; solche Durchstimmung alle 2 Jahren für den gewöhnlichen Preiß.

Wobey ihm dem, wie sonst gewöhnlich, der Bälgentreter, Anhalter, Materialen &c alles von der Kirchen frey gehalten wird.

Urkundlich sind von diesem *Contract* 2 gleichlautende *Exemplaria* ausgefertiget, damit dieses alles getreulich möge nachgelebet und ohne Ausflüchte gehalten werden, von beyden Theilen unterschrieben besiegelt, und jedem Theile ein *Exemplar* zugestellet worden. So geschen Lübeck 1782 d. 16. Mart.

[seal]   Jochim Christoph Kaltschmidt
          Orgelbauer

10. St. Marien, Taufen
1659–1676

1668, 19 March, p. 157:
 Hanß beede Klockenleuter
 Diederich Buxtehude
 Dorothe von Wicken
 Margaretha Tunders

1669, 24 July [June?], p. 163:
 Diederich Buxtehude
 Samuel Franck
 Fr. Catharina Rodde
 Sebastian Spangenbergs Frau

1670, 15 July, p. 185:
 Diedterich Buxtehude
 H. Bürgerm. D. David Gloxins Frau
 H. Caspar von Degens frau
 Thomas Plonnius
 ds Kind [Helena, Margreta,] Magdalena Elisabeth

1672, 8 April, p. 229:
 Diedterich Buxtehude Werckmeister u. Organist, alhie
 H. Matthäus Rodde junior
 H. Pastoris Balemann Liebste
 J. Margreta Catrina Rodden
 ds Kind Anna Sophia

1675, 10 June, p. 313:
 Diedrich Buxtehude Organista
 Margreta Plonnies
 Margreta Janeke
 Johan Christoffer Tunder
 ds Kind Anna Margreta

1676–1693

1678, 30 August, p. 68:
    Diedrich Buxtehude Werckm.
        H. Burgmeist. Ritters Eheliebste
        Sophia Augusta Franken
        Peter Buxtehude
            das Kind Anna Sophia

1683, 25 March, p. 189:
    Diedrich Buxtehud Werckmeister u. Organ.
        D. Henricus Balemann
        Dorothea Tunders
        Elisabeth Roddin
            das Kind Doroth. Catrin

1686, 7 April, p. 253:
    Diedrich Buxtehude Organist alhie
        Anton Brandes
        Maria Fredenhagens
        Engel Rodden
            das Kind Maria Engel

11. St. Marien, Traubuch
1660–1701

p. 84
    Dom: 9. post trinitatis [19 July 1668]
    Dieterich Buxtehude Anna Margarethe Tunders in Johan von Essen Hause. [moon].

1701–1738

p. 44
    9. Trinit: [21 August 1707]
    Organ: u. Werckmeister dieser Kirche Joh: Christian Schieferdecker
    Anna Margarethe Buxtehude
    die Hochzeit in ihre Hause Montag.

    10. Trinit: [28 August 1707]
    Organ: in Braunsewieck Johan Casper Winckler
    Dorothea Catharina Buxdehuden
    die hochzeit in Sehl. Buxdehude Hause Montag

E. Printed Sources

1. Revised Church Order for Mecklenburg

Revidirte Kirchen-Ordnung : wie es mit Christlicher Lehre, Reichung der Sacramenten, Ordination der Diener des Evangelii, ordentlichen Ceremonien in der Kirchen, Visitation, Consistorio und Schulen : im Hertzogthumb Mecklenburg, etc., gehalten wirdt (Lüneburg: In Verlegung Martin Lamprechts, 1650)

fol. 150r–v:

Sonnabends, und andere heilige Abend und Feiertage, Nachmittage, sol der *Cüster* auff den Schlag Eins, zur Vesper leuten, und folgends der *Cantor* und seine zugeordnete, mit den Schülern umb zwey Uhr, fein ordentlich zu Chore gehen, und anfenglich singen, *Veni Sancte Spiritus &c.* Darnach ein *Antiphon de Dominica* oder Fest, und derauff einen, zwen oder drey *Psalmos* singen, und denn das *Responsorium* und *Hymnum,* die da rein sind, und auff die zeit sich schicken.

Darnach sol ein Knabe eine *Lection* auß dem Newen Testament Lateinisch, und ein ander Knabe dieselbige *Lection* Deutsch, oder aber des Sontags Festtages Evangelium lesen.

Nach der *Lection,* singe man das *Magnificat* Deutsch oder Lateinisch, auch mit einer *Antiphon de Dominica* oder *Festo.*

Wo aber Orgeln seyn, sol der Organist einen Verß umb den andern schlagen.

Darauff singe der Priester, *Dominus vobis cum* und eine *Collecten de tempore,* und beschliesse der Chor mit dem *Benedicamus Domino,* und *Da Pacem Domine.*

Zu solchen Alten und Christlichen reinen Choralgesangen, sollen die Schulmeister und *Cantores* die Knaben gewenen, und fleiß anwenden, daß dieselbigen ihnen von jugend auff eingebildet und bekand werden.

2. Text Book for 1682–83 Christmas Season

Natalitia Sacra, Oder Verzeichnüß aller Texte, Welche in bevorstehenden Heiligen Festen, als Weinachten, Neuen Jahr und Heil. drey Könige allhie zu St. Marien sowohl Vor- als Nachmittag, theils vor und nach den Predigten, theils auch unter der Communion mit genugsamer Vocal-Hülffe sollen musiciret werden (Lübeck, 1682):

Feria I.
vor der Predigt.
    Kyrie . . .
    Gloria . . .
Nach der Predigt.
    Credo . . .
    Zur Praefation.
    Sanctus . . .
[all mass movements:] à 10 Strom. 8 Vocalisten 8 zur Capell
Unter der Communion
    Fürchtet euch nicht . . . [STTB; 6 Str.]

Nachmittag vor der Predigt
    I. Corde natus ex parentis . . . 8 Vocum
    II. Uns ist ein Kind gebohren . . . [SSATB; V V Va Va Tr Tr Cn Cn Tn Tn Tn Fg]

Nach der Predigt
    I. Magnificat cum laudibus . . . Sinf. à 10 Strom. 4 Vocalst. 4 zur Capell

[1]	Magnificat anima mea Dominum:	Tutti
[2]	Et exultavit Spiritus meus in Deo, salutari meo.	SAT, Tutti
	Laudes: Vom Himmel hoch da kom ich her . . .	Tutti
[3]	Quia respexit humilitatem ancillae suae:	S, 4 Violae
	Ecce enim, ex hoc beatam me dicent omnes generationes.	
[4]	Quia fecit mihi magna, qui potens est,	ATB
	et sanctum nomen ejus.	
	Laudes: Freut Euch und jubilirt . . .	Tutti
[5]	Et misericordia ejus à progenie in progenies,	T, 4 Violae
	timentibus eum.	
[6]	Fecit potentiam in brachio suo,	SAB
	dispersit superbos mente cordis sui.	
	Laudes: Gloria in excelsis Deo . . .	Tutti
[7]	Deposuit potentes de sede, & exaltavit humiles.	B, 4 Violae
[8]	Esurientes implevit bonis,	SATB, Tutti
	& divites dimisit inanes.	
	Laudes: Virga jessae floruit . . .	Tutti

II.
[9]	Suscepit Israel puerum suum,	A 4 violae
	recordatus misericordiae suae.	
[10]	Sicut locutus est ad patres nostros,	SATB, Tutti
	Abraham & semini ejus in secula.	
	Laudes: Joseph lieber, Joseph mein . . .	
[11]	Gloria patri & Filio, & Spiritui sancto,	SATB, Tutti
[12]	Sicut erat in principio & bunc & semper,	
	& in secula seculorum, Amen.	
	Laudes: Psallite unigenito Christo, Dei Filio . . .	Tutti

    III. Dancksagen wir alle . . . 2 Viol. 4 Violae 2 Corn. 4 Tromb. 2 Clarin. 1 Fag. 6 Vocalist. 6 zur Capel.

Feria II.
Vor der Predigt. 2 Viol. 2 Corn. 4 Tromb. 1 Fagot. 5 Vocalst. 6 zur Capel.
    Kyrie . . .
    Gloria . . .
Nach der Predigt.
    Credo . . .
Unter der Communion.
    O admirabile commercium . . . 4 Tromb. A. A.

Nachmittage vor der Predigt.
    I. Alpha & O. [crossed out: replaced with Ecce quem] Motetta 8. Vocum
    II. Denen zu Zion wird ein Erlöser kommen . . . [ATTB; V V Va Va Va Tr Tr Cn Cn]
Nach der Predigt.
    I. Magnificat absque laudibus. 10 Str. 5 Vocal Stim. 5 zur Capel.
    II. Ich will den Herrn loben allezeit . . . 2 Viol. 3 Viol. 2 Corn. 3 Tromb. 2 Clar. 1   Fag. 5 Vocal-Stim. 5 zur Capell.

Auffs Neue Jahr.
Vor der Predigt. 6 Strom. 6 Vocalst. 6 zur Capell.
  Kyrie . . .
  Gloria . . .
Nach der Predigt.
  Credo . . .
Unter der Communion
  Nun dancket alle Gott . . . 2 Viol. 2 Violdigamb. A.T.B.

Nachmittage vor der Predigt.
  I. Motetta 8. Vocum. Daß Neugebohrne Kindelein.
  II. Aria. O Jesu süß wer dein gedenckt . . . [ATB; V V Vg Vg Vg]
Nach der Predigt.
  I. Herr Gott dich loben wir, Herr Gott, etc. 10 Strom. 5 Vocal-Stim. 5 Zur Capel.
  II. Preise Jerusalem den Herrn . . . 10 Strom. 8 Vocalst. 8 zur Capell.

Auff Heiligen drey König
Vor der Predigt. 9 Strom. 5 Vocalst. 4 zur Capell.
  Kyrie . . .
  Gloria . . .
Nach der Predigt.
  Credo . . .
Unter der Communion
  Bringet her dem Herren . . . 8 Stro. 3 Bass.

Nachmittag vor der Predigt
  I. Motetta 8 Vocum. Ist Gott versöhnt etc.
  II. Ich freue mich des . . . Tenor 2 Viol.
Nach der Predigt.
  I. Magnificat anima mea Dominum. à 6 Strom. und 8 Vocalstim.
    C.C.A.A.T.T.B.B. 6 zur Capel.
  II. Laudate pueri Dominum . . . 12 Violinis 2. Violon A.T.B.
Zu Gedäncken!
Daferne etwas Zeit Vormittage, ehe die Predigt gehet, wird übrig seyn, sollen folgende Texte musiciret werden.
  Fer. I.
    Verbum caro factum est . . . Motet. 6 Voc.
  Fer. II.
    Ach mein Hertzliebes Jesulein . . . 3. Stro. 3 Voc.
  Am Neuen Jahrs-Tage.
    Jesu dulcis memoria . . . Alt. 5 Stro.
  Am Heiligen drey Könige Tage.
    Lobet den Nahmen des Herrn. Ten. 9 Viol.

3. Buxtehude, Sonatas, opus 1, Dedication
Buxtehude, Dieterico. *VII Sonate à doi* . . . *Opera prima* (Hamburg, [1694])

Denen Hoch-Edlen, Gestrengen, Hoch-Gelahrten, Hoch- und Wohl-Weisen Herren, Herren Bürgermeistern und Raths-Verwandten, Der Käyserlichen Freyen und des Heil. Römischen Reichs Stadt Lübeck,

Meinen hochzuehrenden Herren, wehrtesten *Patronis*, und hochgeneigten Beförderern.

Magnifici, Hoch-Edele, Hoch-Gelahrte, Hoch- und Wohl-Weise sonders Großgünstige und Hochgebietende Herren,

Ew. *Magnific.* und Herrlichkeiten geruhen den ersten Theil meiner *Sonaten* mit so beliebigen Händen anzunehmen, als ich denselben mit auffrichtigen und ergebenen Hertzen unterdienstlichst überreiche. Jemand anders diese Blätter zu wiedmen, wäre der reichlich-empfangenen vieljährigen Gutthaten vergessen. Und wie solte diß *Musicali*sche Werck fremde Schutz-Götter wehlen, das es unter Ihrem Schutz, Hochgebietende Herren, bißhero so glücklich verfertiget worden? Zugeschweigen, daß ich Mühe haben würde, andere solche Gönner dieser Edlen Kunst zu finden, vornemlich, da zu diesen, (daß ich so reden mag,) gantz verstimmten, und gar nicht wol übereinstimmenden Zeiten die liebe *Musica* leider! fast verstummen will. Zweiffle demnach im geringsten nicht, Ew. *Magnific.* und Herrlichkeiten werden Ihnen diese gantz unterdienstliche Uberreichung hochgeneigt gefallen lassen, der ich nechst getreuester Empfehlung in des Allwaltenden Gnaden-Obhut nebst den Meinigen Lebens-lang zu verharren gedencke

Ew. *Magnific.* und Herrlichkeiten

unterdienstwilligst-gehorsamster
Dieterich Buxtehude

4. Buxtehude, Sonatas, opus 2, Dedication

Buxtehude, Dieterico. *VII. Suonate à due . . . Opera secunda* (Hamburg, 1696)

Al Molto Illustre, Magnifico e Generoso SIGNORE IL SIGNOR GIOVAN RITTERO, Consule dignisimo della Libera, & Imperiale Città di Lübeca sempre Augusta, &c.

SIGNORE, e PADRON mio sempre Osservandissimo.

Molto Illustre Magnifico & Eccellentissimo Signore,

Essendomi stato concesso dalla sorte l'essere per lo spatio di più anni annoverato frà il fortunato numero di coloro, che vivono sotto il glorioso vessillo della VOSTRA authorevole protettione MOLTO ILLUSTRE, e MAGNIFICO SIGNORE, mi è parso (docendo far comparire alle stampe le qui annesse Sonate, Opera seconda, di quel talento, che mi fà attribuito dal Cielo) presentarli à piedi di VOSTRA MAGNIFICENZA, acciò ammantate col VOSTRO GLORIOSO NOME possino dà per tutto risplendere.

Accetti dunque VOSTRA MAGNIFICENZA con la picciolezza del dono la mia ossequiosa osservanza conquella medema benignità c'hà sempre mai con ogn'uno essercitato, che io all in contro augurandovi ogni bramata felicità resto

a di'

DI VOSTRA MAGNIFICENZA

Humilissimo, & obligatissimo
Servidore
Dieterico Buxtehude

5. Literary Journal of the Baltic Sea

Nova Literaria Maris Balthici et Septentrionis, Collecta Lubecae (Lübeck and Hamburg, 1698–1707)

1700, January, p. 32:

> Sub auspicium novi anni 1700. ipsis Januarii Calendis, finitis Sacris, in Basilica B. Virg. Mariae, moderante Dieterico Buxtehude, Organi musici istius Ecclesiae Directore, anonymi at nobilis Poetae Carmen Seculare vernaculum, de Felicitate Imperialis Liberae Civitatis Lubecae, solenni Musica, interstrepente tympanorum buccinarumque, & omnis generis instrumentorum harmonice concentu, in amplissima panegyri fuit recitatum, cui titulus: Hundertjähriges Gedicht, für die Wolfahrt der Kayserlichen Freyen Reichs Stadt Lübeck, den 1. Jenner des 1700. Jubel-Jahres, in der Haupt-Kirchen S. Marien feyerlichst musiciret von Dieterico Buxtehuden, Compositore und Directore.

1706, April, pp. 123–24:

> *Die II. Decembris, Dietericus Buxtehude*, Organi in aede D. Mariae Director, pietatem suam Gloriosissimae memoriae LEOPOLDI I, supremam probaturus, dicto in loco, Musica quadam lugubri, cui additae cernebantur aliquot, quas vocant, Illuminationes, prentavit, quam solennitatem, sequenti
>
> *Die III. Decembr.* excepit alia, quâ dignissimo Leopoldi nostri Successori & Filio, JOSEPHO I. Imperatoris fastigium denuò publici gaudii interprete Musicâ idem gratulatus est. Ejus rei ergo prodiit, quae Actum hunc plenius paulò sistit, & Odas praesertim in eo cantatas continet, gemina descriptio, altera hâc epigraphe notata: *Castrum doloris* Dero in Gott ruhenden Römisch. Kayserl. auch Königl. Majestäten Leopold den Ersten zum glorwürdigsten Andencken in der Kayserl. Freyen Reichs-Stadt Lübecks Haupt-Kirchen zu S. Marien zur Zeit gewöhnlicher Abend-Music aus allerunterthänigster Pflicht Musicalisch vorgestellet etc. altera hanc ferens inscriptionem: *Templum Honoris* Dero regierenden Römisch. Kayserl. auch Königl. Majestät Joseph dem Ersten zu unsterblichen Ehren etc. glückwünschend gewidmet.

1707, July, p. 224:

> *Die IX. Maji* diem obiit supremum artis Musicae peritissimus si quis, Magister, Organique apud nos in aede Mariana per annos 38. Director, *Didericus Buxtehude*, cujus et caetero quin apud rerum istarum aestimatores nomen notum est, et in *Novis* hisce *nostris* passim servatur memoria. Patriam agnoscit Daniam, unde in nostras delatus oras septuaginta circiter vivendo annos implevit.

6. Instructions on the Lübeck Liturgy

"Kurtze Anweisung. wie künfftighin der Gottesdienst in denen Lübeckischen Kirchen wird anzustellen seyn," in appendix to *Lübeckisches Gesang-Buch . . . Auff Verordnung Eines Hoch-Edlen Hochweisen Raths Von Einem Ehrwürdigen MINISTERIO Ausgegeben* (Lübeck: Christian Ernest Wiedemeyer, 1729 [first printing 1703])

> Von denen Sonn- und Fest-Tags-Vespern [i.e. for the eves of Sundays and feasts]

> Wenn gewöhnlicher massen in denen 5. Haupt-Kirchen geläutet worden, als wird um 2. Uhr ein teutscher Psalm, Komm heiliger Geist &c. gesungen, die Sonn- oder Fest-Tags-Lection auf dem Chore teutsch verlesen, drauf die Orgel, (ohne daß in der Fasten von Dom. Judica an die Orgel stehen bleibt) *intonirt*, das *Magnificat* teutsch, wenn solches gesungen, werden einige (aufs wenigste drey) Buß- oder andere Zeit-Lieder

angestimmet, und wenn ein Prediger wegen derer Leichen zugegen, wird die *Collecte* deutsch gesungen, in dessen Abwesenheit aber mit dem Gesang Nun dancket alle GOtt, p. 170. und mit dem *Benedicamus Domino* beschlossen, und hernach die Orgel gerühret, daß also der völlige Gottesdienst umb 3. Uhr zu Ende gebracht wird. In der Marien Kirchen aber wird von 3. biß 4. Uhr geprediget, und obige Lieder, oder andere, die sich auf die Predigt schicken, gesungen. . . . (pp. 76–77)

Von denen Sonn- und Fest-Tags, Früh- und Haupt-Predigten.

Zu denen Haupt-Predigten aber wird in allen 5. Haupt-Kirchen der Gottesdienst angefangen, mit dem Liede: Komm Heiliger Geist &c, nach diesem das *Symbolum Athanasii* auff dem Chor teutsch abgelesen, und darauff mit Einschlagung der Orgel, gesungen: HERR GOtt dich loben wir. Nach dem intoniret die Orgel das *Kyrie*, für dem Altar folget das *Gloria in Excelsis DEo*, und der Chor respondiret: *Et in terra Pax &c.* Hebet auch an zu singen: Allein GOTT in der Höh sey Ehr, &c. Nach solchen wird für dem Altar die *Collecte* teutsch, und die Epistel verlesen, darauff alsobald der Haupt-Gesang den der *Pastor* ordnet, (an denen Sonntagen nach *Trinitatis* aber zuvor mit Einschlagung der Orgel: *O adoranda Trinitas, O veneranda unitas* gesungen) angestimmet wird, und nach selbigen im Hingang nach der Cantzel eines von denen Liedern: Nun bitten wir den heiligen Geist &c p. 111. Herr Jesu Christ p. 564. Liebster JEsu wir sind hier &c. p. 565. An denen Fest-Tagen, desgleichen an denen Sonntagen, wenn man sonst das *Patrem* zu musiciren pfleget, wird das Kyrie in den Kirchen *figuraliter* gesungen und nach Verlesung der Epistel, wenn Zeit vorhanden ein Stück musiciret. Wenn darauff die Predigt geendiget, so wird die Beichte samt der Absolution, das ordentliche Gebet und die Vorbitten abgelesen, das Vater Unser in der Stille, und der Seegen laut gesprochen, und alsdenn das *Credo* intoni̇ret. . . . Wenn aber zu Ostern, Pfingsten, Michaelis, und Weynachten, die Lateinischen *Praefationes* gesungen werden, so wird noch zuvor ein teutsch Fest-Lied angestimmet, worauf die *Praefation* sich anhebt, das übrige bleibt wie am Sonntage. Unter der Communion aber werden Communion-Lob- und Danck-als auch Paßion-Lieder gesungen, oder, an denen Fest-Tagen *musiciret*, doch aber nach dem Seegen jedesmahl mit einem deutschen Liede, als: sey Lob und Ehr mit hohem Preiß, &c, oder mit einem andern kurtzen Lob-Psalm geendiget. Wenn aber, wie es oftermahls an denen ersten hohen Fest-Tagen zu geschehen pfleget, gar keine Communicanten vorhanden sind, wird entweder *musici̇ret*, oder wo keine Music vorhanden, ein Fest-Lied abgesungen, die teutsche *Collecte* verlesen, und der Seegen über die Gemeine gesprochen, und mit einem Gesang beschlossen. (pp. 79–82)

Von denen Sonn- und Festtäglichen Nachmittags-Predigten

Der Nachmittags-Gottesdienst, wenn man darzu, wie es jede Haupt-Kirche mit sich bringet, geläutet hat, wird also gehalten, daß Anfangs Komm heiliger Geist &c. angestimmet, und darauff Tisch- Lob- und Danck-Lieder gesungen werden, dann wenn die Epistel abgelesen, wird die Orgel gerühret und an denen Sonntagen vom *Directori Chori* teutsch gesungen, biß der Prediger mit dem gewöhnlichen Predigt-Liede zur Cantzel gehet. An denen Fest-Tagen aber wird, wo es üblich, *musici̇ret*, biß der Prediger nach dem Haupt-Gesange und Predigt-Liede zur Cantzel gehet. In der

Fasten aber, für dem Predigt-Liede zu St. Marien, HErr GOtt dich loben wir &c. gesungen. Nach der Predigt wird das allgemeine Gebet und die öffentliche Vorbitte abgelesen, darauf der Seegen gesprochen, und ein teutsches Lied gesungen. Nach diesem *intoniret* die Orgel, und wo die Music verhanden und üblich wird selbige fortgesetzet, in deren Ermangelung aber noch 2. teutsche Lieder mit *Praeludir-* und Einschlagung der Orgel, wie es üblich, angestimmt, alsdenn das teutsche *Magnificat*, die teutsche *Collecte* gesungen und mit dem Gesange: Nun GOtt Lob es ist vollbracht, &c. als an denen Sonntagen, an denen Fest-Tagen aber mit einem Fest-Liede und *Benedicamus Domino* geschlossen. Und weil über dieses in St. Marien am Sonntage *Judica* und *Palmarum* nach der Mittags-Predigt eine Passions-Music pfleget gehalten zu werden, als wird solche jedesmal fleissig mit zu beobachten seyn. . . . (pp. 86–88)

7. Buxtehude, Wedding Aria for Anton Winckler

Buxtehude, Dieter. *Auff Hochansehnlichem Hochzeit-Fest des . . . Herrn Anthonii Winckler . . .* (Lübeck, 1705) [BuxWV 120; original print missing since 1942; vss. 1–3 from Stahl edition; end of vs. 7 from Pirro, 481]:

1. O fröhliche Stunden, o herrlicher Tag,
von welchem muß weichen all traurige Klag.
Frohlocket und jauchzet, ihr Musengesellen,
wie's immer geschiehet in fröhlichen Fällen.
Anstimmet ein lieblich hochzeitlich Getön,
das selbst des Apollinis Kithar verhöhn.

2. O fröhliche Stunden, o lieblicher Tag,
von welchem muß weichen all traurige Klag.
Gott gebe, daß ferner sie mögen erfahren
im Alter die silbergesprengeten Haaren,
vom Himmel den nimmer ablassenden Schutz,
der Stadt und den Zünften zu dienendem Nutz.

3. O fröhliche Stunden, o lieblicher Tag,
von welchem muß weichen all traurige Klag.
Es falle auf beide vom Himmel der Regen
voll Leben und Liebe und heiligem Segen,
daß alles Behagen mit Neumannin sei,
im ruhigen Stande stets munter und neu.

7. . . .
O möcht es gefallen nur was wir hie bringen
Die Gönner zu Ehre, wir treten hervor,
Ich Diener der Orgel, und mit mir das Chor.

8. Johann Moller's Biography of Buxtehude

Moller, Johann. *Cimbria Literata* (Copenhagen, 1744), II, 132–33:

Dietericus Buxtehude, Helsingorae in Zeelandia Danica, patre Johanne, Templi urbani Organoedo, A. 1637. natus, eodemque in aede Mariana Lubecensi, ab A. 1669, functus officio, septuagenarius d. 9. Maji A. 1707. vivis est exemptus.[1] A Lubecensibus[2] *Magister artis* salutatur *Musicae, si quis, peritissimus*, ab Henr. Elmenhorstio[3] ein weitberühmter Musicus und Organiste, & a Wolfg. Casp. Printzio[4] ac Conrado ab Höveln[5] ein fürtreflicher Organiste und Componiste.

Unterschiedliche Hochzeit-Arien. Lubecae 1672. in fol. (*Cat. nund.*)

Fried- und Freudenreiche Hinfahrt des alten Simeons, bey Absterben seines Vaters, Ioh. Buxtehuden, 32jährigen Organisten in Helsingör (der zu Lübeck am 22. Ian. 1674. 72jährig verstorben), in zwey Contrapuncten musicalisch abgesungen. Lub. 1674. in fol.

Abend-Musick in IX. Theilen. Lub. 1678–1687. in 4. (*Catal.*)

Hochzeit des Lammes. Lub 1681 in 4. (*Catal.*)

VII. Sonate a doi, Violino & Viola di gamba, con cembalo. Lub. 1696. in fol.

Anonymi Hundertjähriges Gedichte vor die Wolfahrt der Stadt Lübeck, am 1. Ian. des Jubel-Jahrs 1700. in S. Marien Kirche musicalisch vorgestellt. Lub. 1700. in fol. V. *Nova lit. Lub., M. Jan. A. 1700, p. 32.*

Castrum doloris dem verstorbenen Keyser, Leopoldo, und Templum honoris dem regierenden Keyser, Iosepho I., in zwey Musicken, in der Marien Kirche zu Lübeck, gewidmet. Lub. 1705. in fol. V. *N.L. Lubec., M. Apr. A. 1706, p. 123, 124.*

His addantur *in Catalogo nundin. vern. A. 1684. Lipsiensi, p. 32.*, ab ipso promissa, & a Christ. Hendreichio, *in Pandect. Brandeb.* p. 812., editis, more suo, annumerata:

1. Himlische Seelen-Lust auf Erden über die Menschwerdung und Geburt unsers Heylands IEsu Christi.
2. Das allerschröcklichste und allererfreulichste, nemlich das Ende der Zeit, und der Anfang der Ewigkeit, Gesprächs-weiße vorgestellet.

Notes

1. V. *Nova literaria Lubecensia, M. Jul. A. 1707., p. 224.*
2. l.c.
3. in *Dramatologia antiquo-hodierna p. 100.*
4. in der Historischen Beschreibung der Singekunst, c. 12, p. 148.
5. im beglückten und geschmückten Lübeck p. 114.

Appendix 5

Inventories of Music

A. St. Mary's Church, Helsingør, 1659

Source: Helsingør, Skt. Mariae Kirke Regnskabsprotokol 1659–1760, fol. 3r. Rearranged in alphabetical order by composer; numerals before each entry designate original order. The column on the left contains the original entries; the column on the right, suggested identifications with known publications.

[2] M. Erhardi Bodenschaff Florilegen 9 böger in 4to	Bodenschatz, Erhard, ed. *Florilegium Portense* (Leipzig, 1618) or *Florilegii Musici Portensis . . . Pars altera*, (Leipzig, 1621)
[6] Jacobi Finetti Concerten 5 böger	Finetti, Giacomo. *Concerti ecclesiastici II. III. IIII. vocibus, cum basso generali ad organum* (Antwerp, 1621)
[1] Andreae Hakenbergij 13 böger in 4to	Hakenberger, Andreas. *Harmonia Sacra in qua motectae VI. VII. VII.–IX. X. ET XII. concinnatae vocibus continentur, una cum basso generali pro organo* (Frankfurt, 1617)
[15] Andreae Hammersmedß Madrigalien 5 böger in 4to	Hammerschmidt, Andreas. *Musicalischer Andachten, Ander Theill,* Das ist: Geistliche Madrigalien, Mit 4.5 und 6. Stimmern sambt *einem General-Bass, Benebenst einer fünffstimmigen Capella* (Freiberg, 1641)
[17] Andreae Hammersmedß Geistl Concerten 6 böger in 4to	Hammerschmidt, Andreas. *Musicalischer Andachten, Dritter Theil, Das ist: Geistliche Symphonien, Mit 1. und 2. Vocal-Stimmen, zwey Violinen, sampt einem Violon, Nebenst einem General Baß für die Orgel, Lauten, Spinet, &c* (Freiberg, 1642)
[7] Andreae Hammerschmed dealogus 6 böger in 4to	Hammerschmidt, Andreas. *Geistlicher Dialogen Ander Theil, Darinnen Herrn Opitzens Hohes Lied Salomonis In I. und 2. Vocal-Stimmen, 2 Violinen, einem Instrumental- und General-Bass componiret* (Dresden, 1645)
[16] Andreae Hammersmedß Moteten 10 böger in folio	Hammerschmidt, Andreas. *Vierdter Theil, Musicalischer Andachten, Geistlicher Moteten und Concerten, Mit 5, 6, 7, 8, 9, 10, 12 und mehr Stimmen, nebenst einem gedoppelten General-Baß* (Freiberg, 1646)

[3] Casper Haseleri
8 böger in 4to

Hassler, Caspar, ed. *Sacrae symphoniae* (Nürnberg, 1598), or *Sacrarum symphoniarum continuatio* (Nürnberg, 1600), or *Magnificat octo tonorum* (Nürnberg, 1600), or *Sacrae symphoniae* (Nürnberg, 1613)

[22] Johan Andr.
Herbst Hiertens
Suck
Et blad in 4to

Herbst, Johann Andreas. *Suspiria Cordis. . . Das ist: Hertzens-Seufftzer zu Christo Unserm Heyland. Mit 4 Stimmen. Tre Soprani e Basso, neben den Numeris und Signis pro Basso continuo* (Frankfurt, 1646)

[11] Johann:
Erahm
Kinderman
Dialogus
5 böger in 4to

Kindermann, Johann Erasmus. *Dialogus, Mosis Plag, Sünders Klag, Christi Abtrag, Auff die Passionszeit, und sonsten täglichen, zu musiciren bequemlich. Mit 1. 2. 4. und 6. Stimmen, neben dem General Bass* (Nürnberg, 1642)

[18] Johan Erasmi
Kinderman
4 böger in 4to

Kindermann, Johann Erasmus. *Cantiones Pathetikai* (Nürnberg, 1639) or *Friedens Klag* (Nürnberg, 1640) or *Musicalische Friedens Seufftzer* (Nürnberg, 1642)

[12] Casper
Ketteln Arien
5 böger in 4to

Kittel, Caspar. *Arien und Cantaten mit 1. 2. 3. und 4. Stimmen sambt beygefügtem Basso Continuo* (Dresden, 1638)

[19] Martini
Drenge Concert:
4 böger in folio
er aff 3. Stemmer
General Bass, er
Ubunden, er Doct.
Josuae Stegmans
Klage ofver den
Langewarige Kriegtid

Knabe, Martin. *Concert von drey Stimmen, zusampt dem Basso continuo, uber das bekandte Klaglied dess langwirigen Kriegswesens: Wenn soll doch mein Leid sich enden?* (Halle, 1635)

[24] Movij
Triumph
Psalmer
9 böger in 4to

Movius, Caspar. *Triumphus Musicus Spiritualis: Das ist: . . . Trostreiche Psalmen . . . mit 6. und 8. Stimmen sampt dem Basso Continuo* (Rostock, 1640)

[20] Johan Schopen
Concerten
5 böger in 4to

Schop, Johann. *Erster Theil Geistlicher Concerten, Mit 1. 2. 3. 4. und 8. Stimmen Sambt beygefügtem Basso Continuo vor die Orgel* (Hamburg, 1643)

[8] Monomachia
Thom Selij
8 böger in 4to

Selle, Thomas. *Monomachia harmonico-latina* (Hamburg, 1630) with *Ritornellorum quinis et senis vocibus . . . concinnendorum . . . monomachias* (Hamburg, 1630)

[13] Thom. Selij
Concerten6 böger

Selle, Thomas. *Concertuum latino-sacrorum II. IV. & V. vocibus ad bassum continuum concinendorum* (Rostock, 1646)

[9] Johan Stadlmaÿr
Psalmi
6 böger

Stadlmayr, Johann. *Psalmi integri, a quatuor vocibus concertantibus, quatuor aliis accessoriis ad libitum accinendis cum 2 cornet. sive violin* (Innsbruck, 1641)

[10] Pauli Sÿfert
Palmi
6 böger

Siefert, Paul. *Psalmen Davids, . . . mit 4. und 5. Stimmen zu singen, und mit allerhand Instrumenten zu gebrauchen, nebenst einem General-Baß* (Danzig, 1640)

[14] Johan
Vierdancken
Concerten
7 böger in 4to

Vierdanck, Johann. *Ander Theil Geistlicher Concerten Mit 3. 4. 5. 6. 7. 8. und 9. Stimmen nebenst einem gedoppelten Basso Continuo, Einen vor das Corpus, den andern vor den Directore, oder zu einem Violon, zu gebrauchen* (Rostock, 1643)

[5] Georgij
Vintzij Messae
9 böger in 4to

Vintz, Georg. *Missae ad praecipuos dies festos accomodatae, quinque, sex & octo vocibus, . . . cum basso continuo* (Erfurt, 1630)

[21] Johan Weichman
5 hoffned
Palmen er 3 böger
in 4to

Weichmann, Johann. *Die Fünff Haupt-Stück der Christlichen Lehre in Fünf sonderbare Lieder oder Reimen verfasset . . . mit 5 Stimmen zu singen gesetzet* (Königsberg, 1646)

[4] Otte schreffne
böger variorum
authorum

?

[23] Noch Otte
schreffven Tabulatur
böger in folio

?

B. Helsingør Latin School, 1696

Source: Johnsson, *Den Danske Skolmusiks Historie indtil 1739*, 74. Columns arranged as in A.

Musicalia in Folio:

5. Aureum opus
Missarum
Capricorni 4 vol.

Capricornus, Samuel. *Opus aureum missarum quae ad sex decem & duodecim tonos redactae cum basso ad organum* (Frankfurt, 1670)

3. Hammerschmidths
Motetter 9 vol

Hammerschmidt, Andreas. *Fest, Bus- und Danck-Lieder, mit 5 Vocal-Stimmen und 5 Instr. nach Beliebung. Nebenst dem Basso Continuo* (Zittau, 1658)

2. Havemanni
Opera 8 vol

Havemann, Johannes, ed. *1sten Theil, aus 30 lateinischen Concerten der berühmtesten Italiäner, 1. 2.–7. Stimmen bestehend* (Berlin and Jena, 1659)

1. Rauschii aureus triumphalis 13 Vol	Rauch, Andreas. *Currus triumphalis musici. . .in quo selectiores iubilares, triumphales, ac solennes festivales cantus, 8. 9. 10. 11. 12. pluriumque vocum, cum duplicato generali basso* (Vienna, 1648)
4. I partim blaa bøger med Messer 8 vol.	Possibly the manuscript music purchased in 1675 or that in the copy books purchased 1675
6. I partim bøger med Concerter og Misser 8 vol.	Possibly the manuscript music purchased in 1675 or that in the copy books purchased 1675

In Quarto:

1. Hammersmith in Evangelia 8 vol.	Hammerschmidt, Andreas. *Musicalische Gespräche über die Evangelia, mit 4. 5. 6. und 7. Stimmen nebenst den Basso continuo* (Dresden, 1655)
2. Taffel og Chor Music 8 vol.	Hammerschmidt, Andreas. *Kirchen- und Tafel Musik Darinnen 1. 2. 3. Vocal. und 4. 5. und 6. Instrumenta enthalten* (Zittau, 1662); purchased and bound into 9 volumes in 1674 [see appendix 5]
3. Profii Collectean a 19 vol.	Profe, Ambrosius, ed., selected from *RISM* 1627[8], 1641[2], 1641[3], 1642[4], 1646[3], 1646[4], 1649[6]
4. Partitur 9 vol.	?

C. St. Mary's Church, Lübeck, 1814

Source: Archiv Lübeck, Marienkirche III, Schriften Musik 9: "Verzeichnis von Musikalien, die 1814 nach Wien geschickt worden sind." All titles listed in *RISM* for *Wgm* unless noted. Complete catalogue of individual works forthcoming in Kerala J. Snyder, *The Choir Library of St. Mary's in Lübeck: 1546–1674*.

1. Single Prints

Arnold, Georg. *Prima pars. Quatuor Missae* (Bamberg, 1672)
Bart, Gulielmo. *Missae et Motetta* (Antwerp, 1674)
Belloni, Gioseffo. *Messa e motetti* (Venice, 1606)
Benedictus, a Sancto Josepho. *Missae, litaniae et motetta* (Antwerp, 1666)
Capricornus, Samuel. *Opus musicum* (Nürnberg, 1655)
Capricornus, Samuel. *Jubilus Bernhardi* (Stuttgart, 1660)
Cazzati, Maurizio. *Op. 14. Messa e salmi* (Venice, 1653)
Chinelli, Giovanni Battista. *Missarum . . . liber secundus* (Antwerp, 1651)
Corsi, Bernardo. *Missa ac sacrae cantiones* (Venice, 1618)

Crüger, Johannes. *Meditationum musicarum* (Berlin, 1626)
Dedekind, Constantin. *König Davids Göldnes Kleinod* (Dresden, 1674)
Demantius, Cristoph. *Triades Sioniae* (Freiberg, 1619)
DuMont, Carolus. *Missae et motetta* (Antwerp, 1671)
Freschi, Domenico. *Messa . . . e salmi* (Venice, 1660)
Grandi, Alessandro. *Messa et salmi* (Venice, 1636)
Hammerschmidt, Andreas. *Musikalische Gespräche über die Evangelia* (Dresden, 1655)
Hammerschmidt, Andreas. *Ander Theil geistlicher Gespräche über die Evangelia* (Dresden, 1656)
Hammerschmidt, Andreas. *Fest- Bus- und Dancklieder* (Zittau, 1658)
Hammerschmidt, Andreas. *Kirchen- und Tafel Musik* (Zittau, 1662)
Hammerschmidt, Andreas. *Missae* (Dresden, 1663)
Honorio, Romualdo. *Il secondo libro di messe concertate* (Venice, 1645)
Meiland, Jakob. *Cantiones sacrae* (Nürnberg, 1564)
Nervius, Leonardus. *Missae* (Antwerp, 1618)
Petraeus, Christoph. *Praecationis thuribulum* (Guben, 1669)
Praetorius, Hieronymus. *Liber missarum, qui est operum musicorum tomus tertius* (Hamburg, 1616)
Praetorius, Hieronymus. *Cantiones variae . . . quae sunt operum musicorum tomus quartus* (Hamburg, 1618)
Praetorius, Hieronymus. *Cantiones Sacrae . . . quae sunt operum musicorum tomus primus* (Hamburg, 1622)
Praetorius, Hieronymus. *Canticum B. Mariae Virginis, seu Magnificat . . . quod est operum musicorum tomus secundus* (Hamburg, 1622)
Quagliati, Paolo. *Motecta octonis et psalmus Dixit dominus* (Rome, 1612)
Reina, Sisto. *Novelli Fiori ecclesiastici* (Milan, 1648)
Rovetta, Giovanni. *Messa, e Salmi Concertati* (Venice, 1639), at *LÜh*
Rovetta, Giovanni. *Salmi concertati* (Venice, 1641)
Rovetta, Giovanni. *Delli Salmi* (Venice, 1662)
Schein, Johann Hermann. *Cymbalum Sionium* (Leipzig, 1615)
Scherer, Sebastian Anton. *Musica sacra* (Ulm, 1657)
Schütz, Heinrich. *Symphoniarum sacrarum tertia pars* (Dresden, 1650)
Staden, Johann. *Harmoniae variatae sacrarum cantionum* (Nuremberg, 1632)
Stadlmayer, Johann. *Missae IX vocum* (Antwerp, 1643)
Steelant, Philipp van. *Missa et moteta* (Antwerp, 1656)
Steingaden, Konstantin. *Flores hyemales* (Constance, 1666)
Vecchi, Orfeo. *Salmi intieri* (Milano, 1614)
Verlit, Gaspard de. *Missae et motetta* (Antwerp, 1661)
Verlit, Gaspard de. *Missae et moteta* (Antwerp, 1668)
Vermeeren, Anthonis. *Missae et motetta* (Antwerp, 1665)
Vesi, Simone. *Messa e salmi.* (Venice, 1646)
Vesi, Simone. *Salmi concertati* (Venice, 1656)
Vesi, Simone. *Salmi a otto ariosi* (Venice, 1663)
Vintz, Georg. *Missae ad praecipuos dies festos* (Erfurt, 1630)
Zeutschner, Tobias. *Musicalische Kirchen- und Haus-Freude* (Leipzig, 1661)

2. Collections, with RISM *Sigla*

1546[6]   Susato, Tilman. *Liber primus sacrarum cantionum* (Antwerp, 1546)
1546[7]   Susato, Tilman. *Liber secundus sacrarum cantionum* (Antwerp, 1546)

1547[5] Susato, Tilman. *Liber tertius sacrarum cantionum* (Antwer, 1547)

1547[6] Susato, Tilman. *Liber quartus sacrarum cantionum* (Antwerp, 1547)

1568[2] Giovanelli, Pietro. *Novi thesauri musici liber primu* (Venice, 1568)

1568[3] Giovanelli, Pietro. *Novi atque catholici thesauri musici. Liber secundus* (Venice, 1568)

1568[4] Giovanelli, Pietro. *Novi atque catholici thesauri musici. Liber tertius* (Venice, 1568)

1568[5] Giovanelli, Pietro. *Novi atque catholici thesauri musici. Liber quartus* (Venice, 1568)

1568[6] Giovanelli, Pietro. *Liber quintus & ultimus* (Venice, 1568)

1607[2] Sacchi, Salvatore. *Missa, motecta, Magnificat, et Litaniae* (Rome, 1607)

1611[1] Schadaeus, Abraham. *Promptuarii musici . . . Collectore* (Strasbourg, 1611)

1612[3] Schadaeus, Abraham. *Promptuarii musici . . . Pars altera* (Strasbourg, 1612)

1613[2] Schadaeus, Abraham. *Promptuarii musici . . . pars tertia* (Strasbourg, 1613)

1614[3] Costantini, Fabio. *Selectae cantiones excellentissimorum auctorum* (Rome, 1614)

1615[2] Gruber, Georg. *Reliquae sacrorum concentuum* (Nürnberg, 1615)

1617[1] Vincentius, Caspar. *Promptuarii musici . . . Pars quarta* (Strasbourg, 1617)

1618[1] Bodenschatz, Erhard. *Florilegium Portense* (Leipzig, 1618)

1621[2] Bodenschatz, Erhard. *Florilegii Musici Portensis* (Leipzig, 1621)

1651[1] Floridus, R. *Quatuor missas* (Rome, 1651)

1671[1] Anonymous ed. *Sacrae Sirenes* (Kempten, 1671)
        Set of 8 manuscript partbooks

Appendix 6

Chorale Melodies Set by Buxtehude

Abbreviations: *Dan* = folio in *Den danske Psalmebog* (1569); *MK13* = Archiv der Hansestadt Lübeck, St. Marien I [Bücher] 3 [Musik], 13; *L1703* = number in *Lübeckisches Gesangbuch* [1703] and Pagendarm's chorale book; * = musical setting not present in Pagendarm's chorale book of 1705; † = text varies, but melody present.

Chorale Melody	Zahn	Buxtehude title	BuxWV	Dan	MK13	L1703	Lübeck use
Ach Gott und Herr	2050	Ach Gott und Herr	177	—	66a	104	Penitence
Ach Herr, wie lang willst du jetzt	8138	Herren vår Gud	40	—	—	—	
Auf meinen lieben Gott	2164	Auf meinen lieben Gott	179	—	132b	193	Cross & Consolation
		Wo soll ich fliehen hin	112	—	125	113	Penitence
Aus meines Herzens Grunde	5269e	Gott will ich lassen raten	4	—	—	280*	Morn/evening
Christ, der du bist der helle Tag	384	Befiehl dem Engel, daß er komm	10	323	56b	289	Morn/evening
Christ, unser Herr, zum Jordan kam	7245	Christ, unser Herr, zum Jordan kam	180	123	20	86	Baptism
Danket dem Herren	12	Danket dem Herren	181	text	108b†	128†	
Der Tag der ist so freudenreich	7870	Der Tag der ist so freudenreich	182	9	24	7	Christmas
Du Friedefürst, Herr Jesu Christ	4373	Du Friedefürst, Herr Jesu Christ	20	—	132a	198*	Cross & Consolation
		Du Friedefürst, Herr Jesu Christ	21	—	—	—	
Durch Adams Fall ist ganz verderbt	7549	Durch Adams Fall ist ganz verderbt	183	154	58	121	Justification
		Wer hofft in Gott und dem vertraut	34	—	58	121	

Chorale Melody	Zahn	Buxtehude title	BuxWV	Dan	MK13	L1703	Lübeck use
Ein feste Burg ist unser Gott	7377a	Ein feste Burg ist unser Gott	184	218	60a	226	Church
Erhalt uns, Herr, bei deinem Wort	350a	Erhalt uns, Herr, bei deinem Wort	27	253	102a	227	Church
		Erhalt uns, Herr, bei deinem Wort	185				
Erschienen ist der herrlich Tag	1743	Wir danken dir, Herr Jesu Christ	224		144	57	Ascension
Es ist das Heil uns kommen her	4430	Es ist das Heil uns kommen her	186	151	54	122	Justification
Es spricht der Unweisen Mund wohl	4436	Es spricht der Unweisen Mund wohl	187	150	56a	225	Church
Gelobet seist du, Jesu Christ	1947	Gelobet seist du, Jesu Christ	188	21	28a	4	Christmas
		Gelobet seist du, Jesu Christ	189				
Gott der Vater wohn uns bei	8507	Gott der Vater wohn uns bei	190	111	64b	67	Trinity
Herr Christ, der einig Gottes Sohn	4297a	Herr Christ, der einig Gottes Sohn	191	29	6b	124	Justification
		Herr Christ, der einig Gottes Sohn	192				
Herr Jesu Christ, du höchstes Gut	4489	Herr Jesu Christ, ich weiß gar wohl	193	—	116	245	Death & dying
		So komm ich nun, mein Gott, allhie	112	—	158	103	Penitence
Herzlich lieb hab ich dich, o Herr	8326	Herzlich lieb hab ich dich, o Herr	41	—	118	251	Death & dying
		Ach Herr, mich armen Sünder	178	—	—	115	Penitence
Herzlich tut mich verlangen	5385a	Herzlich tut mich verlangen	42	—	140	254	Death & dying
		Walts Gott, mein Werk ich lasse	103	—	—	—	Death & dying
Ich dank dir, lieber Herre	5354b	Ich dank dir, lieber Herre	194	318	—	278*	Morn/evening
Ich dank dir schon durch deinen Sohn	247b	Ich dank dir schon durch deinen Sohn	195	—	—	279*	Morn/evening
Ich ruf zu dir, Herr Jesu Christ	7400	Ich ruf zu dir, Herr Jesu Christ	196	269	36	145	Christian life
In dulci jubilo	4947	In dulci jubilo	52	16	25a	9	Christmas
		In dulci jubilo	197				
Jesu, meine Freude	8032	Jesu, meine Freude	60	—	166	154	Christian life
Jesus Christus unser Heiland ... Tod	1978	Jesus Christus unser Heiland ... Tod	198	—	78b	47	Easter
Komm, Heiliger Geist, Herre Gott	7445a	Komm, Heiliger Geist, Herre Gott	199	—	98b	60	Holy Spirit
		Komm, Heiliger Geist, Herre Gott	200				
Kommt her zu mir, spricht Gottes Sohn	2496c	Kommt her zu mir, spricht Gottes Sohn	201	231	40	146	Christian life

Chorale tune	No.	Setting					Category
Lobt Gott, ihr Christen allzugleich	198	Lobt Gott, ihr Christen allzugleich	202	—	142	14	Christmas
Meine Seele erhebt den Herrn	1956	Magnificat noni toni	205	303	128	2	Advent
Mensch, willt du leben seliglich	3986	Mensch, willt du leben seliglich	206	114	94b	77	10 Commandments
Mit Fried und Freud ich fahr dahin	2029a	Mit Fried und Freud ich fahr dahin	76	334	48b	260	Death & dying
Nun bitten wir den Heiligen Geist		Nun bitten wir den Heiligen Geist	208	101	98a	59	Holy Spirit
		Nun bitten wir den Heiligen Geist	209				
Nun freut euch, lieben Christen gmein	4427	Gen Himmel zu dem Vater mein	32	52	86	55	Ascension
		Nun freut euch, lieben Christen gmein	210		86	55	Ascension
		Sinfonia [Gott fähret auf]	33				
Nun komm, der Heiden Heiland	1174	Nun komm, der Heiden Heiland	211	1	6a	1	Advent
Nun laßt uns den Leib begraben	352	Ihr lieben Christen, freut euch nun	51	335	—	259*	Death & dying
Nun laßt uns Gott dem Herren	156+	Nun laßt uns Gott dem Herren	81	—	84b	132	Thanksgiving
Nun lob, mein Seel, den Herren	8244+	Nun lob, mein Seel, den Herren	212	—	100	127	Thanksgiving
		Nun lob, mein Seel, den Herren	213				
		Nun lob, mein Seel, den Herren	214				
		Nun lob, mein Seel, den Herren	215				
O Gott, wir danken deiner Güt	4493b	O Gott, wir danken deiner Güt	86	—	108a	287	Morn/evening
Puer natus in Bethlehem	192b	Puer natus in Bethlehem	217	20	30	15	Christmas
Vater unser im Himmelreich	2561	Nimm von uns, Herr, du treuer Gott	78	119	106b	177	Cross & consolation
		Nimm von uns, Herr, du treuer Gott	207				
		Vater unser im Himmelreich	219				Prayer
Verleih uns Frieden gnädiglich	1945b	Gib unserm König	29	255	62	83	Church
		All solch dein Gut wir preisen	3	—	102b	227*	New Year
Von Gott will ich nicht lassen	5264a	Von Gott will ich nicht lassen	220	—	18b	17	Cross & consolation
		Von Gott will ich nicht lassen	221		122	188	
Wachet, auf ruft uns die Stimme	8405a	Wachet, auf ruft uns die Stimme	100	—	16	269	Last judgment
Wär Gott nicht mit uns diese Zeit	4434	Wär Gott nicht mit uns diese Zeit	102	297	—	229	Church
		Wär Gott nicht mit uns diese Zeit	222				
Wie schön leuchtet der Morgenstern	8359	Wie schön leuchtet der Morgenstern	223	—	8	275	Heaven & hell

Notes

Chapter One: Denmark

Basic literature: Butt, *Music Education and the Art of Performance;* Dalsager, *Helsingør St. Mariæ Kirkes Historia;* Friis, *Buxtehude: Hans By og hans Orgel;* Friis, *Diderik Buxtehude;* Friis, *Orgel Bygning in Danmark;* Hagen, *Diderik Buxtehude;* Hammerich, *Dansk Musikhistorie indtil ca. 1700;* Hostrup-Schultz, *Helsingørs Embeds- og Bestillingsmæend;* Hultkvist, "Ny Buxtehudeorgel i Helsingborg"; Hultkvist, "Orglar i 1600-talets Skåne"; Johannesson, *Helsingborg: stad i 900 år;* Johnsson, *Den danske skolemusiks historie indtil 1739;* Kongsted, "Codex Rattus Helsingorensis"; Lundgren, "Nicolajorganisten Johan Lorentz i Köpenhamn"; Mikkelsen, *Helsingør;* Nørfelt, "Sct. Mariæ Kirkes orgelhistorie"; Pirro, *Dietrich Buxtehude;* Preußner, "Die Methodik im Schulgesang der evangelischen Lateinschulen des 17. Jahrhunderts"; *Sancta Maria Kyrka i Hälsingborg;* Schiørring, *Musikkens Historie i Danmark,* vol. I; *Den ved Øresund Beliggende Anseelige Stad Helsingørs Beskrivelse.*

1. Quoted in Follin, *Helsingborgs Historia,* 62.
2. Photograph in Friis, *Diderik Buxtehude,* plate 3.
3. Stahl, "Dietrich Buxtehudes Eltern" (1937); "Dieterich Buxtehudes Geburtsort" (1951).
4. Klüver, *Bürgerbuch der Stadt Bad Oldesloe,* 123.
5. Läpple, "Dieterich Buxtehude und Oldesloe," 26–27.
6. *Florilegium Portense* (1618), no. 57. Handl's original version is published in *Denkmäler der Tonkunst Österreichs* XII, 28.
7. "Organista ipse nulli in Europa secundus," quoted from a travel diary by Lundgren in "Johan Lorentz in Kopenhagen," 184.
8. Wolf, *Encomion Regni Daniae,* 382.
9. Ogier, *Ephemerides, sive iter Danicum, Svecicum, Polonicum,* 81. Ogier does not specifically name Lorentz in this reference, but he had previously referred to the organist of St. Nicholas's who played for an hour on alternate days (p. 50).
10. Friis, "Nikolaj Kirkes Orgler, Organister og Klokkespillere," 441–43.
11. Hagen was the first to undertake biographical research on Buxtehude in the archives of Helsingør and Helsingborg. He communicated his findings by letter to André Pirro in Paris, who published them in his book *Dietrich Buxtehude* (1913); Hagen's own book appeared in 1920.
12. Mårtensson, "Orgelverken i S:ta Maria," 16.
13. Wolf, *Encomion Regni Daniae,* 309.
14. Bruns, "Die Lübecker Syndiker und Ratssekretäre," 110.
15. The title page with this dedication is reproduced in *Werke,* VII, 57. It is not an autograph.
16. *Bibliotheca Marci Meibomii, Frederici tertii, Daniae Regis, olim consiliarii, continens raros libros . . . Qui publica Auctione Vendentur.*

Chapter Two: Lübeck: The City

Basic literature: *800 Jahre Musik in Lübeck*, I, II; Andresen, *Lübeck: Geschichte, Kirchen, Befestigungen*; Asch, *Rat und Bürgerschaft in Lübeck*; von Brandt, *Geist und Politik in der Lübeckischen Geschichte*; Dollinger, *The German Hansa*; Graßmann, ed., *Lübeckische Geschichte*, Hauschild, *Kirchengeschichte Lübecks;* Heidrich, "Andachts- und Erbauungsliteratur"; Hennings, *Musikgeschichte Lübecks: I: Weltliche Musik*; Jaacks, "Trostlose Düsternis;" Karstädt, *Die "extraordinairen" Abendmusiken*; Lindtke, *Alte Lübecker Stadtansichten*; Pirro, *Dietrich Buxtehude*; Ruhle, "An Anonymous Seventeenth-century German Oratorio"; Smither, *A History of the Oratorio*, II; Snyder, "Buxtehude, the Lübeck Abendmusiken, and *Wacht! Euch zum Streit gefasset macht*"; "Franz Tunder's Stock-Exchange Concerts"; Söhngen, "Die Lübecker Abendmusiken"; Stahl, *Franz Tunder und Dietrich Buxtehude*; Stahl, "Die Lübecker Abendmusiken."

1. Stahl, *Franz Tunder und Dietrich Buxtehude*, 37.
2. Carr, *Remarks Of the Government of severall Parts of Germanie*, 159–62.
3. According to Stahl ("Lübecker Abendmusiken," 3), Hermann Lebermann, pastor of the Cathedral, was responsible for the revision, but his name does not appear in the book itself.
4. Hartwig, "Lübeck's Einwohnerzahl," 80.
5. von Brandt, "Thomas Fredenhagen," 246–69.
6. Bugenhagen, *Lübecker Kirchenordnung*, 5.
7. *Ordnung Eines Erbahren Raths* (1619), as modified in 1623.
8. Carr, 153–54.
9. Mattheson, *Ehrenpforte*, 26. Mattheson is not absolutely clear as to whether he is referring here to Peter Bruhns or Nicolaus Bruhns, the subject of the entry. Gerber (*Neues historisch-biographisches Lexikon* I, 528) used the same words with reference to Nicolaus Bruhns.
10. Schwab, "Lübecks Stadtmusikgeschichte," 203.
11. Scheibe, *Critischer Musicus*, 796.
12. Pirro, 479–81. The original print has been missing since 1942; Stahl's edition (Bärenreiter no. 1274) includes only the first three of seven strophes and omits the title of the sonatina.
13. *Die Beglückte und Geschmückte Stadt Lübeck*, 114.
14. Ruetz, *Widerlegte Vorurtheile* (1752), 44–49.
15. Quoted by Carl H. H. Franck, *Nachrichten über die Börse in Lübeck* (Lübeck: H. G. Rahtgens, 1873), 15. For further details see Snyder, "Franz Tunder's Stock-Exchange Concerts."
16. Text complete in Pirro, 175–184; summarized in Smither, II, 89–90.
17. The evidence rests only on a pencilled note in the Copenhagen copy of Moller's *Cimbria literata* (Bolte, "Das Stammbuch Johann Valentin Meder's," 503), but Petersen wrote other *Gelegenheitsgedichte* at this time; see Matthias, *Johann Wilhelm und Johanna Eleonora Petersen*, 385.
18. Göhler, *Verzeichnis*, part 2, p. 12; Moller also lists these works in his article on Buxtehude in *Cimbria Literata* (appendix 4, E8).
19. Elmenhorst, *Dramatologia Antiquo-Hodierna* (1688), 100–101.
20. Titles listed in appendix 1 under BuxWV 133.
21. Published in facsimile in Karstädt, *Die "extraordinairen" Abendmusiken* and in a facsimile edition by the Bibliothek der Hansestadt Lübeck (2002); summarized in Smither, 94–95.

22. *Uu* vok. mus. i hskr. caps. 71. There is no title page, but the wrappers for the parts of each act contain pencil notations in a seventeenth-century hand. The wrapper for the parts of Act I—not included in the microfilm supplied by the Deutsches Musikgeschichtliches Archiv—reads "Actus 1^{mus} / Wacht euch zum Streit / a / Soprano 1mo et 2do / Alto / Tenore 1mo et 2do / Basso / doi Violini / doi Violetti / Basso Cont."

23. Extracted from the parts and supplied with an English translation in Ruhle, 325–68; summarized in Smither, 96–99.

24. The libretto of 1700 bore the name of Dieterich Wulfrath, written in Buxtehude's hand; see illustration in Stahl, *Franz Tunder und Dietrich Buxtehude*, 65.

25. Tesdorpf, *Die Geschichte des Tesdorpf'schen Geschlechts*, 45.

26. Missing since 1942; title page illustrated in Stahl, *Franz Tunder und Dietrich Buxtehude*, 74.

Chapter Three: Lübeck, St. Mary's Church

Basic literature: *Bach Dokumente* I, II, III; von Brandt, *Geist und Politik in der Lübeckischen Geschichte*; Edler, *Der nordelbische Organist*; Geck, *Die Vokalmusik Dietrich Buxtehudes;* Hasse, *Die Marienkirche zu Lübeck*; Hauschild, *Kirchengeschichte Lübecks*; Jannasch, *Geschichte des lutherschen Gottesdienstes in Lübeck*; Jimmerthal, "Zur Geschichte der St. Marien Kirche in Lübeck; Ortgies, "Die Praxis der Orgelstimmung in Norddeutschland," Snyder, "Bach, Buxtehude, and the Old Choir Library of St. Mary's in Lübeck"; Snyder, "Partners in Music-making"; Snyder, "To Lübeck in the Steps of J. S. Bach"; *Speculum aevi: Kirchengesang in Lübeck als Spiegel der* Zeiten; Stahl, *Franz Tunder und Dietrich Buxtehude*; Stahl, *Die große Orgel der Marienkirche zu Lübeck*; Stahl, *Musikgeschichte Lübecks II: Geistliche Musik*; Stahl, *Die Totentanz-Orgel der Marienkirche zu Lübeck*; Vogel, "Tuning and Temperament."

1. Niedt, *Musicalische Handleitung Anderer Theil* (2d edition, ed. Mattheson), 189–90. The third new stop of 1704, Pedal Dulcian 16', appears to have replaced an existing one. For the most recent discussion of the large organ see Ortgies, "Über den Umbau."

2. Jimmerthal, 333. Jimmerthal was the organist and Werkmeister of St. Mary's from 1845 to 1886, and he prepared the catalogue of the St. Mary's archives that is still in use. Even with the return of most archives to Lübeck, Jimmerthal's source for this information concerning the new keyboards is not clear, but in all cases where the original archival sources are available for comparison, his statements have proven accurate.

3. On the Schulze organ, see Walter, *"This Heaving Ocean of Tones,"* 31–65.

4. Jimmerthal, 437.

5. Fock, "Lübeck, Totentanzorgel," penciled notes in the Fock Archiv in the Schnitger Zentrum Golzwarden (Brake).

6. Werckmeister, *Erweiterte und verbesserte Orgel-Probe*, 79, 82.

7. For a catalogue of seventy-seven such organs, see Ortgies, "Subsemitones in Organs Built between 1468 and 1721." To this list should now be added the organ in St. Peter's Church, Hamburg (see Schröder, "Die Orgelgeschichte der Hauptkirche St. Petri," 32).

8. For a useful survey, see Padgham, *The Well-Tempered Organ*.

9. Praetorius, *Organographia*, 155; Werckmeister, *Orgelprobe* (1698), 79.

10. "Joh. Siborch will versuchen so viehl immer müghligen dieselbe Quinta zwischen a vnd d rein zu stimmen vnd die tertien zu schärffen vnd die schwebende Quinta an andere Oerter zu bringen." Quoted by Fritz Piersig, "Die Orgeln der bremischen Stadtkirche," 401; the original document is now lost.

11. BuxWV 146 (in g), 182, and 246, in Dietrich Buxtehude, *Orgelwerke* vol. 5 (Dabringhaus und Grimm, 3425).

12. This instrument is still extant at the St. Annen Museum in Lübeck. Roland Wilson reports that "the maximum possible pitch alteration by using a shorter bocal would be something like 10 Hertz and therefore that Buxtehude's pitch would have been in the region of a = 475. With a normal size bocal the Lübeck instrument plays at standard Chorton ca. a = 465" (Wilson, e-mail to author, 7 December 2005). The figure of a' = 480 comes from Ortgies, "Über den Umbau," 327. This is approximately three quarters of a tone higher than modern a' = 440.

13. Johann Philipp Bendeler referred to it as "*Saccharum des Bleyes*" in his *Organopoeia* ([1690], fol. A1.) Lead corrosion still presents a problem in historic organs; the facade pipes of the Stellwagen organ in St. Jakobi, Lübeck, have suffered greatly from it. The European Union's program COLLAPSE (Corrosion of Lead and Lead-Tin Alloys of Organ Pipes in Europe) is currently addressing this problem; see http://goart.gu.se/cgi-bin/hpslev1/goart.taf.

14. Ruetz, *Widerlegte Vorurtheile* (1752), 152–55 passim.

15. This lost music is listed in the *Buxtehude-Werke-Verzeichnis* as BuxWV 126, but neither Lebermann's description (in *Die Beglückte und Geschmückte Stadt Lübeck*, 108) nor Buxtehude's own entry into the accounts states that he himself composed it.

16. On this hymnal see Kadelbach, "Verloren und wieder entdeckt."

17. *St. Marien I [Bücher] 3 [Musik], 13*; details in Snyder, "Tradition with Variations."

18. His letter of appointment is reprinted in Stahl, *Musikgeschichte Lübecks* II, 193.

19. Hennings, *Musikgeschichte Lübecks* I, 46.

20. Ruetz, *Wiederlegte Vorurtheile* (1752), 47.

21. Stiehl, "Katalog (1893)"; my thematic catalogue of the separate works is forthcoming. For documentation and further information on selected aspects of the choir library, see Snyder, "Bach, Buxtehude, and the Old Choir Library"; "Partners in Music-making"; and "Text and Tone."

22. Cited by Gebler, "Beiträge zur Geschichte der Entwicklung des Kirchengesanges in Lübeck," 84.

23. Mithobius, *Psalmodia christiana*, 376–77.

24. The entire text is printed as Anhang 2 in Stahl, *Musikgeschichte Lübecks* 2: 192.

25. Letter to the church of St. Jakobi, Stettin, quoted in Fock, *Arp Schnitger und seine Schule*, 175.

26. See Hudson, "Franz Tunder, the North-Elbe Music School and Its Influence on J. S. Bach," 20–40.

27. *Bach-Dokumente* 3: 82.

28. *Bach-Dokumente* 2: 19–20.

29. Maul and Wollny, *Weimarer Orgeltabulatur*.

30. von Brandt, *Geist und Geschichte*, 34, 36.

Chapter Four: Beyond the Walls of Lübeck

Basic literature: Braun, *Vom Remter zum Gänsemarkt*; Dirksen, ed., *Orgelmusik av familjen Düben*; Fock, *Arp Schnitger und seine Schule*; Grapenthin, "The Catharinen Organ during Scheidemann's Tenure"; Grapenthin, "'Sweelincks Kompositionsregeln'"; Grapenthin, "The Transmission of Sweelinck's *Composition Regeln*"; Grusnick, "Die Dübensammlung";

Jaacks, *Hamburg zu Lust und Nutz*; Kjellberg, *Kungliga musiker i sverige*; Krüger, *Die hamburgische Musikorganisation*; Schulze, *Die Quellen der Hamburger Oper*; Schwab, "Johannes Voorhouts Gemälde"; Snyder, "Dietrich Buxtehude's Studies in Learned Counterpoint"; C. Wolff, "Das Hamburger Buxtehude-Bild"; H. C. Wolff, *Die Barockoper in Hamburg*.

1. Carr, *Remarks Of the Government of severall Parts of Germanie*, 157–58.
2. Katzschke, "Verkehrswege zwischen Lübeck und Hamburg," 42.
3. Hach, "Schilderungen Lübecks in älteren Reisebeschreibungen," 130.
4. Rist, *Monatsgespräche* II, 167, quoted by Krüger, 98.
5. See Frandsen, *Crossing Confessional Boundaries*, 17–37 and 172–74.
6. Reproduced in color in *300 Jahre Oper in Hamburg*, 79.
7. Christoph Wolff, "Das Hamburger Buxtehude-Bild," first published in *800 Jahre Musik in Lübeck*, 1982.
8. English translation by Thomson Moore in *Boston Early Music Festival & Exhibition* (program book, Boston, 1987), 104–5.
9. This final idea was suggested by Dorothea Schröder (personal conversation, 23 May 2006) and confirmed by Friedemann Hellwig (e-mail, 26 July 2006). Hellwig adds, "It is noteworthy that the third finger and even more so the fourth finger have been set quite carelessly, so as if it would not matter where they are." Heinrich Schwab first mentioned to me in May 1987 that Buxtehude was more likely the gamba player in the painting, an opinion that he had formed prior to Harro Schmidt's publication of this interpretation in *Der Kirchenmusiker* (1987, Heft 5). Wolff responded to Schmidt in his "Nachwort 1988" to the republication of "Der Hamburger Buxtehude-Bild" in *Studien zur Musikgeschichte der Hansestadt Lübeck* (1989). I gratefully acknowledge the help of numerous colleagues who have discussed this painting with me at various times: Judith Colton, Ulf Grapenthin, Friedemann Hellwig, Gisela Jaacks, Wayne Meeks, Dorothea Schröder, David Schulenberg, Heinrich Schwab, Joel Speerstra, and Christoph Wolff.
10. Kremer, *Joachim Gerstenbüttel*, 174.
11. Facsimile of title page in the modern edition, Vereeniging voor Noord-Nederlandische Muziekgeschiedenis, Uitgave, XIII.
12. For a discussion of Theile's treatise see Grapenthin, " 'Sweelincks Kompositionsregeln," 100–107. Note, however, that Grapenthin's dating of manuscript 5823 to the 1690s is not now so secure in view of Peter Wollny's investigations of the origins of the Österreich-Bokemeyer collection (see chapter 9).
13. Mattheson, *Criticae musicae tomus secundus* (1725), 57.
14. Sweelinck, *Werken*, 10: 58; see also Grapenthin, " 'Sweelinck's Kompositionsregeln,' " 81.
15. Quoted in Fock, *Arp Schnitger*, 57.
16. Adlung, *Musica mechanica organoedi* (1768), 288, footnote a.
17. Fock, *Hamburg's Role*, 106.
18. For details see http://www.stiftung-johann-sebastian.de/ (accessed 3/26/06).
19. Braun, *Vom Remter zum Gänsemarkt*, 17.
20. Karl Heller, "Ein Rostocker Schüler," 104.
21. Fock, Arp Schnitger, 173.
22. See Hüschen, "Hamburger Musikdrucker und Musikverleger im 16. und 17. Jahrhundert," 268–69.
23. *Düben Collection Database Catalog*, http://www.musik.uu.se/duben/Duben.php (accessed 10/12/06).

24. BuxWV 7 was composed while Buxtehude was in Helsingør, but the date of its entry into the Düben collection is uncertain. See chapter 10.

25. Walther, *Briefe*, 135, 146, 216.

26. Kjellberg, 205. Illustration of the triumphal arch (from Dahlberg, *Suecia Antiqua*), p. 206.

27. Kjellberg, Appendix 5.10, dated 12 March 1663.

28. Kjellberg, 231.

29. For details of the extensive documentation of this project, see Ericsson, ed., *Övertorneå Projektet.*

30. Kjellberg, 236.

31. *Harmonologia Musica*, 90–93, 102. See also Dodds, "Columbus's Egg."

32. Walther, *Briefe*, 70.

33. Letter to Bokemeyer, 6 August 1729; Walther, *Briefe*, 62–3.

34. Haacke, "Der Buxtehudeschüler Daniel Erich und seine Orgel in Güstrow," 24; also in Fock, *Arp Schnitger*, 176.

35. Fock, *Arp Schnitger*, 171–75.

36. Listed in Freytag, *Musikgeschichte der Stadt Stettin im 18. Jahrhundert*, 143–45. See also Schwartz, "Zur Geschichte der liedlosen Zeit in Deutschland," 15–27.

37. Fuhrmann, *Die an der Kirchen Gottes gebauete Satans-Capelle* (1729), 55.

38. Geck, "Nochmals: Die Authentizität des Vokalwerks Dietrich Buxtehudes," 175.

Chapter Five: Vocal Music

Basic literature: Blume, "Das Kantatenwerk Dietrich Buxtehudes"; Bunners, *Kirchenmusik und Seelenmusik*; Frandsen, *Crossing Confessional Boundaries;* Geck, "Die Authentizität des Vokalwerks Dietrich Buxtehudes"; Geck, *Die Vokalmusik Dietrich Buxtehudes und der frühe Pietismus*; Irwin, "German Pietists and Church Music"; Karstädt, *Der Lübecker Kantatenband*; Kilian, "Das Vokalwerk Dietrich Buxtehudes"; Krummacher, *Die Choralbearbeitung in der protestantischen Figuralmusik zwischen Praetorius und Bach*; Krummacher, "Die geistliche Aria in Norddeutschland und Skandinavien"; Krummacher, "Über das Spätstadium des geistlichen Solokonzerts in Norddeutschland"; Matter, "Buxtehude and Pietism"; Maxton, "Die Authentizität des 'Jüngsten Gerichts' "; Ruhle, "An Anonymous Seventeenth-century German Oratorio"; Sørensen, *Buxtehudes Vokale Kirkemusik*; Sørensen, "Monteverdi—Förster—Buxtehude"; Snyder, "Buxtehude, the Lübeck Abendmusiken, and *Wacht! Euch zum Streit gefasset macht*"; Snyder, "Buxtehude and *Das Jüngste Gericht*"; Snyder, "Musik für den Kenner und den 'gemeinen Bürger' "; Webber, *North German Church Music.*

1. Löhner, *Der Geistlichen Erquickstunden des Fürtrefflichen Theologi H. Doct. Heinrich Müllers . . . Poetischer Andacht-Klang*, XXXIV [p. 199]: "Beständigkeit im Gebet: Anhalten macht Erhalten; Erquick St. CCXLVI Betrachtung." The corresponding meditation in *Dr. Heinrich Müllers geistliche Erquickstunden* [1822 edition] reads in part: "Gott hält mit der Gabe zurück, daß du desto inbrünstiger betest; er verbirgt sich, daß du desto fleißiger suchest; er verschleußt die Himmelsthür, daß du desto heftiger anklopfen sollst. Bittet, suchet, klopfet an!" (p. 560).

2. Irwin, "German Pietists," 39. She discusses this issue at much greater length in her later book, *Neither Voice nor Heart Alone* (1993).

3. Fuhrmann, *Musicalischer-Trichter*, 83–84. Further references to Fuhrmann's discussion of vocal genres are all drawn from pp. 82–84.

4. The three selections from *Musikalische Andachten* IV in volume 40 of *Denkmäler deutscher Tonkunst* (numbers 16–18, pp. 78ff) are all designated "cum & sine Fundamento" in the index of the original print.

5. Five selections published in Vetter, *Das frühdeutsche Lied*, II, 60–64; four selections in Moser, *Corydon*, II, 3–7.

6[Neumeister], *Die allerneueste Art, zur Reinen und galanten Poesie zu gelangen*, 275. Christian Friedrich Hunold unashamedly published Neumeister's lectures under his own pen name, "Menantes," as he acknowledges in his foreword, dated 1706.

7. *Die allerneueste Art*, 284. Although his definition does not refer specifically to sacred music, the examples that follow have sacred texts in both German and Latin.

8. See *Crossing Confessional Boundaries*, 191 and 229–44; for a modern edition of Albrici's *O cor meum* see Frandsen, "The Sacred Concerto in Dresden," 3: 195–222.

9. Fischer-Krückeberg, "Johann Crüger's Choralbearbeitungen," 254.

10. Dietrich Kilian's edition of *Membra* contains a tutti setting of the first strophe of the aria "Salve mundi salutare" from the first cantata (Veröffentlichung des Instituts für Musikforschung, Berlin; Reihe I, Heft 31 [Berlin: Merseburger, 1960], pp. 7–8). Buxtehude in fact set the first strophe for soprano 1, following the opening concerto, which ends on a half cadence. After the three strophes of the aria, the opening concerto is to be repeated, followed by the tutti setting of the first strophe to conclude the entire composition on the tonic. Gustav Düben set the precedent for the modification of Buxtehude's plan by adding a full cadence to the end of the concerto in his copy of Buxtehude's autograph tablature (*Uu* 50:12) and including it in his set of parts for the first cantata (*Uu* 6:2).

11. Grusnick, "Die Dübensammlung," *Stm* 48 (1966): 148. Peter Wollney has recently identified it as belonging to a group of works emanating from Zeitz or Merseburg; see Wollny, "A Source Complex."

12. I should like to thank Professor Dr. Friedhelm Krummacher for bringing this work to my attention and Professor Dr. Hans Rudolf Jung of Weimar for supplying me with a copy of the manuscript and additional information concerning it.

Chapter Six: Works of Learned Counterpoint

Basic literature: Belotti, "'. . . une petite chanson'"; Bernhard, "Tractatus compositionis augmentatus," in Müller-Blattau, *Kompositionslehre*, translated in Hilse, "The Treatises of Christoph Bernhard"; Bolte, "Das Stammbuch Johann Valentin Meders"; Braun, *Deutsche Musiktheorie*; Geck, "Quellenkritische Bemerkungen zu Dietrich Buxtehudes Missa brevis"; Grapenthin, "'Sweelincks Kompositionsregeln"; Grapenthin, "The Transmission of Sweelinck's *Composition Regeln*"; Snyder, "Buxtehude's Studies in Learned Counterpoint"; Yearsley, "Towards an Allegorical Interpretation."

1. The mass and *Prudentia prudentiana* are published in *Das Erbe deutscher Musik*, vol. 90; *Zur selbigigen Zeit* in *Das Chorwerk*, vol. 107. Two masses on the chorale melodies "Christ unser Herr zum Jordan kam" (*Das Chorwerk*, vol. 16) and "Durch Adams Fall" (*Das Chorwerk*, vol. 107) depart only slightly from the dissonance treatment that Bernhard prescribes for *stile antico*; see Fiebig, *Christoph Bernhard*, 195.

2. *Carmina Lugubria quibus obitum D. Menonis Hannekenii Dnn. Doctores Professores, Collegae aliiqu; variis in locis Amici & Fautores Prosequi voluerunt.*

3. *Compositions Tractat*, p. 33, as quoted by Braun, *Deutsche Musiktheorie* II, 281.

4. Photographs from this autograph book, formerly at the Gesellschaft für Geschichte und Altertumskunde in Riga, were made for André Pirro in 1910 and are now found with his literary estate at the Bibliothèque Nationale in Paris (Fonds Pirro, Boîte 60).

5. The "canon duplex" appears in Sweelinck, *Werken*, X, 87 and is reprinted in my article "Buxtehude's Studies in Learned Counterpoint." Note, however, that the work of Braun and Grapenthin has now superceded the information I gave there on the authorship, copyist, and dating of this part of the treatise.

6. Grusnick, "Dübensammlung" (1966), 163; Rudén I, 164.

7. Düben's ink catalogue numbers are listed by Grusnick in "Dübensammlung" (1964), 42–64; see also chapter 10.

8. The use of "nostri" instead of the more usual "nobis" is found in the masses of several other seventeenth-century German composers, including Bernhard, Theile, Selle, and Johann Philipp Krieger.

Chapter Seven: Keyboard Works

Basic literature: Apel, *The History of Keyboard Music*; Archbold, *Style and Structure in the Praeludia of Dietrich Buxtehude*; Breig, "Der norddeutsche Orgelchoral"; Breig, *Die Orgelwerke von Heinrich Scheidemann*; Collins, *The* Stylus Phantasticus *and Free Keyboard Music*; Dirksen, "Dieterich Buxtehude and the Chorale Fantasia"; Dirksen, "The Enigma of the *stylus phantasticus*"; Gable, "Alternation practice and seventeenth-century German organ Masgnificats"; Gustafson, *French Harpsichord Music of the 17th Century*; Hedar, *Dietrich Buxtehudes Orgelwerke*; Kämper, "Die Kanzone in der norddeutschen Orgelmusik des 17. Jahrhunderts"; Krummacher, "Stylus phantasticus"; Kunze, "Gattungen der Fuge in Bachs Wohltemperiertem Klavier"; Lorenz, "Die Klaviermusik Dietrich Buxtehudes"; Palisca, "The genesis of Mattheson's style classification"; Pauly, *Die Fuge in den Orgelwerken Buxtehudes*; Porter, "Johann Herbst's *Arte prattica & poëtica*; Porter, "Observations concerning Contrapuntal Improvisation"; Porter, "Psalm-tone Formulas in Buxtehude's Organ Works?"; Spitta, *Johann Sebastian Bach*, I; Snyder, "The Örgryte Organ as a Work of Musical Scholarship"; Walker, *Theories of Fugue*; Wolff, "Präludium (Toccata) und Sonata."

1. Krüger, "Johann Kortkamps Organistenchronik," 204–6.

2. Ortgies, "Die Praxis der Orgelstimmung," 238–39.

3. Rampe, "Abendmusik oder Gottesdienst?" *SJ* 2004, 155.

4. Rampe, "Abendmusik oder Gottesdienst?" *SJ* 2005, 91–114. Note, however, that the table on p. 109 is hypothetical; Walther did not pay for his copies of Buxtehude's works, but received them as gifts from Werckmeister. See Walther, *Briefe*, 62–63, 70.

5. Fuhrmann, *Musicalischer Trichter*, 90.

6. Rampe, "Abendmusik oder Gottesdienst?" SJ 2005, 93.

7. Archbold, "Towards a Critical Understanding," 93–100; Breig, "Die geschichtliche Stellung," 271–73.

8. Marpurg, part I, p. 129, and Tab. XXXVI, Fig. 3.

9. Staats- und Universitätsbibliothek Hamburg, ND VI 5384, part 1 (see chapter 4), partially reprinted in Sweelinck, *Werken* 10: 23–24, 49–58.

10. Sweelinck, *Werken* X, 54.

11. Brahms to Spitta [Wieden-Wien, 19.] January 1874, *Johannes Brahms im Briefwechsel mit Philipp Spitta*, 53.

12. Weckmann, *Sämtliche Freie Orgel- und Clavierwerke*, ed. Rampe, p. 14, mm. 21–36.

13. Fuhrmann, *Musicalischer Trichter*, p. 86. Further references to Fuhrmann's discussion of instrumental genres are all drawn from pp. 86–87.

14. *Kircherus jesuita germannus Germaniae redonatus*, 158.

15. See Rampe, "Das 'Hintze Manuskript,'" 83; also 104–6, where he gives transcriptions of two letters from Froberger to Kircher, dated 1649 and 1654.

16. Dirksen, "The Enigma," 112.

17. "P.S. Ich hab disen psalmen mit fleiß nit mit aigner handt geschrieben, dan man macht es sonsten kennen, daß ichs gemacht habe. E. E. kennen sagen sie hetten es gemacht." Quoted in Rampe, "Das 'Hintze-Manuskript,'" 105.

18. Walther, *Praecepta der Musicalischen Composition*, 185.

19. Müller-Blattau, *Kompositionslehre*, 83.

20. Butler, "The Fantasia as Musical Image," 609.

21. Dirksen, "Dieterich Buxtehude and the Chorale Fantasia," 162.

22. For a brief description of this organ, see Snyder, "A New Organ for a New Millenium," in Snyder, ed., *The Organ as a Mirror of Its Time*, 339–46; for the complete documentation of its construction, see Speerstra, ed., *The North German Organ Research Project*. Chapter 27, "The Örgryte Organ as a Work of Musical Scholarship," contains my discussion of Buxtehude's *Te Deum* in a performance by William Porter.

23. Quoted in Schwab, "Suitensätze und Tanzmodelle," 191.

24. Küster, "Cembalo und Violinmusik"; Buxtehude, *Suite in d* [*sic*.; *recte* a], ed. Küster.

25. *VI Suittes*, ed Dirksen.; see also Dirksen, "A Buxtehude Discovery."

Chapter Eight: Sonatas

Basic literature: Allsop, *The Italian 'Trio' Sonata;* Defant, *Kammermusik und Stylus phantasticus;* Einstein, *Zur deutschen Literatur für Viola da Gamba;* Jensen, "Nord- und südeuropäische Traditionen"; Linfield, "Dietrich Buxtehude's Sonatas"; Linfield, "North and South European Influences"; Newman, *The Sonata in the Baroque Era.*

1. The *RISM* entry for this publication incorrectly lists the parts as two violins and continuo; an edition of one of Becker's sonatas for violin, viola da gamba, and continuo may be found in Einstein, *Zur deutschen Literatur für Viola da* Gamba, 95–102.

2. See Walker, *Theories of Fugue*, 232–34, together with note 27. According to Walker's definition, a permutation fugue has at least three themes; Reincken's fugues have only two.

3. Translated in Alsop, *The Italian 'Trio' Sonata*, 57.

4. Eva Linfield, in an e-mail of 7 August 2006, reports that Jochen Thesmann found the concordance ascribed to Nicolai in the Düben Collection, *Uu* imhs 5:6a, and the two concordances attributed to Young at the Durham Cathedral library.

5. Kircher, *Musurgia*, 466.

Chapter 9: The Sources of Buxtehude's Music

Basic literature: Beckmann, "Ein anderer Buxtehude?"; Beckmann, "Textkritische Überlegungen zu Buxtehude's Orgelwerken"; Belotti, *Die freien Orgelwerke Dieterich Buxtehudes;* Buxtehude, *The Collected Works*, ed. Snyder (vol. 9), Beckman (vol. 10, in press), Linfield (vol. 14), Belotti (vol. 15, vol. 16 in press); Daw, "Copies of J. S. Bach by Walther & Krebs"; Grusnick, "Die Dübensammlung"; Gustafson, *French Harpsichord Music*; Hedar, *Dietrich Buxtehudes Orgelwerke*; Kjellberg and Snyder, Düben Collection Database Catalogue; Krummacher, *Die Überlieferung der Choralbearbeitungen*; Karstädt, *Der Lübecker Kantatenband Dietrich Buxtehudes*; Kümmerling, *Katalog der Sammlung Bokemeyer*; Maul and Wollny, *Weimarer* Orgeltabulatur; May, "J. G. Walther"; Riedel, *Quellenkundliche Beiträge*; Schulze, *Studien zur Bach-Überlieferung*; Synofzik, "Johann Gottlieb Preller"; Zietz, *Quellenkritische Untersuchungen an den Bach-Handschriften P801, P802 und P803*.

1. Ruetz, *Widerlegte Vorurtheile* (1753), 112–13.
2. Wollny, "Beiträge zur Entstehungsgeschichte der Sammlung Düben," 101. See also Wollny's facsimile edition of *Herr, ich lasse dich nicht*.
3. The Düben Collection Database Catalogue (DCDC) can be accessed at http://www.musik.uu.se/duben/Duben.php
4. Wollny, "Zwischen Hamburg, Gottorf und Wolfenbüttel," 62–63.
5. Listed in Seiffert, "Die Chorbibliothek der Michaelisschule in Lüneburg."
6. Maul and Wollny, *Weimarer Orgeltabulatur*. My thanks to Peter Wollny for sharing information about the Weimar tablatures with me before the appearance of this publication.
7. Schulze, *Studien zur Bach-Überlieferung*, 30–56. See also Schulze, "Johann Christoph Bach."
8. Identified independently by Schulze and Dietrich Kilian: Schulze, *Studien*, 49 (facsimile on the cover); Kilian, "Zu einem Bachschen Tabulaturautograph."
9. Schulze, "Bach und Buxtehude"; Wollny, "Traditionen des phantastischen Stils," note 8; Belotti, ed., *Dieterich Buxtehude Collected Works*, 15B, 15.
10. Dürr, "Zur Chronologie," 63.
11. *B* Mus.ms. Am.462 and 430; also *B* Mus.ms. 2683 and 2681/1.
12. It is listed on p. 144 of Poelchau's copy (*B* Df 132/1) of the catalogue of books and music from Forkel's estate, *Verzeichniß der von dem verstorbenen Doctor und Musikdirector Forkel in Göttingen nachgelassenen Bücher und Musikalien*, and on fol. 41r of Poelchau's manuscript catalogue of his own collection, "Katalog Pölchau, Bd. IV: Handschriften (praktische Musik)" (*B* Mus ms theor K41).
13. Information kindly supplied by Hans-Joachim Schulze.
14. Kobayashi, "Der Gehrener Kantor Johann Christoph Bach," 168–77.
15. It does not appear in the auction catalogue of Kittel's own estate, however, unless the designation "gest." (*gestochen*, "engraved") is incorrect for entry no. 457: "Samml. von Präludien und Fugen, ausgeführte Choräle etc. von berühmten ältern Meistern, gest." Two Buxtehude manuscripts appear in the list: "494: Buxtehude, 2 Präludien in D u. G geschr." and "496: Buxtehude, Präludien und Fugen, geschr." *Verzeichnis derjenigen Musikalien und musikalischen Schriften aus dem Nachlasse des verstorbenen Hrn. Organist Kittel in Erfurt*.
16. Facsimile in Kobayashi, 177.
17. Kilian, NBA IV/5-6, KB 195.
18. Kilian, NBA IV/5-6, KB 204.
19. Quoted in Schulze, *Studien*, 130.
20. Schulze, *Studien*, 74.
21. Information kindly supplied by Dr. Wolfgang Schlieder and Frau Gertraude Spoer, Deutsches Buch- und Schriftmuseum, Leipzig. Three seals with coat of arms of Johann Georg III are illustrated in Karlheinz Blaschke, *Siegel und Wappen in Sachsen*, 51.
22. Information kindly supplied by Jane Greenfield of the Yale University Library.

23. Both Seiffert (*Dietrich Buxtehudes Werke für Orgel*, Ergänzungsband, p. vi) and Riedel (p. 187) demonstrated that Strungk could not be considered the copyist of the Lowell Mason Codex.

24. Vollhardt, *Geschichte der Cantoren und Organisten von den Städten im Königreich Sachsen*, 74, 76, passim.

25. Dresden, Stadtarchiv, D. XXXIV.4, fol. 12r,v: letter dated 19 May 1682; fol. 15r, v: signed specification of defects in the organ.

Chapter Ten: Toward a Chronology of Buxtehude's Music

Basic literature: Archbold, *Style and Structure*; Beckmann, "Zur Chronologie," Belotti, *Die freien Orgelwerke Dieterich Buxtehudes*; Dirksen, "Dieterich Buxtehude and the Chorale Fantasia"; Gerardy, *Datieren mit Hilfe von Wasserzeichen*; Grusnick, "Die Dübensammlung: Ein Versuch ihrer chronologischen Ordnung"; Grusnick, "Zur Chronologie von Dietrich Buxtehudes Vokalwerken"; Kjellberg and Snyder, Düben Collection Database Catalogue; Krummacher, "Orgel- und Vokalmusik"; Riedel, *Quellenkundliche Beiträge*; Rudén, "Vattenmärken och Musikforskning"; Schneider, *Buxtehudes Choralfantasien*.

1. Spitta, "Vorwort" to *Dietrich Buxtehudes Orgelkompositionen*, I, iii. On the Grobe tablature see Belotti, *Die freien Orgelwerke*, 93–98, and Rathey, "Die Grobe-Tabulatur."

2. Beckmann, "Zur Chronologie," 228–34; Schneider, *Buxtehude Choralfantasien*, 185–87; Dirksen, "Dieterich Buxtehude and the Chorale Fantasia," 163–64; Belotti, *Die freien Orgelwerke* (1st ed., 1995), 289–94. In his third edition (2004), Belotti takes account of Ortgies's research on the St. Mary's organs and uses only "ab den 1680er Jahren (Temperatur)" as a criterion in his chronology (302–3).

Chapter Eleven: The Performance of Buxtehude's Music

Boyden, *The History of Violin Playing*; Brock, *Introduction to organ playing in 17th and 18th century style*; Bruggaier, *Studien zur Geschichte des Orgelpedalspiels*; Davidsson, *Matthias Weckmann*; Faulkner, *J. S. Bach's Keyboard Technique*; Hellwig, *Joachim Tielke*; Karstädt, "Die Instrumente in den Kantaten und Abendmusiken Dietrich Buxtehudes"; Karstädt, *Die Sammlung alter Musikinstrumente im St. Annen-Mudseum*; Lindley and Boxall, *Early Keyboard Fingerings*; Lohmann, *Studien Zu Artikulationsproblemen*; Owen, *The Registration of Baroque Organ Music*; Van Dijk, "Aspects of Fingering"; Vogel, "North German Organ Building"; Vogel, "Tuning and Temperament in the North German School."

1. Avison, *An Essay on Musical Expression*, 89–90.

2. Praetorius, *Syntagma musicum* III, 196.

3. *LÜh* A 373, fol. 11b; facsimile in Karstädt, *Lübecker Kantatenband*, Abb. 5.

4. In contrast, Buxtehude's own numerical designation in *Uu* 82:39, "a 13. 16. vel 20," may contain an error, since the addition of neither three nor four parts accommodates the capella. If "16" is read instead as "18," however, the addition of two more parts for a total of twenty can be explained by Buxtehude's autograph addition of the words "doi vel piu violini" before the sonata in the Lübeck tablature.

5. Facsimile in Buxtehude, *Ihr lieben Christen freut euch nun,* ed. Bruno and Barbara Grusnick, Stuttgarter Buxtehude-Ausgabe (Neuhausen-Stuttgart, Hänssler, 1979), 8.

6. The cover title page and the first page of Soprano 2 Concert[ato] are reproduced in *Werke* IV, 21–22.

7. Facsimile in Karstädt, *Lübecker Kantatenband,* Abb. 4 and Collected Works, IX, 267.

8. The only other mass in *stile antico* preserved in the Düben Collection is an anonymous "Missa ex F. alla brevis" (*Uu* 42:24). The head title of the bass part reads "Missa a 4 voc: alla Capella."

9. Petri, *Anleitung zur praktischen Musik,* 206.

10. Mattheson, *Das Neu-Eröffnete Orchestre,* III/3, §18. Further references to Mattheson's discussion of instruments are all drawn from pp. 265–85.

11. Fuhrmann, *Musicalischer Trichter,* 93. Further references to Fuhrmann's discussion of instruments are all drawn from pp. 91–93.

12. According to information from Friedemann Hellwig (e-mail, 6 September 2006), "Two features speak in favour of Tielke, one against him. The double purfling around the edge of the viol front is typical of Tielke and is not found in many other instruments of the time. The shape of the C-holes also reminds one of this master. The pegbox is atypical in that it does not show the peg for the highest string close to the nut as is found in all of his early viols; instead the peg arangement is the one adopted by Tielke in the mid 1680s."

13. In BuxWV 6, only the bass instrumental part calls unambiguously for viola da gamba. The title page of the set of parts (*Uu* 50:3) reads "con tre viole de Gambe overo Tromboni." The original nomenclature for the two upper instrumental parts, however, is Violino 1 and 2, and they are written in the treble clef. A later addition on the upper left corner of each part reads "viola da gamba 1: [2:] 1 8tava niedriger." These instructions have been carried out in *Werke* VII, 49–55, thus suppressing the original scoring.

14. Niedt, *Musicalische Handleitung* II, 115. Further references to Niedt's discussion of instruments are all drawn from pp. 109–15.

15. Speer, *Grundrichtiger Unterricht,* 205. Further references to Speer's discussion of instruments are all drawn from pp. 188–260.

16. Senn, *Jakob Stainer der Geigenmacher zu Absam,* 119.

17. Mersenne, *Harmonie universelle* III, 173–75.

18. The Kuhnau-Mattheson correspondence was published by Mattheson in *Critica Musica* II, 229–50.

19. Burney, *The Present State of Music in Germany, the Netherlands, and United Provinces,* edited by Percy Scholes, II, 148, with editorial note 1.

20. Reproduced in *The New Grove* (second edition, 2001), 11: 341.

21. In the unique source for this work, *LÜh* A 373, fol. 19b, the heading above the opening Sinfonia, in Buxtehude's hand, reads "Sinphonia 3 Violini doppo con Violon e Cymbalo." The five lines of tablature are not individually identified, but it appears that the fourth is for the violone and *cymbalo* and the fifth for the continuo, which is not normally listed in a heading. On the first beat of mm. 2 and 3 an extra voice, on the pitch g′, appears between the third and fourth lines, but marks beneath it clearly indicate that these notes belong to a double stop for the Violin III part above rather than to the violone-*cymbalo* part below.

22. Reproduced in facsimile in Karstädt, *Lübecker Kantatenband,* Abb. 11. Don Smithers discussed the trumpet parts of this work in *The Music and History of the Baroque Trumpet before 1721,* pp. 161–63, apparently without access to the tablature source. His conclusions are nevertheless correct: that the work is scored for natural trumpets, not slide trumpets, and that four measures (mm. 227–30) containing notes unavailable on the natural

trumpet should be an octave higher. Seiffert's edition (*DdT* XIV) is in fact incorrect at this point; this portion of the source is autograph, and Seiffert failed to recognize Buxtehude's idiosyncratic manner of indicating the octave beginning at c″. The f′ in Trumpet II at m. 18 should also be one octave higher.

23. Translated in Strunk, *Source Readings in Music History*, 454–70.

24. The term *Violon* is used for a continuo part in *Uu* 6:14, while *Violon* is used for the bass instrumental part in 51:15, 51:20 and 51:24.

25. The original print is lost; see Pirro, 479–81.

26. Boyden, "Bowing," *The New Grove* (first edition, 1980), 3:131.

27. Tosi, *Opinioni dé cantori antichi e moderni* (Bologna, 1723), 30–31; trans. Mr. Galliard as *Observations on the Florid Song*, 52–53.

28. Brock, *Introduction to organ playing;* Lindley and Boxall, *Early Keyboard Fingerings;* Vogel, ed. Samuel Scheidt, *Tabulatura Nova II.*

29. Seiffert, *Geschichte der Klaviermusik*, 119.

30. C. P. E. Bach, *Versuch*, Mitchell translation, 42.

31. Niedt II, 121f.

Bibliography

Early Printed Sources

Adlung, Jacob. *Musica mechanica organoedi.* Berlin: Friedrich Wilhelm Birnstiel, 1768. Facsimile reprint, edited by Christhard Mahrenholz. Kassel: Bärenreiter, 1961.

Angelus Silesius, Johann [Johann Scheffler]. *Heilige Seelen-Lust, Oder Geistliche Hirten-Lieder Der in ihren JESUM verliebten Psyche.* Breslau, 1657. Also facsimile reprint of 1668 edition, ed. Michael Fischer und Dominik Fugger. Kassel: Bärenreiter, 2004.

Avison, Charles. *An Essay on Musical Expression.* London: C. Davis, 1752.

Bach, Carl Philipp Emanuel. *Exempel nebst achtzehn Probe-Stücken in sechs Sonaten zu Carl Philipp Emanuel Bachs Versuche über die wahre Art das Clavier zu spielen auf XXVI. Kupfer-Tafeln.* Berlin: In Verlegung des Auctoris, 1753.

————. *Versuch über die wahre Art das Clavier zu spielen.* 2 vols. Berlin: In Verlegung des Auctoris, 1753, 1762. Facsimile reprint, ed. Lothar Hoffmann-Erbrecht. Wiesbaden: Breitkopf & Härtel, 1986.

Beer, Johann. *Musikalische Diskurse.* Nürnberg: Peter Conrad Monath, 1719. Facsimile reprint. Leipzig: VEB Deutscher Verlag für Musik, 1982.

Die Beglückte und Geschmückte Stadt Lübeck. Was ist Kurtze Beschreibung der Stadt Lübeck So wol Vom Anfang und Fortgang Derselben In ihrem Bau, Herrschafften und Einwohnern, Als sonderlich Merckwürdigen Begebenheiten und Veränderung. Lübeck: Johann Gerhard Krüger, 1697 [revised verson of von Höveln, 1666, probably prepared by Hermann Lebermann].

Bendeler, Johann Philipp. *Organopoeia.* Franckfurt and Leipzig: Theodor Calvisius, [1690]. Facsimile ed. Rudolf Bruhin. Amsterdam: Frits Knuf, 1972.

Bernhard, Christoph. *Prudentia Prudentiana, Maxime reverendo Doctori et clarissimo Professori Domino Rudolfo Capello Hamburgensi . . . solatio tribus contrapunctis convertibilibus et auctario elaborata.* Hamburg, 1669.

BIBLIA, Das ist: Die gantze H. Schrifft Alten und Newen Testaments, Deutsch D. MARTIN. LUTHER. Lüneburg: Stern, 1672.

Bibliotheca Marci Meibomii, Frederici tertii, Daniae Regis, olim consiliarii, continens raros libros . . . Qui publica Auctione Vendentur. Amsterdam: Boom, 1705.

Bodenschatz, Erhard, ed. *Florilegium Portense, continens CXV. selectissimas cantiones 4. 5. 6. 7. 8. vocum praestantissimorum aetatis nostrae autorum.* Leipzig: A. Lamberg and C. Closemann, 1618.

————, ed. *Florilegii Musici Portensis, sacras harmonias sive motetas V. VI. VII. VIII. X. vocum. E diversis, iisque praestantissimis aetatis nostrae autoribus collectus comprehendentis. Pars altera.* Leipzig: A. Lamberg, 1621.

Brossard, Sebastian de. *Dictionaire de Musique, contenant Une explication des Termes Grecs, Latins, Italiens, & François, les plus usitez dans la Musique.* 2d edition. Paris: Christophe

Ballard, 1705. Facsimile reprint, edited by Harald Heckmann. Hilversum: Frits Knuf, 1965.

Bugenhagen, Johannes. *Der Keyserliken Stadt Lübeck Christlike Ordeninge.* [Lübeck: Johann Balhorn], 1531. Facsimile reprint, under the title *Lübecker Kirchenordnung von Johannes Bugenhagen 1531,* edited and translated into High German by Wolf-Dieter Hauschild. Lübeck: Schmidt-Römhild, 1981.

[Buxtehude, Dieterich?]. *Castrum Doloris, Dero in Gott Ruhenden Römis. Käyserl. auch Königl. Majestäten Leopold dem Ersten, Zum Glorwürdigsten Andencken, In der Käyserl. Freyen Reichs-Stadt Lübecks Haupt-Kirchen zu St. Marien, Zur Zeit gewöhnlicher Abend-Music, Aus Aller-Unterthänigster Pflicht Musicalisch vorgestellet Von Diterico Buxtehuden, Organisten daselbst.* Lübeck: Schmalhertzens Wittwe, 1705. Facsimile reprint in Georg Karstädt, *Die "extraordinairen" Abendmusiken Dietrich Buxtehudes.* Lübeck: Max Schmidt-Römhild, 1962; Facsimile Lübeck: Bibliothek der Hansestadt, 2002.

Buxtehude, Dietrich. *Herr, ich lasse dich nicht. BuxWV 36. Faksimile der autographen Stimmen in der Universitätsbibliothek Uppsala. Mit Partitur im Neusatz.* Edited by Peter Wollny, Kassel: Bärenreiter, 2007.

[Buxtehude, Dieterich?]. *Die Hochzeit des Lamms, Und die Freuden-volle Einholung der Braut zu derselben in den 5. klugen Und die Außschliessung der Gottlosen von derselben in den 5. thörichten Jungfrauen, Welche wie sie Von dem Seelen-Bräutigam Christo selbst beym Matth. 25. an die Hand gegeben, Auch nach Anleitung andrer Orther in der Heil. Schrifft den Frommen und nach der Zukunfft ihres Seelen-Bräutigams hertzlich sehnenden zum innerlichen Seelen-Trost und süssten Freude; den Gottlosen aber zum Schrecken; Beides zu Gottes hohen Ehren; Christwollmeinend in der gewöhnlichen Zeit der Abend-Music am 2. und 3. Advents-Sonntage in der Haupt-Kirchen St. Marien von 4. biß 5. Uhr soll vorgestellet werden von Dieterico Buxtehuden, Organista Marian: Lubec.* Lübeck: Schmalhertzens Erben, 1678.

[Buxtehude, Dieterich?]. *Templum Honoris, Dero Regierenden Römis. Käyserl. auch Königl. Majestät Joseph Dem Ersten, Zu Unsterblichen Ehren, In der Käyserl. Freyen Reichs-Stadt Lübecks Haupt-Kirchen zu St. Marien, Im Jahr Christi 1705. Zu beliebter Zeit bey der gewöhnlichen Abend-Music, Aus Aller-Unterthänigster Pflicht Glückwünschend gewidmet Von Diterico Buxtehuden, Organisten daselbst.* Lübeck: Schmalhertzens Wittwe, 1705. Facsimile reprint in Georg Karstädt, *Die "extraordinairen" Abendmusiken Dietrich Buxtehudes.* Lübeck: Max Schmidt-Römhild, 1962; Facsimile Lübeck: Bibliothek der Hansestadt, 2002.

Buxtehude, Dietrich. For original prints of music, see appendix 3A.

Carmina Lugubria quibus obitum D. Menonis Hannekenii Dnn. Doctores Professores, Collegae aliiqu; variis in locis Amici & Fautores Prosequi voluerunt. Lübeck: Schmalhertz, n.d. [1671?].

Carr, William. *Remarks Of the Government of severall Parts of Germanie, Denmark, Sweedland, Hamburg, Lubeck, and Hansiatique Townes, but more particularly of the United Provinces, with some few directions how to Travell in the States Dominions.* Amsterdam, 1688.

Crüger, Johann, ed. *Praxis pietatis melica.* Berlin: Christoff Runge, 1664.

Diruta, Girolamo. *Il Transilvano. Dialogo sopra il vero modo di sonar organi et istromenti da penna.* Venice: Vincenti, 1593. Facsimile reprint, edited by Luisa Cervelli. Bologna: Forni, n.d.

Ebeling, Johan Georg. *Pauli Gerhardi Geistliche Andachten. Bestehend in hundert und zwantzig Liedern.* Berlin, 1667.

Eler, Franz. *Cantica sacra, partim ex sacris literis desumta, partim ab orthodoxis patribus, et piis ecclesiae doctoribus composita, et in usum ecclesiae et ivventvtis scholasticae Hamburgensis collecta, atque ad duodecim modos ex doctrina Glareani accomodata.* Hamburg: Jacob Wolff, 1588. Facsimile, ed. Klaus Beckmann. Hildesheim: Olms, 2002.

Elmenhorst, Hinrich. *Dramatologia antiquo-hodierna.* Hamburg, 1688.

Franck, Johann Wolffgang. *Arien, Aus dem Musicalischen Sing-Spiel Aeneas Ankunfft in Italien, Mit beygefügten Ritornellen.* Hamburg: author, 1680.

————. *Arien, aus dem Sing-Spiel Diocletian. Mit darzu gehörigen Ritornellen.* Hamburg: author, 1682.

————. *Arien aus dem Sing-Spiel Vespasian Mit ihren Ritornellen.* Hamburg: author, 1681.

————. *Arien Aus den beyden Operen, Von dem Erhöhten und Gestürtzten Cara Mustapha Türckischen Groß-Vezier.* Hamburg: König, 1687.

Fritzsch, Ahasverus. *Himmels Lust und Welt-Unlust oder: zwey und vierzig Himmlische Seelen-Gespräche Von der grossen überschwenglichen Herrligkeit des zukunftigen Ewigen Freuden-Lebens und elenden zeitlichen Welt-Wesens zur Erweckung eines heiligen Verlangens nach dem Himmlischen, und Verschmähung des Irrdischen, mit einigen schönen Himmels-Liedern.* Leipzig: Caspar Lunizius, 1679.

Fuhrmann, Martin Heinrich. *Die an der Kirchen Gottes gebauete Satans-Capelle.* Cologne [Berlin], 1729.

————. *Musicalischer-Trichter.* Frankfurt an der Spree [Berlin], 1706.

Gerber, Ernst Ludwig. *Historisch-biographisches Lexicon der Tonkünstler.* 2 vols. Leipzig: Breitkopf, 1790–92.

————. *Neues historisch-biographisches Lexikon der Tonkünstler.* 4 vols. Leipzig: Kühnel, 1812–14.

Geystliche Lieder. Mit einer newen vorrhede, D. Mart. Luth. Leipzig: Gedruckt durch Valentin Babst, 1545. Facsimile edited by Konrad Ameln. 2d edition. Kassel: Bärenreiter, 1966.

Gerhardt, Paul. *Geistliche Andachten Bestehend in hundert und zwantzig Liedern . . . Dutzendweise mit neuen sechstimmigen Melodeyen gezieret. Hervor gegeben und verlegt Von Johan Georg Ebeling.* Berlin: Chreistoff Rungen, 1667. Facsimile ed. Friedhelm Kemp. Bern: Francke, 1975.

Das grosse CANTIONAL, Oder: Kirchen-Gesangbuch. Darmstadt: Henning Müller, 1687.

Hammerschmidt, Andreas. *Geistlicher Dialogen Ander Theil, Darinnen Herrn Opitzens Hohes Lied Salomonis In I. und 2. Vocal-Stimmen, 2. Violinen, einem Instrumental- und General-Bass componiret.* Dresden: Gimel Bergens Erben, 1645.

————. *Kirchen- und Tafel Music, Darinnen 1. 2. 3. Vocal und 4. 5. und 6. Instrumenta, enthalten.* Zittau in Ober Laußitz: Verlegung des Autoris, 1662.

————. *Vierdter Theil Musicalischer Andachten, Geistlicher MOTETEN und CONCERTEN, Mit 5, 6, 7, 8, 9, 10, 12 und mehr Stimmen, nebenst einem gedoppelten General-Baß.* Freiberg in Meißen: Georg Beuther, 1669.

Herbst, Johann Andreas. *Arte prattica & poetica, Das ist: Ein kurtzer Unterrricht wie man einen Contrapunct machen und Componiren sol lernen (in Zehen Buücher abgetheilet) sehr kürtz- und leichtlich zu begreiffen; So vor diesem von Giov. Chiodino Latein- und Italienisch beschrieben worden. Dessgleichen: II. Ein kurtzer Tractat und Unterricht/ wie man einen Contrapunct à mente, non à penna, Das ist: Im Sinn/ und nicht mit der Feder Componiren und setzen solle: Und Letzlichen: III. Corollarii loco: Eine Instruction und Unterweisung zum General-Bass.* Frankfurt: In Verlegung Thomae Matthiae Götz(e), 1653.

[Hôveln, Conrad von]. *Der Kaiserl: Freien Reichs-Stadt Lübek Glaub- und Besähewürdige Herrligkeit, samt Verhandener Altertums Nüzlichen Gedächtnis, den Einheimisch- und Ausländischen nachrichtlich ausgefärtigt und entworfen von Des Hochlöbl: Swan-Ordens Geselschafter dem Geträuen Candore, Virtute, Honore.* Lübeck: Verlägts Michael Volk, 1666.

Hülphers, Abrah: Abrahs Son. *Historisk Afhandling om Musik och Instrumenter särdeles om Orgwerks Inraettnungen i Allmänhet, jemte Kort Beskrifning öfwer Orgwerken i Swerige.* Westerås, 1773. Facsimile reprint. Amsterdam, 1971.

Jespersøn, Niels. *Gradual.* Copenhagen, 1573. Facsimile reprint, edited by Erik Abrahamsen. Copenhagen: J. H. Schultz Forlag, 1935.

Kauffmann, Georg Friedrich. *Harmonische Seelen Lust.* Leipzig: Author, 1733–36.

Kircher, Athanasius. *Kircherus jesuita germanuus Germaniae redonatus sive artis magnae de consono & dissono ars minor; das ist, Philosophischer Extract und Auszug aus dess Welt-berühmten teutschen Jesuitens Athanasii Kircheri von Fulda Musurgia universali . . .* / ausgezogen und verfertiget . . . von Andrea Hirschen . . . Schwäbisch Hall: Gedruckt bei H. R. Laidigen, 1662. Facsimile, ed. Melania Wald. Kassel: Bärenreiter, 2006.

———. *Musurgia universalis sive Ars magna consoni et dissoni in X. libros digesta.* Rome, 1650. Facsimile reprint, edited by Ulf Scharlau. Hildesheim: Georg Olms, 1970.

Kittel, Johann Christian. *Vierstimmige Choräle mit Vorspielen.* Altona: Johann Friedrich Hammerich, 1803.

Lebègue, Nicolas-Antoine. *Second Livre de Clavesin.* Paris, n.d. [1687].

Löhner, Johann. *Der Geistlichen Erquickstunden des Fürtrefflichen Theologi H. Doct. Heinrich Müllers . . . Poetischer Andacht-Klang: von denen Pegnitz-Blumgenossen verfasset; und in Arien gesetzet durch Johann Löhner der Sing-dichtkunst Beflissenen.* Nürnberg: Felsecker, 1673.

Lübeckisches Gesang-Buch . . . Auff Verordnung Eines Hoch-Edlen Hochweisen Raths Von Einem Ehrwürdigen MINISTERIO Ausgegeben. Lübeck: Christian Ernest Wiedemeyer, 1729.

Marpurg, Friedrich Wilhelm. *Abhandlung von der Fuge nach den Grundsätzen und Exempeln der besten deutschen und ausländischen Meister.* 2 vols. Berlin: A. Haude & J. C. Spener, 1753–54. Facsimile Hildesheim: Georg Olms, 1970.

Mattheson, Johann. *Criticae musicae tomus secundus.* Hamburg, 1725. Facsimile Laaber: Laaber, 2003.

———. *Grundlage einer Ehren-Pforte.* Hamburg: Verlegung des Verfassers, 1740. Reprint, edited by Max Schneider. Berlin: Kommissionsverlag von Leo Liepmannssohn, 1910. Reprint Kassel: Bärenreiter, 1969.

———. *Das Neu-Eröffnete Orchestre.* Hamburg: Benjamin Schillers Witwe, 1713. Facsimile Hildesheim: Georg Olms, 1997.

———. *Der Vollkommene Capellmeister.* Hamburg: Christian Herold, 1739. Facsimile reprint, edited by Margarete Reimann. Kassel: Bärenreiter, 1954.

Merler, Jacob, ed. *PARADISUS ANIMAE CHRISTIANAE.* Cologne: Balth. von Egmondt, 1670.

Mersenne, Marin. *Harmonie universelle contenant la Théorie et la Pratique de la Musique.* Paris, 1636. Facsimile reprint, edited by François Lesure. Paris: Éditions du Centre national de la Recherche scientifique, 1963.

Mithobius, Hector. *Psalmodia christiana. Ihr Christen, singet und spielet dem Herrn Ephes. V. vs 19. Das ist Gründliche Gewissens-Belehrung, Was von der Christen Musica, so wol Vocali als Instrumentali zu halten? Allen alten und neuen Music-Feinden, absonderlich aber der Meinung Sel. H. M. Theophili Grossgebaurs in seiner neulich edirten Wächterstimme Cap. XI entgegen gesetzet. Bey ordentlicher Erklärung der gewöhnlichen Epistel am XX Sontage nach Trinitatis, von weyland Doctore Hectore Mithobio etc. in einer Predigt angefangen; Nachgehends aber in zweyen Predigten continuiret, mit Fleiß weiter ausgeführet, und zur Ehre GOttes, wie auch zur Ehren-Rettung aller Musicorum, Cantorum, Organicorum etc. Cum Censurâ Amplissimae Facultatis Theologicae auff der Weltberühmten Lutherischen Universität Wittenberg.* Jena: Erhard Berger, 1665.

Moller, Johannes. *Cimbria literata.* Copenhagen, 1744.

Musculus, Andreas. *Precationes ex veteribus orthodoxis doctoribus.* Leipzig, 1575 (first published 1553).

Natalitia Sacra, Oder Verzeichnüß aller Texte, Welche in bevorstehenden Heiligen Festen, als Weinachten, Neuen Jahr und Heil. drey Könige allhie zu St. Marien sowohl Vor- als Nachmittag, theils vor und nach den Predigten, theils auch unter der Communion mit genugsamer Vocal-Hülffe sollen musiciret werden. Lübeck: Moritz Schmalhertz, 1682. Reprinted in Geck, *Vokalmusik,* 230–37.

Neidhardt, Johann Georg. *Beste und leichteste Temperatur des Monochordi.* Jena, 1706.

[Neumeister, Erdmann]. *Die allerneueste Art, zur Reinen und galanten Poesie zu gelangen: allen edlen und dieser Wissenschafft geneigten Gemühtern, zum vollkommenen Unterricht, mit überaus deutlichen Regeln, und angenehmen Exempeln und [ans] Licht / gestellet von Menantes.* Hamburg: Johann Wolffgang Fickweiler, 1712.

Niedt, Friederich Erhard. *Musicalische Handleitung, oder Gründlicher Unterricht.* Erster Theil. Hamburg: Benjamin Schiller, 1710 [first edition 1700].

———. *Musicalische Handleitung Anderer Theil, Von der Variation Des General-Basses . . . Die Zweyte Auflage, Verbessert, vermehret, mit verschiedenen Grund-richtigen Anmerckungen, und einen Anhang von mehr als 60. Orgel-Wercken versehen durch J. Mattheson.* Hamburg: Bey Benjamin Schillers Wittwe und Joh. Christoph Kißner im Dom, 1721 [first edition 1706].

———. *Musicalischer Handleitung Dritter und letzter Theil.* Opus posthumum, edited by Johann Mattheson. Hamburg: Benjamin Schillers Erben, 1717. Facsimile reprint of all three parts, under the title *Musicalische Handleitung 1710, 1717, 1721.* Bibliotheca Organologica, vol. 32. Buren: Frits Knuf, 1976.

Nova Literaria Maris Balthici et Septentrionis Collecta. Lübeck and Hamburg, 1698–1707.

Ogier, Charles. *Caroli Ogerii Ephemerides; sive, Iter Danicvm, Svecicvm, Polonicvm, cum esset in comitatu illustriss. Clavdii Memmii Comitis Auauxij, ad septentrionis reges extraordinarij legati.* Paris, 1656.

Ordnung Eines Erbahren Raths der Keiserlichen Freyen, und des heiligen Reichß Stadt LÜBECK Darnach sich hinführo dieser Stadt Bürger und Einwohner bey Verlöbnüssen, Hochzeiten, in Kleydungengen, Kindbetten, Gefatterschafften, Begräbnissen, und was denselben allen angengig sampt ihren Frawen, Kindern und Gesinde, verhalten sollen. Lübeck, 1619.

Pachelbel, Johann. *Hexachordum Apollinis: Sex Arias exhibens Organo pneumatico, vel clavato cymbalo, modulandas, quarum singulis suae sunt subjectae Variationes.* Nürnberg: Cornelis Nicolas Schurtz, 1699. Facsimile ed. Rupert Gottfried Frieberger, Innsbruck: Helbling, 1994; Facsimile Courlay: Éditions J.M. Fuzeau, 1996; Facsimile New York: Performers' Facsimiles, 1998.

Petersen, Johann Wilhelm. *Die Hochzeit Des Lammes und der Braut Bey Der herannahenden Zunkunfft Jesu Christi Durch ein Geschrey in dieser Mitternacht, zur heiligen Wache: Beweglich vorgestellet, und mit vielen Kupffern, auch dreyen Registern außgezieret.* Offenbach am Mayn, Bonaventura de Launoy, n.d. [1706?].

Petri, Johann Samuel. *Anleitung zur praktischen Musik.* 2d edition. Leipzig: J.G.I. Breitkopf, 1782. Facsimile Giebing über Prien am Chiemsee: E. Katzbichler, 1969; Facsimile Munich: B. Katzbichler, 1999.

Praetorius, Michael. *Syntagma musicum II: De Organographia.* Wolfenbüttel: author, 1619. Facsimile reprint, edited by Wilibald Gurlitt. Kassel: Bärenreiter, 1958.

———. *Syntagma musicum III: Termini musici.* Wolfenbüttel: author, 1619. Facsimile reprint, edited by Wilibald Gurlitt. Kassel: Bärenreiter, 1958.

Printz, Wolfgang Caspar. *Historische Beschreibung der Edlen Sing- und Kling-Kunst, in welcher Deroselben Ursprung und Erfindung, Fortgang, Verbesserung, unterschiedlicher Gebrauch, wunderbare Würckungen, mancherley Feinde, und zugleich berühmteste Ausüber von Anfang der Welt biß auff unsere Zeit in möglichster Kürtze erzehlet und vorgestellet werden.* Dresden: In Verlegung Johann Christoph Mieths, 1690. Facsimile ed. Othmar Wessely. Graz: ADEVA 1964.

Ravn, Hans Mikkelsen. *Heptachordum Danicum seu Nova Solsisatio.* Copenhagen, 1646. Facsimile reprint, edited with commentary by Bengt Johnsson. 2 vols. Copenhagen: Gads, 1977.

Rist, Johann. *Der zu seinem allerheiligsten Leiden und Sterben hingeführter und an das Kreütz gehefteter Christus Jesus.* Hamburg: Johann Nauman, 1655.

―――. *Himlische Lieder.* Lüneburg: Johann & Heinrich Stern, 1641–42. Facsimile reprint. Hildesheim: Georg Olms, 1976.

―――. *Neüe Musikalische Fest-Andachten.* Lüneburg: Johann & Heinrich Stern, 1655.

[Ritter, Christian]. *Der erschaffene, gefallene und auffgerichtete Mensch. In einem Singe-Spiel vorgestellet.* [Hamburg, 1678].

Rosenmiller, Giouanni [Johann Rosenmüller]. *Sonate à 2.3.4. è 5. Stromenti da Arco & Altri.* Nuremberg: Endter, 1682. Facsimile reprint. Madrid: Arte Tripharia, 1984.

Ruetz, Caspar. *Widerlegte Vorurtheile von der Beschaffenheit der heutigen Kirchenmusic und von der Lebens-Art einiger Musicorum.* Lübeck: Peter Böckmann, 1752.

―――. *Widerlegte Vorurtheile von der Wirkung der Kirchenmusic und von den darzu erfoderten Unkosten.* Rostock and Wismar: Johann Andreas Berger and Jacob Boedher, 1753.

Scheibe, Johann Adolph. *Critischer Musicus.* Leipzig: Breitkopf, 1745. Facsimile reprint. Hildesheim, 1970.

Sohre, Peter, ed. *Musicalischer Vorschmack Der Jauchtzenden Seelen im ewigen Leben. Das ist: Neu-außgefärtigtes, vollständiges . . . Gesang-Buch.* Hamburg: Hinrich Völcker, 1683.

Speer, Daniel. *Grund-richtiger, Kurtz- Leicht- und Nöthiger, jetzt Wol-vermehrter Unterricht der Musicalischen Kunst. Oder, Vierfaches Musicalisches Kleeblatt.* Ulm: Georg Wilhelm Kühnen, 1697. Facsimile reprint. ed. Isolde Ahlgrimm. Leipzig: Edition Peters, 1974.

Stökken, Christian von. *Klahre Andeutung Und wahre Anleitung Zur Nachfolge Christi Bei Verschmähung der weltlichen Eitelkeiten Und Überstehung der wiedrigen Begebenheiten In Ansehung der göttlichen Süßigkeiten; Aus des Thomas von Kempen dreien Büchern solchen gestalt ausgeführet Auch mit XXXVIII Andachts-Liedern, und fast so viel-neuen Melodein ausgezieret, Daß nunmehr von wahren Evangelischen Christen alles ohn irrung gelesen ohn Hinderung verstanden, und zur Andachtsübung nüzzlich kan gebrauchet werden.* Plön: Tobias Schmidt, 1678.

Teutsch-Englisches Lexicon, Worinnen nicht allein die Wörter, samt den Nenn- Bey- und Sprich-Wörtern, Sondern auch so wol die eigentliche als verblümte Redens-arten verzeichnet sind. Aus den besten Scribenten und vorhandenen Dictionariis mit grossem fleiß zusammen getragen. Das ersto so iemahls gemacht worden. Leipzig: bey Thomas Fritschen, 1716.

Theile, Johann. *Pars prima Missarum 4. et 5. vocum a pleno choro cum et sine basso continuo juxta veterum contrapuncti stylum.* Wismar: Joachim Georg Rhete, 1673.

Thomissøn, Hans. *Den danske Psalmebog.* Copenhagen: Laurentz Benedicht, 1569. Facsimile reprint. Copenhagen: Samfundet Dansk Kirkesang, 1933, 1968.

Tosi, Pier Francesco. *Opinioni de' cantori antichi e moderni, o sieno Osservazioni sopra il canto figurato.* Bologna, 1723. German translation by Johann Friedrich Agricola as *Anleitung zur Singkunst* (Berlin, 1757). Facsimile of both ed. Erwin R. Jacobi. Celle: Hermann Moeck, 1966. English translatlion by Mr. Galliard as *Observations on the Florid Song; or, Sentiments on the Ancient and Modern Singers* (London, 1742).

Den ved Øresund Beliggende Anseelige Stad Helsingørs Beskrivelse Angaaende Dens Navne, Graendser, Skikkelse, private og publique Bygninger Samt Stadens of Egnens Historie og Forandringer fra 70 Aar for Christi Fødsel indtil vore tider. Aalborg: J. P. Holtzberg, 1757.

Verzeichnis derjenigen Musikalien und musikalischen Schriften aus dem Nachlasse des verstorbenen Hrn. Organist Kittel in Erfurt. Erfurt, 1809.

Verzeichniß der von dem verstorbenen Doctor und Musikdirector Forkel in Göttingen nachgelassenen Bücher und Musikalien. Göttingen, 1819.

Voll-ständiges Gesang-Buch. Lüneburg: Stern, 1661.

Walther, Johann Gottfried. *Musicalisches Lexicon.* Leipzig: Wolffgang Deer, 1732. Facsimile reprint, edited by Richard Schaal. Documenta musicologica, Erste Reihe, III. Kassel: Bärenreiter, 1953.

Werckmeister, Andreas. *Erweiterte und verbesserte Orgel-Probe, Oder Eigentliche Beschreibung, Wie und welcher Gestalt man die Orgelwercke von den Orgelmachern annehmen, probiren, untersuchen und denen Kirchen liefern könne; Auch was bey Verdüngniß eines neuen und alten Wercks, so da zu renoviren vorfallen möchte, nothwendig in acht zu nehmen sey.* Quedlinburg: Theodor Philipp Calvisius, 1698. Facsimile reprint, edited by Dietz-Rüdiger Moser. Kassel: Bärenreiter, 1970.

———. *Harmonologia Musica Oder Kurtze Anleitung Zur Musicalischen Composition Wie man vermittels der Regeln und Anmerckungen bey den General-Baß einen Contrapunctum simplicem mit sonderbahrem Vortheil durch drey Sätze oder Griffe Componiren/ und extempore spielen: auch dadurch im Clavier und Composition weiter zu schreiten und zu variiren Gelegenheit nehmen könne: Benebst einen Unterricht, wie man einen gedoppelten Contrapunct und mancherley Canones oder Fugas Ligatas, durch sonderbahre Griffe und Vortheile setzen und einrichten möge, aus denen Mathemathischen und Musicalischen Gründen aufgesetzet.* Quedlingburg: Theodor Philipp Calvisius, 1702. Facsimile, Hildesheim: Georg Olms, 1970; Facsimile ed. Dietrich Bartel, Laaber: Laaber Verlag, 2003.

———. *Musicalische Temperatur, Oder deutlicher und warer Mathematischer Unterricht, Wie man durch Anweisung des MONOCHORDI Ein Clavier, sonderlich die Orgel-Wercke, Positive, Regale, Spinetten, und dergleichen wol temperirt stimmen könne, damit nach heutiger manier alle Modi ficti in einer angenehm und erträglichen Harmonia mögen genommen werden, Mit vorhergehender Abhandlung Von dem Vorzuge, Vollkommen und weniger Vollkommenheit der Musicalischen Zahlen, Proportionen, und Consonantien, Welche bey Einrichtung der Temperaturen wohl in acht zu nehmen sind: Benebst einem darzugehörig in Kupffer vorgebildeten deutlichen und völligem MONOCHORDO beschrieben, und an das Tages-Licht gegeben.* Quedlingburg: Theodor Philipp Calvisius, 1691. Facsimile ed. Rudolf Rasch, Utrecht: Diapason Press, 1983; Facsimile ed. Guido Bimberg and Rüdiger Pfeiffer, Essen: Blaue Eule, 1996; Facsimile ed. Mark Lindley, Oschersleben: Ziethen, 1997.

———. *Orgel-Probe Oder Kurtze Beschreibung Wie und welcher gestalt man Die Orgel-Wercke Von den Orgelmachern annehmen, probiren, untersuchen und den Kirchen liefern könne und solle, Benebst einem kurtzen jedoch gründlichen Unterricht Wie durch Anweiß und Hülffe des Monochordi ein Clavier wohl zu temperiren und zu stimmen sey, damit man nach heutiger Manier alle modos fictos in einer erträglichen und angenehmen harmoni vernehme.* Quedlinburg: Theodorus Phil. Calvisius, 1681.

Wolf, Jens Lauritsøn. *Encomion Regni Daniae, Det er: Danmarckes Riges Loff, oc dets høyloflige Konge Riges tilhørige Provinciers, Øers, Kongelige Slotters oc Festningers, Herre-Sæders, oc andre Præctige Bygningers Beskriffvelse.* Copenhagen: Peter Hake, 1654.

Secondary Sources in Manuscript

Fock, Gustav. "Lübeck, Totentanzorgel." Penciled notes concerning inspection of Totentanz organ, St. Mary's, Lübeck, ca. 1937. Fock Archive at the Schnitger-Zentrum, Golzwarden (Brake), Germany.

Jimmerthal, Hermann. "Zur Geschichte der St. Marien Kirche in Lübeck." Manuscript [1857] at Archiv der Hansestadt Lübeck; Second copy at Nordelbisches Ev.-Luth. Kirchenarchiv, Lübeck.

Schnobel, Johann Hermann. "Lübeckische Geschlechter." 5 vols. Manuscript at Archiv der Hansestadt Lübeck.

Vogt, Theodor. "Orgel-Dispositionen gesammelt von Theodor Vogt, Orgelbaumeister in Lübeck." Manuscript at St. Jakobi Kirchenamt, Lübeck.

Books and Articles

Alain, Marie-Claire. "Why an Acquaintance with Early Organs Is Essential for Playing Bach." In *J. S. Bach as Organist: His Instruments, Music and Performance Practices*, edited by George Stauffer and Ernest May, 48–53. Bloomington: Indiana University Press, 1986.

Allsop, Peter C. *The Italian 'Trio' Sonata from its Origins until Corelli*. Oxford: Oxford University Press, 1992.

Andersen, Poul-Gerhard. *Organ Building and Design*. Translated by Joanne Curnutt. London: George Allen and Unwin Ltd., 1969.

Andersson, Greger. "Musikförbindelser över Öresund: Dietrich Buxtehude och Dübensamlingen. In *1600-Talets Ansikte*, edited by Sten Åke Nilsson and Margareta Ramsay, 147–67. Nyhamnsläge: Gyllenstiernska Krapperupstiftelsen, 1997.

Andresen, Rainer. *Lübeck: Geschichte, Kirchen, Befestigungen*. Das Alte Stadtbild, 1. Lübeck: Verlag Neue Rundschau, n.d.

Anthony, John Philip. "The Organ Works of Johann Christian Kittel." 2 vols. PhD diss., Yale University, 1978.

Apel, Willi. *The History of Keyboard Music to 1700*. Translated and revised by Hans Tischler. Bloomington: Indiana University Press, 1972.

———. "Neu aufgefundene Clavierwerke von Scheidemann, Tunder, Froberger, Reincken und Buxtehude." *Acta musicologica* 34 (1962): 65–67.

Archbold, Lawrence [Larry Leo]. *Style and Structure in the Praeludia of Dietrich Buxtehude*. Ann Arbor: UMI Research Press, 1985.

———. "Towards a Critical Understanding of Buxtehude's Expressive Chorale Preludes." In *Church, Stage, and Studio: Music in its Contexts in Seventeenth-century Germany*, edited by Paul Walker, 87–106. Ann Arbor: UMI Research Press, 1990.

Asch, Jürgen. *Rat und Bürgerschaft in Lübeck 1598–1669*. Lübeck: Schmidt-Römhild, 1961.

Bach, Carl Philipp Emanuel. *Essay on the True Art of Playing Keyboard Instruments*. Translated and edited by William J. Mitchell. New York: Norton, 1949.

Bach-Dokumente I: *Schriftstücke von der Hand Johann Sebastian Bachs*. Edited by Werner Neumann and Hans-Joachim Schulze. Kassel: Bärenreiter, 1963.

Bach-Dokumente II: *Fremdschriftliche und gedruckte Dokumente zur Lebensgeschichte Johann Sebastian Bachs 1685–1750*. Edited by Werner Neumann and Hans-Joachim Schulze. Kassel: Bärenreiter, 1969.

Bach-Dokumente III: *Dokumente zum Nachwirken Johann Sebastian Bachs 1750–1800*. Edited by Hans-Joachim Schulze. Kassel: Bärenreiter, 1972.

Baines, Francis. "What exactly is a violone? A note towards a solution." *Early Music* 5 (1977): 173–76.

Bangert, Friedrich. *Geschichte der Stadt und des Kirchspiels Oldesloe.* Bad Oldesloe: Verlag J. Schüthes Buchdruckerei, 1925.

Beisswenger, Kirsten. "Erwerbungsmethoden von Musikalien im frühen 18. Jahrhunderts: Am Beispiel Johann Sebastian Bachs und Johann Gottfried Walthers." *Fontes Artis Musicae* 45 (1998): 237–49.

Beckmann, Klaus. "Ein anderer Buxtehude? Zur umstrittenen Textfrage bei Buxtehudes Orgelwerken." *Der Kirchenmusiker* 35 (1984): 1–12, 48–59.

————. "Eine bisher unbeachtete Quelle zu Buxtehudes fis-moll-Präludium." *Musik und Kirche* 54 (1984): 271–75.

————. "Randbemaerkninger til musikerfamilien Radeck." In *Dansk Orgelkultur,* edited by Per Kynne Frandsen, Svend Prip, and Claus Røllum-Larsen, 77–83. N.p.: Danske Orgelselskab, 1995.

————. "Reincken und Buxtehude: Zu einem wiederentdeckten Gemälde in Hamburg." *Der Kirchenmusiker* 31 (1980): 172–77.

————. "Textkritische Überlegungen zu Buxtehudes Orgelwerken." *Musik und Kirche* 38 (1968): 106–13.

————. "Zur Chronologie der freien Orgelwerke Buxtehudes." In *Dietrich Buxtehude und die europäische Musik seiner Zeit: Bericht über das Lübecker Symposion 1987,* edited by Arnfried Edler and Friedhelm Krummacher, 224–34. Kieler Schriften zur Musikwissenschaft, 35. Kassel: Bärenreiter, 1990.

Belotti, Michael. "Buxtehude und die norddeutsche Doppelpedaltradition." In *Dietrich Buxtehude und die europäische Musik seiner Zeit: Bericht über das Lübecker Symposion 1987,* edited by Arnfried Edler and Friedhelm Krummacher, 235–41. Kieler Schriften zur Musikwissenschaft, 35. Kassel: Bärenreiter, 1990.

————. *Die freien Orgelwerke Dieterich Buxtehudes: Überlieferungsgeschichtliche und stilkritische Studien.* 3d edition. Frankfurt: Peter Lang, 2004.

————. "'. . . une petite chanson qui vous représente mon humeur . . .': Buxtehude's Kanon für Meno Hanneken" *Musik und Kirche,* 57 (1987): 181–86.

Berglund, Lars. "Studier i Christian Geists vokalmusik." PhD diss., Acta Universalis Upsaliensis, *Studia Musicologica Upsaliensia,* nova series, 21. Uppsala: Uppsala University, 2002.

Birkner, Gerhard Kay. "Woher stammte Franz Tunder? Aus Lübeck und nicht von Fehmarn!" *Lübeckische Blätter* 161 (1996): 248.

Blankenburg, Walter. "Neue Forschungen über das geistliche Vokalschaffen Dietrich Buxtehudes." *Acta musicologica* 40 (1968): 130–54.

Blaschke, Karlheinz. *Siegel und Wappen in Sachsen.* Leipzig: Koehler & Amelang, 1960.

Blume, Friedrich. "Buxtehude, Dietrich." *Die Musik in Geschichte und Gegenwart* I, cols. 548–71. Kassel: Bärenreiter, 1952. Reprinted without list of works and bibliography in Friedrich Blume, *Syntagma musicologicum: Gesammelte Reden und Schriften,* edited by Martin Ruhnke, 1: 302–19. Kassel: Bärenreiter, 1963.

————. "Dietrich Buxtehude in Geschichte und Gegenwart," a lecture delivered in 1957. In *Syntagma musicologicum,* 1: 357–63.

————. "Das Kantatenwerk Dietrich Buxtehudes." *Jahrbuch der Musikbibliothek Peters* 47 (1940). Reprint in *Syntagma musicologicum,* 1: 349–51.

Bolte, Johannes. "Das Stammbuch Johann Valentin Meders." *Vierteljahresschrift für Musikwissenschaft* 7 (1892): 499–506.

Bonta, Stephen. "From Violone to Violoncello: A Question of Strings?" *Journal of the American Musical Instrument Society,* 3 (1977): 64–99.

Borgir, Tharald. "The Performance of the Basso Continuo in Seventeenth Century Italian Music." PhD diss., University of California, Berkeley, 1971.

Boyden, David. *The History of Violin Playing from its Origins to 1761 and its Relationship to the Violin and Violin Music.* London: Oxford University Press, 1965.

Brahms, Johannes. *Briefwechsel mit Philipp Spitta.* Edited by Carl Krebs. Berlin: Verlag der Deutschen Brahms-Gesellschaft, 1920.

Brandt, Ahasver von. *Geist und Politik in der Lübeckischen Geschichte.* Lübeck: Schmidt-Römhild, 1954.

Brandt, Ahasver von. "Das Lübecker Archiv in den letzten hundert Jahren." *Zeitschrift des Vereins für Lübeckische Geschichte und Altertumskunde* 33 (1952): 33–80.

———. "Thomas Fredenhagen (1627–1709): Ein Lübecker Großkauffmann und seine Zeit." In *Lübeck, Hanse, Nordeuropa: Gedächtnisschrift für Ahasver von Brandt,* edited by Klaus Friedland and Rolf Sprandel, 246–69. Cologne: Böhlau, 1979.

Braun, Werner. *Deutsche Musiktheorie des 15. bis 17. Jahrhunderts: Zweiter Teil, von Calvisius bis Mattheson.* Geschichte der Musiktheorie, vol. 8, part 2. Darmstadt: Wissenschaftliche Buchgesellschaft, 1994.

———. *Die Musik des 17. Jahrhunderts.* Neues Handbuch der Musikwissenschaft, IV. Wiesbaden, 1981.

———. *Vom Remter zum Gänsemarkt: Aus der Frühgeschichte der alten Hamburger Oper 1677–1697).* Saarbrücker Studien zur Musikwissenschaft, Neue Folge, Band 1. Saarbrücken: Saarbrücker Druckerei und Verlag, 1987.

Breig, Werner. "Die geschichtliche Stellung von Buxtehudes monodischem Orgelchoral." In *Dietrich Buxtehude und die europäische Musik seiner Zeit: Bericht über das Lübecker Symposion 1987,* edited by Arnfried Edler and Friedhelm Krummacher, 260–74. Kieler Schriften zur Musikwissenschaft, 35. Kassel: Bärenreiter, 1990.

———. "Der norddeutsche Orgelchoral und Johann Sebastian Bach: Gattung, Typus, Werk." In *Gattung und Werk in der Musikgeschichte Norddeutschlands und Skandinaviens,* edited by Friedhelm Krummacher and Heinrich W. Schwab, 79–94. Kieler Schriften zur Musikwissenschaft, 26. Kassel, 1982.

———. *Die Orgelwerke von Heinrich Scheidemann.* Wiesbaden: Franz Steiner, 1967.

———. "Der 'stylus phantasticus' in der Lübecker Orgelmusik." In *800 Jahre Musik in Lübeck. Teil II: Dokumentation zum Lübecker Musikfest 1982,* edited by Arnfried Edler, Werner Neugebauer and Heinrich W. Schwab, 43–51. Lübeck: Senat der Hansestadt Lübeck, Amt für Kultur, Veröffentlichung 21, 1983.

Briquet, Charles Moïse. *Les filigranes: Dictionnaire historique des marques du papier dès leur apparition vers 1282 jusqu'en 1600. A Facsimile of the 1907 Edition.* Edited by Allan Stevenson. 4 vols.; Amsterdam: Paper Publications Society, 1968.

Brock, John. *Introduction to organ playing in 17th and 18th century style = Einführung in das Orgelspiel des 17. und 18. Jahrhunderts.* Deutsche Übersetzung von Christian Hermann Stähr. 2nd ed. Colfax, NC: Wayne Leupold Editions, 2002.

Brooks, Brian P. "The Emergence of the Violin as a Solo Instrument in Early Seventeenth-Century Germany." PhD diss., Cornell University, 2002.

Bruggaier, Eduard. "Studien zur Geschichte des Orgelpedalspiels in Deutschland bis zur Zeit Johann Sebastian Bachs." PhD diss., Frankfurt am Main, 1959.

Bruns, Friedrich. "Die Lübecker Syndiker und Ratssekretäre bis zur Verfassungsänderung von 1851." *Zeitschrift des Vereins für Lübeckische Geschichte und Altertumskunde* 29 (1938): 91–168.

Buelow, George. "Die schöne und getreue Ariadene (Hamburg 1691): A Lost Opera by J. G. Conradi Rediscovered." *Acta musicologica,* 44 (1972): 108–21.

Buelow, George. "Hamburg Opera during Buxtehude's Lifetime: The Works of Johann Wolfgang Franck." In *Church, Stage, and Studio: Music in its Contexts in Seventeenth-century Germany*, edited by Paul Walker, 127–41. Ann Arbor: UMI Research Press, 1990.

Bunners, Christian. *Kirchenmusik und Seelenmusik: Studien zu Frömmigkeit und Musik im Luthertum des 17. Jahrhunderts*. Göttingen: Vandenhoeck & Ruprecht, 1966.

Burney, Charles. *Dr. Burney's Musical Tours in Europe*. Edited by Percy A. Scholes. 2 vols. London: Oxford University Press, 1959.

Butler, Gregory. "The Fantasia as Musical Image. *The Musical Quarterly* 60 (1974): 602–15.

Butt, John. *Music Education and the Art of Performance in the German Baroque*. Cambridge: Cambridge University Press, 1994.

Buxtehude, Dietrich. *Abendmusiken und Kirchenkantaten* [BuxWV 4, 24, 34, 36, 43 (Alleluia only), 51, 101 and 112]. Edited by Max Seiffert. Denkmäler deutscher Tonkunst, XIV. Leipzig: Breitkopf & Härtel, 1903. Revised edition, edited by Hans J. Moser. Wiesbaden: Breitkopf & Härtel, 1957.

———. *Dieterich Buxtehude: The Collected Works*. Volume 9: Works for Four Voices and Instruments. Edited by Kerala J. Snyder. New York: The Broude Trust, 1987.

———. *Dieterich Buxtehude: The Collected Works*. Volume 14: Instrumental Works for Strings and Continuo. Edited by Eva Linfield. New York: The Broude Trust, 1994.

———. *Dieterich Buxtehude: The Collected Works*. Volume 15: Preludes, Toccatas, and Ciacconas for Organ (*pedaliter*). Edited by Michael Belotti. New York: The Broude Trust, 1998.

———. *Dietrich Buxtehudes Werke*. Edited by Wilibald Gurlitt et al. 8 vols. Klecken and Hamburg: Ugrino, 1925–58. Reprint. New York: Broude International Editions, 1977.

———. *Dietrich Buxtehudes Werke für Orgel*. Edited by Philipp Spitta. 2 vols. Leipzig: Breitkopf & Härtel, 1875–76. Revised by Max Seiffert, 1903–4.

———. *Dietrich Buxtehudes Werke für Orgel*. Ergänzungsband. Edited by Max Seiffert. Leipzig: Breitkopf & Härtel, 1939.

———. *Das Jüngste Gericht: Abendmusik in fünf Vorstellungen*. Aufgefunden und für die Aufführung eingerichtet von Willy Maxton. Kassel: Bärenreiter, 1939.

———. *Klavervaerker*. Edited by Emilius Bangert. Copenhagen: Hansen, 1942.

———. *Neue Ausgabe sämtlicher freien Orgelwerke* (vols. 1–3), *Neue Ausgabe sämtlicher Orgelwerke* (vols. 4–5). Edited by Christoph Albrecht. Kassel: Bärenreiter, 1994–98.

———. *Sämtliche Orgelwerke*. Edited by Joseph Hedar. 4 vols. Copenhagen: Hansen, 1952.

———. *Sämtliche Orgelwerke*. Edited by Klaus Beckmann. 2 vols. Wiesbaden: Breitkopf & Härtel, 1971–72. 2d edition, 1995–97.

———. *Sämtliche Suiten und Variationen für Klavier/Cembalo*. Edited by Klaus Beckmann. Wiesbaden: Breitkopf & Härtel, 1980.

———. *Sonaten für Violine, Gambe und Cembalo*. Edited by Carl Stiehl. Denkmäler deutscher Tonkunst, XI. Leipzig: Breitkopf und Härtel, 1903. Revised edition, edited by Hans J. Moser. Wiesbaden: Breitkopf & Härtel, 1957.

———. *Suite in d* [*sic; recte: a*], ed. Konrad Küster. Stuttgart: Carus-Verlag, 2005.

Churchill, W. A. *Watermarks in Paper in Holland, France, etc., in the XVII and XVIII Centuries and their Interconnections*. Amsterdam: Menno Hertzberger, 1935; 3rd ed., 1967.

Collins, Paul. *The Stylus Phantasticus and Free Keyboard Music of the North German Baroque*. Aldershot: Ashgate, 2005.

Conradi, Johann Georg, and Christian Heinrich Postel, *Ariadne*. Boston Early Music Festival Orchestra and Chorus, Paul O'Dette and Stephen Stubbs. CPO 777 073–2.

Cowan, Alexander Francis. *The Urban Patriciate: Lübeck and Venice 1580–1700*. Quellen und Darstellungen zur hansischen Geschichte, 30. Köln: Böhlau Verlag, 1986.

Dalsager, Johannes. *Helsingør St. Mariæ Kirkes Historia, 1450–1950.* Copenhagen: Hagerup, 1950.

David, Hans T. and Arthur Mendel. *The Bach Reader.* Revised edition. New York: Norton, 1966.

David, Werner. *Johann Sebastian Bach's Orgeln.* Berlin: Berliner Musikinstrumenten-Sammlung, 1951.

Davidsson, Hans. *Matthias Weckmann: the Interpretation of his Organ Music.* Skrifter från Musikvetenskapliga institutionen, Göteborg, 22.Göteborg: Gehrmans Musikförlag, 1991.

Daw, Stephen. "Copies of J. S. Bach by Walther & Krebs: A Study of the Manuscripts P 801, P 802, P 803." *The Organ Yearbook* 7 (1976): 31–58.

Defant, Christine. *Instrumentale Sonderformen in Norddeutschland: Eine Studie zu den Auswirkungen eines Theologenstreites auf Werke der Organisten Weckmann, Reincken und Buxtehude.* Frankfurt: Peter Lang, 1990.

———. *Kammermusik und Stylus phantasticus. Studien zu Dietrich Buxtehudes Triosonaten.* Europäische Hochschulschriften, Reihe XXXVI: Musikwissenschaft, vol. 14. Frankfurt: Peter Lang, 1985.

Das deutsche Kirchenlied. Kritische Gesamtausgabe der Melodien. I: Verzeichnis der Drucke von den Anfängen bis 1800. Edited by Konrad Ameln, Markus Jenny, and Walther Lipphardt. Répertoire international des sources musicales [*RISM*], B/VIII/1. Kassel: Bärenreiter, 1975.

Dietrich, Fritz. *Geschichte des deutschen Orgelchorals im 17. Jahrhundert.* Kassel: Bärenreiter, 1932.

Dirksen, Pieter. "A Buxtehude Discovery." http://www.pieterdirksen.nl/Essays/Bux%20Discovery.htm

———. "Dieterich Buxtehude and the Chorale Fantasia." *GOArt Research Reports* 3 (2003): 149–66.

———. "The Enigma of the *stylus phantasticus.*" In *Orphei Organi Antiqui: Essays in Honor of Harald Vogel,* edited by Cleveland Johnson, 107–32. N.p.: The Westfield Center, 2006.

———, ed. Dieterich Buxtehude?, *Nun freut euch, lieben Christen gmein: Choralfantasie für Orgel / Chorale Fantasia for Organ.* Wiesbaden: Breitkopf & Härtel, 2006.

———, ed. *Orgelmusik av familjen Düben.* Bibliotheca Organi Sueciae, Vol. 1. Stockholm: Runa Nototext, 1997.

———, ed. *VI Suittes, divers airs avec leurs variations et fugues pour le clavessin: Amsterdam 1710,* Utrecht: Koninklijke Vereiniging voor Nederlandse Muziekgeschiedenis, 2004.

Diruta, Girolamo. *The Transylvanian.* Translated and edited by Murray C. Bradshaw and Edward J. Soehnlen. 2 vols. Henryville, PA: Institute of Mediaeval Music, Ltd., 1984.

Dodds, Michael R. "The Baroque Church Tones in Theory and Practice." Ph. D. diss., Eastman School of Music, University of Rochester, 1998.

———. "Columbus's Egg: Andreas Werckmeister's Teachings on Contrapuntal Improvisation in *Harmonologia musica* (1702)." *Journal of Seventeenth-Century Music* 12, no. 1 (2006); www.sscm-jscm.org/jscm/v12/no1/dodds.html

Dollinger, Philippe. *The German Hansa.* Translated by D. S. Ault and S. H. Steinberg. Stanford: Stanford University Press, 1970.

Dreyfus, Laurence D. *Bach's Continuo Group: Players and Practices in His Vocal Works.* Studies in the History of Music, 3. Cambridge: Harvard University Press, 1987.

Die Düben Orgel: Festschrift zur Einweihung—Stockholm 9. Mai 2004. Stockholm: St. Gertruds Gemeinde Stockholm, 2004.

Edler, Arnfried. *Der nordelbische Organist: Studien zu Sozialstatus, Funktion und kompositorischer Produktion eines Musikerberufes von der Reformation bis zum 20. Jahrhundert.* Kieler Schriften zur Musikwissenschaft, 23. Kassel: Bärenreiter, 1982.

———. "Fantasie and Choralfantasie: On the Problematic Nature of a Genre of Seventeenth-Century Organ Music." *The Organ Yearbook,* 19 (1988): 53–66.

800 Jahre Musik in Lübeck. [Teil I]: *Zur Ausstellung im Museum am Dom aus Anlaß des Lübecker Musikfestes 1982.* Senat der Hansestadt Lübeck, Amt für Kultur, Veröffentlichung 19. Edited by Antjekathrin Graßmann and Werner Neugebauer. Lübeck, 1982. Teil II: *Dokumentation zum Lübecker Musikfest 1982.* Senat der Hansestadt Lübeck, Amt für Kultur, Veröffentlichung 21. Edited by Arnfried Edler, Werner Neugebauer and Heinrich W. Schwab. Lübeck, 1983.

Einstein, Alfred. *Zur deutschen Literatur für Viola da Gamba im 16. und 17. Jahrhundert.* Publikationen der Internationalen Musikgesellschaft, II/1. Leipzig, 1905. Reprint. Walluf bei Wiesbaden: Sändig, 1972.

Eitner, Robert. *Biographisch-bibliographisches Quellen-Lexikon der Musiker und Musikgelehrten der christlichen Zeitrechnung bis zur Mitte des 19. Jahrhunderts.* Leipzig, 1898–1904; Reprint Graz: ADEVA, 1959–60.

Ericsson, Lena Weman, ed. *Övertorneåprojekte: Om dokumentationen av orgeln i Övertorneå och rekonstruktionen av 1684 års orgel i Tyska kyrkan.* Luleå: Musikhögskolan i Piteå, Luleå tekniska universitet, 1997.

Eschenbach, Gunilla. "Dietrich Buxtehudes Membra Jesu Nostri im Kontext lutherischer Mystik-Rezeption." *Kirchenmusikalisches Jahrbuch* 88 (2004): 41–54.

Faulkner, Quentin. *J. S. Bach's Keyboard Technique: A Historical Introduction.* St. Louis: Concordia, 1984.

Fehling, E. F. *Lübeckische Ratslinie von den Anfängen bis auf die Gegenwart.* Veröffentlichungen zur Geschichte der Freien und Hansestadt Lübeck VII, 1. Lübeck: Schmidt-Römhild, 1925. Reprint Lübeck: Schmidt-Römhild, 1978.

Ferand, Ernest T. "Improvised Vocal Counterpoint in the Late Renaissance and Early Baroque." *Annales musicologiques* 4 (1956): 129–74.

Fernström, John. *Dietrich Orgemester: En Bok om Buxtehude.* Lund: C. W. K. Gleerups Förlag, 1937.

Fiebig, Folkert. *Christoph Bernhard und der Stile moderno: Untersuchungen zu Leben und Werk.* Hamburger Beiträge zur Musikwissenschift, 22. Hamburg: Karl Dieter Wagner, 1980.

Fischer, Bernd. *Hanse-Städte: Geschichte und Kultur.* Cologne: Dumont, 1981.

Fischer-Krückeberg, Elisabeth. "Johann Crügers Choralbearbeitungen." *Zeitschrift für Musikwissenschaft* 14 (1931–32): 248–71.

Fock, Gustav. *Arp Schnitger und seine Schule: Ein Beitrag zur Geschichte des Orgelbaues im Nord- und Ostseeküstengebiet.* Kassel: Bärenreiter, 1974.

———. *Der junge Bach in Lüneburg. 1700 bis 1702.* Hamburg, 1950.

———. *Hamburg's Role in Northern European Organ Building.* Foreword and Appendix by Harald Vogel; transl. and ed. Lynn Edwards and Edward C. Pepe. Easthampton, Mass.,: Westfield Center, 1997.

Follin, Elias. *Helsingborgs Historia.* Uppsala: Wahlström & C., 1851.

Frandsen, Mary E. "Albrici, Peranda und die Ursprünge der Concerto-Aria-Kantate in Dresden." *Schütz-Jahrbuch* 18 (1996): 123–39.

———. *Crossing Confessional Boundaries: The Patronage of Italian Sacred Music in Seventeenth-Century Dresden.* Oxford and New York: Oxford University Press, 2006.

———. "The Sacred Concerto in Dresden, ca. 1660–1680." PhD diss., Eastman School of Music, University of Rochester, 1997.

Freytag, Werner. "Musikgeschichte der Stadt Stettin im 18. Jahrhundert." PhD diss., Greifswald, 1936.

Friis, Niels. *Buxtehude: Hans By og hans Orgel.* Helsingør, 1960.

———. *Diderik Buxtehude.* Copenhagen: Dan Fog-Olsen, 1960.

———. "Nikolaj Kirkes Orgler, Organister og Klokkespillere." *Historiske meddelelser om København,* 4. R, Bd. 2 (1951): 417–81.

———. *Helsingør Domkirke Sct. Olai Kirkes Orgel 1559–1969.* Helsingør: Bogtrykkergården, 1969.

———. *Orgel Bygning in Danmark Renaissance, Barok og Rokoko.* Copenhagen, 1949.

Gable, Frederick K. "Alternation practice and seventeenth-century German organ Masgnificats." *Beiträge zur Musikgeschichte Hamburgs vom Mittelalter bis in die Neuzeit,* edited by Hans Joachim Marx., 131–48. Hamburger Jahrbuch für Musikwissenschaft 18 (2001).

Gebler, H. "Beiträge zur Geschichte der Entwicklung des Kirchengesanges in Lübeck." *Sionia, Monatsschrift für Liturgie und Kirchenmusik* 21 (1896): 83–91.

Geck, Martin. "Die Authentizität des Vokalwerks Dietrich Buxtehudes in quellenkritischer Sicht." *Die Musikforschung* 14 (1961): 393–415.

———. *Nicolaus Bruhns, Leben und Werk.* Cologne, 1968.

———. "Quellenkritische Bemerkungen zu Dietrich Buxtehudes Missa Brevis." *Die Musikforschung* 13 (1960): 47–49.

———. "Nochmals: Die Authentizität des Vokalwerks Dietrich Buxtehudes in quellenkritischer Sicht." *Die Musikforschung* 16 (1963): 175–81.

———. *Die Vokalmusik Dietrich Buxtehudes und der frühe Pietismus.* Kieler Schriften zur Musikwissenschaft, 15. Kassel: Bärenreiter, 1965.

Gerardy, Theodor. *Datieren mit Hilfe von Wasserzeichen.* Schaumburger Studien, IV. Bückeburg: Grimme, 1964.

Gerdes, Gisala, ed. *46 Choräle für Orgel von J. P. Sweelinck und seinen deutschen Schülern.* Mainz: B. Schott's Söhne, 1957.

Glahn, Henrik and Søren Sørensen, eds. *The Clausholm Music Fragments.* Copenhagen: Wilhelm Hansen, 1974.

Godwin, Joscelyn. *Athanasius Kircher: A Renaissance Man and the Quest for Lost Knowledge.* London: Thames and Hudson, 1979.

Göhler, Albert. *Verzeichnis der in den Frankfurter und Leipziger Messekatalogen der Jahre 1564 bis 1759 angezeigten Musikalien.* Leipzig, 1902. Reprint. Hilversum, 1965.

Gorman, Sharon Lee. "Rhetoric and Affect in the Organ Praeludia of Dieterich Buxtehude" (1637–1707). Ph. D. diss., Stanford University, 1990.

Grapenthin, Ulf. "The Catharinen Organ during Scheidemann's Tenure." In: Pieter Dirksen, *Heinrich Scheidemann's Keyboard Music: Transmission, Style and Chronology.* Aldershot: Ashgate, 2006.

———. "Der Hamburger Catharinenorganist Johann Adam Reincken." In *Das Land Oldenburg: Mitteilungsblatt der oldenburgischen Landschaft,* Nr. 103 (2. Quartal 1999): 1–6.

———. "'Sweelincks Kompositionsregeln' aus dem Nachlass Johann Adam Reinckens." In *Beiträge zur Musikgeschichte Hamburgs vom Mittelalter bis in die Neuzeit,* edited by Hans Joachim Marx, 71–110. Hamburger Jahrbuch für Musikwissenschaft, vol. 18. Frankfurt am Main Peter Lang, 2001.

———. "The Transmission of Sweelinck's *Composition Regeln.*" In *Sweelinck Studies: Proceedings of the Sweelinck Symposium Utrecht 1999.* Ed. Pieter Dirksen. Utrecht: STIMU, 2002.

Graßmann, Antjekathrin, ed. *Alte Bestände—Neue Perspektiven: Das Archiv der Hansestadt Lübeck—5 Jahre nach der Archivalienrückführung.* Lübeck: Schmidt-Römhild, 1992.

———, ed. *Lübeckische Geschichte.* Lübeck: Schmidt-Römhild, 1988.

Griffiths, Michael. "Mirrors of Eternity: Genre, *Affekt* and Emblem in Buxtehude's *Te Deum Laudamus.*" *British Institute of Organ Studies Journal* 27 (2003): 10–39.

Grusnick, Bruno. "Die Dübensammlung: Ein Versuch ihrer chronologischen Ordnung." *Svensk tidskrift för musikforskning* 46 (1964): 27–82; 48 (1966): 63–186.

———. "Dietrich Buxtehudes 'Benedicam Dominum': Überlieferung und Kompositionsanlaß." *Lübeckische Blätter* 144 (1984): 74–76.

———. "Zur Chronologie von Dietrich Buxtehudes Vokalwerken." *Die Musikforschung* 10 (1957): 75–84.

Gudewill, Kurt. *Franz Tunder und die nordelbingische Musikkultur seiner Zeit.* Kultusverwaltung der Hansestadt Lübeck, Veröffentlichung I. Lübeck, 1967.

Gustafson, Bruce. *French Harpsichord Music of the 17th Century: A Thematic Catalog of the Sources with Commentary.* Studies in Musicology, No. 11. 3 vols. Ann Arbor: UMI Research Press, 1979.

Haacke, W. "Der Buxtehudeschüler Daniel Erich und seine Orgel in Güstrow." *Musik und Kirche* 39 (1969): 18–24.

Hach, Ad. "Schilderungen Lübecks in älteren Reisebeschreibungen." *Zeitschrift des Vereins für Lübeckische Geschichte und Altertumskunde* 4 (1884): 129–34; 5 (1886): 157–59.

Hagedorn, A. "Briefe von Dietrich Buxtehude." *Mitteilungen des Vereins für Lübeckische Geschichte und Altertumskunde* 3 (1887/88): 192–96.

Hagen, S. A. E. *Diderik Buxtehude (o. 1637–1707): hans Familie og lidet kjendte Ungdom, inden han kom til Lübeck 1668.* Copenhagen: Skou & Madsens Bogtrykkerei, 1920.

Hammerich, Angul. *Dansk Musikhistorie indtil ca. 1700.* Copenhagen: G. E. C. Gads Forlag, 1921.

Harriss, Ernest C. *Johann Mattheson's Der vollkommene Capellmeister: A Revised Translation with Critical Commentary.* Ann Arbor: UMI Research Press, 1981.

Hartwig, J. "Lübeck's Einwohnerzahl in früherer Zeit." *Mitteilungen des Vereins für Lübeckische Geschichte und Altertumskunde* 33 (1917): 77–92.

Hasse, Max. *Die Marienkirche zu Lübeck.* Munich: Deutsche Kunstverlag, 1983.

Hatting, Carsten E. "Sind die Choralvorspiele Buxtehudes mit der Improvisationspraxis verbunden?" In *Zu Fragen der Improvisation in der Instrumentalmusik der ersten Hälfte des 18. Jahrhunderts: Konferenzbericht der 7. Wissenschaftliche Arbeitstagung Blankenburg/Harz, 29. Juni bis 1. Juli 1979.*, 72–76. Studien zur Aufführungspraxis und Interpretation von Instrumentalmusik des 18. Jahrhunderts, 10. Magdeburg: Rat des Bezirkes, 1980.

Hauschild, Wolf-Dieter, *Kirchengeschichte Lübecks: Christentum und Bürgertum in neun Jahrhunderten.* Lübeck: Schmidt-Römhild, 1981.

Hedar, Josef. *Dietrich Buxtehudes Orgelwerke.* Stockholm: Nordiska Musikförlaget, 1951.

Heidrich, Jürgen. "Andachts- und Erbauungsliteratur als Quelle zur norddeutschen Musikgeschichte um 1700: Dieterich Buxtehude, Johann Wilhelm Petersen und die 'Hochzeit des Lamms.'" In *Bach, Lübeck und die norddeutsche Musiktradition: Bericht über das Internationale Symposion der Musikhochschule Lübeck April 2000,* edited by Wolfgang Sandberger, 86–100. Kassel: Bärenreiter, 2002.

Heller, Karl. "Ein Rostocker Schüler Johann Adam Reinkens: der Marienorganist Heinrich Rogge." In *"Critica musica" Studien zum 17. und 18. Jahrhundert. Festschrift Hans Joachim Marx zum 65. Geburtstag.* Stuttgart: J. B. Metzler, 2001. 97–110.

Hellwig, Günther. *Joachim Tielke: Ein Hamburger Lauten- und Violenmacher der Barockzeit.* Frankfurt a. M., 1980.

Hennings, Johann. *Musikgeschichte Lübecks I: Weltliche Musik.* Kassel: Bärenreiter, 1951.

Henningsen, Henning. *Helsingør Domkirke: Sct. Olai Kirke.* Helsingør: Domsogns Menighedsråd, 1973.

Herl, Joseph. *Worship Wars in Early Lutheranism: Choir, Congregation, and Three Centuries of Conflict.* Oxford: Oxford University Press, 2004.

Hill, John Walter. *Baroque Music: Music in Western Europe, 1580–1750.* New York: W. W. Norton, 2005.

Hill, Robert. "The Moller Manuscript and the Andreas Bach Book: Two keyboard anthologies from the circle of the young Johann Sebastian Bach." PhD diss., Harvard University, 1987.

Hilse, Walter. "The Treatises of Christoph Bernhard." *Musik Forum* 3 (1973): 1–196.

Hostrup-Schultz, V. *Helsingørs Embeds- og Bestillingsmaend: Genealogiske Efterretninger.* [Copenhagen]: J. H. Schultz's Universitetsbogtrykkeri, 1906.

Houck, M. E. "J(e)an Adam(s) Reincken." *Tijdschrift der Vereeniging voor Noord-Nederlands Muziekgeschiedenis* 6 (1900): 151–58.

Howard, John Brooks. "The Latin Lutheran Mass of the Mid-Seventeenth Century: A Study of Andreas Hammerschmidt's *Missae* (1663) and Lutheran Traditions of Mass Composition." PhD diss., Bryn Mawr College, 1983.

Hudson, Frederick. "Franz Tunder, the North-Elbe Music School and its Influence on J. S. Bach." *The Organ Journal* 8 (1977): 20–40.

Hultkvist, Mats. "Ny Buxtehudeorgel i Helsingborg." *Orgelforum* 22 (2000): 124–27.

———. "Orglar i 1600-talets Skåne." In *Dansk Orgelkultur,* ed. Per Kynne Frandsen, Svend Prip, and Claus Røllum-Larsen, 169–208. N.p.: Danske Orgelselskab, 1995. Partially translated as "Die Orgel der St. Marien-Kirche zu Helsingborg (Schweden), heutiges Torrlösa." In *Orglet i Sct. Mariæ Kirke i Helsingør—et Festskrift,* edited by Henrik Fibiger Nørfelt, 36–44. [Helsingør, 1999].

Hüschen, Heinrich. "Hamburger Musikdrucker und Musikverleger im 16. und 17. Jahrhundert." In *Beiträge zur Musikgeschichte Nordeuropas: Festschrift Kurt Gudewill zum 65. Geburtstag,* edited by Uwe Haensel, 255–70. Wolfenbüttel: Möseler, 1978.

Irwin, Joyce. "German Pietists and Church Music in the Baroque Age." *Church History* 54 (1985): 29–40.

———. *Neither Voice nof Heart Alone: German Lutheran Theology of Music in the Age of the Baroque.* American University Studies, Series VII, vol. 132. New York: Peter Lang, 1993.

Jaacks, Gisela. *Gesichter und Persönlichkeiten.* Hamburg: Museum für Hamburgische Geschichte, 1992.

———. "Hamburg als Zentrum geistiger und musikalischer Kultur im Barock." In *300 Jahre Oper in Hamburg,* edited by Gisela Jaacks, 36–49. Hamburg: Hans Christians Verlag, 1978.

———. *Hamburg zu Lust und Nutz: Bürgerliches Musikverständnis zwischen Barock und Aufklärung (1660–1760).* Hamburg: Verlag Verein für Hamburgische Geschichte, 1997.

———. "'Häusliche Musikszene' von Johannes Voorhout. Zu einem neu erworbenen Gemälde im Museum für Hamburgische Geschichte." *Beiträge zur deutschen Volks- und Altertumskunde* 17 (1978): 56–59.

———. "Musikleben in Hamburg zur Barockzeit." *Hamburg Portrait* 8 (1978). Hamburg: Museum für Hamburgische Geschichte.

———. "'Trostlose Düsternis' oder 'unvergeßliche Werte'? Lübecks Kultur um 1700." In *Bach, Lübeck und die norddeutsche Musiktradition: Bericht über das Internationale Symposion der Musikhochschule Lübeck April 2000*, edited by Wolfgang Sandberger, 9–26. Kassel: Bärenreiter, 2002.

Jaacks, Gisela, ed. *300 Jahre Oper in Hamburg*. Hamburg: Hans Christians Verlag, 1978.

Jacobson, Lena. "Musical Rhetoric in Buxtehude's Free Organ Works." *The Organ Yearbook* 13 (1982): 60–79.

Jander, Owen. "The Wellesley Organ's 'Breath of Life' as it Affects the Music of Buxtehude." In *Charles Brenton Fisk, Organ Builder*, Volume I: *Essays in his Honor*, 85–92. Easthampton, MA: The Westfield Center for Early Keyboard Studies, 1986.

Jannasch, Wilhelm. *Geschichte des lutherischen Gottesdienstes in Lübeck von 1522 bis 1633*. Gotha: Leopold Klotz, 1928.

Jensen, Niels Martin. "Buxtehudes vokale und instrumentale Ensemblemusik." In *800 Jahre Musik in Lübeck. Teil II: Dokumentation zum Lübecker Musikfest 1982*, edited by Arnfried Edler, Werner Neugebauer and Heinrich W. Schwab, 53–62. Lübeck: Senat der Hansestadt Lübeck, Amt für Kultur, Veröffentlichung XXI, 1983.

———. "Die italienische Triosonate und Buxtehude. Beobachtungen zu Gattungsnorm und Individualstil." In *Gattung und Werk in der Musikgeschichte Norddeutschlands und Skandinaviens*, edited by F. Krummacher and W. Schwab, 107–13. Kieler Schriften zur Musikwissenschaft, 26. Kassel: Bärenreiter, 1982.

———. "Nord- und südeuropäische Traditionen in der Kammermusik Buxtehudes." In *Dietrich Buxtehude und die europäische Musik seiner Zeit: Bericht über das Lübecker Symposion 1987*, edited by Arnfried Edler and Friedhelm Krummacher, 215–23. Kieler Schriften zur Musikwissenschaft, 35. Kassel: Bärenreiter, 1990.

Jimmerthal, Hermann. *Beschreibung der großen Orgel in der St. Marien-Kirche zu Lübeck*. Erfurt & Leipzig: G. W. Körner, 1859.

Jørgensen, Johan. "Denmark's Relations with Lübeck and Hamburg in the Seventeenth Century." *The Scandinavian Economic History Review* 11 (1963): 73–116.

Johannesson, Gösta. *Helsingborg: stad i 900 år*. Stockholm: Almquist & Wiksell Förlag, 1980.

Johnsson, Bengt. *Den danske skolemusiks historie indtil 1739*. Studier fra Sprog- og Oldtidsforskning, vol. 284. Copenhagen: G. E. C. Gads Forlag, 1973.

———. "Hans Mikkelsen Ravn's Heptachordum Danicum 1646." *Dansk Aarbog for musikforskning* [2] 1962, 59–92.

Kadelbach, Ada. "Verloren und wieder entdeckt: *Lübeckisch= Vollständiges Gesangbuch*, Lübeck und Leipzig 1698/99: Ein „geistreiches"Gesangbuch?" in *Pietismus und Liedkultur*, ed. Gudrun Busch and Wolfgang Miersemann, 143–58. Hallesche Forschungen, no. 9. Tübingen: Verlag der Franckeschen Stiftungen Halle im Max Niemeyer Verlag, 2002.

Kadelbach, Ada, and Arndt Schnoor, eds. *Speculum aevi: Kirchengesang in Lübeck als Spiegel der Zeiten*. Lübeck: Schmidt-Römhild, 1995.

Kämper, Dietrich. "Die Kanzone in der norddeutschen Orgelmusik des 17. Jahrhunderts." In *Gattung und Werk in der Musikgeschichte Norddeutschlands und Skandinaviens*, edited by Friedhelm Krummacher and Heinrich W. Schwab, 62–78. Kieler Schriften zur Musikwissenschaft, vol. 26. Kassel: Bärenreiter, 1982.

Kamphausen, Alfred. *Bachstein-Gotik*. Heyne Stilkunde, 13. Munich: Wilhelm Heyne, 1978.

Karstädt, Georg. "Buxtehude und die Neuordnung der Abendmusiken." In *Festschrift für Bruno Grusnick zum 80. Geburtstag*, edited by Rolf Saltzwedel and Klaus D. Koch, 119–27. Neuhausen-Stuttgart: Hänssler, 1981.

———. *Die "extraordinairen" Abendmusiken Dietrich Buxtehudes: Untersuchungen zur Aufführungspraxis in der Marienkirche zu Lübeck*. Lübeck: Max Schmidt-Römhild, 1962.

Karstädt, Georg. "Die Instrumente in den Kantaten und Abendmusiken Dietrich Buxtehudes." In *Beiträge zur Musikgeschichte Nordeuropas. Festschrift Kurt Gudewill zum 65. Geburtstag*, edited by Uwe Haensel, 111–21. Wolfenbüttel and Zürich, 1978.

———. *Die Musiksammlung der Stadtbibliothek, Lübeck*. Lübeck: Senat der Hansestadt, Amt für Kultur, 1979.

———. *Die Sammlung alter Musikinstrumente im St. Annen-Museum*. Lübecker Museumshefte, no. 2 (n.d.).

———. *Der Lübecker Kantatenband Dietrich Buxtehudes: Eine Studie über die Tabulatur Mus. A 373*. Lübeck: Max Schmidt-Römhild, 1971.

———. "Richtiges und Zweifelhaftes in Leben und Werk Dietrich Buxtehudes." *Musik und Kirche* 49 (1979): 163–70.

———. *Thematisch-systematisches Verzeichnis der musikalischen Werke von Dietrich Buxtehude: Buxtehude-Werke-Verzeichnis (BuxWV)*. Wiesbaden: Breitkopf & Härtel, 1974. 2d edition 1985.

Katz, Erich. "Die musikalischen Stilbegriffe des 17. Jahrhunderts." PhD diss., Freiburg/Breisgau, 1926.

Katzschke, Erich. "Verkehrswege zwischen Lübeck und Hamburg." *Postgeschichtliche Blätter Hamburg 1973*, Heft 16, 35–58.

Kelletat, Herbert. *Zur musikalischen Temperatur*. Band I: Johann Sebastian Bach und seine Zeit. 2d edition. Berlin: Merseburger, 1981.

Kilian, Dietrich. "Das Vokalwerk Dietrich Buxtehudes: Quellenstudien zu seiner Überlieferung." PhD diss., Freie Universität Berlin, 1956.

———. "Zu einem Bachschen Tabulaturautograph." In *Bachiana et alia musicologica: Festschrift Alfred Dürr*, edited by Wolfgang Rehm, 161–67. Kassel: Bärenreiter, 1983.

———, ed. *Johann Sebastian Bach: Neue Ausgabe Sämtlicher Werke*, Series IV, vols 5–6, *Kritischer Bericht*. Kassel: Bärenreiter, 1978.

Kjellberg, Erik. "Kungliga musiker i sverige under stormakstiden: Studier kring deras organisation, verksamheter och status, ca. 1620–ca. 1720." 2 vols. PhD diss., Uppsala University, Institutionen för musikvetenskap, 1979.

Kjellberg, Erik, and Kerala J. Snyder, eds. *Duben Collection Database Catalogue*. http://www.musik.uu.se/duben/Duben.php.

Kjersgaard, Erik. *A History of Denmark*. Copenhagen: Royal Danish Ministry of Foreign Affairs, 1974.

Klotz, Hans. *Über die Orgelkunst der Gotik, der Renaissance und des Barock*. Kassel: Bärenreiter, 1975.

Klüver, Theodor. *Bürgerbuch der Stadt Bad Oldesloe*. Bad Oldesloe: Kommissionsverlag L. H. Meyer, 1940.

Kobayashi, Yoshitake. "Der Gehrener Kantor Johann Christoph Bach (1673–1727) und seine Sammelbände mit Musik für Tasteninstrumente." In *Bachiana et alia Musicologica: Festschrift Alfred Dürr*, edited by Wolfgang Rehm, 168–77. Kassel: Bärenreiter, 1983.

Kongsted, Ole. "Codex Rattus Helsingorensis." In *Skt. Olai Kirke: Restaureringen af Helsingør Domkirke 2000–2001*, ed. Lone Hvass et al., 27–34. Helsingør: Kommunes Museer, 2001.

Koopman, Ton. "Dietrich Buxtehude's organworks: a practical help." *The Musical Times* 132 (1991): 148–53.

Krams, Peter. *Wechselwirkungen zwischen Orgelkomposition und Pedalspieltechnik auf den Pedalklaviaturen verschiedener Bauart, untersucht an exemplarischen Orgelkompositionen vom 16. Jahrhundert bis zur Gegenwart (1973)*. Wiesbaden: Breitkopf & Härtel, 1974.

Kremer, Joachim. *Joachim Gerstenbüttel (1647–1721) im Spannungsfeld von Oper und Kirche: Ein Beitrag zur Musikgeschichte Hamburgs*. Hamburg: von Bockel Verlag, 1997.

Krickeberg, Dieter. *Das protestantische Kantorat im 17. Jahrhundert: Studien zum Amt des deutschen Kantors.* Berliner Studien zur Musikwissenschaft, Band 6. Berlin: Merseburger, 1965.

Krüger, Liselotte. *Die Hamburgische Musikorganisation im XVII. Jahrhundert.* Strassburg: Heitz, 1933.

————. "Johann Kortkamps Organistenchronik, eine Quelle zur hamburgischen Musikgeschichte des 17. Jahrhunderts." *Zeitschrift des Vereins für Hamburgische Geschichte* 23 (1933): 188–213.

Krummacher, Friedhelm. *Die Choralbearbeitung in der protestantischen Figuralmusik zwischen Praetorius und Bach.* Kieler Schriften zur Musikwissenschaft, 22. Kassel: Bärenreiter, 1978.

————. "Die geistliche Aria in Norddeutschland und Skandinavien: Ein gattungsgeschichtlicher Versuch." In *Weltliches und Geistliches Lied des Barock: Studien zur Liedkultur in Deutschland und Skandinavien,* edited by Dieter Lohmeier, 229–64. Stockholm: Svenskt visarkiv, 1979.

————. "Individualität und Tradition in der Danziger Figuralmusik vor 1700." In *Musica Antiqua. Acta scientifica,* 5, 339–56. Bydgoszcz: Filharmonia Pomorska im. I. Paderewskiego, 1978.

————. "Orgel- und Vokalmusik im Oeuvre norddeutscher Organisten um Buxtehude." *Dansk Aarbog for musikforskning* 5, 1966/67, 63–93.

————. "Stylus phantasticus und phantastische Musik: Kompositorische Verfahren in Toccaten von Frescobaldi und Buxtehude." *Schütz-Jahrbuch* 2 (1980): 7–77.

————. "Über das Spätstadium des geistlichen Solokonzerts in Norddeutschland: Bemerkungen zu einem Druckwerk von Georg Bronner (1696)." *Archiv für Musikwissenschaft* 25 (1968): 278–88; 26 (1969): 63–79.

————. *Die Überlieferung der Choralbearbeitungen in der frühen evangelischen Kantate.* Berliner Studien zur Musikwissenschaft, 10. Berlin: Merseburger, 1965.

Kümmerling, Harald. *Katalog der Sammlung Bokemeyer.* Kieler Schriften zur Musikwissenschaft, 14. Kassel: Bärenreiter, 1970.

Kunze, Stefan. "Gattungen der Fuge in Bachs Wohltemperiertem Klavier." In *Bach-Interpretationen,* edited by Martin Geck, 74–93. Göttingen: Vandenhoeck & Ruprecht, 1969.

Küster, Konrad. "Cembalo- und Violinmusik im Notenbuch des Johan Kruse (1694/1704): Kompositionen Buxtehude, Reinkens, Pachelbels, Muffats und anderer/" *Schütz-Jahrbuch* 27 (2005): 129–74.

————. "Hamburgs 'zentrale Stellung' in der norddeutschen Orgelkultur: Überlegungen zu einem Forschungsmodell." In In *Beiträge zur Musikgeschichte Hamburgs vom Mittelalter bis in die Neuzeit,* edited by Hans Joachim Marx, 149–75. Hamburger Jahrbuch für Musikwissenschaft, vol. 18. Frankfurt am Main Peter Lang, 2001.

Läpple, Paul. "Dietrich Buxtehude und Oldesloe." In *Festschrift: [der] Oberrealschule zu Bad Oldesloe,* 26–29. [Bad Oldesloe]: Spies, 1937.

Lindberg, Folke. "Katalog över Dübensamlingen i Uppsala Universitets Bibliotek." Typescript [1946] at University Library, Uppsala.

Lindley, Mark. *Lutes, viols and temperaments.* Cambridge: Cambridge University Press, 1984.

Lindley, Mark, and Maria Boxall. *Early Keyboard Fingerings: A Comprehensive Guide.* Mainz and New York: Schott, 1992.

Lindtke, Gustav. *Alte Lübecker Stadtansichten.* Lübecker Museumshefte, Heft 7. Lübeck, 1968.

Linfield, Eva. "Dietrich Buxtehude's Sonatas: A Historical and Analytical Study." PhD diss., Brandeis University, 1984.

————. "North and South European Influences on Buxtehude's Chamber Music: Despite Influences, a Unique Repertory." *Schütz Jahrbuch* 10 (1988): 104–25.

Little, Meredith and Natalie Jenne. *Dance and the Music of J. S. Bach*. Bloomington: Indiana University Press, 1991.

Lohmann, Ludger. *Studien zu Artikulationsproblemen bei den Tasteninstrumenten des 16.-18. Jahrhunderts*. Kölner Beiträge zur Musikforschung, vol. 125. Regensburg: Gustav Bosse, 1982.

Lohmeier, Dieter, ed. *Weltliches und Geistliches Lied des Barock: Studien zur Liedkultur in Deutschland und Skandinavien*. Stockholm: Svenskt visarkiv, 1979.

Lorenz, Helmut. "Die Klaviermusik Dietrich Buxtehudes." *Archiv für Musikwissenschaft* 11 (1954): 238–51.

Lundgren, Bo. "Johan Lorentz in Kopenhagen—organista nulli in Europa secundus." In *Bericht über den siebenten internationalen musikwissenschaftlichen Kongress, Köln, 1958*, 183–85. Kassel: Bärenreiter, 1959.

———. "Nicolajorganisten Johan Lorentz i Köpenhamn." *Svensk tidskrift för musikforskning* 40 (1961): 249–63.

Mackey, Elizabeth Jocelyn. "The Sacred Music of Johann Theile." 2 volumes. PhD diss., University of Michigan, 1968.

Mahrenholz, Christhard. *Die Orgelregister: ihre Geschichte und ihr Bau*. Kassel: Bärenreiter, 1930.

Maier, Michael. *Atalanta fugiens: An Edition of the Fugues, Emblems and Epigrams*. Trans. Joscelyn Godwin. Magnum Opus Hermetic Sourceworks 22. Grand Rapids: Phanes Press, 1989.

Mann, Alfred. *The Study of Fugue*. New York: Norton, 1965.

Mann, Thomas. *Buddenbrooks*. Translated by H. T. Lowe-Porter. Together with "Lübeck as a Way of Life and Thought," a Lecture Delivered by the Author on June 5, 1926, on the 700th Anniversary of Its Founding, translated by Richard and Clara Winston. New York: Alfred A. Knopf, 1965.

Märker, Michael. "'Manches schöne Clavier-Stück von des kunstreichen Buxtehudens Arbeit': Die Suiten und Variationen von Dietrich Buxtehude." *Jahrbuch Ständige Konferenz Mitteldeutsche Barockmusik in Sachsen Sachsen-Anhalt und Eisenach* 1 (2000): 196–204.

———. *Die protestantische Dialogkomposition in Deutschland zwischen Heinrich Schütz und Johann Sebastian Bach: Eine stilkritische Studie*. Cologne: Studio, 1995.

Mårtensson, Torsten. "Orgelverken i s:ta Maria." In *Orgelinvigningen in S:ta Maria Kyrka den 16 dec. 1928*, 15–19. Helsingborg, 1928.

Marx, Hans Joachim. "Geschichte der Hamburger Barockoper: Eine Forschungsbericht." *Hamburger Jahrbuch für Musikwissenschaft* 3 (1978): 7–34.

Marx, Hans Joachim, and Dorothea Schröder. *Die Hamburger Gänsemarkt-Oper: Katalog der Textbücher*. Laaber: Laaber Verlag, 1995.

Marx, Klaus. *Die Entwicklung des Violoncells und seiner Spieltechnik bis J. L. Duport (1520–1820)*. Forschungsbeiträge zur Musikwissenschaft, 13. Regensburg: Gustav Bosse, 1963.

Matter, E. Ann. "Buxtehude and Pietism? A Reappraisal." *The American Organist* 21 (May, 1987): 81–83.

Matthias, Markus. *Johann Wilhelm und Johanna Eleonora Petersen*. Arbeiten zur Geschichte des Pietismus, Band 30. Göttingen: Vandenhoeck & Ruprecht, 1993.

Maul, Michael, and Peter Wollny. *Weimarer Orgeltabulatur: Die frühesten Notenhandschriften Johann Sebastian Bachs sowie Abschriften seines Schüler Johann Martin Schubart. Werke von Dietrich Buxtehude, Johann Adam Reinken und Johann Pachelbel. Faksimile und Übertragung*. Kassel: Bärenreiter, in press [2007].

Maxton, Willy. "Mitteilungen über eine vollständige Abendmusik Dietrich Buxtehudes." *Zeitschrift für Musikwissenschaft* 10 (1928): 387–95.

Maxton, Willy. "Die Authentizität des 'Jüngsten Gerichts' von Dietrich Buxtehude." *Die Musikforschung* 15 (1962): 382–94.

May, Ernest. "J. G. Walther and the Lost Weimar Autographs of Bach's Organ Works." In *Studies in Renaissance and Baroque Music in Honor of Arthur Mendel*, edited by Robert L. Marshall, 264–82. Kassel: Bärenreiter and Hackensack: Joseph Boonin, 1974.

McCredie, Andrew D. "Instrumentarium and Instrumentation in the North German Baroque Opera." PhD diss., University of Hamburg, 1964.

Mersenne, Marin. *Harmonie universelle, vol. III, The Books on Instruments.* Translated by Roger E. Chapman. The Hague: Martinus Nijhoff, 1957.

Mikkelsen, Birger. *Helsingør: Sundtoldstad og borgerby.* Helsingør: Nordisk Forlag, 1976.

———. *Kronborg.* Helsingør: Nordisk Forlag, 1978.

Mills, Isabelle and Walter Kreyszig. *Dietrich Buxtehude and Samuel Scheidt: An Anniversary Tribute: The Proceedings of the International Buxtehude/Scheidt Festival and Conference at the University of Saskatchewan, November 1987.* Saskatoon: University of Saskatchewan, 1988.

Moberg, Carl-Allan. *Dietrich Buxtehude.* Gillet Gamla Helsingborg, Handlingar VIII. Helsingborg, 1946.

———. "Die Musikkultur des Ostseeraumes zur Zeit Buxtehudes." *Der Wagen: Ein Lübeckisches Jahrbuch,* 1958, 52–57.

Mortensen, Otto. "Über Typologisierung der Couranten und Sarabanden Buxtehudes." *Dansk Aarbog for Musikforskning* 6 (1968–72): 5–51.

———. "Ein Vergleich der Couranten und Sarabanden Buxtehudes und Lebègues." *Dansk Aarbog for Musikforskning* 7 (1973–76): 129–39.

Moser, Hans Joachim. *Corydon, das ist: Geschichte des mehrstimmigen Generalbaßliedes und des Quodlibets im deutschen Barock.* 2 vols. Braunschweig: Henry Litolff, 1933.

———. *Dietrich Buxtehude, der Mann und sein Werk.* Berlin: Merseburger, 1957.

Müller, Heinrich. *Dr. Heinrich Müllers geistliche Erquickstunden.* Edited by Joh. Georg Rußwurm. Ratzeburg: J.G.C. Freystatzky, 1822.

Müller, Karl and Fritz Wiegand, eds. *Arnstädter Bachbuch: Johann Sebastian Bach und seine Verwandten in Arnstadt.* 2d edition. Arnstadt: Im Auftrage des Rates der Stadt, 1957.

Müller-Blattau, Joseph. *Die Kompositionslehre Heinrich Schützens in der Fassung seines Schülers Christoph Bernhard.* 2d edition. Kassel: Bärenreiter, 1963.

Die Musik Hamburgs im Zeitalter Seb. Bachs: Ausstellung anläßlich des neunten deutschen Bachfestes zu Hamburg 3.-7. Juni 1921. Hamburg, 1921.

Neubacher, Jürgen. "Drei wieder zugängliche Ariensammelbände als Quellen für das Repertoire der Hamburger Gänsemarkt-Oper." In *Beiträge zur Musikgeschichte Hamburgs vom Mittelalter bis in die Neuzeit,* edited by Hans Joachim Marx, 195–206. Hamburger Jahrbuch für Musikwissenschaft, vol. 18. Frankfurt am Main Peter Lang, 2001.

Neumann, Frederick. *Ornamentation in Baroque and Post-Baroque Music.* Princeton: Princeton University Press, 1978.

Newman, William S. *The Sonata in the Baroque Era.* Revised Edition. Chapel Hill: The University of North Carolina Press, 1966.

Nørfelt, Henrik Fibiger. "Sct. Mariæ Kirkes orgelhistorie." In *Orglet i Sct. Mariæ Kirke i Helsingør—et Festskrift,* edited by Henrik Fibiger Nørfelt, 45–63. [Helsingør, 1999].

Norlind, Tobias. "Was ein Organist im 17. Jahrhundert wissen musste." *Sammelbände der Internationalen Musikgesellschaft* 7 (1905–6): 640–41.

Nyerup, R. *Udkast til en Historie om de latinske Skoler i Danmark og Norge fra Reformationen af og til 1804.* Copenhagen: A.& S. Soldin, 1804.

Olesen, Ole. "Buxtehude-orglet i Torrlösa." Lecture, 31. May 2003. http://www.musikhistoriskmuseum.dk/reg/torrloesa_foredrag.htm

Ortgies, Ibo. "Bartold Hering, Organist und Orgelbauer in Lübeck?" *Ars Organi* 52 (2004): 70–74.

———. "Die Praxis der Orgelstimmung in Norddeutschland im 17. und 18. Jahrhundert und ihr Verhältnis zur zeitgenössischen Musikpraxis." PhD dissertation, Göteborg University, 2004.

———. "Subsemitones in Organs Built between 1468 and 1721: Introduction and Commentary with an Annotated Catalog." GOArt Research Reports 3 (2003): 11–74.

———. "Über den Umbau der großen Orgel der Marienkirche zu Lübeck durch Friedrich Stellwagen, 1637–41." In *Orphei Organi Antiqui: Essays in Honor of Harald Vogel*, edited by Cleveland Johnson, 313–36. N.p.: The Westfield Center, 2006.

Otterstedt, Annette. "Wie deutet man ein Bild?" In *"Pièces de Viole": Fünf Beiträge zur Viola da Gamba*. Jubiläumsschrift zum zehnjährigen Bestehen der Viola da Gamba-Gesellschaft. Winterthur: Viola da Gamba-Gesellschaft, 2004.

Owen, Barbara. *The Registration of Baroque Organ Music*. Bloomington: Indiana University Press, 1997.

Padgham, Charles A. *The Well-Tempered Organ*. Oxford: Positif Press, 1986.

Palisca, Claude. "The genesis of Mattheson's style classification." In *New Mattheson Studies*, edited by George Buelow and Hans Joachim Marx, 409–23. Cambridge: Cambridge University Press, 1983.

Patalas, Aleksandra: *Catalogue of early music prints from the collections of the former Preussische Staatsbibliothek in Berlin, kept at the Jagiellonian Library in Cracow*. Krakow: Musica Iagellonica, 1999.

Pauli, Carl Wilhelm. *Geschichte der Lübeckischen Gesangbücher und Beurtheilung des gegenwärtigen*. Lübeck: In Commission der Buchhandlung Rudolf Seelig, 1875.

Pauly, Hans-Jakob. *Die Fuge in den Orgelwerken Dietrich Buxtehudes*. Regensburg: Gustav Bosse, 1964.

Pedersen, Laurits. "Buxtehuderne og Helsingør." *Dansk Musiktidsskrift* 8 (1933): 41–47.

———. "Fra Didrik Hansen Buxtehudes barndom og ungdom 1636–37 til 1. maj 1668." *Medlemsblad for Dansk Organist og Kantorsamfund af 1905* 3 (1937): 25–37.

———. *Helsingør i Sundtoldstiden 1426–1857*. 2 volumes. Copenhagen: Nyt Nordisk Forlag–Arnold Busck, 1926–29.

Piersig, Fritz. "Die Orgeln der bremischen Stadtkirchen im 17. und 18. Jahrhundert." *Bremisches Jahrbuch* 35 (1935): 379–425.

Pirro, André. *Dietrich Buxtehude*. Paris: Fischbacher, 1913. Reprint. Geneva: Minkoff, 1966.

Planyavsky, Alfred. *Geschichte des Kontrabasses*. Tutzing: Hans Schneider, 1970. 2nd edition 1984.

Porter, William. "Hamburg Organists in Lutheran Worship." In *The Organ as a Mirror of Its Time: North European Reflections, 1610–2000*, edited by Kerala J. Snyder, 60–77. Oxford and New York: Oxford University Press, 2002.

———. "Johann Herbst's *Arte prattica & poëtica*: A Window into German Improvisational Practice in the Mid-seventeenth Century." In *Orphei Organi Antiqui: Essays in Honor of Harald Vogel*, edited by Cleveland Johnson, 251–60. N.p.: The Westfield Center, 2006.

———. "Observations concerning Contrapuntal Improvisation." *GOArt Research Reports* 3 (2003): 135–48.

———. "Psalm-tone Formulas in Buxtehude's Organ Works?" In *Charles Brenton Fisk, Organ Builder, Volume I: Essays in his Honor*, edited by Fenner Douglass et al., 161–74. Easthampton, MA: The Westfield Center for Early Keyboard Studies, 1986.

Preußner, Eberhard. "Die Methodik im Schulgesang der evangelischen Lateinschulen des 17. Jahrhunderts." *Archiv für Musikwissenschaft* 6 (1924): 407–49.

Rampe Siegbert. "Abendmusik oder Gottesdienst? Zur Funktion norddeutscher Orgelkompositionen des 17. und frühen 18. Jahrhunderts. *Schütz-Jahrbuch,* 25 (2003): 7–70; 26 (2004): 155–204; 27 (2005): 53–127.

———. "Das 'Hintze-Manusckript'—Ein Dokument zu Biographie und Werk von Matthias Weckmann und Johann Jacob Froberger." *Schütz-Jahrbuch* 19 (1997): 71–111.

Rathey, Markus. "Die Grobe-Tabulatur: Überlegungen zu ihrer Genese und zur thüringischen Buxtehudeüberlieferung im 17. Jahrhundert." In Ständige Koferenz Mitteldeutsche Barockmusik in Sachsen, Sachsen-Anhalt und Thüringen, *Jahrbuch 2000,* 42–55. Eisenach: Karl Dieter Wagner, 2000.

Reichert, Peter. "Musikalische Rhetorik in den Choralvorspielen von Dietrich Buxtehude." *Acta Organologica* 24 (1994): 145–84.

Reincken, Johann Adam. *An Waßer Flüßen Babÿlon: Choralfantasie für Orgel.* Ed. Ulf Grapenthin. Wilhelmshaven: Heinrichshofen's Verlag, 2001.

Répertoire International des Sources Musicales [RISM]. Series A/I: *Einzeldrucke vor 1800.* 11 volumes. Kassel: Bärenreiter, 1971–86.

Répertoire International des Sources Musicales [RISM]. Series B/I/1: *Récueils imprimés, XVI–XVII siècles: liste chronologique.* Edited by François Lesure. Munich: Henle, 1960.

Riedel, Friedrich Wilhelm. *Quellenkundliche Beiträge zur Geschichte der Musik für Tasteninstrumente in der zweiten Hälfte des 17. Jahrhunderts (vornehmlich in Deutschland).* Kassel: Bärenreiter, 1960. 2nd edition, Munich–Salzburg: Katzbichler, 1990.

———. "Ein Skizzenbuch von Alessandro Poglietti." In *Essays in Musicology: A Birthday Offering for Willi Apel,* edited by Hans Tischler, 145–52. Indiana University School of Music, 1968.

Riemer, Otto. "Erhard Bodenschatz und sein Florilegium Portense." PhD diss., Halle, 1927.

Riemsdijk, J. C. M. van. "Jean Adam Reinken." *Tijdschrift der Vereeniging voor Noord-Nederlands Muziekgeschiedenis* 2 (1887): 61–91.

Ritter, August Gottfried. *Zur Geschichte des Orgelspiels, vornehmlich des deutschen, im 14. bis zum Anfange des 18. Jahrhunderts.* 2 vols. Leipzig: Max Hesse's Verlag, 1884. Reprint Hildesheim: Olms 1969.

Rose, Stephen. "Music, Print and Presentation in Saxony During the Seventeenth Century." *German History* 23 (2005): 1–19.

Rosenquist, Carl E. "Redogörelse för orgeln i Torrlösa kyrka jämte förslag till åtgärder." Unpublished typescript, 1957.

Rowland, Ingrid D. *The Ecstatic Journey: Athanasius Kircher in Baroque Rome.* Chicago: University of Chicago Library, 2000.

Rudén, Jan Olof. "Ett nyfunnet komplement till Dübensamlingen." *Svensk tidskrift för musikforskning* 47 (1965): 51–58.

———. "Vattenmärken och Musikforskning: Presentation och Tillämpning av en Dateringsmetod på musikalier i handskrift i Uppsala Universitetsbiblioteks Dübensamling." 2 vols. Licentiatavhandling i musikforskning, Uppsala University, 1968.

Ruhle, Sara Cathcart. "An Anonymous Seventeenth-Century German Oratorio in the Düben Collection (Uppsala University Library vok. mus. i hskr. 71)." PhD diss., University of North Carolina, 1982.

Sancta Maria Kyrka i Hälsingborg: Minnesbok vid 500-Årsjubiléet 1951. Helsingborg: Sancta Maria Församlings Pastorsexpedition, 1951.

Salmen, Walter. *Musiker im Porträt.* 5 vols. Munich: C. H. Beck, 1982–84.

Sandberger, Wolfgang, ed. *Bach, Lübeck und die norddeutsche Musiktradition: Bericht über das Internationale Symposion der Musikhochschule Lübeck April 2000.* Kassel: Bärenreiter, 2002.

Sanford, Sally Allis. "Seventeenth and Eighteenth Century Vocal Style and Technique." DMA essay, Stanford University, 1979.

Schacht, Matthias Henriksen. *Musicus Danicus eller Danske Sangmester* [1687]. Edited by Godtfred Skjerne. Copenhagen: H. Hagerups Forlag, 1928.

Schäfertöns, Reinhard. "Die Organistenproge: Ein Beitrag zur Geschichte der Orgelmusik im 17. und 18. Jahrhundert." *Die Musikforschung* 49 (1996): 142–52.

Scheidt, Samuel. *Tabulatur-Buch Hundert geistlicher Lieder und Psalmen Herrn Doctoris Martini Lutheri und anderer gottseligen Männer* (Görlitz, 1650). Edited by Gottlieb Harms. Samuel Scheidts Werke, I. Hamburg: Ugrino, 1923.

Scherliess, Volker and Arndt Schnoor, eds. *"Theater-Music in der Kirche": Zur Geschichte der Lübecker Abendmusiken.* Lübeck: Bibliothek der Hansestadt Lübeck—Musikhochschule Lübeck, 2003.

Schieche, Emil. *400 Jahre Deutsche St. Gertruds Gemeinde in Stockholm 1571–1971.* Stockholm, 1971.

Schiørring, Nils. *Musikkens Historie i Danmark; Bind I: Fra Oldtiden til 1750.* Edited by Ole Kontsted and P. H. Traustedt. [Copenhagen]: Politikens Forlag, 1977.

Schleuning, Peter. *Die frei Fantasie: Ein Beitrag zur Erforschung der klassischen Klaviermusik.* Göppinger Akademische Beiträge, No. 76. Göppingen: Alfred Kümmerle, 1973.

Schmidt, Harro. "Das Buxtehude-Bild von Voorhout: Zur Authentizität des einzigen Buxtehude-Bildes." *Der Kirchenmusiker* 1987, Heft 5, 161–63.

Schneider, Matthias. "*Ad ostentandum ingenium, & abditam harominae rationem*—zum Stylus Phantasticus bei Kircher und Mattheson." *Basler Jahrbuch für historische Musikpraxis,* 22 (1998): 103–26.

———. *Buxtehude Choralfantasien: Textdeutung oder "phantastischer Stil"?.* Kassel" Bärenreiter, 1997.

Schröder, Dorothea. "Die Einführung der italienischen Oper in Hamburg durch Johann Georg Conradi und Johann Sigismund Kusser (1693–1696). In *Il melodramma italiano in Italia e in Germania nell'eta barocca/Die italienische Barockoper, ihre Verbreitung in Italien und Deutschland.* Como, Italy: Antiquae Musicae Italicae Studiosi, 1995 p. 43–55.

———. "Die Orgelgeschichte der Hauptkirche St. Petri vom Mittelalter bis 1885." In *Gloria in excelsis Deo: Eine Geschichte der Orgeln in der Hauptkirche St. Petri zu Hamburg,* edited by Dorothea Schröder, 23–42. Neumünster: Wachholtz Verlag, 2006.

———. *Zeitgeschichte auf der Opernbühne: Barockes Musiktheater in Hamburg im Dienst von Politik und Diplomatie (1690–1745).* Göttingen: Vandenhoeck & Ruprecht, 1998.

Schulze, Hans-Joachim. "Bach und Buxtehude: Eine wenig beachtete Quelle in der Carnegie Library zu Pittsburgh/PA." *Bach Jahrbuch* 77 (1991): 177–81.

———. "Johann Christoph Bach (1671–1721), 'Organist und Schul Collega in Ohrdruf,' Johann Sebastian Bachs erster Lehrer." *Bach Jahrbuch* 71 (1985): 55–81.

———. *Studien zur Bach-Überlieferung im 18. Jahrhundert.* Leipzig: Edition Peters, 1984.

Schulze, Theodor. "Die Anfänge des Pietismus in Lübeck: Ein Beitrag zur Geschichte des religiösen Lebens in Lübeck im 17. Jahrhundert." *Mitteilungen des Vereins für Lübeckische Geschichte und Altertumskunde* 10 (1901–2): 68–96, 99–113.

Schulze, Walter. *Die Quellen der Hamburger Oper (1678–1738): Eine bibliographisch-statistische Studie zur Geschichte der ersten stehenden deutschen Oper.* Hamburg/ Oldenburg: Gerhard Stalling, 1938.

Schwab, Heinrich W. "Suitensätze und Tanzmodelle: Zur Rezeption des Menuetts in der norddeutschen Region der Buxtehude-Zeit." In *Dietrich Buxtehude und die europäische*

Musik seiner Zeit: Bericht über das Lübecker Symposion 1987, edited by Arnfried Edler and Friedhelm Krummacher, 183–203. Kieler Schriften zur Musikwissenschaft, 35. Kassel: Bärenreiter, 1990.

Schwab, Heinrich. "Johannes Voorhouts Gemälde 'Häusliche Musikszene' (1674): Zum Problem der Identifikation Dietrich Buxtehudes." In *Festskrift Niels Krabbe*, ed. Erland Kolding Nielsen et al., Copenhagen, 2006.

———. "Lübecks Stadtmusikgeschichte—Gesamtbild und Einzelforschung." In *800 Jahre Musik in Lübeck*, edited by Antjekathrin Graßman and Werner Neugebauer, 201–5. Lübeck: Senat der Hansestadt Lübeck, Amt für Kultur, 1982.

———. "Ratsmusik und Hausmusik—Offizielles und privates Musizieren aus der Zeit zwischen 1600 und 1800." In *800 Jahre Musik in Lübeck. Teil II: Dokumentation zum Lübecker Musikfest 1982*, edited by Arnfried Edler, Werner Neugebauer and Heinrich W. Schwab, 31–42. Lübeck: Senat der Hansestadt Lübeck, Amt für Kultur, Veröffentlichung XXI, 1983.

Schwartz, Rudolf. "Zur Geschichte der liedlosen Zeit in Deutschland." *Jahrbuch der Musikbibliothek Peters* 20 (1913): 15–27.

Seiffert, Max. "Die Chorbibliothek der Michaelisschule in Lüneburg zu Seb. Bachs Zeit." *Sammelbände der Internationalen Musikgesellschaft* 9 (1907–8): 593–621.

———. *Geschichte der Klaviermusik.* (3rd edition of C. F. Weitzmann, *Geschichte des Klavierspiels und der Klavierliteratur.*) Leipzig: Breitkopf & Härtel, 1899.

———. "Matthias Weckmann und das Collegium musicum in Hamburg." *Sammelbände der Internationalen Musikgesellschaft* 2 (1900–1901): 76–132.

———. "Das Plauener Orgelbuch von 1708." *Archiv für Musikwissenschaft* 2 (1919–20): 371–93.

Senn, Walter. *Jakob Stainer der Geigenmacher zu Absam.* Schlern-Schriften, no. 87. Innsbruck: Universitäts-Verlag Wagner, 1941.

Silbiger, Alexander. "The Autographs of Matthias Weckmann: A Reevaluation." In *Heinrich Schütz und die Musik in Dänemark zur Zeit Christians IV*, ed., Anne Orbaek Jensen and Ole Kongsted. 117–44. Copenhagen: Engstrom & Sodring, 1989.

———. "Passacaglia and Ciaccona: Genre Pairing and Ambiguity from Frescobaldi to Couperin." *Journal of Seventeenth-Century Music* 2 (1996) http://www.sscmjscm.org/jscm/v2/no1/Silbiger.html.

———. "The Roman Frescobaldi Tradition." *Journal of the American Musicological Society* 23 (1980): 42–87.

Smither, Howard. *A History of the Oratorio. II: The Oratorio in the Baroque Era—Protestant Germany and England.* Chapel Hill: The University of North Carolina Press, 1977.

Smithers, Don L. *The Music and History of the Baroque Trumpet before 1721.* Syracuse: Syracuse University Press, 1973. 2nd edition, Carbondale: Southern Illinois University Press, 1988.

Snyder, Kerala J. "Bach and Buxtehude at the Large Organ of St. Mary's in Lübeck." In *Charles Brenton Fisk, Organ Builder. Volume I: Essays in his Honor*, edited by Fenner Douglass et al., 175–90. Easthampton, MA: The Westfield Center for Early Keyboard Studies, 1986.

———. "Bach, Buxtehude, and the Old Choir Library of St. Mary's in Lübeck," in *Das Frühwerk Johann Sebastian Bachs*, edited by Karl Heller and Hans-Joachim Schulze, 33–47. Cologne: Studio, 1995.

———. "Buxtehude and *Das Jüngste Gericht*: A New Look at an Old Problem." In *Festschrift für Bruno Grusnick zum 80. Geburtstag*, edited by Rolf Saltzwedel and Klaus D. Koch, 128–41. Neuhausen-Stuttgart: Hänssler, 1981.

Snyder, Kerala J. "Buxtehude, Dietrich." In *The New Grove Dictionary of Music and Musicians*, edited by Stanley Sadie. Vol. 3. London: Macmillan, 1980. Revised reprint in *The New Grove North European Baroque Masters*, edited by Stanley Sadie, 1985, 173–213. London: Macmillan, 1985. Further revision in *The New Grove Dictionary of Music and Musicians*, 2nd ed. Vol. 4. London: Macmillan, 2001. German translation in *Die Musik in Geschichte und Gegenwart*. 2nd ed., edited by Ludwig Finscher. Personenteil, Vol. 3. Kassel: Bärenreiter, 2000.

———. "Buxtehude, the Lübeck Abendmusiken, and *Wacht! Euch zum Streit gefasset macht.*" In *Church, Stage, and Studio: Music in its Contexts in Seventeenth-century Germany*, edited by Paul Walker, 205–30. Ann Arbor: UMI Research Press, 1990. German translation in *Jahrbuch Alte Musik* 1 (1989): 153–81.

———. "Buxtehude's Organ Music: Drama without Words." *The Musical Times* 120 (1979): 517–21.

———. "Buxtehude's Organs: Helsingør, Helsingborg, Lübeck." *The Musical Times* 126 (1985): 365–69, 427–34.

———. "Dietrich Buxtehude's Studies in Learned Counterpoint." *Journal of the American Musicological Society* 33 (1980): 544–64.

———. "Franz Tunder's Stock-Exchange Concerts: Prelude to the Lübeck Abendmusiken, *GOArt Research Reports* 2 (2000): 41–57.

———. "Lübecker Abendmusiken." In *800 Jahre Musik in Lübeck. Teil II: Dokumentation zum Lübecker Musikfest 1982*, edited by Arnfried Edler, Werner Neugebauer and Heinrich W. Schwab, 63–70. Lübeck: Senat der Hansestadt Lübeck, Amt für Kultur, Veröffentlichung 21, 1983.

———. "Music for Church and Community: Buxtehude in Lübeck." In *The World of Baroque Music: New Perspectives*, ed. George B. Stauffer, 78–104. Bloomington: Indiana University Press, 2006.

———. "Musik für den Kenner und den "gemeinen Bürger": Stilistische Varianten in Buxtehudes Vokalmusik." In *Dietrich Buxtehude und die europäische Musik seiner Zeit: Bericht über das Lübecker Symposion 1987*, edited by Arnfried Edler and Friedhelm Krummacher, 108–22. Kieler Schriften zur Musikwissenschaft," 35. Kassel: Bärenreiter, 1990.

———. "The Örgryte Organ as a Work of Musical Scholarship." In *The North German Organ*, ed. Joel Speerstra, 355–61. Göteborg: GOArt, 2003.

———. "To Lübeck in the Steps of J. S. Bach." *The Musical Times* 127 (1986): 672–77.

———. "Partners in Music-making: Organist and Cantor in 17th-century Lübeck," in *The Organist as Scholar: Essays in Honor of Russell Saunders*, edited by Kerala J. Snyder, 233–55. Stuyvesant, NY: Pendragon Press, 1994.

———. "Text and Tone in Hassler's German Songs and their Sacred Parodies." In *Musical Humanism and Its Legacy: Essays in Honor of Claude V. Palisca*, edited by Nancy Kovaleff Baker and Barbara Russano Hanning, 253–77. Stuyvesant, NY: Pendragon, 1992.

———. "Tradition with Variations: Chorale Settings *per omnes versus* by Buxtehude and Bach." In *Music and Theology: Essays in Honor of Robin A. Leaver On His Sixty-Fifth Birthday*, edited by Daniel Zager, 31–50. Lanham, MD: The Scarecrow Press, 2006.

———, ed. *The Organ as a Mirror of Its Time: North European Reflections, 1610–2000*. Oxford and New York: Oxford University Press, 2002.

Söhngen, Oskar. "Die Lübecker Abendmusiken als Kirchengeschichtliches und theologisches Problem." *Musik und Kirche* 27 (1957): 181–91.

Sørensen, Søren. *Das Buxtehudebild im Wandel der Zeit.* Lübeck: Senat der Hansestadt Lübeck, Amt für Kultur, Veröffentlichung VI, 1972.

Sørensen, Søren. *Diderich Buxtehudes vokale kirkenmusik: Studier til den evangeliske kirkekantates udviklingshistorie.* Copenhagen: Ejnar Munksgaard, 1958.

———. "Instrumentalforspillene i Buxtehudes Kantater." *Dansk Aarbog for Musikforskning* [I] 1961, 5–37.

———. "Monteverdi—Förster—Buxtehude. Entwurf zu einer entwicklungsgeschichtlichen Untersuchung." *Dansk Aarbog for musikforskning* [3] 1963, 87–100.

Speerstra, Joel. *Bach and the Pedal Clavichord: An Organist's Guide.* Rochester, NY: University of Rochester Press, 2004.

Spies, Hans-Bernd. "Buxtehude und die finanzielle Musikförderung in Lübeck." *Musik und Kirche* 53 (1983): 5–8.

———. "Vier neuentdeckte Briefe Dietrich Buxtehudes." *Zeitschrift des Vereins für Lübeckische Geschichte und Altertumskunde* 61 (1981): 81–93.

Spitta, Philipp. *Johann Sebastian Bach.* Leipzig, 1873; English translation by Clara Bell and J. A. Fuller-Maitland, London, 1889. Reprint. New York: Dover, 1951.

Sponheuer, Bernd. "Phantastik und Kalkül: Bemerkungen zu den Ostinato-Kompositionen in der Orgelmusik Buxtehudes." In *Dietrich Buxtehude und die europäische Musik seiner Zeit: Bericht über das Lübecker Symposion 1987,* edited by Arnfried Edler and Friedhelm Krummacher, 289–309. Kieler Schriften zur Musikwissenschaft, 35. Kassel: Bärenreiter, 1990.

Stahl, Wilhelm. *Dietrich Buxtehude,* 2nd ed., Kassel: Bärenreiter, 1952.

———. "Dietrich Buxtehudes Eltern." *Lübeckische Blätter* 79 (1937): 477–80.

———. "Dietrich Buxtehudes Geburtsort." *Die Musikforschung* 4 (1951): 382.

———. *Franz Tunder und Dietrich Buxtehude.* Leipzig: Kistner & Siegel, 1926.

———. *Die große Orgel der Marienkirche zu Lübeck.* Kassel: Bärenreiter, [1938].

———. "Die Lübecker Abendmusiken im 17. und 18. Jahrhundert." *Zeitschrift des Vereins für Lübeckische Geschichte und Altertumskunde* 29 (1937): 1–64.

———. *Musikgeschichte Lübecks. II: Geistliche Musik.* Kassel: Bärenreiter, 1952.

———. *Die Totentanz-Orgel der Marienkirche zu Lübeck.* Mainz: Paul Smets, 1932; 2d edition, Mainz: Rheingold, 1942.

———. "Unsere Liturgie." *Lübeckische Blätter* 58 (1916): 26–29.

Stauffer, George. "Bach's Organ Registration Reconsidered." In *J. S. Bach as Organist: His Instruments, Music, and Performance Practices,* edited by George Stauffer and Ernest May, 193–211. Bloomington: Indiana University Press, 1986.

Stiehl, Carl. "Katalog der Musik-Sammlung auf der Stadtbibliothek zu Lübeck." In *Programm des Katharineums zu Lübeck 1893.* Lübeck, 1893.

———. *Lübeckisches Tonkünstlerlexikon.* Leipzig: Max Hesse's Verlag, 1887.

Strunk, Oliver. *Source Readings in Music History.* New York: Norton, 1950.

[Sweelinck, Jan Pieterszon?]. "Compositions Regeln Herrn M. Johan Peterssen Sweeling." *Werken van Jan Piertszn. Sweelinck,* 10, edited by Hermann Gehrmann. The Hague, 1901.

Synofzik, Thomas. "Johann Gottlieb Preller und seine Abschriften Bachscher Clavierwerke: Kopistenpraxis als Schlüssel zur Aufführungspraxis." In *Bach und seine mitteldeutschen Zeitgenossen. Bericht über das internationale musikwissenschaftliche Kolloquium Erfurt und Arnstadt 13. bis 16. Januar 2000,* edited by Rainer Kaiser, 45–65. Eisenach: Karl Dieter Wagner 2001.

Tesdorpf, Oscar L. *Die Geschichte des Tesdorpf'schen Geschlechts bis 1920.* Heidehaus i.d. Göhrde: Verlag des Verfassers, 1921.

Theile, Johann. *Musikalisches Kunstbuch.* Edited by Carl Dahlhaus. Denkmäler Norddeutscher Musik, 1. Kassel: Bärenreiter, 1965.

Thomas, Richard Hinton. *Poetry and Song in the German Baroque.* Oxford, 1963.

Thrane, Carl. *Fra Hofviolonernes Tid: Skildringer af det kongelige Kapels Historie 1648–1848.* Kjøbenhavn: Schønbergske Forlag, 1908.

van Dijk, Pieter. "Aspects of Fingering and Hand Division in Lynar A1." In *Sweelinck Studies: Proceedings of the Sweelinck Symposium, Utrecht 1999.* Edited by Pieter Dirksen. Utrecht: STIMU, 2002.

Vetter, Walther. *Das Frühdeutsche Lied: Ausgewählte Kapitel aus der Entwicklungsgeschichte und Aesthetik des ein- und mehrstimmigen deutschen Kunstliedes im 17. Jahrhundert.* 2 vols. Münster i.W.: Helios Verlag, 1928.

Viderø, Finn. "Buxtehudes Präludium in fis-moll." *Musik und Kirche* 49 (1979): 13–20.

Vogel, Harald. "Mitteltönig—Wohltemperiert: Der Wandel der Stimmungsästhetik im norddeutschen Orgelbau und Orgelrepertoire des 17. und 18. Jahrhunderts." *Jahrbuch Alte Musik* 1 (1989): 119–51.

———. "North German Organ Building of the Late Seventeenth Century: Registration and Tuning." In *J. S. Bach as Organist: His Instruments, Music, and Performance Practices,* edited by George Stauffer and Ernest May, 31–40. Bloomington: Indiana University Press, 1986.

———. "Tuning and Temperament in the North German School of the Seventeenth and Eighteenth Centuries." In *Charles Brenton Fisk, Organ Builder,* Volume I: *Essays in his Honor,* 237–66. Easthampton, MA: The Westfield Center for Early Keyboard Studies, 1986.

———. "Zur Spielweise der Musik für Tasteninstrumente um 1600 / Keyboard Playing Techniques around 1600." In Samuel Scheidt, *Tabulatura nova, Teil II,* edited by Harald Vogel, 145–71. Wiesbaden: Breitkopf & Härtel, 1999.

Vollhardt, Reinhard. *Geschichte der Cantoren und Organisten von den Städten im Königreich Sachsen.* Berlin: Wilhelm Issleib, 1899. Reprint, edited by Hans-Joachim Schulze. Leipzig: Peters, 1978.

Wackernagel, Philipp. *Das deutsche evangelische Kirchenlied von den ältesten Zeiten bis zum Anfang des 17. Jahrhunderts.* 5 vols.; Leipzig: B. G. Teubner, 1864–77. Reprint Hildesheim: Georg Olms, 1964.

Walin, Stig. "Zur Frage der Stimmung von Buxtehude-Orgeln." *Svensk tidskrift för musikforskning* 44 (1962): 13–29.

Walker, Paul. "From Renaissance 'Fuga' to Baroque Fugue: The Role of the 'Sweelinck Theory Manuscripts.'" *Schütz-Jahrbuch* 7–8 (1985–86): 93–104.

———. *Theories of Fugue from the Age of Josquin to the Age of Bach.* Rochester: University of Rochester Press, 2000.

Walter, Joachim. *"This Heaving Ocean of Tones": Nineteenth-Century Organ Registration Practice at St. Marien, Lübeck.* Studies from the Department of Musicology, Göteborg University, no. 60. Göteborg, 2000.

Walther, Johann Gottfried. *Briefe.* Edited by Klaus Beckmann and Hans-Joachim Schulze. Leipzig: Deutscher Verlag für Musik, 1987.

———. *Praecepta der Musicalischen Composition.* Edited by Peter Benary. Jenaer Beiträge zur Musikforschung, vol. 2. Leipzig: VEB Breitkopf & Härtel, 1955.

Webber, Geoffrey. *North German Church Music in the Age of Buxtehude.* Oxford: Oxford University Press, 1996.

Weckmann, Matthias. *Sämtliche Freie Orgel- und Clavierwerke / Complete Freely Composed Organ and Keyboard Works.* Revised edition. Ed. Siegbert Rampe. Kassel: Bärenreiter, 1999.

Wettstein, Hermann. *Dietrich Buxtehude (1637–1707): Bibliographie zu seinem Leben und Werk.* 2nd ed., Munich: Saur, 1989.

Williams, Peter. *The European Organ 1450–1850.* London: Batsford, 1966.

———. *A New History of the Organ from the Greeks to the Present Day.* Bloomington: Indiana University Press, 1980.

Williams, Peter. *The Organ Music of J. S. Bach.* 3 volumes. Cambridge: Cambridge University Press, 1980–84.

Wölfel, Dietrich. *Die wunderbare Welt der Orgeln: Lübeck als Orgelstadt.* Lübeck: Schmidt-Römhild, 1980.

————, ed. *Die kleine Orgel in St. Jakobi zu Lübeck—Stellwagen-Orgel: Festschrift anlässlich ihrer Wiederherstellung 1977/1978.* Lübeck: Kirchenvorstand St. Jakobi, 1978.

Wolff, Christoph. "Das Hamburger Buxtehude-Bild." In *800 Jahre Musik in Lübeck,* edited by Antjekathrin Graßman and Werner Neugebauer, 64–79. Lübeck: Senat der Hansestadt Lübeck, Amt für Kultur, 1982. Reprinted with abbreviated notes in *Musik und Kirche* 53 (1983): 8–19. Reprinted with "Nachwort 1988" in *Studien zur Musikgeschichte der Hansestadt Lübeck,* ed. Arnfried Edler and Heinrich W. Schwab, 44–62. Kassel: Bärenreiter, 1989. Trans. Thomson Moore in *Boston Early Music Festival & Exhibition, 8–14 June 1987,* program book, 102–12.

————. "Johann Adam Reinken und Johann Sebastian Bach: Zum Kontext des Bachschen Frühwerks." *Bach Jahrbuch* 71 (1985): 99–118. Emended translation by the author in *J. S. Bach as Organist: His Instruments, Music, and Performance Practices,* edited by George Stauffer and Ernest May, 57–80. Bloomington: Indiana University Press, 1986.

————. *Johann Sebastian Bach: The Learned Musician.* New York: W. W. Norton, 2000.

————. "Präludium (Toccata) und Sonata: Formbildung und Gattungstradition in der Orgelmusik Buxtehudes und seines Kreises" In *Orgel, Orgelmusik und Orgelspiel: Festschrift Michael Schneider zum 75. Geburtstag,* edited by Christoph Wolff, 55–64. Kassel: Bärenreiter, 1985.

————. "Probleme und Neuansätze der Bach-Biographik." In *Bachforschung und Bachinterpretation heute: Bericht über das Bachfest-Symposium 1978 der Philipps-Universität Marburg,* edited by Reinhold Brinkmann, 9–31. Kassel: Bärenreiter, 1981.

Wolff, Helmut Christian. *Die Barockoper in Hamburg (1678–1638).* 2 volumes. Wolfenbüttel: Möseler, 1957.

Wollny, Peter. "Beiträge zur Entstehungsgeschichte der Sammlung Düben." *Svensk tidskrift för musikforskning* 87 (2005): 100–114.

————. "A Source Complex from Saxony in the Düben Collection." Paper read at the symposium "The Dissemination of Music in 17th-Century Europe: Celebrating the Düben Collection." Uppsala, 7 September 2006.

————. "Traditionen des phantastischen Stils in Johann Sebstian Bachs Toccaten BWV 910–16." In *Bach, Lübeck und die norddeutsche Musiktradition: Bericht über das Internationale Symposion der Musikhochschule Lübeck April 2000,* edited by Wolfgang Sandberger, 245–55. Kassel: Bärenreiter, 2002.

————. "Zwischen Hamburg, Gottorf und Wolfenbuttel: Neue Ermittlungen zur Entstehung der "Sammlung Bokemeyer." *Schütz-Jahrbuch* 20 (1998): 59–76.

Yearsley, David. "Alchemy and Counterpoint in an Age of Reason." *Journal of the American Musicological Society* 51 (1998): 201–43.

————. *Bach and the Meanings of Counterpoint.* Cambridge: Cambridge University Press, 2002.

————. "Towards an Allegorical Interpretation of Buxtehude's Funerary Counterpoints," *Music & Letters* 80 (1999): 183–206.

Zahn, Johannes. *Die Melodien der deutschen evangelischen Kirchenlieder.* 6 vols; Gütersloh, 1888–93. Reprint. Hildesheim: Georg Olms, 1963.

Zarlino, Gioseffo. *The Art of Counterpoint: Part Three of "Le Istitutioni Harmoniche, 1558."* Translated by Guy A. Marco and Claude V. Palisca. New York: Norton, 1976.

Zelm, Klaus. "Die Sänger der Hamburger Gänsemarkt-Oper." *Hamburger Jahrbuch für Musikwissenschaft, Band 3: Studien zur Barockoper*, 35–73. Hamburg: Karl Dieter Wagner, 1978.

Zietz, Hermann. *Quellenkritische Untersuchungen an den Bach-Handschriften P 801, P 802 und P 803 aus dem "Krebs'schen Nachlass" unter besonderer Berücksichtigung der Choralbearbeitungen des jungen J. S. Bach*. Hamburg: Karl Dieter Wagner, 1969.

Ziller, Ernst. *Der Erfurter Organist Johann Heinrich Buttstädt (1666–1727)*. Beiträge zur Musikforschung, 3. Halle/Saale: Buchhandlung des Waisenhauses, 1935.

Index

Pasquini, Bernardo, 331–32, 434;
passacaglia, 117, 207, 238–41, 285, 325,
328, 354–55, 359, 363. *See also* ciaccona
pedal, organ, use of, 51, 229, 239–42,
245, 249, 316, 325, 329–30, 334, 337,
392–96
Pedersen, Laurits, 6
Pedersøn, Mogens, 22
Peranda, Giuseppe, 109, 139, 155,
161–62
Peterman, Tobias, 140
Petersen, Johann Wilhelm, 43, 60,
144–46, 179, 345
Petri, Johann Samuel, 370–71
Pezel, Johann, 219
Pfeiffer, August, 43
Pietism, 43, 146–49
Pinel, Germain, 281
Pirro, André, 21–22, 25–26, 137, 221
Poelchau, Georg, 325
Poglietti, Alessandro, 239, 331–32
Pohle, David, 206, 321, 339, 349
Praetorius, Gesa, 22
Praetorius, Hieronymus, 17, 96, 228
Praetorius, Jacob, 7, 22, 24–25, 45, 85–86,
142, 228, 239, 249, 262, 274, 397–98
Praetorius, Johann, 7, 25, 108
Praetorius, Michael, 152, 187, 313;
Organographia, 82, 85–86; *Syntagma
musicum III*, 149–50, 192, 365, 370;
Theatrum Instrumentorum, 373–74,
377–79, 381
Preller, Johann Gottlieb, 327–28, 392
Printz, Wolfgang Caspar, 133
Prudentius, Aurelius, 215
psalms, 90, 92, 98, 150, 138, 145, 173, 354

Quagliati, Paolo, 96
Quellinus, Thomas, 42
Quelmaltz, Jean Carl, 62, 69
Quintilian, Marcus Fabius, 260

Rabe, Jacob, 79
Radeck, Johan, 35
Radeck, Martin, 219, 239, 331
Rampe, Siegbert, 229–30
Raupach, Christoph, 131
Ravn, Hans Mikkelsen (Corvinus):
Heptachordum Danicum, 13–16, 285
real answer, 236, 256, 290, 358

recitative, 19, 155, 161, 163–64, 166, 169,
197, 211–12, 259, 363
recorder, 61, 377
regal, 61, 97, 230, 255, 381–82, 399
Reincken (Reinken), Johann Adam, 127,
180, 221, 342
and Bach, 262, 104, 286–87, 323
compositions, 239, 262, 264, 277,
279–80, 323, 334, 347, 393
composition treatises, 112–14, 224,
235–37, 256–57, 285
friendship with Buxtehude, 25, 109–19,
213
and Hamburg opera, 116–17
Hortus musicus, 112–13, 284–87, 292
as organist in Hamburg, 108, 114–15,
130, 132
and Theile, 113–14
ricercar, 247, 252, 254–55, 262, 332
Richborn, Joachim, 87–88
Richborn, Otto Dietrich, 87
Richter, Ferdinand Tobias, 128–29
Riemsdijk, J. C. M. van, 118, 222
Rinck, Johann Christian Heinrich, 230,
326
Ringk, Johannes, 327
ripieno, 320, 367, 369, 386–87, 399
Rist, Johann, 52–53, 108–9, 140, 142,
146, 152, 180–81, 183
ritornello, 54, 62, 92, 116, 118, 137, 153,
173, 178–82, 184–86, 188, 199,
210–11, 344–45, 351, 355–59, 366,
368, 380
Ritter, August Gottfried, 347
Ritter, Christian, 323
Ritter, Johann, 48–49, 205
Rodde, Matthäus Jr., 48, 58
Rodde, Matthäus Sr., 48, 56, 58
Roger, Estienne, 278
Rogge, Heinrich, 118–19, 221–23
Roman Catholic church, 17, 38, 40, 89,
96, 139, 142
Rosenmüller, Johann, 138, 284, 287, 314,
321
Rostock, 32, 37, 118, 144, 146, 347
Roth, Johann Philipp, 51, 93–94, 99, 101,
302
Roth, Martin, 17
Rovetta, Giovanni, 96
Rudén, Jan Olof, 340–41

Eastman Studies in Music

This book is a revised edition of the most comprehensive life-and-works study o the great Baroque-era organist and composer Dieterich Buxtehude (ca. 1637-1707), released to celebrate the tercentenary of the composer's death.

Originally published in 1987 and long out of print, *Dieterich Buxtehud Organist in Lübeck* is considered the standard work on Buxtehude in both North America and Europe. In addition to a biography, it includes close description of Buxtehude's compositional output, from trio sonatas to the famed Abendmusiken: Buxtehude's yearly oratorio presentations. The young J. S. Bach traveled to Lübeck on foot in 1705 to learn as much as he could from the great master of the organ and of Lutheran church music.

The revised edition contains new information on the organs that Buxtehude played in Scandinavia and Lübeck, excerpts from the newly available account books from St. Mary's in Lübeck, a discussion of newly discovered sources, including one written by J. S. Bach, an evaluation of recent scholarship on Buxtehude, and an extensive bibliography. Written for both the casual reader and the serious scholar.

The accompanying CD provides examples of all genres discussed in the book—vocal works, a trio sonata, harpsichord music, and organ music newly recorded on the North German meantone organ in Gothenburg, Sweden, by a noted specialist in this repertoire, Hans Davidsson, who is professor of organ at the University of Rochester's Eastman School of Music and the founder of the Göteborg Organ Art Center (GOArt).

Kerala J. Snyder is professor emerita of musicology, Eastman School of Music (University of Rochester).